WORKS OF
FISHER AMES

FISHER AMES

WORKS OF
FISHER AMES

———

AS PUBLISHED BY

SETH AMES

Edited and Enlarged by

W. B. Allen

———

VOLUME I

Liberty Fund

INDIANAPOLIS

1983

*This book is published by Liberty Fund, Inc., a foundation
established to encourage study of the ideal of a society of free
and responsible individuals.*

𒂼𒄀

*The cuneiform inscription that serves as the design motif for our endpapers is
the earliest-known written appearance of the word "freedom" (ama-gi), or
"liberty." It is taken from a clay document written about 2300 B.C.
in the Sumerian city-state of Lagash.*

This edition of the *Works of Fisher Ames* follows the edition by Seth Ames
(1854) published at New York, except for the arrangement, and bears some
corrections carried from the 1809 edition by George Cabot et al., Boston,
and *Speeches of Fisher Ames in Congress (1789–1796)*, edited by Pelham W.
Ames (1871), Boston. It has further been enlarged with essays, speeches,
and correspondence found in manuscripts in various collections.

*Frontispiece photo for Volume I courtesy of the Stanford University Libraries,
Stanford, California.*
*Frontispiece photo for Volume II courtesy of the Independence National Historical
Park Collection, Philadelphia, Pennsylvania.*

LIBRARY OF CONGRESS CATALOGING IN PUBLICATION DATA

Ames, Fisher, 1758–1808.
  Works of Fisher Ames.

  Reprint. Originally published: Boston: Little,
Brown, 1854.
  Includes index.
  1. United States—Politics and government—Constitu-
tional period, 1789–1809—Addresses, essays, lectures.
2. Ames, Fisher, 1758–1808. 3. Statesmen—United States
—Correspondence. I. Allen, W. B., 1944–
II. Ames, Seth, 1805–1881. III. Title.
E302.A52 1983   973.4'092'4   83-13568
ISBN 0-86597-013-0 (set)   ISBN 0-86597-017-3 (pbk.: v. 1)
ISBN 0-86597-016-5 (pbk.: set)   ISBN 0-86597-015-7 (v. 2)
ISBN 0-86597-014-9 (v. 1)   ISBN 0-86597-018-1 (pbk.: v. 2)

00 99 98 97 96 C 6 5 4 3 2
00 99 98 97 96 P 6 5 4 3 2

CONTENTS

VOLUME I

PART ONE

ESSAYS

I. ESSAYS ON SOCIAL CLASS AND CHARACTER

II. FROM CONFEDERATION TO NATION

III. ESSAYS ON FOUNDING AND PATRIOTISM

IV. ESSAYS ON MONARCHICAL VERSUS REPUBLICAN GOVERNMENT

V. ESSAYS ON AMERICA'S POLITICAL PARTIES

VI. ESSAYS ON EQUALITY

VII. DEFENDING THE FEDERALISTS

PART TWO

SPEECHES AND LETTERS

1788

1789

1790

VOLUME II

1791

1792

1793

1794

1795

1796

1797

1798

1799

1800

1803

1804

1805

1806

1807

FOREWORD

———

*Our wisdom made a government and committed
it to our virtue to keep.*

FISHER AMES was one of the most influential Federalist
statesmen of his day, his party's greatest orator, a brilliant
essayist, and perhaps the most accomplished man of letters
among his contemporaries in public service. Ames was active
in public life from 1787 through 1807 and a member of
Congress for the eight years of Washington's presidency.
Though his deeds are now obscured by the passage of time,
once his name was almost as often on the lips of his countrymen
as that of Madison, Jefferson, or Hamilton. By the time of
his retirement from public office, Ames had established
himself as the leader of the Federalist party in the House of
Representatives. It was he, in 1789, who provided the
decisive form for the First Amendment to the Constitution.

Fisher Ames was born on April 9, 1758, in the little town
of Dedham, Massachusetts, a few miles south of Boston. His
father died when Fisher was six. He attended the town school
and at twelve years of age journeyed to Cambridge to apply
for admission to Harvard College. Fisher was pronounced by

his examiner "a youth of uncommon attainments and bright promise." He became the second-youngest member of the class of 1774.

Ames graduated from Harvard at age sixteen and then taught intermittently in the country schools near his home. He devoted his leisure time to rereading the Greek and Latin classics and English literature and history. He thus developed an abundant stock of lore with which to embellish his speeches and writings of a later period. In 1775, he was mustered out to join a detachment of militia that marched toward Boston upon news of the fight at Bunker Hill. His detachment was not involved in the fighting and was dismissed after two days. In 1778, he enlisted in a company that was sent to guard the land approaches to Boston. After fifteen days' service, the men were dismissed, and this turned out to be Ames's final service in the revolutionary war.

In 1777, Ames had begun the study of law on his own. He later entered the law offices of William Tudor, a prominent Boston attorney, completed his training in the autumn of 1781, and opened an office in Dedham.

Although he was not so precocious, perhaps, as Hamilton, Ames gave a hint of his potential in 1779, when he was but twenty-one years old. In that year, prices rose sharply in Massachusetts because of the shortage of goods and the state's excessive printing of paper money. A convention of 175 men from around the state met at Concord on July 14 to look into the matter. This convention devised a system of wage and price controls in an effort to check the runaway inflation. Ames attended a second session of the convention as a delegate from Dedham. Since prices had continued to rise in the months following the first session, the delegates set about revising the price scale upward. Ames delivered a speech, now lost, in which he attacked the very idea of price controls. According to his biographer, writing shortly after Ames's death, it was

> A lucid and impressive speech, shewing the futility
> of attempting to establish by power that value of
> things, which depended solely on consent; that the
> embarrassment was inevitable, and that it must be
> met by patriotism and patience, and not by attempting
> to do what was impossible to be done.

That young Ames would oppose a measure that had been
endorsed by so many respectable men of the state shows that
he possessed more than a common degree of courage and
had already grasped the principles of the new science of
political economy—principles that later guided him through
debates far more momentous.

By the close of the revolutionary war in 1783, the nation's
economy was all but ruined. The Continental Congress and
the states had incurred huge debts during the war. Under
the Articles of Confederation, Congress had no power to put
the nation's finances on a sound basis. A currency shortage
occurred throughout the country at the same time that creditors
began to demand the payment of debts, driving debtors to
extremes. The debtors, in turn, pressured state legislatures
to pass tender acts, making livestock or produce a legal
payment for debts; to pass postponing the collection of debts;
and to issue paper money. In the states that passed such
laws, creditors fled to escape the swarms of debtors descending
upon them to pay debts with produce or worthless paper
money.

In Massachusetts, the debtors were unable to push their
program through the state legislature, which instead put state
finances on a specie basis. When creditors began to exercise
liens on land and livestock for the payment of debts, desperate
farmers, led by Daniel Shays, sought forcibly to prevent the
courts from sitting. The state was compelled to call out the
militia to disperse the farmers and restore order.

Before the militia was called out, the Lucius Junius Brutus
essays appeared in a Boston newspaper. Under this pseu-

donym, Ames argued that the rebels had to be stopped before the Constitution was overthrown. He criticized unnecessary delays and temporizing by state officials; finally, he maintained that while tender acts and paper money might provide relief to one part of the community, they constituted an unjust confiscation of the property of another part.

In February and March 1787, after the rebellion had been suppressed, Ames penned a series of five essays under the pseudonym Camillus. He employed these essays to congratulate the state on the suppression of the rebellion and to expatiate on the fundamental principles of republican government that were at stake, not just for Massachusetts, but for the nation. He warned of errors in public opinion that could lead to future rebellions if not corrected. He chastised "men of speculation and refinement" who were ready to abandon the republican experiment because "the first years of the millenium had fallen far short of the expected felicity" and then closed with a call for constitutional change. "It is time," he said, "to render the federal head supreme in the United States."

These early essays brought Fisher Ames before the public eye at a critical point in the nation's history. The convention, which met in Philadelphia in May 1787, drafted a new constitution. Since his essays proved him energetic, articulate, and federal-minded, Ames was elected to represent Dedham in the state convention called to ratify or reject the new document.

The Massachusetts state ratifying convention met in Boston on January 9, 1788. There gathered 280 of the ablest men in the state, with another eighty-four expected. The delegate list included old revolutionary patriots, delegates to the Constitutional Convention, and other state worthies.

Ames was one of the youngest delegates, but his influence compared favorably with that of the older men. One observer classed Ames among the ablest advocates of the Constitution.

Another stated that the "masterly speeches of . . . Dana, Parsons, King, [and] Ames . . . would add a lustre to any Parliament in Europe."

By fall of 1788, public interest in the upcoming elections for the new House of Representatives began to build. Federalists throughout the country urged the voters to elect proven supporters of the new Constitution.

A candidate was needed to unify the Federalist vote against Samuel A. Adams, the principal anti-Federalist candidate. Barely two weeks before the election, Fisher Ames was presented to the Suffolk voters as the Federalist candidate for representative. Samuel Adams had been a popular figure in Massachusetts since the Revolution, so the Federalists were hoping at best for a good showing by Ames. As the votes came in from around the country, Ames took a slim lead, and he was declared the winner on January 7, 1789. His victory was all the more impressive in that he had garnered a majority even though the votes were eventually split among fifteen candidates.

The United States was entering a new era in its political history, with a strong government formed to raise the country from its "state of imbecility under the Articles of Confederation." The problems to be solved were many. The nation's credit was in ruins. The revolutionary war debt had been left unpaid, and interest on it was accumulating. The federal treasury was empty. There was no federal revenue system. Congress faced the tasks of creating executive departments and delineating their powers and duties, forming the federal judiciary, and determining the extent of the federal government's powers and its relation to the states. None could say how these matters would be handled or whether the new constitution would endure.

James Madison took the lead, introducing in the House of Representatives almost all of the initial measures from revenue bills to constitutional amendments that were needed to launch the government. Ames took his bearings in these early debates from principles on which he consistently relied throughout his congressional career. He had advocated low duties on molasses because he was convinced that "promoting the interests of particular states increases the general welfare." On the other hand, he had voted against Madison's tonnage bill even though it would have benefited New England shipping. He did so because he thought that the disruption of foreign trade would injure the nation as a whole.

While points of difference between Madison and Ames— the principal figures in the House in the First Congress— serve to illuminate the principles initially at stake, more significant in this first session was their cooperation in the overall Federalist project. The tasks they had to perform were large, an instance of which was the need to appeal to anti-Federalists through a "Bill of Rights," as Washington had counseled in his inaugural address. While Ames's judgment on this point differed, he offered no resistance to the project. A further case in point was the bill to establish a treasury department. When some representatives objected to Madison's proposal that the secretary "digest and report plans" to the House improving the nation's finances, Ames delivered a powerful speech supporting the idea.

As the first session of the First Congress ended on September 29, 1789, a federal revenue system and the executive departments had been created; a bill of rights had been proposed to the states for ratification; and a federal judiciary had been formed. But perhaps the greatest problem of all had yet to be faced: how to handle the enormous debt incurred during the war. This question would occupy most of the time of the second and third sessions. It would also give rise to what John Marshall called "[t]he first regular and systematic opposition to the principles on which the affairs of the union were administered. . . ."

The second session of the First Congress began on January 4, 1790. The House soon received word from Alexander Hamilton, now secretary of the treasury, that, agreeably to their request, he had prepared a report on the public credit. The main recommendations of the report were that the revolutionary war debt be provided for in full by a permanent funding system,* that no discrimination be made between original holders of the government securities that constituted the debt and subsequent holders of purchase,† and that the debts that the individual states had incurred during the war be assumed by the federal government. Ames strongly supported each of Hamilton's recommendations.

The House took up Hamilton's report on February 8 and debated three days before deciding to fund the debt in full. At this point, Madison tossed a firebrand into the discussion. In a speech on February 11, he advocated discriminating between original and subsequent holders of the debt in order to conform to "justice and public opinion."

On February 15, Fisher Ames took exception to Madison's proposal with a speech of his own. The securities, he argued, had been transferred by an agreement between the buyer and seller that the government should honor. Moreover, the purchasers had taken upon themselves the risk that the

---

* *Funding meant that Congress would pledge a certain part of each year's revenue for payment of the interest on the debt and for the gradual redemption of the principal.*

† *The original holders were those who had either bought government securities or received them for goods and services during the war. Many of these people had sold their securities at greatly depreciated rates either through necessity or lack of faith that the government would ever redeem them. Discrimination meant that the government would pay subsequent holders not the face value of the securities but only the highest price for which they had sold in the market. The difference would be given to the original holders as compensation for their earlier losses. Original holders retaining their securities would receive the face value of the note.*

original holders had been unable or unwilling to bear—that the government might never redeem the securities. Lastly, Ames doubted that the public favored a discrimination. But even if they did,

> it is more a duty on government to protect right when it may happen to be unpopular; that is what government is framed to do. If, instead of protecting, it assumes the right of controlling property, and disposing of it at its own pleasure, and against the consent of the owner, there is a cheat in the compact.

Ames thought that if the House acted on this occasion as if right depended "not on compact, and sacred faith" but "on opinion, on a major vote," the nation's credit would be destroyed and the very foundations of the government shaken.

Debate continued for several days on Madison's proposal before it was finally rejected by a large majority. Madison's discrimination proposal meant that he had broken with Hamilton and the Federalists, thus abdicating his position as their leader in the House. He gradually assumed the leadership of those men who were opposed to the policies of Washington's administration and who later came to be called Republicans. From this point on, Ames and Madison were found on opposite sides of nearly every major question that came before Congress. Ames was called on time and again to defend Federalist policies against Madison and the Republicans.

The Third Congress was the first to be elected squarely on the basis of the new party labels. In the House of Representatives, the election produced a standoff between the Federalists and Republicans, and in some respects the Republicans prevailed. Madison once again occupied the key leadership position. Working in tandem with Thomas Jefferson, he launched the Third Congress by resurrecting an issue from the First Congress.

On December 19, 1793, shortly before retiring as secretary of state, Jefferson sent to Congress his *Report on the Privileges and Restrictions on the Commerce of the United States in Foreign Countries*. This report was designed to prove that France's commercial policy was friendly toward the United States, while Great Britain's was not. When the House took up the report some days later, Madison introduced a series of coordinated resolutions. The resolutions raised anew the demand for discrimination against the trade of nations not having commercial treaties with the United States. They also sought reciprocal action against nations imposing restrictions on American commerce.

Fisher Ames did not speak at length on Madison's resolutions until they had been debated for several days. At last, on January 27, he rose. The question, as he saw it, was how Congress might put America's trade and navigation on a better footing. For trade to be on a good footing, Ames said, meant for exports to sell dear and imports to be bought cheap. The test of Madison's resolutions, therefore, was the effect they would have on the prices of exports and imports. Ames then ran through a list of the thirteen products that constituted the bulk of American exports to Britain. Only two of the products were dutied in the British market. The other products paid no duty, while the same products from other nations were either prohibited or dutied by the British. It appeared, then, that contrary to Jefferson's assertions, Britain's commercial policy favored the United States.

According to Ames, the bulk of America's exports were sold to England for one of two reasons: either the British paid the highest prices for them, or the French had little use for them. Either way, diverting trade toward France would mean a loss for American producers. The competition that Madison had promised in the supplying of American imports would also be at the expense of Americans. The competition would be promoted by taxing British goods until they sold as dear as French goods. But it was the American consumer who would pay the difference. "We shall pay more for a time," said Ames, "and in the end pay no less; for no object but that one nation may receive our money instead of the other." For the Federalists, Madison's resolutions would have meant the end of the American policy toward Europe that had prevailed since Washington's Proclamation of Neutrality in April 1793. By voting down the resolutions, the House could assert a true "independence of spirit." "[W]e shall be false to our duty and feelings as Americans," Ames concluded, "if we basely descend to a servile dependence on France or Great Britain."

During the debate on Madison's resolutions, news arrived that the British were confiscating American merchant vessels in the Caribbean. At about the same time, reports began circulating that the British in Canada were stirring up the Indians against the Northwest frontier. Since hostilities with Britain now appeared imminent, the Federalists were able to shift debate in the House to preparing the nation's defenses for war. Then, at the height of the crisis, Britain revoked the order in council that had authorized the confiscation of American ships. Seizing upon this opportunity to seek peace, President Washington appointed John Jay as a special envoy to negotiate a settlement of the differences between the two countries.

Debate over making the necessary appropriations to put the treaty into effect began in the House on March 7, 1796. The Republicans at this point adopted the position that whenever a treaty required appropriations of money or any other act of Congress, the House had the discretionary power to carry it into effect or to annul it by refusing its cooperation. The Federalists, for their part, maintained that a treaty was binding on the nation from the moment it was signed by the president. For the House to refuse its cooperation, they reasoned, was to break the treaty and violate the faith of the nation. Debate continued on and off for nearly two months.

By 1796, Fisher Ames had contracted the disease that eventually took his life. Before leaving Dedham to attend the Fourth Congress, he had solemnly promised his doctors to take no part in the debates. But after sitting quietly through almost the entire debate on Jay's treaty, he could be still no longer. On April 28, it became known in the corridors of Congress Hall that Fisher Ames would finally speak. The Senate and the Supreme Court adjourned for the occasion, as would-be auditors rushed for seats in the House galleries. Struggling to his feet, his face pale and thin, Ames began: "I entertain the hope, perhaps a rash one, that my strength will hold me out to speak a few minutes."

For "a few minutes," Ames spoke, with a dramatic and rhetorical effect that did not disappoint his listeners. He meticulously refuted Republican claims to an independent treaty-approving authority in the House. He invoked the rule of law. And he called mounting public opinion to testify in his behalf. Breaking the treaty would leave the British in possession of the Northwest posts. From these posts, the Indians would be incited against the western frontier. It took modest wit to picture the result:

> I would say to the inhabitants, Wake from your false security! Your cruel dangers—your more cruel apprehensions—are soon to be renewed; the wounds, yet unhealed, are to be torn open again. In the day time, your path through the woods will be ambushed; the darkness of midnight will glitter with the blaze of your dwellings. You are a father: the blood of your sons shall fatten your cornfield! You are a mother: the war-whoop shall wake the sleep of the cradle! . . . Who will say that I exaggerate . . . ! Who will answer, by a sneer, that all this is idle preaching? . . . By rejecting the posts, we light the savage fires— we bind the victims! This day we undertake to render account to the widows and orphans whom our decision will make, to the wretches that will be roasted at the

stake . . . To conscience and to God we are answerable
. . . While one hand is held up to reject this treaty,
the other grasps a tomahawk. I can fancy that I listen
to the yells of savage vengeance, and to the shrieks
of torture. Already they seem to sigh in the West
Wind; already they mingle with every echo from the
mountains.

If, in spite of these consequences, the treaty were broken,
Ames concluded, "Even I, slender and almost broken as my
hold upon life is, may outlive the Government and Constitution
of my country."

The effect of the speech was overwhelming. Vice President
Adams and Supreme Court Justice James Iredell sat drained
in the galleries. "My God, how great he is," said Iredell.
"How great he has been." "He has been noble," replied
Adams. "Tears enough were shed," Adams wrote home to
his wife. "Not a dry eye, I believe, except some of the
Jackasses who had occasioned the necessity of the oratory."
Dr. Joseph Priestley, a dedicated Republican who had
listened to Chatham, Pitt, Burke, and Fox, declared the
speech "the most bewitching piece of parliamentary oratory
he had ever listened to." And Jeremiah Smith, one of Ames's
friends, commented that Ames should "have died in the fifth
act; that he never will have an occasion so glorious, having
lost this he will now have to make his exit like other men."*
The Republicans had been confident that they could carry a
vote against the appropriations at any time, but when the
final vote was taken on April 30, the appropriations passed
by fifty-one to forty-nine.

Ames's speech on the Jay Treaty has been declared the
first really great speech delivered on the floor of the House.

---

* Smith's reference doubtlessly and most significantly is a reference to
Joseph Addison's famous play, Cato, whose hero was a popular model
for American Republicans.

One may doubt that, yet take note that it became a standard for American political rhetoric for successive generations of American statesmen. Young Daniel Webster, for one, memorized the speech as a model for his own oratory. Even decades later, when "Federalist" had become a term of reproach in American politics, the speech was fondly remembered. For example, George S. Boutwell, one of Grant's secretaries of the treasury, reported that Abraham Lincoln greatly admired the speech and could recite long portions of it from memory.

At the close of the next session, Fisher Ames retired from Congress and returned home to his family and friends. He resumed his legal practice and attended the sessions of the courts when his health permitted. Farming became an occupation for him, as he experimented with the breeding of dairy cattle and hogs and with the culture of fruit trees. But even when occupied with these various pursuits, public affairs were not far from his mind.

What Ames regarded as the unfinished work of the founding called forth a barrage of essays that appeared in the party presses. These essays aimed to boost the Federalists and to overthrow the Republicans after their victory of 1800. But most of all, they aimed to establish a correct standard of public opinion, echoing the work of the youthful Camillus. Indefatigable as he was, however, his party never revived.

During his congressional career, Ames had kept up a personal correspondence with Massachusetts Federalists in order to keep them abreast of national events. After his retirement, he corresponded with Federalist leaders around the country. His letters constitute the closest thing we have to a deliberate commentary on nearly all the important political events from 1789 to 1807. They give an inside view of the purposes and strategies of his party and interesting assessments of the men from both parties with whom Ames had personal acquaintance.

The last years of Ames's life were plagued by the lung disease that had forced his retirement from Congress. He would grow seriously ill, have fainting spells, and be confined to bed for days at a time. Then he would recover strength enough to go about his business for a while. In 1808, his periods of illness grew more frequent and more severe, and by June he was definitely failing. By the end of the month, he could not rise from bed; at sunrise on Monday, July 4, the thirty-second anniversary of the nation's birth, he died quietly at his home in Dedham.

With the passing of Fisher Ames, federalism as a direct political influence passed into history. After him, there remained but the genius of John Marshall, entrenched on the Supreme Court. But as for a party spokesman, organizer, and theoretician, suited to slugging it out in the arena of democracy, none remained. Washington died in 1799; his ablest lieutenant, Hamilton, was slain in 1804; and Ames, Hamilton's ablest lieutenant, followed four years later. Soon after his death, his friends issued a short edition of his works, meant as a bible for the rising generations. While the party's energy was spent and young men embraced instead the victorious Republicans, the energy of Ames's thought continues to live. With this greatly revised and corrected edition, we offer Ames's thought to a new generation.

W. B. A.

Claremont, California

William B. Allen is Professor of Government at Harvey Mudd College, Claremont, California.

EDITOR'S NOTE

THIS EDITION of the *Works of Fisher Ames* is based on the edition published in 1854 by Seth Ames. It has been substantially enlarged to supply omissions in the earlier version that are material to an understanding of Ames's contribution in the era of founding in the United States.

The "Essays" represent Ames's most extensive public production. Where possible, ellipses from the earlier version have been supplied. Those ellipses that remain, whether on account of deteriorated original texts or our inability to acquire original texts, have been indicated by brackets enclosing a series of end stops, thus, [. . .]. The original headnotes, incorporated from the 1809 edition, have been deleted, save in the case of the posthumously published "Dangers of American Liberty." The series of footnotes incorporates our notes with those of the 1854 edition, which latter are indicated by a bracketed "S. Ames" or "F. Ames," as appropriate. It is also well to note that the essays are not presented in mere chronological order. They have been arranged by themes. Within each theme, the chronological order prevails whenever reasonable. On the whole, a chronological order is noticeable but not exact. We add to this collection twenty-three essays missing from the 1854 edition, and in many instances we correct the bibliographical references to the essays that were published. Such changes are carried silently.

The "Letters and Speeches" stand as a mix of private and public reflections on questions of public moment. The speeches are all public productions, but the occasional element of spontaneity in them often echoes or mimics ideas more freely expressed in private correspondence. We preserve this twilight relationship between the letters and speeches by publishing them as a carefully arranged whole. They have been arranged along two complementary lines, thematic and chronological. The speeches divide easily into seventeen topics, for each of which a lead speech has been selected. The lead speeches have been inserted among the letters in strict chronological order. Other speeches, however, are associated with the lead speech to which they most closely relate thematically. Thus, the secondary speeches following the lead speech violate the overall chronological order, albeit among themselves they are in chronological order. The correspondence is strictly chronological.

Here, too, we enlarge the collection, publishing nearly all of Ames's speeches, whereas before only a few were published, and greatly adding to the correspondence. This edition contains eighty-five new letters while deleting six of minor importance and substantially shortening many others. Furthermore, many of the speeches and letters have been edited against their originals and the resulting corrections silently carried into the previously published text.

Our purpose throughout has been to render Ames as clearly and faithfully as possible. Because Ames was the quintessential Monday-morning quarterback (as well as an effective pregame strategist), his letters, speeches, and essays now offer the foremost *sustained* criticism of the American founding, from the time of the Constitutional Convention through Jefferson's re-election as president. As such, this collection is a tool of inestimable value.

We have relied on the guidance of several sources in preparing this collection, among them the first account of Ames's life by his friend J. T. Kirkland. Kirkland's "Life of Fisher Ames" was prefixed to the *Works of Fisher Ames* (Boston: T. B. Wait, 1809) and also to the Seth Ames edition of the same work (Boston: Little, Brown, 1854). Several other sketches of Ames appeared in magazines and journals in the 1800s, but few added to an understanding of his life or career. Among the few, an article by Mellen Chamberlain appeared in the *Harvard Graduate's Magazine*, 4 (1895–1896). Additionally, the debate between John Quincy Adams (*American Principles*) and John Lowell (*Remarks on Adam's Review of Ames's Works*), occurring on the occasion of the first publication of Ames's *Works*, greatly contributes to an understanding of the context of his political endeavor.

Two more recent articles deserve attention: Samuel E. Morison, "Squire Ames and Doctor Ames," *The New England Quarterly*, 1 (1928) and Elisha P. Douglass, "Fisher Ames, Spokesman for New England Federalism," *Proceedings of the American Philosophical Association*, 103 (1959).

The only full-scale biography of Ames was written in 1965 by Winfred E. A. Bernhard. *Fisher Ames, Federalist and Statesman* (Chapel Hill: University of North Carolina Press, 1965) gives a most balanced account of Ames's life and thus largely supersedes earlier accounts.

Among general histories of the founding era, the following were of value in the effort to situate Ames within the context of the founding: John Marshall, *The Life of George Washington* (Philadelphia: C. P. Wayne, 1804–1807); John C. Miller, *The Federalist Era* (New York: Harper & Row, 1960); Samuel E. Morison, Henry S. Commager, and William E. Leuchtenburg, *The Growth of the American Republic* (New York: Oxford University Press, 1969); Forrest McDonald, *The Presidency of George Washington* (New York: Norton, 1974); and the best of recent sources, James M. Banner, *To the Hartford Convention: The Federalists and the Origin of Party Politics in Massachusetts, 1789–1815* (New York: Knopf, 1970).

We gratefully acknowledge the assistance of, and permission to publish materials from, the following collections: American Antiquarian Society, Worcester, Massachusetts; Boston Public Library, Boston, Massachusetts; the Historical Society of Pennsylvania, Philadelphia, Pennsylvania; the Huntington Library, San Marino, California; the Putnam Papers and the Charles Goddard Slack Collection, Dawes Memorial Library, Marietta College, Marietta, Ohio; Massachusetts Historical Society, Boston, Massachusetts; the New York Historical Society, New York, New York; New York Public Library, New York, New York; the New York Society Library, New York, New York; the Pierpont Morgan Library, New York, New York; the Rhode Island Historical Society, Providence, Rhode Island; the John Rutledge Papers in the Southern Historical Collection of the University of North Carolina Library, Chapel Hill, North Carolina; the Stanford University Libraries Special Collections, Stanford, California; the Fisher Ames Collection (#4217), Manuscripts Department, University of Virginia Library, Charlottesville, Virginia; and the Morse Family Papers (Fisher Ames to Jedediah Morse, Dec. 20, 1792) of Yale University Library, New Haven, Connecticut. The Manuscripts Division of the Library of Congress, whose staff provided great assistance in identifying two heretofore misplaced Ames essays in the Papers of Alexander Hamilton, deserves thanks. From previously published works we acknowledge Columbia University Press's *The Papers of Alexander Hamilton* (1961); G. P. Putnam's Sons *The Life and Correspondence of Rufus King* (1895); Jonathan Elliot's *Debates in the Several State Con-*

ventions (1888); *The Annals of Congress;* from G. Gibbs's *The Federal Administrations,* the "Wolcott Papers"; and *The Memoirs of William Tudor.* We were aided by many others in this endeavor, whose resources enabled us to verify and correct much previously published Ames material. We cannot name them all here, but hereby extend our gratitude.

Finally, we acknowledge our debt to Mrs. Diane Sanchez's secretarial skills. The editor recognizes the important editorial contributions and assistance of graduate assistants Eldon Alexander and Wesley Phelan. We express abiding appreciation of the editorial and managerial contributions of Liberty Fund, Inc., and thank them for the opportunity to peruse these works. We acknowledge, with them, a great debt to Pierre F. Goodrich.

W. B. A.
Claremont, California

PREFACE

TO THE

SECOND EDITION

———

THE EDITOR of these volumes has for some time past had it in contemplation to publish a second edition of his father's writings. The collection originally published in 1809 has long been out of print, and it was hoped that a second edition might be acceptable. Like many other resolutions intended to be carried into effect at some more convenient season, this project has slumbered, and perhaps has been in some danger of a general and indefinite postponement. A few months ago, however, it was his good fortune to receive, from a friend in Boston, a large number of original letters to the late Governor Gore, and they were found, on examination, sufficiently interesting and important to change the half-forgotten purpose into a somewhat urgent and imperative duty. Further inquiries were made in appropriate quarters, and those inquiries have been so kindly received and so faithfully seconded, that it soon became manifest that the original letters, placed at the disposal of the editor, would require that his proposed republication should be, to a considerable extent, a new and a different work. It has been found more convenient to devote the second volume of the present work to the speeches and essays published in 1809. They will be found in that volume with a slight change of arrangement, and with the omission of one essay, entitled "Sketches of the State of Europe," which is now ascertained to have been the work of another author.*

The editor flatters himself that the new volume, containing a collection of his father's letters to his political and personal friends, will be found to be a valuable addition to the original work. It is well known that Fisher Ames was considered by his contemporaries quite as remarkable for his colloquial gifts, as for the eloquence and vigor of his public speeches and written essays. His letters were very numerous, and generally as unpremeditated as his spoken words. They approach, in some degree, to the energy and vivacity of his conversation, and partially supply the want of those personal memorials which have unfortunately perished. He kept no letter-book, and, with only three or four exceptions, no copies of any of his letters, and undoubtedly a large portion of them is irrecoverably lost. None of them appear to have been written with any view to publication, and only two or three seem to have been intended to go beyond the persons to whom they were immediately addressed. Some of them were of an exceedingly delicate and confidential character, and some were accompanied with an injunction that they should be committed to the flames. But the reasons for privacy have long since ceased to exist, and there is nothing in the whole correspondence that will not bear the light of publicity. In some instances names have been suppressed; and occasionally a paragraph has been omitted, which might give annoyance or uneasiness in some quarters if imparted to the public at large. In the letters to his brother-in-law, Thomas Dwight of Springfield, there are of course many domestic details, too trivial and minute to be of any public interest, which are for that reason omitted. No letters to his excellent and most

* See note 58 below.

intimate friend, George Cabot, are contained in this collection, because none could be found. Whatever written correspondence may have passed between them has disappeared, and is lost. The letters to Oliver Wolcott, Jr., Secretary of the Treasury under Washington and Adams, published in Gibbs's History of the Federal Administrations, are omitted, because Mr. Gibbs's absence from this part of the country has rendered it inconvenient to obtain that gentleman's express consent to their republication here.

The editor hardly considers it necessary to apologize for not attempting to connect these letters together by a thread of biographical narrative. He was but three years of age at the time of his father's death, and he has absolutely no materials for such a narrative, except such as are furnished by the letters themselves, and the public history of the country. He may be pardoned also for saying that he cannot remember a time when he did not feel entirely satisfied with the beautiful and touching memoir by the late Dr. Kirkland. The most that he has attempted to do has been so to arrange the letters as to make the writer of them tell his own story, and act as his own biographer. For this reason, a few are included which are important only as furnishing some matter of fact, or going into some detail as to his daily life and occupation, which may not be found in Dr. Kirkland's brief and general sketch.

The correspondence will be found to present the unstudied outpourings of a singularly impulsive and ardent temperament. Sometimes, of course, it is deeply colored with the despondency growing out of habitual ill-health; at other times the writer's gayety and good spirits are too great even for sickness wholly to subdue; and sometimes he suffers himself to be betrayed into expressions which his more deliberate judgment would probably have led him to qualify. The entire series will be found to present as honest an account of his own opinions and impulses for the time being, and as faithful a portrait of himself, as any man ever drew. It is hoped that it will be found valuable and interesting, not only as the history of a leader in the Federal party from its origin, but as a contemporaneous record, by an eye-witness, of a portion of our political history, once very generally neglected, now exciting more of curiosity and interest, but not even yet generally understood. The Federal party has long since ceased to exist, "except in the pages of history," and, for that very reason, the public is in a good position to inquire, without prejudice or passion, what sort of men the early Federalists were, what were their views of public affairs, and in what manner they fought the political battle of their day and generation.

SETH AMES

PREFACE

TO THE

FIRST EDITION

———

An Abridgment of The Life of Fisher Ames

MR. AMES was distinguished among the eminent men of our country. All admitted, for they felt, his extraordinary powers; few pretended to doubt, if any seemed to deny, the purity of his heart. His exemplary life commanded respect; the charms of his conversation and manners won affection. He was equally admired and beloved.

His public career was short, but brilliant. Called into the service of his country in seasons of her most critical emergency, and partaking in the management of her councils during a most interesting period of her history, he obtained a place in the first rank of her statesmen, legislators, orators, and patriots. By a powerful and original genius, an impressive and uniform virtue, he succeeded, as fully perhaps as any political character, in a republic agitated by divisions, ever did, in surmounting the two pernicious vices, designated by the inimitable biographer of Agricola, insensibility to merit on the one hand, and envy on the other.

Becoming a private citizen, he still operated extensively upon the public opinion and feeling, by conversation and writing. When least in the public eye, he remained the object of enthusiastic regard to his friends, and of fond reliance and hope to those lovers of his country who discern the connection between the agency of a few and the welfare of the many; whilst in the breasts of the community at large he engaged a sentiment of lively tenderness and peculiar respect.

The sickness, which diffused an oppressive languor upon his best years, was felt to be a common misfortune; and the news of his death, though not unexpected, gave a pang of distress to the hearts of thousands. Those inhabitants of the capital of Massachusetts who had always delighted to honor him, solicited his lifeless remains for the privilege of indulging their grief, and evincing their admiration by funeral obsequies. The sad rites being performed, those who had cherished his character and talents with such constant regard and veneration, and who felt their own and the public loss in his death with poignant affliction, demanded a publication of his works. They urged that it would gratify their affection, reflect honor on his name, and be a voice of instruction and warning to his country.

In compliance with their general and earnest wish, this volume is given to the world. Some account of the author's life and character is thought due, if not to his fame, yet to the interest which all have in those "who were born, and who have acted, as though they were born for their country and for mankind."

He needs not our praises; he would be dishonored by our flattery; but he was our distinguished benefactor. We owe a record of this kind, though imperfectly executed, to our sense of his merits and services, and to our gratitude to heaven who endues some with extraordinary gifts to be employed for the benefit of others. It is the part of justice to afford, to those who desire it, all practicable lights to guide their judgment of an eminent man, living in times and acting in situations, which expose his character to be imperfectly understood. We must pay respect to that natural and laudable curiosity of mankind, which asks an explanation of the causes that may have contributed to form any peculiar excellence in one of our species, and which takes an interest in the circumstances and events of his life. Examples of great talents diligently exerted, and of shining virtues practised with uniformity, should be preserved and displayed, as furnishing models in conduct and incentives to excellence. By such exhibitions, the timid are encouraged and the inactive roused. Emulation fires generous spirits to endeavor to fill the void made by the loss of the eminent. Are any capable of doing great and durable good to their country and the world, they are stimulated to tread in the fair paths which have been trodden before; and those whom nature and circumstances have confined to a small compass of action, are instructed to place their single talent to the best account.

On the kind or degree of excellence which criticism may concede or deny to Mr. Ames's productions, we do not undertake with accurate discrimination to determine. He was undoubtedly rather actuated by the genius of oratory, than disciplined by the precepts of rhetoric; was more intent on exciting attention and interest, and producing effect, than securing the praise of skill in the artifice of composition. Hence critics might be dissatisfied, yet hearers charmed. The abundance of materials, the energy and quickness of conception, the inexhaustible fertility of mind which he possessed, as they did not require, so they forbade a rigid adherence to artificial guides in the disposition and employment of his intellectual stores. To a certain extent, such a speaker and writer may claim to be his own authority.

Image crowded upon image in his mind; he is not chargeable with affectation in the use of figurative language; his tropes are evidently prompted by imagination, and not forced into his service. Their novelty and variety create constant surprise and delight. But they are, perhaps, too lavishly employed. The fancy of his hearers is sometimes overplied with stimulus, and the importance of the thought liable to be concealed in the multitude and beauty of the metaphors. His condensation of expression may be thought to produce occasional abruptness. He aimed rather at the terseness, strength, and vivacity of the short sentence, than the dignity of the full and flowing period. His style is conspicuous for sententious brevity, for antithesis and point. Single ideas appear with so much lustre and prominence, that the connection of the several parts of his discourse is not always obvious to the common mind, and the aggregate impression of the composition is not always completely obtained. In those respects where his peculiar excellences came near to defects, he is rather to be admired than imitated.

Mr. Ames, though trusting much to his native resources, did by no means neglect to apply the labors of others to his own use. His early love of books has been mentioned; and he retained and cherished the same propensity through his whole life. He was particularly fond of ethical studies; but he went more deeply into history, than any other branch of learning. Here he sought the principles of legislation, the science of politics, the causes of the rise and decline of nations, and the character and passions of men acting in public affairs. He read Herodotus, Thucydides, Livy, Tacitus, Plutarch, and the modern historians of Greece and Rome. The English history he studied with much care. Hence he possessed a great fund of historical knowledge always at command both for conversation and writing. He contemplated the character of Cicero as an orator and statesman with fervent admiration.

He never ceased to be a lover of the poets. Homer, in Pope, he often perused; and read Virgil in the original within two years of his death with increased delight. His knowledge of the French enabled him to read their authors, though not to speak their language. He was accustomed to read the Scriptures, not only as containing a system of truth and duty, but as displaying, in their poetical parts, all that is sublime, animated, and affecting in composition. His learning seldom appeared as such, but was interwoven with his thoughts, and became his own.

In public speaking he trusted much to excitement, and did little more in his closet than draw the outlines of his speech, and reflect on it, till he had received deeply the impressions he intended to make; depending for the turns and figures of language, illustrations, and modes of appeal to the passions, on his imagination and feelings at the time. This excitement continued, when the cause had ceased to operate. After debate, his mind was agitated, like the ocean after a storm, and his nerves were like the shrouds of a ship, torn by the tempest.

He brought his mind much in contact with the minds of others, ever pleased to converse on subjects of public interest, and seizing every hint that might be useful to him in writing, for the instruction of his fellow-citizens. He justly thought, that persons below him in capacity might have good ideas, which he might employ in the correction and improvement of his own. His attention was always awake to grasp the materials that came to him from every source. A constant labor was going on in his mind.

He never sunk from an elevated tone of thought and action, nor suffered his faculties to slumber in indolence. The circumstances of the times in which he was called to act, contributed to elicit his powers, and supply fuel to his genius. The greatest interests were subjects of debate. When he was in the national legislature, the spirit of party did not tie the hands of the public functionaries; and questions, on which depended the peace or war, the safety or danger, the freedom or dishonor of the country, might be greatly influenced by the counsels and efforts of a single patriot.

The political principles and opinions of Mr. Ames are not

difficult to be understood, and should be attentively regarded by those who will estimate the merit of his labors. Mr. Ames was emphatically a republican. He saw that many persons confounded a republic with a democracy. He considered them as essentially distinct and really opposite. According to his creed, a republic is that structure of an elective government, in which the administration necessarily prescribe to themselves the general good as the object of all their measures; a democracy is that, in which the present popular passions, independent of the public good, become a guide to the rulers. In the first, the reason and interests of society govern; in the second, their prejudices and passions. The frame of the American Constitution supposes the dangers of democracy. The division of the Legislature into two branches and their diverse origin, the long duration of office in one branch, the distinct power of the executive, the independence and permanency of the judiciary, are designed to balance and check the democratic tendencies of our polity. They are contrivances and devices voluntarily adopted by the people to restrain themselves from obstructing, by their own mistakes or perversity, the attainment of the public welfare. They are professed means of insuring to the nation rulers, who will prefer the durable good of the whole, to the transient advantage of the whole or a part. When these provisions become ineffectual, and the legislator, the executive magistrate, and the judge become the instruments of the passions of the people, or of the governing majority, the government, whatever may be its form, is a democracy, and the public liberty is no longer safe. True republican rulers are bound to act, not simply as those who appoint them *would*, but as they *ought*; democratic leaders will act in subordination to those very passions which it is the object of government to control; but as the effect of this subserviency is to procure them unlimited confidence and devotedness, the powers of society become concentrated in their hands. Then it is, that men, not laws, govern. Nothing can be more inconsistent with the real liberty of the people, than the power of the democracy thus brought into action. For in this case the government is a despotism beyond rule, not a republic confined to rule. It is strong, but its strength is of a terrible sort; strong to oppress, not to protect; not strong to maintain liberty, property, and right, it cannot secure justice nor make innocence safe.

Mr. Ames apprehended that our government had been sliding down from a true republic towards the abyss of democracy; and that the ambition of demagogues operating on personal, party, and local passions, was attaining its objects. "A quack doctor, a bankrupt attorney, and a renegado from England, by leading the mobs of three cities, become worth a national bribe; and after receiving it, they are not the servants but the betrayers of the state." The only resource against this degeneracy of our affairs, and their final catastrophe, Mr. Ames considered to be the "correctness of the public opinion, and the energy that is to maintain it." Hence his zeal to support the federal administration in the constitutional exercise of its powers, and his fervid appeals to enlighten, animate, and combine the friends of republican liberty. Hence the stress he laid on the principles, habits, and institutions that pertain to the New England state of society. "Constitutions," said he, "are but paper; society is the substratum of government. The New England state of society is the best security to us, and, mediately, to the United States, for a government favorable to liberty and order. The chance of these is almost exclusively from their morals, knowledge, manners, and equal diffusion of property, added to town governments and clergy; all circumstances inestimable."

In conformity to these principles, he considered party as the necessary engine of good, as well as the instrument of evil in a republic. Party, meaning an association or political connection for the public good, is a name of praise; and a "party united and actuated by a common impulse or interest, adverse to the rights of the citizens, and the permanent and aggregate interests of the community," even though it be a majority, is a faction. Accident, as well as vice, would operate strongly on the formation of the one body, and in some small degree of the other: but their prevailing character and views constitute their distinction, and determine them good or bad. Neutrality is not permitted to a good citizen. Indifference about political party is not moderation, but either an insensibility to the public welfare, or a selfish desire of getting favor with both sides, at the expense of the honest. Moderation consists in maintaining the love of country superior to party feeling, and in showing respect to the rights of opponents, not in allowing their wishes, or fearing their enmity, or relaxing in prudent exertions to baffle their designs.

He did not, however, turn his eyes from the favorable side of his situation. "There is a vexation in public cares, but these cares awaken curiosity; an active interest in the event of measures, which gradually becomes the habit of a politician's soul. Besides, the society of worthy and distinguished men, whose virtues and characters are opened and colored by the sympathy of united efforts, is no mean compensation." His health, and perhaps his life, were the costly oblations which he laid on the altar of patriotism. The fine machinery of his system could ill withstand the excitement produced by public speaking, and his keen interest in public affairs.

It is happy for mankind, when those who engage admiration, deserve esteem; for vice and folly derive a pernicious influence from an alliance with qualities that naturally command applause. In the character of Mr. Ames, the circle of the virtues seemed to be complete, and each virtue in its proper place.

The objects of religion presented themselves with a strong interest to his mind. The relation of the world to its Author, and of this life to a retributory scene in another, could not be contemplated by him without the greatest solemnity. The réligious sense was, in his view, essential in the constitution of man. He placed a full reliance on the divine origin of

1

Christianity. If there was ever a time in his life, when the light of revelation shone dimly upon his understanding, he did not rashly close his mind against clearer vision, for he was more fearful of mistakes to the disadvantage of a system, which he saw to be excellent and benign, than of prepossessions in its favor. He felt it his duty and interest to inquire, and discovered, on the side of faith, a fulness of evidence little short of demonstration. At about thirty-five, he made a public profession of his belief in the Christian religion, and was a regular attendant on its services. In regard to articles of belief, his conviction was confined to those leading principles, about which Christians have little diversity of opinion. Subtle questions of theology, from various causes often agitated, but never determined, he neither pretended nor desired to investigate, satisfied that they related to points uncertain or unimportant. He loved to view religion on the practical side, as designed to operate by a few simple and grand truths on the affections, actions, and habits of men. He cherished the sentiment and experience of religion, careful to ascertain the genuineness and value of impressions and feelings by their moral tendency. He insisted much on the distinction between the real and lively, but gentle and unaffected emotions of a pious mind, naturally passing into the life, and that "morbid fanaticism," which consists in inexplicable sensations, internal acts, and artificial raptures, that have no good aspect upon religious obedience. In estimating a sect, he regarded more its temper than its tenets; he treated the conscientious opinions and phraseology of others on sacred subjects with tenderness, and approached all questions concerning divine revelation with modesty and awe. His prudence and moderation in these particulars may, possibly, have been misconstrued into an assent to propositions, which he meant merely not to deny, or an adoption of opinions or language, which he chose merely not to condemn. He, of all men, was the last to countenance exclusive claims to purity of faith, founded on a zeal for peculiar dogmas, which multitudes of good men, approved friends of truth, utterly reject. He was no enemy to improvement, to fair inquiry, and Christian freedom; but innovations in the modes of worship and instruction, without palpable necessity or advantage, he discouraged, as tending to break the salutary associations of the pious mind. His conversation and behavior evinced the sincerity of his religious impressions. No levity upon these subjects ever escaped his lips; but his manner of recurring to them in conversation indicated reverence and feeling. The sublime, the affecting character of Christ, he never mentioned without emotion.

Mr. Ames was married July 15th, 1792, to Frances, third daughter of John Worthington, Esq. of Springfield. He left seven children, six of whom are sons; the eldest fifteen years old. He was gratefully sensible of the peculiar felicity of his domestic life. In his beloved home, his sickness found all the alleviation that a judicious and unwearied tenderness could minister; and his intervals of health, a succession of every pleasing engagement and heartfelt satisfaction. The complacency of his looks, the sweetness of his tones, his mild and often playful manner of imparting instruction, evinced his extreme delight in the society of his family, who felt that they derived from him their chief happiness, and found in his conversation and example a constant excitement to noble and virtuous conduct. As a husband and father, he was all that is provident, kind, and exemplary. He was riveted in the regards of those who were in his service. He felt all the ties of kindred. The delicacy, the ardor, and constancy, with which he cherished his friends, his readiness to the offices of good neighborhood, and his propensity to contrive and execute plans of public improvement, formed traits in his character, each of remarkable strength. He cultivated friendship by an active and punctual correspondence, which made the number of his letters very great, and which are not less excellent than numerous.

When he emerged from comparative obscurity, to fill a large space in the eyes of the public, he lost none of the simplicity of character and modesty of deportment which he had before displayed, and neglected none of the friends of his youth. He never yielded to that aversion to the necessary cares of life, which men, accustomed to high concerns, or fond of letters, sometimes improvidently indulge. Without any particle of avarice, he was strictly economical.

He had no envy, for he felt no personal rivalry. His ambition was of that purified sort, which is rather the desire of excellence, than the reputation of it; he aimed more at desert, than at superiority. He loved to bestow praise on those who were competitors for the same kind of public consideration as himself, not fearing that he should sink by their elevation.

He was tenacious of his rights, but scrupulous in his respect to the rights of others. The obloquy of political opponents, was sometimes the price he paid for not deserving it. But it could hardly give him pain, for he had no vulnerable points in his character. He had a perfect command of his temper; his anger never proceeded to passion, nor his sense of injury to revenge. If there was occasional asperity in his language, it was easy to see there was no malignity in his disposition. He tasted the good of his existence with cheerful gratitude; how he received its evil has been already intimated.

His fears concerning public affairs did not so much depress his spirits, as awaken his activity to prevent or mitigate, by his warnings and counsels, the disorder of the state. He was deeply anxious for the fortunes of his country, but more intent on rendering it all the service in his power; convinced that, however uncertain may be the events of the future, the present duty is never performed in vain.

J. T. KIRKLAND

PART ONE

ESSAYS

I.

ESSAYS ON
SOCIAL CLASS AND
CHARACTER

———

THE MIRE OF A DEMOCRACY

It has been said that every man may be flattered. A fine understanding may make its possessor shrewd to detect the flatterer's art, and great experience in the world may place suspicion as a sentinel at one's door. All this may increase the difficulty of finding access to a man's vanity, but still it is not inaccessible. There are opinions, which every man wishes every other man to entertain of his merit, temper, or capacity, and he is sure to be pleased when he discovers, or thinks he discovers, that his skilful flatterer really entertains them. He indulges a complacency and kindness towards him, who puts him at peace and in good humour with himself.

Previously published as "The Mire of Democracy," by Lewis P. Simpson, in the anthology The Federalist Literary Mind *(Baton Rouge, Louisiana State University Press), this essay appeared originally in the* Monthly Anthology *of the Boston Athenaeum (1805), vol. II, pp. 563–566, from which it is reprinted in this collection. We express our gratitude to the Henry E. Huntington Library and Art Gallery for making its collection available to us.*

But to flatter the ignorant and inexperienced requires no skill, it scarcely requires any thing more than a disposition to flatter; for with that class of people the very disposition is accepted as an evidence of kindness. It is still easier to make flattery grateful to a multitude, and especially an assembled multitude of such men. No arts are too gross, no topicks of praise disgusting. Popular vanity comes hungry to an election ground, and claims flattery as its proper food. In democracies the people are the depositaries of political power. It is impossible they should exercise it themselves. In such states therefore it is a thing inevitable, that the people should be beset by unworthy flatterers and intoxicated with their philtres. Sudden, blind, and violent in all their impulses, they cannot heap power enough on their favourites, nor make their vengeance as prompt and terrible as their wrath against those, whom genius and virtue have qualified to be their friends and unfitted to be their flatterers. The most skilful sort of flattery is that, which exalts a man in his own estimation by ascribing to his character those qualities, which he is most solicitous to be thought to possess. He mellows into complacency when he finds that his pretensions are rightly understood and cheerfully admitted. As nothing so conspicuously lifts one man above every other man in society as power, of course it is of all topicks of praise the most fascinating and irresistible. When therefore a demagogue invites the ignorant multitude to dwell on the contemplation of their sovereignty, to consider princes as their equals, their own magistrates as their servants and their flatterers, however otherwise distinguished in the world as their slaves, is it to be supposed that aristocratic good sense will be permitted to disturb their feast or to dishonour their triumph? Accordingly we know from history, and we might know if we would from a scrutiny into the human heart, that every democracy, in the very infancy of its vicious and troubled life, is delivered bound hand and foot into the keeping of ambitious dema-

4

gogues. Their ambition will soon make them rivals, and their bloody discords will surely make one of them a tyrant.

But the fate of democracies, which every man of sense will deem irreversibly fixed, is not so much the object of these remarks as the complexion of popular opinions while they last.

They will all be such as the multitude have an interest, or which is the same thing a pleasure, in believing. Of these, one of the dearest and most delusive is, that the power of the people is their liberty. Yet they can have no liberty without many strong and obnoxious restraints upon their power.

To break down these restraints, to remove these courts and judges, these senates and constitutions, which are insolently as well as artfully raised above the people's heads to keep them out of their reach, will always be the interested counsel of demagogues and the welcome labour of the multitude. The actual state of popular opinion will be ever hostile to the real and efficient securities of the publick liberty. The spirit of '76 is yet invoked by the democrats, because they, erroneously enough, understand it as a spirit to subvert an old government, and not to preserve old rights. Of all flattery, the grossest (gross indeed to blasphemy) is, that the voice of the people is the voice of God; that the opinion of a majority like that of the Pope, is infallible. Hence it is, that the public tranquillity has, and the democrats say ought to have, no more stable basis than popular caprice; hence compacts and constitutions are deemed binding only so long as they are liked by a majority. The temple of the public liberty has no better foundation, than the shifting sands of the desert. It is apparent then that pleasing delusions must become popular creeds. After habit has made praise one of the wants of vanity, it cannot be expected that reproof will be sought or endured, a stomach spoiled by sweets will loathe its medicines. Prudence and duty will be silent.

An individual rarely passes unpunished, who forms and prosecutes his plan of life under a great mistake of his own qualifications and character. And shall a democracy, which is sure to overstretch its rights, to despise its duties, to entrust its traitors and persecute its patriots, to demolish its own bulwarks and invite the host of its assailants to come in, shall such a system last long, or enjoy any degree of tranquillity while it lasts? It is impossible.

Nevertheless, it is assumed as a position of uncontested authority, that the discontents of the people never ripen into resistance and revolution, unless from the oppression and vices of their government. The people are alleged to be always innocent when they refuse evidence, the government is almost always culpable when it exacts it. It may be admitted that no ordinary pressure of grievances would impel a people to rise against government, when that government is possessed of great strength, and is administered with vigour. It cannot be supposed that men conscious of their weakness will attack a superiour power. Yet oppression may at length make a whole nation mad, and when it is perceived that the physical strength is all on one side the political authority will inspire no terror.

But surely there is no analogy between such a government and a democracy. As the force of this latter depends on opinion, and that opinion shifts with every current of caprice, it will not be pretended that the propensity to change is produced only by the vices of the magistrates or the rigour of the laws, that the people can do no wrong when they respect no right, and that the authority of their doings, whether they act for good cause or no cause at all but their own arbitrary pleasure, is a new foundation of right, the more sacred for being new.

To guard against this experienced and always fatal propensity of republics to change and destroy, our sages in the great Convention devised the best distribution of power into separate departments, that circumstances permitted them to select. They intended our government should be a *republic*, which differs more widely from a democracy than a democracy from a despotism. The rigours of a despotism often, perhaps most frequently, oppress only a few, but it is of the very essence and nature of a democracy, for a faction claiming to be a majority to oppress a minority, and that minority the chief owners of the property and the truest lovers of their country. Already the views of the framers of the Constitution are disappointed. The Judiciary is prostrate. Amendments are familiarly resorted to for the purpose of an election, or to wreak the vengeance of an angry demagogue upon the senate. We are sliding down into the mire of a democracy, which pollutes the morals of the citizens before it swallows up their liberties. Our vanity is the parent of our errors, and these, now grown vices, will be the artificers of our fate.

NO REVOLUTIONIST

The Palladium, NOVEMBER 13, 1801

MANY PERSONS seem to despair of the Commonwealth. They say, it is evident, a violent jacobin administration is begun. The address to the popular passions, they argue, is generally successful; and always very encouragingly rejected, even when it is not. While federalists rely on the sense of the people, the jacobins appeal to their nonsense with infinite advantage; they affect to be entirely on the people's side; and their mistake, if by great good luck it is supposed they err, is ascribed to a good motive, in a manner and spirit that invites fresh attempts to deceive. Thus the deceivers of the people tire out their adversaries; they try again and again; and an attempt that is never abandoned, at last will not fail. What, then, it is asked, can be done? We have an enlightened people who are not poor, and therefore are interested to keep jacobinism down, which ever seeks plunder as the end, and confusion as the means. Yet the best informed of this mighty people are lazy, or ambitious, and go over to the cause of confusion; or are artfully rendered unpopular, because they will not go over to it. The sense, and virtue, and property of the nation, therefore, will not govern it; but every day shows that its vice, and poverty, and ambition will. We have been mistaken. In our affairs, we have only thought of what was to be hindered, and provided sufficiently for nothing that was to be done. We have thought that virtue, with so many bright rewards, had some solid power; and that, with ten thousand charms, she could always command a hundred thousand votes. Alas! these illusions are as thin as the gloss on other bubbles. Politicians have supposed that man really is what he should be; that his reason will do all it can, and his passions and prejudice no more than they ought; whereas his reason is a mere looker-on; it is moderation, when it should be zeal; is often corrupted to vindicate, where it should condemn; and is a coward or a trimmer that will take hush-money. Popular reason does not always know how to act right, nor does it always act right when it knows. The agents that move politics are the popular passions; and those are ever, from the very nature of things, under the command of the disturbers of society. While those who would defend order, and property, and right, the real friends of law and liberty, have a great deal to say to silence passion, but nothing to offer that will satisfy it; nothing that will convince a *sans-culotte* that his ignorance, or vice, and laziness, ordain that he should be poor, while a demagogue tells him it is the funding system that makes him poor, and revolution shall make him rich. Few can reason, all can feel; and such an argument is gained, as soon as it is proposed. While, then, the popular passions are sure to govern, and the reason of the society is sure to be awed into silence, or to be disregarded, if it is heard, what hope is there that our course will not be as headlong, as rapid, and as fatal, as that of every government by mere popular impulse has ever been? The turnpike road of history is white with the tombstones of such republics.

Answer.—If our government must fall, as it may very deplorably, and soon, and as it certainly must with a violent jacobin administration, let the monstrous wickedness of working its downfall really be, and appear, if possible, to the whole people to be chargeable to the jacobins. Let the federalists cling to it, while it has life in it, and even longer than there is hope. Let them be auxiliary to its virtues; let them contend for its corpse, as for the body of Patroclus,[1] and let them reverence its memory. Let them delay, if they cannot prevent, its fate; and let them endeavor so to animate, instruct, and combine the true friends of liberty, that a new republican system may be raised on the foundations of the present government. Despair not only hastens the evil, but renders any remedy unavailing. Time, that soothes all other sufferings, will bring no relief to us, if we neglect or throw away the means in our hands. What are they? Truth and argument. They are feeble means, feeble indeed, against prejudice and passion; yet they are all we have, and we must try them. They will be jury-masts, if we are shipwrecked.

The managers of the plan of confusion, are not numerous; for that reason, they are the better united. They are a desperate gang, chiefly resident in the city of New York, in

---

[1] *See Homer's* Iliad, *books XVII–XVIII.*

Pennsylvania, and Virginia. No men on earth more despise democracy; or are more overbearing in their dispositions; or form vaster plans of personal aggrandizement. Yet, as they have need of the democrats, who are more numerous, are honester, and more in credit than the jacobins, they are obliged to make use of them. They flatter and deceive, and will surely betray them, as Cromwell and the independents did the presbyterians, in 1648, in England.

They will abolish credit, by taxing the funds; they will abolish justice, by transferring the judiciary to the states, that is, to Virginia. They will push on the democratic traders to do violent things, which will surely make them odious; and then they will expect, that the resentments of the honest federalists will assist the jacobins to supplant the democrats. The ruling party contains within itself the seeds of discord; yet, though the revolutionary spirit, once indulged, naturally leads to changes, they are sure to be changes for the worse; a more violent faction will dispossess one that is moderate.

The question, therefore, seems to be, how far we shall probably travel in the revolutionary road; and whether there is any stopping place, any hope of taking breath, as we run towards the bottomless pit, into which the revolutionary fury is prone to descend. France had twenty-three millions poor, and one million rich; America has twenty-three persons at ease, to one in want. Our rabble is not numerous; and a reform in our elections ought to exclude those who have nothing, or almost nothing, from the control of every thing. Our assailants are therefore weaker, and our means of defence greater than the first patriots of France possessed; our good men, instead of running away, like the French emigrants, and giving up their estates to confiscation, must stay at home, and exert their talents and influence to save the country. Events may happen to baffle the schemes of jacobinism; and if New England should not be sleepy or infatuated, of which there is, unhappily, great danger, our adversaries will never be able to push the work of mischief to its consummation.

SCHOOL BOOKS

The Palladium, JANUARY, 27, 1801

IT HAS BEEN THE CUSTOM, of late years, to put a number of little books into the hands of children, containing fables and moral lessons. This is very well, because it is right first to raise curiosity, and then to guide it. Many books for children are, however, judiciously compiled; the language is too much raised above the ideas of that tender age; the moral is drawn from the fable, they know not why; and when they gain wisdom from experience, they will see the restrictions and exceptions which are necessary to the rules of conduct laid down in their books, but which such books do not give. Some of the most admired works of this kind abound with a frothy sort of *sentiment,* as the readers of novels are pleased to call it, the chief merit of which consists in shedding tears, and giving away money. Is it right, or agreeable to good sense, to try to make the tender age more tender? Pity and generosity, though amiable impulses, are blind ones, and as we grow older are to be managed by rules, and restrained by wisdom.

It is not clear that the heart, at thirty, is any the softer for weeping, at ten, over one of Berquin's fables, the point of which turns on a beggar boy's being ragged, and a rich man's son being well clad. Some persons, indeed, appear to have shed all their tears of sympathy before they reach the period of mature age. Most young hearts are tender, and tender enough; the object of education is rather to direct these emotions, however amiable, than to augment them.[2]

[2] *Probably Arnaud Berquin, (ca.) 1749–1791.* The Looking Glass for the Mind . . . Stories and Tales Chiefly translated from L'Ami des Enfants.

Why then, if these books for children must be retained, as they will be, should not the Bible regain the place it once held as a school book? Its morals are pure, its examples captivating and noble. The reverence for the sacred book that is thus early impressed lasts long; and probably, if not impressed in infancy, never takes firm hold of the mind. One consideration more is important. In no book is there so good English, so pure and so elegant; and by teaching all the same book, they will speak alike, and the Bible will justly remain the standard of language as well as of faith. A barbarous provincial jargon will be banished, and taste, corrupted by pompous Johnsonian affectation, will be restored.

HERCULES

The Palladium, OCTOBER, 1801

TO PRINTERS:

IT SEEMS as if newspaper wares were made to suit a market, as much as any other. The starers, and wonderers, and gapers, engross a very large share of the attention of all the sons of the type. Extraordinary events multiply upon us surprisingly. Gazettes, it is seriously to be feared, will not long allow room to any thing that is not loathsome or shocking. A newspaper is pronounced to be very lean and destitute of matter, if it contains no account of murders, suicides, prodigies, or monstrous births.

Some of these tales excite horror, and others disgust; yet the fashion reigns, like a tyrant, to relish wonders, and almost to relish nothing else. Is this a reasonable taste? or is it monstrous and worthy of ridicule? Is the History of Newgate the only one worth reading? Are oddities only to be hunted? Pray tell us, men of ink, if our free presses are to diffuse *information*, and we, the poor ignorant people, can get it no other way than by newspapers, what knowledge we are to glean from the blundering lies, or the tiresome truths about thunder storms, that, strange to tell! kill oxen or burn barns; and cats, that bring two-headed kittens; and sows, that eat their own pigs? The crowing of a hen is supposed to forebode cuckoldom; and the ticking of a little bug in the wall threatens yellow fever. It seems really as if our newspapers were busy to spread superstition. Omens, and dreams, and prodigies, are recorded, as if they were worth minding. One would think our gazettes were intended for Roman readers, who were silly enough to make account of such things. We ridicule the papists for their credulity; yet, if all the trumpery of our papers is believed, we have little right to laugh at any set of people on earth; and if it is not believed, why is it printed?

Surely extraordinary events have not the best title to our studious attention. To study nature or man, we ought to know things that are in the ordinary course, not the unaccountable things that happen out of it.

This country is said to measure seven hundred millions of acres, and is inhabited by almost six millions of people. Who can doubt, then, that a great many crimes will be committed, and a great many strange things will happen, every seven years? There will be thunder showers, that will split tough white oak trees; and hail storms, that will cost some farmers the full amount of *twenty shillings* to mend their glass windows; there will be taverns, and boxing matches, and elections, and gouging and drinking, and love and murder, and running in debt, and running away, and suicide. Now, if a man *supposes* eight, or ten, or twenty dozen of these amusing

13

events will happen in a single year, is he not just as wise as another man, who reads fifty columns of amazing particulars, and, of course, *knows* that they have happened?

This state has almost one hundred thousand dwelling houses; it would be strange if all of them should escape fire for twelve months. Yet is it very profitable for a man to become a deep student of all the accidents by which they are consumed? He should take good care of his chimney corner, and put a fender before the back-log, before he goes to bed. Having done this, he may let his aunt or grandmother read by day, or meditate by night, the terrible newspaper articles of fires; how a maid dropped asleep reading a romance, and the bed clothes took fire; how a boy, searching in a garret for a hoard of nuts, kindled some flax; and how a mouse, warming his tail, caught it on fire, and carried it into his hole in the floor.

Some of the shocking articles in the papers raise simple, and very simple, wonder; some terror; and some horror and disgust. Now what instruction is there in these endless wonders? Who is the wiser or happier for reading the accounts of them? On the contrary, do they not shock tender minds, and addle shallow brains? They make a thousand old maids, and eight or ten thousand booby boys, afraid to go to bed alone. Worse than this happens; for some eccentric minds are turned to mischief by such accounts as they receive of troops of incendiaries burning our cities: the spirit of imitation is contagious; and boys are found unaccountably bent to do as men do. When the man flew from the steeple of the North church fifty years ago, every unlucky boy thought of nothing but flying from a sign-post.

It was once a fashion to stab heretics; and Ravaillac, who stabbed Henry the Fourth of France, the assassin of the Duke of Guise, and of the Duke of Buckingham, with many others, only followed the fashion. Is it not in the power of newspapers to spread fashions; and by dinning burnings and murders in everybody's ears, to detain all rash and mischievous tempers on such subjects, long enough to wear out the first impression of horror, and to prepare them to act what they so familiarly contemplate? Yet there seems to be a sort of rivalship among printers, who shall have the most wonders, and the strangest and most horrible crimes. This taste will multiply prodigies. The superstitious Romans used to forbid reports of new prodigies, while they were performing sacrifices on such accounts.

Every horrid story in a newspaper produces a shock; but, after some time, this shock lessens. At length, such stories are so far from giving pain, that they rather raise curiosity, and we desire nothing so much as the particulars of terrible tragedies. The wonder is as easy as to stare; and the most vacant mind is the most in need of such resources as cost no trouble of scrutiny or reflection; it is a sort of food for idle curiosity that is readily chewed and digested.

On the whole, we may insist that the increasing fashion for printing wonderful tales of crimes and accidents is worse than ridiculous, as it corrupts both the public taste and morals. It multiplies fables, prodigious monsters, and crimes, and thus makes shocking things familiar; while it withdraws all popular attention from familiar truth, because it is not shocking.

Now, Messrs. Printers, I pray the whole honorable craft to banish as many murders, and horrid accidents, and monstrous births and prodigies from their gazettes, as their readers will permit them; and, by degrees, to coax them back to contemplate life and manners; to consider common events with some common sense; and to study nature where she can be known, rather than in those of her ways where she really is, or is represented to be, inexplicable.

Strange events are facts, and as such should be mentioned, but with brevity and in a cursory manner. They afford no ground for popular reasoning or instruction; and, therefore, the horrid details that make each particular hair stiffen and stand upright in the reader's head ought not to be given. In short, they must be mentioned; but sensible printers and sensible readers will think that way of mentioning them the best that impresses them least on the public attention, and that hurries them on the most swiftly to be forgotten.

FALKLAND IV

The Palladium, FEBRUARY 13, 1801

TO NEW ENGLAND MEN:

THE PROJECT of transmuting the classes of American citizens, and converting sailors into backwoodsmen, is not too monstrous for speculatists to conceive and to desire; but it is too vast for such men, and especially in four years, to accomplish. They are not of the race of the Titans. They cannot pluck up the iron-bound shores, with all their towns, and plant them on the Miami; and as long as the sea washes these shores, our citizens will be navigators, and will claim protection in a tone that will not be soothed by the answer, that a navy is expensive, or that the wilderness stretches out its welcome arms to receive them. They will reply, so does death its more welcome arms.

The maritime interest of New England is very essential to the existence of every other. If it really is not, it is pretty extensively believed to be, the root of our prosperity. Laying, or threatening to lay the axe to that root, would excite such an opposition as would deter the most vigorous despotism from its purpose.

In prosperous times, when men feel the greatest ardor in

their pursuits of gain, they manifest the most callous apathy to politics. Those who possess nothing, and have nothing to do but to manage the intrigues of elections, will prevail against five times their number of men of business. Each description is actuated by strong passions, moving in different, but not opposite directions. When, however, some of the great interests of society are invaded, those passions change their direction and are quickened in it. They are then capable of defending themselves with all the vivacity of the spirit of gain and of enterprise, with all the energies of vengeance and despair. These, it must be confessed, are revolutionary resources, for the defence of property and right, which cannot and ought not to be called forth on ordinary occasions. The classes in question will be long in danger, before they will be in fear; and if their adversary forbears to push the attack in so rude a manner as to make that fear overpower all other emotions, he may proceed, unsuspected and unopposed. They will be as much engrossed with their business, as the political projectors with their plans of reforming, till they destroy it. It is probable, therefore, that the maritime interest of the Eastern States is scarcely yet beginning to suffer apprehension, or to think of measures of precaution. It will seem incredible to the concerned, that interests so precious should appear of small value even to illuminists and reformers. They will not believe that the jacobin Catilines could be vile or daring enough to assail them. They will say, supposing the new president to be fond of power, it cannot be the interest of his ambition to prosecute the attack, as it would expose his four years' administration to the most dreadful agitations, and animate against himself, personally, enemies by classes and hosts, whom he could not expect ever to pacify, nor always to overpower. They will, therefore, feel a sanguine confidence, that banks and debts, public and private, manufactures, navigation, and the fisheries, will be sure of tranquility, and almost sure of patronage. It would extend these pages too far to examine in detail the grounds of this confidence. It will be sufficient briefly to observe, that it may be true, and perhaps it is, as the democrats pledged themselves for the event, that the new president will be averse from violent counsels; that he is so from principle, character, and policy, and that the new men will pursue the old measures. Yet it ought to be remembered that the head of the party cannot wholly reject, nor, perhaps, very materially alter, the system prescribed to him by his political supporters. If he does, he will be a federalist. If he will support principles, they will not oppose him; they will not, like the jacobins, oppose for opposition sake. But, to gain their confidence, he must give them the evidence of facts; he must act right. For confidence grows, if at all, without artificial culture; it will not bear the forcing of a hothouse. Like a shrub on the high peak of a mountain, where it seldom rains, it absorbs the dew, and though it grows not much in a year, and is never lofty, its roots striking deeper than its top branches, yet it grows for an age, and braves the tempests; while the weeds of popularity have tall, weak stems, from the rankness of their growth, and perish on the dunghills that they sprout from.

If he should cling with fond zeal to the schemes of his old friends, the president will be strongly impelled by the party current, and if he yields to it, he will soon cease to be their leader and become their instrument. Indeed there are but two divisions of party in the United States; and he is a very weak or very presumptuously vain man, who can think of organizing a third party, that shall rule them both. Those who possess property, who enjoy rights, and who reverence the laws as the guardians of both, naturally think it important, and, what is better, feel the necessity of sustaining the controlling and restraining power of the state; in other words, their interests and wishes are on the side of justice, because justice will secure to every man his own. This is federalism. On the other hand, those who do not know what right is, or if they do, despise it; who have no interest in justice, because they have little for it to secure, and that little, perhaps, its impartial severity would transfer to creditors; who see in the mild aspect of our government a despot's frown, and a dagger in its hand, while it scatters blessings; who consider government as an impediment to liberty, and the stronger the government, the stronger the impediment; that it is patriotism, virtue, heroism to surmount it; that liberty is to be desired for its abstract excellence, rather than its practical benefits, and therefore, that it is better to run the hazard of the greatest possible degree of a perishable liberty, rather than to accept it with those guards and defences, which to insane theorists seem to make it less, but which, on the just analogies of experience, promise to make it immortal; those, in a word, who look on government with fear and aversion, on the relaxation or subversion of it with complacency and hope; all who from credulity, envy, anger, and pride, from ambition or cupidity, are impatient under the restraints, or eager for the trappings of power,—all such reason, when they can, and act, and feel in a manner unfavorable to the support of the Constitution and laws. Their opinions and creeds are various, and many of them are plausible, and seem to be moderate. It is probable they would all, except the leaders, at present incline to stop short of the extremes, to which the first steps are not perceived to tend, but which, when they are taken, are inevitable. They are impelled by a common instinct, as blind as it is steady and powerful in its action. They are, by nature, instinct, habit, and interest, opposers of the government. They consist of four classes, antifederalists, democrats, anarchists, and jacobins, exceedingly unlike in character and in views, yet, while they are all out of power, harmoniously concurring to promote the common cause; once in power, it is probable they would disagree. There can, of course, exist but two political divisions in the country; to help, or to hinder the administration of its government. This description is so comprehensive as to embrace all the active citizens, and leaves, for the formation of a third party, neither materials, artificers, nor object.

Some very vain and some weak men, and some very great hypocrites, pretend to be of no party; while they arrogate to themselves a discernment superior to both parties, they affect to be neutral and undecided between them. They claim the title of the truest patriots, and to love their country with the ardor of passion, yet they inconsistently condemn the violence of both parties, and expect to have both believe that the fire of their zeal subsists, pure and unexpended, in the frost of moderation. Such men are often flattered as federalists, more often used as democrats, but always held in a contempt, that is never more hearty than when it is discreetly suppressed.

Whoever is president will have too much sense to denounce both parties, and to think of poising his weight exactly between two supports, but resting upon neither. We know already that this policy, if it may be called such, will not be adopted by either of the two successful candidates. He will shape his system according to the federal or democratic plan; he will adhere either to the restraining doctrines, or to those which counteract restraint; he must either serve God or Mammon. The Washington and Adams administration proceeded on the basis, that the government was organized, and clothed with power to rule according to the Constitution; the democratic theorists insist, that the people, meaning themselves, have a good right to rule the government.

By exciting the people to govern or to oppose government, these leaders well know, that those who are thus irregularly permitted to act in their behalf, will engross all their power. Against this natural propensity to faction, a regular and vigorous government is the proper and only adequate security. Of course, for that very reason, such a government will be hateful to faction, and will be, if possible, usurped and destroyed by it. For such usurpation the nature of liberty excites the desire, and affords the pretext and the means.

Accordingly we have seen a faction bitter against the Constitution in its passage, against the government in its administering the laws, and the magistrates and officers intrusted with the execution of them. They have struggled for the mastery, and, after a persevering effort for twelve years, they have succeeded in the late great election. Will this party acquiesce, if the mere change of men should be the only fruit of their victory? No, the nature of faction itself, our observation of jacobinism in France, our knowledge of jacobin characters at home, forbid the idea. They will be greater malcontents than ever, if new men should pursue old measures. Few can be so absurd as to expect office; multitudes do expect a political millennium. Taxes are to be abolished; the occasions for taxes are to be forever removed; armies are to be no more raised; navies will be reduced, reduced as soon as it can be made tolerably safe and popular, to nothing; interest on the public debt is to be reduced gradually, but at the pleasure of those who think the principal a fraud and a curse, an avenging devil, and a tempter. Hopes like these are to be disappointed or gratified. The president will know that it is impossible to do all that is expected, but he will readily undertake to do something, that every thing may not be required of him. He will recommend economy, and profess the profoundest reverence for the sense of the people, which the united Irishmen will of course apply to themselves. He will keep in office such federalists as are willing to stay, and lend a prismatic light of contrasted colors to his administration. He will appoint a Livingston and a Gallatin to office.

He will lavish his smiles on federalists, and his confidence on two or three select democrats, and will be very glad, perhaps, to get on his four years' political journey in this seemingly equivocal manner as a president,

> Placed on the isthmus of a middle state,
> A being darkly wise and rudely great.

But if this would do for him it would not answer for his party; they will expect much and attempt every thing.

AMERICAN LITERATURE

FEW SPECULATIVE SUBJECTS have exercised the passions more or the judgment less, than the inquiry, what rank our country is to maintain in the world for genius and literary attainments. Whether in point of intellect we are equal to Europeans, or only a race of degenerate creoles; whether our artists and authors have already performed much and promise every thing; whether the muses, like the nightingales, are too delicate to cross the salt water, or sicken and mope without song if they do, are themes upon which we Americans are privileged to be eloquent and loud. It might indeed occur to our discretion, that as the only admissible proof of literary excellence is the measure of its effects, our national claims ought to be abandoned as worthless the moment they are found to need asserting.

Nevertheless, by a proper spirit and constancy in praising ourselves, it seems to be supposed, the doubtful title of our vanity may be quieted in the same manner as it was once believed the currency of the continental paper could, by a universal agreement, be established at par with specie. Yet such was the unpatriotic perverseness of our citizens, they preferred the gold and silver, for no better reason than because the paper bills were not so good. And now it may happen, that from spite or envy, from want of attention or the want of our sort of information, foreigners will dispute the claims of our preëminence in genius and literature, notwithstanding the great convenience and satisfaction we should find in their acquiescence.

In this unmanageable temper or indocile ignorance of Europe, we may be under the harsh necessity of submitting our pretensions to a scrutiny; and as the world will judge of the matter with none of our partiality, it may be discreet to anticipate that judgment, and to explore the grounds upon which it is probable the aforesaid world will frame it. And after all, we should suffer more pain than loss, if we should in the event be stripped of all that does not belong to us; and especially if, by a better knowledge of ourselves, we should gain that modesty which is the first evidence, and perhaps the last, of a real improvement. For no man is less likely to increase his knowledge than the coxcomb, who fancies he has already learned out. An excessive national vanity, as it is the sign of mediocrity, if not of barbarism, is one of the greatest impediments to knowledge.

It will be useless and impertinent to say, a greater proportion of our citizens have had instruction in schools than can be found in any European state. It may be true that neither France nor England can boast of so large a portion of their population who can read and write, and who are versed in the profitable mystery of the rule of three. This is not the footing upon which the inquiry is to proceed. The question is not, what proportion are stone blind, or how many can see, when the sun shines, but what geniuses have arisen among us, like the sun and stars to shed life and splendor on our hemisphere.

This state of the case is no sooner made, than all the firefly tribe of our authors perceive their little lamps go out of themselves, like the flame of a candle when lowered into the mephitic vapor of a well. Excepting the writers of two able works on our politics, we have no authors. To enter the lists in single combat against Hector, the Greeks did not offer the lots to the nameless rabble of their soldiery; all eyes were turned upon Agamemnon and Ajax, upon Diomed and Ulysses. Shall we match Joel Barlow against Homer or Hesiod? Can Thomas Paine contend against Plato? Or could Findley's history of his own insurrection vie with Sallust's narrative of Catiline's? There is no scarcity of spelling-book makers, and authors of twelve-cent pamphlets; and we have a distinguished few, a sort of literary nobility, whose works have grown to the dignity and size of an octavo volume. We have many writers who have read, and who have the sense to understand, what others have written. But a right perception of the genius of others is not genius; it is a sort of business talent, and will not be wanting where there is much occasion for its exercise. Nobody will pretend that the Americans are a stupid race; nobody will deny that we justly boast of many able men, and exceedingly useful publications. But has our country produced one great original work of genius? If we tread the sides of Parnassus, we do not climb its heights; we even creep in our path, by the light that European genius has thrown upon it. Is there one luminary in our firmament that shines with unborrowed rays? Do we reflect how many constellations blend their beams in the history of Greece, which will appear bright to the end of time, like the path of the zodiac, bespangled with stars?

If, then, we judge of the genius of our nation by the success with which American authors have displayed it, our country has certainly hitherto no pretensions to literary fame. The world will naturally enough pronounce its opinion, that what we have not performed we are incapable of performing.

It is not intended to proceed in stripping our country's honors off, till every lover of it shall turn with disgust from the contemplation of its nakedness. Our honors have not faded—they have not been won. Genius no doubt exists in our country, but it exists, like the unbodied soul on the stream of Lethe, unconscious of its powers, till the causes to excite and the occasions to display it shall happen to concur.

What were those causes that have forever consecrated the name of Greece? We are sometimes answered, she owes her fame to the republican liberty of the states. But Homer, and Hesiod, to say nothing of Linus, Orpheus, Musæus, and many others, wrote while kings governed those states. Anacreon and Simonides flourished in the court of Pisistratus, who had overthrown the democracy of Athens. Nor, we may add in corroboration, did Roman genius flourish till the republic fell. France and England are monarchies, and they have excelled all modern nations by their works of genius. Hence we have a right to conclude the form of government has not a decisive, and certainly not an exclusive influence, on the literary eminence of a people.

If climate produces genius, how happens it that the great men who reflected such honor on their country appeared only in the period of a few hundred years before the death of Alexander? The melons and figs of Greece are still as fine as ever; but where are the Pindars?

In affairs that concern morals, we consider the approbation of a man's own conscience as more precious than all human rewards. But in the province of the imagination, the applause of others is of all excitements the strongest. This excitement is the cause; excellence, the effect. When every thing concurs, and in Greece every thing did concur, to augment its power, a nation wakes at once from the sleep of ages. It would seem as if some Minerva, some present divinity, inhabited her own temple in Athens, and by flashing light and working miracles had conferred on a single people, and almost on a single age of that people, powers that are denied to other men and other times. The admiration of posterity is excited and overstrained by an effulgence of glory, as much beyond our comprehension as our emulation. The Greeks seem to us a race of giants, Titans, the rivals, yet the favorites of their gods. We think their apprehension was quicker, their native taste more refined, their prose poetry, their poetry music, their music enchantment. We imagine they had more expression in their faces, more grace in their movements, more sweetness in the tones of conversation than the moderns. Their fabulous deities are supposed to have left their heaven to breathe the fragrance of their groves, and to enjoy the beauty of their landscapes. The monuments of heroes must have excited to heroism; and the fountains, which the muses had chosen for their purity, imparted inspiration.

It is indeed almost impossible to contemplate the bright ages of Greece, without indulging the propensity to enthusiasm.

We are ready to suspect the delusion of our feelings, and to ascribe its fame to accident, or to causes which have spent their force. Genius, we imagine, is forever condemned to inaction by having exhausted its power, as well as the subjects upon which it has displayed itself. Another Homer or Virgil could only copy the Iliad and Æneid; and can the second poets, from cinders and ashes, light such a fire as still glows in the writings of the first. Genius, it will be said, like a conflagration on the mountains, consumes its fuel in its flame. Not so. It is a spark of elemental fire that is unquenchable, the contemporary of this creation, and destined with the human soul to survive it. As well might the stars of heaven be said to expend their substance by their lustre. It is to the intellectual world what the electric fluid is to nature, diffused everywhere, yet almost everywhere hidden, capable by its own mysterious laws of action and by the very breath of applause, that like the unseen wind excites it, of producing effects that appear to transcend all power, except that of some supernatural agent riding in the whirlwind. In an hour of calm we suddenly hear its voice, and are moved with the general agitation. It smites, astonishes, and confounds, and seems to kindle half the firmament.

It may be true, that some departments in literature are so filled by the ancients, that there is no room for modern excellence to occupy. Homer wrote soon after the heroic ages, and the fertility of the soil seemed in some measure to arise from its freshness: it had never borne a crop. Another Iliad would not be undertaken by a true genius, nor equally interest this age, if he executed it. But it will not be correct to say, the field is reduced to barrenness from having been overcropped. Men have still imagination and passions, and they can be excited. The same causes that made Greece famous, would, if they existed here, quicken the clods of our valleys, and make our Bœotia sprout and blossom like their Attica.

In analyzing genius and considering how it acts, it will be proper to inquire how it is acted upon. It feels the power it exerts, and its emotions are contagious, because they are fervid and sincere. A single man may sit alone and meditate, till he fancies he is under no influence but that of reason. Even in this opinion, however, he will allow too little for prejudice and imagination; and still more must be allowed when he goes abroad and acts in the world. But masses and societies of men are governed by their passions.

The passion that acts the strongest, when it acts at all, is fear; for in its excess, it silences all reasoning and all other passions. But that which acts with the greatest force, because it acts with the greatest constancy, is the desire of consideration. There are very few men who are greatly deceived with respect to their own measure of sense and abilities, or who are much dissatisfied on that account; but we scarcely see any who are quite at ease about the estimate that other people make of them. Hence it is, that the great business of mankind is to fortify or create claims to general regard. Wealth procures respect, and more wealth would procure more respect. The man who, like Midas, turns all he touches into gold, who is oppressed and almost buried in its super-fluity, who lives to get, instead of getting to live, and at length belongs to his own estate and is its greatest encumbrance, still toils and contrives to accumulate wealth, not because he is deceived in regard to his wants, but because he knows and feels, that one of his wants, which is insatiable, is that respect which follows its possession. After engrossing all that the seas and mountains conceal, he would be still unsatisfied, and with some good reason, for of the treasures of esteem who can ever have enough? Who would mar or renounce one half his reputation in the world?

At different times, the opinions of men in the same country will vary with regard to the objects of prime consideration, and in different countries there will ever be a great difference; but that which is the first object of regard will be the chief object of pursuit. Men will be most excited to excel in that department which offers to excellence the highest reward in the respect and admiration of mankind. It was this strongest of all excitements that stimulated the literary ages of Greece.

In the heroic times, it is evident, violence and injustice prevailed. The state of society was far from tranquil or safe. Indeed, the traditional fame of the heroes and demigods is founded on the gratitude that was due for their protection against tyrants and robbers. Thucydides tells us, that companies of travellers were often asked whether they were thieves. Greece was divided into a great number of states, all turbulent, all martial, always filled with emulation, and often with tumult and blood. The laws of war were far more rigorous than they are at present. Each state, and each citizen in the state, contended for all that is dear to man. If victors, they despoiled their enemies of every thing; the property was booty, and the people were made slaves. Such was the condition of the Helots and Messenians under the yoke of Sparta. There was every thing, then, both of terror and ignominy, to rouse the contending states to make every effort to avoid subjugation.

The fate of Platæa, a city that was besieged and taken by the Spartans, and whose citizens were massacred in cold blood, affords a terrible illustration of this remark. The celebrated siege of Troy is an instance more generally known, and no less to the purpose. With what ardent love and enthusiasm the Trojans viewed their Hector, and the Greeks their Ajax and Achilles, is scarcely to be conceived. It cannot be doubted, that to excel in arms was the first of all claims to the popular admiration.

Nor can it escape observation, that in times of extreme danger the internal union of a state would be most perfect. In these days we can have no idea of the ardor of ancient patriotism. A society of no great extent was knit together like one family by the ties of love, emulation, and enthusiasm. Fear, the strongest of all passions, operated in the strongest of all ways. Hence we find, that the first traditions of all nations concern the champions who defended them in war.

This universal state of turbulence and danger, while it would check the progress of the accurate sciences, would greatly extend the dominion of the imagination. It would be deemed of more importance, to rouse or command the feelings of men, than to augment or correct their knowledge.

In this period it might be supposed, that eloquence displayed its power; but this was not the case. Views of refined policy, and calculations of remote consequences were not adapted to the taste or capacity of rude warriors, who did not reason at all, or only reasoned from their passions. The business was not to convince, but to animate; and this was accomplished by poetry. It was enough to inspire the poet's enthusiasm, to know beforehand that his nation would partake it.

Accordingly, the bard was considered as the interpreter and favorite of the gods. His strains were received with equal rapture and reverence as the effusions of an immediate inspiration. They were made the vehicles of their traditions, to diffuse and perpetuate the knowledge of memorable events and illustrious men.

We grossly mistake the matter, if we suppose that poetry was received of old with as much apathy as it is at the present day. Books are now easy of access; and literary curiosity suffers oftener from repletion than from hunger. National events slip from the memory to our records; they miss the heart, though they are sure to reach posterity.

It was not thus the Grecian chiefs listened to Phemius or Demodocus, the bards mentioned by Homer. It was not thus that Homer's immortal verse was received by his countrymen. The thrones of Priam and Agamemnon were both long ago subverted; their kingdoms and those of their conquerors have long since disappeared, and left no wreck nor memorial behind; but the glory of Homer has outlived his country and its language, and will remain unshaken like Teneriffe or Atlas, the ancestor of history, and the companion of time to the end of his course. O! had he in his lifetime enjoyed, though in imagination, but a glimpse of his own glory, would it not have swelled his bosom with fresh enthusiasm, and quickened all his powers? What will not ambition do for a crown? and what crown can vie with Homer's?

Though the art of alphabetic writing was known in the east in the time of the Trojan war, it is nowhere mentioned by Homer, who is so exact and full in describing all the arts he knew. If his poems were in writing, the copies were few; and the knowledge of them was diffused, not by reading, but by the rhapsodists, who made it a profession to recite his verses.

Poetry, of consequence, enjoyed in that age, in respect to the vivacity of its impressions, and the significance of the applauses it received, as great advantages as have ever since belonged to the theatre. Instead of a cold perusal in a closet, or a still colder confinement unread, in a bookseller's shop, the poet saw with delight his work become the instructor of the wise, the companion of the brave and the great. Alexander locked up the Iliad in the precious cabinet of Darius, as a treasure of more value than the spoils of the king of Persia.

But though Homer contributed so much and so early to fix the language, to refine the taste, and inflame the imagination of the Greeks, his work, by its very excellence, seems to have quenched the emulation of succeeding poets to attempt the epic. It was not till long after his age, and by very slow degrees, that Æschylus, Sophocles, and Euripides carried the tragic art to its perfection.

For many hundred years, there seems to have been no other literary taste, and indeed no other literature, than poetry. When there was so much to excite and reward genius, as no rival to Homer appeared, it is a clear proof, that nature did not produce one. We look back on the history of Greece, and the names of illustrious geniuses thicken on the page, like the stars that seem to sparkle in clusters in the sky. But if with Homer's own spirit we could walk the milky-way, we should find that regions of unmeasured space divide the bright luminaries that seem to be so near. It is no reproach to the genius of America, if it does not produce ordinarily such men as were deemed the prodigies of the ancient world. Nature has provided for the propagation of men—giants are rare; and it is forbidden by her laws that there should be races of them.

If the genius of men could have stretched to the giant's size, there was every thing in Greece to nourish its growth and invigorate its force. After the time of Homer, the Olympic and other games were established. All Greece, assembled by its deputies, beheld the contests of wit and valor, and saw statues and crowns adjudged to the victors, who contended for the glory of their native cities as well as for their own. To us it may seem, that a handful of laurel leaves was a despicable prize. But what were the agonies, what the raptures of the contending parties, we may read, but we cannot conceive. That reward, which writers are now little excited to merit, because it is doubtful and distant, "the estate which wits inherit after death," was in Greece a present possession. That public so terrible by its censure, so much more terrible by its neglect, as then assembled in person, and the happy genius who was crowned victor was ready to expire with the transports of his joy.

There is reason to believe, that poetry was more cultivated in those early ages than it ever has been since. The great celebrity of the only two epic poems of antiquity, was owing to the peculiar circumstances of the ages in which Homer and Virgil lived; and without the concurrence of those circumstances their reputation would have been confined to the closets of scholars, without reaching the hearts and kindling the fervid enthusiasm of the multitude. Homer wrote of war to heroes and their followers, to men who felt the military passion stronger than the love of life; Virgil, with art at least equal to his genius, addressed his poem to Romans, who loved their country with sentiment, with passion, with fanaticism. It is scarcely possible, that a modern epic poet should find a subject that would take such hold of the heart, for no such subject worthy of poetry exists. Commerce has supplanted war, as the passion of the multitude; and the arts have divided and contracted the objects of pursuit. Societies are no longer under the power of single passions, that once flashed enthusiasm through them all at once like electricity. Now the propensities of mankind balance and neutralize each other, and, of course, narrow the range in which poetry used to move. Its coruscations are confined, like the northern light, to the polar circle of trade and politics, or like a transitory meteor blaze in a pamphlet or magazine.

The time seems to be near, and perhaps is already arrived, when poetry, at least poetry of transcendent merit, will be considered among the lost arts. It is a long time since England has produced a first rate poet. If America has not to boast at all what our parent country boasts no longer, it will not be thought a proof of the deficiency of our genius.

It is a proof that the ancient literature was wholly occupied by poetry, that we are without the works, and indeed without the names, of any other very ancient authors except poets. Herodotus is called the father of history; and he lived and wrote between four and five hundred years after Homer. Thucydides, it is said, on hearing the applauses bestowed at the public games on the recital of the work of Herodotus, though he was then a boy, shed tears of emulation. He afterwards excelled his rival in that species of writing.

Excellent, however, as these Grecian histories will ever be esteemed, it is somewhat remarkable, that political science never received much acquisition in the Grecian democracies. If Sparta should be vouched as an exception to this remark, it may be replied, Sparta was not a democracy. Lest that however should pass for an evasion of the point, it may be further answered, the constitution of Lycurgus seems to have been adapted to Sparta rather as a camp than a society of citizens. His whole system is rather a body of discipline than of laws whose whole object it was, not to refine manners or extend knowledge but to provide for the security of the camp. The citizens, with whom any portion of political power was intrusted, were a military caste or class; and the rigor of Lycurgus's rules and articles was calculated and intended to make them superior to all other soldiers. The same strictness, that for so long a time preserved the Spartan government, secures the subordination and tranquility of modern armies.

33

Sparta was, of course, no proper field for the cultivation of the science of politics. Nor can we believe, that the turbulent democracies of the neighboring states favored the growth of that kind of knowledge, since we are certain it never did thrive in Greece. How could it be, that the assemblies of the people, convened to hear flattery or to lavish the public treasures for plays and shows to amuse the populace, should be any more qualified, than inclined, to listen to political disquisitions, and especially to the wisdom and necessity of devising and putting in operation systematical checks on their own power, which was threatened with ruin by its licentiousness and excess, and which soon actually overthrew it? It may appear bold, but truth and history seem to warrant the assertion, that political science will never become accurate in popular states; for in *them* the most salutary truths must be too offensive for currency or influence.

It may be properly added, and in perfect consistency with the theory before assumed that fear is the strongest of all passions, that in democracies writers will be more afraid *of* the people, than afraid *for* them. The principles indispensable to liberty are not therefore to be discovered, or if discovered, not to be propagated and established in such a state of things. But where the chief magistrate holds the sword, and is the object of reverence, if not of popular fear, the direction of prejudice and feeling will be changed. Supposing the citizens to have privileges, and to be possessed of influence, or in other words, of some power in the state, they will naturally wish so to use the power they have, as to be secure against the abuse of that which their chief possesses; and this universal propensity of the public wishes will excite and reward the genius, that discovers the way in which this may be done. If we know any thing of the true theory of liberty, we owe it to the wisdom, or perhaps more correctly, to the experience of those nations whose public sentiment was employed to check rather than to guide the government.

It is then little to be expected that American writers will add much to the common stock of political information.

It might have been sooner remarked, that the dramatic art has not afforded any opportunities for native writers. It is but lately that we have had theatres in our cities; and till our cities become large, like London and Paris, the progress of taste will be slow, and the rewards of excellence unworthy of the competitions of genius.

Nor will it be charged, as a mark of our stupidity, that we have produced nothing in history. Our own is not yet worthy of a Livy; and to write that of any foreign nation where could an American author collect his materials and authorities? Few persons reflect, that all our universities would not suffice to supply them for such a work as Gibbon's.

The reasons why we yet boast nothing in the abstruse sciences, are of a different and more various nature. Much, perhaps all, that has been discovered in these, is known to some of our literati. It does not appear that Europe is now making any advances. But to make a wider diffusion of these sciences, and to enlarge their circle, would require the learned leisure, which a numerous class enjoy in Europe, but which cannot be enjoyed in America. If wealth is accumulated by commerce, it is again dissipated among heirs. Its transitory nature no doubt favors the progress of luxury, more than the advancement of letters. It has among us no uses to found families, to sustain rank, to purchase power, or to pension genius. The objects on which it must be employed are all temporary, and have more concern with mere appetite or ostentation than with taste or talents. Our citizens have not been accustomed to look on rank or titles, on birth or office, as capable of the least rivalship with wealth, mere wealth, in pretensions to respect. Of course the single passion that engrosses us, the only avenue to consideration and importance in our society, is the accumulation of property; our inclinations cling to gold, and are bedded in it, as deeply as that precious ore in the mine. Covered as our genius is in this mineral crust, is it strange that it does not sparkle? Pressed down to earth, and with the weight of mountains on our heads, is it surprising, that no sons of ether yet have spread their broad wings to the sky, like Jove's own eagle, to gaze undazzled at the sun, or to perch on the top of Olympus, and partake the banquet of the gods?

At present the nature of our government inclines all men to seek popularity, as the object next in point of value to wealth; but the acquisition of learning and the display of genius are not the ways to obtain it. Intellectual superiority is so far from conciliating confidence, that it is the very spirit of a democracy, as in France, to proscribe the aristocracy of talents. To be the favorite of an ignorant multitude, a man must descend to their level; he must desire what they desire, and detest all that they do not approve; he must yield to their prejudices, and substitute them for principles. Instead of enlightening their errors, he must adopt them; he must furnish the sophistry that will propagate and defend them.

Surely we are not to look for genius among demagogues; the man who can descend so low, has seldom very far to descend. As experience evinces that popularity, in other words, consideration and power, is to be procured by the meanest of mankind, the meanest in spirit and understanding, and in the worst of ways, it is obvious, that at present the excitement to genius is next to nothing. If we had a Pindar, he would be ashamed to celebrate our chief, and would be disgraced, if he did. But if he did not, his genius would not obtain his election for a selectman in a democratic town. It is party that bestows emolument, power, and consideration; and it is not excellence in the sciences that obtains the suffrages of party.

But the condition of the United States is changing. Luxury is sure to introduce want; and the great inequalities between the very rich and the very poor will be more conspicuous, and comprehend a more formidable host of the latter. The rabble of great cities is the standing army of ambition. Money will become its instrument, and vice its agent. Every step, (and we have taken many,) towards a more complete, unmixed democracy is an advance towards destruction; it is treading where the ground is treacherous and excavated for an explosion. Liberty has never yet lasted long in a democracy; nor has it ever ended in any thing better than despotism. With the change of our government, our manners and sentiments will change. As soon as our emperor has destroyed his rivals, and established order in his army, he will desire to see splendor in his court, and to occupy his subjects with the cultivation of the sciences.

If this catastrophe of our public liberty should be miraculously delayed or prevented, still we shall change. With the augmentation of wealth, there will be an increase of the numbers who may choose a literary leisure. Literary curiosity will become one of the new appetites of the nation; and as luxury advances, no appetite will be denied. After some ages we shall have many poor and a few rich, many grossly ignorant, a considerable number learned, and a few eminently learned. Nature, never prodigal of her gifts, will produce some men of genius, who will be admired and imitated.

II.

FROM CONFEDERATION

TO NATION

━━━

LUCIUS JUNIUS BRUTUS I

The Independent Chronicle, AT BOSTON,
OCTOBER 12, 1786

Heu, miseri cives
Non hostes, inimicaque castra,
Vestras spes uritis.[3]

MANY FRIENDS of the government seem to think it a duty to practice a little well-intended hypocrisy, when conversing on the subject of the late commotions in the Commonwealth. They seem to think it prudent and necessary to conceal from the people, and even from themselves, the magnitude of the present danger. They affect to hope, that there is not any real disaffection to government among the rioters, and that reason will soon dispel the delusion which has excited them

---

[3] *Alas! suffering citizens*
Neither enemies, nor hostile camps
have laid waste your hopes.

38

to arms. But the present crisis is too important, and appearances too menacing, to admit of pusillanimous councils, and half-way measures. Every citizen has a right to know the truth. It is time to speak out, and to rouse the torpid patriotism of men, who have every thing to lose by the subversion of an excellent Constitution.

The members of the General Court acquired the esteem of the most respectable part of the community, by their wise and manly conduct during the last session; the task before them is now become arduous indeed; the eyes of their country, and of the world, are upon them, while they resolve, either to surrender the Constitution of their country, without an effort, or by exerting the whole force of the State in its defence, to satisfy their constituents, that its fall (if it must fall) was effected by a force, against which all the resources of prudence and patriotism had been called forth in vain.

It will be necessary to consider the nature and probable consequences of the late riots, in order to determine, whether this alternative, to surrender or to defend the Constitution, is now the question before the General Court.

The crime of high treason has not been always supposed to imply the greatest moral turpitude and corruption of mind; but it has ever stood first on the list of civil crimes. In European states, the rebellion of a small number of persons can excite but little apprehension, and no danger; an armed force is there kept up, which can crush tumults almost as soon as they break out; or if a rebellion prevails, the conqueror succeeds to the power and titles of his vanquished competitor. The head of the government is changed; but the government remains.

The crime of levying war against the state is attended with particular aggravations and dangers in this country. Our government has no armed force; it subsists by the supposed approbation of the majority; the first murmurs of sedition excite doubts of that approbation; timid, credulous, and ambitious men concur to magnify the danger. In such a government, the danger is real, as soon as it is dreaded. No sooner is the standard of rebellion displayed, than men of desperate principles and fortunes resort to it; the pillars of government are shaken; the edifice totters from its centre; the foot of a child may overthrow it; the hands of giants cannot rebuild it. For if our government should be destroyed, what but the total destruction of civil society must ensue? A more popular form could not be contrived, nor could it stand; one less popular would not be adopted. The people then, wearied by anarchy, and wasted by intestine war, must fall an easy prey to foreign or domestic tyranny. Besides, our Constitution is the free act of the people; they stand solemnly pledged for its defence, and treason against such a Constitution implies a high degree of moral depravity.

Such are the aggravations of the crime of high treason against the Commonwealth of Massachusetts.

Is it safe, by our timidity and affected moderation, to afford the principal perpetrators of this atrocious crime the prospect of impunity? There are offences which wise nations have supposed it unsafe to pardon. For their forgeries, the benevolent Dodd, and the ingenious Ryland suffered death; the pardon of the one was refused to the tears of a suppliant nation; nor could a monarch's favor save the other from his punishment. This crime against a free Commonwealth, which has no standing military force, will be repeated if it is not punished; witness the increase of insolence and numbers, with which the late riots have succeeded each other. The certainty of punishment is the truest security against crimes; but if a number of individuals are allowed, with impunity, to support by arms their disapprobation of public measures, though the Constitution should remain, yet we shall be cursed with a government by men, and not by laws. The plans of an enlightened and permanent national policy may be defeated by, and in fact must depend upon, the desperate ambition of the worst men in the Commonwealth; upon the convenience of bankrupts and sots, who have gambled or slept away their estates; upon the sophisms of wrong-headed men of some understanding; and upon the prejudices, caprice, and ignorant enthusiasm of a multitude of tavern-haunting politicians, who have none at all. The supreme power of the State will be found to reside with such men; and in making laws, the object will not be the general good, but the will and interest of the vile legislators. This will be a government by men, and the worst of men; and such men, actuated by the strongest passions of the heart, having nothing to lose, and, hoping from the general confusion to reap a copious harvest, will acquire in every society a larger share of influence, than equal property and abilities will give to better citizens. The motives to refuse obedience to government are many and strong; impunity will multiply and enforce them. Many men would rebel, rather than be ruined; but they would rather not rebel than be hanged. The English government may sometimes treat insurrections with lenity, for they dare to punish. But who will impute our forbearance either to prudence or magnanimity?

It need not be observed, that it is rebellion to oppose any of the courts of justice; but opposing the Supreme Court, whose justices are so revered for their great learning and integrity, is known to be high treason by every individual who has mingled with the mob. Many of them have been deluded with the pretence of grievances; but they well know that the method of redress which they have sought is treasonable; they dare to commit the offence, because they believe that government have not the power and spirit to punish them.

This seems therefore to be the time, and perhaps the only time, to revive just ideas of the criminality and danger of treason; for our government to govern; for our rulers to vindicate the violated majesty of a free Commonwealth; to convince the advocates of democracy, that the Constitution may yet be defended, and that it is worth defending; that the supreme power is really held by the legal representatives of the people; that the county conventions and riotous assemblies of armed men shall no longer be allowed to legislate, and to form an *imperium in imperio;* and that the protection of government shall yet be effectually extended to every citizen of the Commonwealth.

In a free government, the reality of grievances is no kind of justification of rebellion. It is hoped that our rulers will act with dignity and wisdom; that they will yield every thing to reason, and refuse every thing to force; that they will not consider any burdens as a grievance which it is the duty of the people to bear; but if the burden is too weighty for them to endure, that they will lighten it; and that they will not descend to the injustice and meanness of purchasing leave to hold their authority by sacrificing a part of the community to the villainy and ignorance of the disaffected.

It may be very proper to use arguments, to publish addresses, and fulminate proclamations against high treason; but the man who expects to disperse a mob of a thousand men, by ten thousand arguments, has certainly never been in one. I have heard it remarked, that men are not to be reasoned out of an opinion that they have not reasoned themselves into. The case, though important, is simple. Government does not subsist by making proselytes to sound reason, or by compromise and arbitration with its members; but by the power of the community compelling the obedience of individuals. If that is not done, who will seek its protection, or fear its vengeance? Government may prevail in the argument, and yet we may lose the Constitution.

We have been told that the hatchet of rebellion would be buried, at least till another occasion shall call it forth, provided all public and private debts be abolished; or, in lieu of such abolition, that a tender act be passed; or an emission of paper money, as a tender for all debts, should be made; or that the courts of justice should be shut, until all grievances are redressed.

Here naturally arise two questions. In strict justice, ought our rulers to adopt either of these measures? And should they adopt either, or all of them, will the energy of government be restored, and the Constitution be preserved?

As to the first question, who is there that keeps company with honest men that will not give scope to the vehement detestation that he bears the idea? Is there a rogue in the State so hardened against shame and conscience that he would consent to be, alone, the author of either of those measures? It is to be hoped that the time is not yet arrived when the government of a free, new people is worse than the worst man in it.

But should government resolve that a measure which is morally wrong is politically right; that it is necessary to sacrifice its friends and advocates to buy a truce from its foes; will those foes, having tasted the sweets of ruling, intermit their enterprises, while there is a remnant of authority left in the State to inflict punishments and to impose taxes, and that authority is no longer formidable by the support of those men whose rights have been already surrendered? Did cowardice, did injustice, ever save a sinking state? Did any man, by giving up a portion of his just right, because he had not courage to maintain it, ever save the residue? The insolence of the aggressor is usually proportioned to the tameness of the sufferer. Every individual has a right to tell his rulers, "I am one of the parties to the constitutional contract. I promised allegiance, and I require protection for my life and property. I am ready to risk both in your defence. I am competent to make my own contracts; and when they are violated to seek their interpretation and redress in the judicial courts. I never gave you a right to interpose in them. Without my consent, or a crime committed, neither you, nor any individual, have a right to my property. I refuse my consent; I am innocent of any crime. I solemnly protest against the transfer of my property to my debtor. An act making paper or swine a tender, is a confiscation of my estate, and a breach of that compact under which I thought I had secured protection. If ye say that the people are distressed, I ask is the proposed relief less distressing? Relieve distress from your own funds; exercise the virtues of charity and compassion at your own charge, as I do. Am I to lose my property, and to be involved in distress, to relieve persons whom I never saw, and who are unworthy of compassion if they accept the dishonest relief? If your virtues lead you to oppress me, what am I to expect from your vices? But if ye will suffer my life to depend upon the mercy of the mob, and my property upon their opinion of the expediency of my keeping it, at least restore me the right which I renounced when I became a citizen, of vindicating my own rights, and avenging my own injuries."

In fine, the public will be convinced that the designs of the rioters are subversive of government; that they have knowingly incurred the penalties of high treason; that arguments will not reach them; will not be understood; if understood will not convince them; and after having gone such lengths, conviction will not disarm them; that if government should reason and deliberate when they ought to act; should choose committees, publish addresses, and do nothing; we shall see our free Constitution expire, the state of nature restored, and our rank among savages taken somewhere below the Oneida Indians. If government should do worse than nothing, should make paper money or a tender act, all hopes of seeing the people quiet and property safe, are at an end. Such an act would be the legal triumph of treason.

But, before we make such a sacrifice, let us consider our force to defend the State. And to direct that force, at the head of the government is a magistrate[4] whose firmness, integrity, and ability are well known. The senate and house

---

[4] *Governor Bowdoin* [S. AMES]

have hitherto deserved the public confidence. Every man of principle and property will give them his most zealous aid. A select corps of militia may easily be formed, of such men as may be trusted; the force of the United States may be relied upon, if needed. The insurgents, without leaders, and without resources, will claim the mercy of the government as soon as vigorous counsels are adopted.

But if the Constitution must fall, let us discharge our duty, and attempt its defence. Let us not furnish our enemies with a triumph, nor the dishonored page of history with evidence that it was formed with too much wisdom to be valued, and required too much virtue to be maintained by its members.

LUCIUS JUNIUS BRUTUS II

The Independent Chronicle, OCTOBER 19, 1786

Quo res summa loco, Panthu?
quam prendimus arcem?
Venit summa dies et
ineluctabile tempus Americae.[5]

TO THE RESPECTABLE MEMBERS OF THE HONORABLE SENATE AND HOUSE OF REPRESENTATIVES:

You are the depositaries of a sacred trust; the ark of the Constitution is in your custody. It is your task to defend it from sacrilege. If the profane hand of treason touch it, let it

---

[5] *Virgil, Aeneid, book II, l. 324: quo res summa loco, Panthu? quam prendimus arcem? . . . venit summa dies et ineluctabile tempus Dardaniae; "Where is the crisis, Panthus? What stronghold are we to seize? . . . It is come—the last day and inevitable hour for Troy." (Fairclough translation) Ames's adaptation presumably means, "What matter is placed foremost, O Panthus? What citadel are we taking? America's last day and ineluctable hour has come."*

45

wither. We believe that your integrity, like your trust, is above all price. It is not enough, however, that you will not betray the Constitution; convince us, that the wisdom of its keepers cannot be overreached; that their fortitude cannot be shaken. If there are any neutrals in the state, suffer not an hour to elapse, before you give them evidence, that you will not neglect, that you cannot abandon, the public defence. They will perceive that safety and duty are on your side. Pardon the writer's warmth; he is, at the same time, a victim of the agonies of despair and the transports of indignation. He contemplates, and he earnestly invites his countrymen to contemplate with him, what the rebels have done, and what the government has foreborne to do; what ought, and what ought not to be done; and what will be the consequence of doing wrong, or of doing nothing.

Let us consider these subjects distinctly; minutely we cannot.

The insurgents have refused the payment of taxes—have neglected to choose representatives—have instituted conventions to find fault with government, and to interfere between the precept of lawful authority, and the obedience of individuals. They have attempted to change the government, to abolish the Senate, one of the eyes of the Commonwealth, and to make the House of Representatives absolute. They declare their purpose of forming a state convention, that they may *seem lawfully* to subvert the laws. They are said to have chosen committees to hold a regular intercourse, and to agree upon common measures with the disaffected in the several counties, and in other states, and are preparing to assume the powers of government. They have dared to call the fulfillment of the most solemn obligations of common honesty and sound policy a grievance; they have poisoned the minds and absolutely turned the heads of the people with false reports, and absurd and wicked principles; and to accomplish their nefarious machinations, have assembled in arms. It is the first time that the people of this state have men in arms to oppose legal authority. They have stopped the courts of law, not excepting the Supreme Court, with all the insolent parade of war. The distribution of justice is confined to a corner of the state, and the only remedy for the public injuries, is patience, or punishment to the aggressors.

At first, they pretended to aim only at the abolition of the Courts of Common Pleas; next, to defend their leaders against prosecutions; when that object ceased to alarm them, that no civil business should be done, and that the militia should disperse without pay; and at last, they were ready to fight for the possession of their adversary's camp. Ready, thus, progressively, for opinion-sake, for indemnity, for motives of policy, for revenge, as a vain point of honour, to embrue their treacherous hands in blood.

The history of man has furnished but few instances, and our own country but one, of individuals forming a society. We here behold, for the first time, the attempt of a part of this community to unorganize government, preferring ferocious independence to civil liberty, combining to seperate [sic], and forming a decompounded mass of repulsive ingredients.

The existence of society is at hazard, and the insurgents, like the Hottentots, when it has been found impracticable to tame, seem prepared to renounce the institutions and duties of cultivated life.

Upon the whole, we may pronounce the rebellion the most radically wicked in its principles and purposes, and the most rapid and audacious in its progress, that ever disturbed the peace of mankind.

Upon this review of the principal transactions against lawful authority, can we believe that they began in August late? That the middle of October is arrived? That the sword of public justice has not yet been drawn, and that a system, or part of a system, has not been hitherto adopted, to suppress the rebellion? We recollect that our worthy first magistrate directed your attendance on the 18th of October. But as the danger became more pressing, you were convened on the 27th of September. It was natural for the public to infer that there was a necessity, *without delay, and before the 18th of October,* to provide for the public safety; otherwise, the Governor would not have called you together before the last mentioned day.

But the 18th of October is arrived, and the business for which you were convened is no more advanced than it would have been, had the precept for your meeting on that day, continued in force.

Still, however, we remain persuaded, that we may depend upon the strenuous exertions of a large and respectable majority in both houses. Many of that majority are possessed of abilities, of incorruptable [*sic*] integrity—of personal courage.

Respectable fellow-citizens, indulge the expostulations of a subject whose heart is with you.

The ensigns of rebellion having been triumphantly waved in five counties of the state, we expected the day of your meeting with anxiety. We cannot stifle our surprise, that near three weeks of a period, teeming with important events, have passed away, like a common session, with an aspect of tranquility. While the state, within thirty miles round the capital, is in convulsion and may soon be in conflagration, we learn that your philosophy is not disturbed, and that you earnestly engaged in discussing the propriety of a three shilling change in the fee table. The public is not possessed of equal fortitude. Our fears seek the shelter of your patronage. It is still a problem, and every day has rendered it more distressing, whether the continuance of law and government is to be expected from the forbearance of our adversaries, or from the fortitude and wisdom of our rulers. We expected that your first step would have been to form an entire system of vigorous measures. Is it good policy to delay that system? Timid men will incline to that side which they suppose will prevail. Many are now balancing. This time is precious and it behooves government to over-awe treachery, and re-assure the hearts of those who begin to despair of the commonwealth. Many will soon despair of you. You now possess our confidence. Cherish it.

So far from adopting a plan of defence, we do not even hear of an act to suspend the habeas-corpus act, or to revive the suits and to continue in force the attachments, which were lost by the interruption of the courts of law. The session seems to be drawing to a close, and we are not encouraged to hope that any effectual measures to defend the Constitution are likely to be taken.

(Remainder in our next)

LUCIUS JUNIUS BRUTUS III

———

The Independent Chronicle, OCTOBER 26, 1786

Ne cede malis, sed contra audentior ito.[6]

TO THE RESPECTABLE MEMBERS OF THE HONORABLE SENATE AND HOUSE OF REPRESENTATIVES:

(Concluded from the second page of our last, and which was then postponed for want of room.)

To FIND FAULT in government is always easy; to prescribe what ought to be done is more difficult. Perhaps, you will enquire, what ought government, in this emergency, to do?

---

[6] *Virgil: Do not yield to evil, but, on the contrary, proceed more fearlessly against it.*

Indeed, gentlemen, that is not, directly, the writer's business to answer. But if you will indulge his presumption, he will not decline it.

You ought to do something. In the present crisis, the rashest of all counsels is, to do nothing. You ought to do it immediately. A right thing, done in season, is twice done. The rioters grow bold, by your delay. They will strengthen faster than you will. To gain strength, you must appear to have it. You ought to do all that is proper to be done. You are hostile to the state, if you do less than all that you can do to save it. It is trifling with the fate of an empire, to do nothing more than to suspend the habeas-corpus act, and to publish pompous syllogisms to convince the understandings of mad men and knaves. If you have any false members, expel them. Their leprosy might prove contagious. Declare that a rebellion exists, for is it not a fact? is it a time to affect a delicacy upon the subject? or who is to be deceived by it? The Governor will have power in that case to establish martial law. A corps of ten thousand minutemen might be formed. Probably, a sixth part of the number will be more than sufficient. It is not to be expected, that this force will be required many days in the field. We ought not to think of the expence; the pay should be liberal and proportioned to the nature of the service. But it could not be great. To defray that expense, if the zeal of individuals, whose all is at stake, should furnish nothing, rather mortgage your eastern lands, the impost and excise, the house that you sit in, and Castle William, with its ordnance and stores; anything is more eligible than ruin. You have good officers, and many soldiers, who have served in the late army. Accompany your military preparations with an act of indemnity, excepting the most atrocious offenders. As the rabble of offenders are below punishment, they should not be kept in fear of it. But if any persons included in the act of indemnity shall be found in arms in future, it ought to be provided, that the punishment of death or a total or partial confiscation of their estates, real and personal, or imprisonment for life, or a term of years, shall be inflicted, according as the case may require. The whole of the charges incurred ought to be drawn from the traitors. Application should be made to Congress for the aid of the Union; and the neighboring states, upon your request would rigorously interdict all intercourse with the insurgents. Your officers, civil and military should be forbidden to negotiate with them; or to allow the constitution to depend upon the success of a bargain. Many other measures will be suggested by the spur of the occasion. But this is a topic which ought not to be further discussed in a newspaper.

Thus far I have calculated upon the certainty of a formidable opposition to government.

Let us examine more closely the strength of the rebel cause. Berkshire has been the most licentious, for a reason which often occurs in the history of mobs, that their insolence is always most to be dreaded when they meet with neither contradiction nor resistance. We are, however, well informed, that the disaffected do not outnumber the loyal in that county. In Hampshire, the Supreme Court was effectually defended; and in case of a battle, it was not doubted by the judges of the subject that the rioters would have been totally defeated. When proper measures shall be adopted with the militia, it may be supposed that the friends of government will be able to keep the insurgents in awe, in those two counties. In Worcester and Middlesex, we have nothing to fear. Disaffection is confined to very narrow limits in those two counties. We scarce need inquire whether the state is able to wage war with the insurgents of Bristol. We have the remainder of the state and the force of the union to add to the friends of government in the disaffected counties. The writer is no judge of military matters, but, suppose, directly against the truth, their numbers and desperation to be as great as the preachers of terror have asserted, yet the success of govern-

51

ment is to be expected, without much, and most probably without any bloodshed. Our troops, well officered, well appointed and supplied with artillery, under good subordination, (and it will be our own fault, if they are not) may possess themselves of the strongest posts and fortify them. They may decline fighting, without evident advantage, and may spin out war to a length, that must consume the resources and zeal of the insurgents. With such advantages, and the country and the United States open to supply and reinforce them, is it to be conceived that a rabble, though ever so monstrous, without a single dollar to supply their wants, without a single person of any genius to direct their counsels, without government, magazines, artillery, warlike stores, discipline, or object to contend for, in the heart of the United States, all hostile to their treason, is it to be conceived, that such a body are in any condition to support the slow operations of regular war? A newspaper does not admit of a full discussion of the subject, for which moreover, the writer is not qualified. The burdens of war press hard upon the most populous and wealthy nations, and tire out the most patient. Against such odds, it is not to be expected that a very numerous body of insurgents could be collected, and still less probable that they could be detained unpaid, and unprovided with tents, hospitals, and every species of military equipage in the field, during the campaign. They have nothing to hope, everything to dread. Will they quit their harvest and their families, and risk all in such a guilty desperate cause? Scores of young fellows, who have considered a riot as a holiday will be brought to reflection, when the case becomes so serious. Pardoned for their past offences, and threatened with the heaviest penalties, in case they offend in like manner again, every motive must concur to keep them quiet. I am persuaded that government will be in no danger, when you determine to defend it with vigor. The insolent hopes of our enemies are rested on your fears.

But if it is granted that this comparison of force is too favorable to our hopes, what follows? If there is danger, shall we yield to it? Are you, or we, at liberty to surrender the Constitution when its defence becomes hazardous? This state, before the aid of other states was feared, defied and encountered, alone, the power of the first nation in the world. And shall we now, victorious and independent, sue for peace to the despicable insurgents against law, honesty and the Constitution?

Are we to be told that vigorous measures will not be pleasing to the disaffected; and that something must be done to please the people? Nothing can be more displeasing to the guilty than their punishment. Let the advocates of lenient measures to appease the people, explain themselves. What are we to understand by lenient measures? No measures? or wrong measures? That such institutions, as they have called grievances, shall be abolished? Shall the Senate be considered as a grievance? That body, and the Supreme Court, are the two anchors of the state. Shall the governor's salary be reduced, till it is unworthy the acceptance of a man of eminent character and abilities? or shall the salary be subject to frequent alterations, in order to render the first magistrate, as far as possible, dependent? If we thus give up two branches of our government, what will remain? Will you abolish the Courts of Common Pleas? Grant that the jurisdiction of those courts might be beneficially transferred to the Supreme Court, is this tune of confusion well chosen to begin the reformation? Shall we attempt to new model the administration of law, before we provide that we have law to administer? Call the engines; extinguish the fire; when that is done, enlarge or alter the house to your taste. Will you give the jurisdiction of the Common Pleas to the justices of peace? Are those who complain of the Common Pleas as a *grievance*, willing to submit to the jurisdiction of a single Justice, as a *remedy?* If *they* are willing, are *you* willing to subject the property of the people, and the law-records, the evidence of their property, to a class of men, among whom it is not too severe to say, some petty, ignorant, needy tyrants, may be found? Who shall keep, or certify those records, in case of the death, or removal of a Justice? We dread innovations; and we think that if the appointment of justices of the Common Pleas, is judiciously made, we ought to submit to the *grievance;* and from the *remedy,* good Lord defend us!

Shall we say that paper or pork shall satisfy a debt, which both parties have agreed silver or gold only is competent to do? From whence did government derive the powers of a po[lit]ical popery, to release the loaded conscience from a burden, which it had, in vain, struggled to throw off? Are you authorized to interfere in private contracts, or in your own, or to withdraw from property, the protection plighted by the Constitution? Who gave you such authority? Certainly not the Constitution, nor the parties.

Are you willing to do evil, that good may come of it? Shall the public debt be annihilated by an act of government? The tribes of wandering Arabs, whose morality allows of theft, from strangers, would not consent to such an act. Nay, the Rhode-Island Assembly would not go so far.

To redress grievances, then, shall we break up our government, abolish its branches, debase its dignities, destroy our records, and repeal the laws of morality? After this is done, shall we be able to punish individual vice with good consciences? To disperse the rioters, shall government join them? But it is too early to talk of lenient measures. Show your power first; then show mercy. First apprehend, try, convict, and pass sentence; then pardon, if you dare not punish. Shall we forgive before they ask it? while they despise our mercy and defy our power?

Shall we grant their demands, whether just or not? If their demands are just, who will oppose them? If they are not just, and you grant them, it is giving up the government. If you admit unjust demands, you sanction their cause with your authority. They have shown themselves to be bad reasoners already. They will receive it as a justification of their conduct. Suppose that they impute your compliance to your fears; will that opinion make them loyal, or you respectable? A wrong measure must fall heavy somewhere. Will it comfort and encourage the friends of government to see the schemes of the mob prevail, even more than their power? What can they expect to gain, by defending you with success, if they lose the protection of law? It is time to set a value upon your friends; they are of as much importance to you as your foes.— What is there that we support and esteem government for, unless it be for those privileges which the rioters and conventions have called grievances?

We have stated what it is conceived government ought to do—and what ought not to be done—and what will be the consequence of your measures,—let us now put a fair question, resulting from the former observations: What will vigorous measures lose, that lenient measures will preserve? If you can neither punish guilt, nor shelter innocence, if you must ask leave to govern, and are most obnoxious when you govern well; if your vengeance is a jest to your adversaries, your protection a snare to your friends, your honor in the dust,—your legal existence, if lenient measures should protract it, will be irksome to yourselves; and what can it avail your constituents? Is this preserving the Constitution? No longer the guardians and ministers of that Constitution, is there no safety but in dishonor? If all that treachery has propagated and cowardice believed of the rebel force were true, rather than become tenants at the sufferance of the mob, rather than be justly scorned by the contemptible, and reproached by the profligate, rather than confess that you are overmatched by the weak, and renounced by all good men, take the magnanimous resolution, worthy of your country and your station, to collect all the force of the state to your standard, against any odds, in spite of any obstacles; resolve to do your duty, and to trust to your courage for your safety.

If that resource should fail, trust them to flight; and if hospitable Algiers, or the more hospitable wilderness, will receive you, your persecuted virtue, even there, would find a safer shelter than this wretched state could afford. It would be some consolation to reflect, that the miseries from which you had fled, were neither produced by your tyranny, nor merited by your cowardice.

Everything depends upon your wisdom and firmness during this session. The fact ought not and cannot be concealed—our constitution is in jeopardy. It was the work of philosophy and patriotism—it is the glory of our age and country—it gives us rank above the [brutal] peasants of other countries—it is with you to transmit the fair inheritance to our children.

The obligation to preserve it ought to be sacred. But if we lose it; if we have not the virtue to sustain freedom, surely we shall not have the patience to endure servitude, and we shall sink to irretrievable debasement. Our fall would involve a species of national infamy which could not be aggravated. The crisis approaches. Even the future interests of society depend on your measures.

It is for you to say whether man shall fall a second time—from glory to infamy—from liberty to anarchy—from the rank of a citizen, to the wretchedness of the savage.

CAMILLUS I

The Independent Chronicle, FEBRUARY 15, 1787

(Omitted in our last for want of room)

MESS'RS PRINTERS:

PERHAPS THERE IS NOT any country of the world, where the people have more weight in the Government, nor where politicians more abound, than our own. They are not more distinguished by their numbers, than by the precipitation with which they form, and the arrogance with which they pronounce their opinions, upon partial or perverted information; and often upon no information at all, our sauntering statesmen express the most unqualified contempt for the decision of the proper and best informed constitutional judges of a subject, and who had perhaps, been determined by the force of reasons, which *they* had never considered. This is only ridiculous. But when [. . .] not only presume to dissent from lawful authority, but in effect to countermand and resist its precepts, our disposition to deride their presumption and perverseness is suppressed by our concern for the infection of their example. There is no language of reproach sufficiently pungent to reprehend their temerity. I shall therefore, forbear.

However, in order that their own feelings may supply the full measure of their chastisements, I shall endeavour to convince, even their prejudiced minds, of the fitness and expediency of the Governor's call upon the militia, which they have so undutifully and precipitately condemned, and so audaciously refused. At present, it is necessary that the public counsels should have the public approbation. This is peculiarly necessary at a time when the Constitution of the people's own choice is in danger. Every man is called to his post, his services and influence are due to the community, and there is no person so insignificant upon whom some portion of active duty to the public, is not devolved. I shall presume that the right of the Governor to call out the militia, not only by the Constitution, but by the resolves of the General Court, can require no proof; every well meaning man will enquire before he denies it. And when he has enquired, he cannot deny it.

I further premise, that the resolution of supporting government, by arms, having been already adopted, it becomes the duty of every good citizen, to afford his honest aid, although his mind may not be fully convinced of the expediency of the measure, for all that is dear to the people is at hazard. And the man, who, by pretending doubts, shall withhold his services, is either a disaffected man, or if by accident he is not, the reasoning which must be bestowed to gain such an untoward proselyte, will not be rewarded by the success.

First it will be easy to show, that the suppression of the rebellion could not have been postponed, till another election should be made by the people, without the extremest hazard and injury to the state.

It is very singular, that a petition for delay, from a body of men, in arms, and in open rebellion, should have had any weight, with the well-affected; I should have inferred the very reverse, and should have supposed, that a jealousy and aversion would have arisen against their design. The rebels request delay, and why? Because their schemes are not ripe, and they are not so ready for war, as they expect that they shall be. This is one good reason why the state should take them unprepared.

It is highly probable, that many reasons, arising from our federal connections, subsisted to influence the Governor and Council, which have not been laid before the public.

We are acquainted, however, with reasons sufficient to satisfy any honest man, that no time ought to have been lost.

In the winter, men may be spared, and can be engaged for moderate wages. The state troops, being better paid, fed, and provided with camp equipage, than the mob, have an advantage of the first importance. The insurgents cannot now take shelter, nor hide in the leafless woods, and swamps, nor carry on a predatory war, nor raise cavalry, nor form ambuscades. A speedy decision may now be expected, and of course, a great saving of blood and treasure, as there is a clear superiority on the side of government.

After another election, wages will be high, and the loss to agriculture would then be immense. Men half clothed, may keep the field, in the summer, and half provided, may subsist on [trifles] and vegetables. Their military operations will be less impeded by the want of money, and every pasture will refresh their cavalry. Their [. . .] will be rapid, and the country exposed to the most ruinous depredations.

By delay, the rebel influence would, doubtless, increase in the three disaffected, and perhaps, in the loyal counties. Unprotected by government, the loyalists would be delivered up, for [. . .], to the arts, and the power of the public enemies. Men are more alert to do mischiefs than to do good. The defence of government is a cold appeal to the understanding; its benefits are speculative, its burdens are palpable. The bold startling creed of rebellion, addressed to the passions and feelings of mankind, has novelty to recommend it, especially to young citizens, and the zeal of the insurgents has, accordingly been twenty fold greater, in making proselytes, than their opponents; for the duty of the loyalist, has been, till of late, to do nothing.

The first impression of horror against a great crime, is the deepest. The aversion to a rebel is abated by frequent intercourse. We become reconciled, by the habits of many months, not only to the criminal, but the crime. The idea of the punishment is removed, by the dealing, and imposes a very feeble restraint upon the mind. We begin to wish well to the opinions of *our* friends. The arts of insinuation are employed. Lies, without number, are invented, so very apropos, and supported, for the good of the cause, by such superabundant testimony, that the new disciple is perplexed and amazed. Threats against the property and persons of the friends of government, are in due season, thrown out. Treason becomes the fashion. Loyalty is pointed at as singular and ridiculous; and many, who would disdain threats, and reply to arguments, will yield to ridicule. There is a sympathy in our opinions, without a single argument, or a single person able to form one; the social mob, and their half-converted pupils, stand hand in hand, while sedition, they know not how, nor why, like a stroke of electricity (if I may be allowed the comparison) passes through their elbows, without reaching their understandings. They yield to the wishes of their companions, what they had refused to their reasonings.

Wearied by importunity, intimidated by menaces, influenced by shame, by lies, by friends, by the fallacious hopes of advantage, and by a thousand inexplicable causes, which incline the human heart to vice and folly, how many scores of weak and tolerably honest men, particularly young men, have joined the insurgents, whose first ideas teemed with abhorrence against the crime of rebellion! The delay of government, by raising the presumption of their final success, and weakening the sense of their actual guilt, would have given an accession of converts to their cause, while the friends of government would have been in total despair. Two other dangers, of the most menacing aspect, forbade delay—the danger of foreign interference—and of rebel representatives.

The corruption of our representation is even more formidable than foreign force. When the enemies of our government are seated in the Senate, and Representatives chambers, it will be time for honest men to remove out of the commonwealth.

Reason so plainly dictates that insurrections should be crushed in embryo; the experience of six months has been so decisive against delay, and so much has been already lost by it, for which there is no compensation or equivalent, that I cannot believe there is now a man, who would expect, by a further delay, to save the money, blood or laws of his country. For my own part, I am fully persuaded, that the ruin of the Constitution, and of the federal government, would ensue.

But, happily for the State, our rulers have done their duty, and if the people are not delinquent, we shall soon be able to prevail against the machinations of our secret, and the violence of our open enemies.

In the present moment, therefore, of peril and expectation, it is incumbent upon the friends of government, to combine as a band of brothers, for the preservation of the best Constitution, with which Heaven has ever rewarded the prayers of a pious, or the sufferings of a magnanimous people.

It is time to call forth the zeal of honest men, to restrain the activity of incendiaries, though less inflammable than their adversaries, it's time for patriots to take their side, and to evince, that they are as ardently resolved to preserve, as they have been to establish the public liberty.

The pretensions to neutrality are usually false. In the present instance, they are criminal: And the man who shall make them ought to be remembered with contempt, when the aversion of one party will be no title to favour with the other. We may fairly conclude, that he who knows any thing, and yet expects to be free under the power of a triumphant mob, discerns his own advantage, in the revolution. He favors the rebellion, in his heart. Let that man be marked; if his head is sound, his heart is hollow. The subject is not hard to understand. Without the aid of metaphysics, an honest man, will determine as readily against committing rebellion as theft: He will decide against so infamous a crime, almost by instinct! He that is obliged to ask his judgment, and to deliberate whether he shall be a radical, is already one. He will feel his duty to his fingers' ends; and if his muscles do not instruct him, he never will learn it from his understanding.

Disaffection, however, is less surprising than neutrality. The aniphibious hypocrite, who pretends to be cool between the [. . .] of two parties, who affects to view, with unconcern, as a philosopher, the ruin of a system which was held inestimable to the *real* philosophers who formed it; who kindles into vehemence, while he condemns the effusion of blood, in self defence, and yet mediates to secure impunity, for those by whose aggressions it was shed; certainly he is more likely to dupe himself than mankind. It is a species of legerdemain, which he persists in exhibiting, after every bystander is possessed of the secret of the performance. For the time is come when characters are assayed, and duplicity brought to the test. The disembodied soul of intriguing villainy stands naked—sore with [. . .], and vulnerable to scorn—it shrinks from the bar of an abused public. The sword of government, like the spear of Ithurial, has a transforming power;[7] the whisperers at the ear of credulity, are forced to assume their proper shape.

It has been pretended, that government has invaded the rights of the people. The conduct of some towns has evinced a disposition to encroach upon the just limits of authority. Considering the supreme power as a derelict property, they have seized a portion, and have proceeded to erect themselves into petty commonwealths. As if government was not competent, they propose a method of their own. Accordingly, they have offered their mediation to heal the contention, and to induce the parties to accommodate. What could the king of Prussia do more to prevent the civil war between the Dutch and the Stadtholder? To cover their disaffection, and to sanctify it with the nature of a virtue, they express great horror against shedding blood, and yet very inconsistently refuse their quota of men for government, and to contribute to that superiority of force, which will prevent resistance. Time will convince them; they will find it necessary to shift the disgace of their votes from one to another, till no body

---

[7] *The infallible test of genuineness or truthfulness, immortalized in Milton's* Paradise Lost, *book IV, l. 810. Ithurial is one of the three deputy sarim (princes) of the holy sefiroth serving under the ethnarchy of the angel Sephuriron.*

appears to be responsible. They will then believe that those who were not for the government, were against it.

This, therefore, is the time for men to exert, and to risk their influence—now let the men, who have a sense of obligation in virtue and their country, who feel a just independence of sentiment, and as just contempt for the sneaking hypocrisy of those, who whisper doubts, and foment intrigues, at this period of popular distraction; let such give aid to government, by the promptitude of their services, and the untemporizing energy of their zeal.

CAMILLUS II

The Independent Chronicle, FEBRUARY 22, 1787

MESS'RS. ADAMS & NOURSE:

As THE SUPREME POWER resides in the General Court, it is their duty to exercise it, according to their best discretion, for the common good, without being deterred by the factious clamor of individuals, however numerous, much less by the intrigues of the disaffected. To support this inference, may seem superfluous in the opinion of those who have not heard it denied. But infinite mischief has been disseminated, by appealing to public clamor, as a public authority. And it has become necessary to expose two favorite topics of incendiary declamation:—

That all government is properly controlled, and is actually held by the majority of individuals;—

And that the support of government, by arms, ought to have been delayed, till another election. The former is subversive of all government; the latter, tending to the evident destruction of our own, has been already discussed.

Government is produced by necessity; there is not any community, or collection of individuals, without it—and every man who has the disposition, and wit enough to be seditious, allows the necessity, in order, with the more plausibility, to condemn the exercise of its powers. It is an unguarded expression, to say, that we part with a portion of our natural liberty, to secure the remainder—for what is the liberty of nature? Exposed to the danger of being knocked on the head for an handful of acorns, or of being devoured by wild beasts, the melancholy savage is the *slave* of his wants and his fears. There is no other liberty than civil liberty.—It is in every man's mouth—we we [*sic*] cannot live without government. How then, can it be affirmed, that the majority of individuals must rule, and that their sense ought to control authority?

This assertion goes too far. If it is true, then a majority, who have neither assembled to hear each other's reasons, nor the objections of the discerning minority, divided by factions, and (disoriented) by falsehoods, after having parted will all their authority, still retain a controlling power over those rulers, whom the public voice, including that very majority, has made supreme. So far the assertors seem inclined to go. But this assertion not only proves, that the supreme power is not supreme, but that any delegation of power, was originally *unnecessary;* because, freely, the majority of individuals can govern the people, as well and as wisely, as they can govern their rulers; but that is admitted to be impossible.

More than once I have renounced the pen, apprehensive that judicious persons will censure these observations as superfluous.

But it has been argued, that ours is a government, *by consent,* and that it is highly improper to use force to support it; others have represented the people as the proprietors of the government, and seem to think, that they may rightfully, though perhaps very unwisely, and even ruinously, dispose of their own. This is a dreadful idea of a republic, if the major part of individuals have a right to destroy not only themselves, but the minority, and their rulers. Many with a keen appetite for mischief, and a total ignorance of their subject, have maintained, that government was opposed to the great body of the people, with whom all power resides; and have wickedly and seditiously represented the most wise and necessary exercise of authority, as an usurpation of their rights. They have been incited to vindicate those rights, which, said the missionaries of Satan, they had no sooner rescued from British power, than they were alarmed by rulers of their own choice. It is well known, that in a certain venerable Assembly, the expressions, "the people will not hear it," "the people will rise," "something must be done to *please* the people," have been heard, while the most momentous questions of policy have been under discussion.

Therefore, as it has been the unfortunate fashion of the day, to dispute against first principles, those who do *not* doubt them, will excuse me for the sake of those who *do*, if I attempt a concise explication of the subject.

It is true, that all lawful government is derived from the people; they are [the] source and origin of power. This truth has been the basis of a thousand observations; it has been, for the incendiary, such a place to stand upon, as some philosophers have desired, who have boasted, that with a packthread, they could move the world from its center. But when the people had consented to a form of government, the social compact was compleat. The state of nature was at an end; free to give, or to withhold, their consent, they became bound when they gave it. Every man knows that contract shall bind the contracting parties. The whole people have expressly contracted with each individual, and each individual with the whole people. Certain rights are expected out of the contract, which, it is declared, are not the subjects of delegation. The powers of the servants of the public, are accurately defined, and comprehend every subject, not excepted in the Bill of Rights; and in the exercise of those powers, by a common, but bold figure of speech, they are constitutionally omnipotent. It has been very properly demanded, what residue of power is there left for the majority of individuals to exercise themselves, or to delegate to conventions?

Individuals are silent [. . .] the only method of collecting [. . .] people, is by their Representatives [. . .] General Court. It is there, and there only, that the majority shall govern. The minority are bound by the social compact to submit, but if they refuse obedience, force may be lawfully used to extort it.

If there is any government which can legitimate, and even sanctify force, it is the government which is founded on consent. And it may well be doubted, whether any other foundation of power will justify it. A free republic necessarily subsists by the force of the whole community, represented by the body politic, applied to repel foreign invasion, or to procure domestic obedience. It is precisely the force that is used every day, by the sheriff, to carry into effect the precepts of law. The right of the Governour and General Court to suppress the rebellion, is as evident, as the right of taking a debtor's goods by execution, which, in fact, are taken by his own consent, first given to the law. But as we have repented of the contract, and withdraw our consent, it is asked, are we bound by the contract still? Certainly. But we are a free sovereign people, it is again insisted. All power is with us. If the Constitution is above the people, then we are not free—we are slaves. I reply, honest men hold themselves bound by their own bargains; they think it for their own advantage to be so. This doctrine of calling the strict observation of our own promises, slavery, is only of a few years standing. If consent once given, can be withdrawn at pleasure, then there is a lawful contract, without any lawful obligation: An absurdity which refutes itself. If the contract is binding upon the people, what right have the majority of individuals to annul or change it? Is there no basis to support the ponderous fabric of government, but opinion—mere air? Then we have all been deceived; and the boasted liberty of this very majority is nothing—a mere whim. But know, profane dunce, government is founded on nature and necessity; it is a firm compact, sanctified from violation, by all the ties of personal honor, morality, and religion.

I have known these remarks put a man in a passion: What! Are we slaves then, to the General Court? Is all power out of the people's hands? Had they known it, they would not have parted with it all; they would have kept back some part to defend their privileges. But now you say, that there is no remedy for the people, if their rulers mistake or abuse their powers, and become tyrants.

Hold, friend. We shall soon agree. The better our constitution is understood, the more it will be admired. The people are not slaves to the General Court. *They* are themselves part of the people. The heavy burdens they impose, they likewise bear. They are liable to mistake. But the people have a right to instruct; and if the experience of their mistakes should not make them wiser, they may find wiser men.

As to actual tyranny, it is merely the cant word of a faction. There is not on earth, and ancient Greece did not boast, a set of public men less chargeable with corruption and tyranny, than those, who since the revolution, have swayed the councils of this country. This is not intended as flattery; it is only the just eulogium of our political institutions.

But as public trust may be abused, what security have the people against it? The right of annual elections, and instruction. Will a man, in one year, set up a tyranny, which, in the following, another may exercise over himself? Public men are not above the laws. They are liable to impeachment for their misconduct. The fear of punishment is a restraint upon them, in common with other men. But the grand security of the public liberty, is the independence of the judicial authority. If the Bill of Rights is violated, there every injured citizen may expect, and will have more complete redress, than an army of insurgents could give him. No act can have the force of law against the Bill of Rights. Every farmer ought to read it, and to learn its nature and value. He will prize it more than his acres; for without it, another might reap where he sows. By the wise and equitable distribution of power under our excellent constitution, that oppression is prevented, or redressed, in the first instance, which, in every other country of the world, is borne till it is intolerable, and then flames out in rebellion. A rebellion, therefore, is as unnecessary in our government, for the redress of grievances, as it is fruitful to produce them.

For every purpose of tyranny, our rulers are mere citizens. They are disarmed by the constitution. Nay more, they are criminals; and are delivered over to the law, for punishment.

To promote the common good, they have all power; and there is no majority of individuals, or convention of men, who may dispute their commands.

People of Massachusetts!

Cherish your Constitution. Let it be dear to your hearts, because they bled to defend it. Let it be dear, because it was the *peculiar act* of the *people*. Let it be dear, for its equity and wisdom, and still dearer for its danger. Favoured by Heaven that ye have it, be bold in its defence. Its preservation will reward you. But let the weight of your united execration fall upon these incendiary miscreants, who have defamed its excellence, and excited its children to parricide.

Stand acquitted by the world, if it must fall; nor let the sigh of *compassion,* which the nations will breathe for your *misfortune,* be suppressed by their *contempt* for your cowardice.

CAMILLUS III

The Independent Chronicle, MARCH 1, 1787

THE LATE EVENTS have been so interesting and so rapid, that the public mind has been confounded by the magnitude and oppressed with the variety of the reflections which result from them. The season of the most useful observation for statesmen and philosophers is not yet arrived. Their decisions are made upon facts, as they appear in their simplicity, after faction has ceased to distort, and enthusiasm to adorn them. It is otherwise with the public. Their judgment is formed while the transactions are recent, while the rage of party gives an acumen to their penetration and an importance to their discoveries, which, however, are soon cheerfully consigned to oblivion. This seems therefore to be the time to reconsider the state of parties, and to examine the opinions, which have lately prevailed. Perhaps some fruit may be gathered from our dear experience; and we may in some measure succeed in eradicating the destructive notions which the seditious have infused into the people.

But experience, which makes individuals wise, sometimes makes a public mad: judging only by their feelings, disastrous events are usually charged to the agency of bad men; and in the bustle, excited by their vindictive zeal, the precious lessons of adversity are lost. It belongs to the sage politician to draw from such events just maxims of policy for the future benefit of mankind; and it belongs to mankind to keep these maxims accumulating, by repeating the same blunders and pursuing the same phantoms, with equal ignorance and equal ardor, to the end of the world. This disposition is so obvious that proof cannot be needed. But if it be desired, it is furnished so abundantly by the history of every nation that it requires some taste to select judiciously the most pertinent evidence. It is most useful to advert to our own times.

In spite of national beggary, paper money has still its advocates, and probably of late its martyrs. In spite of national dishonor, the continental impost is still opposed with success. Never did experience more completely demonstrate the iniquity of the one and the necessity of the other. But in defiance of demonstration, knaves will continue to proselyte fools, and to keep a paper money faction alive. The fear of their success has annihilated credit, as their actual success would annihilate property. For many years we may expect that our federal government will be permitted to languish, without the powers to extort commercial treaties from rival states, or to establish a national revenue. All this is notorious. It is the common language of the people, not excepting the least informed. But it is vain to expect that schemes plainly unjust and absurd will therefore want advocates. Our late experience forbids this confidence. Hitherto invention has not equalled credulity; and the next pretence for rebellion will more probably fail of rousing the disaffected to arms, because it is not monstrous and absurd enough, than because its repugnance to reason and common justice are palpable. The love of novelty and the passion for the marvellous have ever made the multitude more than passive; they have invited imposture, and drunk down deception like water. They will remain as blind, as credulous, as irritable as ever; ambitious men, and those whose characters and fortunes are blasted, will not be wanting to deceive and inflame them openly or by intrigue. The opposition to federal measures, and the schemes of an abolition of debts and an equal distribution of property, with their subdivisions and branches, will be pursued with unremitting industry, till they involve us again in general confusion, unless government, by system, energy, and honesty, shall render the laws from this period irresistibly supreme.

But success never fails to produce good humor, and to procure for government a season of popularity. The public attention is now awake, and this is the favorable moment to induce the people, by a retrospect of their errors, to renounce them, to place confidence in their rulers, and in the permanency and energy of our republic, and to unite in the patriotic sentiment, that it is indispensably necessary to the general prosperity, and to the very existence of government, that the reins should be resumed and held with a firmer hand; and that palliatives and half expedients, and the projects of factious ignorance, will not avail.

To a philosophic observer, indeed, the present confusion will afford an inexhaustible fund of astonishment and concern.

He will behold men who have been civilized returning to barbarism, and threatening to become fiercer than the savage children of nature, in proportion to the multitude of their wants, and the cultivated violence of their passions. He will see them weary of liberty, and unworthy of it, arming their sacrilegious hands against it, though it was bought with their blood, and was once the darling pride of their hearts; complaining of oppression because the law, which has not forbidden, has not also enforced cheating; endeavoring to oppose society against morality, and to associate freemen against freedom. He will call this a chaos of morals and politics, in which are floating and conflicting, not the first principles and simple elements, out of which systems may be formed, but the fragments which have escaped the wreck of institutions and opinions; not the embryo, but the ruins of a world. When he turns his eye from this landscape of barrenness and horror, so painful to the senses and the imagination, he will be led to contemplate the rigorous wisdom of Providence, which has so palpably ordained that the guilt of this rebellion shall be punished by its folly.

It is no less true than singular, that our government is not supported by national prejudice. The people of every country but our own, though poor and oppressed, bear a patriotic preference to their own laws and national character. They will not suffer any one to revile them. The Briton who sells his vote, and is sold by his representative, glories in that freedom which is his birthright; without the smallest knowledge of the principles and institutions by which that freedom is secured, he relies upon the fact, and takes rank of a Frenchman, whom he stigmatizes as a slave. To defend that rank, his ardent valor is always devoted to his country. Every Frenchman is equally prompt to maintain the glory of his king. This prejudice is useful, and bears to just political knowledge the relation of instinct to reason; its decisions are quick; its influence uniform and certain. It is the cement of political union. The government of Turkey is doubtless applauded at Constantinople. Tyranny receives the homage of its dupes and its victims; but liberty among us cannot preserve the reverence of her sons. We have no national character, no just pride in the glorious distinction of freemen, which elevates a Massachusetts beggar above the despots of Asia. We have, it is true, our portion of common follies; and we are not exceeded by any people in the zeal to maintain them; but unfortunately they tend to vilify and to destroy the public liberty. The people have turned against their teachers the doctrines, which were inculcated in order to effect the late revolution. With more privileges and more information than are possessed by the inhabitants of any other country, our citizens, either because they have not learned the value of those privileges by the loss of them, or by a comparison with the nations subject to despotism, or because they have not been accustomed to think that any change will be unfavorable to them, appear to have no more attachment to the Constitution than to the rules of the Robinhood society. The admirers of our government are beyond the Atlantic. It is extolled by the sages of Europe, as giving the sanction of law to the precepts of wisdom, and investing philanthropy with the power to legislate for mankind. But far from contemplating its excellence with partial fondness and implicit reverence, the people arraign the institution of the senate, the exactness and multiplicity of the laws, and the Constitution itself. Devoted folly! Will they continue to destroy the pillars of their security till they are buried in the ruins!

CAMILLUS V

———

The Independent Chronicle, MARCH 15, 1787

WE cannot look back without terror upon the dangers we have escaped. Our country has stood upon the verge of ruin. Divided against itself; the ties of common union dissolved; all parties claiming authority, and refusing obedience; every hope of safety, except one, has been extinguished; and that has rested solely upon the prudence and firmness of our rulers. Fortunately they have been uninfected with the frenzy of the times. They have done their duty, and have shown themselves the faithful guardians of liberty as well as of power. But much remains to do. Sedition, though intimidated, is not disarmed. It is a period of adversity. We are in debt to foreigners. Large sums are due internally. The taxes are in arrears, and are accumulating. Manufactures are destitute of materials, capital, and skill. Agriculture is despondent; commerce bankrupt. These are themes for factious clamor, more than sufficient to rekindle the rebellion. The combustibles are collected; the mine is prepared; the smallest spark may again produce an explosion.

This is a crisis in our affairs which requires all the wisdom and energy of government; for every man of sense must be convinced that our disturbances have arisen more from the want of power than the abuse of it; from the relaxation and almost annihilation of our federal government; from the feeble, unsystematic, temporizing, inconstant character of our own state; from the derangement of our finances, the oppressive absurdity of our mode of taxation; and from the astonishing enthusiasm and perversion of principles among the people. It is not extraordinary that commotions have been excited. It is strange, under the circumstances which we have been discussing, that they did not appear sooner, and terminate more fatally. For let it be remarked, that a feeble government produces more factions than an oppressive one; the want of power first makes individuals legislators, and then rebels. Where parents want authority, children are wanting in duty. It is not possible to advance further in the same path. Here the ways divide; the one will conduct us first to anarchy, and next to foreign or domestic tyranny; the other, by the wise and vigorous exertion of lawful authority, will lead to permanent power and general prosperity. I am no advocate for despotism; but I believe the probability to be much less of its being introduced by the corruption of our rulers, than by the delusion of the people. Experience has demonstrated that new maxims of administration are indispensable. It is not, however, by six-penny retrenchments of salaries; nor by levying war against any profession of men;

nor by giving substance and existence to the frothy essences and fantastic forms of speculation; nor is it by paper money, or an abolition of debts; nor by implicit submission to the insolence of beggarly conventions; nor by the temporary expedients of little minds, that authority can be rendered stable, and the people prosperous. A well-digested, liberal, permanent system of policy is required; and when adopted, must be supported, in spite of faction, against every thing but amendment. The confederation must be amended.

While the bands of union are so loose we are no more entitled to the character of a nation than the hordes of vagabond traitors. Reason has ever condemned our party prejudices upon this important subject; now that experience has come in aid of reason, let us renounce them. For what is there now to prevent our subjugation by foreign power but their contempt of the acquisition? It is time to render the federal head supreme in the United States. It is also time to render the general court supreme in Massachusetts. Conventions have too long, and indeed too unequally, divided power. Until this is effected we cannot depend upon the success of any plans of reformation. When this is done we ought to attempt the revival of public and private credit. With what decency can we pretend that republics are supported by virtue, if we presume, upon the foulest of all motives, our own advantage, to release the obligation of contracts?

Some measures to provide for the common safety and defence are necessary. It ought to be considered how far, and in what manner, this may be accomplished, by perfecting the discipline of the militia, or by calling them into actual service by rotation. Taxation is a subject of the greatest nicety and difficulty. When men of the first information have devised a plan, experience only can give it the stamp of excellence. The established mode is despicable in the extreme. It is arbitrary, uncertain, and unequal; the smallest possible sum is taken out of the pockets of the people, and it is kept the longest possible time out of the hands of the commonwealth.

These important subjects deserve a distinct investigation. Perhaps at some future period the writer may be seduced, by his zeal for the stability of the government, or by his vanity, to attempt it.

But in the mean time he would warn his countrymen that our commonwealth stands upon its probation. If we make a wise use of the advantages which, with innumerable mischiefs, the rebellion has afforded, our government may last. This is the tide in our affairs which, if taken at the flood, will lead to glory. If we neglect it ruin will be inevitable. It is in vain to expect security in future, merely from the general conviction that government is necessary, and that treason is a crime. It is vain to depend upon that virtue which is said to sustain a commonwealth. This is the highflown nonsense of philosophy, which experience daily refutes. It is still more absurd to expect to prevent commotions by conforming the laws to popular humors, so that faction shall have nothing to complain of, and folly nothing to ask for.

There is in nature, and there must be in the administration of government, a fixed rule and standard of political conduct, and that is, the greatest permanent happiness of the greatest number of the people. If we substitute for these maxims the wild projects which fascinate the multitude in daily succession, we may amuse ourselves with extolling the nice proportions and splendid architecture of our republican fabric, but it will be no better than a magnificent temple of ice, which the first south wind of sedition will demolish.

Anarchy and government are both before us, and in our choice. If we fall, we fall by our folly, not our fate; and we shall evince to the astonished world of how small influence to produce national happiness are the fairest gifts of heaven,—

a healthful climate, a fruitful soil, and inestimable laws,—
when they are conferred upon a frivolous, perverse, and
ungrateful generation.

"HISTORY IS PHILOSOPHY TEACHING BY EXAMPLE"

The Palladium, FEBRUARY 2, 1802

AMONG STATES and nations the law of the powerful is
despotism. Yet there are, perhaps, of more than two hundred
thousand heads of families in New England, ten or twenty
thousand who sincerely believe that the power of France is
favorable to general liberty. The opinion is shallow, but a
great many hundreds of the persons who entertain it are no
fools. The error, gross as it is, lies in want of thought, and
want of information.

A nation which has made almost every sacrifice for its
ambition to rule other nations, will not, now it is victorious,
be very modest in requiring from them like sacrifices. France
affects to be the imitator of ancient Rome: never was there
a more abominable original, or a more servile copy.

There was almost no evil that Rome did not inflict, scarcely
any humiliation that she did not impose on her allies. The
people of Latium were denominated her confederates, and
entitled to what was called, as a kind of eminence in slavery,
the *jus Latinum;* the other states claimed only the *jus Italicum.*
These were degrees in slavery. For when the Latins insisted,
as well they might, that they would not follow the Romans
in their wars, their refusal was called treason; a war ensued,
and the Latins yielded on the terms of having the excellent

privilege of the *jus Latinum*. After Latium was thus humbled, Rome extended her sway over the twelve states of Etruria. Those nearest to her, and the most afraid of her power, were tempted by all the offers of citizenship that tyranny could hold forth; and they were offered with effect; they were neutral. Etruria did not combine to resist Rome, till Rome was not to be resisted. Samnium was next attacked. Seventy years of war, and more than twenty triumphs, were necessary to subdue the Samnites, who were as brave and as warlike as the Romans, but not half so well united. The Romans never failed to use one set of slaves to conquer another. The Campanians were called allies, and under that name, entitled to fight the Samnites; and, during a century of the most vigorous oppression, they were incessantly reproached with their ingratitude to the Romans, because they winced a little, when their chains galled to their marrow. The Samnites were reduced; and then Pyrrhus came. The people of Tarentum, who called him over, had little power, and his own state had none, for a distant expedition. He failed. The Carthaginians next disputed the dominion of Sicily with the Romans. They loved money better than glory; and the Romans sought money by winning glory. The men of the sword prevailed in combat against the shopkeepers.

Two extraordinary men raised up Carthage from the dust. Hamilcar, a great man, reduced Spain, where he was cut off in early life; Hannibal, his son, a greater man, perhaps the greatest of men, trained the armies and led them into Italy against the Romans. Much has been said, and more might be said on this subject. Hannibal never met with his equal, and the reason why he did not finally conquer was, that the institutions of Carthage were inferior to those of Rome. The policy of Carthage was to make money; that of Rome to make conquests. In consequence of this defect, Carthage lost both money and conquests; while Rome accumulated both. Carthage stood in fear of her allies; the allies of Rome were afraid of her. The conquests of Rome were old, and well consolidated with her empire; those of Carthage recent and still turbulent. Accordingly, Spain, as soon as Hannibal left it, blazed out with wars, that made her the slave of Rome. Italy was more advanced in slavery, and felt an emulation among her states in their obedience to their mistress. She used her own allies as slaves, and the subjects of Carthage as allies.

Rome courted the great; Hannibal the populace. This was one cause of the ardor and perseverance of the allies in the service of Rome, who courted the oligarchy of every state to assist in oppressing it. Another impediment to Hannibal's success was in the government of Carthage. It was popular, and therefore, a prey to faction. Hanno prevented the supplies being sent to Hannibal, that would have given him the superiority. The jacobins of Carthage destroyed her independence; they hated their rivals more than they loved their country.

The Romans dissembled their anger against Philip, king of Macedon, as long as they had the Carthaginians to deal with. When Carthage was subdued, they picked a quarrel with Philip. Even then they allied themselves with the Ætolians, the Virginians of ancient Greece, and used them as tools to subdue Philip. Philip was beaten at Cynocephale, and the Ætolians were greatly disappointed on the peace that ensued. For they expected that Rome would allow them to domineer as despots in Greece; but Rome very discreetly chose to domineer herself.

Indeed ancient history has a great deal to say to America; but America will not hear it.

The Ætolians, disappointed in their ambition, then said a great many things that were true; but they said all from spite, and were not regarded. Flamininus, the conqueror of Philip, proclaimed at the Isthmian games, liberty to the states of Greece; that is to say, anarchy; that all should be weak, and Rome stronger than all.

He, and the ten ambassadors, told the Roman senate that, unless Lacedæmon were reduced, Nabis, the king of that state, would be lord of all Greece; and yet he told the assembled states of Greece, at Corinth, that it was wholly their affair and nothing to the Romans. The duplicity and profligacy of this transaction are exhibited even by Livy, who is a very Roman in his history.

By dividing, the Romans conquered. Weak confederacies are so many strong factions and crazy governments.

These old examples show what France has already done in Europe, where she has destroyed every one of its republics; and what she will do, if she and her allies, the jacobins, can, in America. They have begun their work—they have made progress.

III.

ESSAYS ON

FOUNDING AND

PATRIOTISM

—————

CAMILLUS IV

—————

The Independent Chronicle, MARCH 8, 1787

IN OUR LAST SPECULATION we expressed our surprise, that a government, which is free almost to excess, should want the love and veneration of that class of the people, whose rights and privileges are so peculiarly connected with its preservation. But it is to be considered, that they have once subverted and again formed a Constitution. Their complete success in both attempts has extinguished all their ideas of the difficulty and hazard of this operation; and accordingly, they seem to think it as easy and safe to change the government as the representatives. We have already considered some of the causes which have produced this perversion of opinions. It is not strange, that people with little information or leisure, with violent prejudices and infinite credulity, should make indifferent politicians. But it remains a subject of amazement, that the men of speculation and refinement have wandered still more widely from the path of duty and good sense. It will be amusing to review the extravagances of these framers of hypothesis. They considered the contest with Britain, as involving the fate of liberty and science. To animate and recompense their sufferings and toils during the conflict, their ardent enthusiasm had anticipated a system of government too pure for a state of imperfection. When they found, that for the first time in the history of man, a nation was allowed by Providence to reduce to practice the schemes, which Plato and Harrington had only sketched upon paper, they expected a constitution which should be perfect and perpetual. Politics has produced enthusiasts as well as religion; and in the theory of our Constitution they could trace their fancied model of perfection. To the mind of the dreamer in speculation the government was a phantom; and to adorn it his fancy had stolen from the evening cloud the gaudiest of its hues; he had dipped his pencil in the rainbow to portray a picture of national felicity for admiration to gaze at. Then was the time to tell of virtue being raised from the dungeon, where priests and tyrants had confined her; and that science had been courted from the skies to meet her; then was the time to talk of restoring the golden age, without being laughed at; and many seemed to believe that a political millennium was about to commence.

But here end our heroes. When they quitted the theory to attend to the administration of government, they descended to vulgar prose. They found, that their admired plan of freedom of election had produced a too faithful representation of the electors; and that something more, and something worse than the public wisdom and integrity were represented. They often heard the unmeaning din of vulgar clamor excited to make that odious which was right, and that popular which was wrong.

They well knew, that the laws were made supreme, and

that politics should have no passions. Yet it was soon perceived, that the legislators themselves sometimes felt, and too often feared and obeyed, the sudden passions and ignorant prejudices of their constituents. They expected a government by laws, and not by men; and they were chagrined to see, that the feelings of the people were not only consulted in all instances, but that in many they were allowed to legislate. They had hoped, that the supreme power would prove, to all legal purposes, omnipotent; and they were thrown into absolute despair, when they found, that not only individuals, but conventions, and other bodies of men, unknown to the Constitution, presumed to revise, and in effect to repeal, the acts of the legislature. Besides, the first years of the millennium had fallen far short of the expected felicity. But when a mad people flew to arms; when they found, that, in spite of the indocile and impenetrable stupidity of the insurgents, there was so much meaning in their wickedness; and that the reasonings of great numbers, who espoused the cause of government, were almost as hostile as the violence of the other party, they gave way to their spleen and disappointment, and declared their conviction, that a republican government was impracticable and absurd. They argued, as they said, from facts as well as from principles, that such a government was cursed with inherent inefficiency; and that property was more precarious than under a despot; a despot, they said, is a man, and would fear the retaliation of his tyranny; but an enthusiastic majority, steeled against compassion, and blind to reason, are equally sheltered from shame and punishment. The theory of the Constitution has not escaped the havoc of their fastidious criticism; and they have seen, with complacency, the stupid fury of Shays and his banditti employed to introduce a more stable government, whose powers, they predicted, would soon be lodged in the hands of abler men. They raved about monarchy, as if we were ripe for it; and as if we were willing to take from the plough-tail or dram-shop some vociferous committee-man, and to array him in royal purple, with all the splendor of a king of the gypsies. So far as we may argue from the sympathy which fools and knaves have for their fellows, and from the fact of Luke Day's influence in the rebellion, the presumption is, that our king, whenever Providence in its wrath shall send us one, will be a blockhead or a rascal.

The sons of science, who have adopted this reprehensible mode of reasoning, are notwithstanding the most sincere lovers of their country; they are not the men to subvert empires. I will repeat, for their consideration, some observations which, though trite, are not unreasonable.

The idea of a royal or aristocratical government for America is very absurd. It is repugnant to the genius, and totally incompatible with the circumstances of our country. Our interests and our choice have made us republicans. We are too poor to maintain, and too proud to acknowledge, a king. The spirit of finance, and the ostentation of power would create burdens; these would produce the Shayses and the Wheelers. The army must be augmented; discontent and oppression would augment of consequence. But this is mere idle speculation; for every honest man is surely bound to give his support to the existing government, until its power becomes intolerable. A change, though for the better, is always to be deplored by the generation in which it is effected. Much is lost, and more is hazarded. Our republic has not yet been allowed a fair trial. The rebellion has called forth its powers, and pointed out, most clearly, the means of giving it stability; let us therefore cherish and defend our Constitution; and when time and wealth shall have corrupted it, our posterity may perform the melancholy task of laying in human blood and misery, as we have done, the foundations of another government. We, who are now upon the stage, bear upon our memories too deep an impression of the miseries of the last revolution to think of attempting another.

It is an Herculean labor to detail our political absurdities.

Since the days of Cromwell there has not been an instance of such general infatuation. But while almost every tavern and conversation circle were infested with the harangues of the emissaries of treason, who without fear or measure reviled the government, and without shame perverted the truth, the opinions of the people at large were inevitably tainted with the impurity of the source from which they were derived.

Nor was the agency of rebel emissaries the only cause of popular error. Where so much uneasiness prevailed against government, they could not be persuaded that all was right. The sufferers, many supposed, were the best able to decide upon the reality of their grievances; and so many honest men would not combine to deceive them. The general court, in their last session, had given some color to these presumptions, and no small consequence to the party, by the minute attention which they paid to their complaints, before they adopted measures to suppress the rebellion, and by the laws of an unprecedented nature, enacted for their relief. Great numbers took their fears for their counsellors, and thought it rashness to contend against the invincible host of insurgents. Another state tax was more dreaded by many, than the subversion of government. Some said, very gravely, Shays himself is for government; while others, as absurdly, in the zeal of their philanthropy against shedding blood, seemed wholly to forget that the right of self-defence belongs to rulers as plainly as to private men. In matters of etiquette and punctilio, the apostles of mischief seemed agreed, that it was more proper for the rulers of a great commonwealth than for the leaders of a ragged banditti, to make concessions. Disappointed men have hoped to gratify their ambition or their revenge; the abolition of public and private debts has been a favorite object with some; others (such has been the extreme of frenzy) have contended for an equal distribution of property; while the giddy multitude have enjoyed the bustle of parties, and have found amusement in destruction.

With what impressions will the impartial world peruse the

record of these facts? They will be ready to affirm, with the lunatic, that all the world had gone mad except a few, who, for their sobriety, were confined in bedlam.

THE REPUBLICAN I

Repertory, JULY, 1804 Reprinted in the
Boston Gazette, JULY 19, 1804

WE ENJOY, or rather till very lately we did enjoy, liberty, to as great an extent as it has ever been asserted, and to a much greater than it has ever been successfully maintained. Kind Heaven, that gave it, best knows how frail the tenure, and how short its date! Vanity, our only national passion that is never cloyed with its feasts, nor tired with its activity, rates high enough the pride of our distinction as a free people, without once regarding the perils which environ this, as every other sort of preëminence. We have absurdly and presumptuously considered our condition as citizens, not as a state of probation for the trial of our virtues, but the heaven where their indolence is to find rest, and their selfishness an everlasting reward. We have dared to suppose our political probation was over, and that a republican constitution, when once fairly engrossed in parchment, was a bridge over chaos that could defy the discord of all its elements. The decision of a majority, adopting such a constitution, has sounded in our ears like a voice saying to the tempestuous sea of liberty, thus far shalt thou go, and here shall thy proud waves be stayed.

Hence it is, that the unthinking and least informed of our citizens have been so ready to look with levity and distrust on senates, courts, and judges, the bulwarks of our liberty, and with complacency on the licentious faction that is destined to subvert it. We have read ourselves, or have been told by those whom ancient history has instructed, that republics breed factions, and that factions breed tyrants. We have seen this faction, and its favorites who are thirsting to be tyrants, but we have sought and found comfort in our vanity, when it asserts that we have the sense to unmask our flatterers, and the virtue that will scorn their bribes; we therefore shall stand, though the liberty of Greece has perished. All this we continue to say, while we see an election carried against a majority of freemen, and an administration that has prostrated the Judiciary and the Constitution, that has its hirelings and emissaries scattered over the face of the land, and that has unconstitutionally annexed to the United States an empire, as a fund for patronage, and in which executive despotism is established by law. We see ourselves in the full exercise of the forms of election, when the substance is gone. We have some members in Congress with a faithful meanness to represent our servility, and others to represent our nullity in the union; but our vote and influence avail no more, than that of the Isle of Man in the politics of Great Britain. If, then, we have not survived our political liberty, we have lived long enough to see the pillars of its security crumble to powder. If the Middle and Eastern States still retain any thing in the union worth possessing, we hold it by a precarious and degrading tenure; not as of right, but by sufferance; not as the guarded treasure of freemen, but as the pittance, which the disdain of conquerors has left to their captives.

While we look round with grief and terror on so much of the work of destruction as three years have accomplished, we resolve to hope and sleep in security for the future. We will not believe that the actual prevalence of a faction is any thing worse than an adverse accident, to which all human affairs are liable. Demagogues have taken advantage of our first slumbers, but we are awaking and shall burst their "Lilliputian ties;"[8] and as we really do expect that the jacobins will divide, and that McKean and others will turn State's evidence to convict their accomplices, we resolve to indulge our hopes and our indolence together, and leave it to time, no matter what time, and truth, to do their slow but sure work, without our concurrence. We still cherish the theories that are dear to our vanity. We still expect that men will act in their politics as if they had no passions, and will be most callous or superior to their influence at the very moment when the arts of tyrants, or the progress of public disorders, have exalted them to fury. Then, yes then, in that chosen hour, reason will display her authority, because she will be free to combat error. Her voice will awe tumult into silence; revolution will quench her powder when it is half exploded; the thunder will be checked in mid volley.

Such are the consolations that bedlam gives to philosophy, and that philosophy faithfully gives back to bedlam; and bedlam enjoys them. The *Chronicle*, with the fervor of scurrility, and all the sincerity of ignorance, avers that there is no danger—our affairs go on well; and Middlesex is comforted. They can see no danger; if Etna should blaze, it would not cure the moles of their blindness.

But all other men who have eyes are forced to confess, that *the progress of our affairs is in conformity with the fixed laws of our nature, and the known course of republics. Our wisdom made a government and committed it to our virtue to keep; but our passions have engrossed it, and they have armed our vices to maintain their usurpation.*[9]

---

[8] *An allusion to Jefferson's letter to Mazzei. The entire sentence reads as follows: "We have only to awake and snap the Lilliputian cords with which they have been entangling us during the first sleep which succeeded our labours."*

[9] *Ames was strongly taken with this formulation and, beginning with "Republican IV" and continuing through the end of the series, he employed it as an epigram at the head of each essay.*

What then are we to do? Are we to sit still, as heretofore, till we are overtaken by destruction, or shall we rouse now, late as it is, and show, by our effort against a jacobin faction, that if we cannot escape, we will not deserve, our fate?

THE REPUBLICAN II

Boston Gazette, JULY 26, 1804

WE JUSTLY CONSIDER the condition of civil liberty as the most exalted to which any nation can aspire; but high as its rank is, and precious as are its prerogatives, it has not pleased God, in the order of his providence, to confer this preëminent blessing, except upon a very few, and those very small, spots of the universe. The rest sit in darkness, and as little desire the light of liberty, as they are fit to endure it.

We are ready to wonder, that the best gifts are the most sparingly bestowed, and rashly to conclude, that despotism is the decree of heaven, because by far the largest part of the world lies bound in its fetters. But either on tracing the course of events in history, or on examining the character and passions of man, we shall find that the work of slavery is his own, and that he is not condemned to wear chains till he has been his own artificer to forge them. We shall find that society cannot subsist, and that the streets of Boston would be worse than the lion's den, unless the appetites and passions of the violent are made subject to an adequate control. How much control will be adequate to that end, is a problem of no easy solution beforehand, and of no sort of difficulty after some experience. For all who have any thing to defend, and all indeed who have nothing to ask protection

89

for but their lives, will desire that protection; and not only acquiesce, but rejoice in the progress of those slave-making intrigues and tumults, which at length assure to society its repose, though it sleeps in bondage. Thus it will happen, and as it is the course of nature, it cannot be resisted, that there will soon or late be control and government enough.

It is also obvious, that there may be, and probably will be, the least control and the most liberty there, where the turbulent passions are the least excited, and where the old habits and sober reasons of the people are left free to govern them.

Hence it is undeniably plain, that the mock patriots, the opposers of Washington and the Constitution, from 1788 to this day, who, under pretext of being the people's friends, have kept them in a state of continual jealousy, irritation, and discontent, have deceived the people, and perhaps themselves, in regard to the tendency of their principles and conduct; for instead of lessening the pressure of government, and contracting the sphere of its powers, they have removed the field-marks that bounded its exercise, and left it arbitrary and without limits. The passions of the people have been kept in agitation, till the influence of truth, reason, and the excellent habits we derive from our ancestors is lost or greatly impaired; till it is plain, that those, whom manners and morals can no longer govern, must be governed by force; and that force a dominant faction derives from the passions of its adherents; on that alone they rely.

Take one example, which will illustrate the case as well as a hundred; the British treaty was opposed by a faction, headed by six or eight mob leaders in our cities, and a rabble, whom the arts of these leaders had trained for their purpose. Could a feeble government, could mere truth and calm reason, pointing out the best public interest, have carried that treaty through, and effected its execution in good faith, had not the virtue and firmness of Washington supplied an almost superhuman energy to its powers at the moment? No treaty made by the government has ever proved more signally beneficial. The nature of the treaty, however, is not to the point of the present argument. Suppose a mob opposition had defeated it, and confusion, if not war, had ensued, the confusion that every society is fated to suffer, when, on a trial of strength, a faction in its bosom is found stronger than its government; on this supposition, and that the conquering faction had seized the reins of power, is it to be believed that they would not instantly provide against a like opposition to their own treaties? Did they not so provide, and annex Louisiana, and squander millions in a week? Have we not seen in France, how early and how effectually the conqueror takes care to prevent another rival from playing the same game, by which he himself prevailed against his predecessor?

Let any man, who has any understanding, exercise it to see that the American jacobin party, by rousing the popular passions, inevitably augments the powers of government, and contracts within narrower bounds, and on a less sound foundation, the privileges of the people.

Facts, yes facts, that speak in terror to the soul, confirm this speculative reasoning. What limits are there to the prerogatives of the present administration? and whose business is it, and in whose power does it lie, to keep them within those limits? Surely not in the senate: the small States are now in vassalage, and they obey the nod of Virginia. Not in the judiciary: that fortress, which the Constitution had made too strong for an assault, can now be reduced by famine. The Constitution, alas! that sleeps with Washington, having no mourners but the virtuous, and no monument but history. Louisiana, in open and avowed defiance of the Constitution, is by treaty to be added to the union; the bread of the children of the union is to be taken and given to the dogs.

Judge then, good men and true, judge by the effects,

whether the tendency of the intrigues of the party was to extend or contract the measure of popular liberty. Judge whether the little finger of Jefferson is not thicker than the loins of Washington's administration; and, after you have judged, and felt the terror that will be inspired by the result, then reflect how little your efforts can avail to prevent the continuance, nay, the perpetuity of his power. Reflect, and be calm. Patience is the virtue of slaves, and almost the only one that will pass for merit with their masters.

BRITISH ALLIANCE

The Repertory, NOVEMBER, 1806

THOSE are not the wisest of men who undertake to act always by rule. In political affairs there are no more self-conceited blunderers than the statesmen who affect to proceed, in all cases, without regard to circumstances, but solely according to speculative principles.

Politics is the science of good sense, applied to public affairs; and as those are forever changing, what is wisdom to-day would be folly, and perhaps ruin to-morrow. Politics is not a science so properly as a business. It cannot have fixed principles, from which a wise man would never swerve, unless the inconstancy of men's views of interest and the capriciousness of their tempers could be fixed.

We make these remarks, because we are sometimes sorry, and sometimes diverted, at the dispute about an alliance offensive and defensive with Great Britain. If ever there was a question of moonshine this is one. There is no more probability that Mr. Jefferson will conclude such a treaty, than that he will breakfast to-morrow morning upon gunpowder; and it is the prevailing opinion, that he is fonder of hominy. We might as well speculate upon our probable condition, "if angels in the form of presidents should come down to the federal city to govern us;" or who would get or lose a fat commission, if the time had come when Mr. Jefferson would make no other inquiry than, "Is he capable, is he honest?" It is a pity that our printers should argue, and contend, and explain about *any* of these matters of moonshine.

If the time should ever come (and a new race of men must be let down from the sky before it can come) when an honest spirit of patriotism will have such a question to decide, our Catos, and our Ciceros, and Favonii would say, the decision must depend on circumstances, not on principles deduced *à priori. Salus reipublicæ suprema lex esto.*[10] To serve and save the commonwealth controls all maxims.

It is absurd to say Washington made no such treaty, and therefore Mr. Jefferson ought not to make it. The times never required it of Washington; and if they had, that firm and tempered soul, that heard reproach in the huzzas of popularity, unless conscience sanctioned its applause, would have impelled him to a treaty offensive and defensive with Great Britain. The heart swells and convulses at the mention of his name (in contrast even) with Jefferson's. But even Jefferson ought not to be reproached for negotiating such a treaty when the circumstances may require it. We are not disposed to assert that at present they do require it. We hope, but while they negotiate with France we scarcely know why we hope, that British hearts, such stout hearts as our ever-renowned ancestors wore, will resist Bonaparte, till his despotism has spent its fury, or the subject nations of Europe have recovered their spirit. Nevertheless, if American independence could not be preserved, without joining Great Britain to resist its great enemy, the coward world's master, is there an American

---

[10] *The well-being of the republic is the supreme law.*

93

who would object to such an alliance? An alliance of this sort with any nation is an evil; but to say there is no condition of our affairs, in which it would not be a less evil than subjugation, or than the increased peril of subjugation, without such a concert of counsels and of efforts, is book wisdom. It is that sort of folly and infatuation, which every nation that now wears French chains has fitted itself for slavery by first adopting.

Whenever, therefore, a miracle is about to be publicly wrought, and Mr. Jefferson grows so careless of his popularity and so careful of his country, as to act the great part, which the reduction of the British power would justify and require, let not the federalists take off from his shoulders to their own the reproach of suffering our liberties to be seized by France as a prey.

If Britain falls in fighting our battles, we must fight our own; and what law of sound policy or true wisdom is there, that we should choose to fight them, unassisted and alone? We do not say that the time has come—heaven forbid it should; but it may come, and that speedily, when the opposition to a British alliance would be treason against American independence. Let French emissaries cavil, but let Americans ponder.

HINTS AND CONJECTURES CONCERNING
THE INSTITUTIONS OF LYCURGUS

———

WRITTEN IN 1805

THE INSTITUTIONS of Lycurgus have engrossed, and, perhaps, have deserved the praises of all antiquity. Even the Athenians, the rivals and enemies of Sparta, do not withhold or stint their admiration of the sublime genius and profound wisdom of this legislator. Such a general concurrence of opinions, and for so many ages, in favor of the laws of Lycurgus, can scarcely be imagined to proceed from error, accident, or caprice.

When to this we add, that for seven hundred years, the Lacedæmonian state continued to respect, if not rigidly to observe, these laws, we are not permitted at this late day to arraign their wisdom, especially by attempting to ridicule their singularity. We are the less authorized to pronounce their condemnation, as the ancients have taken more pains to make them appear admirable than intelligible. A complete and satisfactory view of the Spartan policy, if any such were exhibited of old, has not reached our times. Besides, so unlike are our manners and institutions to those of Greece, and particularly of Sparta, that the representations of Xenophon, Aristotle, Polybius, and Plutarch, though amply sufficient for the information of their countrymen, cannot fail to appear defective and obscure to us.

The chief articles of the system of Lycurgus seem so much more extraordinary than any thing else that has happened in the world, except their political consequences, that we should be induced to deny the facts, if the historical evidence of them were not complete. As we are not permitted to do this, we submit to the authority of history, with a sort of vague and uninstructed astonishment at the strangeness of its testimony.

Sparta or Lacedæmon, ancient writers tell us, was rent with factions, one of the two kings being at the head of each, without laws, and so deeply corrupted, that neither morals nor manners could supply their place. In this exigency Lycurgus appeared, and by his genius took the ascendant over the kings and demagogues, and indeed over all the men of his age and nation, as the pasture oak towers above the shrubs, or like a giant among dwarfs. The oracle of Delphi gave him, moreover, all the authority that superstition can maintain over ignorance. Thus far all is easy of comprehension.

But when we are required to believe that a whole people readily submitted to give up their property to be divided anew; that they renounced luxury, ostentation, and pleasure, and even the use of money, except iron; that they were obliged, under severe penalties, from which their kings were not exempted, to dine in public and on wretched fare; that their children were taken from them and exposed to death, if adjudged weakly and infirm, or if permitted to live, placed under the tutelage of public officers; and that such was the intolerable rigor of their regulations, that actual service in camp was a welcome relaxation;—when we read all this, surely, if there is nothing to justify our doubts, there is nothing that can suppress our wonder. We yield our faith at once, that the Lacedæmonians immediately became a nation of heroes, who had extinguished nature, and silenced appetite and passion, save only the passion to live and die for their country.

By this expedient, we make the Spartan story somewhat more credible. As we can know nothing of what demi-gods would do, we may imagine just what we please. But men now-a-days, we are sure, would not be brought to adopt such laws, nor, if they did, long to observe them.

Nevertheless, we know, that the success of the system of Lycurgus did not arise from the superiority of his race of Spartans. On the contrary, so far were they from being superior to other men, that he found them, we are told, worse. This we are forced to believe; for he found them factious; and faction, we know, is as sure to degrade and corrupt the citizens, as to bewilder and inflame them. Indeed he left them as he found them, and as they are represented by all antiquity, faithless, ferocious, and cruel, yet loving their country with an ardor of passion, and with a disregard of justice, that made it hateful and terrible to the rest of mankind.

We are driven back, then, to consider how men, and very bad men, could be prevailed on to establish, and what is still more surprising, for many hundred years to maintain, such self-denying and odious institutions. It would be absurd to suppose, that the enthusiasm kindled by Lycurgus spread so far and lasted so long. This sort of fire, which seldom catches any thing but light combustibles, only flashes and expires. We find, on the contrary, that the institutions of Lycurgus had a sort of awful authority, to fix the popular caprice and overcome their disgust, to charm their sages and animate their heroes, to form the manners and control the policy of the nation for many ages. The mere popularity of his system would not have lasted for a year; and though superstition might do much, nature in the end would do more, and resume her violated rights. So many painful exercises, such endless and unsufferable privations and constraints, would soon exhaust the patience of the most passive wretches that ever existed. It was said, with almost as much truth as wit, by the Athenian Alcibiades: "no wonder the Spartans cheerfully encounter death; it is a welcome relief to them from such a life as they are obliged to lead."

It is therefore, after all, extremely difficult to conceive, that the discipline of this famous legislator was intended for the body of the inhabitants of the city of Lacedæmon, much less for the whole country of Laconia, or that it was ever so applied. Human nature has not changed for the worse by the lapse of twenty-six hundred years; and we may venture to say, that there is no people now on the face of the earth, who could be persuaded or forced to submit to such a discipline.

The Jews, it is true, adopted a very singular body of laws; but it is equally true, that they were infinitely less obnoxious to the sentiments and feelings of nature than those of Lycurgus.

It is also true, that under the immediate government of God himself, manifested by signs and wonders, by awful warnings and signal punishments, the Hebrews repeatedly yielded to their natural repugnance, and departed from the law of Moses. Yet Lycurgus, without any divine, and even without the regal authority in Sparta, is commonly supposed, not only to have wielded the political power of the state, a thing not in the least difficult to suppose, but to have changed or extinguished the inclinations of every Lacedæmonian heart, and to have substituted in their stead a passion for self-denial, restraint, and suffering.

Yet all the writers of antiquity represent the discipline of Lycurgus, no less than his political constitution, as being in full force over all the citizens; that food, dress, sports, conversation, and even the intercourse of the sexes, were restricted by law; in short, that a system of regulations unspeakably more minute, vexatious, disgusting, and tyrannical than we can find prescribed for the fraternity of La Trappe, or the monks of the order of St. Francis, was inflexibly imposed on a nation, and quietly obeyed for many ages. All this may possibly be true; and we must yield our belief, if we cannot help it; but it would be almost as hard to command our faith in this extent of the story, as our obedience to the laws of Sparta.

In this exigency, and with this hard alternative before us, it is hoped that those who are profoundly versed in classic learning will not deem it treason against the ancients, if we propose some hints and conjectures tending to throw light upon the subject, and which, if well grounded, may somewhat better reconcile the long unquestioned miracles of Spartan legislation with common sense and the unchangeable uniformity of the human character.

Now, though it is inconceivable, that a whole nation should submit to the numberless, endless, intolerable vexations and rigors of the Spartan discipline, it is by no means incredible, that two or three thousand of them should. The wandering

Tartars, who live encamped in tents, might possibly be subjected to a pretty strict military regulation; although it is certain that they are not; but a people dispersed over a whole territory, living in houses, and cherishing, as from their situation they must, the delights that a fixed home affords, cannot be made monks, and be cut off from society, while they are suffered to remain warm in its bosom.

Why then are we not permitted to suppose that the system of Lycurgus, so far as it regulated the meals, education, dress, and indifferent actions of the citizens, was made for a particular class, and enforced only upon them, and not upon the mass of the free inhabitants; that this class was formed exclusively of the Spartan or noble families; that the object of this system was not, as is generally believed, by changing or expelling human nature, to raise a whole nation above it, but to raise a governing aristocracy above that nation? To illustrate the conjecture, may we not imagine these Spartans to have been to the rest of the free citizens of the state, in point of rank, privilege, power, and numbers, what the knights of St. John lately were to the people of Malta? It is probable, there was a system of *education* extremely rigid for the nobles; and a system of *discipline* for the national militia quite distinct from the former. Lycurgus distributed the lands to these latter in thirty-nine thousand lots, or shares, of which less than five thousand were assigned to the citizens of Sparta. Now, as we read of no education of the youth according to the rules of Lycurgus out of that city, we can scarcely refrain from adopting both the before mentioned conjectures, viz. that the famous plan of Spartan education was only for the nobles or their sons who were in the city; and that the military system, if there was one, (which we cannot doubt,) was distinct from it, and embraced the whole feudal tenants or national militia.

Admitting these suppositions to be well-founded, our difficulties disappear at once.

The rules for a patrician academy, and for a fixed militia,

though severe, might be enforced by the public authority. The former had power and rank, and the latter had lands to stimulate and reward their obedience. The very circumstance of setting apart a class of young men for the noblest of all professions, the profession of arms, would naturally inspire the young Spartans with the *esprit du corps,* with the lofty pride that would more cheerfully seek than shun the occasions to make efforts and sacrifices. In framing the rules for the education and discipline of this noble class, there was ample scope for the genius of Lycurgus, and for the display of his deep insight into the secrets of the human heart. Instead of extinguishing nature, and acting, as it is generally thought he did, without means, or at least without any that we can believe to be adequate, he had only to act with the aid of one of the strongest passions, and to apply that love of distinction, which is one of the most powerful agents in the transactions of mankind. Hence it was, that every Spartan thought it better not to live at all than live a coward. Hence, Leonidas and his little troop, at Thermopylæ, did all that human nature could do—but they did no more; no more than British sailors do now; no more than American sailors are capable of doing, and will certainly do, whenever our government shall feel somewhat of their spirit. The military character, which causes a generous devotion of life to honor, is no prodigy; it is the familiar business of every day of modern warfare.

On examining these conjectures of the restricted, instead of the universal application of the discipline of Lycurgus, their conformity with the known laws of human action will afford ground to admit them, as at least plausible. Let us review the history of the Lacedæmonians, and see if we cannot find matter of corroboration.

Less than one hundred years after the war of Troy, the descendants of Hercules, who had been exiled, and in a long course of years had greatly increased in numbers, renewed the attempt to recover possession of the Peloponnesus. With the assistance of a body of Dorians, then the most ferocious barbarians in all Greece, they succeeded, expelled most of the inhabitants, who took refuge in Attica and on the coast of Asia Minor, as well as in the islands of the Ionian sea. The Heraclidæ subverted the thrones of the princes of the Peloponnesian states, seized on the lands for themselves and such of their Dorian allies as chose to remain with them, and reduced to slavery such of the old stock of inhabitants as did not betake themselves to flight. Two sons of Aristodemus, of the race of Hercules, were placed on the throne of Lacedæmon.

It is well known, that Hercules for his exploits was deified; and as long as paganism was the popular religion of Greece, which it continued to be fifteen hundred years after this event, his name was adored with the most enthusiastic devotion. He was most emphatically the hero and the deity of the Greeks. Now, as the return of the Heraclidæ caused one of the most thorough and sweeping revolutions recorded in all history, so complete as in a great measure to change the inhabitants, and entirely to change the governing classes, and as they came back to Peloponnesus with the double claim of being conquerors and the progeny of a god, it is plain there was a patrician, heaven-descended class existing in the state long before the age of Lycurgus, engrossing to themselves a great part of the lands, and all the powers and advantages of the government.

It is impossible to say positively, whether this class consisted only of the race of Hercules, or whether it included also some of the chiefs of the Dorians. As Lycurgus is said to be only the tenth in descent from Hercules, the Heraclidæ, though sufficiently numerous for an order of nobility, could have been scarcely numerous enough to keep the remains of a conquered people in subjection. It is probable, that a large part of the holders of the conquered lands were not of that

101

heroic race. This is the more readily to be supposed, as Laconia is represented in very early times as a populous country, and containing a hundred cities. These no doubt were inconsiderable towns; yet, after allowing for a very great emigration in consequence of the conquest, we may believe that the native inhabitants still outnumbered their conquerors. The descendants of Hercules, being princes, were exclusively allowed the command of the armies, the exercise of all the powers of government, and their hereditary rank as an order of nobles, afterwards called, by way of distinction, Spartans. The rest of the citizens, who became distinguished by the appellation of Lacedæmonians, were the conquering soldiery, to whom lands were assigned in reward for their past services, and as a pledge of their future obedience. Thus, we may believe, a governing aristocracy and a national militia, in subordination to that body, were called into existence at the time and by the circumstances of the conquest.

It is also to be remembered, that all the governments of Greece were originally formed by the confederacy of cities; and in all of them the capital city aspired to the chief, and in every case where it was practicable, to the sole authority over the rest. In several of the confederacies this ambitious project was resisted with success. But in the earliest antiquity and immediately after the return of the Heraclidæ, we learn that Sparta was chosen as the residence of the kings and seat of government, and that the domination of that city was stretched over all the towns of Laconia. Helos alone resisted and was subdued;[11] and its inhabitants were reduced to a sort of qualified slavery, by which they were fixed to the soil as peasants to labor for their Spartan landlords. Now, as Sparta governed the state, and the aristocracy governed Sparta, for the kings, except in time of war, were ciphers, we cannot hesitate to admit, that these nobles were chiefly

---

[11] *See Strabo, Book VIII, for the derivation of* Helots *from* Helos.

collected as residents in the city of Sparta. The very fact, that there were two kings, must have annihilated their authority, if any had been intrusted to them. That circumstance and every other that has been transmitted to us by history proves, that the government was in the hands of an aristocracy.

Hence we discern the best reasons in the world, why Lycurgus did, and Solon did not, establish an aristocracy. Neither of them could create or annihilate the materials of their respective governments. The people of Attica, who called themselves with no little vanity, α'υτόχθο νες, or the original people, constituted a democracy, which could not be forced, and would not be persuaded, to establish a body of governing nobles. Lycurgus, on the contrary, found a numerous and powerful race of the first conquerors, outnumbered by slaves who were kept in subjection by an aristocracy with two kings at their head. Accordingly, it seems to have been the utmost extent of his undertaking, to new model the government rather than the nation. The aristocracy was itself in danger of degenerating into an oligarchy, and was exposed to perish by its own inevitable factions, as well as by the silent growth and consequent encroachments of the unprivileged classes of the citizens. Already the extreme disorders of the state portended convulsions and revolution.

In this emergency, he devised such expedients as would give, not liberty to the people, which seems not to have been in the least degree his concern, but stability and perpetuity to the aristocracy. He formed, or perhaps only revived, a senate of twenty eight members, elected for life by the numerous body of the noble Spartans. These Spartans had also their assemblies monthly, in which they exercised very important functions of the government. Thus two bodies were formed, who may be thought to bear some resemblance to the houses of Lords and Commons in England.

Having thus placed the government in the hands of the

Spartans, much was still necessary to enable them to maintain it. In that age preëminence could neither be gained, nor secured by commerce or arts, but only by arms. Here then, we see the obvious necessity of the case, that Lycurgus should, by his system of education and his discipline, make these Spartans really superior to the men they governed. This was the more necessary, as we are informed by ancient writers, that they were detested by the rest of the inhabitants.

This being admitted, and it can scarcely be denied, we can no longer so much as conceive, that it was the policy or any part of the plan of Lycurgus to include all the free citizens of Laconia, or even of the city of Sparta, in his great system of education. It was his object to establish an incontestable superiority in favor of the Spartans. By infusing into the other citizens the pride and desperate fanaticism of the nobles, the former, being also perfectly well trained to arms, would have been as incapable of submission and as capable of rule as their superiors.

Admitting that nothing is so much for the interest of a class of men as power, and they are very apt to think that nothing is, then surely nothing could be more for the interest of the aristocracy than the laws of Lycurgus, for in consequence of them they maintained their authority over the state for many ages. The power of the Roman patricians was from the first balanced, imperfectly enough we confess, by the people; but the whole power of the Lacedæmonian state was engrossed by the Spartans. Until the establishment of the ephori, one hundred and thirty years after Lycurgus, it does not appear, that, in respect to political power, there was any other people; the rest of the inhabitants of Laconia and Sparta were nothing.

If Lycurgus met with infinite difficulty in getting his laws established, it is certain he had vast means of influence in the pride and ambition of the nobles, who were so greatly interested in their adoption. In so great a length of time as had elapsed since the return of the Heraclidæ, many of these nobles, and probably still more of the soldiery, had diminished or alienated their original lots of land. The poor members of the aristocracy and of the militia would, of course, insist upon restoring the ancient division of lands by a new assignment. Lycurgus, knowing that power follows property, and especially property in lands, and intending to prevent all rivalship with the aristocracy, by giving to that body and their military dependents a monopoly of the lands, was inclined and enabled to restore the original division.

It cannot be believed, that without such reasons and helps, he could have originated a plan for an arbitrary assignment of the territory. On the contrary, it may be fairly presumed, that very few, and those great proprietors, were dispossessed, and very many were accommodated. By thus creating a stock of popularity with one class of men, and those the most numerous, he could use it to compel the submission of another and the most refractory. This, we are informed, is precisely what he did. Thus he established a perpetual fund for the support of this ruling aristocracy.

That it might be perpetual, he made the lands unalienable though inheritable; he proscribed all trade, manufactures, and luxury, and even gold and silver coins. He foresaw, that industry and trade would bring in wealth; and that wealth would confer distinction. In this event the military spirit would decline, and the unprivileged orders of the state would rise into importance. To guard against this disturbance of the operation of his system, he exerted all his great abilities to provide every political expedient possible to keep Sparta poor and warlike.

It will never be imagined, when he gave the purse to one set of men, or, in other words, all the lands to the aristocracy and the military, that he gave the sword to another set. On the contrary, we shall find that he established a complete monopoly of power and property in favor of the Spartans. It has been already observed, that this governing order resided chiefly in the *city;* and that we nowhere read of a Spartan education out of it. The inhabitants of Laconia, we are told, were deemed inferior to those of the city, not having the same education.

Are we to suppose, that the inhabitants of even the city of Sparta, or all such as were free, were indiscriminately fed at the public tables, and daily subjected to the whole discipline of Lycurgus? Even this is incredible. It cannot be imagined, that the landholders, of whom the number in Sparta and its immediate territory was at first nine thousand, were thus assembled and fed. If we take half that number for the city alone, we shall not readily admit, that they were educated and trained in this manner.

We should confine our calculation to the noble Spartans only; for Sparta was undoubtedly a great city, though we know not the extent of its population. But, as it contained inhabitants enough, though wholly unfortified and without walls, twice to repulse Epaminondas with his victorious army, we may reckon Sparta to be equal to Thebes or Athens. It was accounted one of the great cities of Greece, and might have fifty or sixty thousand inhabitants, certainly ten times too many to be fed in the public halls or in the barracks. As the landholders were a militia, and not a regular standing army, it is on that account the less to be admitted, that they were daily drawn out, exercised, and fed. Xenophon says, he has seen five thousand Lacedæmonians assembled together, and was scarcely able to pick out thirty Spartans. The Lacedæmonian armies often marched on expeditions with less than one hundred of this order.

This distinction was not merely nominal; if it had been, it would have soon disappeared from its frivolousness; and it must have been frivolous to the last degree, if these Spartans had not received a different sort of education, and claimed a very superior rank and authority in the state. When one hundred and thirty Spartans were shut up and besieged in the little island of Sphacteria, the government was extremely agitated, and offered to make the most extraordinary concessions to Athens to procure the release of these men. To the aristocracy, their destruction seemed like a dismemberment of their body.

This governing class, being also the fighting class, was continually diminishing. On the defeat of the Lacedæmonians at Leuctra, the government was thrown into the deepest consternation, because so unusual a number of Spartans and the king Cleombrotus were slain. They saw with pain and terror the reduction of the numbers, and the proportionate reduction of the influence and power of their order.

It may after all be said, although these facts prove, that all the free inhabitants of Sparta were not Spartans, yet it still remains a question, whether all the former did not receive the strict education prescribed by Lycurgus.

It is true, there is no express evidence to that point; but we may take these facts as evidence of the spirit of the government, and conclusive evidence, that from its very nature it could have no other spirit. That being premised, it would be truly surprising, that the strict discipline and education of the great legislator should be enforced upon all the citizens. As a common education makes men, could it be, that a Spartan education, which made heroes, was lavished upon the tradesmen of the city; (for the necessary trades were allowed from the first, and, no doubt, many more had got footing there,) upon the strangers, who might happen to reside in the city; and, above all, upon the numerous description of the sons of Helots, who had been made free for their services to the state?

As a mortal hatred subsisted between those freedmen and the nobles, it cannot be allowed that these latter had permitted, much less required, an exact equality as to the use of arms and every admired accomplishment that could be derived from education. On that supposition, ten or twenty thousand base-born heroes would have snatched the sway from the hands of less than one thousand heaven-descended heroes of the blood of Hercules. The education that conferred glory and distinction, for its chief object was to make every thing else seem vile, would have made power tempting, too tempting to remain for ages within reach, yet untouched.

On these grounds we seem to be authorized to conclude, that the Spartan education and discipline were not imposed on all the free inhabitants, although the language used by all the ancient writers on the subject scarcely admits of their restriction to the noble and military classes. Polybius, who is as remarkable for his gravity as for his good sense, warmly exclaims in praise of Lycurgus, as a sort of divinity, who had created a nation anew by his system of education.

We may conjecture, that the noble class, being the only one that attracted much notice, was put for the nation; or it might be, that while the sons of the nobles were educated by the State, great numbers of an inferior order were trained as soldiers; and these distinctions being known to everybody in the time of Xenophon, were not deemed to require a minute explanation. However that may be, Herodotus, whose notion of the universality of the Spartan system seems to be like that of all succeeding writers, uses an expression that will countenance our restriction of it, as we have before suggested. Giving an account of the dignity of the Spartan kings, he says: "If they dine at the public feasts, as they are obliged to do, unless specially excused, they are allowed a double portion of the food, as also if they are feasted by a private citizen." How could a private citizen invite a Spartan king to dine with him, if he were himself obliged to dine in the public hall? May we not, then, infer from this passage of Herodotus, that the citizens of Sparta dined and supped in their own houses?

That the regulations of Lycurgus for the education of youth, and for convening the citizens at the public meals, were not extended to all the inhabitants of the city of Sparta and its territory, may be inferred from some of the facts transmitted to us by Xenophon and Plutarch. When a male child was born, and after being examined by public officers, pronounced sound and worth the bringing up, one of the nine thousand lots was immediately assigned to him. Now if a trademan's, a slave's, or a stranger's son should happen to be born of as good a shape as a noble Spartan's, is it to be supposed a lot would be given to the former and refused to the latter, who might come into the world the day after they were all disposed of? A populous city, like Sparta, would have more healthy male children than lots. But supposing the distribution confined to the continually diminishing military class of Spartans, there would be more lots than children; and this was in fact the case. The lands assigned as a fund for the military class, proved more than sufficient for the number of Spartans. Supposing it liable to be absorbed by other children, it would not only have proved insufficient, but it would have been employed to defeat its original use and destination, to raise the degraded classes, and to stint or starve the military class.

Another fact is worth observation. As the messes or tables of the public meals, which, we are told, admitted fifteen, no person was received without the consent of the whole company. Can we then suppose, for a moment, the law required every inhabitant to eat at these tables, and yet authorized every citizen to exclude him? Where was he to dine? And where, let it be asked, were those persons to dine, who having lost their arms, or turned their backs in battle, were stigmatized and shunned by all citizens?

Again, we are told, the very children were obliged to attend those meals, because they heard only wise and solid discourse on such occasions. If the ignorant, sordid rabble of a great city were really seated at those tables, will any man think, that Lycurgus himself, if he had lived as long as his institutions, could have kept order? or that, without a miraculous inspiration, as often as the tables were spread, the conversation could have been edifying? It is incredible and absurd.

The sons of noble Spartans were, no doubt, educated by the state, were kept in an academy, dined and supped together, and probably it was the official duty of the kings to superintend their education. They were trained, not as citizens, but as rulers; not simply as soldiers, but as generals. To perpetuate the aristocracy, the government took care to exclude accident, caprice, and folly as much as possible from all influence on the young nobles. It is obvious, that the stability of the government depended on its transmitting its peculiar identity of perfection from generation to generation. All this makes it natural, that the rulers should be educated by the state, and that the citizens who had only to obey, should not be. This idea derives some further force from the observation of Plutarch, who says: "The chief object of Lycurgus being a system of education, and to establish habits and manners, he would not permit his laws to be reduced to writing." This can hardly be supposed, if they were intended for a whole nation. The class of Spartans, though amounting to several thousands originally, were reduced in the time of Xenophon to about seven hundred; and even of these the greater part were in a state of poverty. Agis and Cleomenes, two kings of Lacedæmon, successively attempted to restore the strict discipline of Lycurgus. Plutarch informs us, that Cleomenes, when attempting to enforce a new division of the lands, alleged, in recommendation of the measure, that it would provide means for admitting foreigners of merit to citizenship. The state in that case, he said, would no longer want defenders, alluding to the reduced number of Spartans. This government had ever been to the last degree averse from granting citizenship, precisely because the exclusive possessors of power are ever unwilling to admit partners. Now, if there were many thousand able-bodied brave men in Sparta, as Cleomenes knew they were, for he led a gallant army of them into the field, why did he lament the want of defenders of the state? Why did he speak of admitting foreigners to take lands and become citizens, when it was so easy a thing to raise Lacedæmonians to be Spartans, especially too, if they had received the same public education? It is however evident, from this passage of Plutarch, that they had not received such an education, that they did not hold so high a rank in the state, and that it could not be gratuitously conferred upon them. *Noble* foreigners might be made citizens without any degradation of the Spartan pride; but the admission of the plebeian inhabitants of Sparta to a higher rank would be a source both of individual mortification and of public disorder; the partition between ranks would be broken down.

We shall be further confirmed in our opinion of the exclusive aristocratical policy of the Spartan government by a closer observation of its effects.

In the Lacedæmonian state there were two descriptions of slaves, the Helots, who were an oppressed, degraded peasantry, the cultivators of the soil on a fixed rent for their Spartan landlords; and the domestic slaves, who were treated with still greater rigor. These two classes are supposed to have amounted to nearly one half the population. The free citizens may be also placed in two classes, the Spartans and the Lacedæmonians. These latter must at all times have greatly exceeded the Spartans in number, yet by the original plan of Lycurgus their political power was next to nothing.

The kings and their wives, the senators and all magistrates, except the ephori, and it is believed all military officers of high rank, must have been Spartans. The Spartans were electors also of the senators for life; but, as the choice was determined by a computation of the number of suffrages by the noise of the acclamations, in favor of a candidate, it may be conjectured, the senate in effect filled up the vacancies in its own body. A Spartan assembly was held once a month. Thus we see the powers of government were engrossed by a senate, and its dignities and privileges by an hereditary aristocracy.

There was, indeed, a general assembly of the Lacedæmonian nation to determine on peace, war, and alliances. To this assembly deputies from the several cities and from the allied states were admitted. Yet, as it was convened at Sparta, as its objects concerned chiefly the external policy, and as the effective government was in the hands of the aristocracy, it was not found to disturb or divide their monopoly of power.

To perpetuate this order of things, Lycurgus was not more solicitous by his institutions to elevate one class, than to depress and disarm every other. We must repeat it, for this reason it was, he forbade all arts, except such as could not be dispensed with; even learning itself was denied its honors; he did not allow his Spartans to travel into foreign countries, nor foreigners to be admitted to Sparta; he interdicted trade, luxury, and gold and silver; he would have his Spartans wholly intent on military distinction; arms, and only arms should confer glory. His Spartans did not labor themselves, but the Helots labored for them. Not only was the monopoly of power complete, but the roots and seeds of future rivalship by the depressed classes of the society seemed to be exterminated.

Here let us pause to make a reflection. For more than two thousand years the world has been loud and violent in its panegyric of Spartan virtue, because Lycurgus had bestowed all possible care to make his nobles brave, without having employed the least to make them honest; because he had made them love power better than labor; because they loved their country, while they owned and governed it; and because, when riches did not command honor, and titled poverty did, they sought honor in the only way in which it was to be had, and held that preferable which everybody in that age actually preferred. Spartan virtue did not, most certainly, include morals. The Roman Cincinnatus was proud of his birth, and probably much the prouder for his poverty. It is not at this degenerate day at all essential to the glory of a great general, that he should have a great estate.

Effectual as for some ages this policy of Lycurgus was, time and the revolution of human affairs at length gradually subverted it. The depressed classes of the state slowly rose from the ground, and from the feet of the aristocracy, and claimed and took their station in society.

It may be supposed the Spartans exacted at first from the Helots, who cultivated the soil, as large a part of the produce as they possibly could. It was easier to require than to get much; indeed, by requiring too much, they would get nothing. Despair would baffle rapacity. It is also to be conceded that the proportion once fixed must remain fixed. This, ancient writers inform us, was the case. Now as the Spartans were a body continually diminishing, their power to extort must have declined with their numbers. Time also must have made great changes in the value of the rents, though payable in kind. Accordingly, we are told that most of the Spartan families fell into poverty, and many of the Helots became very rich. Their rise to some share of political and personal importance was the necessary consequence.

It was only one hundred and thirty years after Lycurgus that the operation of these principles was made manifest, and their progress accelerated, by the establishment of the ephori. These five annual magistrates resembled the Roman tribunes of the people, were elected by the mass of the nation, and in fact were often selected from the dregs of the people. At first their power and their pretensions were moderate; but as the aristocracy continued to decline, and the democracy, whose favorites and champions they were, made haste to raise itself, they gradually subverted the original system of the government, and engrossed its powers. They deposed kings, and exercised the functions of sovereignty themselves.

Hence it is that all antiquity bewails the decay of Spartan virtue. The citizens had not declined from virtue, for the Spartan morals were ever bad; but the aristocracy had fallen from power. Polybius assures us that the institutions of Lycurgus were admirably adapted to Sparta, while it was content to remain a small state, and refrained from ambitious wars to conquer Greece and Asia. Their degeneracy is dated from the time when Lysander took Athens, and when Agesilaus made his expedition against the Persian king. Sparta was then filled with rich spoils, and corruption entered, they say, with riches. The laboring classes had always loved property, but were deprived as much as possible by Lycurgus of all chances to amass it. The governing class had not, until these wars, enjoyed many opportunities to get it, nor had it then become an object of personal influence and consideration.

But too much influence seems to be allowed to these victories. In a very early age, the Lacedæmonians, after an obstinate and long protracted contest, had subdued Messene, a state little less considerable than their own, and made slaves of the people. The property was the booty of the conquerors; yet they maintained their laws for many hundred years after that event. The Romans were conquerors from the days of Romulus, if we except the peaceful reign of Numa; yet the greatest boasts of Roman simplicity and virtue, of love of country and contempt of wealth, are made in the very crisis of their most dangerous wars with Pyrrhus and the Samnites, which gave them the dominion of Italy.

Had the Lacedæmonians abstained from wars of ambition, they would have changed, or as it is the fashion to term it, degenerated. The wars of Lysander and Agesilaus furnished the occasions, but were not the causes of the change. When property and power, once a Spartan monopoly, had passed into other hands, the change was inevitable.

Spartan equality has been the everlasting boast of declamation. It was not Lycurgus's view to make his nobles better, but to raise them higher than other men; and that they might to the end of time be sustained at that point of elevation, he contrived to sink all other classes to servitude or insignificance. The nobles were a sort of perpetual garrison for Sparta. Lycurgus did not intend to train all the inhabitants to be nobles.

Having made this accurate distinction of orders in the state, and removed, as far as human wisdom could do it, all the causes that might revive their rivalships and struggles, he may be pronounced the friend of the independence and of the tranquillity of his country, but without excessive absurdity he cannot be allowed to be the founder of equal liberty. The Lacedæmonians had all the liberty, and most of the virtues and vices of a camp, which is always quiet, and generally has reason to be, as long as subordination is maintained.

Is it wonderful then that a state, thus admirably organized for its own peculiar purposes, was able, for so many centuries, to preserve itself unsubdued by its hostile neighbors? or that the aristocracy, who engrossed all political power, as well as the command of armies, should be able so long to hinder the excluded orders of the state from obtaining a share in the government of it?

IV.

ESSAYS ON
MONARCHICAL
VERSUS REPUBLICAN
GOVERNMENT

═══

THE REPUBLICAN XI

Boston Gazette, SEPTEMBER 10, 1804
Reprinted from the *Repertory*

> *The progress of our affairs is in conformity with the fixed laws of our nature, and the known course of Republics. Our wisdom made a government, and committed it to our virtue to keep, but our passions have engrossed it, and they have armed our vices to maintain their usurpation.*

The will of the people ought to prevail. This is the cant of all demagogues. But, we demand, What is meant by this will? It is understood that their reasonable, their honest, their deliberate will ought to prevail—then who denies it? Surely not the federalists? It is no part of their political creed to maintain that such will of the people ought to be opposed.

116

The federalist, however, never considered the miserable banditti, the lazaroni, who walked in procession at Philadelphia, on the funeral of Dr. Rittenhouse, as the Democratic Society—they never considered these ignorant, needy, vicious, French *sans cullottes* [*sic*], as the people, though their resolves in opposition to Washington and the laws, frequently used and abused the authority of that name.

The will of the people, to claim authority, must be rightful—and to be rightful, it must be reasonable. If it should ever happen, in a moment of rage and blindness, that the people desire a wicked thing to be done, the demagogues, who desire nothing else, would of course say, and emphatically on such an occasion, their voice is the voice of God. But ought any honest man, or true patriot, to obey or approve such will of the people? Is there any one man without passions, and when these domineer, is that man's will a proper rule even for the government of his own conduct? Still less is it a safe or fit role in any case that affects the rights of another person. Would it not then be absurd beyond measure, to pretend that a million of men, in a transport of fury, can do no wrong? that their will is as superior to law and right as it is to the resistance of its innocent victims? On the contrary, is there one of the million who would not look the next day with horror and remorse on the devastations of his madness, and lament that it was not possible to restrain the work of men while it was doing, nor to repair it after it was accomplished. Such bitter, such useless regrets, are all that even one in a million will bestow on the havoc of a day. For Revolution has no eyes for foresight, no time for repentance. Assuming the name of the people, and acting by the wonder-working power of their passions, none of the agents are allowed leisure or opportunities to look round or look forward. Each day has its peculiar excitements. A rabble animated by praise as heroes and reformers, delighted with scenes in which all is bustle, and all shifting, themselves risking nothing, and expecting, and being promised everything, are the instruments of revolution, the more formidable for being blind and passive. They foresee nothing, they dread nothing; but kindle in their course, for it is downhill.

Yet even at the bottom, and after the crash of their fall, the democrats are still amused with sounds, still consoled for the loss of liberty, a loss which the licentious passions of the multitude fatally ensures; by the currency of the empty words of its false friends. Liberty, equality, and the rights of man, the sovereignty of the people, the republic, &c. &c. are scarcely less in use in France than they were in 1793.

It is a curious and not uninstructive comment upon the sense and sincerity with which our demagogues affect to employ these phrases, that the French tribunate, and the new Emperor Bonaparte, have not renounced them. The will of the people ought to prevail, says, the pamphlet of "anonymous slander." The national will, says a tribunate in the decree making Bonaparte emperor, the national will, when it could manifest itself with the greatest freedom, declared for the unity of the supreme power, and for its hereditary succession; that is, that the French have ever been royalists, while our democratic dupes have exulted in the accession of thirty millions to the republican cause. This monarchical opinion, they rather say, has been the first wish of the French people. By this arrangement, they add, France may earnest the maintenance of the rights and liberties of the people. And it is no bad hint to us, Americans, when the tribunate proceed in virtue of the 29th Article of their Constitution to proclaim Bonaparte emperor. It is not, they say, a change, but the perfecting and establishing of the republic, that is accomplished by this formal institution of monarchy. We have seen an amendment, as it is called, of our Constitution, by which a dominant [. . .] President for life. Is this copied, we ask, from the aforesaid 29th Article of the French Constitution? It will show how easily paper republican constitutions are torn, when a consul wished to be emperor.

Bonaparte, in his reply to the Conservative Senate, tells that body that all his thoughts and cares have been long occupied for the people—and he goes on to observe, at least as well as the pamphlet says the late Samuel Adams observed, that the people have the sovereignty. We have been constantly guided by this grand truth, says the pious, equality loving Emperor, that the sovereignty resides in the French people. He also speaks of improving their institutions so as to secure the triumph of equality and public liberty forever. Hence, for the people's sake, he mounts a throne. Is not this edifying? Can any man, of sense enough to take care of his farm, in Berkshire, read the pamphlet, so secretly circulated, like counterfeit bank money, to influence the election of governor and senators—can any man read that pamphlet, and note the cant, the stale imposture of love for the people, which pervades it, without scorn and contempt for the baseness of it? Is it possible that we shall go on boasting of our sense and information, when the people are addressed with flattery so coarse and nauseous, and when they are deceived too by such tricks as scarcely deserve the praise of sleight of hand. Yet on this ground of difference, the pamphleteer pretends to exhibit the democratic and federal parties; the former as those who respect the national will, the latter as its opposers.

This topic is too fruitful as well as too interesting, to be fully discussed in one number of these essays. But as the delusion, that the demagogues are for the people, and the federalists against them, constitutes the chief strength of the jacobins, it will be necessary to return to the subject on some future occasion.

119

THE DANGERS OF AMERICAN LIBERTY

WRITTEN IN THE BEGINNING OF
THE YEAR 1805

In February, 1805, the following sketch of a dissertation of "The Dangers of American Liberty," accompanied with a short familiar letter,[12] was sent by Mr. Ames to a friend for his perusal. It was soon returned, for the purposes expressed in the author's letter, with a hope that he would reconsider, revise, and complete it; and especially that he would fulfill his original design of applying his argument in a manner that would lead the people to preserve as long as possible the civil blessings they enjoy, and not sacrifice them to delusive theories.

It does not appear that the author ever resumed his subject, or that the manuscript was opened after that period, until since his death. Yet it is thought

---

[12] *The following is the letter of Mr. Ames, mentioned above.*

MY DEAR FRIEND,

You will see the deficiencies and faults of this performance. You will see that the conclusion, if your life and patience should hold out to the end, is incomplete. There is, I dare say, tautology, perhaps contradiction. It is an effusion from the mind of the stock that was laid up in it, without any resort to books. Of course it wants more facts, more illustrations, more exact method, to change its aspect of declamation and rhetorical flourish into a business performance. I know it is unequal. When the children cried, or my head ached, the work flagged. To be of value enough for the author to own it, he must be allowed time, must bestow on it more thought, search for facts and principles in pamphlets and larger works, and in short make it entirely over again.

Therefore, it is not shown to you for publication, or approbation, as a thing that is written, but a subject proposed to be written upon, for which you will furnish hints and counsels.
1805.

Yours, truly
[S. AMES]

not improper to gratify the public with a work,
which, though quite imperfect, would, if it had
been finished, have been found deeply interesting to
its welfare.

Sic tibi persuade, me dies et noctes
nihil aliud agere, nihil curare, nisi ut mei
cives salvi liberique sing. *Ep. Famil.* 1.24.
Be assured, therefore, that neither day
nor night have I any cares, any labors, but for
the safety and freedom of my fellow citizens.

I AM NOT positive that it is of any immediate use to our country that its true friends should better understand one another; nor am I apprehensive that the crudities which my ever hasty pen confides to my friends will essentially mislead their opinion in respect either to myself or to public affairs. At a time when men eminently wise cherish almost any hopes, however vain, because they choose to be blind to their fears, it would be neither extraordinary nor disreputable for me to mistake the degree of maturity to which our political vices have arrived, nor to err in computing how near or how far off we stand from the term of their fatal consummation.

I fear that the future fortunes of our country no longer depend on counsel. We have persevered in our errors too long to change our propensities by now enlightening our convictions. The political sphere, like the globe we tread upon, never stands still, but with a silent swiftness accomplishes the revolutions which, we are too ready to believe, are effected by our wisdom, or might have been controlled by our efforts. There is a kind of fatality in the affairs of republics, that eludes the foresight of the wise as much as it frustrates the toils and sacrifices of the patriot and the hero. Events proceed, not as they were expected or intended, but as they are impelled by the irresistible laws of our political existence. Things inevitable happen, and we are astonished, as if they were miracles, and the course of nature had been overpowered or suspended to produce them. Hence it is, that, till lately, more than half our countrymen believed our public tranquillity was firmly established, and that our liberty did not merely rest upon dry land, but was wedged, or rather rooted high above the flood in the rocks of granite, as immovably as the pillars that prop the universe. They, or at least the discerning of them, are at length no less disappointed than terrified to perceive that we have all the time floated, with a fearless and unregarded course, down the stream of events, till we are now visibly drawn within the revolutionary suction of Niagara, and every thing that is liberty will be dashed to pieces in the descent.

We have been accustomed to consider the pretension of Englishmen to be free as a proof how completely they were broken to subjection, or hardened in imposture. We have insisted, that they had no constitution, because they never made one; and that their boasted government, which is just what time and accident have made it, was palsied with age, and blue with the plague-sores of corruption. We have believed that it derived its stability, not from reason, but from prejudice; that it is supported, not because it is favorable to liberty, but as it is dear to national pride; that it is reverenced, not for its excellence, but because ignorance is naturally the idolater of antiquity; that it is not sound and healthful, but derives a morbid energy from disease, and an unaccountable aliment from the canker that corrodes its vitals.

But we maintained that the federal Constitution, with all the bloom of youth and splendor of innocence, was gifted with immortality. For if time should impair its force, or faction tarnish its charms, the people, ever vigilant to discern its wants, ever powerful to provide for them, would miraculously restore it to the field, like some wounded hero of the epic, to take a signal vengeance on its enemies, or like Antæus, invigorated by touching his mother earth, to rise the stronger for a fall.

There is of course a large portion of our citizens who will not believe, even on the evidence of facts, that any public evils exist, or are impending. They deride the apprehensions of those who foresee that licentiousness will prove, as it ever has proved, fatal to liberty. They consider her as a nymph, who need not be coy to keep herself pure, but that on the contrary, her chastity will grow robust by frequent scuffles with her seducers. They say, while a faction is a minority it will remain harmless by being outvoted; and if it should become a majority, all its acts, however profligate or violent, are then legitimate. For with the democrats the people is a sovereign who can do [no] wrong, even when he respects and spares no existing right, and whose voice, however obtained or however counterfeited, bears all the sanctity and all the force of a living divinity.

Where, then, it will be asked, in a tone both of menace and of triumph, can the people's dangers lie, unless it be with the persecuted federalists? They are the partisans of monarchy, who propagate their principles in order, as soon as they have increased their sect, to introduce a king; for by this only avenue they foretell his approach. Is it possible the people should ever be their own enemies? If all government were dissolved to-day, would they not reëstablish it to-morrow, with no other prejudice to the public liberty than some superfluous fears of its friends, some abortive projects of its enemies? Nay, would not liberty rise resplendent with the light of fresh experience, and coated in the sevenfold mail of constitutional amendments?

These opinions are fiercely maintained, not only as if there were evidence to prove them, but as if it were a merit to believe them, by men who tell you that in the most desperate extremity of faction or usurpation we have an unfailing resource in the good sense of the nation. They assure us there is at least as much wisdom in the people as in these ingenious tenets of their creed.

For any purpose, therefore, of popular use or general impression, it seems almost fruitless to discuss the question, whether our public liberty can subsist, and what is to be the condition of that awful futurity to which we are hastening. The clamors of party are so loud, and the resistance of national vanity is so stubborn, it will be impossible to convince any but the very wise, (and in every state they are the very few,) that our democratic liberty is utterly untenable; that we are devoted to the successive struggles of factions, who will rule by turns, the worst of whom will rule last, and triumph by the sword. But for the wise this unwelcome task is, perhaps, superfluous: they, possibly, are already convinced.

All such men are, or ought to be, agreed that simple governments are despotisms; and of all despotisms a democracy, though the least durable, is the most violent. It is also true, that all the existing governments we are acquainted with are more or less mixed, or balanced and checked, however imperfectly, by the ingredients and principles that belong to the other simple sorts. It is nevertheless a fact, that there is scarcely any civil constitution in the world, that, according to American ideas, is so mixed and combined as to be favorable to the liberty of the subject—none, absolutely none, that an American patriot would be willing to adopt for, much less to impose on, his country. Without pretending to define that liberty, which writers at length agree is incapable of any precise and comprehensive definition, all the European governments, except the British, admit a most formidable portion of arbitrary power; whereas in America no plan of government, without a large and preponderating commixture of democracy, can for a moment possess our confidence and attachment.

It is unquestionable that the concern of the people in the affairs of such a government tends to elevate the character, and enlarge the comprehension, as well as the enjoyments

of the citizens; and supposing the government wisely constituted, and the laws steadily and firmly carried into execution,
these effects, in which every lover of mankind must exult,
will not be attended with a corresponding depravation of the
public manners and morals. I have never yet met with an
American of any party who seemed willing to exclude the
people from their temperate and well-regulated share of
concern in the government. Indeed it is notorious, that there
was scarcely an advocate for the federal Constitution who
was not anxious, from the first, to hazard the experiment of
an unprecedented, and almost unqualified proportion of
democracy, both in constructing and administering the government, and who did not rely with confidence, if not blind
presumption, on its success. This is certain, the body of the
federalists were always, and yet are, essentially democratic
in their political notions. The truth is, the American nation,
with ideas and prejudices wholly democratic, undertook to
frame, and expected tranquilly and with energy and success
to administer, a republican government.

It is and ever has been my belief, that the federal
Constitution was as good, or very nearly as good, as our
country could bear; that the attempt to introduce a mixed
monarchy was never thought of, and would have failed if it
had been made; and could have proved only an inveterate
curse to the nation if it had been adopted cheerfully, and
even unanimously, by the people. Our materials for a
government were all democratic, and whatever the hazard of
their combination may be, our Solons and Lycurguses in the
convention had no alternative, nothing to consider, but how
to combine them, so as to insure the longest duration to the
Constitution, and the most favorable chance for the public
liberty in the event of those changes, which the frailty of the
structure of our government, the operation of time and
accident, and the maturity and development of the national
character were well understood to portend. We should have

succeeded worse if we had trusted to our metaphysics more. Experience must be our physician, though his medicines may kill.

The danger obviously was, that a species of government in which the people choose all the rulers, and then, by themselves or ambitious demagogues pretending to be the people, claim and exercise an effective control over what is called the government, would be found on trial no better than a turbulent, licentious democracy. The danger was that their best interests would be neglected, their dearest rights violated, their sober reason silenced, and the worst passions of the worst men not only freed from legal restraint, but invested with public power. The known propensity of a democracy is to licentiousness, which the ambitious call, and the ignorant believe to be, liberty.

The great object, then, of political wisdom in framing our Constitution, was to guard against licentiousness, that inbred malady of democracies, that deforms their infancy with gray hairs and decrepitude.

The federalists relied much on the efficiency of an independent judiciary, as a check on the hasty turbulence of the popular passions. They supposed the senate, proceeding from the states, and chosen for six years, would form a sort of balance to the democracy, and realize the hope that a federal republic of states might subsist. They counted much on the information of the citizens; that they would give their unremitted attention to public affairs; that either dissensions would not arise in our happy country, or if they should, that the citizens would remain calm, and would walk, like the three Jews in Nebuchadnezzar's furnace, unharmed amidst the fires of party.

It is needless to ask how rational such hopes were, or how far experience has verified them.

The progress of party has given to Virginia a preponderance that perhaps was not foreseen. Certainly, since the late amendment in the article for the choice of president and vice-president, there is no existing provision of any efficacy to counteract it.

The project of arranging states in a federal union has long been deemed, by able writers and statesmen, more promising than the scheme of a single republic. The experiment, it has been supposed, has not yet been fairly tried; and much has been expected from the example of America.

If states were neither able nor inclined to obstruct the federal union, much indeed might be hoped from such a confederation. But Virginia, Pennsylvania, and New York are of an extent sufficient to form potent monarchies, and of course are too powerful, as well as too proud, to be subjects of the federal laws. Accordingly, one of the first schemes of amendment, and the most early executed, was to exempt them in form from the obligations of justice. States are not liable to be sued. Either the federal head or the powerful members must govern. Now, as it is a thing ascertained by experience that the great states are not willing, and cannot be compelled to obey the union, it is manifest that their ambition is most singularly invited to aspire to the usurpation or control of the powers of the confederacy. A confederacy of many states, all of them small in extent and population, not only might not obstruct, but happily facilitate the federal authority. But the late presidential amendment demonstrates the overwhelming preponderance of several great states, combining together to engross the control of federal affairs.

There never has existed a federal union in which the leading states were not ambitious to rule, and did not endeavor to rule by fomenting factions in the small states, and thus engross the management of the federal concerns. Hence it was, that Sparta, at the head of the Peloponnesus, filled all Greece with terror and dissension. In every city she had an aristocratical party to kill or to banish the popular faction that was devoted to her rival, Athens; so that each city was inhabited by two hostile nations, whom no laws of war could control, no leagues or treaties bind. Sometimes Athens, sometimes Sparta took the ascendant, and influenced the decrees of the famous Amphyctionic council, the boasted federal head of the Grecian republics. But at all times that head was wholly destitute of authority, except when violent and sanguinary measures were dictated to it by some preponderant member. The small states were immediately reduced to an absolute nullity, and were subject to the most odious of all oppressions, the domination of one state over another state.

The Grecian states, forming the Amphyctionic league, composed the most illustrious federal republic that ever existed. Its dissolution and ruin were brought about by the operation of the principles and passions that are inherent in all such associations. The Thebans, one of the leading states, uniting with the Thessalians, both animated by jealousy and resentment against the Phocians, procured a decree of the council of the Amphyctions, where their joint influence predominated, as that of Virginia now does in congress, condemning the Phocians to a heavy fine for some pretended sacrilege they had committed on the lands consecrated to the temple of Delphi. Finding the Phocians, as they expected and wished, not inclined to submit, by a second decree they devoted their lands to the god of that temple, and called upon all Greece to arm in their sacred cause, for so they affected to call it. A contest thus began which was doubly sanguinary, because it combined the characters of a religious and civil war, and raged for more than ten years. In the progress of it, the famous Philip of Macedon found means to introduce himself as a party; and the nature of his measures, as well as their final success, is an everlasting warning to all federal republics. He appears, from the first moment of his reign, to have planned the subjugation of Greece; and in two-and-twenty years he accomplished his purpose.

After having made his escape from the city of Thebes, where he had been a hostage, he had to recover his hereditary kingdom, weakened by successive defeats, and distracted with factions from foreign invaders, and from two dangerous competitors of his throne. As soon as he became powerful, his restless ambition sought every opportunity to intermeddle in the affairs of Greece, in respect to which Macedonia was considered an alien, and the sacred war soon furnished it. Invited by the Thessalians to assist them against the Phocians, he pretended an extraordinary zeal for religion, as well as respect for the decree of the Amphyctions. Like more modern demagogues, he made use of his popularity first to prepare the way for his arms. He had no great difficulty in subduing them; and obtained for his reward another Amphyctionic decree, by which the vote of Phocis was forever transferred to Philip and his descendants. Philip soon after took possession of the pass of Thermopylæ, and within eight years turned his arms against those very Thebans whom he had before assisted. They had no refuge in the federal union which they had helped to enfeeble. They were utterly defeated; Thebes, the pride of Greece, was razed to the ground; the citizens were sold into slavery; and the national liberties were extinguished forever.

Here let Americans read their own history. Here let even Virginia learn how perilous and how frail will be the consummation of her schemes. Powerful states, that combine to domineer over the weak, will be inevitably divided by their success and ravaged with civil war, often baffled, always agitated by intrigue, shaken with alarms, and finally involved in one common slavery and ruin, of which they are no less conspicuously the artificers than the victims.

If, in the nature of things, there could be any experience which would be extensively instructive, but our own, all history lies open for our warning,—open like a churchyard, all whose lessons are solemn, and chiselled for eternity in the hard stone,—lessons that whisper, O! that they could thunder to republics, "Your passions and vices forbid you to be free."

But experience, though she teaches wisdom, teaches it too late. The most signal events pass away unprofitably for the generation in which they occur, till at length, a people, deaf to the things that belong to its peace, is destroyed or enslaved, because it will not be instructed.

From these reflections, the political observer will infer that the American republic is impelled by the force of state ambition and of democratic licentiousness; and he will inquire, which of the two is our strongest propensity. Is the sovereign power to be contacted to a state centre? Is Virginia to be our Rome? And are we to be her Latin or Italian allies, like them to be emulous of the honor of our chains on the terms of imposing them on Louisiana, Mexico, or Santa Fe? Or are we to run the giddy circle of popular licentiousness, beginning in delusion, quickened by vice, and ending in wretchedness?

But though these two seem to be contrary impulses, it will appear, nevertheless, on examination, that they really lead to but one result.

The great state of Virginia has fomented a licentious spirit among all her neighbors. Her citizens imagine that they are democrats, and their abstract theories are in fact democratic; but their state policy is that of a genuine aristocracy or oligarchy. Whatever their notions or their state practice may be, their policy, as it respects the other states, is to throw all power into the hands of democratic zealots or jacobin knaves; for some of these may be deluded and others bought to promote her designs. And, even independently of a direct Virginia influence, every state faction will find its account in courting the alliance and promoting the views of this great leader. Those who labor to gain a factious power in a state, and those who aspire to get a paramount jurisdiction over it, will not be slow to discern that they have a common cause to pursue.

In the intermediate progress of our affairs, the ambition of Virginia may be gratified. So long as popular licentiousness is operating with no lingering industry to effect our yet unfinished ruin, she may flourish the whip of dominion in her hands; but as soon as it is accomplished she will be the associate of our shame, and bleed under its lashes. For democatic license leads not to a monarchy regulated by laws, but to the ferocious despotism of a chieftain, who owes his elevation to arms and violence, and leans on his sword as the only prop of his dominion. Such a conqueror, jealous and fond of nothing but his power, will care no more for Virginia, though he may rise by Virginia, than Bonaparte does for Corsica. Virginia will then find, that, like ancient Thebes, she has worked for Philip, and forged her own fetters.

There are few, even among the democrats, who will doubt, though to a man they will deny, that the ambition of that state is inordinate, and unless seasonably counteracted, will be fatal; yet they will persevere in striving for power in their states, before they think it necessary, or can find it convenient to attend to her encroachments.

But there are not many, perhaps not five hundred, even among the federalists, who yet allow themselves to view the progress of licentiousness as so speedy, so sure, and so fatal, as the deplorable experience of our country shows that it is, and the evidence of history and the constitution of human nature demonstrate that it must be.

The truth is, such an opinion, admitted with all the terrible light of its proof, no less shocks our fears than our vanity, no less disturbs our quiet than our prejudices. We are summoned by the tocsin to every perilous and painful duty. Our days are made heavy with the pressure of anxiety, and our nights restless with visions of horror. We listen to the

131

clank of chains, and overhear the whispers of assassins. We mark the barbarous dissonance of mingled rage and triumph in the yell of an infatuated mob; we see the dismal glare of their burnings and scent the loathsome steam of human victims offered in sacrifice.

These reflections may account for the often lamented blindness, as well as apathy of our well-disposed citizens. Who would choose to study the tremendous records of the fates, or to remain long in the dungeon of the furies? Who that is penetrating enough to foresee our scarcely hidden destiny, is hardy enough to endure its anxious contemplation?

It may not long be more safe to disturb than it is easy to enlighten the democratic faith in regard to our political propensities, since it will neither regard what is obvious, nor yield to the impression of events, even after they have happened. The thoughtless and ignorant care for nothing but the name of liberty, which is as much the end as the instrument of party, and equally fills up the measure of their comprehension and desires. According to the conception of such men, the public liberty can never perish; it will enjoy immortality, like the dead in the memory of the living. We have heard the French prattle about its rights, and seen them swagger in the fancied possession of its distinctions long after they were crushed by the weight of their chains. The Romans were not only amused, but really made vain by the boast of their liberty, while they sweated and trembled under the despotism of the emperors, the most odious monsters that ever infested the earth. It is remarkable that Cicero, with all his dignity and good sense, found it a popular seasoning of his harangue, six years after Julius Cæsar had established a monarchy, and only six months before Octavius totally subverted the commonwealth, to say, "It is not possible for the people of Rome to be slaves, whom the gods have destined to the command of all nations. Other nations may endure slavery, but the proper end and business of the Roman people is liberty."

This very opinion in regard to the destinies of our country is neither less extensively diffused, nor less solidly established. Such men will persist in thinking our liberty cannot be in danger till it is irretrievably lost. It is even the boast of multitudes that our system of government is a pure democracy.

What is there left that can check its excesses or retard the velocity of its fall? Not the control of the several states, for they already whirl in the vortex of faction; and of consequence, not the senate, which is appointed by the states. Surely not the judiciary, for we cannot expect the office of the priesthood from the victim at the altar. Are we to be sheltered by the force of ancient manners? Will this be sufficient to control the two evil spirits of license and innovation? Where is any vestige of those manners left, but in New England? And even in New England their authority is contested and their purity debased. Are our civil and religious institutions to stand so firmly as to sustain themselves and so much of the fabric of the public order as is propped by their support? On the contrary, do we not find the ruling faction in avowed hostility to our religious institutions? In effect, though not in form, their protection is abandoned by our laws and confided to the steadiness of sentiment and fashion; and if they are still powerful auxiliaries of lawful authority, it is owing to the tenaciousness with which even a degenerate people maintain their habits, and to a yet remaining, though impaired veneration for the maxims of our ancestors. We are changing, and if democracy triumphs in New England, it is to be apprehended that in a few years we shall be as prone to disclaim our great progenitors, as they, if they should return again to the earth, with grief and shame to disown their degenerate descendants.

Is the turbulence of our democracy to be restrained by preferring to the magistracy only the grave and upright, the men who profess the best moral and religious principles, and whose lives bear testimony in favor of their profession, whose virtues inspire confidence, whose services, gratitude, and whose talents command admiration? Such magistrates would add dignity to the best government, and disarm the malignity of the worst. But the bare moving of this question will be understood as a sarcasm by men of both parties. The powers of impudence itself are scarcely adequate to say that our magistrates are such men. The atrocities of a distinguished tyrant might provoke satire to string his bow, and with the arrow of Philoctetes to inflict the immedicable wound. We have no Juvenal; and if we had, he would scorn to dissect the vice that wants firmness for the knife, to elevate that he might hit his object, and to dignify low profligacy to be the vehicle of a loathsome immortality.

It never has happened in the world, and it never will, that a democracy has been kept out of the control of the fiercest and most turbulent spirits in the society; they will breathe into it all their own fury, and make it subservient to the worst designs of the worst men.

Although it does not appear that the science of good government has made any advances since the invention of printing, it is nevertheless the opinion of many that this art has risen, like another sun in the sky, to shed new light and joy on the political world. The press, however, has left the understanding of the mass of men just where it found it; but by supplying an endless stimulus to their imagination and passions, it has rendered their temper and habits infinitely worse. It has inspired ignorance with presumption, so that those who cannot be governed by reason are no longer to be awed by authority. The many, who before the art of printing never mistook in a case of oppression, because they complained from their actual sense of it, have become susceptible of every transient enthusiasm, and of more than womanish fickleness of caprice. Public affairs are transacted now on a stage where all the interest and passions grow out of fiction, or are inspired by the art, and often controlled at the pleasure of the actors. The press is a new, and certainly a powerful, agent in human affairs. It will change, but it is difficult to conceive how, by rendering men indocile and presumptuous, it *can* change societies for the better. They are pervaded by its heat, and kept forever restless by its activity. While it has impaired the force that every just government can employ in self-defence, it has imparted to its enemies the secret of that wildfire that blazes with the most consuming fierceness on attempting to quench it.

Shall we then be told that the press will constitute an adequate check to the progress of every species of tyranny? Is it to be denied that the press has been the base and venal instrument of the very men whom it ought to gibbet to universal abhorrence? While they were climbing to power it aided their ascent; and now they have reached it, does it not conceal or justify their abominations? Or, while it is confessed that the majority of citizens form their ideas of men and measures almost solely from the light that reaches them through the magic-lantern of the press, do our comforters still depend on the all-restoring, all-preserving power of general information? And are they not destitute of all this, or rather of any better information themselves, if they can urge this vapid nonsense in the midst of a yet spreading political delusion, in the midst of the "palpable obscure" that settles on the land, from believing what is false, and misconstruing what is true? Can they believe all this, when they consider how much truth is impeded by party on its way to the public understanding, and even after having reached it, how much it still falls short of its proper mark, while it leaves the envious, jealous, vindictive will unconquered?

Our mistake, and in which we choose to persevere because

our vanity shrinks from the detection, is, that in political affairs, by only determining what men ought to think, we are sure how they will act; and when we know the facts, and are assiduous to collect and present the evidence, we dupe ourselves with the expectation that, as there is but one result which wise men can believe, there is but one course of conduct deduced from it, which honest men can approve or pursue. We forget that in framing the judgment every passion is both an advocate and a witness. We lay out of our account, how much essential information there is that never reaches the multitude, and of the mutilated portion that does, how much is unwelcome to party prejudice; and therefore, that they may still maintain their opinions, they withhold their attention. We seem to suppose, while millions raise so loud a cry about their sovereign power, and really concentre both their faith and their affections in party, that the bulk of mankind will regard no counsels but such as are suggested by their conscience. Let us dare to speak out; is there any single despot who avowedly holds himself so superior to its dictates?

But our manners are too mild, they tell us, for a democracy—then democracy will change those manners. Our morals are too pure—then it will corrupt them.

What, then, is the necessary conclusion, from the view we have taken of the insufficiency or extinction of all conceivable checks? It is such as ought to strike terror, but will scarcely raise public curiosity.

Is it not possible, then, it will be asked, to write and argue down opinions that are so mischievous and only plausible, and men who are even more profligate than exalted? Can we not persuade our citizens to be republican again, so as to rebuild the splendid ruins of the state on the Washington foundation? Thus it is, that we resolve to perpetuate our own delusions, and to cherish our still frustrated and confuted hopes. Let only ink enough be shed, and let democracy rage, there will be no blood. Though the evil is fixed in our nature, all we think will be safe, because we fancy we can see a remedy floating in our opinions.

It is undoubtedly a salutary labor to diffuse among the citizens of a free state, as far as the thing is possible, a just knowledge of their public affairs. But the difficulty of this task is augmented exactly in proportion to the freedom of the state; for the more free the citizens, the bolder and more profligate will be their demagogues, the more numerous and eccentric the popular errors, and the more vehement and pertinacious the passions that defend them.

Yet, as if there were neither vice nor passion in the world, one of the loudest of our boasts, one of the dearest of all the tenets of our creed is, that we are a sovereign people, self-governed—it would be nearer truth to say, self-conceited. For in what sense is it true that any people, however free, are self-governed? If they have in fact no government but such as comports with their ever-varying and often inordinate desires, then it is anarchy; if it counteracts those desires, it is compulsory. The individual who is left to act according to his own humor is not governed at all; and if any considerable number, and especially any combination of individuals, find or can place themselves in this situation, then the society is no longer free. For liberty obviously consists in the salutary restraint, and not in the uncontrolled indulgence of such humors. Now of all desires, none will so much need restraint, or so impatiently endure it, as those of the ambitious, who will form factions, first to elude, then to rival, and finally to usurp the powers of the state; and of the sons of vice, who are the enemies of law, because no just law can be their friend. The first want to govern the state; and the others, that the state should not govern them. A sense of common interest will soon incline these two original factions of every free state to coalesce into one.

So far as men are swayed by authority, or impelled or

excited by their fears and affections, they naturally search for some persons as the sources and objects of these effects and emotions. It is pretty enough to say, the republic commands, and the love of the republic dictates obedience to the heart of every citizen. This is system, but is it nature? The republic is a creature of fiction; it is everybody in the fancy, but nobody in the heart. Love, to be any thing, must be select and exclusive. We may as well talk of loving geometry as the commonwealth. Accordingly, there are many who seldom try to reason, and are the most misled when they do. Such men are, of necessity, governed by their prejudices. They neither comprehend nor like any thing of a republic but their party and their leaders. These last are persons capable of meriting, at least of knowing and rewarding their zeal and exertions. Hence it is, that the republicanism of a great mass of people is often nothing more than a blind trust in certain favorites, and a no less blind and still more furious hatred of their enemies. Thus, a free society, by the very nature of liberty, is often ranged into rival factions, who mutually practise and suffer delusion by the abuse of the best names, but who really contend for nothing but the preëminence of their leaders.

In a democracy, the elevation of an equal convinces many, if not all, that the height to which he is raised is not inaccessible. Ambition wakes from its long sleep in every soul, and wakes, like one of Milton's fallen angels, to turn its tortures into weapons against the public order. The multitude behold their favorite with eyes of love and wonder; and with the more of both, as he is a new favorite, and owes his greatness wholly to their favor. Who among the little does not swell into greatness, when he thus reflects that he has assisted to make great men? And who of the popular favorites loses a minute to flatter this vanity in every brain, till it turns it?

The late equals of the new-made chief behold his rise with

very different emotions. They view him near, and have long been accustomed to look behind the disguises of his hypocrisy. They know his vices and his foibles, and that the foundations of his fame are as false and hollow as his professions. Nevertheless, it may be their interest or their necessity to serve him for a time. But the instant they can supplant him, they will spare neither intrigues nor violence to effect it. Thus, a democratic system in its very nature teems with faction and revolution. Yet, though it continually tends to shift its head, its character is immutable. Its constancy is in change.

The theory of a democracy supposes that the will of the people ought to prevail, and that, as the majority possess not only the better right, but the superior force, of course it will prevail. A greater force, they argue, will inevitably overcome a less. When a constitution provides, with an imposing solemnity of detail, for the collection of the opinions of a majority of the citizens, every sanguine reader not only becomes assured that the will of the people must prevail, but he goes further, and refuses to examine the reasons, and to excuse the incivism and presumption of those who can doubt of this inevitable result. Yet common sense and our own recent experience have shown, that a combination of a very small minority can effectually defeat the authority of the national will. The votes of a majority may sometimes, though not invariably, show what ought to be done; but to awe or subdue the force of a thousand men, the government must call out the superior force of two thousand men. It is therefore established the very instant it is brought to the test, that the mere will of a majority is inefficient and without authority. And as to employing a superior force to procure obedience, which a democratic government has an undoubted right to do, and so indeed has every other, it is obvious that the admitted necessity of this resort completely overthrows all the boasted advantages of the democratic system. For if obedience cannot be procured by reason, it must be obtained by compulsion; and this is exactly what every other government will do in a like case.

Still, however, the friends of the democratic theory will maintain that this dire resort to force will be exceedingly rare, because the public reason will be more clearly expressed and more respectfully understood than under any other form of government. The citizens will be, of course, self-governed, as it will be their choice as well as duty to obey the laws.

It has been already remarked, that the refusal of a very small minority to obey will render force necessary. It has been also noted, that as every mass of people will inevitably desire a favorite, and fix their trust and affections upon one, it clearly follows that there will be of course a faction opposed to the public will as expressed in the laws. Now, if a faction is once admitted to exist in a state, the disposition and the means to obstruct the laws, or, in other words, the will of the majority, must be perceived to exist also. If then it be true, that a democratic government is of all the most liable to faction, which no man of sense will deny, it is manifest that it is, from its very nature, obliged more than any other government to resort to force to overcome or awe the power of faction. This latter will continually employ its own power, that acts always against the physical force of the nation, which can be brought to act only in extreme cases, and then, like every extreme remedy, aggravates the evil. For, let it be noted, a regular government, by overcoming an unsuccessful insurrection, becomes stronger; but elective rulers can scarcely ever employ the physical force of a democracy without turning the moral force, or the power of opinion, against the government. So that faction is not unfrequently made to triumph from its own defeats, and to avenge, in the disgrace and blood of magistrates, the crime of their fidelity to the laws.

As the boastful pretensions of the democratic system

cannot be too minutely exposed, another consideration must be given to the subject.

That government certainly deserves no honest man's love or support, which, from the very laws of its being, carries terror and danger to the virtuous, and arms the vicious with authority and power. The essence, and in the opinion of many thousands not yet cured of their delusions, the excellence of democracy is, that it invests every citizen with an equal proportion of power. A state consisting of a million of citizens has a million sovereigns, each of whom detests all other sovereignty but his own. This very boast implies as much of the spirit of turbulence and insurbordination as the utmost energy of any known regular government, even the most rigid, could keep in restraint. It also implies a state of agitation that is justly terrible to all who love their ease, and of instability that quenches the last hope of those who would transmit their liberty to posterity. Waiving any further pursuit of these reflections, let it be resumed, that if every man of the million has his ratable share of power in the community, then, instead of restraining the vicious, they also are armed with power, for they take their part; as they are citizens, this cannot be refused them. Now, as they have an interest in preventing the execution of the laws, which, in fact, is the apparent common interest of their whole class, their union will happen of course. The very first moment that they do unite, which it is ten thousand to one will happen before the form of the democracy is agreed upon, and while its plausible constitution is framing, that moment they form a faction, and the pretended efficacy of the democratic system, which is to operate by the power of opinion and persuasion, comes to an end. For an *imperium in imperio* exists; there is a state within the state, a combination interested and active in hindering the will of the majority from being obeyed.

But the vicious, we shall be told, are very few in such an honest nation as the American. How many of our states did, in fact, pass laws to obstruct the lawful operation of the treaty of peace in 1783? and were the virtuous men of those states the framers and advocates of those laws? What shall we denominate the oligarchy that sways the authority of Virginia? Who is ignorant that the ruling power have an interest to oppose justice to creditors? Surely, after these facts are remembered, no man will say, the faction of the vicious is a chimera of the writer's brain; nor, admitting it to be real, will he deny that it has proved itself potent.

It is not however the faction of debtors only that is to be expected to arise under a democracy. Every bad passion that dreads restraint from the laws will seek impunity and indulgence in faction. The associates will not come together in cold blood. They will not, like their federal adversaries, yawn over the contemplation of their cause, and shrink from the claim of its necessary perils and sacrifices. They will do all that can possibly be done, and they will attempt more. They will begin early, persevere long, ask no respite for themselves, and are sure to triumph if their enemies take any. Suppose at first their numbers to be exceedingly few, their efforts will for that reason be so much the greater. They will call themselves the people; they will in their name arraign every act of government as wicked and weak; they will oblige the rulers to stand forever on the defensive, as culprits at the bar of an offended public. With a venal press at command, concealing their number and their infamy, is it to be doubted that the ignorant will soon or late unite with the vicious? Their union is inevitable; and, when united, those allies are powerful enough to strike terror into the hearts of the firmest rulers. It is in vain, it is indeed childish to say, that an enlightened people will understand their own affairs, and thus the acts of a faction will be baffled. No people on earth are or can be so enlightened as to the details of political affairs. To study politics, so as to know correctly the force of the reasons for a large part of the public measures, would stop the labor of the plough and the hammer; and how are these million of students to have access to the means of information?

When it is thus apparent that the vicious will have as many opportunities as inducements to inflame and deceive, it results, from the nature of democracy, that the ignorant will join, and the ambitious will lead their combination. Who, then, will deny that the vicious are armed with power, and the virtuous exposed to persecution and peril?

If a sense of their danger compel these latter, at length, to unite also in self-defence, it will be late, probably too late, without means to animate and cement their union, and with no hope beyond that of protracting, for a short time, the certain catastrophe of their destruction, which in fact no democracy has ever yet failed to accomplish.

If then all this is to happen, not from accident, not as the shallow or base demagogues pretend, from the management of monarchists or aristocrats, but from the principles of democracy itself, as we have attempted to demonstrate, ought we not to consider democracy as the worst of all governments, or if there be a worse, as the certain forerunner of that? What other form of civil rule among men so irresistibly tends to free vice from restraint, and to subject virtue to persecution?

The common supposition is, and it is ever assumed as the basis of argument, that in a democracy the laws have only to command individuals, who yield a willing and conscientious obedience; and who would be destitute of the force to resist, if they should lack the disposition to submit. But this supposition, which so constantly triumphs in the newspapers, utterly fails in the trial in our republic, which we do not denominate a democracy. To collect the tax on Virginia coaches we have had to exert all the judicial power of the nation; and after that had prevailed, popularity was found a greater treasure than money, and the carriage tax was repealed. The tax on whiskey was enforced by an army, and no sooner had its receipts begun to reimburse the charges of government, and in some measure to equalize the northern and southern burdens, but the law is annulled.

With the example of two rebellions against our revenue laws, it cannot be denied that our republic claims the submission, not merely of weak individuals, but of powerful combinations, of those whom distance, numbers, and enthusiasm embolden to deride its authority and defy its arms. A faction is a sort of empire within the empire, which acts by its own magistrates and laws, and prosecutes interests not only unlike, but destructive to those of the nation. The federalists are accused of attempting to impart too much energy to the administation, and of stripping, with too much severity, all such combinations of their assumed importance. Hence it is ridiculously absurd to denominate the federalists, the admirers and disciples of Washington, a faction.

But we shall be told, in defiance both of fact and good sense, that factions will not exist, or will be impotent if they do; for the majority have a right to govern, and certainly will govern by their representatives. Let their right be admitted, but they certainly will not govern in either of two cases, both fairly supposable, and likely, nay sure, to happen in succession: that a section of country, a combination, party, or faction, call it what you will, shall prove daring and potent enough to obsruct the laws and to exempt itself from their operation; or, growing bolder with impunity and success, finally by art, deceit, and perseverance, to force its chiefs into power, and thus, instead of submitting to the government, to bring the government into submission to a faction. Then the forms and the names of a republic will be used, and used more ostentatiously than ever; but its principles will be abused, and its ramparts and defences laid flat to the ground.

There are many, who, believing that a penful of ink can impart a deathless energy to a constitution, and having seen with pride and joy two or three skins of parchment added, like new walls about a fortress, to our own, will be filled with astonishment, and say, is not our legislature divided? our executive single? our judiciary independent? Have we not amendments and bills of rights, excelling all compositions in prose? Where then can our danger lie? Our government, so we read, is constructed in such a manner as to defend itself and the people. We have the greatest political security, for we have adopted the soundest principles.

To most grown children, therefore, the existence of faction will seem chimerical. Yet did any free state ever exist without the most painful and protracted conflicts with this foe? or expire any otherwise than by his triumph? The spring is not more genial to the grain and fruits, than to insects and vermin. The same sun that decks the fields with flowers, thaws out the serpent in the fen, and concocts his poison. Surely we are not the people to contest this position. Our present liberty was born into the world under the knife of this assassin, and now limps a cripple from his violence.

As soon as such a faction is known to subsist in force, we shall be told, the people may, and because they may they surely will, rally to discomfit and punish the conspirators. If the whole people in a body are to do this as often as it may be necessary, then it seems our political plan is to carry on our government by successive, or rather incessant revolutions. When the people deliberate and act in person, laying aside the plain truth, that it is impossible they should, all delegated authority is at an end; the representatives would be nothing in the presence of their assembled constituents. Thus falls or stops the machine of a regular government. Thus a faction, hostile to the government, would ensure their success by the very remedy that is supposed effectual to disappoint their designs.

Men of a just way of thinking will be ready to renounce the opinions we have been considering, and to admit that liberty is lost where faction domineers; that some security must be provided against its attacks; and that no elective government can be secure or orderly, unless it be invested by the Constitution itself with the means of self-defence. It is enough for the people to approve the lawful use of them. And this, for a free government, must be the easiest thing in the world.

Now the contrary of this last opinion is the truth. By a free government this difficulty is nearly or quite insuperable; for the audaciousness and profligacy of faction is ever in proportion to the liberty of the political constitution. In a tyranny individuals are nothing. Conscious of their nothingness, the spirit of liberty is torpid or extinct. But in a free state there is, necessarily, a great mass of power left in the hands of the citizens, with the spirit to use and the desire to augment it. Hence will proceed an infinity of clubs and associations, for purposes often laudable or harmless, but not unfrequently factious. It is obvious, that the combination of some hundreds or thousands for political ends will produce a great aggregate stock or mass of power. As by combining they greatly augment their power, for that very reason they will combine; and as magistrates would seldom like to devolve their authority upon volunteers who might offer to play the magistrate in their stead, there is almost nothing left for a band of combined citizens to do, but to discredit and obstruct the government and laws. The possession of power by the magistrate is not so sure to produce respect as to kindle envy; and to the envious it is a gratification to humble those who are exalted. But the ambitious find the public discontent a passport to office—then they must breed or inflame discontent. We have the example before our eyes.

Is it not evident, then, that a free government must exert a great deal more power to obtain obedience from an extensive combination or faction than would be necessary to extort it from a much larger number of uncombined individuals? If the regular government has that degree of power which, let

it be noted, the jealousy of a free people often inclines them
to withold; and if it should exercise its power with promptness
and spirit, a supposition not a little improbable, for such
governments frequently have more strength than firmness,
then the faction may be, for that time, repressed and kept
from doing mischief. It will, however, instantly change its
pretexts and its means, and renew the contest with more art
and caution, and with the advantage of all the discontents
which every considerable popular agitation is sure to multiply
and to embitter. This immortal enemy, whom it is possible
to bind, though only for a time, and in flaxen chains, but
not to kill; who may be baffled, but cannot be disarmed; who
is never weakened by defeat, nor discouraged by disappointment, again tries and wears out the strength of the government
and the temper of the people. It is a game which the factious
will never be weary of playing, because they play for an
empire, yet on their own part hazard nothing. If they fail,
they lose only their ticket, and say, draw your lottery again;
if they win, as in the end they must and will, if the Constitution
has not provided within, or unless the people will bring,
which they will not long, from without, some energy to hinder
their success, it will be complete; for conquering parties
never content themselves with half the fruits of victory. Their
power once obtained can be and will be confirmed by nothing
but the terror or weakness of the real people. Justice will
shrink from the bench, and tremble at her own bar.

As property is the object of the great mass of every faction,
the rules that keep it sacred will be annulled, or so far
shaken, as to bring enough of it within the grasp of the
dominant party to reward their partisans with booty. But the
chieftains, thirsting only for dominion, will search for the
means of extending or establishing it. They will, of course,
innovate, till the vestiges of private right, and of restraints
on public authority, are effaced; until the real people are
stripped of all privilege and influence, and become even

147

more abject and spiritless than weak. The many may be deluded, but the success of a faction is ever the victory of a few; and the power of the few can be supported by nothing but force. This catastrophe is fatal.

The people, it wll be thought, will see their error and return. But there is no return to liberty. What the fire of faction does not destroy, it will debase. Those who have once tasted of the cup of sovereignty will be unfitted to the subjects; and those who have not, will scarcely form a wish, beyond the unmolested ignominy of slaves.

But will those who scorn to live at all unless they can live free, will these noble spirits abandon the public cause? Will they not break their chains on the heads of their oppressors? Suppose they attempt it, then we have a civil war; and when political diseases require the sword, the remedy will kill. Tyrants may be dethroned, and usurpers expelled and punished; but the sword, once drawn, cannot be sheathed. Whoever holds it, must rule by it; and that rule, though victory should give it to the best men and the honestest cause, cannot be liberty. Though painted as a goddess, she is mortal, and her spirit, once severed by the sword, can be evoked no more from the shades.[13]

Is this catastrophe too distant to be viewed, or too improbable to be dreaded? I should not think it so formidably near as I do, if in the short interval of impending fate, in which alone it can be of any use to be active, the heart of every honest man in the nation, or even in New England, was penetrated with the anxiety that oppresses my own. Then the subversion of the public liberty would at least be delayed, if it could not be prevented. Her maladies might be palliated, if not cured. She might long drag on the life of an invalid, instead of soon suffering the death of a martyr.

---

[13] *This short paragraph explains the writer's motive for presenting such a gloomy picture of the affairs of our country. He hoped, by alarming the honest part of our citizens, to defer, or mitigate our fate.* [S. AMES]

The soft, timid sons of luxury, love liberty as well as it is possible they should, to love pleasure better. They desire to sleep in security, and to enjoy protection, without being molested to give it. While all, who are not devoted to pleasure, are eager in the pursuit of wealth, how will it be possible to rouse such a spirit of liberty as can alone secure, or prolong its possession? For if, in the extraordinary perils of the republic, the citizens will not kindle with a more than ordinary, with a heroic flame, its cause will be abandoned without effort, and lost beyond redemption. But if the faithful votaries of liberty, uncertain what counsels to follow, should, for the present, withhold their exertions, will they not at least bestow their attention? Will they not fix it, with an unusual intensity of thought, upon the scene; and will they not fortify their nerves to contemplate a prospect that is shaded with horror, and already flashes with tempest?

If the positions laid down as theory could be denied, the brief history of the federal administration would establish them. It was first confided to the truest and purest patriot that ever lived. It succeeded a period, dismal and dark, and like the morning sun, lighted up a sudden splendor that was gratuitous, for it consumed nothing, but its genial rays cherished the powers of vegetation, while they displayed its exuberance. There was no example, scarcely a pretence of oppression; yet faction, basking in those rays, and sucking venom from the ground, even then cried out, "O sun, I tell thee, how I hate thy beams." Faction was organized sooner than the government.

If the most urgent public reasons could ever silence or satisfy the spirit of faction, the adoption of the new Constitution would have been prompt and unanimous. The government of a great nation had barely revenue enough to buy stationery for its clerks, or to pay the salary of the door-keeper. Public faith and public force were equally out of the question, for as it respected either authority or resources,

149

the corporation of a college, or the missionary society were greater potentates than Congress. Our federal government had not merely fallen into imbecility, and of course into contempt, but the oligarchical factions in the large states had actually made great advances in the usurpation of its powers. The king of New York levied imposts on Jersey and Connecticut; and the nobles of Virginia bore with impatience their tributary dependence on Baltimore and Philadelphia. Our discontents were fermenting into civil war; and that would have multiplied and exasperated our discontents.

Impending public evils, so obvious and so near, happily roused all the patriotism of the country; but they roused its ambition too. The great state chieftains found the sovereign power unoccupied, and like the lieutenants of Alexander, each employed intrigue, and would soon have employed force, to erect his province into a separate monarchy or aristocracy. Popular republican names would indeed have been used, but in the struggles of ambition they would have been used only to cloak usurpation and tyranny. How late, and with what sourness and reluctance, did New York and Virginia renounce the hopes of aggrandizement which their antifederal leaders had so passionately cherished! The opposition to the adoption of the federal Constitution was not a controversy about principles; it was a struggle for power. In the great states, the ruling party, with that sagacity which too often accompanies inordinate ambition, instantly discerned, that if the new government should go into operation with all the energy that its letter and spirit would authorize, they must cease to rule—still worse, they must submit to be ruled, nay, worst of all, they must be ruled by their equals, a condition of real wretchedness and supposed disgrace, which our impatient tyrants anticipated with instinctive and unspeakable horror.

To prevent this dreaded result of the new Constitution, which by securing a real legal equality to all the citizens, would bring them down to an equality, their earliest care was to bind the ties of their factious union more closely together; and by combining their influence and exerting the utmost malignity of their art, to render the new government odious and suspected by the people. Thus, conceived in jealousy and born in weakness and dissension, they hoped to see it sink, like its predecessor, the confederation, into contempt. Hence it was, that in every great state a faction arose with the fiercest hostility to the federal Constitution, and active in devising and pursuing every scheme, however unwarrantable or audacious, that would obstruct the establishment of any power in the state superior to its own.

It is undeniably true, therefore, that faction was organized sooner than the new government. We are not to charge this event to the accidental rivalships or disgusts of leading men, but to the operation of the invariable principles that preside over human actions and political affairs. Power had slipped out of the feeble hands of the old congress; and the world's power, like its wealth, can never lie one moment without a possessor. The states had instantly succeeded to the vacant sovereignty; and the leading men in the great states, for the small ones were inactive from a sense of their insignificance, engrossed their authority. Where the executive authority was single, the governor, as for instance in New York, felt his brow encircled with a diadem; but in those states where the governor is a mere cipher, the men who influenced the assembly governed the state, and there an oligarchy established itself. When has it been seen in the world, that the possession of sovereign power was regarded with indifference, or resigned without effort? If all that is ambition in the heart of man had slept in America, till the era of the new Constitution, the events of that period would not merely have awakened it into life, but have quickened it into all the agitations of frenzy.

Then commenced an active struggle for power. Faction

resolved that the new government should not exist at all, or if that could not be prevented, that it should exist without energy. Accordingly, the presses of that time teemed with calumny and invective. Before the new government had done any thing, there was nothing oppressive or tyrannical which it was not accused of meditating; and when it began its operations, there was nothing wise or fit that it was not charged with neglecting; nothing right or beneficial that it did, but from an insidious design to delude and betray the people. The cry of usurpation and oppression was louder then, when all was prosperous and beneficent, than it has been since, when the judiciary is violently abolished, the judges dragged to the culprit's bar, the Constitution changed to prevent a change of rulers, and the path plainly marked out and already half travelled over, for the ambition of those rulers to reign in contempt of the people's votes, and on the ruins of their liberty.

He is certainly a political novice or a hypocrite, who will pretend that the antifederal opposition to the government is to be ascribed to the concern of the people for their liberties, rather than to the profligate ambition of their demagogues, eager for power, and suddenly alarmed by the imminent danger of losing it; demagogues, who leading lives like Clodius, and with the maxims of Cato in their mouths, cherishing principles like Catiline, have acted steadily on a plan of usurpation like Cæsar. Their labor for twelve years was to inflame and deceive; and their recompense, for the last four, has been to degrade and betray.

Any person who considers the instability of all authority, that is not only derived from the multitude, but wanes or increases with the ever changing phases of their levity and caprice, will pronounce that the federal government was from the first, and from its very nature and organization, fated to sink under the rivalship of its state competitors for dominion. Virginia has never been more federal than it was, when, from considerations of policy, and perhaps in the hope of future success from its intrigues, it adopted the new Constitution; for it has never desisted from obstructing its measures, and urging every scheme that would reduce it back again to the imbecility of the old confederation. To the dismay of every true patriot, these arts have at length fatally succeeded; and our system of government now differs very little from what it would have been, if the impost proposed by the old congress had been granted, and the new federal Constitution had never been adopted by the states. In that case, the states being left to their natural inequality, the small states would have been, as they now are, nothing; and Virginia, potent in herself, more potent by her influence and intrigues, and uncontrolled by a superior federal head, would of course have been every thing. Baltimore, like Antium, and Philadelphia, like Capua, would have bowed their proud necks to a new Roman yoke. If any of her more powerful neighbors had resisted her dominion, she would have spread her factions into their bosoms, and like the Marsi and the Samnites, they would at last, though perhaps somewhat the later for their valor, have graced the pomp of her triumphs, and afterwards assisted to maintain the terror of her arms.

So far as state opposition was concerned, it does not appear that it has been overcome in any of the great states, by the mild and successful operation of the federal government. But if states had not been its rivals, yet the matchless industry and close combination of the factious individuals who guided the antifederal presses would, in the end, though perhaps not so soon as it has been accomplished by the help of Virginia, have disarmed and prostrated the federal government. We have the experience of France before our eyes to prove that, with such a city as Paris, it is utterly impossible to support a free republican system. A profligate press has more authority than morals; and a faction will possess more energy than magistrates or laws.

On evidence thus lamentably clear, I found my opinion, that the federalists can never again become the dominant party; in other words, the public reason and virtue cannot be again, as in our first twelve years, and never will be again the governing power, till our government has passed through its revolutionary changes. Every faction that may happen to rule will pursue but two objects, its vengeance on the fallen party, and the security of its own power against any new one that may rise to contest it. As to the glory that wise rulers partake, when they obtain it for their nation, no person of understanding will suppose that the gaudy, ephemeral insects, that bask and flutter no longer than while the sun of popularity shines without a cloud, will either possess the means or feel the passion for it. What have the Condorcets and Rolands of to-day to hope or to enjoy from the personal reputation or public happiness of to-morrow? Their objects are all selfish, all temporary. Mr. Jefferson's letters to Mazzei or Paine, his connection with Callender, or his mean condescensions to France and Spain, will add nothing to the weight of his disgrace with the party that shall supplant him. To be their enemy will be disgrace enough, and so far a refuge for his fame, as it will stop all curiosity and inquiry into particulars. Every party that has fallen in France has been overwhelmed with infamy, but without proofs or discrimination. If time and truth have furnished any materials for the vindication of the ex-rulers, there has nevertheless been no instance of the return of the public to pity, or of the injured to power. The revolution has no retrograde steps. Its course is onward from the patriots and statesmen to the hypocrites and cowards, and onward still through successive committees of ruffians, till some one ruffian happens to be a hero. Then chance no longer has a power over events, for this last inevitably becomes an emperor.

The restoration of the federalists to their merited influence in the government supposes two things, the slumber or extinction of faction, and the efficacy of public morals. It supposes an interval of calm, when reason will dare to speak, and prejudice itself will incline to hear. Then, it is still hoped by many, *Nova progenies cœlo demittitur alto*,[14] the genuine public voice would call wisdom into power; and the love of country, which is the morality of politics, would guard and maintain its authority.

Are not these the visions that delight a poet's fancy, but will never revisit the statesman's eyes? When will faction sleep? Not till its labors of vengeance and ambition are over. Faction, we know, is the twin brother of our liberty, and born first; and as we are told in the fable of Castor and Pollux, the only one of the two that is immortal. As long as there is a faction in full force, and possessed of the government, too, the public will and the public reason must have power to compel, as well as to convince, or they will convince without reforming. Bad men, who rise by intrigue, may be dispossessed by worse men, who rise over their heads by deeper intrigue; but what has the public reason to do but to deplore its silence or to polish its chains? This last we find is now the case in France. All the talent of that country is employed to illustrate the virtues and exploits of that chief who has made a nation happy by putting an end to the agitations of what they called their liberty, and who naturally enough insist that they enjoy more glory than any other people, because they are more terrible to all.

The public reason, therefore, is so little in a condition to reëstablish the federal cause, that it will not long maintain its own. Do we not see our giddy multitude celebrate with joy the triumphs of a party over some essential articles of our Constitution, and recently over one integral and independent branch of our government? When our Roland falls, our Danton will be greeted with as loud a peal and as

---

[14] *New offspring descending from heaven on high.*

155

splendid a triumph. If federalism could by a miracle resume the reins of power, unless political virtue and pure morals should return also, those reins would soon drop or be snatched from its hands.

By political virtue is meant that love of country diffused through the society, and ardent in each individual, that would dispose, or rather impel every one to do or suffer much for his country, and permit no one to do any thing against it. The Romans sustained the hardships and dangers of military service, which fell not, as amongst modern nations, on the dregs of society, but, till the time of Marius, exclusively on the flower of the middle and noble classes. They sustained them, nevertheless, both with constancy and alacrity, because the excellence of life, every Roman thought, was glory, and the excellence of each man's glory lay in its redounding to the splendor and extent of the empire of Rome.

Is there any resemblance in all this to the habits and passions that predominate in America? Are not our people wholly engrossed by the pursuit of wealth and pleasure? Though grouped together into a society, the propensities of the individual still prevail; and if the nation discovers the rudiments of any character, they are yet to be developed. In forming it, have we not ground to fear that the sour, dissocial, malignant spirit of our politics will continue to find more to dread and hate in party, than to love and reverence in our country? What foundation can there be for that political virtue to rest upon, while the virtue of the society is proscribed, and its vice lays an exclusive claim to emolument and honor? And as long as faction governs, it must look to all that is vice in the state for its force, and to all that is virtue for its plunder. It is not merely the choice of faction, though no doubt base agents are to be preferred for base purposes, but it is its necessity also to keep men of true worth depressed by keeping the turbulent and worthless contented.

How then can love of country take root and grow in a soil,

from which every valuable plant has thus been plucked up and thrown away as a weed? How can we forbear to identify the government with the country? and how is it possible that we should at the same time lavish all the ardor of our affection, and yet withhold every emotion either of confidence or esteem? It is said, that in republics majorities invariably oppress minorities. Can there be any real patriotism in a state which is thus filled with those who exercise and those who suffer tyranny? But how much less reason has any man to love that country, in which the voice of the majority is counterfeited, or the vicious, ignorant, and needy, are the instruments, and the wise and worthy are the victims of oppression?

When we talk of patriotism as the theme of declamation, it is not very material that we should know with any precision what we mean. It is a subject on which hypocrisy will seem to ignorance to be eloquent, because all of it will be received and well received as flattery. If, however, we search for a principle or sentiment general and powerful enough to produce national effects, capable of making a people act with constancy, or suffer with fortitude, is there any thing in our situation that could have produced, or that can cherish it? The straggling settlements of the southern part of the union, which now is the governing part, have been formed by emigrants from almost every nation of Europe. Safe in their solitudes, alike from the annoyance of enemies and of government, it is infinitely more probable that they will sink into barbarism than rise to the dignity of national sentiment and character. Patriotism, to be a powerful or steady principle of action, must be deeply inbued by education, and strongly impresssed both by the policy of the government and the course of events. To love our country with ardor, we must often have some fears for its safety; our affection will be exalted in its distress; and our self-esteem will glow on the contemplation of its glory. It is only by such diversified and

157

incessant exercise that the sentiment can become strong in the individual, or be diffused over the nation.

But how can that nation have any such affinities, any sense of patriotism, whose capacious wilderness receives and separates from each other the successive troops of emigrants from all other nations, men who remain ignorant, or learn only from the newspapers that they are countrymen, who think it their right to be exempted from all tax, restraint, or control, and of course that they have nothing to do with or for their country, but to make rulers for it, who, after they are made, are to have nothing to do with their makers; a country, too, which they are sure will not be invaded, and cannot be enslaved? Are not the wandering Tartars or Indian hunters at least as susceptible of patriotism as these stragglers in our western forests, and infinitely fonder of glory? It is difficult to conceive of a country, which, from the manner of its settlement, or the manifest tendencies of its politics, is more destitute or more incapable of being inspired with political virtue.

What foundation remains, then, for the hopes of those who expect to see the federalists again invested with power?

Shall we be told, that if the nation is not animated with public spirit, the individuals are at least fitted to be good citizens by the purity of their morals? But what are morals without restraints? and how will merely voluntary restraints be maintained? How long will sovereigns, as the people are made to fancy they are, insist more upon checks than prerogatives? Ask Mr. . . . and Judge Chase.

Besides, in political reasoning it is generally overlooked, that if the existence of morals should encourage a people to prefer a democratic system, the operation of that system is sure to destroy their morals. Power in such a society cannot long have any regular control; and, without control, it is itself a vice. Is there in human affairs an occasion of profligacy more shameless or more contagious than a general election?

Every spring gives birth and gives wings to this epidemic mischief. Then begins a sort of tillage, that turns up to the sun and air the most noxious weeds in the kindliest soil; or, to speak still more seriously, it is a mortal pestilence, that begins with rottenness in the marrow. A democratic society will soon find its morals the encumbrance of its race, the surly companion of its licentious joys. It will encourage its demagogues to impeach and persecute the magistracy, till it is no longer disquieted. In a word, there will not be morals without justice; and though justice might possibly support a democracy, yet a democracy cannot possibly support justice.

Rome was never weary of making laws for that end, and failed. France has had nearly as many laws as soldiers, yet never had justice or liberty for one day. Nevertheless, there can be no doubt that the ruling faction has often desired to perpetuate its authority by establishing justice. The difficulties however lie in the nature of the thing; for in democratic states there are ever more volunteers to destroy than to build; and nothing that is restraint can be erected without being odious, nor maintained if it is. Justice herself must be built on a loose foundation, and every villain's hand is of course busy to pluck out the underpinning. Instead of being the awful power that is to control the popular passions, she descends from the height of her temple, and becomes the cruel and vindictive instrument of them.

Federalism was therefore manifestly founded on a mistake, on the supposed existence of sufficient political virtue, and on the permanency and authority of the public morals.

The party now in power committed no such mistake. They acted on the knowledge of what men actually are, not what they ought to be. Instead of enlightening the popular understanding, their business was to bewilder it. They knew that the vicious, on whom society makes war, would join them in their attack upon government. They inflamed the ignorant; they flattered the vain; they offered novelty to the restless;

159

and promised plunder to the base. The envious were assured that the great should fall; and the ambitious that *they* should become great. The federal power, propped by nothing but opinion, fell, not because it deserved its fall, but because its principles of action were more exalted and pure than the people could support.

It is now undeniable that the federal administration was blameless. It has stood the scrutiny of time, and passed unharmed through the ordeal of its enemies. With all the evidence of its conduct in their possession, and with servile majorities at their command, it has not been in their power, much as they desired it, to fix any reproach on their predecessors.

It is the opinion of a few, but a very groundless opinion, that the cause of order will be reëstablished by the splitting of the reigning jacobins; or, if that should not take place soon, the union will be divided, and the northern confederacy compelled to provide for its own liberty. Why, it is said, should we expect that the union of the bad will be perfect, when that of the Washington party, though liberty and property were at stake, has been broken? And why should it be supposed that the Northern States, who possess so prodigious a preponderance of white population, of industry, commerce, and civilization over the Southern, will remain subject to Virginia? Popular delusion cannot last, and as soon as the opposition of the federalists ceases to be feared, the conquerors will divide into new factions, and either the federalists will be called again into power, or the union will be severed into two empires.

By some attention to the nature of a democracy, both these conjectures, at least so far as they support any hopes of the public liberty, will be discredited.

There is no society without jacobins; no free society without a formidable host of them; and no democracy whose powers they will not usurp, nor whose liberties, if it be not absurd to suppose a democracy can have any, they will not destroy. A nation must be exceedingly well educated, in which the ignorant and the credulous are few. Athens, with all its wonderful taste and literature, poured them into her popular assemblies by thousands. It is by no means certain that a nation, composed wholly of scholars and philosophers, would contain less presumption, political ignorance, levity, and extravagance than another state, peopled by tradesmen, farmers, and men of business, without a metaphysician or speculatist among them. The opulent in Holland were the friends of those French who subdued their country, and enslaved them. It was the well dressed, the learned, or at least the conceited mob of France that did infinitely more than the mere rabble of Paris to overturn the throne of the Bourbons. The multitude were made giddy with projects of innovation, before they were armed with pikes to enforce them.

As there is nothing really excellent in our governments, that is not novel in point of institution, and which faction has not represented as old in abuse, the natural vanity, presumption, and restlessness of the human heart have, from the first, afforded the strength of a host to the jacobins of our country. The ambitious desperadoes are the natural leaders of this host.

Now, though such leaders may have many occasions of jealousy and discord with one another, especially in the division of power and booty, is it not absurd to suppose, that any set of them will endeavor to restore both to the right owners? Do we expect a self-denying ordinance from the sons of violence and rapine? Are not those remarkably inconsistent with themselves, who say, our republican system is a government of justice and order, that was freely adopted in peace, subsists by morals, and whose office it is to ask counsel of the wise and to give protection to the good, yet who console themselves in the storms of the state with the fond hope that order will spring out of confusion, because innovators will grow weary of change, and the ambitious will contend about their spoil? Then we are to have a new system exactly like the old one, from the fortuitous concourse of atoms, from the crash and jumble of all that is precious or sacred in the state. It is said, the popular hopes and fears are the gales that impel the political vessel. Can any disappointment of such hopes be greater than their folly?

It is true, the men now in power may not be united together by patriotism, or by any principle of faith or integrity. It is also true, that they have not, and cannot easily have, a military force to awe the people into submission. But on the other hand, they have no need of an army; there is no army to oppose them. They are held together by the ties, and made irresistible by the influence of party. With the advantage of acting as the government, who can oppose them? Not the federalists, who neither have any force, nor any object to employ it for, if they had. Not any subdivision of their own faction, because the opposers, if they prevail, will become the government, so much the less liable to be opposed for their recent victory; and if the new sect should fail, they will be nothing. The conquerors will take care that an unsuccessful resistance shall strengthen their domination.

Thus it seems, in every event of the division of the ruling party, the friends of true liberty have nothing to hope. Tyrants may thus be often changed, but the tyranny will remain.

A democracy cannot last. Its nature ordains, that its next change shall be into a military despotism, of all known governments, perhaps, the most prone to shift its head, and the slowest to mend its vices. The reason is, that the tyranny of what is called the people, and that by the sword, both operate alike to debase and corrupt, till there are neither men left with the spirit to desire liberty, nor morals with the power to sustain justice. Like the burning pestilence that

destroys the human body, nothing can subsist by its dissolution but vermin.

A military government may make a nation great, but it
cannot make them free. There will be frequent and bloody
struggles to decide who shall hold the sword; but the conqueror
will destroy his competitors and prevent any permanent
division of the empire. Experience proves, that in all such
governments there is a continual tendency to unity.

Some kind of balance between the two branches of the
Roman government had been maintained for several ages,
till at length every popular demagogue, from the two Gracchi
to Cæsar, tried to gain favor, and by favor to gain power by
flattering the multitude with new pretensions to power in the
state. The assemblies of the people disposed of every thing;
and intrigue and corruption, and often force disposed of the
votes of those assemblies. It appears, that Catulus, Cato,
Cicero, and the wisest of the Roman patriots, and perhaps
wiser never lived, kept on like the infatuated federalists,
hoping to the last, that the people would see their error and
return to the safe old path. They labored incessantly to
reestablish the commonwealth; but the deep corruption of
those times, not more corrupt than our own, rendered that
impossible. Many of the friends of liberty were slain in the
civil wars; some, like Lucullus, had retired to their farms;
and most of the others, if not banished by the people, were
without commands in the army, and of course without power
in the state. Catiline came near being chosen consul, and
Piso and Gabinius, scarcely less corrupt, were chosen. A
people so degenerate could not maintain liberty; and do we
find bad morals or dangerous designs any obstruction to the
election of any favorite of the reigning party? It is remarkable,
that when by a most singular concurrence of circumstances,
after the death of Cæsar, an opportunity was given to the
Romans to reëstablish the republic, there was no effective

disposition among the people to concur in that design. It seemed as if the republican party, consisting of the same class of men as the Washington federalists, had expired with the dictator. The truth is, when parties rise and resort to violence, the moment of calm, if one should happen to succeed, leaves little to wisdom and nothing to choice. The orations of Cicero proved feeble against the arms of Mark Antony. Is not all this apparent in the United States? Are not the federalists as destitute of hopes as of power? What is there left for them to do? When a faction has seized the republic, and established itself in power, can the true federal republicans any longer subsist? After having seen the republic expire, will it be asked, why they are not immortal?

But the reason why such governments are not severed by the ambition of contending chiefs, deserves further consideration.

As soon as the Romans had subdued the kingdoms of Perseus, Antiochus, and Mithridates, it was necessary to keep on foot great armies. As the command of these was bestowed by the people, the arts of popularity were studied by all those who pretended to be the friends of the people, and who really aspired to be their masters. The greatest favorites became the most powerful generals; and as at first there was nothing which the Roman assemblies were unwilling to give, it appeared very soon that they had nothing left to withhold. The armies disposed of all power in the state, and of the state itself; and the generals of course assumed the control of the armies.

It is a very natural subject of surprise, that when the Roman empire was rent by civil war, as it was perhaps twenty times from the age of Marius and Sylla to that of Constantine, some competitor for the imperial purple did not maintain himself with his veteran troops in his province; and found a new dynasty on the banks of the Euphrates or the Danube, the Ebro or the Rhine. This surprise is augmented by considering the distractions and weakness of an elective government, as the Roman was; the wealth, extent, and power of the rebellious provinces, equal to several modern first rate kingdoms; their distance from Italy; and the resource that the despair, and shame, and rage of so many conquered nations would supply on an inviting occasion to throw off their chains and rise once more to independence; yet the Roman power constantly prevailed, and the empire remained one and indivisible. Sertorius was as good a general as Pompey; and it seems strange that he did not become Emperor of Spain. Why were not new empires founded in Armenia, Syria, Asia Minor, in Gaul or Britain? Why, we ask, unless because the very nature of a military democracy, such as the Roman was, did not permit it? Every civil war terminated in the reunion of the provinces, that a rebellion had for a time severed from the empire. Britain, Spain, and Gaul, now so potent, patiently continued to wear their chains, till they dropped off by the total decay of the Western empire.

The first conquests of the Romans were made by the superiority of their discipline. The provinces were permitted to enjoy their municipal laws, but all political and military power was exercised by persons sent from Rome. So that the spirit of the subject nations was broken or rendered impotent, and every contest in the provinces was conducted, not by the provincials, but by Roman generals and veteran troops. These were all animated with the feelings of the Roman democracy. Now a democracy, a party, and an army bear a close resemblance to each other; they are all creatures of emotion and impulse. However discordant all the parts of a democracy may be, they all seek a centre, and that centre is the single arbitrary power of a chief. In this we see how exactly a democracy is like an army: they are equally governments by downright force.

A multitude can be moved only by their passions; and these, when their gratification is obstructed, instantly impel them to arms. *Furor arma ministrat*.[15] The club is first used, and then, as more effectual, the sword. The disciplined is found by the leaders to be more manageable than the mobbish force. The rabble at Paris that conquered the Bastile were soon formed into national guards. But from the first to the last, the nature, and character, and instruments of power remain the same. A ripe democracy will not long want sharp tools and able leaders; in fact, though not in name, it is an army. It is true, an army is not constituted as a deliberative body, and very seldom pretends to deliberate; but whenever it does, it is a democracy in regiments and brigades, somewhat the more orderly as well as more merciful for its discipline. It always will deliberate when it is suffered to feel its own power, and is indiscreetly provoked to exert it. At those times, is there much reason to believe it will act with less good sense, or with a more determined concept for the national interest and opinion, than a giddy multitude managed by worthless leaders? Now though an army is not indulged with a vote, it cannot be stripped of its feelings, feelings that may be managed, but cannot be resisted. When the legions of Syria or Gaul pretended to make an emperor, it was as little in the power as it was in the disposition of Severus to content himself with Italy, and to leave those fine provinces to Niger and Albinus. The military town-meeting must be satisfied; and nothing could satisfy it but the overthrow of a rival army. If Pompey, before the battle of Pharsalia, had joined his lieutenants in Spain, with the design of abandoning Italy, and erecting Spain into a separate republic or monarchy, every Roman citizen would have despised, and every Roman soldier would have abandoned him. After that fatal battle, Cato and Scipio never once thought of keeping Africa as an independent government; nor did Brutus and Cassius suppose that Greece and Macedonia, which they held with an army,

---

[15] *Passion serves arms.*

afforded them more than the means of contesting with Octavius and Antony the dominion of Rome. No hatred is fiercer than such as springs up among those who are closely allied and nearly resemble each other. Every common soldier would be easily made to feel the personal insult and the intolerable wrong of another army's rejecting his emperor and setting up one of their own—not only so, but he knew it was both a threat and a defiance. The shock of the two armies was therefore inevitable. It was a sort of duel, and could no more stop short of destruction than the combat of Hector and Achilles. We greatly mistake the workings of human nature when we suppose the soldiers in such civil wars are mere machines. Hope and fear, love and hatred, on the contrary, exalt their feelings to enthusiasm. When Otho's troops had received a check from those of Vitellius, he resolved to kill himself. His soldiers, with tears, besought him to live, and swore they would perish, if necessary, in his cause. But he persisted in his purpose, and killed himself; and many of his soldiers, overpowered by their grief, followed his example. Those whom false philosophy makes blind will suppose that national wars will justify, and therefore will excite, all a soldier's ardor; but that the strife between two ambitious generals will be regarded by all men with proper indifference. National disputes are not understood, and their consequences not foreseen, by the multitude; but a quarrel that concerns the life, and fame, and authority of a military favorite takes hold of the heart, and stirs up all the passions.

A democracy is so like an army that no one will be at a loss in applying these observations. The great spring of action with the people in a democracy is their fondness for one set of men, the men who flatter and deceive, and their outrageous aversion to another, most probably those who prefer their true interest to their favor.

A mob is no sooner gathered together than it instinctively feels the want of a leader, a want that is soon supplied. They may not obey him as long, but they obey him as implicitly, and will as readily fight and burn, or rob and murder, in his cause, as the soldiers will for their general.

As the Roman provinces were held in subjection by Roman troops, so every American State is watched with jealously, and ruled with despotic rigor by the partisans of the faction that may happen to be in power. The successive struggles to which our licentiousness may devote the country, will never be of state against state, but of rival factions diffused over our whole territory. Of course, the strongest army, or that which is best commanded, will prevail, and we shall remain subject to one indivisible bad government.

This conclusion may seem surprising to many; but the event of the Roman republic will vindicate it on the evidence of history. After faction, in the time of Marius, utterly obliterated every republican principle that was worth any thing, Rome remained a military despotism for almost six hundred years; and, as the reëstablishment of republican liberty in our country after it is once lost is a thing not to be expected, what can succeed its loss but a government by the sword? It would be certainly easier to prevent than to retrieve its fall.

The jacobins are indeed ignorant or wicked enough to say, a mixed monarchy, on the model of the British, will succeed the failure of our republican system. Mr. Jefferson in his famous letter to Mazzei has shown the strange condition both of his head and heart, by charging this design upon Washington and his adherents. It is but candid to admit, that there are many weak-minded democrats who really think a mixed monarchy the next stage of our politics. As well might they promise, that when their factious fire has burned the plain dwelling-house of our liberty, her temple will rise in royal magnificence, and with all the proportions of Grecian architecture, from the ashes. It is impossible sufficiently to elucidate, yet one could never be tired of elucidating the matchless absurdity of this opinion. An unmixed monarchy, indeed, there is almost no doubt, awaits us; but it will not be called a monarchy. Cæsar lost his life by attempting to take the name of *king*. A president, whose election cannot be hindered, may be well content to wear that title, which inspires no jealousy, yet disclaims no prerogative that party can usurp to confer. Old forms may be continued till some inconvenience is felt from them; and then the same faction that has made them forms can make them less, and substitute some new organic decree in their stead.

But a mixed monarchy would not only offend fixed opinions and habits, but provoke a most desperate resistance. The people, long after losing the substance of republican liberty, maintain a reverence for the name; and would fight with enthusiasm for the tyrant who has left them the name, and taken from them every thing else. Who, then, are to set it up? and how are they to do it? Is it by an army? Where are their soldiers? Where are their resources and means to arm and maintain them? Can it be established by free popular consent? Absurd. A people once trained to republican principles will feel the degradation of submitting to a king. It is far from certain that their opposition would be soothed, by restricting the powers of such a king to the one half of what are enjoyed by Mr. Jefferson. That would make a difference, but the many would not discern it. The aversion of a republican nation to kingship is sincere and warm, even to fanaticism; yet it has never been found to exact of a favorite demagogue, who aspired to reign, any other condescension than an ostentatious scrupulousness of regard to names, to appearances, and forms. Augustus, whose despotism was not greater than his cunning, professed to be the obsequious minister of his slaves in the senate; and Roman pride not only exacted, but enjoyed to the last, the pompous hypocrisy of the phrase, the majesty of the Roman *commonwealth*.

To suppose, therefore, a monarchy established by vote of the people, by the free consent of a majority, is contrary to the nature of man and the uniform testimony of his experience. To suppose it introduced by the disciples of Washington, who are with real or affected scorn described by their adversaries as a fallen party, a despicable handful of malcontents, is no less absurd than inconsistent. The federalists cannot command the consent of a majority, and they have no consular or imperial army to extort it. Every thing of that sort is on the side of their foes, and of course an unsurmountable obstacle to their pretended enterprise.

It will weigh nothing in the argument with some persons, but with men of sense it will be conclusive, that the mass of the federalists are the owners of the commercial and moneyed wealth of the nation. Is it conceivable that such men will plot a revolution in favor of monarchy, a revolution that would make them beggars as well as traitors if it should miscarry; and if it should succeed ever so well, would require a century to take root and acquire stability enough to ensure justice and protect property? In these convulsions of the state, property is shaken, and in almost every radical change of government actually shifts hands. Such a project would seem audacious to the conception of needy adventurers who risk nothing but their lives; but to reproach the federalists of New England, the most independent farmers, opulent merchants, and thriving mechanics, as well as pious clergy, with such a conspiracy, requires a degree of impudence that nothing can transcend. As well might they suspect the merchants of a plot to choke up the entrance of our harbors by sinking hulks, or that the directors of the several banks had confederated to blow up the money vaults with gunpowder. The Catos and the Ciceros are accused of conspiring to subvert the commonwealth—and who are the accusers? The Clodii, the Antonies, and the Catilines.

Let us imagine, however, that by some miracle a mixed

monarchy is established, or rather put into operation; and surely no man will suppose an unmixed monarchy can possibly be desired or contemplated by the federalists. The charge against them is, that they like the British monarchy too well. For the sake of argument, then, be it the British monarchy. To-morrow's sun shall rise and gild it with hope and joy, and the dew of to-morrow's evening shall moisten its ashes. Like the golden calf it would be ground to powder before noon. Certainly, the men who prate about an American monarchy copied from the British, are destitute of all sincerity or judgment. What could make such a monarchy? Not parchment. We are beginning to be cured of the insane belief that an engrossing clerk can make a constitution. Mere words, though on parchment, though sworn to, are wind, and worse than wind, because they are perjury. What could give effect to such a monarchy? It might have a right to command, but what could give it power? Not an army, for that would make it a military tyranny, of all governments the most odious, because the most durable. The British monarchy does not govern by an army, nor would their army suffer itself to be employed to destroy the national liberties. It is officered by the younger sons of noble and wealthy parents, and by many distinguished commanders who are in avowed opposition to the ministry. In fact, democratic opinions take root and flourish scarcely less in armies than in great cities, and infinitely more than they are found to do, or than it is possible they should, in the cabals of any ruling party in the world.

Great Britain, by being an island, is secured from foreign conquest; and by having a powerful enemy within sight of her shore is kept in sufficient dread of it to be inspired with patriotism. That virtue, with all the fervor and elevation that a society which mixes so much of the commercial with the martial spirit can display, has other kindred virtues in its train; and these have had an influence in forming the habits and principles of action, not only of the English military and nobles, but of the mass of the nation. There is much, therefore, there is every thing in that island to blend self-love with love of country. It is impossible that an Englishman should have fears for the government, without trembling for his own safety. How different are these sentiments from the immovable apathy of those citizens, who think a constitution no better than any other piece of paper, nor so good as a blank on which a more perfect one could be written!

Is our monarchy to be supported by the national habits of subordination and implicit obedience? Surely when they hold out this expectation, the jacobins do not mean to answer for themselves. Or do we really think it would still be a monarchy, though we should set up, and put down at pleasure, a town-meeting king?

By removing or changing the relation of any one of the pillars that support the British government, its identity and excellence would be lost, a revolution would ensue. When the house of commons voted the house of peers useless, a tyranny of the committees of that body sprang up. The English nation have had the good sense, or more correctly, the good fortune, to alter nothing, till time and circumstances enforced the alteration, and then to abstain from speculative innovations. The evil spirit of metaphysics has not been conjured up to demolish, in order to lay out a new foundation by the line, and to build upon plan. The present happiness of that nation rests upon old foundations, so much the more solid, because the meddlesome ignorance of professed builders has not been allowed to new lay them. We may be permitted to call it a *matter of fact* government. No correct politician will presume to engage, that the same form of government would succeed equally well, or even succeed at all, anywhere else, or even in England under any other circumstances. Who will dare to say that their monarchy would stand, if this generation had raised it? Who indeed will believe, if it did stand, that the weakness produced by the novelty of its institution would not justify, and even from a regard to self-preservation, compel, an almost total departure from its essential principles?

Now is there one of those essential principles, that it is even possible for the American people to adopt for their monarchy? Are old habits to be changed by a vote, and new ones to be established without experience? Can we have a monarchy without a peerage? or shall our governors supply that defect by giving commissions to a sufficient number of nobles of the quorum? Where is the American hierarchy? Where, above all, is the system of English law and justice, which would support liberty in Turkey, if Turkey could achieve the impossibility of supporting such justice?

It is not recollected that any monarchy in the world was ever introduced by consent; nor will any one believe, on reflection, that it could be maintained by any nation, if nothing but consent upheld it. It is a rare thing for a people to choose their government; it is beyond all credibility, that they will enjoy the still rarer opportunity of changing it by choice.

The notion, therefore, of an American mixed monarchy is supremely ridiculous. It is highly probable our country will be eventually subject to a monarchy, but it is demonstrable that it cannot be such as the British; and whatever it may be, that the votes of the citizens will not be taken to introduce it.

It cannot be expected that the tendency towards a change of government, however obvious, will be discerned by the multitude of our citizens. While demagogues enjoy their favor, their passions will have no rest, and their judgment and understanding no exercise. Otherwise it might be of use to remind them, that more essential breaches have been made in our constitution within four years than in the British in the last hundred and forty. In that enslaved country every executive attempt at usurpation has been spiritedly and

173

perseveringly resisted, and substantial improvements have been made in the constitutional provisions for liberty. Witness the habeas corpus, the independence of the judges, and the perfection, if any thing human is perfect, of their administration of justice, the result of the famous Middlesex election, [16] and that on the right of issuing general search warrants. Let every citizen who is able to think, and who can bear the pain of thinking, make the contrast at his leisure.

They are certainly blind who do not see that we are descending from a supposed orderly and stable republican government into a licentious democracy, with a progress that baffles all means to resist, and scarcely leaves leisure to deplore its celerity. The institutions and the hopes that Washington raised are nearly prostate; and his name and memory would perish, if the rage of his enemies had any power over history. But they have not—history will give scope to her vengeance, and posterity will not be defrauded.

But if our experience had not clearly given warning of our approaching catastrophe, the very nature of democracy would inevitably produce it.

A government by the passions of the multitude, or, no less correctly, according to the vices and ambition of their leaders, is a democracy. We have heard so long of the indefeasible sovereignty of the people, and have admitted so many specious theories of the rights of man, which are contradicted by his nature and experience, that few will dread at all, and fewer still will dread as they ought, the evils of an American

---

[16] *John Wilkes, a London radical, published the* North Briton, *containing insulting remarks about the king, in April, 1763. He was arrested and expelled from the Commons. The "General Warrants" used in his case became an issue and were declared illegal by the chief justice. Wilkes was then outlawed. In 1768 he returned and was again elected to Commons from Middlesex. After expulsion by the "king's friends," he was thrice elected and thrice rejected. The affair finally resulted in establishing "freedom of election of the House of Commons," ultimately enlisting such worthies as Pitt in defense of the principle.*

democracy. They will not believe them near, or they will think them tolerable or temporary. Fatal delusion!

When it is said, there may be a tyranny of the *many* as well as of the *few*, every democrat will yield at least a cold and speculative assent; but he will at all times act, as if it were a thing incomprehensible, that there should be any evil to be apprehended in the uncontrolled power of the people. He will say arbitrary power may make a tyrant, but how can it make its possessor a slave?

In the first place, let it be remarked, the power of individuals is a very different thing from their liberty. When I vote for the man I prefer, he may happen not to be chosen; or he may disappoint my expectations if he is; or he may be outvoted by others in the public body to which he is elected. I may then hold and exercise all the power that a citizen can have or enjoy, and yet such laws may be made and such abuses allowed as shall deprive me of all liberty. I may be tried by a jury, and that jury may be culled and picked out from my political enemies by a federal marshal. Of course, my life and liberty may depend on the good pleasure of the man who appoints that marshal. I may be assessed arbitrarily for my faculty, or upon conjectural estimation of my property, so that all I have shall be at the control of the government, whenever its displeasure shall exact the sacrifice. I may be told that I am a federalist, and as such bound to submit, in all cases whatsoever, to the will of the majority, as the ruling faction ever pretend to be. My submission may be tested by my resisting or obeying commands that will involve me in disgrace, or drive me to despair. I may become a fugitive, because the ruling party have made me afraid to stay at home; or, perhaps, while I remain at home, they may, nevertheless, think fit to inscribe my name on the list of emigrants and proscribed persons.

All this was done in France, and many of the admirers of French examples are impatient to imitate them. All this time the people may be told, they are the freest in the world; but what ought my opinion to be? What would the threatened clergy, the aristocracy of wealthy merchants, as they have been called already, and thirty thousand more in Massachusetts, who vote for Governor Strong, and whose case might be no better than mine, what would they think of their condition? Would they call it liberty? Surely, here is oppression sufficient in extent and degree to make the government that inflicts it both odious and terrible; yet this and a thouand times more than this was practised in France, and will be repeated as often as it shall please God in his wrath to deliver a people to the dominion of their licentious passions.

The people, as a body, cannot deliberate. Nevertheless, they will feel an irresistible impulse to act, and their resolutions will be dictated to them by their demagogues. The consciousness, or the opinion, that they possess the supreme power, will inspire inordinate passions; and the violent men, who are the most forward to gratify those passions, will be their favorites. What is called the government of the people is in fact too often the arbitrary power of such men. Here, then, we have the faithful portrait of democracy. What avails the boasted power of individual citizens? or of what value is the will of the majority, if that will is dictated by a committee of demagogues, and law and right are in fact at the mercy of a victorious faction? To make a nation free, the crafty must be kept in awe, and the violent in restraint. The weak and the simple find their liberty arise not from their own individual sovereignty, but from the power of law and justice over all. It is only by the due restraint of others, that I am free.

Popular sovereignty is scarcely less beneficent than awful, when it resides in their courts of justice; there its office, like a sort of human providence, is to warn, enlighten, and protect; when the people are inflamed to seize and exercise it in their assemblies, it is competent only to kill and destroy. Temperate liberty is like the dew, as it falls unseen from its own heaven; constant without excess, it finds vegetation thirsting for its refreshment, and imparts to it the vigor to take more. All nature, moistened with blessings, sparkles in the morning ray. But democracy is a water-spout that bursts from the clouds, and lays the ravaged earth bare to its rocky foundations. The labors of man lie whelmed with his hopes beneath masses of ruin, that bury not only the dead but their monuments.

It is the almost universal mistake of our countrymen, that democracy would be mild and safe in America. They charge the horrid excesses of France not so much to human nature, which will never act better, when the restraints of government, morals, and religion are thrown off, but to the characteristic cruelty and wickedness of Frenchmen.

The truth is, and let it humble our pride, the most ferocious of all animals, when his passions are roused to fury and are uncontrolled, is man; and of all governments, the worst is that which never fails to excite, but was never found to restrain those passions, that is, democracy. It is an illuminated hell, that in the midst of remorse, horror, and torture, rings with festivity; for experience shows, that one joy remains to this most malignant description of the damned, the power to make others wretched. When a man looks round and sees his neighbors mild and merciful, he cannot feel afraid of the abuse of their power over him; and surely if they oppress me, he will say, they will spare their own liberty, for that is dear to all mankind. It is so. The human heart is so constituted, that a man loves liberty as naturally as himself. Yet liberty is a rare thing in the world, though the love of it is so universal.

Before the French Revolution, it was the prevailing opinion of our countrymen, that other nations were not free, because their despotic governments were too strong for the people. Of course, we were admonished to detest all existing govern-

177

ments, as so many lions in liberty's path; and to expect by their downfall the happy opportunity, that every emancipated people would embrace, to secure their own equal rights for ever. France is supposed to have had this opportunity, and to have lost it. Ought we not then to be convinced, that something more is necessary to preserve liberty than to love it? Ought we not to see that when the people have destroyed all power but their own, they are the nearest possible to a despotism, the more uncontrolled for being new, and tenfold the more cruel for its hypocrisy?

The steps by which a people must proceed to change a government, are not those to enlighten their judgment or to soothe their passions. They cannot stir without following the men before them, who breathe fury into their hearts and banish nature from them. On whatever grounds and under whatever leaders the contest may be commenced, the revolutionary work is the same, and the characters of the agents will be assimilated to it. A revolution is a mine that must explode with destructive violence. The men who were once peaceable like to carry firebrands and daggers too long. Thus armed, will they submit to salutary restraint? How will you bring them to it? Will you undertake to reason down fury? Will you satisfy revenge without blood? Will you preach banditti into habits of self-denial? If you can, and in times of violence and anarchy, why do you ask any other guard than sober reason for you life and property in times of peace and order, when men are most disposed to listen to it? Yet even at such times, you impose restraints; you call out for your defence the whole array of law, with its instruments of punishment and terror; you maintain ministers to strengthen force with opinion, and to make religion the auxiliary of morals. With all this, however, crimes are still perpetrated; society is not any too safe or quiet. Break down all these fences; make what is called law an assassin; take what it ought to protect, and divide it; extinguish, by acts of rapine and vengeance, the spark of mercy in the heart; or, if it should be found to glow there, quench it in that heart's blood; make your people scoff at their morals, and unlearn an education to virtue; displace the Christian sabbath by a profane one, for a respite once in ten days from the toils of murder, because men, who first shed blood for revenge, and proceed to spill it for plunder, and in the progress of their ferocity, for sport, want a festival—what sort of society would you have? Would not rage grow with its indulgence? The coward fury of a mob rises in proportion as there is less resistance; and their inextinguishable thirst for slaughter grows more ardent as more blood is shed to slake it. In such a state is liberty to be gained or guarded from violation? It could not be kept an hour from the daggers of those who, having seized despotic power, would claim it as their lawful prize. I have written the history of France. Can we look back upon it without terror, or forward without despair?

The nature of arbitary power is always odious; but it cannot be long the arbitrary power of the multitude. There is, probably, no form of rule among mankind, in which the progress of the government depends so little on the particular character of those who administer it. Democracy is the creature of impulse and violence; and the intermediate stages towards the tyranny of one are so quickly passed, that the vileness and cruelty of men are displayed with surprising uniformity. There is not time for great talents to act. There is no sufficient reason to believe, that we should conduct a revolution with much more mildness than the French. If a revolution find the citizens lambs, it will soon make them carnivorous, if not cannibals. We have many thousands of the Paris and St. Domingo assassins in the United States, not as fugitives, but as patriots, who merit reward, and disdain to take any but power. In the progress of our confusion, these men will effectually assert their claims and display their skill. There is no governing power in the state but

179

party. The moderate and thinking part of the citizens are without power or influence; and it must be so, because all power and influence are engrossed by a factious combination of men, who can overwhelm uncombined individuals with numbers, and the wise and virtuous with clamor and fury.

It is indeed a law of politics, as well as of physics, that a body in action must overcome an equal body at rest. The attacks that have been made on the constitutional barriers proclaim, in a tone that would not be louder from a trumpet, that party will not tolerate any resistance to its will. All the supposed independent orders of the commonwealth must be its servile instruments, or its victims. We should experience the same despotism in Massachusetts, New Hampshire, and Connecticut, but the battle is not yet won. It will be won; and they who already display the temper of their Southern and French allies, will not linger or reluct in imitating the worst extremes of their example.

What, then, is to be our condition?

Faction will inevitably triumph. Where the government is both stable and free, there may be parties. There will be differences of opinion, and the pride of opinion will be sufficient to generate contests, and to inflame them with bitterness and rancor. There will be rivalships among those whom genius, fame, or station have made great, and these will deeply agitate the state without often hazarding its safety. Such parties will excite alarm, but they may be safely left, like the elements, to exhaust their fury upon each other.

The object of their strife is to get power *under* the government; for, where that is constituted as it should be, the power *over* the government will not seem attainable, and, of course, will not be attempted.

But in democratic states there will be factions. The sovereign power being nominally in the hands of all, will be effectively within the grasp of a few; and therefore, by the very laws of our nature, a few will combine, intrigue, lie, and fight to engross it to themselves. All history bears testimony, that this attempt has never yet been disappointed.

Who will be the associates? Certainly not the virtuous, who do not wish to control the society, but quietly to enjoy its protection. The enterprising merchant, the thriving tradesman, the careful farmer, will be engrossed by the toils of their business, and will have little time or inclination for the unprofitable and disquieting pursuits of politics. It is not the industrious, sober husbandman, who will plough that barren field; it is the lazy and dissolute bankrupt, who has no other to plough. The idle, the ambitious, and the needy will band together to break the hold that law has upon them, and then to get hold of law. Faction is a Hercules, whose first labor is to strangle this lion, and then to make armor of his skin. In every democratic state, the ruling faction will have law to keep down its enemies; but it will arrogate to itself an undisputed power over law. If our ruling faction has found any impediments, we ask, which of them is now remaining? And is it not absurd to suppose, that the conquerors will be contented with half the fruits of victory?

We are to be subject, then, to a despotic faction, irritated by the resistance that has delayed, and the scorn that pursues their triumph, elate with the insolence of an arbitrary and uncontrollable domination, and who will exercise their sway, not according to the rules of integrity or national policy, but in conformity with their own exclusive interests and passions.

This is a state of things which admits of progress, but not of reformation; it is the beginning of a revolution, which must advance. Our affairs, as first observed, no longer depend on counsel. The opinion of a majority is no longer invited or permitted to control our destinies, or even to retard their consummation. The men in power may, and no doubt will give place to some other faction, who will succeed, because they are abler men, or possibly, in candor we say it, because they are worse. Intrigue will for some time answer instead of force, or the mob will supply it. But by degrees force only will be relied on by those who are *in*, and employed by those who are *out*. The vis major will prevail, and some bold chieftain will conquer liberty, and triumph and reign in her name.

Yet it is confessed, we have hopes that this event is not very near. We have no cities as large as London or Paris; and of course the ambitious demagogues may find the ranks of their standing army too thin to rule by them alone. It is also worth remark, that our mobs are not, like those of Europe, excitable by the cry of no bread. The dread of famine is everywhere else a power of political electricity, that glides through all the haunts of filth, and vice, and want in a city, with incredible speed, and in times of insurrection rives and scorches with a sudden force, like heaven's own thunder. Accordingly, we find the sober men of Europe more afraid of the despotism of the rabble than of the government.

But as in the United States we see less of this description of low vulgar, and as in the essential circumstance alluded to, they are so much less manageable by their demagogues, we are to expect that our affairs will be long guided by courting the mob, before they are violently changed by employing them. While the passions of the multitude can be conciliated to confer power and to overcome all impediments to its action, our rulers have a plain and easy task to perform. It costs them nothing but hypocrisy. As soon, however, as rival favorites of the people may happen to contend by the practice of the same arts, we are to look for the sanguinary strife of ambition. Brissot will fall by the hand of Danton, and he will be supplanted by Robespierre. The revolution will proceed in exactly the same way, but not with so rapid a pace, as that of France.

REVIEW OF A PAMPHLET ON THE
STATE OF THE BRITISH CONSTITUTION

FROM THE SIZE of this pamphlet,[17] and from its title-page, it was natural to expect profound investigation and accurate and important results. The design of the work is announced with uncommon parade in an introduction of sixteen pages; but we do not hesitate to say, these are sixteen pages too much; for the object of the writer is sufficiently unfolded in what follows.

The work is divided into two parts. In the first part, he proposes to discuss the theory of the British Constitution, and to examine how the theory differs from the practice. This part extends from the seventeenth to the ninety-ninth page, inclusive. It is very verbose, and contains nothing new. After a long display of old historical facts, which he seldom applies, and which are not always applicable to his subject, he abruptly and unexpectedly concludes, that the security of the people under the present British Constitution, is owing to the freedom of the press. We confess, we have been ready to prove the remarkable strength and stability of that constitution, and of course the security of the people, by its having stood so long in spite of the abuses of the press. For where the press is free, it will be abused.

We are, heart and soul, friends to the freedom of the press. It is, however, the prostituted companion of liberty, and somehow or other, we know not how, its efficient auxiliary. It follows the substance like its shade; but while a man walks erect, he may observe that his shadow is almost always in

---

[17] Present State of the British Constitution Historically Illustrated *(London: Longman, Hurst, Rees, & Orme, 1807).*

the dirt. It corrupts, it deceives, it inflames. It strips virtue of her honors, and lends to faction its wildfire and its poisoned arms, and in the end is its own enemy and the usurper's ally. It would be easy to enlarge on its evils. They are in England, they are here, they are everywhere. It is a precious pest and a necessary mischief, and *there would be no liberty without it.* We expected that the author would have attempted profoundly to trace its useful operation, but he has not done it; and this rare task remains for some more acute inquirer into the obscure causes of its salutary influence.

In the second part, he undertakes to prove that this is the great safeguard of that constitution. For this purpose, he resorts again to history. But in the instances he adduces to show the influence of a free press, he only demonstrates the power of public opinion. The nation would have an opinion, if it had not a press; and that opinion would have weight and authority. Before the art of printing was known, bad ministers were crushed by public odium. The favorites of Edward the Second, of England, were as effectually overpowered by it as if the press had been used. The freedom of the press cannot hinder its being venal. Had it then existed, those odious favorites would have used it to palliate their crimes. They would have bought the press; and no doubt they would have been patriots in type, till they were stripped of the means of corruption; and then again they would have been odious monsters. In our time this boasted luminary vents more smoke than light; so that the circumstances of transactions, and the characters of men, are to be clearly known only by waiting for the evidence of history in a future age, when it will be of very little comparative importance whether the subject be understood or mistaken.

Though nobody will deny the influence of public opinion upon government, still it is a distinct question, what is the boasted salutary influence of the press? It might help the cause of truth and liberty; it might produce, as well as gratify a thirst for inquiry. But who pretend to be the instructors of the people? men who are themselves instructed? or needy, ignorant profligates? The use of the press must be supposed to lie in helping a nation to discern and to judge. Experience seems to show, that the press makes every thing more apparent than the truth; and by eternally pretending to judge, the public opinion is without authority or influence; it is counterfeited by fools, and perverted by knaves. But a plain people without a press, would know oppression when they felt it; and there is no government, which is not supported by military force, that would disregard the complaints of an indignant nation. By the help of the press we see invisible things; we foresee evils in their embryo, and accumulate on the present moment all that is bitter in the past or terrible in the future. A whole people are made sick with the diseases of the imagination. They see a monarch in Washington, and conspirators in their patriots. They turn their best men out of office on the strength of their suspicions; and trust their worst men in spite of their knowledge of them. It is the press that has spoiled the temper of our liberty, and may shorten its life.

Still, we repeat, we would by no means wish to see the liberty of the press abridged. But how it is that we are dieted upon poisons and yet live, we pretend not to say, nor has this author instructed us.

From these deductions we venture to pronounce, that the freedom of the press is not the cause of the security of the British people, or of the duration of their constitution. It is not our business to make a theory, but only to expose that of the author, which indeed is scarcely worth confuting. But we should think, that the freedom of that constitution arises rather from the distinct existence and political power of three orders, than from the press. The press could tell of oppression, if it had happened; but the lords and commons could remove and punish it.

But though we cannot possibly discover how the freedom of the press can secure the constitution of an hereditary government, we can easily see, how in a popular state the abuse of the press may fortify a faction in power. It is not merit, it is not wisdom, that in such a state can confer power; it is faction which has an interest in accumulating wealth and privilege upon its members, and persecution on its rivals. We know a country where the press is successfully used for the concealment of the truth. Newspapers written all on one side are read all on one side; and the truth and argument of the adverse party are as little known, and have less chance of being understood by the other, than the language of Hindostan, or the religion of Thibet.

V.

ESSAYS ON
AMERICA'S POLITICAL
PARTIES

———

LAOCOON I

———

Boston Gazette, APRIL, 1799

SOME LABOR has been recently bestowed on the proposition, that the sect of jacobins is not to be converted, and in enforcing the obvious duty on all honest men to unite with energy to resist them. This alarm, it will be objected, is forever sounding; and it is replied, forever sounding to the deaf. Honest men, it is allowed, reasonably expect to enjoy tranquillity under the protection of government; instead of which, it is not denied that they are incessantly summoned to their posts to afford to government the protection they had hoped it would be in a condition to bestow. The cry of danger disturbs their beloved and promised ease, disappoints their fond hopes, disgraces their splendid theories, and saddens that futurity which fancy had adorned like the millennium. To the inhabitants of a besieged town fatigue renders repose more welcome and more necessary; the roar of cannon does not awake them. Familiar dangers lose half their terror, and we yield, with a weakness which we will not detect and cannot resist, to the delusions of every rumor without evidence, and every hope that rises up to console us against it. The federalist rises like the sluggard from his bed at the cry of fire, hoping that a little more water will quench it, and that he may then return to sleep undisturbed. It is not easy, perhaps it is not possible, to make the citizens political soldiers; to persuade them to sleep on their arms, ready at the beat of drum to repel the assaults of the jacobins on law and liberty. It will even sink their estimate of the value of civil liberty to know that it gives joy, gives safety, honor,— gives every thing but sleep. They will be apt, in obedience to the suggestions of spleen and weariness, to say, that the single thing it denies is worth more than the million it bestows, and joyfully to embrace a political condition which would somewhat abate the pretension of each individual to be a sovereign, and require a less painful effort to maintain it.

It is, indeed, exceedingly obvious, that many, if not most persons, have chosen the state of the highest liberty without having counted how much it must cost to preserve it. The calumnies vented against President Adams's book[18] are signal proofs of the crude and indocile state of popular opinion amongst us. He has ingeniously described evils, and faithfully and wisely pointed out their remedies; yet he is accused of being no friend to republics because he well understands their nature, and seriously dreads their dangers. The very factions who create and aggravate those dangers, and who neither understand nor desire those remedies, honor their own ignorance with the name of principle, and claim for their licentiousness the exclusive title of republicanism. If it fails

[18] Discourses on Davila, *a series of essays on the British constitution.*

it is they who make it fail. The impediments to its success, which arise from the structure of the human heart, create surprise, though they were obviously inevitable, and something like despair, though we know that they may be surmounted.

> Faction will freedom, like its shade, pursue;
> Yet, like the shadow, proves the substance true.

We have to sustain an everlasting conflict with faction; a foe, destined to be the companion of liberty, and, at last, its assassin. However we may flatter ourselves with the idea that our blows will prove fatal to this foe, yet, though smitten to the ground, it will rise again like Anteus, untired, invulnerable, and immortal. Nothing can more strikingly illustrate the folly of the jacobins, in their pretensions to a superior vigilance for the people, than the natural and indeed experienced tendency of their turbulence to strengthen the powers of government. The danger these men create must be repelled by arming our rulers with force enough, and appointing them to watch in our stead. Thus good citizens find that they must submit to laws of the more rigor, because the desperate licentiousness and wickedness of the bad could not be otherwise restrained. If the laws they complain of really abridge liberty, as they pretend, which however is positively denied, it is their own wickedness that has supplied to government the pretext, and varnished it over with the appearance of necessity. Quiet, satisfied people, need the least law; but as the jacobins are of a very different character, it is clear that all the fruit of their perverseness must be to abridge the liberty of the people; and this too if they fail of success. But if they should prevail, the people would be crushed, as in France, under tyranny more vindictive, unfeeling, and rapacious, than that of Tiberius, Nero, or Caligula, or any single despot that ever existed. The rage of one man will be tired by repetition of outrage, or it may be eluded by art or by flight. It seldom smites the obscure, who are many, but like a gust uproots chiefly the great trees that overtop the forest. A mobocracy, however, is always usurped by the worst men in the most corrupt times; in a period of violence by the most violent. It is a Briareus with a thousand hands, each bearing a dagger; a Cerberus gaping with ten thousand throats, all parched and thirsting for fresh blood. It is a genuine tyranny, but of all the least durable, yet the most destructive while it lasts. The power of a despot, like the ardor of a summer's sun, dries up the grass, but the roots remain fresh in the soil. A mob-government, like a West India hurricane, instantly strews the fruitful earth with promiscuous ruins, and turns the sky yellow with pestilence. Men inhale a vapor like the sirocco, and die in the open air for want of respiration. It is a winged curse, that envelops the obscure as well as the distinguished, and is wafted into the lurking-places of the fugitives. It is not doing justice to licentiousness to compare it to a wind which ravages the surface of the earth; it is an earthquake that loosens its foundations, burying in an hour the accumulated wealth and wisdom of ages. Those who, after the calamity, would reconstruct the edifice of the public liberty, will be scarcely able to find the model of the artificers, or even the ruins. Mountains have split and filled the fertile valleys, covering them with rocks and gravel; rivers have changed their beds; populous towns have sunk, leaving only frightful chasms, out of which are creeping the remnant of living wretches, the monuments and the victims of despair. This is no exaggerated description. Behold France, that open hell, still ringing with agonies and blasphemies, still smoking with sufferings and crimes, in which we see their state of torment, and perhaps our future state. There we see the wretchedness and degra dation of a people, who once had the offer of liberty, but have trifled it away; and there we have seen crimes so

monstrous, that, even after we know they have been perpetrated, they still seem incredible.

If, however, the real people will wake, when their own
government is in danger; if, like a body of minute-men, they
will rally in its defence, we may long preserve our excellent
system unimpaired in the degree of its liberty; we may
preserve every thing but our tranquillity.

It is however difficult, if not impossible, to excite and
maintain as much zeal and ardor in defence of government,
as will animate the jacobins for its subversion; for to them
action is ease, to us it is effort; to be at rest costs them more
constraint, than us to stir. The machinery of our zeal is
wrought by a feeble and intermitting momentum, and is
impeded by its own friction; their rage beats like the pulse
of life, and to stop it would be mortal. Like the whirlwind,
it clears away obstacles, and gathers speed in its progress.
Any great exertion not only tires, but disgusts the federalists;
their spirit, after flaming brightly, soon sleeps in its embers;
but the jacobins, like salamanders, can breathe only in fire.
Like toads, they suck no aliment from the earth but its
poisons. When they rest in their lurking-places, as they did
after the publication of the despatches,[19] it is, like serpents
in winter, the better to concoct their venom; and when they
are in action, it is to shed it. Without digressing to make an
analysis of the jacobin character, whether it is envy that
sickens at the fame of superiors, cupidity that seeks political

---

[19] *The X Y Z despatches, as they were called, disclosing an attempt on
the part of French officials to obtain bribes from our envoys.* [S. AMES]

*John Marshall, Charles Cotesworth Pinckney, and Elbridge Gerry
were the American peace commissioners in France in late 1797. Agents
"X," "Y," and "Z" of the French foreign minister, Talleyrand, had
demanded a bribe for their superior and an American loan to France
as precondition to peace negotiations. The affair eventuated in the
coining of the slogan, "Millions for defense, but not one cent for
tribute."* [ED.]

power for the sake of plunder, or ambition that considers plunder as the instrument to get power; whether their characters are formed by the weak facility of their faith, or their faith determined by the sour, malignant, and suspicious cast of their temperament, yet all agree in this one point, all are moved by some fixed prejudice or strong passion, some powerful spring of action, so blended with self-interest, or self-love, and so exalted into fanaticism, that the ordinary powers of the man, and the extraordinary powers conferred on the enthusiast, are equally devoted to their cause of anarchy. Hatred of the government becomes a mania, a *dementia quoad hoc,* and their dread of all power but their own, resembles the hydrophobia, baffling our attempts to describe its nature or its remedies. These are the fanatics whom the federalists must oppose; and what in common times is to excite their zeal and secure the constancy of their opposition? A sense of duty, which a few men of abstraction will deduce from just principles, and the foresight of a few more, who will be terrified by the tendencies of democracy to anarchy? But sober duty and a timorous forecast are feeble antagonists against jacobinism; it is flat tranquillity against passion; dry leaves against the whirlwind; the weight of gunpowder against its kindled force. Such federalists may serve as weathercocks to show how the wind blows, but are no shelter against its violence. The quiet citizens may be compared to the still water in the lake; the jacobins to that part of it which falls over a cataract at its outlet; the former having a thousand times the greatest mass, but no energy, and scarcely motion enough to keep it sweet; the latter dashed into foam, and scooping deeper channels in the rocks of adamant. To weight we must impart motion; correct good sense must acquire the energy of zeal. A score of absurd cant opinions must be scouted, all which tend to make us like the jacobin designs a little more, and to dread and abhor their agents a little less. Take a specimen of the proselyting logic; the jacobins, they tell us, are many of them honest men, but misled. Whether they will long remain honest, yet the associates of knaves and their fellow workers of iniquity, may be doubted. If the invectives against those who insist on being called honest, among the jacobins, are "too harsh and acrimonious" to-day, they will by to-morrow, or the next day, be sufficiently assimilated to the company they keep, and the designs they pursue, to merit them; they get a character for life only one day too soon. Besides, it is not the character of an odd man or two, or at most of half a dozen in a state, that happens to have a head too thick to admit, or too hot to yield to the principles of the party that is to denominate the exact dark hue of the vice, or the precise measure of infamy that belongs of right to the party. Look at France; see jacobinism at home, where, neither ashamed of its character, nor afraid of its punishment, it indulges the unrestrained propensities of its nature, and then decide, reader, if you can, that the victims of law are a worse set of men than its conquerors.

It must be remembered, too, that public opinion is the great auxiliary of good government. Where can its weight fall so properly as on the conspirators who disturb its tranquillity and plot its subversion? The man who, from passion or folly, or bad company, happens to believe, that liberty will rise when government sinks, may be less criminal, but little less contemptible, for his sincerity. If a madman should poison a spring, because he fancies that all who drink and die will go to heaven and be happy, is he to be soothed and indulged? Will you let him have his way? Are you not to tell those who are thirsty, and about to drink the poisonous water, that it is death? Will it be against "candor and decency" to tell them that the man is mad? The gentle critics on the style of federal writers would have that scorn withheld, which is almost the only thing that actually restrains the jacobins from mischief; that scorn, which makes those who might be misled ashamed to join them. The factious have the cunning to say, that the bitterness of their spirit is owing to the harsh and acrimonious treatment they receive; as if reproach had made them jacobins; whereas it is jacobinism that extorts reproach. Our government has not armies, nor a hierarchy, nor an extensive patronage. Instead of these auxiliaries of other governments, let it have the sword of public opinion drawn in its defence, and not only drawn but whetted by satire to an edge to hew its adversaries down. Let jacobin vice be seen as a monster, and let not a mock candor pity, till we embrace it. Other governments may stand, though not very steadily, if public opinion be only neuter; but our system has so little intrinsic energy, that this soul of the republic's soul must not only approve but coöperate. The vain, the timid, and trimming must be made by examples to see that scorn smites, and blasts, and withers like lightning the knaves that mislead them. Then let the misled many come off and leave the party if they will; if not, let them club it with them for the infamy.

A frame of government less free and popular might perhaps have been left to take some care of itself; but the people choose to have it as it is, and therefore they must not complain of the burden, but come forward and support it; it has not strength to stand alone without such help from the wise and honest citizens. The time to do this, is at the elections. There, if anywhere, the sovereignty of the citizen is to be exercised; and there the privilege is open to the most excessive and most fatal abuse.

Here at last the jacobins have taken their post, and here they have intrenched themselves to assail our sober and orderly liberty. Here we see of late, indeed within a single year, an almost total change in the tactics and management of parties. The jacobins have at last made their own discipline perfect; they are trained, officered, regimented, and formed to subordination, in a manner that our militia have never yet equalled. Emissaries are sent to every class of men, and

194

even to every individual man, that can be gained. Every threshing-floor, every husking, every party at work on a house-frame or raising a building, the very funerals are infected with bawlers or whisperers against government. In one of our towns, it is a fact, that the vote would have been unanimous for our worthy chief magistrate; but a turbulent man who kept two great dogs, but could not keep his estate, had influence enough to gain five or six votes for the anti-candidate; the only complaint he had to urge against the governor was, that he had signed the act for the dog-tax.

The extreme industry of this faction shows the extent of their designs; even the town governments are not below their scheme of influence. It is plain, that they intend to get the state government into their hands. They will make the attempt, and if they get only one fifth jacobin members, they will try again next year, never despairing of their final success; should they succeed, they would use the power of Massachusetts against the laws and government of the United States. No longer hoping much aid from the fleets and armies of France, which they but lately declared they wished to see on our shores and coast, they rely on themselves. In every state they are exerting themselves rather more like an armed force beating up for recruits, than a sect of political disputants; and it is as certain as any future event can be, that they will take arms against the laws as soon as they dare; probably within a year, if they get the countenance of the New England state governments. They are already in arms in Pennsylvania, and Virginia holds forth all possible encouragement to their rising, by resolutions and remonstrances calculated to excite civil war,[20] and to infuse into the bosoms of the factious all the fury with which such wars are carried on.

If they would rise and try the issue in the field, they would

---

[20] *The Kentucky and Virginia resolutions, drafted by Thomas Jefferson and James Madison, respectively, in 1799, in response to the Alien and Sedition laws, and raising the prospect of nullification.*

be beaten. Let them then come out; but while they depend on lies and industry in spreading them, they will beat us.

They are overmatched by the federalists in argument. Every public question that has been keenly investigated and sifted by the political writers and debaters on both sides, has been clearly decided against them. In the resources of money, and that sort of credit which grows out of confidence in the virtue and morals of political men, the jacobins are weak indeed. The federalists, throughout New England at least, probably pay nineteen shillings in the pound of the taxes; and as to credit, the chiefs of the party would consider an inquiry into their title to any as a cruel irony. For talents as statesmen, the New England jacobin leaders are despicable; their ignorance of commerce, of finance, and of the "diplomatic skill" of France, is not only obvious, but they are concerned to urge the last as an excuse, for if they are not ignorant, they are wicked; it is possible they are both. As to talents in the field, on which side do they appear? The reader may be left to look up jacobin generals and heroes.

With all these undoubted titles to contempt, are the jacobins to be despised? Individually, it may be so; though great numbers are rather to be pitied; but, collectively, they are formidable, and a party is never more to be feared than when it is despised. Then they are let alone to undermine the pillars of the public order; then it happens, as at the present moment, that they bestir themselves to get jacobins elected into the general court; and the friends of government, despising their foe, sleep in a dangerous security.

The jacobins know that they are as yet weak in force, though powerful in lies and low cunning. They will not appear in arms at present, for that would make their weakness the antagonist of our strength. But lies and cunning are always formidable at elections; thus they oppose their strength to our weakness; we cannot and will not resort to lies. But we can overmatch them when we take the alarm in season, and rouse the federal zeal; that zeal has more than once saved the country. Now is the time and the occasion again to display it, for the faction turns its evil eyes to the elections of the house of representatives of the state; and if they obtain even a large minority, they will spread the infection with more ardor than even a majority, as minorities are ever the most industrious and most firmly united. So large a mass of poison in the general court, lying in fermentation for a year, would vitiate and corrupt our political health; and by another year a jacobin majority would appear there to overturn, and overturn, and overturn, till property shall take wings, and true liberty and good government find their graves. By getting a majority of jacobins into the New England state legislatures, they would make civil war, disunion, and perhaps a foreign yoke, the lot of the present generation. Friends of virtue, if you will not attend the election, and lend to liberty the help of your votes, within two years you will have to defend her cause with your swords.

LAOCOON II

To some the warmth of the preceding number of Laocoon will appear excessive, and to others altogether superfluous; excessive, because, they urge, the feelings of the jacobins ought to be treated with more tenderness, and their designs with more candor; and superfluous, because the political sky is bright and unclouded, promising the long continuance of fair weather. The adoption of either of these opinions would have an influence with the writer; the first would change his style, the latter impose silence. Faction is an adherence to interests foreign to the interests of the state; there is such a faction amongst us devoted to France. He believes that the jacobin faction is composed, like every other, of ambitious knaves who mislead, and of a weak and infatuated rabble who are misled. Among the latter are numbers who set out honest, and while they continue so they are deserving of some indulgence, and there is some hope of reclaiming a very few of them; but if they travel far on the party road, or associate long with the desperadoes in the van, who explore the thorny and crooked by-ways, they will not remain honest. They will be corrupted, and so deeply, that in every approach towards civil war and revolution, the dupes who sincerely believe the whole creed of their party, will be found ready to go the farthest. After they have thrown off all political duty, the remains of other moral principles which the philosophers would call the prejudices of education, will be just sufficient to prevent remorse or to stifle it. There is a sophistry in all the passions, and that of every strong one is almost always convincing. We see, accordingly, that men of some morals, when they run politically mad, far from flinching from the debasing company of knaves, whom party dubs patriots, make open profession of their monstrous principles, and hardily vindicate their most desperate designs. It is a fact, the talk of the jacobins, and even their printed threats are to demolish bank property and funded debt, and to wreak vengeance on the aristocrats, meaning the possessors of property. How many professors of the christian religion have seen with complacency, nay with joy and exaltation, the downfall of priests and creeds and churches in France? The unspeakable cruelties and crimes exercised against catholics, they tell us will introduce the true worship, and that they admire, and we are bound to approve, proceedings that are so wicked, because they will be so useful. The sophistry that can thus silence conscience and varnish crimes, has no less succeeded in blinding the understandings of these honest jacobins (so called) to the absolute falsehood of their political notions. France has confessedly lost liberty, and the spirit and love of it, and has become infatuated with the passion for rapine and conquest; yet they still insist, that though France has not liberty at present she will have it. After the revolutionary storm there will be a delightful calm, when reason only will be heard, and nothing but the equal rights of man desired or regarded; and as to the conquest of other nations, aristocracies or corruptions of democracy fell in Switzerland, and the universal domination of France will multiply republics and demolish thrones. Is the writer to blame if he feels contempt for opinions like these? If, notwithstanding their absurdity, and indeed for the very reason that they are absurd, he sees that they are contagious, and knows that they are dangerous; if he sees their propagators formidable by their zeal, and the more formidable for its blindness, digging their mines and laying their trains of gunpowder to blow up the temple of liberty, is it possible for him to feel contempt in silence, or can he express it without a mixture of detestation and abhorrence? The party who thus labor to destroy all that we have toiled and fought for, and sworn to preserve, is surely, collectively speaking, the proper object of our considerate indignation; nor can there be any unfitness, any want of candor, any departure from the line of policy, in exhibiting the picture of this party as it is. The inevitable effect of this picture is to excite aversion, scorn, and terror; the fault of rousing these unpleasant emotions in all their strength is not in the painter; it is in the subject. Let the soft seekers of popularity dream of soothing parties into moderation. When they see a faction devoted to our foreign enemy, putting their all in jeopardy, let them counsel us again as they have often done before, to bestow upon the factious all our charity, and more than half our esteem, and upon the government that is struggling to preserve us, all our jealousy, and as much of our support as we can afford it without making enemies. Let them compose new homilies for hypocrisy, to inculcate upon citizens brotherly love towards amiable patriotic traitors, and upon government forbearance to make or execute laws against inoffensive conspiracies. But let such discourses issue only from the *Chronicle*. Let all but its readers and patrons abstain from censuring the asperity with which the jacobins as a party are treated. The scorn that is poured upon them is the greatest obstacle they encounter in their more than jesuit labors of making converts to jacobinism; and the dread and abhorrence in which the party and their schemes are held, is the chief auxiliary of good government in preventing their success. It is the squeamishness, the trimming, half-way, selfish spirit of too many federalists that keeps the faction encouraged to prosecute its pestilent designs. The British nation is now united as one man, and the force of public opinion is combined; the voice of the real nation is heard, and faction is of consequence in the mire of contempt. Till our spirit is in like manner roused, all things will seem to be possible to party, and therefore all evil things will be attempted. If we allow ourselves to hope any respite from the assaults of the French faction, it is by animating the zeal of the friends of virtue and government, and persuading them to come forth and to speak out, and thus we shall discourage and disarm the factious; their affected moderation must not rob the cause of half its support. It is indeed evident, that the spirit of the friends of order is at all times weak, excepting only when the danger is so near and obvious to rouse an universal alarm and a common exertion. A correct view of the character of jacobinism, if once clearly taken and profoundly impressed upon the public, would keep those well-grounded apprehensions constantly awake, which in effect are the guardians of our political safety.

I will not therefore admit, that the task of delineating the true character of the deluded mass of the jacobins is unnecessary, or that by adhering to truth there will be a deviation from urbanity and candor. I will raise my feeble voice to expose the frailty of those hopes, which too many repose on the honesty of the factious, and which incline them to behold the desperation of their measures without much fear, because they trust that the individuals of the party will flinch as soon as things approach towards extremities. This trust is a vain one. I am as ready as others to make excuses for the deluded of all parties. Of all the causes of seduction from virtue, perhaps none is so powerful as the fellowship of party. But what then? Are we still to maintain that party men are honest, when they have been long exposed to an influence, which we know is almost irresistibly corrupting? We may, and we ought, on this account, the more deeply to deplore the ravages of the spirit of faction upon morals and the sentiments of humanity. We are not, however, to deny the fact, and insist upon reposing our confidence in the correct moral discernment of men, whom we know to be deluded, nor in the restraints of shame and principle upon those minds which have already overcome the shame of their principles and their associates. We may be sure that more than half the utmost corrupting work of political vice is already done, and that the reputed honest men of the faction have either renounced their old principles, or dismissed them as the guides of their conduct. It is a cruel mercy that would spare the party, because some of the individuals mean well. The plain truth should be told; it may alarm a few, and save them from being traitors.

Some labor to exhibit a brief analysis will be proper, as it will tend to excite federalists to a sense of their actual danger, and disarm the host of trimmers and political hypocrites of a topic which they never fail to urge upon our politeness and good nature, whenever they would abate the scorn that is thrown upon one party, or quench the sparks of that zeal which is too rarely excited in the other.

Supposing the honest among the jacobins to possess the ordinary degrees of self knowledge, on looking inward they will find there a consciousness of some moral principle, of some integrity of heart. This will make them less distrustful of themselves, less apprehensive of the reproaches of others; and having adopted erroneous political maxims, they will pursue their dark mazes with a fearless step. The ill consequences, though natural, not being foreseen, will seem to proceed from accident, and only stimulate their perseverance, or to be owing to the malice of the concealed aristocrats, and inflame with a tenfold heat the rancor of their hostility. What was error becomes passion. The honest man thinks that he is summoned to the combat; the casuistry of a jacobin conscience spreads a mist before his eyes, which he thinks renders him invisible; obstinacy cases him in mail; French humanity puts a dagger into one hand, and party zeal, calling itself patriotism, a firebrand into the other. Thus the honest jacobin, equally misled by what he knows, and by the nature of his own principles and their tendencies, goes forth to assist knaves in what he deems the cause of virtue. He has so many excuses in the good motives, which he is sure he does feel, and in the happy consequences, which he thinks he certainly does foresee, that he makes haste to spread ruin without compunction, and to perpetrate crimes without remorse. Every intelligent politician knows, that in all party affairs, the unthinking dupes and honest fools are the rashest. The crimes they can excuse, and even persuade themselves to call virtues, they do not blush to commit. They are not afraid of shame, because they adopt the creed of their teachers and glory in it. They dance on the edge of a precipice, and think it a firm plain all round their feet. They foresee but little, and dread little of what they foresee. Little deterred by unforeseen danger, and strongly allured by imaginary good, that will be the sure reward of their patriot labors if successful, the duty to struggle for that success appears to be superior to every other. The best institutions, the great safeguards of order, seem to them abuses; government is an obstacle and must be removed; magistrates are enemies and must be conquered. They at last make conscience of committing the most shocking atrocities, and learn to throw their eyes beyond the gulf of revolution, confusion, and civil war, which yawns at their feet, to behold an Eden of primitive innocence, equality, and liberty in blossom on the other side. There these tigers of revolution, their leaders, are to lie down with the lamb-like multitude, sometimes suffering hunger yet forbearing to eat them. The rights of man are to be established by being solemnly proclaimed, and printed, so that every citizen shall have a copy. Avarice, ambition, revenge, and rage will be disenchanted from all hearts and die there; man will be regenerated; by slaying half a million only once, four millions will be born twice, and the glorious work of that perfectibility of the species, foretold by Condorcet and the Mazzei sect in America, will begin.

The knaves, however, who lead this infatuated, honest multitude, indulge no such extravagant delusions. They have no faith in this splendid hereafter, this happy future state for jacobins in this world. They have as little taste for it. They propose other rewards for their patriotic virtue, than this heaven of metaphysics has laid up for them. Turning to their own base hearts, they shrink from themselves, and are more likely to feel remorse, than their honest disciples; they are conscious that they ought to be suspected, and they act with the caution that this consciousness inevitably inspires; their dupes act with a fervor, and rage, and thirst for innovation, which render the prospects of all possible confusion insufficient to satisfy them. The cold-thinking villains who lead, "whose black blood runs temperately bad," desire, on the contrary, no more confusion than just enough to answer their own ends; their ambition would naturally desire to preserve the powers of government to usurp them, and their rapacity would spare the wealth of the state to plunder it. A fresh set would indeed succeed, as in France, and rob the first despoilers, till the state, successively a prey, would be reduced to beggary and ruin. It is seldom that the leaders of revolutions have much profited by them; and this shows the shortsightedness even of their policy, and that, as it relates to their own personal advantage, they are nearly as much deluded as their dupes. But the possession of the sovereign power, however precarious, is too great a temptation for their prudence to withstand. Accordingly we see, that for such a prize competitors are never wanting; and they struggle for the imperial purple with as much ardor and fierceness, as if it were not wet and dropping with the blood of its last usurper. Robespierre's fall incited more pretenders than it intimidated.

It will be objected, that this open avowal of contempt and detestation of the jacobins, and this unreserved exhortation to all friends of government to inculcate these sentiments, can only exasperate party animosities and augment their mutual virulence. I ask, in reply, would my silence, or the most soothing style of address I could choose, prevent or compose these animosities? Is it in the nature of free governments to exist without parties? Such a thing has never yet been and probably never will be. Is it in the nature of party to exist without passion? or of passion to acquiesce, when it meets with opposers and obstacles? Is it owing, do the vapid declaimers really think in good faith, to the intemperance or indiscretion of federal writers, that jacobins are restless and malignant? or that, by changing epithets or lavishing lying praises on their honesty, they would change their nature and renounce their designs? No, it is absurd to expect faction cold in the pursuit of great objects, reasonable in selecting means for gratifying inordinate designs, retarded by moral doubts and perplexities, when led by philosophers, soft to persuade, when it is callous to pity, and fearless of consequences. Party moderation is children's talk. Who has ever seen faction calmly in a rage? Who will expect to see that carniverous monster quietly submit to eat grass?

The critics on this performance may be assured, therefore, that if no good is done by it, it will not do the mischief they apprehend. Parties will hate each other a little less for mutual plain dealing and freedom of speech; for they never hate with more inveteracy than when they condescend to soothe and to flatter.

There are some who will admit, that the spirit of party is virulent, and its principle and designs utterly profligate, who will nevertheless scruple to say, that the present state of affairs is such as to demand an alarming appeal to the patriotism of the citizens. France, our dangerous foe, they will tell us, is baffled and detected in her arts, and deprived by the victories of the English navy of her arms; that all fear of invasion may be dismissed; and even if a few thousand negroes should be landed from Guadaloupe, the citizens would rally round the standard of lawful government, and crush the invaders; that the rebellion in Pennsylvania is feeble in force, and cowardly in spirit;[21] that the government never before had such power of arms, of credit, of treasure, and what is more than arms and treasure, of duty and affection in the hearts of all good citizens; that it appears the fairer, for having been falsely accused; that its friends have more zeal and confidence than ever, and the jacobins now feel their own weakness, and know that they can depend little on themselves, and none at all on France. This is, therefore, they will insist, a time for exultation, not of alarm; a time tranquilly to enjoy the blessings of our free Constitution, not to suffer anxiety, and to mount guard as heretofore for its defence. These are pleasing illusions, but they are illusions.

When we look at Europe, and contemplate its political

---

[21] *Fries's Rebellion. See note 25.*

state, we seem to be treading on the crater of a half-extinguished volcano. Here, scarcely cool from their fusion, are the cinders of one republic, and there still smoke the brands of another. On this side, see a little Italian state beginning to belch revolutionary fires; on that, another lies like a little mount on the great French volcano, a jumbled mass of lava and ruins. Can we think there is a decree for the immortality of our republic, when every gazette from Europe is blackened with the epitaphs of nations once independent, now no more. Lately they had life and being; now they lie like little mangled birds to digest in the French tiger's maw. One nation alone resists these new Romans, and prevents the establishment of a universal domination, and a despotism over the whole civilized world. Surely, if we contemplate only external danger, this is no time for security and presumptuous confidence. That single nation, though magnanimous, though powerful in wealth as well as spirit, may grow very weary of standing in the gap, or possibly may imitate the wretched policy of the emperor, and in compensation for a respite to the strong foes of France, may permit her to finish the conquest of her weak ones. The power of France, though checked at sea, is still gigantic, far exceeding that of the Roman empire in the days of Trajan; and before the end of the year, she will probably incorporate all Italy, Spain, and Portugal, with her vast territory, which takes the Rhine for a boundary, and includes Holland. It is more than a thousand years since the world has seen a power any thing near so overwhelming and terrific as that of France. Dreadful as her force is, her arts are still more dreadful, and here our danger lies.

A faction, whose union is perfect, whose spirit is desperate, addressing something persuasive to every prejudice, putting something combustible to every passion, granting some indulgence to every vice, promising those who dread the law to set them above it, to the mean whispering suspicion, to the ambitions offering power, to the rapacious, plunder, to the violent, revenge, to the envious, the abasement of all that is venerable, to innovators, the transmutation of all that is established, grouping together all that is folly, vice, and passion in the state, and forming of these vile materials another state, *an imperium in imperio*. Behold this is our condition, these our terrors. And what are the resources for our safety?

They all exist in the energy and correctness of the public opinion. A thousand proofs exist, but the fact is so notorious, it is needless to vouch them, to show that our government has been, and is supported only by the appeal to the virtue, zeal, and patriotism of the body of the citizens. Genet assumed upon himself the powers of a sovereign, and exercised them too, till the government cried out for help to the people, and they came to help in season.[22] The treaty contest stopped the wheels of government for a time; and the effective sovereignty was first actually assumed and exercised by the town meetings, and then divided between the executive and senate on one side, who adhered to the treaty, and the house who showed a disposition to annul it.[23] This was an instance of the government being near its death, by the benumbing stroke of a factious apoplexy, without a resort to arms, without taking the sense of the people. But again in that case, the real people took the alarm, and saved the

---

[22] *Edmund Genet became French minister to the United States in early 1793. He sought, however, to recruit armies for republican France within the country. He meant to take Florida and Louisiana (Spain's possessions) for France. He also fitted out privateers to sail against British commerce from American ports. Washington requested Genet's recall in August, 1793.*

[23] *The Jay Treaty with Britain. Although ultimately signed by the president and ratified by the Senate, the treaty was the subject of heated partisan campaigning and lobbying. There was also a concerted effort in the House of Representatives in 1796 to deny the appropriations requisite to executing the treaty.*

country from the terrible convulsions, which never fail to ensue, when the political house is divided against itself. With less intelligence of the citizens, or a fortnight's less speed in rallying, all would then have been lost.

When the instances are so recent, that the pulse of alarm has scarcely yet ceased to flutter, will any man of common sense pretend to say, that our government stands unshaken upon a foundation of rock? that the sounds of alarm are counterfeit or imaginary? that faction is impotent and contemptible?

No nation can rely on the sufficiently clear and early political discernment of its citizens, to discover and repel the danger to its liberty and independence; they may discover their danger too late, as all the people of the fallen European states did; they may mistake, too, and think, as the Swiss did, that it is safer to trust the foe than to resist him. Opinion is everywhere fickle, and our political situation is awkward and unprecedented; hard now to change, impossible to maintain a strange middle state, not easy to be understood or approved. It is peace without tranquillity; it is war without action; it is peace, yet it is dangerous; it is war, yet it deadens all the fervors of patriotism, all the energies of valor; it is peace, so far only as to lay our bosoms bare to the poisoned darts of our foe, and to the hostility of his ally, our intestine faction; it is war to every extent, that can expose us to alarm, to depredation, and to expense. Such a state cannot be maintained longer than just to afford to the nation some few months to decide which they will prefer, a foreign or a civil war.

The malady of a foreign faction has grown inveterate by time and by palliatives; it has burrowed deep in the flesh, and mingled a corrosive lymph with the marrow of the bones. Every common observer may be sure it is approaching a violent crisis. The jacobins have been everywhere in movement, preparing every engine of power and influence, to transfer the country, its liberty, and property, at the next election of president and vice-president, into the hands of men equally destitute of private virtue and of public spirit.

At this day, so fatal to the independence of free states, the sound of alarm ought not to surprise, it should animate. Republican liberty is held by the tenure of continuing worthy to hold it; we have to choose between the burden of its duties and its destiny. It has ever been deemed the Hesperian fruit, but since the days of fable it was never yet guarded by dragons. Why, then, will any one reprove the writer for attempting to rouse the vigilance of the citizens? It is for them as a body, and individually, to form a lifeguard to protect it from assassination.

FALKLAND I

The Palladium, FEBRUARY 3, 1801

TO NEW ENGLAND MEN:

THE CHANGE of the American administration is an event to create surprise and alarm.

How will it be considered, and what will be its effects? In Europe, it will certainly discredit republican principles. Those who did not reason deeply, but took their opinions of America as they found them most prevalent, will exclaim, Paine and Barlow, and half the book-makers, and more than half the expatriated American travellers have told us that republican principles were pure in the new world, as they flowed from the fountain head, the people, and the rights of man, and that plenty, contentment, and equality reigned, as in the golden age.

Whatever interest our national vanity may take in these representations, however land-jobbers may try to prolong their credit by painting Kentucky and Tennessee as a new Arcadia, the evidence of facts will prevail. It will be known that the government had enemies, and that our political millennium has bred thousands of malcontents. They will see that the men who said the Constitution ought not to have had being, are intrusted with its life and authority.

They are to be bound by duty and by oath to recommend to confidence what they have blasted with suspicion; to enforce what they have resisted; and to spare the prey they have so long hunted, and at last taken. As the party in power has called the government a bastard of monarchy, a government already rotten, though not ripe, foreigners will conclude, from the event of the election, that this is the public sentiment of the nation, and that the Americans are sick of their republican experiment.

Is it not to all the European world the evidence of facts, that we are at length fully convinced that the antifederalists, who were against trying it, were very much in the right? Republican principles will hold, therefore, in Europe, nearly the same rank with the principles of swindling. Nothing, they will insist, can be so bewitching as their promise; nothing so bitter or so sure as their disappointment. Perhaps, as Europe is not fit for republican forms of government, it is best that they should not any longer admire what they ought not to adopt, and what, if adopted, they could not maintain.

Foreigners, who examine events with an eye of scrutiny, will not hesitate to foretell, that the change is no little cabinet scene, where one minister comes into power and another goes out, but a great moral revolution proceeding from the vices and the passions of men, shifting officers to-day, that measures, and principles, and systems, may be shifted to-morrow. They will say, we know something of Mr. Monroe, his astonishing complaisance to the tyrants of Paris, and the no less astonishing rudeness and insult thrown by Barras on this minister's government. By such a sample we may judge, they will cry, of the spirit and character of the new American rulers; for he is in credit, and his party associates are coming into power. The Washington and Adams policy has built up much. What have they built, that the artificers of ruin have not already denounced, and meditated to destroy? Will Mazzei's correspondent cherish what he hates, or in the day of democratic wrath, spare what he dreads?[24]

The banks and public paper, the *"sceleris vestigia nostri,"* will be expected speedily to fall. Commerce will be represented, as in the days of opposition, when the first frigates were voted against the Algerines, as too expensive to be protected by a naval force. Down, then, with the navy. Down goes commerce, the fruitful mother of British debts, the grandmother and nurse of British influence. Why should we maintain soldiers? Colonel Fries is now attached to the administration, and, therefore, we may depend on him, and on men like him, and on some generals and brigadiers of the militia, to defend the excise and land-tax laws from being repealed by the sovereigns of a whiskey congress, convened at a sedition pole.[25] Down, then, with the army—that is already down; down with the diminutive image of an army

---

[24] *Thomas Jefferson. A letter to Jefferson's Italian correspondent, Philip Mazzei, worked its way through French, back into English, and was published in American newspapers in May of 1797. It was a standard attack on the "Anglo-monarchical-aristocratic faction" but scandalized public opinion with remarks taken as directly disparaging George Washington among those "men who were Samsons in the field and Solomons in the council, but who have had their heads shorn by the harlot England."*

[25] *John Fries, 1750(?)–1818. Leader of Fries's Rebellion, 1798–99, in opposition to federal property tax. Assembled an army of Pennsylvania Germans to resist assessors. Arrested and sentenced to death by federalists, he was pardoned in 1800. The Fries Rebellion was apparently a reprise of the Whisky Rebellion, which broke out in western Pennsylvania in 1794. Protesters from four backwoods counties refused to pay the excise on whisky. The national militia, on orders from President Washington and under the supervision of Alexander Hamilton, marched through the state and quickly restored order.*

on the frontiers, a miniature that preserves deformity and loses the grace and resemblance. Let the sons of Logan[26] come and help us to establish the happy state of nature and primitive virtue. What need of revenue more than impost will yield? Retrench expenses; get rid of the vermin that fatten upon it, and very little revenue will answer. The bloodsuckers will grow thin, perhaps die, but the people will thrive; they will be freed from exaction and guarded against corruption. So long as their lands, and houses, and distilleries pay tribute, they are not free; so long as this tribute goes to pamper an insolent upstart race of funding-system lords, they are not equal.

Wise Europeans will ask, what can protect the rights of the few, when the rage of the many is thus directed against them? We have seen the French clergy stripped in a night. One vote of congress would put the funded debt into the family tomb with paper money. What will be the security of right that is unpopular? and what shall prolong the life of the creatures of popularity? You cannot keep the insects, that buzz in the August sunshine, over winter.

To European observers the prospect of America will appear to sadden, and its horizon to lower.

There is scarcely any evil that has not been foretold in our own gazettes, and that good men do not unfeignedly apprehend from the change.

If the violent jacobins should have it in their power to do what they wish, there is not a shadow of doubt that they would make smooth work of all the most cherished systems

---

[26] *Presumably Dr. George Logan, Philadelphia physician, republican and French sympathizer. He inspired the famous Logan Act, which prohibits diplomatic intercourse between private United States citizens and foreign powers without specific authorization. Logan had intervened in United States–French tensions in 1798, travelling to France at his own expense with the hope of averting a war and preserving the prospect of an alliance.*

of the administrations of Washington and Adams. When they heard of the success of their ticket, it is certain they thought all this would be in their power, and they began to make feasts and to exclaim:

Aggredere O magnos, aderit jam tempus, honores,

which, in English is, now is the glorious time for jacobins to get offices.[27]

If they should administer the government according to the principles they have avowed in the gazettes of the party, and the examples in France which they have so much admired, and if they should abolish and new model all that they have so much professed to detest in the laws of congress, there is indeed no curse of a thorough-going revolution, with which we are not threatened.

FALKLAND III

———

The Palladium, FEBRUARY 10, 1801

TO NEW ENGLAND MEN:

Before evils have happened, it is the part of wisdom to exhibit their worst aspects. When they are known to be inevitable, or have actually occurred, it is no less the office of wisdom to display their palliations or their remedies. It would be cowardly, in despair, to aggravate their weight, or to sink under its pressure. No; bad as our prospects are,

---

[27] *Literally, "the time has now arrived to lay claim to ambitions O! Great One!"*

they are not hopeless. There is a sure resource for hope in ourselves; the steady good sense of New England will be a shield of defence. *Tu ne cede malis, sed contra audentior ito.*[28] The public spirit and opinion of this division of the union constitute a force which the enemies of our constitutions and fundamental interests will labor to corrupt, but will not dare to withstand.

For New England is not inhabited by a conquered people. Their opinions will have some influence on the policy, if their commerce, navigation, and credit should have no hold on the hearts of their rulers. Even conquerors, unless they were willing to have their fighting work to do over again, would choose to mask, under the most specious disguises, the violation of rights and the contempt of opinions.

There is evidence enough, that the party expected to rule is not friendly to the commerce of any of the states, and especially to the fisheries and navigation of the Eastern states. We do not want, they argue, an expensive navy for the sake of these; nor these for the sake of a navy. Navies breed wars, and wars augment navies, and both augment expenses, and this brings forth funding systems, banks, and corrupt influence.

These few words contain the system of our new politicians, which it is probable they will be in future, as in times past, complaisant enough to one another to call philosophy. Such illuminism, such visions of bedlam, have visited some famous heads that do not repose within its cells, and condensed their thin essences into schemes of political reform, projects of cheap governments, that are to be rich without revenue, strong without force, venerable with popular prejudice directed by faction against them. Learned fools are of all the greatest as well as the most indocile. Accordingly, in despite

---

[28] *Virgil: You do not yield to evil, but on the contrary proceed more fearlessly against it.*

of the experience of all the world and of our own, in despite of common sense and the dictates of obvious duty, such men, high in reputation, and expected to be high in office, have insisted that we do not want a single soldier, nor a single armed ship; that credit is an abuse, an evil to be cured only by having none, a cancer that eats, and will kill, unless cut or burnt out with caustics; that if we have any superfluity foreigners will come for it, if they need it, and if they do not it would be a folly and a loss for us to carry it to them. They tell us with emphasis, and seem to expect our vanity will gain them credit for saying, that America ought to renounce the sea and to draw herself closely into her shell; let the mad world trade, negotiate, and fight, while we Americans live happily, like the Chinese, enjoying abundance, independence, and liberty.

This is said by persons clad in English broadcloth and Irish linen, who import their conveniences from England, and their politics from France. It is solemnly pronounced as the only wise policy for a country, where the children multiply faster than the sheep, and it is, inconsistently enough too, pronounced by those who would have all farmers, no manufacturers.

Notions of this stamp of sublimated extravagance have been often in the heads of book-makers and projectors. Some Frenchman suggested a scheme of like wisdom, to bind kings and princes, not republics, to keep the peace, and be of good behavior; and there are some declaimers who would have the Indians on the frontiers enter into recognizance, and thus get rid of the expense and danger of a standing army of four regiments. But they would have a militia, half a million strong, made expert soldiers by training them, unpaid, till they become equal to veterans. A militia system is right; these reformers, however, never touch truth but to distort it, nor any sound principle but to drive it to extremes; they would therefore make a militia system burdensome,

215

unwieldy, and corrupt; a standing army for faction, distinguished by a strange badge, and arrayed against the government.

It is indeed probable that these wild theories have never yet much disturbed the world by addling the brains of any man who had its business to do. Such political sophists, till lately, have been calmly despised, but never trusted with power. Into the hands of such children it has never before been thought prudent to put knives.

If, to punish the manifold sins of this nation, God's displeasure dooms it to be delivered over to projectors and philosophists, the first of the sort who ever had the chance to play the statesman, will they have the temerity to undertake, and will they accomplish their plans?

In free states, so long as they preserve their laws and their tranquillity, the public opinion is the efficient ruler. In times of convulsion it is probably less regarded in such states than under a despotism, because it can be counterfeited better. Suppose Mr. Jefferson should come into office; with all his refinements, he is reputed a man of genius. His experience and caution, we hope, will forbid his pushing schemes against the clear sense of the people, or even of a very large part of them. If the reformers should cry, perish commerce, fisheries, and navigation, live and prosper agriculture; yet the conception of this precious project would be found easier than its execution. Reformers make nothing of old establishments, of interests that have taken root for ages, and of prejudices, habits, and relations, rather less ancient and rather more stubborn than they.

New England now contains a million and a half of inhabitants, of all colonies that ever were founded, the largest, the most assimilated, and to use the modern jargon, nationalized, the most respectable and prosperous, the most truly interesting to America and to humanity, more unlike and more superior to other people, (the English excepted,) than the old Roman race to their neighbors and competitors. This people, whose spirit is as lofty as their destiny, is settled on an extensive coast, and by situation and character, has a greater proportion of its inhabitants engaged in navigation and maritime affairs than France or England, perhaps than even Holland. In spirit and enterprise no nation exceeds them. It is in vain to say things ought not to have been so, it would have been better to have had half as many farmers. It is absurd to say any such thing.

The question for a new administration is not, what ought to have been preferred three ages ago, but what must now be destroyed. These great interests are too precious to be sacrificed, they are too powerful even to be neglected. They will demand, and well they may, the effectual, zealous, assiduous protection and fostering care of government; and no President will ever repel the claim with defiance or contempt. Protection will be promised, and, perhaps, with the design to afford it.

It is right for the public to suppose, that Mr. Jefferson's administration must be tried before it can be known. It is fair and candid to make every presumption in favor of his intentions, that may not be discredited by his conduct. It is, however, an effort of candor (but we must make it) to allow that, like most men of genius, he has been carried away by systems, and the everlasting zeal to generalize, instead of proceeding, like common men of practical sense, on the low, but sure foundation of matter of fact. It is the forte, and it is also the foible of genius, to be under the dominion of the imagination; and such men often judge of a law as they would of a picture, by the rules of taste. They can decide in such a case only as the mob do, by acclamation. What ought to be the result of experience, that a blockhead could both feel and express, is comprehended in the province of sentiment; and, for the curse and confusion of a state, the plodding business of politics becomes one of the fine arts. The statesman is bewildered with his own peculiar fanaticism; he sees the stars near, but loses sight of the earth; he sails in his balloon into clouds and thick vapors, above his business and his duties, and if he sometimes catches a glimpse of the wide world, it seems flattened to a plain, and shrunk in all its proportions; therefore, he strains his optics to look beyond its circumference, and contemplates invisibility, till he thinks nothing else is real. New worlds of metaphysics issue from his teeming brain, and whirl in orbits more elliptic than the comets. Man rises from the mire, into which aristocracy has trodden him, shakes off the sleep of ignorance and the fetters of the law, a gorgeous new being, invested with perfectibility, a saint in purity, a giant in intellect, and goes to inhabit these worlds. Condorcet and Roland, and men like them, will be there, and Paine, and Duane, and Marat, and Burroughs. There virtue will celebrate her triumphs; there patriotism will be inebriated with the ecstasy of her fellow-ships.

I know as little of the political illuminists as of the sect of the Swedenborgians; but to me it has ever appeared, that the former are a new sect of fanatics. They manifest a strange heat in the heart, but no light in the brain, unless it be a feeble light, whose rays are gathered in the lens of philosophy, to kindle every thing in the state that is combustible, into a blaze. A statesman of this sect will poise himself in his chair, like an alchemist in his laboratory, pale with study, his fingers sooty with experiments, eager to make fuel of every thing that is precious, and sanguinely expecting that he shall extract every thing precious from the cinders and dross that must be thrown away.

Yet if we ascribe to Mr. Jefferson these vagaries, so dear if they happen to be his own, so confidently trusted because they have not been tried, it is natural enough to expect that, nevertheless, he will desist from his experiments as soon as the results become too complicated and too uncertain for the satisfaction of a philosopher. He may think it prudent to wait till the world is more enlightened, before he prosecutes his schemes to hasten the progress of its absolute perfectibility. He will stoop to the prejudice that will not rise with him. The family of labor, brown with West India suns, or glistening and rancid with whale oil, will tell him, that they had rather tread a ship's deck than the wilderness, and prefer the conflict with the storms of Spitzbergen, and the chase of the spermaceti, where there is danger and glory, and associates to share the one and to bestow the other, to scalping Indians, or skinning otters, in roaming over an immeasurable waste, where the silence is broken only by the howlings of the famished wolves, and where the sight, even of these animals is less dreaded and less dangerous than that of their fellows. They will tell him, they cannot change their element, nor will they submit, when politicians, with hearts colder than that element at the pole, prove, on calculation, it is best that they should perish in it.

FALKLAND V

The Palladium, FEBRUARY 17, 1801

TO NEW ENGLAND MEN:

To abolish the funding system is neither necessary nor decorous. But there are as many ways to slay this enemy as to destroy human life; by violence, by poison, by neglect. By violence the interest may be reduced; by taxing the holders of public debt, as much may be drawn back in taxes as is paid in the name of interest: this is poison. Or the laws for enforcing the revenue and carrying into effect the engagements of the government may be delayed, and finally not passed. The Gallatin doctrine in regard to treaty appropriations furnishes theory enough for all the paper-money iniquity that ever was practised or imagined.[29] The children of the public faith may come to a democratic government, and say, in the name of justice and plighted honor, give us bread; and such a government may say, as the state government of Rhode Island have heretofore said of their war debts, *take your bread,* offering a stone.

The new president will have a part of no common difficulty to act. He will desire to conciliate the federalists, and, without respecting their systems, might be willing to let them alone. The democrats really wish to see an impossible experiment fairly tried, and to govern without government. It is to be expected that they will applaud their chief, who is believed to be their true disciple, if he should take a fancy to try it.

They consider government as a strange sort of self-moving mill, or a ship, that, while it is acted upon by one element, goes the better for the resistance of another. It is an even chance, therefore, that they may deem the opposition of the federalists as harmless and even as salutary as their own. In pursuance of their plan, they will let the government alone to go by its own inscrutable momentum. They will, as heretofore, deem it proper to be lookers-on, not coöperators, unless when it shall want either force or treasure, or even countenance and approbation; and then they will summon each other to their old post of opposition. Treasure corrupts, and force oppresses, and therefore government shall have neither. The immediate evil to be apprehended to our government is the denial of its daily bread; that sort of

---

[29] *Gallatin spearheaded efforts in the House of Representatives to deny authorization for carrying provisions of the Jay Treaty, which republicans considered too generous to England, into effect, in spring, 1796.*

consumption which preys on the balsamic parts of the blood, and leaves a residuum of vitriol. The body politic, though bloated with a show of health while it perishes, and alive with double-concocted poisons, will shed a corroding and mortal venom on all it touches. The laws will be jacobin; for as soon as the democrats have wasted their first energies, and their system falls into decrepitude, (and a year of democratic government is old age,) they will crowd themselves into power. They are a race distinct from the democrats, and as much worse in their designs, as the independents, in Oliver Cromwell's time, than the presbyterians.

Then expect amendments, that will make the Constitution a confederation. Then expect commercial regulations, which will profess to cramp British commerce, and will cramp our own. First revenue, wealth, and credit will take flight; then peace.

The danger, therefore, to all the interests and institutions of New England, is not so much to be ascribed to the character or designs of the new president, whoever he may be, or to be feared in the first year of the new administration, as from the progress of time, and the natural developments of faction. There is universally a presumption in democracy that promises every thing; and at the same time an imbecility that can accomplish nothing, nor even preserve itself.

There is in jacobinism all the vigor, audacity, and intelligence requisite to take advantage of this state of things. The democrats will be their journeymen to do the work, while they claim the wages; the pioneers, who will clear the way for the procession of the jacobin triumph. The jacobins and democrats are, in fact, less agreed in their objects and principles, though these latter do not know it, than the federalists and the democrats.

It would be improper as well as tedious to pursue, in a newspaper essay, all the illustrations and details that these observations may seem to require. They are not, however, so much addressed to men who are no federalists, but who might be convinced to become such, nor to men who already wish well to the good old cause of order, law, and liberty, yet who are weak enough to think it will be safe in jacobin hands, as to the old federalists, the true and intelligent, who rightly conclude that if our excellent government, in this the day of its humiliation and imminent peril, is to be saved, it must be by the correctness of the public opinion and the energy of the public spirit that is to impress it.

This is no day for despondency, or servility, or trimming. It is as little to the purpose to trust implicitly to the moderation of a jacobin administration, or to those smooth professions with which it will attempt in the beginning to make the federalists supine or treacherous in the cause, to make them cold in its defence, or go over to the enemy.

That cause, though endangered, is not desperate. The jacobins have pretended that the people approve their designs; but their partial success has been owing to the concealment of those designs. They have played the part of hypocrisy with an audacity of impudence that is unparalleled; they have affected to be federalists, republicans, friends, admirers, and champions of the Constitution; they have recommended jacobin members of congress, as better watchmen for it than its known friends; they have assured us that Mr. Jefferson will not subvert or neglect to preserve those institutions and interests which he is known, and, it is believed, well known to condemn and abhor as much as his adherents. These protestations have had effect, and jacobins have been pre-ferred, not because they were such, but because it was believed that they were what they pretended to be. The wolves in sheep's clothing have not yet been stripped: they are in the sheepfold.

Let them not, however, imagine that the people, especially of the Eastern states, are ready to coöperate in the work of jacobinism. If, after having with some success deceived the people, they should become such dupes as to act on the credit of their own tales, let them beware. They will find it is easier to deceive a high-spirited people than to enslave them, and safer to insult them by the imputation of political principles that they abhor, than to plunder and beggar them by carrying such principles into effect.

MONITOR

———

The Palladium, APRIL 17, 1804

ACCIDENT may give rise and extent to republics, but the fixed laws that govern human actions and passions will decide their progress and fate. By looking into history and seeing what has been, we know what will be. It is thus that dumb experience speaks audibly; it is thus that witnesses come from the dead and testify. Are we warned? No. Are we roused? No. We lie in a more death-like sleep than those witnesses. Yet let us hear their testimony, though it should not quicken our stupidity, but only double the weight of our condemnation.

The experiment of a republic was tried, in all its forms, by the Romans. While they occupied only one city, and a few miles of territory near its walls, they had all the virtues and sustained all the toils and perils of a camp. Every Roman was born a soldier, and the state intrusted arms to the hands of those only who had rights and rank as citizens. But when Rome extended her empire over all Italy, and then over all Asia Minor, her size rendered her politics unmanageable; and power in her town-meetings, where the rabble at length outvoted the real citizens, corrupted all virtue, extinguished all shame, and trampled on all right, liberty, and justice. Our Constitution, as Washington left it, is good; but as amendments and faction have now modelled it, it is no longer the same thing.

We now set out with our experimental project exactly where Rome failed with hers; we now begin where she ended. We think it wise to spread over half this western hemisphere a form, and it is only a form, of government that answered for Rome, while Rome governed a territory as narrow as the District of Columbia. The Romans were awed by oaths, and restrained by the despotism of a camp; for in every camp where there is not mutiny there must be despotism. We Americans, who laugh at the difference, if difference there be, between twenty gods and no god; we, who have lost our morals, prate about our liberty.[30] We think that what the Romans, with the Scipios, and Catuli, and Catos, could not keep, we with our Jeffersons cannot lose. Those great Romans thought it better not to live at all than to live slaves; but we care more for our ease than our rights. We can bear injustice better than expense; and we dread war infinitely more than dishonor. Hence, when we had our election we chose infamy and paid fifteen millions for it; we compensated the aggressor for the fatigue of kicking us; and we celebrate, as a jubilee, that treaty that has made our debasement an article of the law of nations. If Rome had ever tamely borne the wrongs that we took, not merely patiently, but thankfully, joyfully, from Spain and Bonaparte, Rome would never have been more than a walled town, where valiant robbers secured their booty. But we who take insults from slaves, and think it victory and glory to buy the forbearance of a tyrant, we talk of Roman liberty as if we were emulous of it. The Romans

---

[30] *This is an allusion to Query 17 of Jefferson's* Notes on the State of Virginia. *The passage reads: "But it does me no injury for my neighbour to say there are twenty gods or no god. It neither picks my pocket nor breaks my leg."*

honored virtue, and loved glory, and thought it cheaply purchased with their blood: we love money, and if we had glory we should joyfully truck it off for more money, or another Louisiana. With such a difference of spirit, are we to hold the republican sceptre that is to sway a million square miles of territory? If we resemble any thing Roman, it is such a domination as Spartacus and his gladiators and slaves would have established if they had succeeded in their rebellion. The government of the *three fifths* of the ancient dominion,[31] and the offscourings of Europe, has no more exact ancient parallel.

The plebeians of Rome asserted their right to serve in the highest offices, and at length obtained it; but the people still chose the most able and eminent men, who were patricians, and rejected their worthless tribunes. But we see our tribunes successful; the judges are at the bar, and the whisky leaders sit in judgment upon them. Surely that people have lost their morals who bestow their votes on those who have none; surely they have lost their liberties, when their judges tremble more than their culprits.

The Romans maintained some barrier about popular rights, as long as the tribunes were sacred; but when Tiberius moved the people to depose Octavius, a fellow tribune, then violence ruled the assemblies, and even the shadow of liberty was lost. We have seen the judiciary law repealed, and the judges, though made sacred by the Constitution, in like manner deposed.

The Romans, in the days of their degeneracy and corruption, set no more bounds to their favor than to their resentments. While Pompey was their idol, they conferred unlimited authority upon him over all the Mediterranean sea,

---

[31] *An allusion to the "three-fifths" clause of the Constitution, in which slaves are counted for purposes of taxation and representation as three-fifths of a free person.*

and four hundred stadia (about forty-five miles) within land. We in like manner devolve on Mr. Jefferson the absolute and uncontrolled dominion of Louisiana. It was thus the Romans were made by their own vote familiar with arbitrary power.

In the contests of their factions, the conquerors inflicted all possible evils on the fallen party; and thus they tasted and liked the sweetness of revenge. Except in removals from office and newspaper invectives, in this point our experience is yet deficient; but, from the spirit of ardent malice apparent in the dominant faction, it is manifest that we have men who, though sparing enough of their own blood, would rival Marius or Anthony in lavishing that of their enemies.

The Romans were not wholly sunk from liberty, till morals and religion lost their power. But when the Thomas Paines, and those who recommended him, as a champion against "the presses" of that day, had introduced the doctrines of Epicurus, the Roman people became almost as corrupt as the French are now, and almost as shameless as the favored patriots of our country, who are the first to get office.

Gradually all power centered in the Roman populace. While they voted by centuries, (the *comitia centuriata*,) property had influence, and could defend itself; but at length the doctrine of universal suffrage prevailed. The rabble, not only of Rome, but of all Italy, and of all the conquered nations, flowed in. *In Tiberim, defluxit Orontes.*[32] Rome could no more be found in Rome itself than we can see our own countrymen in the Duanes, and Gallatins, and Louisianians of the present day.[33] The senate of Rome sunk to nothing;

[32] *The Orontes descends to the Tiber. Juvenal.*

[33] *William Duane was the editor of the Philadelphia* Aurora, *a republican newspaper that slanderously attacked the leaders of the federalist party. Albert Gallatin was a prominent republican from Pennsylvania, elected to but not seated in the federalist-controlled United States Senate in 1796, member of the House of Representatives, and ultimately Jefferson's secretary of the treasury.*

the owners of the country no longer governed it. A single assembly seemed to govern the world, and the worst men in it governed that assembly.

Thus we see the passions and vices of men operate uniformly. What remains, and there is not much of this resemblance that remains unfinished, will be completed.

The chief hazard that attends the liberty of any great people lies in their blindness to the danger. A weak people may descry ruin before it overwhelms them, without any power to retard or repel its advance; but a powerful nation, like our own, can be ruined only by its blindness, that will not see destruction as it comes; or by its apathy and selfishness, that will not stir, though it sees it.

Our fate is not foretold by signs and wonders; the meteors do not indeed glare in the form of types, and print it legibly in the sky; but our warning is as distinct, and almost as awful, as if it were announced in thunder by the concussion of all the elements.

THE REPUBLICAN XII

Boston Gazette, SEPTEMBER 20, 1804
Reprinted from the *Repertory*

The progress of our affairs is in conformity with the fixed laws of our nature, and the known course of Republics. Our wisdom made a government, and committed it to our virtue to keep, but our passions have engrossed it, and they have armed our vices to maintain their usurpation.

Bonaparte, the venerable Samuel Adams and "the anonymous slanderer" have observed, and since they all concur in the sentiment, they have equally "well observed," that the *sovereignty is derived from the people*. This sage remark, so gravely commended by the pamphleteer, was not made by this famous trio for its novelty, for it has been made these two thousand years, and a million times a year by every false hearted, selfish, popularity hunter throughout the whole period. It is made oftenest by those who respect it least, and most solemnly of all in the moment of its violation. It is a cheap commodity that demagogues make for their customers, the multitude, who gape with wonder and gratitude when great men condescend so dearly to love them—and those great men who do, or who will take the trouble to *say* they do love the people, are of course rewarded by a return of love and confidence, for which the people's false friends care nothing, and of votes and power for which they care a great deal.—This small talk of the will of the people and their sovereignty is almost a sure mark of a demagogue and impostor. A true friend of the people scorns to be their flatterer, he will speak the truth and he will pursue it, and as it is his business to serve, it is inevitable that he should sometimes offend them.—His popularity, if he ever gets any, he gets late, and after a life of experience has proved to the people that he is more anxious for their interests than their votes.

But this affected anxiety for the will and the power of the multitude is almost sure to effect two purposes which demagogues have exceedingly at heart. One is to conciliate trust and confidence in those, infamous as they may be in private life, who hold opinions so sound, so meritorious, and the other is that when such men are once uppermost in the strife of parties, all is safe. Liberty sleeps a virgin in her seducer's arms, safe from insult, pure from violation. Such is the prevailing opinion of the New England democrats at this moment. Mr. Jefferson reigns—the man of the people is their President—who cares whether courts are independent or Constitutions whole and sound? The will of the people prevails, and their friends, those who have ever called themselves their friends, triumph over federalists, the enemies of the people and the enemies of those whom they delight to honor.

This is so far from being exaggerated, that nine-tenths of the ardent democrats, who may happen to read this essay, will exult as if the matter of it were an indiscreet but proper confession of the fact, that the friends of the people are in power, and therefore that liberty is safe, therefore the will of the people *will* prevail.

It has already been remarked that the democrats really suppose when it is generally agreed and publically declared that the people's will ought to prevail, it will of course prevail, and also that when the mob favorites are in power it actually does prevail. Yet both these notions are confuted by an examination of human nature, which shows that democracy never can, and of history which solemnly attests that it never did, answer the purpose; it never preserved the power of the people from usurpation, on the contrary, it has been the sure forerunner and the irresistible engine of tyranny; and it is democracy and not republicanism, that the ruling party contend for and mean to establish; woe to America if they do!

It is overlooked or forgotten by the Democrats that when all power is in the hands of the people individually, if indeed that could ever be, there is not the least security for its remaining in their hands. And as their favorites will surely get it, the people will surely loose [*sic*] it. It has been more than once conceded that the honest, reasonable, deliberate will of the people ought to prevail, and where the government is well constituted and is firm and stable, it is probable it will discern and carry into effect the will of the nation. It is the people's best, and their only chance. But in this work of government the opposition of a faction is sure to be encountered—and nothing so certainly sets at nought and holds in scorn and contempt the sense and virtue and best interests of a society, as the faction that is scrambling to engross and usurp its powers. Precisely this sort of impediments, the administrations of Washington and Adams experienced. The passions of the multitude were incessantly roused to obstruct measures demanded by reasons, duty and interest of the quiet solid mass of the nation. When such a faction gets into power, it will still address the passions, it will pursue an interest of its own in disregard of the general interests. As in free states there will be parties or factions, and as the worst description of parties will court the worst passions of the lowest, most ignorant and vicious part of the society, they will necessarily use the language after they have risen which they used before, they will still depend on the violent rabble, whose fists and pikes they have occasion for, and will disregard the sense and principles of the wise and good and wealthy, whom they will of course wish to banish, rob, and kill.

(To be continued)

THE REPUBLICAN XIII

Boston Gazette, SEPTEMBER 27, 1804
Reprinted from the *Repertory*

> *The progress of our affairs is in conformity with the fixed laws of our nature, and the known course of Republics. Our wisdom made a government and committed it to our virtue to keep, but our passions have engrossed it, and they have armed our vices to maintain their usurpation.*

AFTER having endeavored in a cursory manner to expose to merited derision and contempt, the system and principles of democracy, and surely these ought to be the scorn and dread of every true republican, it will be in place to exhibit in contrast the leading principles of the federalists. A newspaper is not indeed spacious enough to contain all the ideas, which it might be necessary to unfold, to make those principles clear in their nature and details, and to distinguish them from the plausible but fallacious dogmas of democracy with which they are too often confounded. This clear exposition would be the more necessary, because without extreme precaution the whole host of jacobin cavillers will not understand and will pervert them. Writers would be wanting as readers, if so much labor should be exacted in discussions of this nature. The mass of the people to whom essays of the ephemeral cast that appear in the gazettes are addressed, cannot be made students, nor detained from their business and their pleasures to endure days and weeks of the headache till they have entirely satisfied their minds as to the right construction of a commonwealth.

In stating therefore the principles of federalists, the reader will of course expect only general outlines, still those outlines should be so well defined as to vindicate the slandered Federalist from the accusations of their enemies, and to mark the thread-line of distinction between them and those enemies.

One of the first articles then, in the political creed of every federalist, is that the Union should be maintained. It is very possible that it may be dissolved, but the work of its dissolution, if done, will be done by the jacobins. On this subject much might be said, and more must be left to the imagination.—It is not discreet to discuss before they happen, the crises in which real patriots would wish for a dissolution of the Union. Extreme cases when they occur make their own law. Extreme indeed must those public evils be which could justify resort to the tremendous evil of a separation. Vain [. . .] those hopes which many repose on the superior good order of a northern confederacy over the turbulent Parisian license of Southern jacobinism. They forget that by erecting a northern republic, the seeds of intestine commotion, sown thick in human nature, and sprouting up to rankness in all the existing institutions of our country, would bear a plentiful crop of revolutions and civil wars. We should take jacobinism home into our bosoms. Instead of having it as now in the model of Pennsylvania, every state would teem with factions which a hostile neighbor would preserve and foment, and in the event of their [. . .] for the superiority, she would side with the weaker of the two. A faction devoted to Sparta and another leaning on Athens filled all the republics of Greece with turbulence and blood.

All these evils being however speculative and distant, it is confessed the force of events may impel the states to a separation whenever a jacobin administration should feel itself strong enough, to venture to sacrifice everything to Virginia, and one of the s[trong] and serious grounds of Federal opposition to Mr. Jefferson's measures is that no sacrifice seems to be too great for her interest or even for her pride. It is seen that the systematic policy of the government is to throw back to the states almost everything, and though not in form yet by this, to renew the old Confederation. In one of his messages, Mr. Jefferson expressly stated that the state governments engross the cognizance of almost every important interior subject of legislation, while Congress has only to concern itself about foreign affairs, or such as concern the alliance of the states with one another. This theory, by leaving the states as the federal compact found them, unequal, of course raises Virginia, as her pride has ever claimed to be raised, above the small states, and above the feeble federal head. The unequal system of taxes, excusing coaches and whisky, and throwing the burden on trade and navigation is another source of complaint and irritation.

But of all federal systems, that Virginia most detested, is federal justice. Justice, of course, treats all as equals, and hence it has been the unceasing endeavor of that proud injurious debtor state to demolish federal justice. It lies now so on the ground that every planter can set his foot on his enemy's neck, and say, I will enjoy today and I will not pay tomorrow.

If the tendency of the partial system, of the jacobin system, should be to make real patriots weary and afraid of the Union, we repeat it, the remedy by separation will be worse than the disease. Violence and injustice may nevertheless drive men against their better and cooler judgments to choose the remedy.

A republican government for the Union is another federal article of faith. No man of sense will believe that an American monarchy can be introduced by consent; and if it should be established by usurpation, like that of France, it would be military despotism. Even the jacobins will acquit their enemies of this departure from their principles, for their accusation against the federalists has ever been that they were attached to a British form of government. Now that government is a mixed monarchy, so says the pamphlet of slander, it is a free government also, let them deny it if they can. Now let it be repeated again and again, usurpation could not introduce a mixed monarchy. The proposition is puerile and absurd. If then there is any class of men in America whose principles eminently bound them to oppose monarchy, it is the calumniated federalists. Not only their principles, but their interests are involved. For in New England certainly almost nineteen shillings in the pound of the property is holden by federalists, and violent revolutions of government are sure to make property change hands.

Besides, the merchants are generally federal, and it is a fact beyond all controversy that the spirit of commerce was in ancient times republican. Witness Carthage, Athens, Corinth, and in Europe since the revival of trade, liberty first took refuge in the trading cities. The great lords of the soil, Virginia planters of thousands of acres and hundreds of negroes are infinitely more inclined to submit to a king who would want a nobility than the federal merchants. There is no end to the absurdity of the charge that the federalists are for erecting an American monarchy. What could support it? Not free popular consent. Surely not. What then? an army! As before observed it would not then be a mixed monarchy, but a simple despotism, from which gracious heaven preserve us!

The monarchy of England stands not by the force of arms, but by the force of habits. If it had been introduced by a popular majority, it would not have lasted to the end of the year in which it was adopted.

The fools of the democratic party are at liberty to prate about a federal monarchy, but any man of sense ought to feel the meanness of the dirty work he does for his party when he repeats the charge.

The federalists believe also that the particular form of a republican government for the Union ought to be very nearly such as was agreed on in 1788, not because it is the best possible, but because it is as good as the people will bear—perhaps better than they would maintain. They are almost cured of their trust in paper constitutions; it is not pen and ink that can infuse energy and stability into constitutions. The spirit of democracy, so prevalent in our nation, would nullify or pervert all the strong amendments that the boldest politician would annex to it. Our political habits and experience are forming, and this constitution is perhaps as good as any other until they are formed.

The "anonymous slanderers" have been indeed in the habit of insisting that the federalists have been uniformly earnest for every interpretation that would enlarge its powers, and the Virginians, on the contrary have been, they say, advocates for the people, to reserve as much power as possible in their hands. It is very true the democratic writers have had this invincible foolish way of arguing, and there is no help for it, unless one could lend them both honesty and discernment.— Every man of only common sense knows that to keep a free republican government from licentiousness requires all possible exertion, and apparently all that honest men can make is sufficient for the patriotic purpose. Down all such governments go, and have ever gone, as if the efforts of Washington and other patriots with wings of paste board kept them up, and mobs and their leaders like so many mill-stones dragged them down. Besides the idea of gradually leading and coaxing a people towards monarchy, is absurd beyond measure. On speculative reasons every mass of people is opposed to monarchy. If they subscribe to it, if they finally prefer it, as they often do in the event, the reasons for the preference are always personal. The mob has its leader, he, if a cunning fellow, flatters much and promises everything and becomes a favorite. His elevation then is the business of all. Blindly and outrageously the king-making mob go to work to make their favorite a Director, a Protector, a Consul, an Emperor. This is the progress.

When therefore the shallow teachers of the rabble pretend that the federalists are disposed to slide by the present Constitution into a monarchy, they betray their ignorance as much as their malignity. No federalist has such expectations or desires.

On the contrary, if the federalists really were monarchists, and were willing to have a king or emperor; for a limited monarch and a mass of privileges, for the nation, are out of the question; then they would of course join the democrats.— They would run the race of folly with them, and would as much as possible quicken the speed of the racers. They would say to each other, the only way to introduce monarchy, simple, absolute monarchy, is by democracy. Let us join the violent and be more violent than they. Let us pull down all that is now standing of judges, courts, and Constitution; let the people be every thing, and let the secret committee or committees of safety be the people, and the chairman of that committee will be president, consul and king.

If after carefully weighing these considerations, any democrat will persevere in accusing the federalists as intriguers, to sap and subvert this Constitution to introduce a monarchy, he will certainly be despised among all fair, honorable men, but it will be exceedingly difficult to find a proper measure of contempt for his understanding.

VI.

ESSAYS ON

EQUALITY

EQUALITY I

The Palladium, NOVEMBER 17, 1801

THERE ARE some popular maxims which are scarcely credited as true, and yet are cherished as precious, and defended as even sacred. Most of the democratic articles of faith are blended with truth, and seem to be true; and they so comfortably soothe the pride and envy of the heart that it swells with resentment when they are contested, and suffers some spasms of apprehension even when they are examined. Mr. Thomas Paine's writings abound with this sort of specious falsehoods and perverted truths. Of all his doctrines, none perhaps has created more agitation and alarm than that which proclaims to all men that they are free and equal. This creed is older than its supposed author, and was threadbare in America before Mr. Paine ever saw our shores; yet it had the effect, in other parts of the world, of novelty. It was news that the French Revolution scattered through the world. It made the spirit of restlessness and innovation universal. Those who could not be ruled by reason resolved that they would not be restrained by power. Those who had been governed by law hungered and thirsted to enjoy, or rather to exercise, the new prerogatives of a democratic majority, which, of right, could establish, and, for any cause or no cause at all, could change. They believed that by making their own and other men's passions sovereign, they should invest man with immediate perfectibility, and breathe into their regenerated liberty an ethereal spirit that would never die. Slaves grew weary of their chains and freemen sick of their rights. The true liberty had no charms but such as the philosophists affirmed had been already rifled. The lazaroni of Naples, fifty thousand houseless, naked wretches, heard of their rights and considered their wants as so many wrongs.[34] The soldiers of Prussia were ready for town-meetings. Even in Constantinople it seemed as if the new doctrine would overpower the sedative action of opium, and stimulate the drowsy Turks to a Parisian frenzy. It is not strange that slaves should sigh for liberty as for some unknown good. But England and the United States of America, while in the full fruition of it, were almost tempted to renounce its possession for its promise. Societies were formed in both countries which considered and represented their patriotism as the remnant of their prejudices; and the old defences of their liberty as the fortresses of an enemy, the means and the badges of their slavish subjection.

All men being free and equal, rulers become our servants, from whom we claim obligation, though we do not admit their right to exact any. This generation, being equal to the last, owes no obedience to its institutions; and, being wiser, owes

---

[34] *In Naples, Italy, idlers who have no homes and live by odd jobs and begging; named after their place of refuge, the Hospital of St. Lazarus.*

them not even deference. It would be treachery to man, so long obstructed and delayed in his progress towards perfectibility, to forbear to exercise his rights. What if the existing governments should resist this new claim of the people, yet the people, to be free, have only to will it! What if this age should bleed, the next, or the twentieth after this, will be disencumbered from the rubbish of the gothic building that we have subverted, and may lay the foundations of liberty as deep, and raise the pillars of its temple as high, as those who think correctly of its perpetuity and grandeur can desire.

With opinions so wild, and passions so fierce, the spirit of democracy has been sublimated to extravagance. There was nothing in the danger that affected other men's persons or rights that could intimidate, nothing in their sufferings that could melt them. They longed to see kings, and priests, and nobles, expiring in tortures. This humane sentiment Barlow has expressed in verse. The massacres of Paris, the siege of Lyons, the drownings of Nantes, the murders in the name of justice, that made hosts of assassins weary of their work, were so many evils necessary to bring about good, or only so many acts of just retaliation of the oppressed upon their oppressors. The "enlightened" philosophists surveyed the agitations of the world as if they did not live in it; as if they occupied, as mere spectators, a safe position in some star, and beheld revolutions sometimes brightening the disk of this planet with their fires, and at others dimming it with their vapors. They could contemplate, unmoved, the whirlwind, lifting the hills from their base and mixing their ruins with the clouds. They could see the foundations of society gaping in fissures as when an earthquake struggles from the centre. A true philosopher is superior to humanity; he could walk at ease over this earth if it were unpeopled; he could tread, with all the pleasure of curiosity, on its cinders the day after the final conflagration.

Equality, they insist, will indemnify mankind for all these

apprehensions and sufferings. As some ages of war and anarchy may pass away before the evils incident to the struggles of a revolution are exhausted, this generation might be allowed to have some cause to object to innovations that are certainly to make them wretched, although, possibly, the grandchildren of their grandchildren may be the better for their sufferings. This slender hope, however, is all that the illuminists have proposed as the indemnity for all the crimes and misery of France, and all the horrors of the new revolutions that they wish to engender in Europe from the Bosphorus to the Baltic. What is meant by this boastful equality? and what is its value?

EQUALITY II

The Palladium, NOVEMBER 20, 1801

THE PHILOSOPHERS among the democrats will no doubt insist that they do not mean to equalize property, they contend only for an equality of rights. If they restrict the word equality as carefully as they ought, it will not import that all men have an equal right to all things, but, that to whatever they have a right, it is as much to be protected and provided for as the right of any persons in society. In this sense nobody will contest their claim. Yet, though the right of a poor man is as much his right as a rich man's, there is no great novelty or wisdom in the discovery of the principle, nor are the French entitled to any preëminence on this account. The *magna charta* of England, obtained, I think, in the year 1216, contains the great body of what is called (and our revolutionists of 1776 called it) English liberty. This they claimed as their birthright, and with good reason; for it enacts that justice shall not be sold, nor denied, nor delayed; and as soon afterwards the trial by jury grew into general use, the subjects themselves are employed by the government to apply remedies when rights are violated. For true equality and the rights of man, there never was a better or a wiser provision, as in fact it executes itself. This is the precious system of true equality, imported by our excellent and ever to be venerated forefathers, which they prized as their birthright. Yet this glorious distinction of liberty, so ample, so stable, and so temperate, secured by the common law, has been reviled and exhibited to popular abhorrence as the shameful badge of our yet colonial dependence on England.

As the common law secures equally all the rights of the citizens, and as the jacobin leaders loudly decry this system, it is obvious that they extend their views still farther. Undoubtedly they include, in their plan of equality, that the citizens shall have assigned to them new rights and different from what they now enjoy. You have earned your estate, or it descended to you from your father; of course, my right to your estate is not as good as yours. Am I then to have, in the new order of things, an equal right with you? Certainly not, every democrat of any understanding will reply. What then do you propose by your equality? You have earned an estate; I have not; yet I have a right, and as good a right as another man, to earn it. I may save my earnings and deny myself the pleasures and comforts of life till I have laid up a competent sum to provide for my infirmity and old age. All cannot be rich, but all have a right to make the attempt; and when some have fully succeeded, and others partially, and others not at all, the several states in which they then find themselves become their condition in life; and whatever the rights of that condition may be, they are to be faithfully secured by the laws and government. This, however, is not the idea of the men of the new order of things, for, thus far, the plan belongs to a very old order of things.

They consider a republican government as the only one in which this sort of equality can exist at all. A tyrant, or a king, which all democrats suppose to be words of like import, might leave the rights of his subjects unviolated. The grand seignor is arbitrary; the heavy hand of his despotism, however, falls only on the great men in office, the aristocrats, whom it must be a pleasure to the admirers of equality to see strangled by the bowstring. The great body of the subjects of the Turkish government lead a very undisturbed life, enjoying a stupid security from the oppressions of power. To enjoy rights without having proper security for their enjoyment, ought not indeed to satisfy any political reasoners, and this is precisely the difficulty of the democratic sect. All the rights and equality they admire are destitute of any rational security, and are of a nature utterly subversive of all true liberty. For, on close examination, it turns out that their notion of equality is, that all the citizens of a republic have an equal right to political power. This is called republicanism. This hastens the journey of a demagogue to power, and invests him with the title of the man of the people. This, the people are told, is their great cause, in opposition to the coalesced tyrants of Europe and the intriguing federal aristocrats in America.

Let me cut out the tongue of that blasphemer, every democratic zealot will exclaim, who dares to deny the rightful and unlimited power of the people. It is indeed a very inveterate evil of our politics that popular opinion has been formed rather to democracy than to sober republicanism. The American Revolution was in fact, after 1776, a resistance to foreign government. We claimed the right to govern ourselves, and our patriots never contemplated the claim of the imported united Irish, that a mob should govern us. It is true that the checks on the power of the people themselves were not deemed so necessary, as on the temporary rulers whom we elected; we looked for danger on the same side where we had been used to look, and suspected every thing but ourselves. Our dread of rulers devoted them to imbecility; our presumptuous confidence in ourselves puffed all the weak, and credulous, and vain, with an opinion that no power was safe but their own, and therefore that should be uncontrollable, and have no limits. This is democracy and not republicanism. The French Revolution has been made the instrument of faction; it has multiplied popular errors and rendered them indocile. Restraints on the power of the people seem to all democrats foolish, for how shall they restrain themselves? and mischievous, because, as they think, the power of the people is their liberty. Restraints that make it less, and on every inviting occasion for mischief and the oppression of a minority, make it nothing, will appear to be the abandonment of its principles and cause.

EQUALITY III

The Mercury and New England Palladium,
NOVEMBER 27, 1801

POLITICS:

THE MULTITUDE everywhere, but especially in European countries, are instructed to believe that equality is some *new* state of society, in which all that is will cease to be, the high are to be brought low and all are to stand on an exact level. It is hard to make ignorance clearly comprehend the doctrine, but it is of all things the easiest to excite vice and want to carry it into practice. However it may be intended or however explained, it is understood by the mere rabble as the levelling principle. It is inconsistent no less with the sense of a just subordination, than with security for property or indeed of any social right whatever. It stirs up those who are unfit to exercise power to claim it, and to enlist under ambitious demagogues, who pretend to assert their claim. The very step, therefore, of a rabble, to vindicate and augment their power, is to part with it, by entrusting it in the hands of the most treacherous of all impostors. All experience shows that the mob leaders betray this trust; they form factions; as soon as these prevail over the laws and regular government, they quarrel about the division of the spoil; and the chief of the prevailing faction becomes master of the state and its tyrant. He may be said in the French style, and with emphatical propriety, to conquer liberty. The foresight of this event will be expected to restrain the multitude from the steps that lead to it; and is it really believed that those who foresee nothing, will descry this danger, which is even hidden from the presumption of philosophists?

The writer of the letter to Mazzei, and the Worcester and Farmer, seem not to have the smallest comprehension of this political danger, which has happened as regularly as the seasons of the year. Democracy, or in other words, the uncontrolled power of the people as it seems, but of a faction as it proves to be, tends with a fatal instinct, that cannot see and will not hear, to tyranny. Yet the Mazzei philosopher considers the government of the United States as the enemy of liberty, and the obstacle to its establishment, and that the removal of the restraints on the people, and of all impediments to their acting according to their arbitrary good pleasure, will ensure its safety and long life. "We shall prevail, we shall," he says, in that letter, "break these Lilliputian ties." At this crisis, therefore, it is exceedingly important to know how the new rulers understand the principle of equality and how it will be understood by the rabble of their adherents. To prevent the group of little snarlers from their usual success in perverting the meaning of words—it is here explicitly declared, that the householders, tradesmen, and yeomanry of the nation are not considered as mere rabble and incendiaries. The men who live by labor, and who get a regular livelihood, though they may lay up nothing, are nevertheless for the most part orderly, quiet, useful citizens.

But all large towns have rabble and mobs. London has perhaps one hundred thousand, and Paris has many of the vilest mob on earth. Wretches destitute of morals, knowledge or property, the standing army of vice and who feed in every European state another army in public pay to keep them from plunder and murder. In 1792, it is probable the United States had not as many as either London or Paris. Since that time Governor McKean probably obtains ten thousand new votes of rabble ejected within the last nine years from London or Dublin. Within the last ten years our mob has doubled in the southern states. It has not increased one-tenth in New England. The squalid tribe of vice and want, and ignorance are everywhere rabble, unfit for liberty and fit for ambitious demagogues to inflame and combine into a regular force, with which to menace government, and in the end to usurp its powers.

Whatever interpretation the philosophers put upon the word equality, the people, as the democrats call this very rabble, understand it as entitling them to power, and to uncontrolled power. Now, it is not in the nature of man to suppose that he is to rule, without instantly turning his thoughts and rousing all his desires to use his power in such a way as to serve some of those desires. Destitute of all things, entitled by the Rights of Man to unlimited power that will command all things, will there be any longer patience in his slavish submission to a government hostile to liberty and to the people's power; will there be any moderation in his appetite for the yet untasted dainties of his sovereignty? No, on the contrary we know that such a multitude will be violent as often as their leaders can make use of their clamors, their votes, or their force. It has been as easy in Paris, and for the democrats in this country, to kindle rage, as to kindle a fire.

The philosophers will complain, that it is uncandid to ascribe the errors of the multitude to their teachers. It might be answered, that it is at least as fair to charge the actual and enormous abuses of the doctrine of equality to democratic leaders, as for these leaders to oppose government, as they did for twelve years, on account of abuses that had not happened but which possibly might happen, because they are incident to the very nature of power. It might be said again, that as popular mistakes on this point, are inevitable, so the teachers are answerable for a doctrine so sure by creating mistakes to work mischief. Yet, as inquisitive and fair-minded men will desire to take other views of the subject, it will be proper to exhibit it somewhat more in detail.

EQUALITY IV

The Palladium, DECEMBER 4, 1801

ALL DEMOCRATS maintain that the people have an inherent, unalienable right to power; there is nothing so fixed that they may not change it; nothing so sacred that their voice, which is the voice of God, would not unsanctify and consign to destruction; it is not only true that no king, or parliament, or generation past, can bind the people, but they cannot even bind themselves; the will of the majority is not only law, but right; having an unlimited right to act as they please, whatever they please to act is a rule. Thus virtue itself, thus public faith, thus common honesty, are no more than arbitrary rules which the people have, as yet, abstained from rescinding; and when a confiscating or paper-money majority in congress should ordain otherwise, they would be no longer rules. Hence the worshippers of this idol ascribe to it attributes inconsistent with all our ideas of the Supreme Being himself, to whom we deem it equally impious and absurd to impute injustice. Hence they argue that a public debt is a burden to be thrown off whenever the people grow weary of it; and hence they somewhat inconsistently pretend that the very people cannot make a constitution authorizing any restraint upon malicious lying against the government. So that, according to them, neither religion, nor morals, nor policy, nor the people themselves can erect any barrier against the reasonable or the capricious exercise of their power. Yet, what these cannot do, the spirit of sedition can; this is more sacred than religion or justice, and dearer than the general good itself. For it is evident, that if we will have the unrestricted liberty of lying against our magistrates, and laws, and government, we can have no other liberty; and the clamorous jacobins have decided that such liberty, without any other, is better than every other kind of liberty without it.

Is it true, however, (if it be not rebellion to inquire,) that this uncontrolled power of the people is their right, and that it is absolutely essential to their liberty? All our individual rights are to be exercised with due regard to the rights of others; they are tied fast by restrictions, and are to be exercised within certain reasonable limits. How is it, then, that the democrats find a right in the whole people so much more extensive than what belongs to any one of their number? In other cases, the extremes of any principle are so many departures from principle. Why is it, then, that they make popular right to consist wholly in extremes, and that so absolutely, that without such boundless pretensions they say it could not subsist at all? Checks on the people themselves are not merely clogs, but chains. They are usurpations which should be abolished, even if in practice they prove useful; for, they will tell you, precedent sanctions and introduces tyranny. Neither Commodus nor Caligula were ever so flattered with regard to the extent of their power, and the impiety of setting bounds to it, as any people who listen to demagogues.

The writings of Thomas Paine and the democratic news-papers will evince that this representation of their doctrine is not caricatured; it is not more extravagant than they represent it themselves. They often, indeed, affirm that they are not admirers of a mere democracy; they know it will prove licentious; they are in favor of an energetic government.

It is both more satisfactory and more safe to trust to the conduct of a party than their professions. What says the conduct of the party? Either the power of the people in the United States is absolutely uncontrolled, or the executive authority, the senate, and the courts of law, are the branches constituted to check it. Now, is it not notorious that one great complaint of the jacobins against the federalists is, that the latter are friendly to the executive department. They are, on the contrary, the friends of the people, and on all occasions bold and eager to enlarge their privileges and influence in the government. It is not amiss to notice, though it is somewhat of a digression, that of late the jacobins vindicate, in their own president, an extent of executive power and patronage such as neither Washington, nor Adams, nor their friends, ever thought of claiming or exercising. They say it is right that the president should displace all federalists, and thus all officers become his creatures and dependents. Thus, a standing army of corruption is to be formed, to be drawn out in array on every election. When the British treaty was depending, these men contended that no treaty was binding, after being ratified by the president and senate, until the immediate representatives of the people had approved it. This was Mr. Gallatin's disorganizing and unconstitutional doctrine. Yet every democrat extols Mr. Jefferson for delivering up the Berceau, and carrying the French treaty into full effect, before congress has even met to consider it.[35] Even this house of representatives, that was thus to be supreme over the supreme treaty-making power, was nevertheless to be subject to a power superior to itself. The people of any district could instruct their members, and such instructions bind him against the plain dictates of his honor and conscience: he must be a rebel to the people, if he will not be perjured.

Besides, the remonstrances of any description of citizens are so many expressions of the will of the sovereign, and, being his will, ought to become law. Thus congress is to be, in all its branches, somewhat less than a mother jacobin club, which has ever been allowed to prescribe rules of conduct to its affiliated clubs. The senate is as little spared in this plan of apportionment of power by the democrats; they uniformly denominate this body the dark divan, the conclave, the aristocratic branch of the government. The famous Virginia amendments proposed, when democracy was in its zenith, to render this branch null, and to make it less a barrier against licentiousness than its convenient instrument. Let every thinking man read those amendments with attention, and he will see that to reform our government was not the object, but to subvert it.

In point of theory, notions somewhat more correct have pevailed in regard to the judiciary. Yet even on this point, at this moment, the democratic gazettes assure us that their

---

[35] *The Treaty of 1800 (Morfontaine), which concluded the quasi-war with France, waged on the seas, which ensued following the XYZ Affair.*

majority will abolish the new judiciary by repealing the law. Thus the judges are to hold their offices during good behavior; they cannot be removed at pleasure; but, as they stand upon the law, that very foundation, the democrats tell us, can be torn up. So that one great barrier of the Constitution, erected to answer the ends of justice and public safety, when either government or the people themselves "feel power and forget right," may be subverted indirectly; though not directly. The democrats cannot get over it; but they say they will get round it. Instead of stopping the flood of democratic licentiousness, this dam is to be the first obstacle that is swept away.

Let the considerate friends of rational liberty decide then, from facts, from the most authentic and solemn transactions of the democratic party, whether there be any check, limitation, or control that they would impose on the people; or any now existing that they would not first weaken and then abolish. If the sober citizens really wish for a simple democracy, and that the power of the people shall be arbitrary and uncontrollable, then let them weigh the consequences well before they consent to the tremendous changes that the federal government must undergo before it will be fit for a democracy. Let them consider the sacrifices of liberty, as well as order, of blood, as well as treasure, that this sort of government never fails to exact; and if, on due reflection, they choose these consequences, then let them elect and let them follow in arms the men who are so much infatuated to bring them about; for "infuriated man will seek his long-lost liberty through desolation and carnage."[36] If, however, they prefer the Constitution as it was made, and as it has been honestly administered, they will cling to the old cause and

---

[36] *A play upon Jefferson's "First Inaugural Address," which actually reads: ". . . during the agonizing spasms of infuriated man, seeking through the blood and slaughter his long lost liberty, it was not wonderful that the agitation of the billows should reach even this distant and peaceful shore. . . ."*

the old friends of federal republicanism, which they have tried in trying times, and, of course, know how to value and to trust.

EQUALITY V

The Palladium, DECEMBER 11, 1801

THERE IS, perhaps, no country in the world where visionary theory has done so much to darken political knowledge as in France, nor where facts appear at length so conspicuously to enlighten it. The doctrines of equality, and the rights of man, and the uncontrolled power of the people, whose voice is, rather unintelligibly, said to be the voice of God, have been so prevalent, that most persons have allowed the French to be political discoverers; and that they were, certainly, not God's, but some other being's chosen people, selected to preserve the true faith in politics from corruption and oblivion. These lofty claims French modesty urged in every country, as if they were Romans, and the others barbarians. Our patriotic sophists very meekly admitted their claim.

Time is as little a friend to folly as to hypocrisy. It obliges the intemperate sometimes to be sober, and makes knavery tired of its mask. The French revolutionary government is now in its teens, and we are compelled, with some steadiness of attention, to behold those features which democratic fondness shut its eyes to imagine were divine in its cradle. Never was popular admiration more extravagant; never were its disappointments more signal or complete. The French Revolution is one of those dire events that cannot happen without danger, nor end without advantage to mankind. It is

251

a rare inundation, whose ravages show the utmost high-water mark; an earthquake, that has laid bare a mine; a comet, whose track through the sky, while it scatters pestilence, excites the curiosity of astronomers, and rewards it.

When the French Revolution began, many of the best, and even some few of the wisest, rejoiced in some of the most pernicious and most absurd of its measures. Down with the nobles, was the cry of the *Tiers Etat*, or third estate, and it was echoed here; let all the three orders vote in one chamber; in other words, let there be but one order, the democratic—that will rule and the others bleed. Down with the priesthood, was the next cry; abuses so great have been tolerated too long: we reform too late, and therefore we cannot reform too much. The many millions of church property were of course, by a simple vote of a majority, reannexed, as they called robbery, to the nation. The nobles were next dismounted in an evening's sitting, and in a fit of emulation in extravagance. All was done without reasoning, and by acclamation. The sovereign mob of the suburbs of Paris, called St. Antoine and Rue Marcel, were next employed. The Bastile was taken; liberty celebrated her triumphs, she trod upon a plain, on the rubbish of her tyrants' palaces, whose ruins were not left as high as their foundations. Her path seemed to be smooth; all obstacles were removed; all men were free and equal; those who had rescued liberty by their blood were ready to shed it in her defence. Where are her friends? Behold them arrayed in armies, brandishing their pikes. Where are her enemies? See their heads dropping gore on those pikes. Is not the danger over? Is not the victory won? Are not the French free, and perfectly secure in their freedom?

Every sagacious democrat answered all these questions in the affirmative.

Nobody seemed any longer to have power but the people. They had all power, and of course unbounded liberty. How little is it considered that arbitrary power, no matter whether of prince or people, makes tyranny; and that in salutary restraint is liberty. A stupid, ferocious multitude, who are unfit to be free, may play the tyrant for a day, just long enough to put a sceptre of iron into their leader's hand. To use quaint language, in order to be the more intelligible, it may be said, that when there is no end to the power of a multitude, there can be no beginning to their liberty.

Review the transactions in France since 1789, and it will appear that there is no condition of a state in which it is more impossible that liberty should subsist, or more nearly impossible that, after being lost, it should be retrieved, than after order has been overthrown, and popular licentiousness triumphs in its stead.

The old government of France was a bad one; but the new order of things was infinitely worse. Most persons suppose this is to be ascribed to the excess of liberty; they think there was too much of a good thing. Now the truth is, there was no liberty at all—absolutely none from the first, no reasonable hope, scarcely a lucky chance for it. Who had liberty? Clearly not the king, the nobles, nor the priests, nor the king's ministers—all these were in jeopardy from the 14th July, 1789; not the rich—they were robbed and driven into banishment; not the great military officers who had gained glory in the American war—they were slain; not the farmers— their harvests and their sons were in requisition; not the merchants—they were so stripped that their race was extinct; they were known only on the grave-stones of Nantes and Lyons; they were remembered in France, like the mammoth, by their bones. But, say the democrats, the people, the many, in other words, the rabble of the cities, were free; bread was issued to them by the public. Yes, but it was the bread of soldiers, for which they were enrolled as national guards to uphold the tyranny of robbers and usurpers; and as soon as this very rabble relucted at their work, the more

253

desperate cutthroats from Marseilles were called for, to shoot them in the streets.

It is often said that the monarchy of France was forcibly upheld by the army. There is much incorrectness in the prevailing notions on this point. Without pausing to consider them, it may be sufficient to say that the leaders of the revolution, apprehending that they should have an army against them, very early determined that they would have also an army on their side. By a simple vote, raising the pay of the king's soldiers, they detached the troops from his side to their own; and, still further to augment their military force, they enlisted the rabble of all the cities as national guards. Thus France was still governed by an army, but this army was itself governed by new chiefs. The people were more than ever subject to military power.

Now, it would be a pleasant task for the democratic declaimers to show that martial law is liberty; and as there never was a half hour since July, 1789, when a man in France had any other rights but such as that law saw fit to spare, they ought now to tell us, as they gave no reason at the time, why they roasted oxen on account of the triumphs of French liberty.

The nature of that precious liberty deserves some further consideration.

EQUALITY VI

————

The Palladium, DECEMBER 15, 1801

THE FRENCH are very unjustly accused of having lost their liberty; they never had it. The old government was not a free one, and the violence that demolished it was not liberty. The leaders were, from the first, as much the sovereigns as the Bourbon kings. A mob would disperse in an hour without a leader, and that leader has immediately an authority, of all despots the most absolute, though the most precarious. To destroy the monarchy, the resort was to force, not to the people; and who, in those times of violence, had any liberty but the possessors of that force? No liberty was then thought more valuable than that of running away from mob tyranny.

Accordingly, the standing army, which had been only two hundred thousand strong, was suddenly increased to half a million. The ruin of trade and manufactures compelled scores of thousands to become soldiers for bread. All France was soon filled with terror, pillage, and massacre. It is absurd, though for a time it was the fashion, to call that nation free, which was, at that very period of its supposed emancipation, subject to martial law, and bleeding under its lash. The rights of a Frenchman were never less, nor was there ever a time when he so little dared to resist or even to complain.

The kings of France, it is true, had a great military force, but the new liberty-leaders had as much again. They used it, avowedly, to strike terror into those they were pleased to call counter revolutionists; in other words, to drive into exile nearly a million nobles, priests, rich people, and women; every description of persons, whom they hated, feared, or wished to plunder, was placed on the proscribed list. All the kings of France, from the days of Pharamond and Clovis, down to the last of the Bourbon race, did not exercise despotic power on so great a scale, nor with such horrid cruelty. If the French were slaves under their kings, their masters did not try to aggravate the weight of their chains; the people were sometimes spared because they were a property; because their kings had an interest in their lives, and some in their affections, but none in their sufferings. The republican French have not whispered their griefs, without hazard of a spy; they have not lingered in their servile tasks, without bleeding under the whips of their usurpers.

Yet this extremity of degradation and wretchedness has been celebrated as a triumph. Americans have been made discontented with their liberty, because it was so much less an object of desire, a condition so inferior in distinction to that of the French.

While the kings reigned, they permitted the laws to govern, at least as much as their quiet and security would allow; and when they used military force to seize the members of the parliament of Paris, and to detain them prisoners for their opposition to their edicts, the ferment in the nation soon induced them to set them at liberty. Thus, it appears that the rigors of despotism once had something existing to counteract and to soften them; but since the revolution, the popular passions have been invariably excited and employed to furnish arms to tyrants, and never to snatch them out of their hands; to overtake fugitive wretches, and to invent new torments.

This, bad as it is, is the natural course of things. Liberty is not to be enjoyed, indeed it cannot exist, without the habits of just subordination; it consists, not so much in removing all restraint from the orderly, as in imposing it on the violent. Now, the first step in a revolution is to make these restraints appear unjust and debasing, and to induce the multitude to throw them off; in other words, to give daggers to ruffians, and to lay bare honest men's hearts. By exalting their passions to rage and frenzy, and leading them on, before they cool, to take bastiles, and overturn altars and thrones, a mad populace are well fitted for an army, but they are spoiled for a republic. Having enemies to contend with, and leaders to fight for, the contest is managed by force, and the victory brings joy only as it secures booty and vengeance. The conquering faction soon divides, and one part arrays its partisans in arms against the other; or, more frequently, by treachery and surprise cuts off the chiefs of the adverse faction, and they reduce it to weakness and slavery. Then more booty, more blood, and new triumphs for liberty!

It is not because there are not malcontents, it is not because tyranny has not rendered scores of thousands desperate, that civil war has not, without ceasing, ravaged that country. But the despotism, that continually multiplies wretches, carefully disarms them; it so completely engrosses all power to itself, as to discourage all resistance. Indeed, the only power in the state is that of the sword; and while the army obeys the general, the nation must obey the army. Hence it has been, that civil war has not raged. The people were nothing, and, of course, no party among them could prepare the force to resist the tyrants in Paris. Hence France has appeared to be tranquil in its slavery, and has been forced to celebrate feasts for the liberty it had not. They have often changed their tyrants, but never their tyranny, not even in the mode and instruments of its operation. An armed force has been the only mode from the first, which free governments may render harmless, because they may keep it subordinate to the civil power. This despotic states cannot do.

The mock "republican" leaders, as they affect to call themselves, but the jacobin chiefs in America, as they are known and called, are the close imitators of these French examples. They use the same popular cant, and address themselves to the same classes of violent and vicious rabble. Our Condorcets and Rolands are already in credit and in power. It would not be difficult to show, that their notions of liberty are not much better than those of the French. If Americans adopt them, and attempt to administer our orderly and rightful government by the agency of the popular passions, we shall lose our liberty at first, and in the very act of making the attempt; next we shall see our tyrants invade every possession that could tempt their cupidity, and violate every right that could obstruct their rage.

Nothing will better counteract such designs than to contemplate the effects of their success in the government of Bonaparte. Of that in the next number.

EQUALITY VII

The *Palladium*, DECEMBER 22, 1801

THE NATURE AND BASIS OF BONAPARTE'S POWER

EVERY DEMOCRAT more or less firmly believes that a revolution is the sure path to liberty; and therefore he believes government of little importance to the people, and very often the greatest impediment to their rights. Merely because the French had begun a revolution, and thrown every thing that was government flat to the ground, they began to rejoice, because that nation had thus become the freest nation in the world. It is very probable many of the ignorant in France really thought so; it is lamentable that many of the well-informed in America fell into a like error.

It is essential, therefore, to review the history of that revolution, at least with so much attention as to deduce a few plain conclusions. Popular discontents naturally lead to a forcible resistance of government. The very moment the physical power of the people is thus employed to resist, the people themselves become nothing. They can only destroy; they cannot rule. They cannot act without chiefs; nor have chiefs, and keep rights. They are blind instruments in the hands of ambitious men; and of necessity act merely as they are acted upon. Each individual is nothing; but the chief, having the power of a great many to aid him, can overpower, and will destroy, any mutinous citizen who presumes to find fault with his general's conduct. Thus a revolution produces a mob. A mob is at first an irregular, then a regular army; but in every stage of its progress, the mere blind instrument of its leaders. The power of an army, of necessity, falls into the hands of one man, the general-in-chief, who is the sole despot and master of the state.

Every thing in France has gone on directly contrary to all the silly expectations of the democrats, though most exactly in conformity with the laws of man's nature, and the evidence of history. If this kind of contemplation could cure Americans of their strange, and perhaps it will prove fatal, propensity to revolutionary principles, and induce them, in future, to prefer characters fitter to preserve order than to overthrow it, then we should grow wise by the direful experience of others. We might stop with our Rolands, without proceeding to our Dantons and Robespierres.

After many convulsions, we behold Bonaparte the undisputed master of France, of new France, whose vast extent, whose immense populousness, whose warlike spirit, and arrogance in victory, invest her with the means, as well as the claim, like old Rome, to parcel out kingdoms, and to sit in judgment upon nations. A nine years' war has left those nations enfeebled. They are too much afraid of France to resist her singly; and unhappily for the repose and security of mankind, too much afraid of each other to join in self-defence.

A position of things so tempting to ambition would awaken it in France, even if it ever slept there. But it never sleeps. Great Britain, though not weakened, is wearied and discouraged by the selfishness and discord of the continental powers, and will not resume her arms, unless compelled by absolute necessity.

Russia alone is not afraid of France; but Russia has views on Turkey, which she will not, by any hostile measures, rouse France to obstruct.

In reality, the European states are, by a singular concurrence of circumstances, more than ever exposed, at this moment, as a prey to the French; and even more exposed to their arts in peace, than to their arms in war. There is little doubt that the power of the French consul would prove irresistible; but the important doubt exists, is it stable?

Bonaparte reigns by military power. There is not, as formerly, a body of nobles, an order of priests, a jealous parliament of Paris, a system of wise municipal laws, that deserved respect, and of provincial customs and claims of separate sovereignty, that extorted it from their kings. The new monarchy is without any such checks. There is no exterior impediment to the power of an army; its obstacles are to be sought for within itself. And simple as its machinery seems to be, military force requires the management of a skilful hand, and it is kept in order, by rightly touching many little wheels and springs.

It is indeed true, that discipline is the ruling principle of armies; but what is discipline more than the fear of the general? While they know they have every thing to suffer from disobedience, and nothing to hope, the troops will obey. If, however, a state of things should exist, that admitted of much to hope from mutiny, and little to dread, there is nothing in the principle of discipline to restrain the soldiers from revolt any more than citizens.

Suppose, for instance, the great lieutenant-generals, especially if they command separate armies, distant from the general, should conspire to place a new commander at their head; in that case, it is evident, the power of discipline would be turned against the general, and converted into an instrument of insurrection. Everybody knows, that the troops would greatly incline to the side of their particular commander. As the thirst for rank is the very soul of an army, the great officers will be hindered from aspiring at the chief command only by the difficulty, and almost impossibility, of attaining it; for as to the danger, men of daring spirits, habituated to think life worth little, and honor worth every thing, will not make much account of the danger.

To guard against this mischief, inherent in the very life, and bone, and muscle of his power, Bonaparte must watch his great officers much, and trust them as little as possible. He must guard most vigilantly every avenue by which a rival might enter his army to tamper with it; he must be jealous of every great military genius in his camp, and ready to meet every unforeseen event; he will prevent their being collected in great force in the distant provinces, and under popular lieutenant-generals; he will not let the honor of victories fall to the share of any commander but himself; and for that reason, he will hurry to Marengo, that everybody may be forced to ascribe the event to his superior talents and fortune. While he keeps the troops in dread of punishment, if they disobey, (and the odium of such punishments he will throw on his lieutenant-generals,) he will spare nothing that taxes or that exactions, without any formality, can obtain, to bestow in largesses on his soldiers. Thus, he will be the dispenser of all bounties, and unite in his favor the sentiments of both fear and affection. Nobody will be able to do others so much evil, nor, before a nation's wealth is at his disposal, can any rival appear to be so willing to do them good as he.

It is obvious, however, that this is a system both of jealousy and rigor. It is equally clear, that to reward the soldiers will be the chief thing; to spare the people a very subordinate consideration.

It will indeed, for other reasons, be nearly impossible, under such a government, greatly to favor the people. The military class, holding the chief power, will claim the first place, in point of rank and honor. Soldiers would grow weary of their condition if they were despised by the citizens, whom they are employed to keep in subjection. Besides it would not be practicable, nor perhaps would it be good policy in the general, to allow the state of a citizen to be greatly preferable to that of a soldier.

It follows also, that the inferior kind of liberty, which many arbitrary governments venture to let their subjects enjoy, and which, prior to this revolution, all the European states seemed desirous to enlarge, will be denied to the French. For if they pretend to be free, they would soon corrupt the soldiery with their doctrines of equality. Hence it is, that the liberty of the press has been tried in France, and really found to be inconsistent with their plan of government. We call it their tyranny, to abridge it; the fact is, self-preservation is the first law of every government; and the liberty to make Bonaparte odious, and to combine all his enemies into a regular body against him, would soon oblige him to draw the sword in self-defence. The liberty of the press, under a military government, is, indeed, only the liberty to kindle a civil war.

For the same reason, martial law must be universal; the government will defend itself; and it cannot defend itself unless it everywhere watches its enemies, and hinders them from acting as soon as they begin to stir. Free governments may consider many libels and lies as idle words; many others as worthy only of moderate fines; but there is no safety in permitting your town-meeting orators to tamper with an army. The government must be jealous, and is scarcely permitted to be either magnanimous or merciful; its fears will make it always strict, and often cruel.

It is not possible, therefore, that the French should enjoy one half of the little liberty they had under their kings. Their revolution will lessen it throughout Europe. But it is certain that the most rigorous governments are the hardest to maintain in tranquillity. Trivial risings of the people are not to be expected; the certainty that any small insurgent force would be instantly crushed by the great force of the army, will prevent any risings but such as are serious struggles for empire, and these are to be expected.

A great commander, with a hundred thousand men to second his designs, is crowned with success. The decision is made by the comparison of hostile forces, and the conqueror, having the greater force, claims the admiration of his countrymen and despotic authority over them. He obtains it. But in peace he has fewer to aid his designs, and more to obstruct them. Those whom he gratifies will not be grateful; those whom he denies will be vindictive. Extravagant hopes are formed, and even great success in a peaceful administration will not be splendid. Few will admire; many will repine and be disappointed.

The circumstance, that his claim to reign is merely personal, will insure disturbances. Tranquillity will not be expected to last longer than his life, and that expectation will abridge it. His indisposition, his old age, his mistakes, and his disasters, will all engender those forebodings of change, that will hasten changes. His ambitious lieutenants will aspire to his place, and will cabal in the army to gain a party to be ready to salute them emperors, as soon as he is dead, or has become odious.

Another consequence worth remark is, that these changes have no tendency to establish liberty. A new struggle, like the old one, must be by violence, which can only give the sceptre to the most violent. The leaders will aim only at the power to reign, and it will not be their wish to lessen that power, which they hope to gain as a prize. The supreme power would not tempt them to such efforts, if it was to be made cheap and vile in their eyes, by bestowing it on the despised rabble of the cities and the common soldiery. These men are unfit for liberty; and if they had it gained for them, would give it away to a demagogue, who would have, in six weeks, another army, and a new despotism, as hard to bear and to overturn, as that which they had subverted. Nor could the leaders establish liberty if they tried; the supreme power being military, the contest can only determine what general shall hold it. A military government in fact, though often changing its chief, is capable of very long duration. Rome, Turkey, and Algiers are examples; France may prove another.

Thus the progress of mob equality is invariably to despotism, and to a military despotism, which, by often changing its head, embitters every one of the million of its curses, but which cannot change its nature. It renders liberty hopeless, and almost undesirable to its victims.

THE REPUBLICAN X

Boston Gazette, AUGUST 30, 1804
Reprinted from the *Repertory*

The progress of our affairs is in conformity with the fixed laws of our nature, and the known course of Republics. Our wisdom made a government, and committed it to our virtue to keep, but our passions have engrossed it, and they have armed our vices to maintain their usurpation.

THE WILL of the people ought to prevail, is the cant of the jacobins, when they tamper with their credulity, in order to engross their power and violate their rights. As there is an abundant stock of credulity that is hungry for imposture, and as there ever will be demagogues to make this credulity, first their dupe and then their prey, its seems useless to contend. Why resort with arguments to the understanding, when passion is sure to decide the controversy?

It is our duty to maintain the federal government as long as we can; and if it must degenerate into a turbulent democracy, it is still our duty, and our prudence too, to delay, if we cannot prevent, its fate. Truth, the plain truth, if we could make it reach the people, would have some temporary effect, at least, to unmask their deceivers, and to protract the term of their liberty, for he must be blind indeed, who does not already see, that the violence of ours is a sure prognostic of its brevity.

The will of the people ought to prevail. But who are the real people, and what is it to be considered as their will, which ought to prevail?

The French solemnly decreed that no government is legitimate that is not founded on equality, and the rights of man. Our ruling party are as loud as the French ever were, and just as sincere in this clamor about equality and the rights of man.

Yet Virginia holds her preponderance, as mistress of the Union!—a title most dear to the lazy arrogance of her plantation barons, by an avowed inequality—an inequality fiercely contended for in 1788, as the very condition of her coming into the Union. An inequality so dear that she would have committed the fates of America to the decision of anarchy and the sword of civil war, rather than not extort it from the prudence and patriotism of the northern and middle States. And now that the amendment to the Constitution, altering the manner of voting for president and vice-president, has been adopted,[37] to gratify a single man, for the urgency of profound considerations was undeniable, and lest denied, has been adopted, we repeat, to make Jefferson president as long as he shall live, and after he is dead, to make some

---

[37] *The Twelfth Amendment, to eliminate the necessity for presidential electors to split their ballots between presidential and vice-presidential candidates, was ratified on June 5, 1804.*

other Virginian president, as long as our union, or its present principles shall last, surely it is right and reasonable, and equal, to make another alteration to abolish the black votes. Some offset, some indemnification is due to the northern states for renouncing forever any chance of a president out of Virginia. Yet the amendment proposed by Massachusetts, was opposed by every servile Virginia-hearted jacobin in our legislature, and hence we may infer, as those people never act without orders from Washington, the Massachusetts amendment will be opposed by Virginia in Congress. And whatever Virginia opposes fails of course. It was right and necessary, however, to propose the amendment; we cannot always give effect to our just claims, but it would be cowardice, folly, treachery toward the people of Massachusetts, by our silence and inaction to surrender or rather to renounce them.

Be the success of the amendment what it may, the fact already is clear, that our government, as the jacobins will have it subsist, is not founded on equality and the rights of man. Let them be forever silent, or if they will, as they must break silence to deceive, let none but the stupidest of the rabble be deceived by their hypocrisy, when they dare to say, the will of the people ought to prevail. They know that without the black votes, Mr. Jefferson would not have been president; they know that these black votes are given in contempt of the rights of man; for the Virginia negroes have no more political will or power than the cattle on the Kennebec.

This is not all; they know that we, the yeomen of the north, the sons of liberty and labor, ae doomed to obey the will of these slave chosen rulers.

On this theme, let jacobin impudence be discreetly silent, or if it will speak, let it be only in the midnight caucus, such as that, (for such will be again convened) where the pamphlet of anonymous slander was agreed to be framed, and a committee chosen to frame, and secretly to distribute it. In the face of day, and in the hearing of men born free, and who have sworn to live free, let shame, let fear, tie their tongues, for it's enough to be oppressed, too much to be insulted by our oppressors. It is too much, to be told, when we are nothing, the will of the people ought to prevail.

Again, let us ask who is meant by the word people? This very lying pamphlet absurdly and insolently complains of the violation of the constitutional right of a jury trial by the federal rulers, because they were authorized to send dangerous aliens out of the country. A constitution is a compact, a high and solemn expression of the will of the people who adopt and ratify it, an engagement which each man makes with the whole society, and the whole society with each man. Yet this miserable pamphleteer, complains of a breach of the constitutional right of ten thousand Cape Francois murderers, and house burners, who are discouraged from coming here, or hindered from following their business after they have come, by the alien act. Are all the incendiaries, who are yet lurking in Ireland, ready to affect the French in setting fire to the four corners of their country, are they possessed of a constitutional right to come here and become members of our society? Are these the people whose will is to be our law? Must we import our masters; is it not enough that they are bred in the tobacco fields on the James and the Rappahannock rivers?

The aliens then, whenever come, or coming here, according to the pamphlet, are the people, and as they preach, so it must be confessed they have prevailed. It is a fact notorious, that an alien rabble has decided the election in several of our cities. It is a fact that in the liberties of Philadelphia, such a lawless, shameless rabble, gathered from the four winds of Heaven, marched to the [parade] ground with the French flag waving; yet this is the will of the people, according to the pamphlet, and to our infinite shame and sorrow, we must act according to the fact.

For, householders, tradesmen, farmers of New England, you are nothing; your vote weights no more in deciding who shall possess the Union, or how the Union shall be governed, or who shall be purchased and added to the Union, than the sentiments of a majority of the blacks. Their vote, or that which is given in the vote of their masters, is of a thousand times more effect than your own, and solemnized, by now. All you have to do is to find money and patience. And money you must find, patience you will probably find, unless you should at length feel the edge of the sarcasm, a great one it is, when you are told the will of the people ought to prevail. Mere injuries are but so much weight that a slave's muscles may support. But insults, like the whip of the negro driver, are sure to produce feeling. The camel patiently bears in pain its master on its back, but he winces when he suffers from the spur in his heel.

VII.

DEFENDING THE

FEDERALISTS

PHOCION I

The Palladium, APRIL 17, 1801

BRITISH INFLUENCE

THERE IS scarcely anything more vehemently talked, or less correctly inquired or reasoned about, than British influence. It seems a paradox, but it is never the less true, that the subject has proved of a nature almost equally to control the faith of the weak, and to elude or bewilder the discernment of the wise. It is not, however, strange that on this point, the arts of demagogues should mislead the multitude. The very phrase, "British Influence," has magic in it, because there is mystery in it. It supposes a malevolent and invisible [*sic*] agency, whose power cannot be resisted, yet whose action cannot be endured. The vulgar, whose imagination has so much power to feel, and so little to resist the impulse to action, the vulgar in silk stockings, who call themselves the enlightened, instantly feel their hair stiffen with the dread of an imaginary political devil, whom no higher deity than such as visibly rules a mob, watches or will bind in chains. Thus their fears are excited, their confidence gained. Thus the former see invisible things in the twilight; the latter is blind in the sunshine. On certain subjects, all men remain children through life; and the mere mob of all countries are children. No wonder then that bugbears terrify them; no wonder that opinions or rather prejudice, which were not reasoned into them cannot be reasoned out of them.

If the evil stopped here it would be great enough, yet as it springs from human infirmity, which is so much more under the dominion of prejudice than of the understanding, we should acquiesce because we should know that it is incurable. If those, who are raised by education above the vulgar, had escaped the prejudices which seemed to be nearly equally allied to meanness and blindness of birth, should say that things were in their natural state, that those were made slaves by prejudice who were made first blind by ignorance, we should say that the weakness which cannot form a creed, nevertheless will not be content without one, and that it had accepted one ready made from the democrats, who, on such occasions are always officious and often obtrusive. If the base and the ignorant only, had charged the federalists with being liable to British influence, there would indeed be nothing to disturb the tranquillity of our contempt, nothing to quicken the pulse of our pity into anger.

But men of a better sort have sometimes been found, in a moment of supposed necessity, trying to borrow influence from this miserable popular prejudice—such men seem to forget that the fears of a British faction, which they counterfeit for temporary or personal purposes, are used by others for permanent public mischiefs—they seem to be insensible that a sacrifice of their party and of their principles would not serve them, for although the jacobins would be delighted with the victims, they would certainly distrust those who furnish them.

It is not clear that any enquiry into the grounds of the

opinion that British influence has prevailed in our federal councils will undeceive those who entertain it. Prejudice must govern those whom reason cannot, and even among those whose minds have been cultivated by education, there is greater proneness to believe than to inquire. The process of credulity is summary, that of inquiry is slow and tedious; and such is the instability and infirmity of human character, that even virtue will sometimes descend to court prejudice instead of attempting to enlighten it.

Faction has ever had an interest in maintaining that British influence was great, was increasing, and ought to be diminished. The French and all their partisans have manifested in all their conduct and writings, a fixed belief, that all in America who were not lovers of France were devoted to Britain. They could discern no medium, and accordingly, their gazettes have proceeded on the supposition, that we were divided between France and her rival. There is no French opinion that the jacobins have not adopted, and therefore, the insolent classification of Americans into French and English, has not allowed them to suppose it possible that we should have the feelings and sentiments of an independent nation, or that we should abhor the one and be jealous of the other. The French have ever despised America, the jacobins have ever been strangers to it in heart and affection. Hence it is, that our jacobins adopted their errors and propagated them.

The federalists, they say, are no friends to France, and therefore they must be partisans of Britain. To their base and servile souls it was incomprehensible that any class of citizens should be American.

It may be said, perhaps, that in free states no opinions strike a deep root but such as party has planted or cultivated. Political principles, that are learned by study and observation, grow lofty indeed like the forest trees; but in great storms the top is a lever to pry up the roots. The base prejudices of party on the contrary are like the shrub oaks, the sign of barrenness, and the cause of it, their chief growth is underground, they defy alike the plow and the tempest. It is not to be expected, therefore, that knaves would yield so much deference to a better argument than the writer could urge, as to renounce that power over fools that the dread of a British influence has given them. No proof would satisfy party so little as demonstration, because that would disappoint and disarm its rage. It seeks weapons not light. Jacobins are not scrupulous or inquisitive as to what they ought rationally to believe, their case is to know what the weakest of the multitude are prone to believe, and then to urge that as a fact.

If an enquiry into the existence of a supposed British influence is to be pursued, who is to be gained by it? Party is deafer than the adder. The jacobins will not be convinced— the federalists do not need it. It is indeed far from certain that truth produces much effect in party contests. But though it is ever treated by jacobins as an odious and suspected stranger, the federalists will ever take satisfaction, and perhaps courage in its company. Another essay shall, therefore, further prosecute the subject.

PHOCION II

The Palladium, APRIL 21, 1801

BRITISH INFLUENCE

BRITISH INFLUENCE is a phrase commonly enough used by the jacobins without any meaning, or without any that is precise. They hate the federalists, and they have some unknown and incommunicable reasons for it, which are at once conveyed, without being defined, by charging them with acting under British influence.

Correct inquirers will however ask for definitions. Influence, then, let it be said, is political power, and is exerted to modify or control, or prevent the public measures of the American nation. It may be the private opinion of a few scholars that the English government is excellent in its principles, and favorable to that sort of healthful, long-lived liberty, that grows hardy by braving labors, and perils, and storms, and that it will probably survive and be in its youth twenty ages after the ephemeral despotisms of France are lost in oblivion. These individual opinions, if they are erroneous, or extravagant, or obnoxious to popular prejudices, are not of a sort to influence the public measures of this country. They never have done it; they have never been popular opinions, and of course have never had political influence. Nor is it material that some persons still respect England as the land of our fathers' sepulchres.

They may think that the early principles and institutions in which the first settlers of New England were educated in England, and which they brought over and planted here, entitle that nation to our respectful remembrance. If even the English character should impress some respect, as being sincere, generous, and benevolent; if their magnanimous spirit in war, their strict and impartial administration of justice, their enterprise in commerce, their ingenuity in the arts, and the renown of their poets, statesmen, and philosophers should, in the eyes of some admirers, throw a lustre over the British name, yet, let it be remembered, those admirers are not numerous. They dare not avow that such are their sentiments. No; though we sprung from English parents, the only language that can be used, without the risk of persecution, is that of rage, abhorrence, and contempt. At the hazard of disgracing our own pedigree, we are summoned six times a week, in the jacobin gazettes, to treat the British subjects as the slaves of a tyrant, whose spirit is as wretched as their lot. The public opinion is certainly not that of attachment to England; and it is the prevailing popular sentiment only that can influence the measures of our government.

If Britain, then, has influence, or in other words, political power, it must be exerted in some other way, and by some other instruments than such as we have mentioned.

The base will say, and the base will believe, that Britain has gold enough to buy friends and to carry a vote in congress as often as her interests require the expense. A charge of this nature seldom needs proof, or is much shaken by confutation. The base will believe it without proof. They will consider congress as a market, where virtue is for sale, and if they look into their own hearts, they will find nothing there to discredit the evidence of such a traffic, or to enhance the terms of the bargain. Integrity and honor are sounding words, and they who would pay a price according to the sound, are welcome to the substance. They consider all virtue as a thing not wanted for their own use, but as a false jewel to be disposed of to the best customers. Of all men I have ever known, the jacobins have the worst opinion of human nature. An honest discharge of duty in any station, is a thing incredible, because with them it is incomprehensible. Accordingly, they begin with accusations and calumnies of the foulest sort, and call upon us to show that they are not true; as if the burden of proof did not rest on the accusers, but the accused.

After having charged Washington, Adams, Hamilton, Pickering, Wolcott, and others, with being British partisans, they assume the charge as a sentence judicially pronounced and established, and affect to consider all solicitude to repel it as an indication of a consciousness of guilt; the galled jade winces, they will say. But even this burden of proof, however unfairly imposed, may be fearlessly assumed by the friends of the federal administration of our government.

It is proper to remark, to the men who are observers of human nature, that of all kinds of influence the first for ignorant and vulgar minds to suspect, is downright bribery and corruption; it is, nevertheless, the last for even the profligate and shameless to yield to. It is so coarse an instrument, that it seldom answers the purpose. There are instances, and one is said to have happened during our revolution, where a man, who wanted integrity, made an outcry, when he had it in his power to brag that it had been tempted. More than half the indictments for rapes are founded on the charges of women of no virtue. There is so much shame in yielding to the offer of a bribe, and so much glory in refusing it, that the latter is often the better and more tempting bribe, which determines the conduct.

Sir Robert Walpole, the celebrated English minister, is said to have been a master in the art of corruption; but when public opinion was decided strongly for or against a measure, as in the cases of the excise, the Jew bill, if I mistake not, and the cruelties of the Spanish *guarda-costas*, his gold and his art failed to secure a majority in parliament. In the late attempt to unite Great Britain and Ireland, the project, in spite of ministerial influence, was at first rejected by the Irish commons. The public reasons were strong, the public good plainly called for the union; yet passion and prejudice opposed the measure. Ireland, by the union, seemed to be lost and swallowed up; and this secret dread, this inward horror, of sinking into nothing, outweighed all the forcible national arguments in favor of the measure. It may be added, that the members felt a like decline of their own weight and influence. It may therefore be said, with Sir Robert Walpole, that it is hard to bribe members even to do their duty, and to vote according to their consciences; much less can they be bribed to vote against them, or rather against the known voice of the nation.

All experience shows, that to get a bad measure adopted when it is popular, is easy; to get a good one is ever hard, against the current of even the most absurd and groundless popular clamor. The side, therefore, to look for corrupt influence is ever the popular side, because that is the unsuspected, and yet the dark side: members, in that case, can be praised for acting against duty. As many are willing to yield their principles, who cannot part with their reputation, the occasions are frequent when members prefer acting so as to please the people instead of serving them.

The current of popularity has ever been anti-British, it has ever been dangerously French. From hence it follows, that bribes could not have been employed without great difficulty, nor with much effect on the British side, nor without a great deal of effect on the French side; there was a general willingness to be deceived in regard to France. Mr. Monroe's unexampled assurances, that Americans would submit to captures, and rejoice in their losses, if it would serve the republic,[38] and Mr. Gerry's unaccountable, and yet unexplained lingering in Paris,[39] are proofs how deep-rooted and general the prejudice is in favor of the French.

It will be asked, also, if bribes were given by England, who was bribed? Washington ratified the treaty; was he bribed? Was the senate and a majority of the house of representatives? If that is true, or only suspected, the democrats who suspect it ought to go to France to enjoy "the pure morals of the republic," instead of living in a country so corrupt, and as Fauchet[40] said, so early decrepit.

---

[38] *Monroe was American minister in Paris from 1794 to 1796. He replaced arch federalist, Gouvernor Morris, to whom the French had a decided antipathy. Monroe, a thoroughgoing republican, went above and beyond the call of duty in exchanging "civilities" with the French republicans, creating some tension and embarrassment for the sensitive negotiations under way in London between Jay and British representatives.*

[39] *Although Marshall and Pinckney responded to Talleyrand's attempted extortion (see note 19 above) by demanding their passports and returning to the United States, Gerry, the republican, remained in Paris six months longer, against State Department orders, seeking a reconciliation.*

[40] *Joseph Fauchet, French minister from whom Edmund Randolph, secretary of state, reputedly solicited a bribe. The minister's confidential*

It is confessed these are observations which tarnish a newspaper; they dishonor America, and yet the files of the democratic gazettes repeat their audacious slanders of British influence, in a style to extort a careful and circumstantial examination of the charge. What will foreigners think, what will honest and yet uncorrupted Americans believe of their new government, such as free elections have made it, such as Washington administered and left it, that, after twelve prosperous years, it is scarcely tolerated; nay, it is not tolerated, for it is taken from the hands of its old friends to put it into other hands; it is arraigned at the bar like a culprit, and called to plead to a charge of bribery and corruption. If those who will rail could reason, the scandalous necessity of this vindication would not be wholly useless; it would come out of the fire of accusation the brighter for the trial. But there is as much levity as malice in the jacobins; they forget the lie and the confutation, and when the *Chronicle* repeats the lie, it is ever fresh and unconfuted.

PHOCION III

The Palladium, APRIL 24, 1801

BRITISH INFLUENCE

BRITISH INFLUENCE, it has been shown, could scarcely operate at all in the way of bribes. Even if members would sell themselves to a British emissary, let it be considered

---

account to his superiors fell into British hands when H.M.S. Cerberus captured the Jean Bart. They then made their way into American hands, and surfaced in July, 1795, discrediting Randolph and decisively influencing Washington's signing of the Jay Treaty, despite reservations.

how few occasions could be sought or found to earn the wages of iniquity. Unless their conduct was popular, they would lose their seats, and it would be necessary every two years to buy a fresh set. It is therefore clear, that British gold could not buy influence against the course of popular prejudices; and if popularity were once gained, there would be no need of bribing votes. Pretty good sort of men, we know, will work for popularity; very bad men could not work to any effect for wages against it. Let it be remembered, that a famous democratic member on the floor of congress once said, when the French minister applied for anticipation of an instalment of the French debt, before it was due, and there was no money in the United States' treasury to pay more than the current expenses and the interest of the public debt.—There would be no merit in paying only when it was due, and when it was convenient to pay; he rejoiced, he said, that America could strain her means, and hazard something to show her gratitude. Bribery did not buy this sentiment, base as it was; nor, had it been unpopular, could money have bought it, for then its intrinsic baseness would have blasted the speaker.

It is the people who are to be bribed, influenced, and corrupted. It is their folly, their prejudice, their best feelings, and their worst, that are to be tampered with. A lie in the *Chronicle* goes farther than a guinea, and ten can be coined and pushed into currency before even Randolph could be enlisted. This is the lever to pry the world out of its orbit. This is the power of necromancy that can conjure spirits from the deep, and they will come and dwell in Marlborough and in Cambridge. The passions of the people are the engines of influence; and he who can move them seems to have the faculty of working miracles. A stupid *Chronicle*, whose history is false, whose argument is sophistry, seemingly too flimsy to gull the mob, whose sneers always want wit, and whose malice seems to be too blind to choose or to exercise its weapons, even this wretched *Chronicle,* which one would think has not vivacity enough to interest fools, nor talent enough to satisfy its knaves, has influence, and it is French influence. Somniferous as it is, yet like the wand of Mercury it has the power to compel the spirits of a multitude.

But from speculative reasoning let us turn our attention to facts. Is there one measure of the government in which British influence has manifested itself: it would be silly to suppose that votes were bought to be lost. In what act has a partiality for Great Britain appeared? Surely our impost act affords no such proof; American manufactures are deservedly preferred. This would be a tender point for British partisans to push. And be it remembered, the opposers of such preference of our own manufactures were, first to last, the Southern jacobins. Had British gold been used for British purposes, the federalists could have gratified their opposers by yielding this point; but they did not and would not yield it. A point no less dear to Great Britain is her carrying trade. That was carried by federal votes to prefer American bottoms, and the preference was carried so far that some sound friends to our navigating interest were afraid of making a counteraction by the British government. Does this look like British influence? If Britain had any thing at heart, it was this; yet the very clamorers about British influence were the opposers of these measures. What did they do? They wished to prefer French fabrics and French bottoms to British; and this would have placed the burden of encouraging French manufactures and shipping, as a tax on the consumers and shippers in America. Does not this look like foreign influence with a vengeance? When Britain captured our vessels in 1794, the

---

[41] *The 1793–1794 war hysteria, brought on by British impressment practices and maritime depredations, was averted by the opening of Jay's negotiations.*

federalists were the only men who said, negotiate first, prepare revenue, ships, and troops, and if we cannot get justice, then fight.[41] This was Hamilton's plan, and all the federal members acted upon it. The opposers of this plan were the accusing jacobins. They said, no ships, nor troops, nor taxes; let New England fit out privateers; we will confiscate; that is our sort of resolution and patriotism. Does not this fact, so authentic and solemn, as well as recent, speak to the memory of the people that if foreign influence prevails, it is not among federalists that it prevails? There is not a naked tribe in Guinea whose spirit is baser, or has yielded with more servile cowardice to foreign influence, than the conduct of the democrats has manifested towards France; yet these are the accusers. Shame, if it had not lost its power on these men, would strike them dumb with confusion. Is there any point that any administration, even Washington's, could have yielded to Britain, so debasing as the surrender of the ships captured from France? There is no condition of disgrace below it; without being vanquished we agree to pass under the yoke.

On a review of the long series of public measures, there is none that bears the aspect of British influence. There has been no attempt even to prefer any foreign nation to America, except in favor of France. That shameless attempt, always baffled, is still renewed; and Bonaparte and his admirers still hope that we shall be French enough to enter the lists against Great Britain, to assert the absurd novelties called the modern law of nations.

Facts do not lie. They speak plainly that there has been no political power to control or prevent the measures of our government possessed or exercised by Britain. Yet this evidence will not silence or abash the impudence of the democratic slanderers of our government; credulity will still be a dupe, nor will detection spoil the game of imposture.

PHOCION IV

The Palladium, MAY 1, 1801

POLITICS — BRITISH INFLUENCE

FOREIGN INFLUENCE will be gained, if money or art can gain it, in every free state. But the suspicion of the democrats has been directed to the wrong avenue for its entrance. They suspected Washington and the chiefs among the federalists. Men who are obnoxious to clamor because they insist that principles should be heard, and passions be silent, are not the men to buy.—They are not for sale. If they have any weight or influence they owe it to their steady adherence to great public interests and sound public principles, and that is all the influence they possess. And happy is that nation where such men have so much. For the democrats are armed with lies and *Chronicles* to strip them of that. If such men would sell themselves they could not assert anything in favor of their corruption against their old principles. No, the men to corrupt with money are those who are already corrupted with a thirst for popularity, and those most obsequious and servile to all popular prejudices and passions, must be blind to all principles. The men who can, influence those who influence the politics of the nation. The men who can, whistle for a mob meeting against the treaty, who can rival Washington in the fulness of his reputation, and say to him with authority, "reject this treaty." The editors of *Chronicles* and *Auroras* are the men worth buying, for they boast of having turned one administration out and put another in. Federal newspapers may enlighten the sense and instruct the virtue of the nation, but these jacobin gazettes have the power to keep its prejudices in a state of constant irritation and at the most critical periods, setting its passions in a blaze. In democratic states, therefore, public opinion will be impetuous and sudden, and before it can have light it will have authority. Passion will legislate, and those who can kindle it will govern the country. If wise and virtuous men, like Washington, are elected, they will find, as Trinculo says in the play,[42] that they are viceroys by the Constitution; but the demagogues and the mob-leaders in the interest if not in the pay of France, are viceroys over them. Washington issued a proclamation of neutrality, but Genet levied troops, fitted out ships, and waged war, and his armed mobs paraded through the streets of Philadelphia in triumph, while the government was glad that it could enjoy a truce by leaving the laws unexecuted. Afterwards Gen. Gideon Henfield was tried by a jury picked by a democratic sheriff, and the scandalous result is remembered. There was a power devoted to France and superior to the laws. The anti-treaty mob meetings affected astonishment that Washington should dare to ratify the treaty in disregard of their authority. France, when she wants influence, is not so destitute of "diplomatic skill," as to corrupt those whom the jacobins suspect to have yielded to foreign intrigue. No, she goes directly to the demagogues or mob-leaders, or rather prime ministers or cabinet counsellors of the sovereign. There, they say, is the seat and source of power, meaning the very rabble and scum of great cities, meaning the vice and ignorance, the bankruptcy, knavery, and profligate ambition of the society—and after power is regularly committed to our rulers, there, say they, in that rabble, whose voice is the voice of God, is the sovereign power, unfettered by chains, ready for instant display. The *real* people, who consist of householders, solid farmers and mechanics, are content to exercise their right of voting for their rulers, and then they quietly leave the matter

---

[42] *One of the characters in Shakespeare's* The Tempest.

to them. Their inaction affords the opportunity for these usurpers to address a *mock* people, as ignorant, as turbulent, as much machines as the lazarroni of Naples, and to overawe and influence the laws and the legislators. Let the appeal be made to facts well remembered since 1793. Has not the turbulent ambition of the Livingstons and Dallases and Clodius (not Cicero), Pinkneys, and Honestuses, been busy to stir up the weakest minded, most destitute and vicious part of our citizens? Have not the sober citizens, the householders, the thrifty journeymen, been federal, and have not the body of the clergy, the merchants, the great mass of substantial yeomanry, been supporters of Washington and federalism?

These are facts, and to profit by them we should reason upon their nature and consequences.

Wretched is that country where its mere mob governs. The people, give them time for it, will display good sense, for they are enlightened and honest—and that will, duly formed and maturely considered, will prevail—and it ought to prevail. But no other will ought to prevail. No counterfeit sense of the people expressed in mob meetings, and dictated by the loudest bawls of the man who happens to rise upon a hogshead, ought to control or prevent the measures of the nation and its government. For then the sovereign political power would be placed not where its sense and virtue, and interest be but with its folly, its passion, and its vice. The owners of property would not have the control of it, but the ragged sanculottes, who would exercise their power as their leaders or their necessities would prompt. They would intimidate the owners of property till they ran away. Then they would confiscate it, as the forfeiture of emigration. This has happened exactly in France. The rabble were numerous, and could carry pikes. They were used as their envy and their poverty dictated, first to terrify, then to strip the rich. Is there a town in New England where the assessment of taxes was in defiance of a plain law managed in like manner?

If there is, we may see how proscription can be begun and conducted. In democracies, it is no matter who is chosen to rule. Demagogues, though not chosen, will rule. It is the prettiest thing in the world to say, the whole people have a right to rule, they have the fountain of power, and being intelligent they will exercise it with discretion, and defend it with vigilance. Easy as all this appears in theory, it is found in practice the most difficult of all things, so to model a government, that its sense and virtue, and interest shall govern, and that its vice and passion shall not. All that is vice and passion will be combined and disciplined by the mob leaders to usurp its powers.

A strong executive, with the aid of an independent judiciary, will form some check, and will struggle to maintain it. But that executive magistrate will be assailed as Washington was, with the utmost intemperance of rage, and lies, and slander, and *Chronicles* and *Auroras* will be used to make him bend to their base and corrupt schemes.

An honest and able chief magistrate, will think that he owes it to the *real* people, before described, to maintain the laws and to hold in restraint the turbulence of these usurping demagogues. Such a discharge of duty ought to endear him to the wise and good, but it will invigorate the factious to exclude him at the next election. As foreign influence will be used in democratic states to stir up the democracy, not to gain the rulers, there will be a strict alliance formed between the mob leaders and the agents of foreign corruption. They will counteract the constituted authorities, exactly as the jacobins have done for twelve years past. It is therefore, obvious, that the constitutional authorities will not be the agents of foreign influence as they are to be the victims of it. The weaker the executive the more audacious, active and pernicious will foreign influence be. The demagogues will have the true power and the laws have less or none at all. It will be a mob rule in which the exercise of sovereignty, no matter who appears to rule, will be for sale, because it will be worth more to sell than to exercise for the public good. Liberty, property and life will be insecure; the removal of wholesome restraints will produce profligacy of manners, the people will become unfit for liberty and careless of it even, while they clamor for the blood of those who are called its enemies.

The natural obstacle to foreign influence is the executive, because a faction, devoted, as faction will be, to a foreign interest, will try to govern, by stripping him of his powers. On the principle of human nature, therefore, that a president had rather govern than be governed, he will try to defend himself by calling on the *real people* to assist him and sustain his authority in doing his duty.

If, however, a magistrate comes into power by the strength of a foreign faction, he must hold his power as he gained it, by giving strength to that faction. He comes in not to be first, but second. He is only the lieutenant of a foreign government.

The weaker the executive the baser and more corrupt will be the faction opposed to it. The obstacles to the usurpation of the whole power of the office will be few, and when the popular ferment is accidentally or artificially raised, these will disappear. Then the demagogues will be able to do for a foreign government all that its views, however hostile to the general interest of the betrayed nation, may demand, and the men who owe their elevation and support to a foreign agent will not be inclined or able to stop short. Having yielded their integrity and virtue for the sake of their ambition, they cannot and will not save their patriotism. Faction is found, accordingly, the most vile in democracies.

A strong executive, by restraining the turbulence of demagogues, obliges them to moderate their views. They will not struggle for things unattainable. They will content themselves with raising clamors that will delay or modify public measures. Ambition, thus fettered, will seek power, not over the government and the laws, but by taking office under it. There selfishness will look for its rewards. The struggle is no longer so dangerous, nor is it for life. Faction sinks into party, which, is a milder form of that evil, which adheres to the very nature of popular liberty. Foreign governments will no longer attempt to buy what is not to be sold, because their partisans could not sell laws or the rejection of treaties. There will be patriotism because there will be a concentration of all the objects of respect and desire within the country, instead of the expectation of them from France.

Let the observers of human nature, the men well read in the history and principles of free commonwealths, reflect on these things, and let them decide if they can, that foreign influence could operate in America except in favor of France.

PHOCION V

———

The Palladium, MAY 8, 1801

POLITICS — BRITISH INFLUENCE

FOREIGN INFLUENCE has been shown, we think on the evidence both of facts and principles, to find auxiliaries in the very nature of democracy. From peculiar circumstances, no less decisive in their application, it will appear, that British influence can meet with nothing but impediments.

It is often insisted that a commercial connection produces political dependence. Our chief commerce, they say, is with Britain, we trade on their capitals, we buy and sell in their marts—we wear their fabrics, we adopt their fashions, their language, their habits, their laws. Even American legislation and finance is but a *facsimile* of the British. It is however in seeming resemblance that we are to meet the greatest diversity; it is in plausible mistake that we find the most radical error, and the most stubborn perverseness.

There is no doubt that Great Britain is the best customer of our principal exports—our pot and pearl ashes, our tar, pitch and turpentine, our flour and grain, our rice, tobacco, masts, spars and lumber. She supplies us with woolen, cotton and iron manufactures on better and cheaper terms than any other nation. Thus we buy and sell to advantage, in her ports. It would call for some detail to prove the preference she allows us in many important points—and the more complete the proof, the more loudly would the jacobins exclaim that the industry in furnishing it was a clear indication of British influence. It would be a digression from the principal purpose of the discussion, and therefore it is waved [*sic*].

The small politicians will seize the statements just made as if they were confessions of the substance of the point in controversy. They will say, the intimate commercial connection admitted to subsist between the two countries is a decisive proof of influence. It should be remembered that nothing is so hard to maintain, or requires so nice rules, or so much habitual good temper as intimacy.—The appearances and the mutual professions of friendship are often discredited by the keen competition in bargains. Partners are seldom long friends, and those who have much to do with each other find or make many occasions of complaint and recrimination. They begin with too much confidence and end their transactions with too much jealousy. Let it be added, that the connection in question is purely commercial: It is confined to a few hundred merchants, nine-tenths of whom live in five of our largest towns. The farmers, mechanics, and other classes have none of this intimacy—no share in the correspondence—not even a knowledge of the names of the

Dickasons and Champions who make so great a figure on the exchange of London. Besides it is proverbially true, that there is no friendship in trade.

If there is nothing more than the interested but necessary correspondence of British and American merchants to contemplate, it falls short of political influence in its nature, for it has no affinity with politics. It falls short of it also in degree, because it can affect only a thousandth or ten-thousandth part of our citizens.

If more than this customary connection is understood to subsist, if mutual friendship, confidence and regard are the fruits of drawing bills and shipping pitch and tobacco, and the correspondence of merchants is carried on as the jacobins at the south ward suppose, in the style and in the spirit of love letters—so much the worse for influence. Mutual claims and expectations, beyond the necessity or reason of their mutual dealings, would surely in the end embitter the correspondence of the merchants. Extravagant expectations would lead to disappointments—anger and hatred would ensue.

But is not all this hypothesis extremely ridiculous? The loquacious idlers at a tavern, who talk and drink themselves into a dread of the corrupting effects of our intercourse with England, and who hiccup their concern for our morals, they, perhaps, may fancy that the merchants have leisure and as great an itch as themselves for scribbling politics. The real merchants will smile at this suggestion. Their pithy letters are too much occupied with bales and packages to afford much space even for common occurrences of news. It will be said, however, that British merchants are singularly men of probity, punctuality and honor, and that few occasions of dispute arise, and many of mutual regard and good will are embraced and cherished. This will not be denied, and if the worth of any class of men is known and respected, is that to be condemned? Is it anything more than the influence of virtue, which one would think could not hurt the jacobins?

How often is the pride of America addressed because we depend on Britain for supplies of clothing, etc.? This influence we are assured still holds us in subjection—we are yet colonies. A column could be filled with like quotations of common place eloquence. But is this a source of political influence?

On the contrary admitting the fact to be true, is such dependence a tie on our affections, or an incentive to popular prejudice and clamor? Experience has settled this point. The violent hatred of Great Britain has been incessantly excited and diffused by such appeals to the pride and to the fears of our citizens. If a man is generous to his dependants, his generosity will cost him less effort than their gratitude. It is easier to do favors well than to receive them well. But if a man stands in the relation to others as a superior to inferiors, if those who are his dependants feel that they are so from necessity, there are no men in the world by whom he will be more heartily hated. The supposed dependence of America on Great Britain is of this latter sort. In the manner that it is represented for popular impression, it both humbles and alarms. It excites envy, rage and hatred. Whatever the degree of political influence may be that Britain derives from her traffic with us, it will be safe to assert, that the counter influence, arising from this appeal to the popular passions is ten times as great.

It is somewhat curious to remark, that this very topic of a slavish dependence of the citizens on those who supply their necesssaries, has been often considered for a different application. The southern planters have been told that they are scandalously in dependence on New England for hats, shoes, and nails—and their laziness and unthriftiness have been often lamented because they do not manufacture for themselves. The southern planters employ labor in their rice and their cotton fields at an exorbitant profit, and yet they inconsiderately wish that they could engross the piddling wages of our nail and shovel makers.

In the like spirit we complain of our dependence because we are not weavers and wool-combers. The wages of labor are higher in New England than in Old England, and higher in Carolina than here. Our citizens, being at liberty in the choice, very rationally prefer the most profitable employment. It has been justly remarked that the superfluity of a necessary is not a necessary. If we depend on Britain for her fabrics, she depends on us for potash and naval stores. The dependence is mutual and beneficial, it consists in exchanging what is not wanted for what is, but it is absurd to call it political or colonial. Such cant phrases are auxiliary to party but not to truth.

The number of British factors in some of the southern seaports is often mentioned as a convincing fact to denominate how much influence Britain possesses in our country. Suppose three of four hundred such persons occupied with invoices and accounts of sale, busy to court new customers and to collect old debts. Their influence certainly will not much exceed their number. But to balance it, remark the hosts of Irishmen who have nothing in the world to do, but, with the utmost condescension, to instruct Americans in the theory and practice of United Irish Liberty. Let it be asked whether Irish influence be not a full set off for British influence!

Our trade is not confined to the British dominions, though a large part of it is invited to them. The intercourse with the Baltic states, with Hamburg, Holland, France and Spain is very considerable. It will be allowed that the various influences of this intercourse will be very far from aiding the politics of England. They may be deemed powers moving in a direction opposite to that of the British commerce, and therefore must destroy or diminish its effect. It is not indeed without some repugnance, that these puerilities are noticed. But as they are gravely assumed as important, and used to inflame and deceive, there is some apology for the prolixity of the inquiry.

PHOCION VI

The Palladium, MAY 19, 1801

BRITISH INFLUENCE

IT IS NOT their only reason, but it is one of very great efficacy with the politicians of the Virginia school, for exciting and diffusing an aversion to the commercial system, that our commerce is carried on by the help of British capital, and that, as the trade increases, the mass of debt due to British merchants goes on augmenting. Hence they assure us that our trade with England is a fruitful source both of corruption and dependence. Nay, these apostles from the race-ground and the cock-pit tremble for our republican morals, so much exposed to the contagion of our intercourse with the manners and fashions, the books and institutions of a corrupted monarchy. The word monarchy is of course a substitute for argument, and its overmatch; many hundreds will condemn the task, as equally bold and mischievous, of the writer who shall presume to think that we may deal with the subject of a king, and make estates, without making a set of king, lords, and bishops for ourselves.

There is a previous question: Are we more likely to become, from observation, monarchy-men, than the citizens of London are to adopt the maxims of our democracies? Perhaps it will appear that our danger is not so great as theirs. Democracy, by indulging the fervors of the popular spirit, is more disposed to imbibe a zeal for proselytism. The everlasting bustle of our elections, the endless disputations and harangues of demagogues, keep our spirits half the time smoking and ready to kindle, and the other half in a blaze. Zeal is ever contagious, and accordingly the only political propagandists now in the world are the democrats. The monarchists have less to do in the concerns of their government, and talk and wrangle less about it. The spirit of subordination they have; that of proselytism they have not. When life, liberty, and property are protected, they are contented, although their system should appear to speculatists inferior in its theory to the best of all possible governments. Some men among us, and some of our scribbling countrymen abroad, have been modest and wise enough to imagine that all the kings and ministers in Europe were watching our republican administration with eyes of fear and jealousy. The jacobin newspapers have assured us that all kings sleep unquietly, and are visited with horrid dreams, because we are republicans. In 1794, "the Solomons in council" then advised us to cling to sister France, as the only power able, and, being a republic, willing to save us from a royal coalition. The fact is, foreign statesmen have not regarded America as much as they ought. We can see more evident marks of their neglect than their dread of us.

But the other part of this commonplace threadbare proof of the preponderance of British influence remains to be considered. We employ British capitals, and therefore, as the borrower is servant to the lender, they say we are but passive instruments in the hands of our creditors. There is no country where capital is employed to so manifest and lasting advantage as in the United States, because there is none where the objects of employment so much exceed the amount of capital to be employed. When we give five or six per cent, for British capital, and employ it at eight, ten, or in some branches of trade at twenty, or when it is occupied in clearing a wilderness almost boundless, and filling it with houses and settlers, the augmentation of our wealth is obvious. The real estate of the nation, that which must belong to posterity, is also prodigiously increased. Every year some hundred thousand acres of new cleared land are added to the pasturage and wheat fields. Yet these advantages, great as they are, would be too dearly purchased if Great Britain derived a political influence over our government from the operations of her wealthy capitalists. It is not easy to see how she obtains a control over our public measures from her subjects permitting our merchants, and speculators, and landjobbers to acquire a control over their wealth. Of all men the jacobins ought to abstain from saying that this is the influence of Britain over our government. They avow principles in regard to public faith and the rights of British creditors that manifestly place British property, intrusted to the safe-keeping of our laws, at the mercy of a confiscating majority of Congress, if, to the scandal of America, such a majority should be there. British capital deposited in Algiers would be considered as a pledge held by the Dey, liable to forfeiture in case the British government should give him occasion of offence. With ideas so honorable to America, principles so truly Algerine that they would be nets to catch unwary Englishmen, it is truly astonishing that the jacobins should mistake so grossly as to call this a source of British influence. One of their objections to the treaty was, that it stipulates security to this booty, and restrains Congress from privateering ashore and before a declaration of war.

The British creditor who claims his debt against a citizen, is dependent on the justice of our laws. All the influence that he or his government can desire in the case is just payment; if more is demanded, surely our juries will be protectors of the rights of the debtor. Any honest American will blush if it is suggested that British influence will be necessary to prevent the denial of justice.

This brings us to consider the supposed influence arising from the claims of British creditors. This is a question to be tested by experience. If political power has followed British debts, then the greatest display and most flagrant abuse of that power is to be expected in the states where there is the largest arrear of debt. Yet in Virginia, which owes fifty times as much as Connecticut, the British influence has never been great enough to obtain payment, while Connecticut allows an Englishman to exact it without reluctance or impediment. So far is Virginia from having been enslaved by the British creditors, that her state laws have been framed and administered so as to exclude lands, and I believe in effect, if not expressly, negroes, from the operation of process. A man might be a debtor there thousands of pounds more than his estate would discharge, and live a life of ease and luxury, defying British creditors and cursing British influence, and go to Congress a patriot fiercer than a dragon for liberty and equal rights. Who does not know that many of the states were in the hands of debtors, who made laws to keep off creditors? Who is ignorant that the Constitution contains an article to restrain such laws, and that this article soured into fermentation the leaven of antifederalism at first, and of jacobinism since? The great planters could not endure it, that equal justice should strip them of the preëminence that they derived from their lands, and that the laws, made for their own convenience, had so long secured to them. So far have British debts been from creating British influence, that they have given rise to the most rancorous hatred. Happy will it be if the Northern people are not in the end made victims of that hatred; if a system of irritation should not be cunningly devised and blindly adopted, that New England may be stripped of its earnings by captures, and that Virginia debts may be wiped off by an unnecessary British war.

PHOCION VII

The Palladium, MAY 26, 1801

BRITISH INFLUENCE

THE FIRST SETTLERS of the British Northern colonies were Englishmen. Most new settlements are first peopled by the outcasts and scum of the mother country; but New England can boast that its ancestors were Englishmen, which, I confess, I consider as matter of boasting, and that they were the best of Englishmen. They were serious, devout Christians, of pure, exemplary morals, zealous lovers of liberty, well educated, and men of substantial property. There was never a new colony formed of better materials; never was one more carefully founded on plan and system, and no plan or system has discovered more foresight, or been crowned with more splendid success. Our forefathers immediately displayed a zeal and watchfulness, that the new society should be of the best sort, rather than of the largest size. Instead of building a Babel of wild Irish, Germans, and outlaws of all nations, such as would be suitable for a McKean to govern, and such as would have preferred his government, they excluded not only foreigners, but immoral persons, from political power, and even from inhabitancy. This has been called meanness and narrowness of spirit. New England, however, owes its schools, colleges, towns, and parishes, its close population, its learned clergy, much of its light and knowledge, its arts

295

and commerce, and spirit of enterprise, to this early wisdom of our ancestors. Even its growth and prosperity, though later, will not ultimately prove less than if it had been settled on what many call a liberal plan.

In consequence of our extraction and the institutions of our ever to be remembered ancestors, New England has a distinct and well-defined national character, the only part of the United States that has yet any pretensions to it. There are many truly enlightened citizens in the other states, who have tried to introduce into them the schools, town divisions, and other institutions of New England. But if they could do it, these institutions would be novelties, whose authority would be for an age or two feeble and limited, in comparison of old habits and institutions. Besides, most of the southern men of sense have prejudices in respect to the establishment of a learned clergy, and obliging every small district to support a minister. Without this precious security for the support of good morals and true religion, the attempt will be vain to adopt the laws and institutions of our ancestors.

Nay, popular prejudices against these institutions are fixed, and have been cherished in most of the Southern states. They, perhaps sincerely, consider these as burdensome and tyrannical restraints, and, without very well knowing what they are, unite in disclaiming them as English, and remnants of bigotry. Hence the laws and customs of England are so much represented in Virginia as inconsistent with republicanism, that they have voted to instruct their members in Congress to procure their formal abolition. Hence it is, that they are stated to be the badges and the instruments of British influence. They say, an Englishman from the midland counties, suddenly transplanted into New England, would scarcely know he was not in his own country; he would hear the same language, he would observe the same manners. This close affinity and resemblance, they say, is the occasion of a partiality for England that is dangerous to our republicanism.

Trite observations of this kind make impression, on the twofold account, that they are plausible, and that they are so loose and indefinite that they are not precisely understood. It seems to be very possible that we should reverence the English common law, and the customs and institutions we derive from our English ancestors, without loving or trusting Lord North, or William Pitt, or any other minister of the British government. This distinction was made very exactly in the year 1775, when hostilities began. The New England states are closely allied in affection, as well as by resemblance of character and manners; yet it has never been the case, that Massachusetts was able to exercise an inconvenient influence over the affairs of Connecticut. It is, perhaps, to be lamented, that the good sense and good order of Connecticut, in its elections, have not had influence enough to procure the adoption of their laws by their neighbors.

Thus it seems that fact stands, as it often does, in opposition to plausible theory.

We adopt the rules of justice from Great Britain, and as long as we are allowed to enjoy good order, we shall desire to provide for the administration of justice, and we shall continue to think it a precious advantage, that we can adopt so many important rules and principles to regulate its distribution, after England has tried them, and proved that they will answer. Surely this is a different thing from political influence. As well might it be said, that by copying their books, or even imitating their new invented labor-saving machines, we augment their influence.

Next to the power of religion, a strict administration of justice is the best security of morals. Foreign influence will not greatly prevail, as long as morals remain uncorrupted. The British common law is, therefore, one of the bulwarks against that corruption of manners, which will invite foreign influence, in spite of all the frothy harangues that will ascribe it to the wrong causes. A people thoroughly licentious and corrupt, (and democracy will make them such,) will be betrayed, and foreign states will reward demagogues for managing their passions to mislead them. It is by practising on their hopes and fears, that such men gain an influence over the people, and after they have gained, they have it for sale.

But, for the very reason that we nearly resemble the English, it will be peculiarly difficult to acquire that popular influence. Let this be examined.

Nothing is so odious or offensive as comparisons. When we find that we are compared with others, we are uneasy and displeased with the result of the comparison, unless we find that the preference is assigned to ourselves. We consider those as our enemies who thus degrade us, and we revenge ourselves by noting the defects of their judgment and the malignity of their dispositions, who have thus deeply wounded our self-love. Comparisons that are thus frequently made, render this angry spirit rancorous and habitual. But comparisons of this kind are not made, unless with persons who pretty nearly resemble us. It is believed to be hard for two beauties to be friends. Our pride is never hurt by our being compared with those who are very unlike us, and even if the superiority is assigned to the other party, the decision is rendered inoffensive by the manifest dissimilarity of the subjects of the comparison. In like manner, we know that Americans resemble Frenchmen so little, that there is no ground for invidious comparison; but Englishmen we are like, and the painful question to national pride is, which nation is superior. Partial as we are and ought to be to the American nation, we cannot despise the English nation, we will not prefer them, all that is left is to hate them. I ask with emphasis, is not this done? Is not the pride of Great

Britain the theme of popular irritation? Is not their power held up as a bugbear? Is not this fear an instrument to work upon the passions of our citizens? and which of our demagogues could hold his authority without using it? We are too much like the English to love them, because we love ourselves better, and we hate all comparisons that mortify our self-love.

The fact is, the hatred of England is excessive, and, as popular passions are the agents of our political good or evil, exposes our government to the extreme hazard of confusion and French fraternity, and our peace to the shock of a British war.

THE REPUBLICAN IV

Boston Gazette, AUGUST 6, 1804
Reprinted from the *Repertory*

> *The progress of our affairs is in conformity with the fixed laws of our nature, and the known course of Republics. Our wisdom made a government and committed it to our virtue to keep, but our passions have engrossed it, and they have armed our vices to maintain their usurpation.*

IT HAS BEEN remarked of the factions which have succeeded each other in France, that every one on coming into power, though itself red with murder, has begun its career by denouncing the crimes of its immediate predecessor. This practice, like everything that is French, has been adopted by the jacobins who now rule the United States. It is not strange, therefore, that a pamphlet, the joint work of the heads of the party in Massachusetts, or at least the fruits of their caucus, should be chiefly occupied in calumniating the

Federalists, and the administration of Washington and Adams. By attending to the nature of the charges, and the proofs alleged, we shall be able to see whether the accusers really believe them to be well grounded; or whether they made them merely to gull the stupidity of the multitude. This inquiry will not undeceive the multitude, but it will oblige the deceivers in future to look for reputation only to their dupes, and to wear, to their lives end, the execration and contempt of the virtuous and wise.

It is impossible to withhold, or to measure that contempt for the author of the pamphlet, when we note his specious sophistry in perverting truth, and the vulgar malevolence of his falsehoods.

There is a sort of talent which a man of sound sense can neither exercise nor respect—the pettifogging art of twisting the truth, and telling a lie with solemnity and method. It has been sometimes called casuistry, and sometimes chicane. It is a compound of that confusion or weakness of mind that cannot discern the truth, and of that baseness that eludes or defies its authority. In arguing it makes a man a sophist, in dealing a knave—it makes him, if in politics, prefer popularity because it is within his reach and disregard reputation, because it is beyond it. No really great man is a quibbler or a chicanist—this art, which is the infirmity of the mind, is the strength of a demagogue.

Let any reader of plain sense—let any fair minded farmer read attentively the pamphlet of "anonymous slander," as Mr. Bacon and Mr. Bidwell had the pleasure to hear it called in the Senate, and he will be forced to apply these remarks to the writer of that base publication.

This "anonymous slanderer" undertakes to shew the difference between the principles of the democrats, whom he foolishly calls republicans, and the federalists. He first affirms it as a basis for his distinction of party principles, that the democrats are for having the will of the people prevail. "This," he says, "is the true theory of our government, in which, as the venerable Samuel Adams well observed, the people have the whole sovereignty."

Now let Mr. Bacon and Mr. Bidwell determine for us, whether even Old South ever made a more insipid observation. Was this observation, pray, original with Samuel Adams? did nobody ever say so good a thing before? and is it, again, be it demanded, peculiar to his politics? When he was in power, and when Shays's insurrection was to be quelled, he was as ready to use force, and to shed blood, as any body. This is not said by way of reproach, for we confess it is right and lawful to resort to force in defence of our Constitution and laws. But it is proper to remind these poor spirited pamphlet makers, that once Samuel Adams carried this notion of government as high as any federalist has ever done.

But let me return to the main subject. Is the principle, that from the people is derived the sovereignty of the government, peculiar to the Democrats? If the "anonymous slanderer" asserts this, he will be disregarded with every man of any sense among his own associates. It is notorious that the Federalists are now, and ever have been Republicans, that they have argued, written and struggled hard to make a republican system successful, and Mr. Jefferson took it from their hands, in the face of the nation and the world, despairing that it was in the full tide of successful experiment. Washington's last address to the people is the solemn creed of federalists, which they approve in their hearts, which they have read, admired, printed and diffused as extensively as possible, and which they devoutly pray may be admitted by every honest citizen to his heart and affections. Would to heaven every voter would make conscience of it to give his suffrage for no candidate who was not sincere and hearty in his approbation of the principles, and all the principles of

301

that excellent address justly called a legacy to our nation. Let General Hull say as much—let Mr. Bidwell, if he can, and I have no ordinary opinion of what this last gentleman can say. He will not say it—for if that address were to govern the votes of the electors, all jacobinism, if not all democracy, would be banished from our legislatures.

Notorious as these facts are, this base pamphleteer has pretended to decide for fair and honorable men, what their inmost thoughts and wishes are—and to decide too against the evidence not merely of their language, but of their whole lives. "To render the senate and executive independent and irresponsible," that is to have a monarchy, he says "is the favorite object of the leaders" of the Federalists. This is false, he knows it is false, and he is called upon to vouch a tittle of proof in support of his assertion. He is challenged to support this foul charge. This surely he can do, when he says this system, (monarchy) "has many open advocates." I am a Federalist, I have known those of the party who have been the most distinguished; and therefore the most calumniated, not a man of them, in the hour of select company, or of private confidence, avows this system, but much less avows it openly to such base "anonymous slanderers" as this pamphleteer. Not a man of sense believes that a monarchy would answer here, not a man, worth a thousand dollars, who would expose them to the terrible shock of a monarchical revolution, still less would any father venture the destinies of his children to such scenes of blood and devastation as the establishment of an American first consul, or Emperor of Louisiana, would introduce, and this the jacobins are in train to establish. Again and again be it said the writer of the pamphlet is a base slanderer. That which he pretends is openly avowed, was never avowed at all.

Judge, then, men of Berkshire, is this creeping prevaricating slanderer, worthy of your votes, or your confidence? Remember April.

THE REPUBLICAN V

Boston Gazette, AUGUST 9, 1804
Reprinted from the *Repertory*

> *The progress of our affairs is in conformity with the fixed laws of our nature, and the known course of Republics. Our wisdom made a government and committed it to our virtue to keep, but our passions have engrossed it, and they have armed our vices to maintain their usurpation.*

EUROPEANS, who think it impossible that the American people should ever cease to reverence the memory of Washington, or that they should continue to reverence his memory, and yet depart from his wise and noble maxims of policy, are ready to wonder; that the friends of Washington, the disciples of his school, the supporters of his principles and counsels should be ignominiously driven from power by the votes of that same people. The wonder rises still higher when they find the writer of the letter to Mazzei, in which Washington is grossly, basely and virulently calumniated, the writer of the letter to the Berkeley Farmer, the writer of the letter to the infamous Tom Paine, whom all Europe despises and abhors, the man who takes that loathsome reptile to his friendship and bosom, who hired Callender to abuse Washington and his administration—the man who gave Philip Freneau a salary for his abominable *National Gazette*, the man, in short, who hated Washington *and* the Constitution, and who has made haste to persecute and displace every officer who was their friend—that man is Washington's successor.

If the world should consider the history of American events, and the causes that produced them, worth inquiring into, they will be anxious, and finally they will be successful in the search of the circumstances that will clear up so great a mystery. Time is indeed the friend of truth, but a friend out of season.

We have told all the world that our people have so much virtue, and so much sense and information, that the first step of Europeans in their inquiry will be to lay out of the case almost every thing that is in it, and belongs to it, and to assume it as a thing impossible that so wise a people should be either ill disposed or deluded. They will not advert at first to the prejudice that multiplies dupes, or to the factious profligacy that has lent the power of necromancy to deceivers. In Europe, they would say, we know very well it is the easiest thing in the world to flatter and inflame the rabble, and if the desperadoes who do it there were let alone for a week, no man's house would escape pillage, no honest man would sleep in his bed. But in America things are on a different footing. The sense and information of the citizens arm them against the arts of faction. As all live in abundance and liberty is not to be fought for, as the people well know they cannot have more than all, there is no possibility of faction, there can be no discontents, no risings against government, for the people will not rise against the [. . .], the laws are their will, and surely the people will not fly in the face of that, nor murmur.

Those opinions are too dear to our vanity, and are supported in Europe by the love of the marvellous, and the spirit of revolution, too strongly to fall immediately into discredit, though they are as nonsensical as they are fallacious; though we have had three rebellions in seventeen years, though we have been once, while the choice of president was pending, nearly without an elected magistracy, and though since the repeal of the Judiciary [Act] and the tampering of amendments we are nearly without a Constitution.

Is it not time then, that our nation should dismount its

vanity from riding any longer the high horse, and admit, mortifying as it may be, that we are not as a people, quite celestial, but very much like other nations, who are made up of men and women, and these men and women, compounded of the same sort of ingredients, the same passion, prejudice, vice and folly that have made some of the nations of Europe wretched in their chains, and still more wretched when they have knocked them off.

If after having quitted our sphere, and pushed into the skies, we return again to our sphere, and pursue the inquiry into our errors, precisely as if we were mortal men, who are liable to them, we shall not find it difficult to develop the causes that have shifted power from federal to jacobin hands. Among these causes we ought to reckon that very delusion of our national vanity. Our people have been fed with praise till it has become a part of their diet. The relish for flattery is one of their appetites—and, of course, the candidate for an election, who did not fall down and worship the idol power and excellence of the people, was doomed to be cast into the furnace. This work of flattery, naturally fell to the jacobin seekers of office. They felt no scruples or qualms, none of that honest pride which will no more offer adulation than endure insult. Besides, the Federalists, who had the government to administer, the laws to enact, the taxes to raise, the courts to establish, had no flattering work to do. It was impossible for those to flatter, whose business it was to restrain. They did not want to raise, and could not employ the passions of the people. It was their part to satisfy their consciences and understandings that what seemed strange, was nevertheless right—that what was irksome, was salutary and necessary.—Thus it is evident the passions of the people and their prejudices, were the armoury of the jacobins and not of the Federalists.

And is it strange, that when one party addresses the understanding, which often refuses its attention, and is always slow in its help, and the other appeals to the popular passions, which are gunpowder, and throws fire brands, that an explosion has happened—is it strange that thousands and tens of thousands of well disposed but credulous citizens, have been inflamed to rage and dread and hatred of the Washington men and measures, when, for ten years past, incendiary presses have garbled and distorted all the evidence that has reached them, and on which they have formed their political opinions. Would it be thought strange, that an honest and capable jury of twelve men, should bring in a verdict against law and right, when all the witnesses who offer their testimony are perjured?

That this is in fact the case, let it be repeated, that the back parts of Pennsylvania, prior to the whiskey insurrection, scarcely read an article concerning the federal government that did not come from Freneau's *National Gazette*. Ought not a North Carolinian or Georgian to detest the Federal system of policy, who forms all his notions of that system on the information of Duane or Matthew Lyon? Yet these base lying wretches, are the oracles, who dictate politics to a large part—it is confessed, the most ignorant part of our nation. The voice of the people, we are told, is the voice of God. Without inquiring into the folly and blasphemy of this maxim, let it be considered, that this voice is first pronounced by Lyon or Cheetham or Duane, and the echo only by the poor alien ridden dupes, who read and believe their lies.

When, therefore, we hear it said exultingly, the people are sovereign over the government, and their prejudices, we see, are sovereign over them, are we not obliged to confess that we live under a monarchy, rather than a republic? and that Duane and Cheetham and those who inflame and manage those prejudices, are our kings? Surely of all conditions of servitude, ours is the lowest, when the tyrants whom we see elevated above our control, are still more mean than terrible, and are scarcely to be raised to a level with our contempt.

THE REPUBLICAN IX

Boston Gazette, AUGUST 27, 1804
Reprinted from the *Repertory*

*The progress of our affairs is in conformity with the
fixed laws of our nature, and the known course of
Republics. Our wisdom made a government and
committed it to our virtue to keep, but our passions
have engrossed it, and they have armed our vices
to maintain their usurpation.*

IT MAY TIRE and probably will disgust the reader to pursue
the political reflections we have begun to unfold. It may be,
however, useful, and therefore we beg his patience.

It will not be pretended that there is no difference between
the federal and democratic creeds. It is for Mr. Jefferson,
when he would enlighten the multitude, to tell us that we
are all federalists, all republicans. Federalists are republicans, but they are not jacobins or democrats, as he would
be understood.

It is, for these reasons, already assumed, no easy task to
state the distinctions of parties with desirable precision.—
But the creed of democracy, it may be safely asserted,
consists chiefly in this: that the will of the people right or
wrong, ought to prevail, and therefore they consider the
business done, and it will prevail.

Or, they maintain, that the uncontrolled power, is liberty,
and in this way that the public will does prevail. They think
that executives and senates and judges and the solemn
compacts of the Constitution, are only forms and expedients
which the unresponsible, arbitrary, Heaven inspired sovereign, the people, has adopted for convenience, not checks
or restraints or obligations that he has taken upon himself.

Both these opinions are apparently adopted in the pamphlets of "anonymous slander," and they are both so palpably and ridiculously false, that the honorable libeller will no doubt disown them. What is written is written, and will remain to fix the stigma on the author that is merited by his principles, so worthy of Paris, and so like it.

Admitting to any extent that a Democrat will ask, his favorite principle, that the will of the people ought to prevail, still we beg leave to ask how, by what means, by what arrangement of the powers of government is the will of the people to be made to prevail? Is it by writing a pamphlet to prove that it ought, and falsely insinuating that the federalists are not willing it should, that this great work is to be achieved? Or is the solution of this problem, which Lycurgus, Solon, Plato and Aristotle, which Cicero and Locke could not solve, to be picked by miracle out of a chest of counterfeiter's tools?[43]

Let it be supposed that Mr. Gallatin's meeting at Cannonsburg had voted all the public magistracies down—and they had accordingly deposed themselves so that no form of government remained. Surely then the people would be equally free as the Indians. Pray how long, honorable sir, do you think their will would prevail? Would not Gallatin's meeting reassemble, and if any State attempted to restore the authority of the laws, would they not fulminate death and slaughter against the aristocracy of funding systems and senates, and tax compelling courts? What would hinder the whisky men from governing the Union, but an association to counteract their associations, and would not the nation be split into [. . .] or great factions, called confederacies, as [. . .] was thirty years ago in the time of the famous confederacy of Bar? Civil war would ensue, and the will of

---

[43] *It is a fact that copies of the pamphlet so often mentioned in this essay were found among the papers and implements seized in the possession of the counterfeiters lately arrested.*

the people would certainly prevail on the side of the conqueror, for he would call his will the people's will, as Bonaparte does. Suppose the citizens actually assembled in a plain to frame a government, all could not speak, all could not hear if they did. A multitude are supposed to have a will, but that will is never formed by deliberating. A multitude cannot deliberate—they can only act and they can act only according to the impulses they receive from their leaders, and those impulses are incapable to and unwilling to preserve, and only prompt to destroy. Chance may often decide who those leaders shall be. The man who happens on this plan to mount on a hogshead, or be a head taller, or to have a louder voice than the rest, may be a leader. But it is probable that as a mere multitude can begin no impulse, but necessarily yields to every strong one, the most audacious and violent of the assembly would take the lead. That moment all equality ends. That moment the will of the leaders becomes or passes for the will of the multitude. An oligarchy or committee, or directory begins, and the first consul or emperor ends the farce.

The federalists have ever been aware of this tragical and inevitable fate of democracy. To keep the people from being devoured by demagogues, who spring to being, they would so distribute the powers of the society, that the portion which the people retain in their own hands shall be sufficient for self defense. By electing the government and being necessary agents of its powers to carry the laws into effect, as jurors, etc., they render it difficult for them ever to encroach upon them, or if they do, they must spend so long time to prepare and give much warning, of their tyrannical design, so that it may be defeated by the election of better men. And if the people will choose none but good men friendly to order and law, whose private lives bear testimony to their public merit, this system might build such a government as would prove the best champion of the public liberty. But if the people can be deluded to reject such worthy men, and to elect atheists and knaves in their place, then the public liberty must die. What shall save the ark from profanation when the Levites themselves abandon or betray their trust.

It is to make liberty safe and perpetual, to make it an inheritance for posterity, that the federalists have wished to restrain us from licentiousness, and to guard it from profanation. The democrats think on the contrary, that without excess there is no liberty; if anything is restrained or dammed, nothing is granted. They would have us like the tempestuous sea, without sources, without bottom, treachery in its calms and destruction in its tempests.

VIII.
ATTACKING THE
REPUBLICANS

═══

FALKLAND II

────

The Palladium, FEBRUARY 6, 1801

POLITICS:

(Continued from our last)

As TO the violent dispositions of the jacobins and anarchists, there can be no doubt. Let us examine the grounds of their hopes, and see whether they are rested on as stable a foundation as they have imagined.

They will act at first, and until they have brought things into the confusion that democrats ever do, and, perhaps, as the first orderly step toward confusion, all Virginia, Kentucky, and Pennsylvania have carried their destroying amendments, they will act according to the forms of the Constitution. The legal powers of a president are not too great, and unless a majority in Congress should co-operate in the abuse of them, we have more to apprehend immediately from their neglect. The executive department will probably be suffered to droop in imbecility, and to struggle with embarrassments. The men who have hitherto opposed order, have not understood nor respected its principles, and it is expected they will more frequently obstruct than enforce them. The Secretary of the Treasury will be treated as a head clerk—his reports and plans will not be asked for nor tolerated—much less adopted. No department of power will be allowed to be safe except that of the House of Representatives—nor that in opposition to a rabble. What if the pipe should get choked up, through which the funding system is nourished, what is that to the people?

If merely by neglect, the work of destruction, though sure, should appear to be too slow, and they should be impatient to hasten it by projects of innovation, there must be a majority in Congress. At present, the Senate of the United States is disposed to stand as a barrier against the democratic flood, the very office for which it was erected. Accordingly, we see that the imported patriots of Pennsylvania are already armed to assail the Senate of that State, as a useless and dangerous branch of government. The like attempt will be made against the Senate of the United States. Indeed Virginia proposed, some years ago, so to amend that branch that it should become in future a tool in the hands of faction, not a defense against it. All barriers against the licentiousness of democracy will be called usurpations on the *people*—meaning always the vile, and ignorant, and needy, and be rendered odious in order to being broken down. Demagogues found their influence on the popular passions—they are certainly sincere, therefore, when they execrate senates and courts, and Sedition Laws, and all other impediments to the current of those passions. They pretend to be the friends of liberty, but all demagogues are the rivals and the enemies of free government.

The most conspicuous of the new men are demagogues. New York and Pennsylvania were subjected to such influence, and Virginia was trained and disciplined according to its tactics. Hence their victory.

The leading men of the ruling party will certainly endeavor to support and exercise their power in the way that they gained it, by soothing the meanest of the vulgar prejudices, and exciting and assuming the direction of their passions. Things that are to be destroyed must be made unpopular, and whatever is popular in Virginia must be attempted. What is popular then? Is credit—is finance—is impost or excise, or the carriage tax, or the stamp act, or the compulsory payment of debts, is trade, and especially trade with the British dominions, popular among those lazy fuedal [*sic*] barons? But regulations and restrictions on the commerce of other states, projects and visionary schemes to make France rich and to starve British manufactures, projects of finance to pay debts by discrimination, pretending to give to original holders what we do not owe, and denying to purchasing holders what we do. Projects to administer the government without departments, without banks, and without compulsion, have been popular, and we are to expect they will be resumed. Impracticable theories will be recommended, and if possible established by law, because they are not British, and because they *seem* to be philosophy.

It is very much to be apprehended that the next House of Representatives in Congress will be hurried away by a democratic impulse. If the majority should be great, they will feel incited to execute the most extravagant of their plans, for which they have long sought the opportunity, conscious that this may not last long, and that they may never enjoy another. What will they do? is the question. It has been already hinted, as one equally momentous, what will they not neglect to do? Waving [*sic*] that consideration, however, for the present, it is material to inquire into the state of their inclinations and of their power; in other words, what they will desire, and what they will be able to do.

They will desire to reduce their darling theories to practice. There is in the democratic sect, which will be the prevailing one, a fanaticism, that disdains argument, and is mad with zeal to make converts; a presumption, that disdains experience; and is blind to difficulties. Every thorough democrat, who is perfect by book, scorns to tread any but "the high pr[iory] road." The people are deemed to be perfect in their intelligence, and all rulers corrupted by their power. The will or the caprice, or, if that could be, the vice of the people, whether regularly and distinctly known, or only guessed at, is a law paramount to all laws, not excepting those of public faith and honor, of God and virtue. Hence the instructions of a representative bind him more than the constitution or his oath, his duty or conscience. With all democrats, the state of nature is still assumed as existing, each man being a sovereign invested with power which he has delegated to his representative in Congress as his ambassador, but no man is a subject even of the laws. The very name subject stinks of slavery, and is disdainfully disclaimed in the gazettes of the democrats.

There is no temperate man of sense, who will take the trouble to examine these gazettes for the last twelve years, who will say, that any sensible or safe system of administration could be extracted from them. He will pronounce with decision, that their principles are absolutely chimerical and impracticable. It is observable that the machine of our government has moved with a great deal of friction, and a very feeble and intermitting momentum. Sensible men have seriously dreaded that it would stop or drop to pieces. The government has not been obeyed in the back country: It has not dared to enforce obedience nor to punish rebellion. Yet the democrats have professed unfeignedly to fear this nerveless government, that could not stand up, but was ever to be held up, as a necromancer whose magic would bind the people in chains of slavery; a giant whose colossal tread would crush them into the earth. Accordingly, for twelve years there is no measure, now a law, that they did not obstruct in its passage; and not one of any importance, that is a law, that they originated. Mr. Madison's abortive commercial resolutions were projected and urged against the opinion of every well-informed merchant in the United States. There is no other plan or system that has even been so much as proposed by the democratic party in Congress. It has been their sufficient employment to *oppose* all business but to do none. It has even been avowed as a salutary principle of duty thus to check the proneness of our government to extremes, unfavourable to the liberty of the people. That our farmers may at once comprehend the usefulness and good sense of this democratic principle of opposing, let them apply a like rule in their own business. Instead of trying to make it easier to do, what would they think of schemes to make it harder. What would they say, if while two of their laborers were getting a load of hay, a third should *think it his duty* to pitch it off? Would they like to have their axle-trees made square or eight sided, in order that the wagon wheels might not turn so fast, and perhaps not turn at all? For it is not the fault of this party that the wheels of the government have not stood still.

In a word, the fundamental principle of the democratic system is to consider *their own power* as liberty, and all other power, even that ordained by the constitution, as despotism.

Accordingly, we may expect that they will feel neither affection nor reverence for the Senate nor the departments, nor even for their democratic president, except as the head of their party, but not as president. They will profess to obey the popular prejudices and passions, and rely on their co-operation to sustain their power. Of course, it will be a system of demagogy. Let it be repeated, the power gained

315

by flattering the prejudices of the whisky, the treaty, the French, the house tax and the stamp act and sedition-act mobs and mob-meetings, must be supported as it was obtained. It is hostile to law, order, property and government, in feeling, principle, tendency and object.

This is the general description of the party. The detail of the measures that they will probably pursue, is only a matter of conjecture. But the most fearful conjecture is corroborated by the analogy of the party here with the principles and examples of France. If they should exercise power, now they are in, with the same spirit that they have opposed while they were out, revolution and confusion have no terrors that would deter, no extremes that would stop them. Is there one principal head of legislation on which their ideas have been temperate, rational and salutary? On the contrary, is there one on which they have not avowed and urged the wildest and most disorganizing theories of their own, and like objections to the systems devised by others? Banks, credit, finance, revenue, commerce, manufactures, fisheries, army and navy, are subjects that have afforded so many classes of absurdities. *Within* they would restore chaos by the jumble of committees, instead of the heads of departments:—*Without*, they would court the curse of a French alliance, while they inconsistently affect to separate America from Europe and its politics. They have tried on all momentous questions to interpret the Constitution to mean nothing, and to pervert it with amendments that would make it mean less—and worse.

What then are we to expect from such men but the execution of their systems? But will they be able to do it?

There will be impediments. Let us examine their nature. It is not the nature of democracy to stop short of extremes, and least of all in the delirium of newly acquired power. The Senate of the United States will be truly republican, and a barrier against licentiousness. Such will be its disposition.

But its firmness will much depend on the energy of the true federal republicans dispersed through the nation. We are to expect every method of intimidation will be used by the jacobins, as in Pennsylvania, to bend the Senate from virtue. Finding, as they will find, that these men will not change their principles, they will raise a clamor in all the federal States to change the men. This, however, will take time that is precious, because it is short—for such the reign of democracy will be. In Massachusetts we have had experience of the noble firmness of our Senate when they saved the state from Shays, perhaps the union from civil war and confusion.

The Judiciary is another rampart against the foes of all right. There is no question of the virtue of the judges. But when jacobin juries have to determine on great contested cases, we have seen enough to make us dread their perversion of the law. The best things, when misapplied, are the worst. Jacobin verdicts for damages might prove proscriptions and confiscations to the federalists.

There will be also a spirited and able minority in Congress, who will expose the bad principles and tendencies of the democratic measures. There public opinion will discern a centre of light and heat. The old republican principles, the wise and tried measures and institutions of the federal administrations, will there have skillful advocates and bold champions. It cannot be that such champions will not be strongly reinforced from the sound and enlightened part of the public. New England is not democratic, and many who now think the system of the party delightful in prospect, will abhor it in the trial. It cannot be tried without shaking New England to its centre. All its interests and systems and even its institutions, political and religious, are such as are detested by the democrats, because they are the strong entrenchments of an enemy. Expect then to see them often mined and at last battered in breach.

THE REPUBLICAN III

Boston Gazette, AUGUST 2, 1804
Reprinted from the *Repertory*

IN EVERY free state, the care of watching over the public liberty, which in some measure is the right of all, and the duty of many, will be the business of very few. The multitude will listen with a curious but vacant levity to political events, as they pass, and allow to them the same momentary interest, and short remembrance, that are claimed by the most trivial topics of the weekly news. What is intended for their instruction, and should be their warning, is made their amusement, and hastens into oblivion with the years beyond the flood.

Hence it will happen, that the whole host, and a host they are, of careless readers, will consider the dangers which have been pointed out as chimerical, as visions that haunt a sick imagination. They will persist in considering our political liberty as a state of sinless perfection, from which we cannot fall—that we are capable of folly; but [not] that it is in the power of folly to undo us. How, they will ask, should liberty, so amiable, so beneficent, so divine, have enemies, and how should these enemies alienate from her cause the hearts of her votaries?

See then how all this has been done.

No sooner has the new Constitution gone into operation, than every anti-federal press hissed like a serpent's hole, with the work of slander. Neither the Constitution, nor Washington himself, not an act of Congress, not a federal officer or member escaped detraction. The *National Gazette* was set up by Philip Freneau, then a clerk under Mr. Jefferson, with an extra salary for doing nothing as a clerk;

and which enabled him, for a time, to buy and blot paper with lies, that had a prodigious currency in the back woods of Pennsylvania, Virginia, and North Carolina. No other paper was read in those extensive Districts, and truly if those poor whisky men really believed the administration of the government to be as bad as all they knew or read about its measures represented it, no wonder it produced nothing but curses and combination, to oppose the excise, and to cut off from the comforts of life, all who were disposed to give it effect. No wonder the back woodmen paid nothing for whisky, while the revenue raised on the spirits consumed in New England was all spent in quelling their insurrection.

Is this statement chimerical, is it the wire drawn speculation of a dreamer? Go then, to Mr. Gallatin, and ask for the minutes of the Cannonsburg meeting, ask Mr. Smilie, ask Mr. Findley, the faithful historian,[44] who when he slipped his neck out of the noose of one whisky rebellion, wrote a book calculated to engender another. Ask boldly for the records of that rebellion are now by the elevation of its chiefs, mingled with the archives of the government.

Whether any government can withstand a corrupt press is a problem. This is certain, neither the "enlightened Republic" of France nor any one of the military governments of Europe, has ventured on the experiment, for its solution. A stream of unanswered, and from its audacity, and still more its repetition, perhaps unanswerable slander was poured from the jacobin presses, pestilential, turbid, and copious as the Nile. The Federal administration was notoriously *lied* down, and the attempt is now making by the very same means, and some of the very same men, to change the government of Massachusetts. Rumour indeed has ventured to say that the

---

[44] *William Findley, 1741 or 2–1821.* History of the Insurrection, in the Four Western Counties of Pennsylvania, in the Year MDCCXCIV. *[Member of the H. of Rep.] (Philadelphia: printed by Samuel Harrison Smith, 1796.)*

jacobin candidate was not at first agreed on by the jacobin faction in the state. They resolved to adhere to Mr. Gerry; but after this resolution, positive orders came on from Washington to substitute a new champion in his place. These orders were obsequiously, though with hearty discontent obeyed.

To support this new arrangement, and to effect, if possible, a Parisian revolution in the state, it was necessary that the party should closely combine together, and lay in secret the plan of their operations. A caucus of the jacobin members of the General Court accordingly took place. Be it remembered, however, that the *Chronicle,* which in candor we acknowledge, has for all its offences some color to plead in excuse, *non compos;* the *Chronicle,* four years ago, loudly condemned Federal caucuses as anti-republican and dangerous; yet behold how tame and silent now. How ready to print a lying pamphlet, which the jacobin caucus agreed to frame, and to spread, guarding with the utmost caution against Federal inspection, through all the distant and dark corners of the Commonwealth, where truth would not go at all, or not in season for the election; and even now, when the election is over, that same *Chronicle* office is still prudently shut against all Federal purchasers of that infamous fabrication. The pamphlet was carefully secured against general distribution; it was not entrusted to its intrinsic merits, and offered to the public; but confined to scenes where such falsehood would find a ready market, and circulated exclusively among credulous and unsuspecting citizens.

Accordingly the pamphlet claims attention in the name, and as the work, not of an individual writer, but of a legislative caucus, composed of men who hunger and thirst to get rid of our legitimate rulers, and to reign alone. This association for calumny and intrigue, organized to give color and currency to statements, the most deceptive, and to men and measures, the most worthy of our aversion and dread, is a proof that if we have any morals left, we have little shame. Surely this combination to give authority to lies, by assuming to them the credit of growing out of a "conference of gentlemen from all the respective counties," is novel and highly reprehensible. We have felicitated ourselves on our superior purity, we have considered our elections as the result of an enlightened and just discrimination; but if falsehood is thus to be secretly and systematically diffused, for the purpose of influencing suffrage, our elections will be a mockery, a fair or market, in which the vilest of mankind will be the most successful dealers, and virtue a commodity. To the profligate arts, and matchless industry of this combination, it is owing, that their votes increased.—Will not the insulted yeomen of Massachusetts, at the next election, withdraw all confidence from their disgraced deceivers? Ought not their secrecy to create distrust?

THE REPUBLICAN VI

Boston Gazette, AUGUST 13, 1804
Reprinted from the *Repertory*

> *The progress of our affairs is in conformity with the fixed laws of our nature, and the known course of Republics. Our wisdom made a government, and committed it to our virtue to keep, but our passions have engrossed it, and they have armed our vices to maintain their usurpation.*

It has often been insisted on by the anti-federalists, that they no longer subsist as a distinct sect, and therefore, those who were once distinguished by that denomination might now with propriety adopt the exclusive and insulting title of republicans; exclusive, as if they were the only republicans; insulting, because it is saying, in every company, where this

321

title is thus usurped, we are better men than you. The President has said, and clearly enough, we confess, but no doubt with design to fix a good name on a base faction, "we are all Federalists, all Republicans."—It would be absurd therefore, even according to Mr. Jefferson, to use by way of distinction, a term which the highest official authority has pronounced to distinguish no party, because it comprehends all. The anti-federalist party have however taken that name, because it is in credit, and have laid aside their old one, because it was out of credit, as any name they wear certainly will be. The federalists have been in many instances abject and low spirited enough to allow them to take their good name, as if it belonged to them exclusively. To steal a man's teeth out of his head, or to rob him of his Christian name, is a proof of no ordinary dexterity. Yet this latter is what the jacobins have impudently done. But no true spirited federalist will sanction the theft, or submit to the insult.

It is true they show, in their eagerness about names, a shrewd discernment of their influence over the multitude. To understand principles requires that a party should understand something. But a name is to a party a labor saving machine; it saves both fluff and work; it needs only strength of lungs to vociferate that name. Thinking and reasoning are out of the question. I will enter my protest, said an English Lord, on the journals and appeal to the sense of the nation. Do it, said Lord Chesterfield archly, do it, if you please, and I will appeal to their nonsense and baffle your protest. The jacobins in March last, took counsel from this witty Lord.

Accordingly they used names and principles, as catch words of party, as countersigns for the order of their camp. To tell a profligate rabble that they are sovereign, to bow before their majesty, and to pronounce their voice the voice of God, is a species of flattery the base and ignorant cannot resist, and that even the wise sometimes listen to with complacency, for it is said that in some form or other every man may be flattered. Hence it is, that the doctrine of the power of the people, which nobody denies, and the just authority of the people's will, which, when the sober, real people pronounce it, everybody will respect, is a theme on which every demagogue affects to be fervid and eloquent. The possession of power is sure to inspire vanity and jealousy both, and woe be to him who is supposed to be hostile to the possessor.

The democratic writers therefore first endeavor to breathe all the ardour of vanity into the multitude, about the extent and majesty and divinity of their sovereign power; which for any cause, or no cause at all, but to show its omnipotence, may, and of right too, set up and pull down governments and constitutions, judges and churches, rights and institutions, and woe be to him who then says nay; for the next work, and it is not easy work, is to kindle rage against the federal political heretics, who are willing to treat the people as worthy of a rational and well-guarded confidence and esteem, but who will neither flatter nor worship the mere multitude, which the demagogues have ever affected to adore, and have in the end succeeded to enslave. No federalist thinks the decisions of even the majority of the people perfect, merely because they are irresistible. He thinks they may do wrong, and they will do nothing else, when their vanity is flattered, and they blindly put themselves into the leading strings of their flatterers.

It certainly is not possible wholly to cure any people of their vanity; perhaps it is not desirable. However that may be, the nation has not yet been found, that does not greatly overrate its own merits, and underrate or scorn the merits of strangers. Of all societies, those which are free are the most prone to vanity. Indeed, they have the most to be proud of; and on that side where a man places his own merits, there he is open to flattery. Thus it is that a free people value themselves, not so much on their liberty, which is a thing that men of science have never yet well defined, and the multitude have never, in the least comprehended, as in their power. In fact, few men have any other idea of liberty than their own power. In despotic states, a government is, they well know, everything, and the subjects nothing. Hence they argue that in free states, the subjects are everything, and the government nothing; and in spite of sophistry, in spite of the deception of fine words without meaning, this is the idea the American democrats have formed both of liberty and government.

The least exercise of rational thought would convince each democrat, when they ever were asked, they would not be democrats; that where the government is nothing, liberty is nothing. There is anarchy whose office it is only to light the fire, out of whose ashes springs despotism; say rather, it is a salamander, breathing his natural element. It is impossible that there can be any liberty where individuals have the possession of all power; and it is only for a moment, and in the act of destroying, that they can have it.—There may be liberty where they have no power, though there can be no adequate security for it, but where the power has no restraint, it is despotism at the instant, despotism in the end. Liberty in the extreme, is not liberty any more than the last convulsive spasm, that separates soul and body, can be called life. Liberty consists in restraint, and by removing that restraint, as the democrats are now foolishly and fatedly doing, in order to get more liberty, they will give it its quietus. All their remedies, for the body politic, are extremes. They would cure the headache by beating out the brains. They pretend to abate a slight inflammation, and they would lay open with the knife, one of the ventricles of the heart. Such, as can be demonstrated, is their system of amendments; such are their soberest notions of the right administration of a free state. Democracy, in its best state, is but the politics of

Bedlam; while kept chained, its thoughts are frantic, but when it breaks loose, it kills the keeper, fires the building, and perishes.

THE REPUBLICAN VII[45]

Boston Gazette, AUGUST 16, 1804
Reprinted from the *Repertory*

> *The progress of our affairs is in conformity with the fixed laws of our nature, and the known course of Republics. Our wisdom made a government and committed it to our virtue to keep, but our passions have engrossed it, and they have armed our vices to maintain their usurpation.*

THE SCIENCE of politics, though one of the most important to the tranquility of mankind, is unfortunately hitherto the least capable of precision in its principles, or certainty in the application of them to human affairs. The greatest lights or discoveries in this science are indeed derived merely from political experience. Our knowledge is no better than empirical; we find that certain distributions of power have answered well and therefore we have assumed it as a maxim of truth that such must be their distribution. To divide the legislature into at least two branches, to render the judiciary independent, and the executive single, with the appointment of representatives, constitute nearly the whole body of *rules* yet ascertained and fixed. But no human being in his sense can be presumptuous enough to say, with confidence, I have so contrived a plan of government, in conformity with these rules, as with certainty to ensure the liberty and welfare of

---

[45] *This essay was mistakenly numbered VI in the* Gazette.

the society. The influence of manners, which are laws that are not enacted, yet cannot be evaded, that of events which though they should happen in their ordinary course, are nevertheless unforeseen, and that of accidents and foreign revolutions often confound wisdom, and discredit prudence. In this uncertainty of the science of politics, the ship of state is often governed more by the elements, than the pilot; there is of course, in all societies, almost infinite opportunity for the excitement of the hopes and fears, the prejudices and the imagination of the people—and this agitation is greatest in free states; for under despotisms there is a darkness that hides and buries everything. But in free states, there is not light enough to make anything quite clear to all yet just enough to render every real object monstrous, and to people every grove with hideous phantoms. It is a twilight, so dim, that fancy can see and hear nothing but spectres. Every citizen's shadow, lengthening as he walks, seems to brandish a giant's arms and defy him. The leaves rustle like so many spears—he feels himself like a spy in the camp of the Prince of Darkness, and if a briar happen to touch the skirt of his coat, he starts as if he were arrested. The object of popular dread must be, of course, any political power that is superior to an individual's own. Hence, the hypochondriac terror of the democrats, as soon as the federal government went into operation, a terror which argument and explanation could not cure, and if medicine could, they would not take it. The quiet trust and confidence of the federalists in Washington had no effect on the democrats—they deemed such courage almost impiety towards liberty, whose most acceptable offering they maintained was jealousy.

The jacobins, instructed by the example of France and the lessons of Genet, very early took skilful advantage of the confusion and ambiguity of political ideas, and of the nervous disease of the popular mind. They endeavored to set up and maintain profligate printers in all parts of the Union, to disseminate suspicions and slanders. In this pious labor, Philip Freneau's clerkship in the office of the Department of State proved an important assistance. His *National Gazette* was the mint where the lies were coined, and the *Chronicle*, the New York *Argus*, Babcock's Hartford *Mercury*, and the underlings, who had malice, but wanted any original wit or invention, were faithful in the distribution. Their system was very like that which the counterfeiters of bank bills have since adopted, and probably enough imitated, from having been concerned in the original scheme; for these honest people have been, to a man, jacobins. The late pamphlet of "anonymous slander" we are told, was found with the implements for counterfeiting, a natural association we confess.—If the pamphlet principles prevailed, these associated patriots could command the true bank bills, and those who are now foolish enough to think themselves securely the owners. And if Federal men should still, in despite of them, be able to protect property, they could then get their pamphlets and their false bills into circulation together.—Thus they have two strings to their bow.

But over and above the advantage the jacobins derived, in their work of deception, from the looseness and obscurity of political principles and ideas, they found some circumstances favorable to their cause, from very unexpected sources.

Nothing so surely excites the most desperate efforts of ambition, as the accessibility of the sovereign power. That apple of death grows so fair, that, if it only hang within reach, blind man will pluck and eat, though in that day he shall die.—While the British government subsisted, no man, in the then colonies, would aspire to any but a subordinate share of power, and that, too, under legal superiors. But no sooner was independence established, than every man was told he was sovereign—and he felt inspired with a royal ambition to try his eloquence at the dram shop, to gain subjects. What theme could his tongue find, so ready, or so fruitful, or so animating, as the abuses and blunders of that government, which dared to usurp a sovereignty over him? In fact, this idea of usurpation, absurd as it is, has been applied, while our sedition law was in force, to the acts of Congress. The dealers in sedition who claimed to be exempt from the troublesome encroachment of our rulers, their servants, upon individual sovereignty.

Independence, like every great political event, had the effect to confound and subvert old habits and ideas. That due subordination, without which no society, whether monarchical or republican, can or ever did subsist, was shaken and nearly overthrown. The little men who could not aspire to be leaders, disdained to be subjects of the laws; and it is a singular and characteristic specimen of arrogance and folly, that the Virginians, to this day, deem it a degradation to be called subjects; as if it were not the boast of a republic, that the laws reign and as if the laws could reign, where men are not subject to them.

But the great men, or those whom popular favor, from being by nature little, could make great, instantly claimed to be superior to the laws. In Virginia, the laws had been framed by such men, in exact conformity with what they deemed the interests of the state aristocracy—for such the jacobin chiefs of the dominion really are.

Mr. Jefferson's *Notes* show clearly with what injustice and inequality they have apportioned representatives, so that the settlers beyond the Blue Ridge, who have few slaves, are stripped of power, as the New England states now are, by the black representation in Congress. Their laws are also framed so as to protect the plantation lords from creditors. This is notorious—and one of the earliest, fiercest, and most stubborn reinforcements to anti-federalism, was drawn from the Virginia debts. Hence it was that Philip Freneau's *Gazette*, from Mr. Jefferson's office of state, seemed to fight the battles of Virginia—it kept the Scotchmen off, and the coach wheels on. They could live bankrupts, yet in luxury, and defy their creditors.

From the hour, therefore, that the Constitution began, a faction was bred and trained in Virginia, to contest its power, and to destroy its life. Alas! Reader, with what fatal success!!

THE REPUBLICAN VIII

Boston Gazette, AUGUST 23, 1804
Reprinted from the *Repertory*

> *The progress of our affairs is in conformity with the fixed laws of our nature, and the known course of Republics. Our wisdom made a government, and committed it to our virtue to keep, but our passions have engrossed it, and they have armed our vices to maintain their usurpation.*

IT WILL be obvious to every reflecting mind, that from the causes which have been already unfolded, the administration of a free republican government, was from the beginning, peculiarly difficult, if not absolutely unmanageable. The state of Virginia was an organized faction, strongly entrenched, and formidably armed against the general government. It will be replied, perhaps, that Virginia is now a loud declaimer for the Union; true, because she weilds [*sic*] it, because no longer her rival or superior, it is her instrument, and the better to answer as her instrument, she has made its justice a shadow, and confined the revenue to impost. Is not the new government then very like the old confederation? But while the administration was in federal hands, the journals of both houses of Congress, will show that her whole weight was thrown into the scale of opposition—and not merely opposition to a few obnoxious measures, but generally to every one that would disembarrass the operations of the government, or give effect to the great objects it was created to accomplish. Judge then is not Virginia now, as ever, most utterly antifederal?

It would be easy, if we are not sunk too low in licentiousness, that wide yawning grave of republics, it might be useful to trace other causes arising from prejudice, passion, or accident, that have contributed to give power to the profligate and base, and covered the virtuous with mourning.

It is cheerfully and unreservedly admitted, that our government is, and ought to be, representative, deriving its sovereignty from the people.—But, as before intimated, the everlasting flattery of the people as sovereigns, has done a great deal, has done almost all that is necessary to be done to make them slaves. For it has invested their flatterers with power. But this incessant contemplation of their power cannot fail to intoxicate them. A despot, who is saluted as our multitude are from sunrise to sunset, with, O Great King, live forever, will think of nothing else. They will prize their power as if it was their liberty, and their demagogue favorites will use the whole power, that the multitude always blind, and always in extremes in their love and hatred, can bestow.— This foreseen, this experienced, this fatal progress which has carried all republican liberty to that bourn from which no republic has yet returned, has filled every true federal patriot with grief and anxiety. Washington has died with words to this import of solemn warning on his lips.

It is for this reason, and on this evidence only, and the conscience of every honorable man among the federalists, will bear testimony with mine, when I say it, we are slandered as enemies of the people—monarchists, aristocrats. It is for this cause, the base pamphleteer, whom the Senate of Massachusetts have, perhaps to his face, stigmatized as an "anonymous slanderer" has dared to represent the federalists as intriguers to subvert the Constitution. Yes, the very men who watched and prayed for its adoption, are stigmatized as its enemies by the refuse of our learned professions, by the miserable tools of Genet, by the disgraced remnants of the antifederal faction. That honest warmth of indignation which these reflections cannot fail to inspire, has in some measure led me a stage beyond the present point of my argument.

I return to it.

The popular mistake, that their power is their liberty, and the jealousy, that ever grows out of excessive love, and which produces hatred and a thirst for revenge, augmented the jacobin faction in all the states. The flatterers, who stick at nothing, had an easy access to the affections and confidence of the multitude. They called themselves the people's friends— champions for their rights and power. Mr. Jefferson's adherents very early tried to stick upon his name the mountebank, impostor title of *The Man of the People.*

When, therefore, the most malignant and profligate opposition was made to the laws, the multitude indulged no little joy to find of how great weight the people were. Mr. Gallatin called county meetings against the excise laws, and the people voted that they were unconstitutional, oppressive, and ought to be resisted. This was encouraged in the *National Gazette* and in all the jacobin newspapers, as the noble spirit of liberty, the revival of the spirit of '76. When the British treaty was in its passage, not a few, who on other subjects, thought and acted with correctness, took pleasure in the dignity and interest that were thrown upon a town meeting, by having national affairs to decide.—So that when government was hindered and obstructed, when it was openly resisted, and when faction was spreading its combinations to become its rival and its conqueror, there was still in every event something to comfort democratic pride in the moment, and to blind its unforeseeing folly to the event.

No extreme of licentiousness alarmed the unthinking, for the excess to which popular power, as it was deceitfully called, was carried, only showed that its extent was greater than was known or exercised before, and who that holds power is sorry to see it augmented? And surely they say, the people can never be their own enemies. Who so fit to keep power as the people themselves, and, who, it may be added, so certain the next moment to usurp it as their ambitious tyrannical demagogues.

Thus it has happened, that the progress of licentiousness was seen with complacency, if not joy, and the operations of the government with coldness, jealousy or rage.

Was it possible then, and ought we to have expected, the prevalence of reason and virtue? Could we expect the public sense would govern, longer than Washington ruled, as the passions, vices, and folly of the nation were dexterously seized and employed, to obstruct the administration of his successor? The jacobin presses sweated with their labor of "anonymous slander." All that was abominable was invented and propogated [sic], and all that was shallow and base gave it currency without evidence, and the friend and disciple of Condorcet rose with his system to power.

Let us look back, and say, with a mournful, perhaps useless emphasis, the federal administation had nothing but its integrity to rely on. With the purest intentions it pursued the wisest measure, and looked for support to the reason and virtue of the citizens.

But what support could reason and virtue afford? When the rage of party had drowned every voice, but its own; those who excited those passions, and those who have an interest in deceiving, have prevailed.

We are subject to a government by the caprice of the alien or thoughtless multitude, and those who blow their impure breath into that multitude by nature have the disposal of our destinies.—They call it their liberty to nullify our Eastern power and influence, and they have engaged a faction in the bosom of Connecticut, Massachusetts and New Hampshire to second their designs. Their success will quench the last faint ray of hope that a republican system can be supported. Mob violence must follow our sad disappointment, and the reign of king mob, though always violent, is ever short; and after some bloody agitations, the Emperor of Louisiana will reign alone. People of New England, so often deceived, so much insulted, be warned, and be saved.

DANGEROUS POWER OF FRANCE I

Repertory, MAY, 1806

THE POLITICAL SKY has seldom remained long unclouded; but it may be doubted, whether it was ever charged with a blacker tempest than that we have lately seen burst upon Europe. France has accomplished, in twelve years, as much as Rome did in five hundred. The Samnites, who occupied a little province, that is now a part of the kingdom of Naples, resisted the Roman arms for half a century; and it was not till after four-and-twenty Roman triumphs, and twice that number of pitched battles, that they were subdued.

King Pyrrhus landed in Italy too late, after the Samnites had lost their spirit no less than their force. He proved an enemy worthy of Roman discipline and courage, yet he was unsuccessful.

The Romans, after five hundred years of incessant war with the petty nations around them, at length aspired to extend their dominion beyond the bounds of Italy. First Sicily, and then Spain were disputed in arms with the Carthaginians. Fifty years were passed in battles and alarms, before this great controversy was decided in favor of Rome.

When Carthage had fallen, Greece, the mistress of Rome in arts, her rival in arms and renown, fell an almost unresisting prey to Roman ambition. She fell with all her confederated republics, as ours will certainly fall, if France should continue to wield our factions, and our factions to dispose of our government; for factions in a democracy are sincere only in their hatred and fear of each other. Whether the Jeffersons and Madisons stand or fall, our rulers can have no patriotism. Their emulation is too fierce, and their objects of ambition too fugitive and too personal, to allow them to take the views, still less to cherish the sentiments of statesmen. Old Rome had patriots, but who would expect to find them in the amphitheatre among the gladiators? Those who love power, will seek it in the contests of party. The lovers of their country will be found nursing their griefs and their despair among the discarded disciples of Washington. To return from this seeming digression, Rome availed herself of the divisions of the Grecian republics to subjugate them all. Affecting a zeal for their liberty, she offered her alliance; and the allies of Rome, like those of France, were her slaves. The Greeks joyfully aided Rome to conquer Macedonia; and Philip, the Macedonian king, was employed against Antiochus, called the Great, the Syrian monarch. Egypt was too base to make any resistance, but submitted to tribute, as quietly as we do.

Thus every independent republic and powerful prince fell a prey to Rome. Beyond the Euphrates, the Parthians, at length, formed a mighty empire, which the distance and the deserts rendered, like the modern Russia, inaccessible to the Roman arms. It was remarkable, that Rome seldom had more than one enemy to fight at a time; they fell in succession;

and their servitude was concealed, thought it was embittered by the title of allies.

France has achieved her purpose—the struggles of liberty are over; and the continental nations of Europe are now sleeping in their chains.

If France possessed the British navy, those chains would be adamant, which no human force could break. French tyranny, like the great dragon, would have wings, and the remotest regions of the civilized world would be near enough to catch pestilence from his breath. Yet we are infatuated enough to think America a hiding-place for liberty, where her assassins will not seek her life; or an impregnable fortress that would protect it.

On what reasonable foundation do these presumptuous expectations rest? When France is master of both land and sea, will distance preserve us? With eight hundred ships in the department of the Thames, distance would be nothing to Bonaparte. He could transport an army of sixty thousand men to occupy New York, which could not make one hour's resistance. He could transport them with more expedition and ease than Mr. Jefferson could asssemble our standing army of two regiments from the frontiers to oppose them. Yet this standing army, so potent to command the types, the exclamations, and the silly fears of the democrats, though it assisted as a bugbear to make Mr. Jefferson president, would no better protect his house, at Monticello, from a French squadron of horse, than the army of the imperial Virginia formerly defended its assembly from Colonel Tarleton.

But our myriads of militia might defy the world in arms. Excellent hopes these! When Austria in vain opposes two hundred thousand veterans to the progress of Bonaparte; when Russia is repelled in the pitched battle of Austerlitz; when Prussia, with its armies complete in numbers and discipline, stands still, not daring to stir, and waiting to acknowledge Bonaparte conqueror; or, to come more plainly to the point, when we see half a million of English volunteers, as formidable and as stiff in buckram as it is in the power of tailors to make uniforms, parading the coasts of Sussex, Essex, and Kent, and yet trusting only to the vigilance of the British navy to hinder the French from crossing the channel; surely, when we see these things, we must be unwilling to reflect, or utterly incapable of reflection, if we can suppose that the array of the militia in the secretary's office would transplant fear from Mr. Jefferson's bosom into Bonaparte's.

To say nothing of the improbability of the militia's obeying the call for actual service, or if they should appear promptly and in sufficient numbers, of the impossibility of detaining them in service long enough to make their arms of the least imaginable use, direful experience has at length instructed nations, that when they are in danger, they are to be preserved from it by their real soldiers. These are made, not in a tailor's shop, by facing blue cloth with red or yellow, but by learning in the field that subordination of mind that will make men do, and insure their doing, all that men possibly can do.

Old Rome did not outnumber her enemies. Two legions, each of less than six thousand men, and as many of the Latin or other Italian allies, made a complete consular army. Such an army routed the numberless forces of Mithridates and Antiochus. It cost the Romans more exertions to subdue Perseus, king of Macedon, than to conquer all the East; his phalanx, of sixteen thousand men, was harder to break than all the millions of militia of the other successors of Alexander. Rome, by the perfection of her discipline, became mistress of the world.

Would Bonaparte calculate on the vigor of our government as an insuperable obstacle to his military attempt on the United States? Would the congress majority, like a Roman senate, create means and employ them with a spirit that would prefer death to servitude or tribute? The French Hannibal, surely, with our fifteen millions of tribute money already in his treasury, would have no discouraging fear of this sort.[46] When he reads our treaty with Tripoli, by which it appears that we chose tribute, when victory was within our reach; when he sees that the Bey of Tunis presumes to say, by his minister at Washington, pay or fight,[47] what can Bonaparte conclude, but that honor is a name, and in America an empty one; and that our national spirit can never be roused to a higher pitch than to make a calculation. With us honor is a coin, whose very baseness confines it at home for a currency. "Such a people," he will say, "are degraded before they are subdued. They are too abject to be classed or employed among my martial slaves. Let them toil to feed their masters, and to replenish my treasury with tribute."

Is there a spirit in our people that would supply the want of it in our rulers? Our total unpreparedness, both by land and sea, to make even the show of resistance against an attack, is certainly not from the want of military means in the United States, but from a dread of the loss of popularity, if they should call them forth.

Why is it unpopular? Because the progress of French domination is not seen at all, or is seen with a fatal complacency; because we love our money better than our country; because we enjoy our ease almost as much as we love our money; and because by shutting our eyes to our public dangers, we escape the insupportable terror of their approach, and the toils of an efficient preparation to resist them.

It is a thing incomprehensible, that even the childish

---

[46] *The purchase price for the Louisiana territory was 80 million francs ($11,250,000).*

[47] *The Tripolitan War, June, 1805; the agreement included the demand that the United States ransom the crew of the captured frigate* Philadelphia *for $60,000.*

babble of the *Chronicle* is not dumb. Admitting the stupidity, admitting the baseness of the democrats, yet without admitting that they are both stupid and base in a miraculous degree, it is unaccountable that they should not see, in the victories of Bonaparte, the stride, and almost feel the gripe of a master. If a storm should sink, or a fire-ship burn the British navy, we should feel that gripe in a month; General Turreau would quietly exercise all the authorities at Washington. Considering how tamely we give up our millions, while that navy still renders America inaccessible to France, is any man alive so absurd as to suppose, that our subjugation to French despotism would cost the great nation a single flask of powder? Take away the British navy, or give it to France, and we free Americans, so valiant of tongue, tie up in our stalls as tamely as our oxen. The pen of Talleyrand would be found a sharper weapon than General . . .'s sword. It is preposterous to suppose, that a military resistance to France would be attempted. Her faction in this country would revive the clubs and the maxims of 1794; and Genet would again summon the enemies of British influence to rally under his banner. We should be called the allies of France, and our loyal addresses would accompany our tribute to conciliate the friendship of the great nation, and to claim a share in its glories. The men who could be nothing without France, would be invested with the titles and powers of magistracy; and property would be made to shift hands, till it rested with those who would be really interested to support France, that France might support them in keeping it. Thus, she would avoid the odium of a violent revolution, and yet would reap all the advantage of it, to rivet our dependence on her power. The distance of the Roman provinces, at length, favored their emancipation from her yoke; but with the sole possession of a navy, the trans-Atlantic provinces of France would not be distant.

With these irrefragable proofs of the fatal certainty with

which the power of France would reach us, and of the unresisting tameness with which we should endure it, if France should ruin the British naval power, what comments shall we make on the sense or spirit of the non-importation project of congress, which, though ineffectual for its purpose, is intended to impair the force and resources of that navy? How deep and considerate will be our scorn and execration of the Armstrongs, and Livingstons, and Monroes, who, to make their flattery welcome to a tyrant's ear, have blended it with American invectives against that navy. We seem to be emulous of the spirit of slavery, before we descend to its condition; as if we were resolved to merit their contempt by an earlier claim, and even by a juster title, than their yoke; for as long as the British navy may triumph, that yoke is not inevitable.

The most successful way to prevent our servitude, is faithfully to expose our dangers. So far as our fate may depend on our wisdom or our choice, it is proper to call the attention of our citizens to the fact, that Bonaparte, though he has done much, has done it in vain, unless he can do one thing more. Give him the British navy, and he will govern the United States as absolutely, and certainly with as little mercy as if our territory were a French department, and actually lay between the Seine and the Loire. Let our scribblers then extol the long-foreseeing wisdom of the Jeffersonian administration. Let them boast of their devotedness to the cause of the people. The man, whose chief merit is grounded on his having penned the Declaration of Independence, has done more than any other man living to undo it. He has made conventions to pour the fulness of our treasury into the coffers of Bonaparte; he has dictated laws in aid of, and to carry into effect, French authority over the blacks of St. Domingo—a degree of servile condescension beneath the independent spirit of those blacks; and now his minions in Congress have begun a warfare against the British trade, as if, without our own active coöperation to cripple the maritime resources of England, Bonaparte might meet with too great obstruction and delay in subverting the independence and liberty of our country.

If we love our country as we ought, we cannot but wish that the conquered nations of Europe may break their chains; we cannot but wish that Great Britain may courageously and triumphantly maintain her independence against France. But on this point what are we to expect? A military opposition on the continent of Europe has proved unavailing. Will France, now mistress of the land, become mistress of the sea also, and establish her iron domination over the civilized world? This is a question of life or death to American independence, and the awful decision is near.

DANGEROUS POWER OF FRANCE II

IT IS a subject of fearful curiosity to inquire into the causes, which have so rapidly conducted France to the conquest of the continental part of Europe. By carefully tracing their operation, we may be the better enabled to calculate the chances of her triumph over England, and, of necessary consequence, over America.

It was a long time the fashion to ascribe French victories to the republican fanaticism of her citizens. When France ceased to be republican in name, and it was only in name that she ever was republican, the superior personal bravery of the French soldiers, and the superior genius of Bonaparte were deemed to be the two adequate causes of her triumphs.

There is probably little ground for these opinions; or the influence of these causes is much overrated. The body of American democrats are no doubt the greatest political bigots in the universe; they are accustomed to believe that no tenets can be true or wise but their own. That all power is derived from the people, and should be exercised for their benefit, is a principle of which they fancy the world was ignorant, till it was discovered in the course of our revolution. Considering themselves the sole depositaries of political truth; having in their hands her casket, where she keeps liberty, the most precious of her jewels, they think our country is entitled to be not a little vain of the office. They feel, too, as if all patriotic merit consists in propagating their principles through the world with a rage of proselytism. They would rejoice, if not only France, but the grand Turk, and the bey of Algiers should gather their unlettered rabble into primary assemblies, and make them swear, with all the zeal and sincerity of opium and brandy, to maintain the rights of man with their daggers and their pikes.

Accordingly when France said, and sung, and swore the words of their republican creed, they were sure the grovelling world was very near being hoisted from its centre; it would be launched into the sky and glitter among the brightest of the stars. The reign of perfectibility was beginning; man, so long a reptile trodden in the mire, was rising to overtop the tallest of the seraphs. Their teeming fancies had made a creation of their own, and lighted it with a new sunshine. Above all things it delighted their hearts, and seemed to realize all their hopes, to see the low vulgar, the squalid hosts of vice and ignorance, issue from the opening cellars of the Fauxbourg of St. Antoine, and from the jails, to exercise the sovereignty of the people, by a signal vengeance on the magistrates, their enemies. They were sure the structure of society must have risen, when they saw its low foundations already higher than its roof. It was not long before this rabble army was arrayed as a body of Marseilles patriots, and as a part of the national guards. The splendid virtues of France were attributed to the exalted heroism of these men, who, it was said, fought well, not because they were soldiers, but because they were citizens. More than a million of the grown people of America believed, that the liberty-loving passion of Frenchmen made them an overmatch for the disciplined mercenaries of Austria and Prussia; and that the citizens were the better for their ignorance of discipline. The French generals were not the dupes of our silly opinions; they drilled and punished their *citizens*, till they would stand fire and push bayonet; and if they would not, they shot them.

The notion, that the political opinions of the common men will make them any better soldiers, is strangely absurd; they are more likely to effect a mutiny than a triumph. Men may fancy they are soldiers; but they are not really such until discipline and habit have new moulded their thoughts and inclinations. The reviews of peaceable tradesmen are no more than the solemn foppery of a pantomime, acted in the open air instead of the theatre. We would not be understood to say, that the militia has not both its merit and its use—both, we confess, are great; but we do say, that their proper use is not to face a veteran enemy. It is indeed very possible, that political enthusiasm, as well as religious fanaticism, may inspire a sudden fury into the bosoms of a raw, undisciplined multitude; but a veteran corps would surely defeat such a multitude.

If the inhabitants of France ever felt the republican enthusiasm, which is indeed very questionable, there is not much reason to believe, that it contributed to fill the ranks of their own army, or to make those of their enemy give way. Experience, which brings plausible theories to the test, and a correct knowledge of human nature, have abundantly confuted the notion, that the common men are the better soldiers for the soundness of their logic or their politics. Men are very much alike, in all the European countries, in respect to their capacity of being trained for war. When so trained, the difference between two hostile armies, of equal numbers, will be found to lie in the talents of their subaltern officers and principal commanders.

Common soldiers are soon trained; but it is the work of art and time to form officers. There is not the least reason in the world to suppose that the Austrians or Russians are inferior to the French soldiers, in steady, persevering valor; but there is ample evidence of the superiority of the French officers over those of their enemies. War has become, indeed it ever was, among civilized nations, a science. It excites and employs the utmost vigor and extent of human intellect. Though it is a science, it is such only for the officers, not for the common men. For two centuries past France has devoted more attention and more money to the perfection of this science than all the rest of Europe. Louis XIV. established such military schools as the great Cyrus would have desired for the education of the officers of that army that achieved for him the conquest of Asia. Bonaparte and Moreau, both undoubtedly great generals, are indebted for their triumphs to these schools. It is often said, the common men will dare to do whatever their officers will lead them on to do. It is no less proper to say, the officers will seldom flinch from leading the men, if they but know how to lead them.

Nothing is more certain than that the military institutions of France supplied the first revolutionary armies with an infinite number of accomplished young officers, who glowed with impatience to gain glory and promotion in that profession which had, from their infancy, engrossed their thoughts and kindled all their passions. The revolution furnished only sparks, and not the fuel for their combustion.

Nor is there the least reason to pretend, that the first French armies were composed of raw recruits. An immense standing army was maintained; and when it is considered, that on the side of the Low Countries, and on the Rhine, France guarded what has been emphatically called her iron frontier, with a double row of fortified towns, and that every one of these was occupied by a veteran garrison, that would figure as a respectable American army, we see plainly that France possessed every advantage for success in war, from the very first day of her military operations.

The democrats, to a man, believe that France was entirely defenceless, when the "coalition of despots" secretly entered into the treaties of Pilnitz and Pavia for the dismemberment. Those treaties, it has been a thousand times proved, are forgeries. Austria was taken by surprise; the Emperor Joseph had levelled the ramparts of his towns in the Netherlands, Luxembourg excepted; and his troops in that country were no more than a feeble corps of observation. The Austrians had a larger proportion of raw recruits in their armies than the French.

Be it remembered too, that the revolution supplied the French with an unexhausted superfluity of men and means, that no regular government in the world could countervail. That man must be strangely disordered in mind, who can now look back on French affairs, and say that the revolutionary leaders, possessing such means, left any option to the governments of England or Austria to remain at peace. As well might they say, when a whole street is burning, that a man, by sitting calmly in his elbow chair, might save his house from the flames. The English government, in particular, was near the scene, and could not see the revolution, like Ætna, vomit fire, without some natural fears and some prudent measures of precaution. Who is now ignorant that Brissot, and Barras, and Danton, and Robespierre would choose to understand those fears and those precautions, as signs of the inveterate hostility of kings to the French liberty? If the English could have shunned the war in February, 1793, it would have been forced upon them before June.

It is childish prattle to charge the enemies of France with the commencement of the war. The nature of the revolution was war against mankind. Its vital principle was a burning passion for power within the state; and when they had gained that, to establish by arms the power of France over every other state. Why is the vulture carnivorous? Why does not the tiger of Bengal eat grass? We might with as much good sense inquire, why does not the torrent stay upon the hills? Why are the collected waters of the revolutionary storm precipitated from the height of the Alps, to desolate the plains and to bury men and their labors under masses of barrenness and ruin?

The military means of Austria were stinted; those of France unlimited. In almost every battle the French had the advantage. The officers, even the subalterns, had been educated so as to qualify them to be generals; the generals were fit for nothing else; they understood their trade and aspired to no other sort of distinction. The French, always well commanded by their officers, well supplied by their enemies' countries which they ravaged, have rapidly overrun all Europe.

Another cause of the French superiority, and which has grown out of the real superiority of their military science, is to be found in the excellence of their artillery. The number and the manageableness of the French field artillery, must have given them a decisive advantage over the Russians in the late battle of Austerlitz. It is not to be supposed that the Russians have equally improved their artillery; nor, if they had, would they have encumbered their march of eight hundred leagues, especially when they had so many reasons for haste, with an immense train of field pieces. They would be the less disposed to do this, as the Austrians must have been relied upon to supply them in sufficient number. The French by the celerity of their movements had, however, obtained possession of a great part of the Austrian artillery. The deficiency of the Russians in this point, was probably a material cause of their loss of the battle.

When gunpowder and great guns were first brought into use, they were more capable of striking an enemy with a panic, than of breaking his line; the cannon were unwieldy machines, and the management of them was unskilful. Still the army which had them must have possessed a great advantage over that which had none. In the time of the famous duke of Marlborough, the event of a battle depended on the expertness and resolution of infantry in discharging their muskets. In still more modern wars, the bayonet has been considered the arbiter of victory. But the French have introduced another revolution in the science of war, the lightness and prodigious number of their horse-artillery enabling them to disorder and break an enemy's ranks, without coming to close fight, by raining upon them an intolerable tempest of grapeshot.

By means of their innumerable field pieces, and of their unusual proportion of cavalry, it has become impossible for their enemy to defend a country by lines of field intrenchment. It has been stated that Bonaparte's grand army was attended by fifty thousand horse. Such a body, always on the alert, could strike an enemy at almost any distance, and in every mortal part at once. If he contracted his posts, his flanks would be turned; if he spread out his troops to prevent it, his lines would be forced. By resisting, he met his fate; and if he retreated, it was swift, and overtook him.

Thus we have seen the French maintain the same invariable superiority over the Austrians, and lately over the Russians, in the field, that the Spaniards possessed over the Mexicans. The Russians and Austrians are as brave as the French; but the French are really superior in the science of their officers, in the number and management of their cannon, and in their cavalry. They will continue therefore to beat their enemies, as the Romans did. Even the Grecian phalanx, supposed to be the perfection of military science, and absolutely invincible, was found unequal to the contest with the Roman legion.

The French victories have happened in such a series that

we cannot rationally suppose them to happen by chance. They are the inevitable results of superior numbers, and of the French military advantages we have mentioned. They would happen again, if their dejected, beaten adversaries could rise again to resistance.

From these positions, this melancholy inference is to be drawn: the continental enemies of France are totally incapable of resisting her in the field; she has taken a permanent ascendant over them. Austria, humbled and beaten, is in no condition to learn the conquering art of her masters. Prussia, without risking the combat, has fallen prostrate with her useless arms in her hands. Russia, like the ancient Parthia, is invincible, but insignificant to the system of enslaved Europe.

If the French armies could pass the channel, there seems to be no sort of reason to hope that Great Britain could resist them. The regular army is spread over all the empire, and, if it were all collected, it would be a handful against the French hosts; and surely no military man would place the smallest dependence on the volunteers of England.

It is one of the inveterate, perhaps incurable evils of Mr. Pitt's administration, and the greatest blemish in the fame of that truly illustrious statesman, that, instead of forming an efficient army of two hundred thousand men, who could be sent wherever they might be wanted, he was either the schemer or the dupe of the useless, expensive, and, if the French should land in England, fatal project of volunteers. By equipping volunteers, he not only had no army, but it was out of the power of England to have one. The men were all engaged in acting the comedy of an army; and the finances were exhausted in getting up the decorations of the piece.

The sole protection of Great Britain, then, is in her navy. The writer has been brought very late, and loath, to believe that the military resistance of the continental nations of Europe would be ineffectual. Events have at last convinced

347

him that the French actually possess a greater and more decisive military superiority over those nations than the old Romans did over the forces of Antiochus, Mithridates, and Jugurtha, and especially over the Carthaginians, Greeks, and Macedonians. Nothing is wanting to the solid establishment of a new universal empire by France, that should spread as far, last as long, and press as heavily on the necks of the abject nations, as that of Rome, but the possession of the British navy. France, whenever she can get access to her enemy, is already irresistible. If Mr. Gregg would give her that navy, he would impart a kind of ubiquity to her power. The soft winds that wake the spring in the remotest regions of the globe would waft there the ministers of French rapacity to blast it. France would enjoy every thing that Rome wanted, to make the plundered world her province.

Are these ideas chimerical? or are the inferences drawn beyond the admitted truth of the premises? Is India more capable of resisting France than an English merchant company, its present sovereign? Spain and Italy are provinces already. Greece, Egypt, the Turkish empire, and all the shores of the Mediterranean were once the patrimony of the Cæsars, and for many hundred years slept soundly in their chains, till they were rudely waked by the Goths, the Heruli, the Huns, and the Arabs. Africa is a quarter of the globe that could be governed by factories; and America is another, that would yield, not merely with tameness, but alacrity, to imperial rescripts. If, by miracle, force should be needed, France could employ Spain, or Dessalines,[48] or slaves still more abject than they, to use it with infallible success. We should be ready not merely to take, but to buy our chains, and to pay our last dollar as a fine for the temerity of our resistance. We should patiently sow our fields, and see our kindly seasons ripen the harvest for French reapers. Our

[48] *One of Toussaint L'Ouverture's chief officers.*

posterity, born in servitude, would inherit our baseness, and bear the yoke from the infancy to the old age of their dishonored lives, without sorrow or repining.

Suppose the whip of the oppressor should at length tear off the callous skin from the slaves' backs, and rage should be kindled by pain, and courage engendered by despair; yet our resistance would only avail to exasperate our tyrants, and to embitter the sense and aggravate the pressure of our calamities. France would not fail to array an army of base Americans, and to place them in the strongest positions of our country; and if these should be insufficient to crush the first movements of rebellion, her ships would transport reënforcements from Europe with greater celerity than the American insurgents could collect and train forces to resist them. Our independence then must be renounced, or we must betake ourselves to the fastnesses of the wilderness to enjoy it, like the revolted negroes of St. Domingo, in peril, want, and barbarism.

The preservation of even this condition would then appear to exact and merit the display of all our energies. Comfortless and desperate as that savage independence may seem, it would nevertheless be preferable to the horrid stillness of our servitude under the power of French tyrants, exercised by their deputies, the Jeffersons and Nicholsons,[49] the present artificers of our ruin.

It is very seldom that the events of war turn out according to the predictions of speculatists on their probabilities. Futurity is no doubt wisely and mercifully hidden from our view. Yet the issue of the contest between France and Great Britain is so momentous to America, it is impossible to

---

[49] *A republican representative from Maryland, Joseph Nicholson introduced into the House of Representatives a resolution seeking to appropriate money for the purchase of West Florida and New Orleans (the mouth of the gulf). The money was eventually applied toward the purchase of the Louisiana Territory.*

·estrain our curiosity from examining the position and relative ;trength of the combatants.

Grant that Great Britain possesses adequate means to cope with France, it is an interesting previous question to decide, or rather to conjecture, whether there is a spirit in her government and people to persevere in the employment of them.

The death of Mr. Pitt has made a complete change in the ministry. He discerned, and it is strange that Mr. Fox, his supposed equal in talents, should not have discerned, the necessity of opposing France in arms, and the fatal consequences of a delusive peace; and any peace that should leave France a giant among pigmies would be delusive. But as Mr. Fox has been the opposer of the war ever since 1793, and as he and a large number of his most strenuous adherents are admitted to power, it may be expected that he will insist on proposing a negotiation. Proud as Bonaparte is, he would joyfully accept the proposal. He may be as liberal as Englishmen can ask in his terms, for any peace will make him their master. Nothing could make it safe, but that France should reduce her power. That is a condition Mr. Fox will not prescribe, nor Bonaparte concede.

We will not undertake to say that Mr. Fox is bound, in point of consistency, now to propose peace. He may say with plausibility, perhaps with strict truth, that the circumstances of the two countries are changed; that he was a friend to peace, while Europe stood independent and powerful in arms to secure the observance of it by the French emperor; but that now peace would lessen none of the burdens of the nation, while it would put its commercial and naval resources, inaccessible in war, within reach of the power and intrigues of Bonaparte.

What is Mr. Fox's present opinion or disposition we know not. We have no hesitation in saying, that as a faithful member of his majesty's councils, it is his duty to prosecute the war, till England can be safe in peace; and she cannot be safe, unless she is great in comparison with France.

Are there not probable grounds of conjecture that Mr. Fox came into the ministry on the terms of supporting the war measures of the government. Before the peace of Amiens, the fruitless negotiation at Lisle had opened the eyes of the English nation to the immeasurable ambition and profligacy of the French rulers. Mr. Fox then persisted in condemning the war. After the peace of Amiens he paid a visit to Bonaparte in Paris, and received and permitted such attention from the French chief as raised the wonder and disgust of all men, and the suspicions of many. His motives for making that visit have never yet been explained.

This is certain, his parliamentary influence had surprisingly dwindled; and perhaps he owes it as much to his frank, open disposition, so unused to and incapable of duplicity, as to his splendid talents, that the nation, with its characteristic generosity, has been willing to forget and forgive his strange visit and strange conduct in Paris.

There is reason to believe that when Mr. Pitt last came into office, the English king had neither forgiven nor forgotten it. He considered Mr. Fox as a jacobin, and resolved to deny the importunities of both parties to admit Mr. Fox to his counsels. Lord Grenville thought himself bound, in consequence, to stand with Mr. Fox, and to decline office.

When the death of Mr. Pitt and the desertion of the allies in Germany seemed to force Mr. Fox upon the king, for all men agreed it was necessary to drop party divisions, and to unite against the common danger, we are told Lord Grenville was closeted with his majesty, and finally arranged the ministry to mutual satisfaction. As Lord Grenville is an honest man, and as able as he is honest, we cannot believe such a man would recommend a jacobin to the king, or that he could prevail over his majesty's aversion to Mr. Fox, without being personally responsible for his conduct and principles.

When it is considered also that those two eminent men formerly acted in opposition to each other, and that, for three years past, they have come to a mutual good understanding, the grounds of division in the present ministry must have been fully explored, and such engagements mutually required and given, as will prevent their collision. Those who had always acted together, before they came into the ministry, we think more likely to fall out afterwards.

The union of the present ministry is the more probable too, when we advert to the known sincerity and amiable temper of Mr. Fox. The attachment of no man's friends has been stronger than Mr. Fox's have ever manifested towards him; and those who remember his famous coalition with Lord North, will believe that too much stubbornness to maintain the appearance of consistency is not one of that gentleman's faults.

Mr. Fox is the only member of the new administration who can be the champion of peace measures. Lord Grenville and Mr. Windham love their country too well, and its dangers are too imminent, to permit us to believe that they are disposed to adopt the fatal counsels of the old opposition.

On these grounds, therefore, we presume to conjecture that the English ministry will be united in favor of a prosecution of the war.

We have not yet inquired whether there is sense and magnanimity enough in the nation to support the ministry in such a resolution. The nation, no doubt, is weary of the war, and staggers under the weight of its burdens; but peace can scarcely cheat the blind multitude with the delusive hope of a respite from those burdens. A vigorous and able opposition to war in parliament might afford aliment to the popular discontent; but the men who used to lead that opposition are now in the ministry. They may say they did not choose, and have not made the war; their predecessors, whom they were accustomed to oppose, left it a sad necessity on their hands.

Besides, peace has once been tried, and proved not only delusive but almost fatal; Bonaparte gained more territory in peace than in war; and England voluntarily gave up her conquests, except Malta, Trinidad, and Ceylon. Such another peace would ruin her.

Under these circumstances, it may be expected that even the populace will see that the continuance of the war is the hard, but inevitable condition, of English liberty and independence. If we are not deceived in these speculations, the British ministry and nation will concur in pursuing the war. With what hope of ultimate success they will pursue it, is a more difficult problem.

DANGEROUS POWER OF FRANCE III

THE SUFFICIENCY of the British finances to supply the enormous expenditures of the war is usually the first inquiry. We cannot, however, refrain from remarking, that the bankruptcy of the French government has been incessantly expected to prove the boundary of the French power. It has happened, on the contrary, that power has made its own resources. No government, certainly no arbitrary government, will sit still and die for want of means when they are to be found within its grasp; it will put forth the hand of violent injustice and reach them. The rulers of France found wealth enough within and without, and they have never hesitated to use it. Their armies flourished while their artisans starved and their farmers desponded. The decline of all employments but that of arms, so far from stopping the course of their victories, materially contributed to accelerate it.

The free government of England is less disposed and less qualified for these extremes; but it will not be equally under the necessity of resorting to them. The wealth of individuals is incalculable, and the machinery of the English laws and government for extracting it in loans and taxes, with some degree of equality, and without popular opposition, is probably adequate to a great annual augmentation. We forbear to say what is the utmost that machinery could effect. An urgent public necessity, so palpable as to confound all doubts and cavils, we should conceive, would enable government to draw from the people larger supplies, by equal laws, than could be obtained by arbitrary violence. It is however, we confess, a frightful prospect for an honest English minister, that he must spend for the public defence more than he can raise by taxes. Hitherto, we believe, he has not been able to produce by his ways and means more than thirty-five or forty millions sterling, nor to bring his expenditures under seventy.

In this extremity, some men have asked, whether the government ought not, without further hesitation, to sponge off their national debt. The jacobin members of our administration will wonder why they have delayed it so long. The English government would long trust and painfully try the public spirit of the nation rather than destroy the debt. We have men in power among us who would sooner destroy any debt, public or private, than hazard their popularity; nay more, they would sponge off all debts for its sake; but in England, nothing short of dire necessity will bring the rulers to touch the property that has so long been confided to the safeguard of the public faith and morals; nor will they, of choice, withhold a penny of the interest.

It is true, necessity, though it is the tyrant's plea, is a sufficient one, when it exists, for the best government. There is no reasoning against necessity; but when there is any reasoning about its existence, it is manifest that it does not exist; it not only makes its own law, but its own evidence. It comes like the fire, or flood, or pestilence, and renders doubt as much impossible as resistance.

Admitting, then, the sufficiency of the plea of necessity to vindicate the withholding of the interest of the British national debt from the public creditors, the fact that such necessity exists is still to be made out. We have already said, this sober argumentative making out of a necessity is inadmissible. Though it is better the national debt should perish than the nation, still it is no less true that the sponging off the national debt is a measure of violence, which needs all the justification that an irresistible necessity can afford. Necessity is a law that makes all other laws silent. It would vindicate the stoppage of the interest of the national debt— it is equally manifest that nothing short of actual necessity will justify such an act.

Now, while the English government is in the regular course of paying the interest, and it is only inconvenient to proceed in that course because new expenses arise, and it is an unpopular task to provide taxes to supply them, it is absolutely a relinquishment of the plea of necessity to pretend that the government is forced to stop the interest.

We know so little of the difficulties of the English government and nation, because we feel none of them, that it is not a little hazardous for any American speculatist to decide upon the proper degree of boldness with which they should impose taxes, or the measure of ability or patience of the subjects to pay them. Nevertheless we should imagine, and we presume to hope it is the case, that by new arrangements of the land tax, by the assessed taxes, by improvements in the mode of collection of the imposts, and by a reform of the all-consuming poor rates, the public revenue may be even yet considerably augmented. The power to tax, no doubt, has its limits; and when a government has multiplied its taxes till it has reached those limits, a new imposition will only give a new form to the public receipts without adding to their amount. We may be mistaken, but we sincerely hope it will prove that the wealth of the English subjects is abundantly adequate to all the enormous expenditures of this necessary war. The time we believe has come to justify all practicable reforms of expenditure and improvements of the revenue, rather than a resort to violent and arbitrary remedies of any sort; especially such as sponging off the debt.

For it can scarcely escape remark, that Great Britain has been, from the first, contending against revolutionary principles. How can Great Britain, the champion of faith, and law, and order, with consistency or advantage adopt, as a remedy, the very measure that is the first badge and sure forerunner of the evil?

For what is revolution? what is its favorite work, but first, and with most malignant ardor, to destroy what faith, and law, and morals, have established and guarded? The English debt of six hundred millions sterling is spread all over the kingdom; it has taken root for a century. To pluck that root from the soil, we believe, would shake the security of all property; and in the event, it might possibly subvert the monarchy.

When the convenience of relieving the nation from this mountain of debt is once admitted, where will the government stop? Will not the progress be, as in France, to make one convenient sacrifice a precedent and argument for another? The clergy will stand next on the black list; the nobles will follow. Will the many continue patient under the pressure of taxes when the plunder of the few is so familiar a substitute? In a revolution, as in a shipwreck, one part of the crew is kept alive by eating the other.

The national debt is in fact private property. We cannot see why the public should seize and appropriate to itself that description of private property rather than the ships in the Thames or the goods in Bond street. The seizure may be less unpopular, and may be more surely carried into effect than the capture of the ships or goods; but we cannot see that the plea of necessity will better justify the act in one case than the other. Indeed, the preference seems to be due to the property in the funds, as the government has solemnly renounced its power of control over it, and chosen to stand in no other relation to the owner of stock than as an equal contracting party.

To those, however, who may consider this last idea a mere refinement, too flimsy to be examined or regarded when the existence of a nation is at stake, another reflection may be suggested.

Many persons may be led, by their abhorrence of jacobinism and of French tyranny, to think favorably of sponging off the tremendous mass of English debt which cripples all their exertions in the war. England, once free from this mill-stone, they imagine, would be in no danger of sinking. The usefulness of such an act of injustice tolerably well reconciles them to its principle.

The most successful answer to the measure will be, to question its utility. The whole taxes fall far short of the expenditures of the nation. Suppose the debt sponged off, and all the products of the present taxes applied to necessary expenses, how shall the deficiency be made up? By new loans? Shall the British chancellor of the exchequer, with the sponge in one hand, hold out a subscription paper in the other? Who would lend? or escape the mad-house if he did? If loans could be obtained, a new national debt would be scored up at the rate of thirty-five or forty millions a year; and as soon as the size of the debt had begun to terrify some by its effect to cripple the energies of the government, and to tire others by the pressure of taxes, it must be sponged off again. Be it remembered, the violent remedies of great evils are almost always aggravations of those evils. If the minister, unable or unwilling to borrow, should raise taxes within the year, equal to the expenditures of war, what becomes of the plea of necessity?

On the whole, is it not right that the property of a nation should defend its liberty? and is this to be done to the extent that the public safety may require, unless the government can obtain loans in its necessity, that it will provide for in its prosperity? A great public debt is no doubt a great evil; but the loss of liberty and independence is one infinitely greater. It is some alleviation of that evil, for any government (for all are prone enough to become corrupt) habitually to guide its measures and its counsels by the experience that its good faith is its good policy. It ought to make men better to contemplate the example of a state, tried and tempted by adversity, and groaning under the load of taxes, yet still faithful to its engagements, and enjoying an ample resource in the confidence of its creditors by deserving their confidence and keeping their property sacred from violation. Such a state gives an illustrious lesson of morality to its subjects. It fulfils the great duty of all governments, which is to protect property. This is not all. It will seem, to some practical men, still more to the purpose, that such a state will have the control, in the extreme exigencies of the public affairs, of the last shilling of private property. Such is the spectacle of the British government.

It is left to others to compute how essential a part of the national wealth consists of property in the national debt, and how much poorer the nation would be by sponging it off. Such a measure would aggravate necessity; but we cannot conceive how it would supply means. As this violation of the public faith would be the most tremendous, as also the most unequal and unfair tax that ever was levied on a state, it is natural to suppose the dread of it and the dread of the enemy would sanction other very strong measures to get at the wealth of the subjects by taxes, and that they would cheerfully acquiesce, at least in their temporary adoption.

It is therefore, we confess, beyond our comprehension, how the stoppage of the interest of the public debt, in other words the sponge, for such it would prove, could relieve the distresses of Great Britain, or supply the resources for the prosecution of the war. It might ensure an English revolution. The work of destruction may be begun by choice, but it never stops while there is any thing left to destroy. Its hostility would be felt by the British government, and derided by that of France.

We know not how the British ministry can find money for their enormous charges; but nevertheless we believe they will find it, because it exists, and enough of it, in the hands of the opulent subjects of that monarchy.

We believe, too, they justly dread the terrible and incalculable evils of a bankruptcy, and that they will find means to avoid it. If a sense of common danger ever unites men, the British nation will be united; and if united and wisely governed, we hope they will prove unconquerable.

Admitting, then, that Great Britain will not be forced to submit to peace, which is to submit to the yoke of France, from the failure of her finances, it remains to inquire, how long and with what prospect of success she can pursue the war.

It does not appear that she could not prosper in commerce and private wealth, if the war should last half a century; and to those who fear the war may last forever, and therefore seem to think a bad peace ought to be chosen now, unless some definite time or some precise object could be proposed, as the end of the war, it is a sufficient answer to say, that war is a hard condition of national existence, but preferable to their subjugation by France. Base are Englishmen, unlike their ancestors, if they would not sooner toil for taxes to support the war, or bleed on a ship's deck, than sweat under the dominion of a French prefect. Perhaps we may wonder at their ideas; but Englishmen will dread ignominy more than taxes or wounds.

While the British navy continues mistress of the seas, it is scarcely possible that Bonaparte should execute his threat of an invasion. If, then, the English cannot make war on the land, nor the French on the sea, it would seem that military operations and military spirit must languish. There is reason to fear that this state of defensive languor will engender discontent in England. But though the expenses might be diminished, if Britain should have no allies, and should fit out no expeditions, they would still be enormous. When the fashionable folly of the volunteer army shall be no longer in vogue, an efficient and large regular army would enable Great Britain to strike her enemy in many vulnerable points. She ought to provide such an army, on which alone she could depend to expel the French, if they should ever land on the island. The distant colonies of France are vulnerable, and would yield to an attack. The employment of the forces would cherish the military spirit of her subjects; and conquests are among the best expedients to preserve harmony and union in the nation.

A solicitude about the ability of Great Britain to resist France, will be understood by some of the weak, and will be misrepresented by all the base and unprincipled, as implying a desire that the United States, in respect to maritime rights and national dignity, should lie at the mercy of the mistress of the ocean. On the contrary, let every real American patriot insist that our government should place the nation on its proper footing as a naval power. With a million tons of merchant shipping, and a hundred thousand seamen, equally brave and expert, it is the fault of a poor-spirited administration, that we are insignificant and despised. It is their fault that our harbors are blockaded, by three British ships, and that outrages are perpetrated within the waters that form part of our jurisdiction, such as no circumstances can justify. Can there exist a stronger proof that our insignificance is to be ascribed to a bad administration, than this single fact; with the greatest merchant marine in the world except one, and of consequence, capable of being soon the second naval power, (in our own seas the first,) we are utterly helpless; that, in the opinion even of our rulers themselves, our only mode of redress, when our commerce is obstructed, is *to destroy our commerce!* We have the means for its protection, which our administration, unhappily, think it would prove more expensive to use, than its protection would be worth. They would provide against the violation of our territory by tribute, and of our commerce by non-importation.

While, therefore, we explicitly disclaim all apology for the abuses of the British naval power; while we strongly reprobate the cowardice, or folly, or both, that leaves our country defenceless, when it is injured, we must view it as an interesting inquiry, whether England can resist France; for if she cannot, it is certain we shall not.

What could France do to annoy Great Britain? Nothing; but to create expense to her government. What could Great Britain do to annoy France? Much; enough to make the distress of war reach her subjects; to cut off nearly all her maritime trade; and to spread want, discontent, and despair from the Baltic to the Adriatic.

The colonies of the enemies of Great Britain would shrivel, like plants and flowers on the Arabian desert, if they were no longer moistened by the rills of commerce. We may assist our conjectures of what Great Britain may do, by asking ourselves what we should do in such a case, if we possessed the British navy, and were contending, as she is, for liberty and life against France.

DANGEROUS POWER OF FRANCE IV

The Repertory, MARCH, 1808

WHEN MEN indulge their passions, they seldom stop where they should; excess breeds more excess. Party hatred surpasses all other, as if fiends from the bottomless pit had breathed their fell inspiration into the human heart. Their virulence strikes the understanding blind, and blindness augments their virulence, till a civil war rages in the state, and without resort to arms, quenches half the joys and all the charities of life. In this condition, liberty is ejected from her temple and stripped of her ornaments and her charms. And as impunity is not often long indulged to habitual vice and folly, whether in a public or an individual, the enemy of the state seldom neglects the inviting opportunity to make a fatal progress, while the attention of the magistrate, who ought to be our common parent and protector, is wholly engrossed by a contest with his enemy. The chief ruler is in that case degraded from his exalted station. He is a man, and when such passions blind him, a weak and bad man too, a magistrate for disorder, and our guardian to betray us.

In these observations we should suppose every man would concur, who is capable of understanding them; and in this great crisis, we should think he could apply them too. Possibly, so predominant are party feelings, those will refuse assent to their truth, who can foresee their just political application. Nevertheless, let us presume to apply them.

Mr. Jefferson has wrapped up all diplomatic communications from France in mystery. Yet we believe it is unjust, on that account, to accuse him of a partial foundness for Bonaparte. Love Bonaparte! No human being ever loved him.

Love the crocodile; love the shark, who feeds upon the dead; or the royal tiger of Bengal, who snatches your children from the cradle, and cracks their bones in your sight. Mr. Jefferson may fear Bonaparte, but he cannot love him. Nor is it possible that he should wish to give him power in the United States. From the inestimable sacrifices he made to get his present power, we may be certain that he loves it. Nor can we admit that Mr. Jefferson, a veteran, and many choose to say an oracle in politics, can be blind to the formidable danger of the present day. He knows that France is not now in the political world what she was, when he was a public minister to Louis XVI. Excepting England, she has absorbed that world into her own limits. A change of fourteen centuries has passed over her head. She has gone back so much, and Attila, "the scourge of God," has come again.

Mr. Jefferson knows that there is but one obstacle to the progress of French power, and that is the hated British navy. The immortal spirit of the wood nymph liberty, dwells only in the British oak. Suppose that navy destroyed, would our liberty survive a week? The wind of the blow that should destroy British independence, would strike our own senseless to the earth. Boastful and vain as we are, the very thought of independence would take flight from our hearts.

We have a curiosity to know whether Mr. Jefferson and Mr. Madison do really believe we could support our liberty, if Great Britain had lost hers. Without intending to indulge in the too common rudeness and disrespect of party addresses, we should deem it a signal work of patriotism, if, by any thing we shall offer, we could induce those gentlemen to examine, with the precision and acuteness of mind that they are allowed to possess, this awful question for America, "If Great Britain falls, will not America fall? Shall we not lie in the dust at the conqueror's foot, and with servile, affected joy receive our chains without resistance?"

It will be ever fashionable to boast of the invincible spirit of freemen, as long as power is to be won by flattery. We remark, that some speakers in Congress assume it as a thing impossible, that an invading foe could make any progress in our country. Others, in party opposition to them, either blind to the truth, or afraid to speak it, readily assent to the assertion that the United States are unconquerable. Thus a dangerous delusion acquires not only a plausible authority, but it seems to be a violation of the sanctity of the national faith to expose it.

This is no time to trifle—let it be exposed.

If Great Britain were conquered, Bonaparte could have her fifteen hundred ships; if only humbled, he could have the ships of all the rest of Europe to transport an army under one of his lieutenants to our shores, as numerous as he might think necessary to ensure conquest. Power seldom long wants means. He could send over twenty thousand, and more, if wanted, of his dismounted horsemen, with their saddles, bridles, and equipments. He would not fail to secure horses from our islands, such as Long Island, and the extensive necks and promontories which could not be defended against him.

Being master of the sea, he could make large and frequent detachments from his camp to defenceless regions, which he would strip. To this, let it be added, the American army, if we should have an army, being concentred to some well-chosen mountainous place, would of course leave the cities a prey.

Thus, it cannot be doubted that he would have horses to remount his cavalry. Suppose a numerous French army, having two fifths of its force cavalry, with all the formidable thousands of light artillery that brought Austria and Prussia to his feet in a day. Would the American militia face this army? Suppose they do not—then our cities, our whole coast, and all the open cultivated country are French. Would the millions on and near the coast take flight to the mountains?

Could they subsist, or would they remain long unmolested there? Mountains, when no equal army was in the field, never did stop the soldiers of Bonaparte.

Let us come back, then, to our militia army, since we are obliged to see that the French would effectually conquer our country, if our army should not be able to check their rapid progress. Could we collect an army? On all the coast would be terror, busy concern to hide property, and to shelter women, helpless age, and infancy. The seaports would not only retain their own men, but call in those of the neighboring country to defend them. Probably they would ask an addition of troops from government.

It would, therefore, be a difficult and very slow work to collect a militia army equal in numbers to the French. Near fifty thousand men were sent to Egypt, and as many more to St. Domingo. Had either of those armies landed here, could we have faced them with an equal force, equal in numbers? We think not.

Let Mr. Jefferson ask any skilful old continental officer, whether our army of militia would push bayonet with the French. No military man would say that our militia would stand the tug of war, and defeat the French.

Did we not, cries some wordy patriot, contend with the British? The answer would be long, to make it as decisive as we think it really is. The British were cooped up in Boston a year. In 1778, Sir William Howe had only four or five hundred cavalry, and he moved as if he was more afraid of our beating him, than resolved to beat us.

At Long Island, Washington was totally defeated, and might have been made prisoner with his whole army. He was not pursued. In the third year of the war, his troops, and even the militia of the States in the scene of the war, had become considerably disciplined. It is not denied, that with three years' preparation we could have an army; but we make no preparation; and unless we enlist our men, the parade of militia is a serious buffoonery. When Sir William Howe forced our men from the field, he had no cavalry, and our men could flee faster than his could pursue. But the French— experience has shown, that when they win battles, they decide the war. Myriads of cavalry press upon the fugitives, and in half a day the defence of a nation is captive or slain. Defeat is irremediable destruction.

Would our stone walls stop their horse? Then the pioneers would pull down those walls. Shooting from behind fences would not stop an army; nor would our militia venture on a measure that would be fatal; the numerous and widely extended flanking parties would cut off all such adventures to a man. No, Mr. Jefferson, do not lull your fears to sleep, do not aggravate our public dangers by a mistake of our situation. There are times, and the case of invasion would be a time, when the mistakes of our rulers could not be committed with impunity.

With an army less than two hundred thousand, but with double the common proportion of cavalry, Bonaparte has overrun the German empire, Austria, Prussia, and all continental Europe from the Adriatic to the Baltic, rich, populous, and computed formerly to arm a million of soldiers.

The democratic gazettes have uniformly maintained, that Bonaparte's unvaried success was not owing to chance, but to the real, irresistible superiority of the French arms, to their newly improved tactics, and to the impetuosity of their attack. All this, rare as our agreement with the democrats may be, all this we believe; and we solemnly warn Mr. Jefferson not lightly to reject the long habitual opinion of his party. We firmly, though unwillingly, believe that as the old Romans were superior to their enemies, so the French are at least as much superior to their enemies by land. The vast extent of both empires, Roman and French, grew out of this superiority.

Hence we conclude, that if our militia army should fight

a battle, they would lose it. They would inevitably lose it, and the loss of the battle would be the loss of the country. The French would hold the coast by their fleet, and the interior by their army. Be it remembered, too, that Canada would be French, if Great Britain should be subdued, and the Floridas and Louisiana, though she should not. Where, then, would be the security of the mountains? Much dreadful experience and more dreadful fears would follow the conquest, till at length, like the rest of the world, we should enjoy the quiet of despair and the sleep of slavery. Popularity, as dear perhaps as liberty, will be sought no more; and we shall place our happiness, if slaves may talk of happiness, in the smiles, or, still better, in the neglect of a master.

We have purposely omitted an infinity of proofs in corroboration of our melancholy conclusion, that, in case of a French invasion, the country would be literally conquered. We should tamely accept a Corsican prince for a king, and in virtue of our alliance with France, agree by treaty to maintain French troops enough to keep down insurrection. Far be it from us to believe, that our fellow-citizens in the militia are not brave. Their very bravery, we apprehend, would ensure their defeat; they would dare to attempt what militia cannot achieve. Nor let the heroic speech-makers pretend that our citizens would swear to live free or die; and that they would resist till the country was depopulated or emancipated. There is no foundation in human nature for this boast. The Swiss were free, and loved their liberty as well as men ever did; yet they are enslaved, and quiet in their chains. Experience shows, that men are glad to survive the loss of liberty. They must be mad, to continue to resist the power that on trial has been found superior and irresistible. Myriads of persons, we see, are glad on pecuniary encouragement, to go into the army, where every democrat will insist there cannot be liberty because there is restraint.

Our readers might soon be tired, if they are not already,

but we should never be tired ourselves to diversify our argument to prove, in contradiction to the groundless and perhaps treacherous pretensions of faction, that our country is absolutely defenceless against Bonaparte, when master of the sea. We could urge, that the French troops marched through countries having three or four times as many people as the United States, with the quietness of a procession. Does he not confide in the conquest of Great Britain, if he could only reach the shore with his troops? Yet Great Britain has twice our population, in a narrow compass too, and nearly one hundred times our military force.

With so many proofs, after so decisive experience of the resistless march of the French, is it not presumption, folly, madness to suppose we could be free, if France had the British fleet? To our minds the proof is demonstration.

We do not urge this fearful conclusion because we despise our countrymen, or wish to see America dishonored. Far, far from our hearts are such abominable wishes. Look, look, fellow-countrymen, as we do, to your dear, innocent children. Ask your hearts, if they can bear so racking a question, whether a shallow confidence, in our unarmed security against Bonaparte, in case Great Britain should fall, does not tend to devote them to the rage of a restless, unappeasable tyrant. We tremble at the thought that our own dear children will be in Bonaparte's conscription for St. Domingo, in case the Gallican policy of our government should be pursued, till its natural tendencies are accomplished.[50]

To fools we say nothing, nothing to traitors, with whom a troubled republic is always cursed; but we would ask Mr. Jefferson, we would ask all sober citizens, whether, if the danger of an invasion be considered as really impending, we

---

[50] *The writer could scarcely speak of his children, during the last few months of his life, without expressing his deep apprehensions of their future servitude to the French.* [S. AMES]

ought not to have an army to meet it? We ask further, would a raw army, raised when the foe is on our shores, be fit to oppose him? Would you stake the life of our liberty upon the resistance that paper could make against iron?

No; every man would say, that if we are to fight an invading enemy, sixty thousand strong, in 1810 or 1812, we have no time to lose in raising an army, by enlistment, stronger than the invaders, and training them to an equality of subordination, discipline, and confidence in themselves and their officers. Such an army, with cavalry, artillery, engineers, &c., would be too expensive for our means, or for the temper of our citizens, who have been studiously taught to hold taxes as grievances and wrongs. The thing, we grant, is impossible. To depend on a militia not enlisted nor disciplined, as before mentioned, is madness.

It follows, then, we think, irresistibly, demonstratively, that our single hope of security is in the triumphs of the British navy. While that rides mistress of the ocean, the French can no more pass it to attack us, than they could ford the bottomless pit.

Hitherto we have designedly avoided all party topics. We have gone upon the supposition that the democrats do not wish their children slaves to Bonaparte any more than our own. We take it for clear, that it is of more national importance to be free than to carry coffee to Amsterdam. If then we have so great interests depending, we cannot but wonder that Mr. Jefferson should endanger them for the sake of minor interests, which are, in comparison, but as the small dust of the balance. He professes to aim his measures at the destruction of the British "tyranny of the seas;" and he seems to exult in the thought that they are adequate to his end. God forbid that they should be! God, of his mercy, forbid, that after having led our forefathers by the hand, and as it were, by his immediate power planted a great nation in the wilderness, he should permit the passions or the errors of our chief to plunge us into ruin and slavery! Shall this French Magog be allowed to pluck our star from its sphere, and quench its bright orb in the sea?

It is apprehended that Mr. Jefferson is entirely convinced that Great Britain is now making her expiring efforts. It is said he holds it impossible that she should resist Bonaparte two years longer. Then let him wear sackcloth. Let him gather a colony, and lead them to hide from a conqueror's pursuit in the trackless forest near the sources of the Missouri. Frost, hunger, and poverty, will not gripe so hard as Bonaparte.

But if he expects the speedy destruction of Great Britain, what motive has he to exert himself to hasten it? He knows mankind, he knows Bonaparte too well to hope that the tyrant's hand will be the lighter for that merit. That bosom, so notoriously steeled against pity, will not melt to friendship. Among the infinite diversity of a madman's dreams, was there ever one so extravagant, as that a republic might safely trust its liberty to the sentiment of a master? Every moon-beam at Washington must have shot frenzy, if such a motive among politicians could have influenced action. If liberty should fall, as it will if France prevails, at least let us have the consolation to say, our hands have not assisted in the assassination.

But is it so very clear that Great Britain will fall in the conflict? A youthful conqueror, scorning all doubts of the unlimited efficiency of his power, has prohibited the use of British manufactures, and all intercourse even of neutrals with her merchants. He expects to cut off the roots of her greatness, or to see her wither like a girdled oak, and her tall trunk, nodding to its fall, making it dangerous to approach her. He seems, like many of our politicians, to suppose that her greatness is factitious, and that her foreign trade is the aliment and life of its support. For our part, we deem her grandeur intrinsic, the fair fruit of her constitution, her justice, her arts, and her magnanimity. But, as we mean to avoid contested points, we restrain ourselves to consider the effect of Bonaparte's decrees to ruin her. He is neither omnipotent nor omniscient. Of course, we imagine that distance, art, avarice, and necessity, will conspire to elude his vindictive blockading orders.

If he succeeds, we hope he will not conquer England. If he fails, as we trust he will fail, his attempt will furnish her with augmented means of a perpetual resistance. British goods will be clandestinely admitted into the continent after they have been charged with British duties. The scarcity will augment the price, so that the duty will not prevent the sale; on the contrary there will be the strongest allurements of profit. The French government will be so far from able to suppress the traffic that we are rather to expect it will be itself under the necessity of occasionally relaxing the rigor of its decrees. After having for some time contemplated the effect of Bonaparte's decrees, we have gradually subdued our fears of the impoverishment of Great Britain from their operation.

Nor let Mr. Jefferson imagine that our country can derive any temporary advantage from our coöperation in his decrees. He disdains to wait for the slow progress of art to accomplish his purposes. He now expects to win allies only by terror. Let them hate, if they do but fear, is his maxim. If Great Britain enforces her countervailing orders, our neutrality cannot longer assist to supply his wants. Enraged to be thus met by Great Britain, nothing remains but for him to intimidate Mr. Jefferson into an alliance. The world's master allows no neutrality. In fact there are no neutrals. The maritime law supposes a society of nations bound together by reciprocal rights and duties. That society is dissolved; and it is chimerical, if not unwarrantable, for the United States to claim singly the aggregated and supposed residuary rights devolved upon us by the departed nations. The old system is gone; and it is a mockery, or worse, for one nation to affect to represent a dozen once independent States now swallowed up by a conqueror. Ambition will violate our moonshine rights; and if we submit to his decrees, we ourselves violate our neutral duties. What tyranny will do in contempt of right, self-preservation permits the other belligerent to do in strict conformity with it. Where then is neutrality? Let us be ashamed of a petulant strife about lost and irrecoverable pretensions. It is a sort of posthumous wisdom, that when the public dangers thicken, always looks back, and never looks round our actual position. Why should we not look our condition in the face? The question is not about the profits of navigation, but the security of our existence.

Why do our public men wilfully blind themselves, and regard no dangers but such as they apprehend from the hostility of party? The earth we tread on holds the bones of the deceased patriots of the revolution. Why will the sacred silence of the grave be broken? Will the illustrious shades walk forth into public places, and audibly pronounce a warning to convince us that the independence, for which they bled, is in danger? No; without a miracle, the exercise of our reason would convince us that our independence is in danger from France; and if Great Britain falls by force, terror alone would bring us into subjection.

We do not love or respect our country less than those who inconsiderately boast of its invincible strength and prowess. As the destroyer of nations has enslaved Europe, and as only one nation, Great Britain, has hindered his coming here to conquer us, they have no ears to hear, they have no hearts to feel for our country, who would break down that obstacle and let him in.

This is not a party effusion; it proceeds from hearts that are ready to burst with anxiety on the prospect of the political insanity that seems ready to join the foe. It is republican suicide, it is treachery to the people, to make them an innocent sacrifice to the passions of our rulers.

Let Mr. Jefferson avail himself of the power that his weight with his own party gives him, and stop the progress of our fate. We do not ask him to go to war with France. Consult prudence, and renounce the affection of that false honor which has been late so much upon our lips. He will find the federalists love their country better than their party. Let there be peace, merely peace, we say nothing of alliance with Great Britain; and if our champion falls in the combat, let us not, when we perish, deplore the fatal folly of having contributed to hasten his and our destruction.

NON-INTERCOURSE ACT

The Repertory, AUGUST, 1806

Our anti-commercial rulers seem to think still that the non-intercourse act will bring Great Britain to terms. Sometime in December, the gun which Congress primed and loaded must go off, unless John Bull, who is so notoriously afraid of a gun, shall, before the day fixed for his fate, turn from the error of his ways, and by repentance obtain Mr. Jefferson's mercy.

No one will deny the great importance of this subject; or that the question in respect to our maritime rights, which we have decided so much off-hand, may possibly have two sides to it; that Great Britain contests our doctrine, and believes, or affects to believe, her admission of it would be fatal to her naval greatness and independence. When, therefore, she is so loath and so much afraid to yield the point, it seems as if her finally yielding must depend on her being still more afraid of our resentment than of every other ill consequence.

The matter will, of course, undergo examination in England, how much reason she has to be afraid of us; and if our resentment shall appear to be of two evils the greatest, we, who lay national honor out of the account, are naturally enough ready to expect she will humble herself in the dust before Mr. Monroe, to avert our wrath, that "distant thunder" which the *National Intelligencer* so distinctly heard in December last.

But that typographical thunder, which was expected to shake the plates and porringers on the shelves at St. James's, has been muffled on this side of the Atlantic. Our public will not break its nap on the apprehension of Mr. Wright's, or Mr. Gregg's, or Mr. Nicholson's breaking the peace with Great Britain. Nothing can exceed our apathy. Whether it be that we are a stupid people, or that we feel to excess and to frenzy as party men, so that as patriots we feel and fear nothing; or that our mortified pride takes some delight in blustering and threatening Great Britain, while France empties her vessels of honor on our heads; or that evils in prospect for the next year have no terrors to the politicians, who never look so far; whatever it may be owing to, the fact is, we behave on the question, whether we shall have any trade, even more strangely careless than the Dutch do in respect to the matter of having a French king or a republic. It seems as if our rulers had reason to be bold when they are preparing to make us suffer, by our defiance of their power to make us think. Says Moses to the vicar, "the corpse can't take cold." Our indifference may not be a shield of defence, but it is opium against our dread of blows.

If our indifference did not surpass belief, the subject would have been long ago eagerly discussed. We should have scrutinized, much more closely than Mr. Nicholson is capable of doing, the grounds of our assumed opinion, that Great

Britain has such great reason to be afraid of us; and probably we should have found occasion to suspect that party has deceived our expectations on this question, as on almost every other. Everybody knows that Mr. Jefferson dare not go to war; the federalists are the only enemies whom he ventures to defy; and even their accusations are not to be encountered in close fight. He cannot fight Spain without first asking leave of France; of course a Spanish war is out of the question.

To fight Great Britain, is equally so; yet, as great complaint is made of captures, and as Bonaparte will be soothed by a show of hostility against England, the show is resolved upon. But be it noted, the show may lead to the thing itself! He begins to bully. Great Britain scorns to yield to his paper bullets. New acts must be passed, still more angry than Nicholson's. Popular rage grows out of commercial distress, and war follows. If this course be only foreseen, will Mr. Jefferson's admirers stick to him? Certainly not.

The federalists say, and really believe, that Mr. Nicholson's act is a feeble measure. Suppose, on trial, it proves feeble, what is to be done? Is some new act to be passed, that will not be feeble? What act, short of war or reprisals, can it be?

Wise nations, foreseeing the ordinary progress of such hostile acts, will stop short, and compute their force before they resort to them. Pride and passion once up, interest weighs little; and our threats will raise either British resentment or contempt. If we put them on their mettle, they will no doubt show how little they regard their commercial profits, even if we could seriously diminish them. Mr. Nicholson's act is avowedly of the nature of compulsion; and we know how the attempt at compulsion will affect a government, which, we choose to say, has at least as much pride as power.

If anybody in America cared about the consequences of this commercial warfare, which does not seem to be the case, it would be proper to point out the futility of the system adopted by our Solomon in council. The two countries are, no doubt, in a condition to do each other a good deal of harm. We forbear to enter at length on the inquiry, which can do the most. Let our southern wiseacres consider carefully what would be the consequence, if Great Britain, in retaliation for Mr. Nicholson's act, should prohibit, after December next, the importation into Great Britain of American rice, cotton, and tobacco. They will no doubt say, these articles are a monopoly; they cannot get them elsewhere. It is easy to say so; but is it true? Bluster, gentlemen; but before it be too late, try likewise to think.

LESSONS FROM HISTORY I

The Repertory, OCTOBER, 1806

CHARLES II., King of Great Britain, was secretly a catholic; and his subjects were, ninety-nine out of a hundred, protestants. He was fond of arbitrary power; and his people passionately fond of liberty. The times required a close application to public business; and his temper drove him headlong into licentious pleasures. His revenue had narrow limits; and his prodigality no limits at all.

He was one of the most pleasant gentlemen in England, and as much of a scholar as our Mr. Jefferson, though less of a pedant and a *quidnunc*. Yet, after being possessed of unbounded popularity, he lost it all, and deserved to lose it, because in every thing, as a king, he acted in the meanest subserviency to his prejudices and pleasures as a man.

Accordingly, through his whole disgraceful reign, the English nation suffered much, and apprehended every thing, from his corrupt and treacherous policy; treacherous, because he pursued an interest of his own, separate from the general interest. Indeed, that nation still suffers from his misconduct; for Charles basely accepted a pension from Louis XIV., the Bonaparte of the seventeenth century, in consideration of which he not only forbore to act against the schemes of universal empire, that Louis XIV. had then begun to pursue, but he hindered the parliament from disturbing the conquering career of France; nay, to the astonishment of all Europe, he joined Louis in attacking the Dutch. It was then in the power of England to have prevented the aggrandizement of France; and such was the desire of the English parliament and nation, such was their true policy.

By neglecting that opportunity, oceans of blood have since been shed in vain. In 1672, the renewal of the triple alliance, negotiated by Sir William Temple, would have confined France to her ancient limits, probably without a war. But, though it would have been easy to prevent her from growing great, it has proved hard, indeed impossible, after she had become great, to reduce her to her former size. The errors of 1672 are visited on the heads of Englishmen in 1806.

Every democrat will exclaim, kings are base creatures, who have no interest in the good of the people. This vile example is not to our purpose.

A king can be nothing else but a king; when he loses his throne, he cannot expect to preserve his life. But a magistrate, chosen to play the part of a king for four years, may have, and if he feels a low ambition, will certainly think he has, an interest as a man, very little connected with the temporary splendor of his office. He is to the full as unwilling to be dethroned as any other king, and therefore he will think much of the popularity that will secure his reëlection at the end of four years, and very little of the public evils that will lie hidden from the eyes of the people for the next seven.

It would be childish to think a demagogue will be a disinterested patriot. It would be absurd to expect that anybody but a patriot of the loftiest elevation of soul, would prefer the public to himself, and would turn himself out of office by doing thankless and unpopular acts of duty.

A demagogue, then, if, for the punishment of the sins of our nation, any future president should prove to be such, would certainly dismantle our ships, and leave the forts of our harbors to crumble into ruins. He would disband our feeble regular regiments, and make haste to repeal taxes, that he may grow rich in popularity, while the government is ostentatiously made to decline in resources. He will bluster to show the spirit that he does not possess, and pay tribute to hide the insults and wrongs that he dare not revenge. In this way, his own shame will be exposed three or four years the later; and the public evils will happen at last, with all the aggravation that improvidence and folly can bring.

We make no comparisons; we leave the reader to apply facts as he may think them applicable. But we must confess, the spirit of party has found our countrymen base, or has made them so, if they can behold the all-conquering progress of French ambition, and then think, with any temper, that our country has not only been left, but for five years artificially and systematically made, defenceless, as if it was intended for a prey.

LESSONS FROM HISTORY II

THE STUART FAMILY kept possession of the English throne from 1603, when Queen Elizabeth died, to 1688, when James II. abdicated the government, a period of eighty-five years. Though not very bad men, they were bad kings. Their notions of government were such as have been since called tory. They were sincere in their principles of arbitrary power, which were no doubt utterly inconsistent with English liberty. We would not be understood to justify all the conduct of the parliament against Charles I.; nevertheless, we hold the English in grateful respect for their spirit and good sense, by which they nobly asserted their own liberty, the ever-glorious, fundamental principles, of which our ancestors, God bless their memory! brought over to New England.

But the ambition and hypocrisy of the parliamentary leaders, and the tyranny which inevitably grew out of their democracy, produced an abhorrence of levelling notions, and an attachment to the church and monarchy, which gave rise, or at least credit and currency, to the doctrines of passive obedience and non-resistance; doctrines subversive of all liberty.

Hence it was that, when the infatuation of James II. had assisted William, Prince of Orange, to dethrone him, (and the folly of James did more towards it than the arms of William,) the English parliament cautiously and timidly admitted the principles of the revolution. To unmake kings, seemed to them a work that might be repeated successively, with less and less necessity, and at length licentiousness, such as followed the beheading of Charles I. would ensue. When, therefore, Queen Mary, wife of King William and daughter of the exiled King James, died, William remained king by no right of blood, but only by virtue of an act of parliament, which might be repealed by any change of the majority. In this perilous state of things, men's minds were agitated with the fears of a renewal of those bloody dissensions, which the contest for the crown between the rival houses of York and Lancaster, had engendered and protracted for more than a century.

At length King William died, and also his rival, King James; and Anne, another daughter of King James, succeeded to the crown, according to the act of parliament. The death of the Duke of Gloucester, the only child of Anne, happened before the death of King William; and as there was no hope of her having more children, men began to turn their eyes to her brother, the pretender, so called. He was an infant, when the bigotry of his father, King James, obliged him to take refuge in the court of Louis XIV. It seemed, therefore, to many lovers of their country, a needless and merciless persecution of this young prince, to visit his father's follies on his innocent head, and to prefer the Princess Sophia of Hanover, one of the most distant relations of the royal family, to the pretender, who, in right of blood, was heir to the British crown. Yet the whig party got the famous Act of Settlement passed in favor of the Princess Sophia, by virtue of which King George III. now holds his power.

In these singular circumstances, it was not strange that there was a secret intestine agitation of parties and opinions throughout the whole of Queen Anne's reign. She herself, no doubt, wished that her brother, the pretender, might succeed her, in preference to the house of Hanover, whom she deemed strangers. Nevertheless, as she held her crown in prejudice of her brother's right, by an act of parliament, and as the nation had an unconquerable dread of popery and arbitrary power, to which James and his son were supposed to be wedded, she was forced to conceal her inclination and intentions. This was the more necessary, as her whig ministry, men of vast abilities, were possessed of unbounded popularity, and the victories of the Duke of Marlborough threw a glory over her reign and nation.

But so inconstant is popularity, that the credit of the whigs began to decline, in the midst of successes and triumphs. The queen seized the moment to dismiss her ministers, of whom she was weary, and to introduce the tories in their stead.

The new tory ministry affected great zeal for the prosecution of the war against France, though in their hearts they wished for peace, because the war supported the popularity of the whigs and the power of Marlborough, their leader, and because it was the interest of their party to have peace. Peace, on many accounts, was indispensable to them, especially before France was reduced in her power, because they looked forward to the death of Queen Anne, when they might need the powerful help of France to place the pretender on the throne.

The Duke of Marlborough had been continued in command; and such was his superior talent, that he had every reason to expect to strip Louis XIV. of all his conquests, and to reduce him to a condition of weakness, which would forever defeat the enormous project of aggrandizement which had agitated Europe for fifty years, and which has lately overturned it from its foundation. So far the views of Marlborough and his former whig associates seem to be justified by the wisest policy and the truest patriotism. But the tories made a clamor about the expenses of the war; they preached economy, they affected to prefer the arts and the benefits of peace to the glitter of triumphs and to the delusive acquisitions of war; delusive, they said, for, while England gained nothing, her allies were aggrandizing themselves by conquests, which were won by English arms. The finest writers of almost any age joined the tory cause with their pens; and at length the new ministers dismissed the Duke of Marlborough, and privately signed preliminary articles of peace with France. This dishonorable transaction was not long a secret. It produced jealousy and discord among the allies, as might be expected, and at length a wretched peace, which somewhat humbled France, but stripped her of little of the means, and of none of the disposition, at a more convenient season, to become the mistress of Europe. This she has at length effected.

Thus we see that a party invested with power, when it has an interest distinct from the national interest, will be carried on by its hatred of its political enemies to sacrifice the public cause to its own. Heaven forbid that France should at last triumph over the United States by the operation of such a party interest in America!

LESSONS FROM HISTORY III

GREAT BRITAIN, whose name and independence, whose king and people every jacobin thinks it a debt of gratitude to France to abhor, was once the sovereign of the territory now called the United States of America.

Mr. Jefferson's wise, vigorous, and pacific conduct has been so much puffed by his friends, it has become of importance, and will be of more and more, to scrutinize it. If Mr. Jefferson, now we are independent, has done less for our honor and safety than Great Britain did when we were colonies; if he has done that little later, and in a manner to make it rather worse than doing nothing at all, our respect for Mr. Jefferson's policy ought to decline, or his friends ought to look out for some other more solid props to support it.

It would seem strange, if on inquiry it should appear that our tyrant and oppressor, as the democrats hold it orthodoxy to consider Great Britain; it would seem strange that she should have acted with more spirit, promptness, and liberality in asserting our rights, than our government is now willing that we, independent States, should act for ourselves.

Facts, which often spoil the work of party, facts will show, that no sooner had the war for the succession of the daughter of the Emperor Charles VI. to the dominion of the house of Austria ended, by the peace of Aix-la-Chapelle, in 1748, than France began to extend her forts on our frontiers from the St. Lawrence to the Mississippi. She pretended that her colonies, Canada and Louisiana, extended to the Alleghany mountains, and included the Mississippi, the Ohio, the Monongahela, and other rivers, as well as the great lakes. France did not merely claim the territory—she proceeded to occupy it with military posts, and to expel the few English settlers that she found within her pretended limits.

Did the English king tell his parliament that these aggressions sprung from the wantonness of subalterns, unauthorized by their government, and that he relied on the justice of his most christian majesty for redress? Did he send a humble embassy to Paris to beg for it? and, when it could not be had for begging, did he get an appropriation of two millions, and then spend fifteen to buy it? and, after finding that he had paid for it in vain, did he send to Paris two millions more for leave only to talk about buying it again? When Spain encroached upon us, when she stopped the navigation of the Mississippi, in avowed violation of our solemn right by treaty, what did we leave undone that baseness, crawling on its belly, like a reptile on the ground, could possibly do to prevail on the proud aggressor to forbear treading upon us? We asked his contempt, as if it was our interest, by obtaining it, to quiet his groundless fears of retaliation.

In 1754, Great Britain reasoned and acted very differently. She might have said, these encroachments of France will make the factious colonists feel their dependence upon the mother country a little more than they do. The acts of La Galissoniere, the French governor of Canada, are not the acts of Louis XV. I may wink at these wrongs, and postpone my vengeance till I have refreshed my wasted strength after the disastrous war that I have just terminated; an unpopular, and perhaps impolitic war, which has increased the burdens of my people, and their impatience in bearing them. If parliament had sitten with closed doors, the king might have talked two languages, like Mr. Jefferson, war and peace.

Great Britain said nothing of the sort. She looked at these

aggressions, and she saw in the whole aspect of affairs, as in a looking-glass, blotches of dishonor, like leprosy in her face, if she should bear these wrongs with a tameness that she foresaw would multiply them. She did not hesitate— orders were immediately sent to all the governors to repel force by force; and Major Washington, a name sacred to honor and patriotism, was sent out to repel the French on the Ohio. Nevertheless, though war was waged in America, it was not declared in Europe. To the spirit of Great Britain, so promptly and powerfully roused in our cause, we owe the expulsion of the French from Canada; an event which has saved us from a war with France to maintain our independence.

Here then are two cases, their circumstances not unlike, the policy of Great Britain and Mr. Jefferson totally unlike. Compare them.

LESSONS FROM HISTORY IV

Rome was a republic from its very birth. It is true, for two hundred and forty-four years it was subject to kings; but the spirit of liberty was never more lofty at any period of its long troubled life than when Rome was governed by kings. They were, in war, generals; in peace, only magistrates. For seven hundred years Rome remained a republic; and during every minute of that time the spirit of conquest excited and ruled every Roman breast.

For thirty years America has been a republic; and during every minute of those thirty years the only question has been, how could she make independence cheap, and not for one minute how could liberty be made durable and glorious.

Liberty has rocked the cradle and suckled the infancy of

both republics. They are different; but why they are different, and how different they are, it would take an octavo volume to tell.

Glory was the object of the Roman republic; and gain is of ours. A Roman felt as if the leprosy had broken out in his cheek when his country was dishonored; and *we charge it in our ledger.* To Rome it cost blood; to us, ink or tribute.

Soon or late every great nation will act out its character. As we do not aspire to glory, we shall never reach it; and our short-sighted policy, which will not provide by the expense of to-morrow for the danger of the day after, will be overwhelmed at last by the destruction of the sordid interests for which we have sacrificed more precious ones.

Without forces, ships, or revenue, we get tallow on our ribs like the oxen, we make honey like the bees, we carry fleeces like the sheep, and we build nests like the birds, not for ourselves, but for others, for Bonaparte.

LESSONS FROM HISTORY V

MACHIAVEL, in his History of Florence, has shown that the rivalship of the great men and the common people is the everlasting source of discord in republics. In Rome, he says, it led to dominion; in Florence, to slavery and dependency. Whence, he asks, was the difference? In Rome, every thing was settled by reason and expostulation; and in Florence by the sword. In Rome they wished to employ their great men; and in Florence to exterminate them. Accordingly, Rome grew from little to great; and Florence dwindled from great to little.

The disciples of the school of equality would learn by studying Machiavel, who studied nature, how wide those men run from the principles of liberty, who carry those principles to impracticable extremes.

But what avails federal truth? If every gravestone of a departed republic bore a lesson of wisdom and of warning, the democrats would shut their eyes rather than look upon it. They have no idea of any principles, except in their extremes, when they are no longer principles. We not only seem to choose our own destiny, but to control it. By our extravagance we render every thing impossible, but our degradation.

It may please God, in the course of his providence, to train our nation by misfortune, and to fit it for greatness by some ages of adversity; but if we should be left to train ourselves, we must be abject and base.

WAR IN DISGUISE

THE WRITER of this pamphlet[51] introduces his subject with some remarks on the importance of the British navy, which few persons in America, and none in England, will be inclined to controvert. Bonaparte's naval efforts, he says, have been great and unremitted, and far more formidable than could have been expected, considering the destruction of French commerce. "The loss of the British superiority at sea," he adds, "would remove from before the ambition of France almost every obstacle, by which its march to universal empire could be impeded." The truth of this position also seems to be clear.

---

[51] *James Stephen,* War in Disguise; or, the frauds of the neutral flags *(London, New York: Hopkins & Seymour, 1806). This review is reprinted from the* Monthly Anthology *of the Boston Athenaeum (1806), vol. III, pp. 47–53.*

To show the possibility that Great Britain may finally lose, and France acquire the sovereignty of the seas, he proposes, as the chief design of this pamphlet, to prove, "that by the encroachments and frauds of the neutral flags France has found a nursery and a refuge for her navy, and that of her Dutch and Spanish allies, as well as secret conduits for those resources, by which she has nourished and augmented it."

Here again, no doubt will exist, that neutral commerce is of great and indispensable advantage to France and her allies, without which they could scarcely draw a single dollar from their colonies. This position of things furnishes a very strong inducement to Great Britain to disturb the commerce of neutrals with her enemies' colonies, and to trump up new and specious principles to vindicate her aggressions. The principles of this pamphlet writer ought therefore to be examined with some suspicion in America, but they ought to be carefully examined.

The pamphlet proceeds to state the singular fact, that, destitute of all active commerce, as France certainly is, and of all means of affording naval protection to her commerce, nevertheless her resources appear to be unimpaired in consequence. This, it is truly said, is a different result from what ever happened in all former wars. Only the *partial* stoppage of the French commerce by the superiority of the British fleets used to produce the last extremity of distress to the people and government of France; so that, strong as the French ever were on land, "the house of Bourbon was vanquished by the masters of the sea."

He accounts for this strange circumstance by ascribing its cause to the use of the neutral flags. If he supposes, that the great mass of the cargoes of the colonial produce, freighted on board American vessels is not, *bona fide*, the property of Americans, we believe he is grossly mistaken. American capital is adequate to the purchase of these products, and this is what Englishmen cannot easily be made to believe.

Nevertheless the purchase of the crops of Martinique and Guadaloupe by American merchants obviously relieves the French planters from the pressure of the war. How is their prosperity retarded or obstructed, if they can have a full price for their crops, the superiority of the British navy notwithstanding? It is true, not a French merchant flag is seen on the ocean. But as the French planter owns no ships, and is interested directly only in the sale of his rum, coffee, cotton, sugar, &c. if the neutral will buy these articles and pay for them at a good price, it is plain the war does not reach the colony to cramp its growth, or to obstruct its supplies, which are abundantly furnished by neutrals.

This state of things, which is verified by the most ample experience, produces no little disappointment and vexation to the belligerent. Hence, as the British arms and our commercial gains mutually obstruct each other, it is extremely natural, that angry invectives and recriminations should ensue between the American and British nations. The usual progress of popular passions, when so excited, is to insult, retaliation, and war. This is a course, which it is incredible the government of either of the two countries should wish to pursue.

Supposing that there is not on either side a disposition to fight, there ought to be a mutual willingness to argue.

The pamphlet writer proceeds to examine, 1st, the origin, nature, and extent of what he calls the evils and abuses of neutral flags. 2d, the remedy and right of applying it. 3d, the prudence of that resort.

Under the first head, "the origin, nature, and extent of the evil," he premises, "that a neutral has no right to deliver a belligerent from the pressure of his enemy's hostilities, by trading with his colonies in time of war, in a way that was prohibited in time of peace." Here we find the marrow of the great question, at present depending between the belligerent and neutral nations.

To support the negative, i.e. that a neutral has no right in time of war to any other trade with an enemy's colonies, than what is permitted in time of peace, he quotes at length the opinion of Sir William Scott, in the case of the Emanuel, Nov. 1799. This, he asserts, was the doctrine of the war of 1756. One of the leading points decided against the Dutch in that war was, we believe, that French colonial property on board Dutch vessels was liable to condemnation; in other words that free ships did not make free goods. That they do, is indeed pretended by the French, and we believe only by the French, or those under their influence; but there is demonstrably no ground for such a doctrine, either as they pretend to derive it from the law of nations, or from a just regard to the commercial advantage of neutrals. By establishing such a doctrine the French, while inferior at sea, would gain much, but the neutral American would certainly be a loser.

If the principle, that "free ships make free goods," had been established, as was vainly attempted, twenty-five years ago, neutrals would have been deprived of immense pecuniary advantages, which they have hitherto enjoyed, and would, in exchange, have derived from the innovation no benefit, to which they are not fully entitled by the acknowledged law of nations. By the operation of the laws of maritime war, the commerce of belligerents is subject to heavy losses and expenses, from which neutrals are exempt. This gives to the latter an advantage over the former, equal, at the least, to the full amount of those losses and expenses; or it drives the belligerent merchant from the sea, and thus leaves to the neutral a virtual monopoly of the whole commerce, which both had carried on. It in effect, therefore, enables the neutral to trade with the belligerent, without the possibility of the latter being an equal competitor; of course *it enables the neutral to sell unusually dear, and buy unusually cheap.* He sells dear in the country of the belligerent, because a part of the supply is cut off, and a part carried at an extremely dear rate. He buys the products of the belligerent cheap, because a part of the usual buyers withdraw from the market, and others cannot afford the accustomed price. Thus the insecurity and increased expense of the belligerent's own trade, augment the profits of the neutral, whose trade is safe. But if free ships made the goods free, *all the commerce would be equally safe,* and the neutral would have no new reward, but simple freight (always the lowest of mercantile wages) to compensate him for the various inconveniences, to which the war exposes him; that is, he would be confined to the earnings of a mere porter, instead of superadding the profits of a merchant, and the income of a capitalist.

We have great doubts, however, whether the decisions of 1756 afford any very clear authority, either for the present British principles, or for the claims of neutral nations. The state of things now in existence is totally unlike any thing that ever was in 1756, or in any war before 1793. Laws, to be of any use or authority, must be founded on their adaptation to existing circumstances. The controversy is a new one, because there never was, till 1793, any room for agitating it. Never, till that time, were France and her allies stripped of all active commerce, and literally banished from the ocean. Of course, never till then were they obliged to use the aid of neutrals, or forego entirely the benefit of their colonial commerce. It is our duty to state the fact. It is the duty of others, more adequate to the task, to draw from it the proper inferences.

The author of the pamphlet proceeds through nearly one hundred pages, to enlarge upon the principle of the war of 1756, and to explain and vindicate the conduct of the British government, and the decisions of the admiralty courts. We have not room to exhibit an abstract of the argument, which nevertheless we recommend to our American statesmen to peruse and confute. We have already hinted at a reason for our forbearing to do this. We believe the ultimate settlement of the controversy will depend more on the actual situation of the parties at the present day, than upon the course of their former conduct and opinions, when their situation was exceedingly dissimilar.

The author supposes fraud on the part of neutrals, in covering enemy's property, to a much greater extent than American merchants will believe is the fact.[52] Yet he undertakes, p. 102, to say, that his conclusion does not depend on the fact assumed. For

> "If the hostile colonies are supplied with all necessary imports, and their produce finds its way to market, the enemy is effectually relieved from the chief pressure of the war, even though both branches of the trade should pass into foreign hands, in reality as well as in form." He adds, that "the produce of the West-Indies sells cheaper at present, clear of duties, in the ports of our enemies than in our own."— P. 105.

If this be true, we cannot see why the French colonies should not prosper beyond those of England. He tells us this is the fact; and repeats, as well founded, the boast of Bonaparte,

> "That Guadaloupe and Martinique are flourishing so much beyond all former experience, that since 1789 they have doubled their population."

---

[52] *There is probably some misrepresentation, and certainly some exaggeration of the conduct of neutrals, in this part of the pamphlet. There is also an evident want of correct information concerning the consumption of sugar and coffee in the United States. These errors seem to be less excusable, because accurate knowledge was easy to be procured, and it is admitted, by the writer himself, that the force of his main argument does not depend on their truth.* [F. AMES]

That colonies should thrive in produce and wealth, because the mother country is driven from the sea, and abandons them to shift as they can without naval protection, and that the English colonies should droop and decline, in consequence of the empire of the British navy on every sea, is certainly a strange assertion. The author strenuously insists, that this is the fact. English vessels are exposed to the peril of capture, and to war freights and premiums, and of course English West India produce goes dearer to market than the products of the enemy's colonies in neutral vessels. In this way, he says, the commerce of England, in West India products, is every where obstructed, and is nearly lost. But he insists, that the tendency of this system, to augment and man the marine of France, and to cramp and discourage that of Great Britain, is a still more disheartening and urgent consideration.

Having in detail treated of the origin, extent, and nature of the evil, he proceeds, page 137, to consider *"the remedy, and the rights of applying it."*

"If," he continues, "neutrals have no right, but through our concession, to carry on the colonial trade of our enemies, we may, *after a reasonable notice,* withdraw that ruinous indulgence." One of the chief topics of complaint in America has been the condemnation of our vessels, without any such *notice* of their being liable to condemnation. Indeed, if Great Britain could make out a right to seize them, it appears, that it has been exercised with an unwarrantable precipitancy and unnecessary harshness. As booty, the prizes go to the captors; and even if the government of England participated in the proceeds, it cannot be supposed to be of magnitude enough to operate as a motive for the captures.

"Nothing," says the author, "can be more advantageous to England, than the suppression of the fraudulent commerce of neutrals. But if it requires a breach of justice, let us inflexibly abstain." These are honourable sentiments, whether the author really feels them, or thinks fit, in order to give force to his reasoning, to affect them.

He professes to think, there is no doubt of the British *right* to stop this trade.

> "Neutral ships (he observes) when taken in a *direct* voyage to or from the hostile countries and their colonies, or in a trade between the latter and any other neutral country, but their own, have been always condemned by our prize courts, both in the last and the present war. These restrictions can be warranted by no other principle, than the unlawfulness of trading with the colonies of a belligerent in time of war, in a way not permitted in time of peace."

> He asks, "whether it is possible that neutral states, in peace and amity with Great Britain, should have *a right* to persevere in conduct, which may, in its natural consequences, make *England a province of France?*"

Supposing this to be the natural consequence, it would be difficult to prove, that a neutral has any such right: for the right of the belligerent to exist, is to be preferred to the right of neutrals to make gain.

> "With what intention," he asks, "did the enemy open his colonial ports to neutrals? The single, manifest, and undissembled object was, to obtain protection and advantage in the war, to preserve his colonial interests without the risk of defending them, and to shield himself, in this most vulnerable part, from the naval hostilities of England."

> "I see not," he continues, "how any mind can doubt, that a co-operation in such an expedient, by powers in amity with England, is a violation of the duties of neutrality."

He adds, that "this very motive for opening the colonial ports is avowed in the public instruments, by which they were opened. With the first news of a war the orders of the mother country to open those ports are dispatched, as of course. Neutrals can show no treaty, no convention with the enemies of Great Britain, as a title to these privileges, that grow out of war, begin and end with it."

Page 183. He considers the probability of a quarrel with the neutral powers, in consequence of the resort to the remedy he has recommended, i.e. of withdrawing the indulgence hitherto allowed to this trade; and he endeavours, 3dly, to vindicate the *prudence of the remedy* by showing, that the neutral powers will not quarrel with England on that account. He firmly believes they will not, because he is sure they ought not. On this head, the writer seems disposed to speak of the United States with some respect. He thinks the Americans are a sagacious people, who will not fail to discern their interest; that they respect justice, and therefore will acquiesce in the exercise by Great-Britain of her just rights, as a belligerent; and that, being lovers of liberty, they will not like to see France lord of the navies, as well as of the armies of Europe.

"But (he goes on to say, page 196) he would not recommend a total prohibition of the colonial trade, though he maintains the *right* of Great Britain to interdict it without reserve. We might extend to all the French colonial ports the privileges, enjoyed by Americans at some of those ports in time of peace (which privileges he specifies); nay, we might allow such an intercourse with the colonies of Spain and Holland." "The farmers of America would in that case find the same market for their produce, and of course they would be on the side of conciliation and peace."

But even a war with the neutral powers, bad as he admits such a war to be, would be a less evil than the abuses of neutrality.

"Peace with the neutral powers is more likely, after all, (he says) to be preserved by a firm than a pusillanimous conduct."

"To conclude: a temperate assertion of the true principles of the law of war, in regard to neutral commerce, seems, as far as human foresight can penetrate, *essential to our public safety.*"

On the soundness of the doctrine of this writer, it belongs to the ablest American jurists and statesmen to pronounce a decision. As the pamphlet is written with considerable ability, and no little labour of research; as it is thought by many to convey the sense of the English government, and probably expresses the opinion of the nation too, it is obvious, that it will signify nothing on our side, to attempt an answer either by sophistry or invective. Indeed the answer will no less disgrace than disappoint America, if it should prove deficient either in candour or solidity. What can be plainer, than that nations, when they disagree, must appeal to reason, if they will not resort to force? If they do not choose to fight, they must negotiate; and if they negotiate, they must argue. Though our first magistrate assures us, that reason is the umpire between just nations, yet with his unfortunate and very unphilosophical antipathy against the British nation and government, and after all the false and silly things his adherents have said against the British treaty, negotiation is understood to be the last expedient, to which our administration will think of resorting. It is palpably clear to common sense, that it should have been the first. For had an attempt been made to negotiate when the British treaty was near expiring; when the British cabinet wished to make friends; and was discouraged to see itself without any; there is no doubt the dispute might have been prevented. At any rate, it would have been anticipated; and if our merchants had anticipated it, they would have saved some millions of dollars, which have since been captured and condemned. Thus it is, that the people have to pay for the national partialities and aversions of their rulers.

If our administration should attempt to frame a new treaty, they will not find in the federalists, we hope, the same want both of sense and principle, that fostered and protracted the opposition to Mr. Jay's. The negociation, it must be confessed, will be attended with great, we hope not insurmountable difficulties; and no man of sense will expect from it the recovery of every lucrative, neutral advantage, that we have at some times enjoyed. Our commercial and political situation would be much mended, if it were better ascertained; if our merchants knew what was safe, instead of conjecturing in the dark, what is right, what is permitted, or what will be maintained.

Great Britain most certainly is averse to a war with America. She is not only interested in our commerce and friendship, but dearly concerned to conciliate the exercise of her naval supremacy, if it be possible, with the judgment and conviction of the wise and able men among the neutral nations. Popular clamour, unsupported by that judgment, will soon expire; but the serious and steady censure of the wise will, in the end, augment the hatred and resentment, naturally engendered by her power, which will seek all opportunities to obstruct its energies, and will surely find some at last to subvert its foundations. Nothing, we know from observation and experience, proves so fatal to the duration of any sort of dominion, as the wantonness of its abuse. Great Britain, strong, by her navy, by her insular position, by her liberty, and, perhaps, not less so by her justice, will desire, will endeavour, and *ought really* to make considerable sacrifices, rather than not succeed to gain, in favour of her maritime principles, the acquiscence, if not the applause of the well informed and fair minded classes of men in the neutral states.

The American re-impression of this pamphlet is executed in a style of great typographical elegance, and prefaced with the following short notice.

> "It was intended to have prefixed to this edition, an introduction of some length, exposing, in a succinct manner, some of the sophistries with which this singular work abounds, by way of putting the reader on his guard against them; but as it is now proposed to follow it shortly with a formal answer, nothing more is thought necessary here, than merely to apprize the reader of this circumstance."

IX.

ESSAYS ON
THE FRENCH REVOLUTION
AND EUROPEAN POLITICS

———

FOREIGN POLITICS I

———

The Palladium, OCTOBER 9, 1801

PRELIMINARY OBSERVATIONS

EUROPEAN EVENTS have long had such a monopoly of the attention of Americans, that we scarcely find leisure or disposition to backbite and persecute each other, as much as the rage of party spirit requires. Our pride is often offended, that our country makes a figure in the world so little conspicious, that others overlook it; and we almost forget ourselves, while we suffer our sympathy and reflections to be exclusively engrossed by the events of the foreign war.

Yet the champions of party ought to be consoled, for the diversion of any part of our patriotic energies from the domestic scene of controversy, by their own success in rendering foreign politics subservient to their design. France, though nerve all over, does not feel the dread nor the shame of her defeats, nor the insolent joy of her victories, with more emotion than our jacobins. They can allege, in excuse for the deep concern they take in all the confusion and all the injustice of France, that they are not mere speculatists, nor subject to impulses that are blind and without object; but that their pure love for the people never ceases to animate them enough to imitate what they admire, and to introduce what they so long have studied, and so well understand.

The men of sense and virtue have excuses too for their anxious solicitude about European affairs; there, they may say, faction culls her poisons; and in that bloody field, at length, we can perceive the antidote is sprouting. Already the *Aurora* tells us, it is nonsense to talk of liberty under Bonaparte. Nevertheless, if France should be superior in the war, and should dictate the terms of peace, our inbred faction, her faithful ally, would be superior here. The civilized world can enjoy neither safety nor repose, if the most restless and ambitious nation in it obtains what it has struggled for, a more than Roman sway, and a resistless power to render the interests of all other states as subservient to its own, as those of her Cisalpine allies. The forest that harbors one wild cat should breed many squirrels. Ambition like that of France requires, for its daily sustenance, tameness like that of Spain or Holland; if all her neighbors were like Britain, where could this royal tigress find prey?

So far indeed is the attention paid by Americans to the affairs of Europe from being a subject of reproach, that, on the contrary, no period of history will be deemed more worthy of study by our statesmen, as well as our youth, than that of the last twelve years.

In France we behold the effects of trying, by the test of experience, the most plausible metaphysical principles, in appearance the most pure, yet the most surprisingly in contrast with the corruption of the national manners. Theories fit for angels, have been adopted for the use of a multitude, who have been found, when left to what is called their self-government, unfit to be called men; as if the misrule of chaos or of pandemonium would yield to a little instruction in singing psalms and divine songs; as if the passions inherent

399

in man, and a constituent part of his nature, were so many devils that even unbelievers could cast out, without a miracle, and without fasting and prayer. By stamping the rights of man on pocket-handkerchiefs, it was supposed they were understood by those who understand nothing; and by voting them through the convention, it would cost a man his life and estate to say that they were not established.

On grounds so solid Condorcet could proclaim to the enlightened, the fish-women, and the mob of the suburbs of St. Antoine, all disciples of "the new school of philosophy;" Mr. Jefferson could assure Thomas Paine, and even the circumspect Madison could pronounce in Congress, that France had improved on all known plans of government, and that her liberty was immortal.

Experience has shown, and it ought to be of all teaching the most profitable, that any government by mere popular impulses, any plan that excites, instead of restraining, the passions of the multitude, is a despotism; it is not, even in its beginning, much less in its progress, nor in its issue and effects, liberty. As well might we suppose that the assassin's dagger conveys a restorative balsam to the heart, when it stabs it; or that the rottenness and dry bones of the grave will spring up again in this life, endued with imperishable vigor and the perfection of angels. To cure expectations, at once so foolish and so sanguine, what can be more rational than to inspect sometimes the sepulchre of French liberty? The body is not deposited there, for indeed it never existed; but much instruction is to be gained by carefully considering the lying vanity of its epitaph.

The great contest between England and France, also shows the stability and the resources of free governments, and the precariousness and wide-spreading ruin of the resort to revolutionary means. We shall not, therefore, hesitate to present, from time to time, the most correct and extensive views we can take of events in Europe.

We have made these observations, and we address them

with the more deliberation to the good sense of the citizens, because it has been a part of the commonplace of democratic foppery to say, what have we to do with Europe? we are a world by ourselves. This they have said a thousand times, while they told us the cause of France was the cause of liberty, and inseparably our cause. Everybody knows that the mad zeal for France was wrought up with the intent to influence American politics; and it did influence and yet influences them. A trading nation, whose concerns extend over the commercial world, and whose interests are affected by their wars and revolutions, cannot expect to be a merely disinterested, though by good fortune it may be a neutral, spectator. Unless, therefore, we survey Europe as well as America, we do not "take a view of the whole ground." And if we must survey it, and our interests are concerned in the course of foreign events, it is obviously important that we should understand what we observe, and separate, as much as possible, error from the wisdom that is to be gleaned by experience.

We invite our able patrons and correspondents to assist us in our labors; and to exercise their candor, if, at any time, we should present an imperfect or mistaken view of European affairs; we shall not wilfully misrepresent.

FOREIGN POLITICS II

————

The Palladium, OCTOBER 13, 1801

GREAT BRITAIN and France are the primary nations; it is evident that all the rest play a subordinate and secondary part. The French adopt this opinion, and call France, Rome, and Great Britain, Carthage. If this similitude were exact,

401

Britain would sink in the contest. But the British government is more stable than that of Carthage; and, therefore, faction is a little less virulent and a great deal less powerful. Besides, the British superiority on the seas is more clearly, as well as more durably established, and more effectively displayed than that of Carthage. The naval art was rude and imperfect in ancient times; and those who then understood it best were little the better for that advantage. Duilius, the Roman consul, gained a naval victory with mere landsmen. The reason was, that the ships of war were rowed alongside their antagonists, and being grappled firmly together, the combat was maintained, as in fights on land, by a body of soldiers on each side. This being the ordinary event of a sea-fight, no wonder the Roman soldiers, whose valor was the steadiest and the best trained in the world, prevailed over the mercenaries of Carthage. Every thing is different between England and France. So superior are the English seamen to the French, so little now depends on the number of men, and so much upon naval art, that the crowd of Frenchmen on board their vessels are rather an encumbrance than an effective force. There is seldom a sea-fight in which the French escape, although their crews are far more numerous than those of their conquerors. Great Britain, too, enjoys a durable superiority. There must be commerce before there will be seamen; there must be a stable government before there will be a general spirit of enterprise and industry to create commerce. The hands of labor will be weak while its earnings are exposed to rapine, as in France. It will be an age or two before that nation will get rid of her military tyrants, and her revolutionary spirit; and, till she does, her prosperity will be precarious, and her naval power will be displayed, like that of Turkey, by forcing awkward landmen on board ships. Despotism will waste men and wealth, and in vain, to imitate the spontaneous energies of industry and commerce, fostered by a free and stable government. It may be added, that a naval power is exerted with infinitely more effect now than it was in ancient times; every nation almost is now vulnerable in its commerce and in its colonies; the ruin of these produces a decay of the revenues and resources for war.

If then France affects to be Rome, she will not find in Great Britain a Carthage. Nay, even in the military spirit of her people, Britain, with the exercise of one brisk campaign, would not be found inferior to her boastful antagonist. The campaign in Egypt evinces that Englishmen can be good soldiers as well as seamen. Carthage, on the contrary, was too much torn by factions to maintain a good infantry of her own citizens; she hired strangers. But her cavalry, as that was not a despised service like the infantry, but attended with honor, was excellent, and so superior to that of Rome, that the Numidian horse, under Hannibal, won every battle in the open plains.

Carthage was rich, and England is richer; Carthage was called free, England is really so; and if the government of Great Britain were either a democracy or a despotism, it, in the first case, would have been shivered to pieces by faction, and in the latter, by France, within the first four years of the war. None but free governments are stable; and none that are purely democratic are free. We hope that public opinion will so effectually counteract the seduction and the threatened preponderance of a violent jacobin administration, that our own government, so wisely and happily combined, and so well adapted to our circumstances and sentiments, will be found, after some trials and agitations, to be both stable and free.

In point of resources, it does not appear that Britain experiences any want; nor that France has, except in the violence of force and tyranny, any sort of security for a supply. It was foretold, years ago, that Great Britain was to be ruined and beggared, and must have peace if she took servitude with it. The opposition assured the nation of the event; yet time has confuted these predictions; wealth goes on augmenting; credit is the steadier for the shocks that have waved its branches, but could not stir its roots. The war is chiefly naval; and the seamen are now formed, and indeed have grown up in the war, in sufficient numbers. The expenses, great as they are, are not increasing, nor are they lavished in Germany, as they were in 1794 and 1795. A long war creates a sort of commerce for itself, and, as it were, makes a part of its own means. There cannot, therefore, exist a doubt, that Britain is able to continue the war. Her land never produced more; and its products never before were worth so much. Her industry never was greater; and the demands for its fabrics were never so little divided with competitors. Her tons of shipping and her trade are greater than at any former period. Her capital is doubled; and it is as sure to create employment, as employment is to accumulate capital. These are the fountains of wealth, and they flow with an unexhausted and progressively increasing stream. France is more nearly beggared by revolution, and Spain by the pride and laziness of her people, than Great Britain is by the war. It is a great evil to a nation to be obliged to exert all its energies to preserve itself from French fraternity; but it would be an evil a hundred times greater to fall under it.

The proper test of the justness of these observations is not, that they may appear to offend against some popular prejudices, or that the jacobin gazettes will interpret them into the most abominable meanings; no one expects that the jacobins will content themselves with the truth on this subject. Inquisitive persons, and fair-minded citizens, are desired to examine before they decide; and even if they expose the errors of our judgment, they will advance our purpose, inasmuch as we wish, and it shall be our endeavor, to extract from foreign events the sound materials for political instruction. We leave it to the jacobin editors to cook for their readers a mawkish aliment for prejudice and faction.

Such readers believe, that, while Great Britain is on the

verge of bankruptcy and ruin, while she is loathsome in her corruptions, and humbled by her fears and her defeats, France is renewing her youth and vigor, happy in her liberty, and strong by her victories. An European would scarcely believe there was in America enough of what, in other countries, is called mob, to give currency to such glaring falsehood.

France has used, from the first, revolutionary means, in other words, all that violence could procure. While England with difficulty taxed income, her rival could, by a decree, seize the capital; and after it had been sold to revolutionary buyers, the next men in power could decree that these were royalists, and seize it a second time; every change brought the whole stock to the new mint. One would expect that France was of all nations the richest in resources, since it could spend all, and then attack the new holders of property, and spend it as often as the necessities of liberty might require. By a formal decree, all property in France has been declared in a state of requisition. The whole people were also enrolled and in requisition; and death, or confiscation of the offender's property, ensued on disobedience. Never did eastern despotism claim more tremendous power, or actually exercise so much. Yet violence is ever a temporary resource; it is a fire, whose splendor is brilliant ruin. France is now destitute of credit, of revenue, of all the ordinary means to extract resources from her people; and she has used and abused the extraordinary, till they are almost as unproductive as they are odious. She looks for means abroad; she looks to Portugal, to Italy, to Spain, and to Holland. The field of plunder will not bear two crops, and it is already barren. Bonaparte, of course, sees the varnish of his popularity wearing off, and the hopes of his slaves fading into disappointment. Already he fears the effects of that temper of the French, which is ever patient under tyranny, but ever eager to establish a new tyrant. He sees Egypt nearly wrested from his domination; his splendid promises of wealth and glory, in an expedition to subvert the British dominion in India, vanish into air; the powers of the north, whom he duped and betrayed, beaten into a better understanding of the law of nations, and embittered against their deceiver; Germany, though too discordant to oppose him in the field, yet too powerful to submit to his dictates. The secularization of the ecclesiastical states is too much the concern of Russia and Prussia, to be carried along on the terms of the treaty of Luneville. He also needs peace to consolidate his power, and to give a breathing spell to his exhausted subjects, and also to induce his triumphant enemy to disarm. But, if the English populace have bread, and the English minister has sense and spirit, the affair of peace will be decided on other grounds than Bonaparte's desire to obtain it. It will be asked, what has England to fear from war? What has she not to fear from peace? War brings no burdens, of which they have not had experience; no evils, but such as they have surmounted. Peace will be a new and untried state of being, requiring all the burdens of war taxes and war forces, and giving no respite to Englishmen, while it affords one to France. The revolutionary fire is not quenched; and peace would leave it to blaze out again in three years, with a fiercer conflagration and a wider ruin than ever.

FOREIGN POLITICS III

The Palladium, OCTOBER 16, 1801

FEW SUBJECTS are considered with so little care, and so much party feeling and prejudice, as the political situation of France. In respect to her neighbors, she is supposed to possess a power as durable as it is preponderant; and, with respect to her own citizens, she is deemed to be as happy as victory, plenty, and liberty can make her. The grounds of these darling errors might be explored with advantage; but it would fill all the columns of a newspaper, and, indeed, the pages of an octavo volume, to exhibit the subject in detail. Men more competent than we pretend to be, must write books; and persons more at leisure than the majority of our readers, will read them. A brief and rapid summary of the most signal facts and principles, is all that we presume to undertake, and even for that, the materials are scanty, and the rage of party has confused and mutilated them. Every booby democrat from France comes home to brag of the power and splendor of the court of Bonaparte, and of the pure republicanism and equality of that nation, as if he had exactly the same measure of understanding as of patriotism. It is well recollected, that while Robespierre reigned, and the blood ran in Paris, Bordeaux, Lyons, and Nantes, in streams that would have turned corn-mills, every ship's captain arrived with such a tale for the jacobin newspapers as would suit the fashion of our market; it seemed as if lies were bespoke and made for customers. All was then represented as peace and order, a stable government, and a contented, happy, prosperous people. The zeal for France invited deception, and sheltered it from scrutiny. The jacobins still prefer France to America, and try very hard to "cover her with glory," when she is defeated, and to represent the "cowardly English" as ruined, when they conquer. Accordingly, Egypt is still, in the *Chronicle,* a burying-ground for the English, where they die of the plague, and by the sword of Menou, and by that of the Mamelukes and Arabs, and thus the *Chronicle* thrice slays the slain; yet, probably, Egypt is now in the full possession of the English and Turks. In this case, one of the supposed difficulties in the way of peace is removed; for if Bonaparte holds Egypt, it can only be to make it a military post, from which, within two years from the signing of a peace, to send forth armies against the British possessions in India. A peace, on such terms, would be a truce altogether favorable to Bonaparte, unfavorable to England. If the spirit of the British nation is up, the minister will not feel himself obliged to submit to any such insidious, and indeed hostile arrangement. The loss of Egypt will remove this bone of contention.

Yet, as France is too powerful to allow her neighbors any repose, the only question seems to be, not whether England shall lay aside her arms, for that is impossible, even in peace, but whether they shall be idle in her hands. While she is in danger, she must make all her efforts in self-defence; and surely every jacobin has enough of the Frenchman in his heart to allow, if he will speak out, that he would use the opportunity of peace to prepare the force, and the first moment of sedition or insurrection in England, or the decease of King George, or any other favorable event, to employ force to overturn that cursed monarchy, and to strip that nation of its navy, commerce, and power. In this state of things, it seems justifiable for the British minister to ponder well, whether, if safety lies, as it certainly does, in arms, which is the best time to employ them, the present, or some future, and not distant time, that France shall seize, when England is in a state of division and dismay. The question is important, and concerns her political life or death.

It has been already observed, that the British land and naval forces cannot be much reduced on a peace. Austria is recruiting her armies, and will soon have need of them, especially if she is believed to be unprepared for war. Peace will lessen the energies of war, but not its burdens. It will, at least in some degree, restore the commerce and navy of Britain's great rival, while her own trade and industry, now secure in a monopoly, will then have to struggle with competition. France is now nearly stripped of all allies, except such as she has conquered. The independent powers are her foes in fact, or in sentiment and policy. Would it not then be strange, if Britain should purchase for herself a short truce, full of treachery and danger, that would refresh her enemy, and leave to her neither a respite nor the hope of advantage? The clamor for peace, so loud, while bread was scarce, ought now to subside in England; and if they are not willing to be Dutchmen or Cisalpines, they ought to be willing to be soldiers and seamen.

War is, indeed, a great evil, but peace, with danger and dishonor, is a greater. It has been the fashion to make it a merit for any man to desire peace; as if the question of peace was to be considered in the abstract, and as if the war that rages was not a case, like every other, to be examined and pronounced upon according to its existing circumstances.

Supposing, then, the war should continue, because the ambition of France still thirsts for conquest and plunder, and because the English government seeks, what peace would deny her, security and repose, what are the chances of this mighty and long-protracted contest? England is all powerful at sea; France has hitherto proved victorious on land. Thus far the odds are in favor of England, because she can annoy France, she can insult her coasts, she can prevent her commerce from reviving, and thus she can distress her enemy in his supplies and his finances. France threatens England with invasion; is not the threat ridiculous? Two or three hundred English ships and frigates will almost touch one another in the channel, and effectually prevent a fleet of French flat-bottomed boats from landing an army by surprise. An English army of three hundred thousand men, fighting for life, liberty, and property, would destroy any hostile force that might be disembarked. The immense land force of France seems to be, therefore, nearly useless in the war with England. It serves, however, to consume her own resources, and to keep alive the jealousy and hatred of her neighbors. Rome subsisted her armies by plunder; a war found its own means of supply; and from the time of Perseus to the consulship of Hirtius and Pansa, the spoils of Macedon and other conquered states, supplied all expenses; so that, for more than one hundred years, no taxes were imposed on the Roman people. Let it be noted, however, that modern wars glean infinitely less from the field of plunder; while they cost, for artillery, sieges, and cavalry, infinitely more. To this add, the Roman soldiers feared the gods and religiously kept their oath to bring all the plunder into the public stock; the Roman senate faithfully and frugally administered this treasure. France plunders Europe; and her tyrants plunder France; it is easier for her to beggar Italy, than to satisfy her commissaries. Her trade is war, and in a maritime strife this cannot be a gainful trade. The confusion of twelve years is not to be retrieved by establishing martial law for eighteen months. The first consul may issue his general orders, that the revolution is over; all France may be hushed to silence, like a camp; yet it will not cease to suffer, while it trembles. With a fruitful territory, a vast addition of subjects by her conquests, and an energy of military government that can take the last dollar, and a man's life, if he seems to give it loathly, it might appear that her pecuniary means are not to be exhausted. Let it, however, be noted, that these very conquests require a large part of her force and treasure to preserve them. Perhaps they now require as much as they supply. Already plundered, they cannot soon yield any great amount of regular revenue, or even of plunder. The immense territory, nominally or effectively conquered by France, obliges her to keep on foot two hundred thousand men, nearly as many as her peace establishment under Louis the Sixteenth. Three hundred thousand other troops absorb more than all the surplus of her means, after providing for other essential objects of government. How is she to defray this enormous charge, so much augmented by revolutionary confusion and fraud? The expedients she has resorted to, sufficiently prove the extremity of her distress on this account. She has had paper money; she has in effect blotted out her old debt; she has repeatedly stopped payment of her new debt, which she pretended to call the sacred price of her liberty; she has sold an hundred thousand square miles of confiscated estates, the property of men whom she forced to run away to save their lives; she has seized the Caisse d'Escompte and the other banks; she has violently extorted money from the Jews and bankers of Paris; she has stript the churches of the Austrian Netherlands, and of Italy; taxed the Dutch six per cent. of all their property; and forced a loan from all her own subjects. The conduct of this forced loan shows both her poverty and her tyranny; her poverty, because it yielded little of what was expected from it; and her tyranny, because no Eastern despot ever adopted more arbitrary means of compulsion. The *sans culottes,* or rabble, and people of small property, who were violent revolutionists, paid nothing; while the rich were arbitrarily, and without any estimation or rule, assessed at pleasure. The tax was a decree of confiscation, with such exceptions in its collection, as to make it robbery. There never was a moment when the government did not use all the rigors of tyranny to procure money; nor one, when the collection of it supplied any adequate resources; the people have ever suffered oppression, and the government want.

Let it be well considered, then, how desperate the contest must be for France, provided the English be able to maintain it for some years longer. The English are not a stupid people, nor have they a feeble government; they will discern the almost certainty of their success, and will persevere to ensure it. The civilized world, long endangered by France, will then be again in security.

PHOCION VIII

The Palladium, MAY 29, 1801

BRITISH INFLUENCE

FOREIGN INFLUENCE has been traced with some attention to the impediments and auxiliaries of its operation, within our country. It remains to look without it, and to consider the political situation of France and England, and to determine, which of the two will be disposed and invited to employ her influence in the control of our affairs.

The counsels of both will be guided by their views of political good and evil. It is not believed, that France, insolent with victory, and crimson with revolutionary crimes, will regard either shame or principle. It is not believed that England will wholly disregard the maxims and rules of civilized states. But without really admitting that France is on a footing in point of morals or deference to the laws of nations, even with Algiers, it shall, for argument sake, be conceded to those who love her better than America, that France and England will exactly alike pursue what their interest dictates. Be it so.

England then is commercial. Her commerce thrives by the immense superiority of her skill, industry, and capital. She has capital enough to employ and to trust. Her interest, as a trading nation, is to have good customers; her interest is, that those who owe should pay. But the essence, and almost the quintessence, of a good government, is to protect property and its rights. When these are protected, there is scarcely any booty left for oppression to seize; the objects and the motives to usurpation and tyranny are removed. By securing property, life and liberty can scarcely fail of being secured;

where property is safe by rules and principles, there is liberty. It is precisely such a government that Great Britain wishes to find and to sustain, wherever her commerce and credit extend. She is, of course, so far as her commercial interest extends, the friend of all governments that are friends to justice and protectors of honest creditors. Where justice ceases, there her credit stops. Stable governments, and especially such as have a portion of liberty to give them enterprise and to make them large consumers, are her best customers. If Turkey in Europe had as much law and liberty as the United States, it would demand, perhaps, as much manufactures as Britain could supply. Britain is obviously and demonstrably interested, not in the overthrow, but in the support of the regular governments in existence, no matter whether monarchies or republics. Governments that will compel debtors to be just, are all, in their form and administration, that British influence, in this point of view, could be employed to make them. Accordingly, we do not find that the trade of England with Holland was ever disturbed, because the latter was a republic, and for half a century destitute even of a stadtholder; we do not find that Englishmen were set at work to preach democracy in Cadiz, though surely English liberty is as unlike Spanish despotism as our republicanism. No, she was well content to clothe the colonists of Spain, and to receive their gold, silver, and diamonds, without stirring up a faction in Lisbon or Madrid to call first town meetings and then parliaments. Experience has fully shown, that commerce, with democratic and aristocratic republics, with monarchies and simple despotisms, has been alike cherished and prosecuted for ages, without a suspicion, and certainly without an attempt on the part of Great Britain to revolutionize their governments. It is not difficult to show, that stable liberty is the best condition of nations for the advancement of her commercial interest; yet no attempt is recollected even to introduce this blessing insidiously among her customers. The subjects of despots consume little and pay less; the diffusion of true and stable liberty would augment her commerce and manufactures.

It must be urged also, that the genuine liberty of Englishmen is unfavorable to the fanatical spirit of conquest. Every able-bodied man at the plough or in the workshops of Birmingham and Sheffield, is worth scarcely less than one hundred guineas. A free nation will be prosperous, and a prosperous nation cannot employ a man as a soldier without diverting his industry from husbandry or the arts. It costs too much for free thriving nations to be soldiers; the military spirit is no more to be indulged, than a taste for luxuries by the poor, because the objects of gratification are, in both cases, equally out of reach. Rich states can poorly afford to wear armor; the sword is the dearest of all tools. The ragged peasantry of France, half employed, less than half paid, were ever ready to listen to the enchanting eloquence of a recruiting sergeant. War has ever been in France the trade first in credit and least of all in rivalship with any other.

Britain, with a moderate population, has, therefore, never been in a condition to indulge the spirit of conquest. Territorial aggrandizement has, indeed, been her object in Bengal and the peninsula of India; but it was there in subservience to her commerce; and, let it be remarked, that the unwarlike Gentoos offered little resistance to her arms; she employed but a handful of Europeans to subject empires to the India Company. This seeming exception from the observation before made is, nevertheless, a strong illustration of its truth; she contended for territory for the sake of her commerce, and great as the prize was, the means she could employ were feeble.

It may be said, therefore, on the ground of experience, that the territorial ambition of Great Britain is limited and checked by her situation, character, and means; her insular situation, her commercial character, and her pecuniary means. Being an island, she cannot annex provinces to her empire; being commercial, she aims rather at profit than power; and being prosperous and industrious, her citizens are too dear to be hired as soldiers. Britain cannot raise great land armies, and therefore she cannot be so mad as to effect conquests that would require them. Admitting that the United States would submit a little sourly to her government, it would take forty or fifty thousand men in camps and garrisons to keep any show of authority over America; and on the first symptoms of resistance they must be doubled. Great Britain, as she is, is not rich enough to afford to accept of the sixteen states as provinces. If a spirit, as restless and turbulent as Pennsylvania has shown, should accompany and succeed our submission, we should certainly drain her treasury and finally baffle her arms.

Great Britain pursues a policy of more moderation, justice, and wisdom. Her naval superiority is employed to extend her commerce; if she carries her sword in one hand, it is to offer her commodities with the other. Her ships of war cannot conquer extensive territories, nor preserve them in subjection. Thus the means she possesses, and those she wants, almost equally exclude her from territorial power. Perhaps the increase of her soldiers would necessarily exhaust the funds for the support of her ships, and, therefore, we are certain that she will not ordinarily attempt impossibilities; she will not try to gain the possession of territory that she could not keep.

The application of these remarks is easy. We conceive that Britain has no motive, nor has she means to disturb the government of the United States, by attempting to excite the popular passions to control its measures. She cannot have influence, because those passions will forever run counter to her wishes; those wishes, conformable to her interests, will be to support the government, that the government may support justice. The very nature of her power ensures an irreconcilable hostility with popular feeling in the United

States. She is commercial, and so are we. Excluded from some of her ports in our own ships, rivals and competitors in all marts, inferior in all seas, and made especially in time of war sensible by her arrogance and injustice, painfully sensible of our inferiority, we shall hate her power and suspect her influence when she has none, when she cannot have any, and when the hatred gives influence to her rival, France.

PHOCION IX

The Palladium, JUNE 2, 1801

FRENCH INFLUENCE

FRENCH INFLUENCE has found, and will long find, both motives and means to disturb and control the measures of any honest and truly national government in America.

Since Rome, no state has ever manifested such exorbitant ambition as France. Whether this arises from the nature of her power, which has ever been military, or the extent of it, which, for two centuries, has proved an overmatch for any European state; whether two centuries spent in efforts for aggrandizement have formed martial habits, or whether the national character be the cause rather than the effect of those struggles, the fact is certain, that France is of all modern states the most military, intriguing, and ambitious. Since the revolution all traces of every other passion have disappeared, and the sword is the only utensil to occupy industry or to carve out its recompense. With that, Frenchmen reap where they have not sowed; by waving that, they command the diamonds of Brazil and strip the churches of Italy. Good fortune, scarcely less than Roman, has kindled a passion for conquest, and blown up a pride which the hostile force of the civilized world would not intimidate, the empire of the world would not satisfy. The avarice of a commercial nation calculates its means and reckons up the value of them; a conquering nation disdains both gold and arithmetic, and computes the presumption and audacity of its attempts as surprises on its plodding neighbors, and as the resources to ensure its triumphs. Behold France, conducting her intrigues and arraying her force between the arctic circle and the tropics; see her in Russia, the friend of despotism, preparing to subvert the empire of the Turks; in Ireland, the auxiliary of a bloody democracy; in Spain and Italy, a papist; in Egypt, a mussulman; in India, a brahmin; and at home, an atheist; countenancing despotism, monarchy, democracy, religion of every sort, and none at all, as suits the necessity of the moment. It may be said that it is nothing to the people of France whether their armies win or lose a battle; glory is not bread.

It is incredible to many that a nation should perform labors and make efforts of the most perilous and astonishing kind merely for glory. Those, however, who reason against the military passion as a chimera, arraign the authority of history. What was it to the Romans that Mithridates, or Tigranes, or Antiochus, or Perseus, or Arsaces, did not respect the majority of the Roman people? Surely that did not affect the markets or amusements of Rome. Yet never was there an objection in the forum, never was there any repugnance to the enrolment of the legions for chastising the rebellious insolence of any king who had never heard of the Roman name, or who did not tremble when he heard it. Accordingly the soldier citizens cheerfully engaged to march across deserts and mountains to the extremities of the then known world, to assert the glory of the Roman name, and to fix the statue of the god Terminus[53] as far east as the shore of the Euphrates. The sons of business, who do not feel this spirit, will be slow to believe that others feel it; but Frenchmen are animated with as large a portion of it as the soldiers of Paulus Emilius, Lucullus, or Crassus.

France is, probably, the most populous of European states, if we except the wandering tribes subject to Russia. It is the only state in which the sword is the only trade. Commerce has not a single ship; arts and manufactures exist in ruins and memory only; credit is a spectre that haunts its burying-place; justice has fallen on its own sword; and liberty, after being sold to Ishmaelites, is stripped of its bloody garments to disguise its robbers. A people, vain enough to be satisfied with the name of liberty, are called free, and the fervors of its spirit are roused to bind other nations in chains.

From all these circumstances, thus singularly combined, the whole physical force of France is its political force. There is not a vein nor a purse that its gigantic despotism cannot open at pleasure.

It is impossible that means so vast should be possessed without the desire to employ them. The obstacle to their succesful employment is England; in all her ambitious attempts she stands in her way. She stands like a necromancer, herself invulnerable, and by her spells the giant France is smitten with a palsy. With a spirit less generous than her courage, and sometimes with an attention to objects unworthy of her situation, England stands the bulwark of the civilized world, the only obstacle to the universal despotism of France.

Every thing, therefore, concurs to give activity to French influence. Her ambition, that seeks territorial aggrandizement in all parts of the earth, and the impediments that the naval power of Great Britain everywhere throws in her way, create

---

[53] *See Ovid*, Fasti, *2.669 ff.*

the necessity, the motive, and the means of influence. Being inferior at sea, she tries to gain friends or to subdue allies on the shore of every sea. Accordingly, in Italy she obliges the Genoese, the Tuscans, and the Romans, to exclude the ships and manufactures of England from their ports. She will exact the like terms from the emperor and from Portugal. She will never cease to stir up the jealousy and ambition of the emperor Paul till he has forced the Turks to banish the English from the Mediterranean. Egypt is seized to secure a station on the land that may finally expel the English from India. Popular passions are courted in America that they may obstruct first, and then subvert and revolutionize the government. Credit, public and private, is an anti-Gallican interest: by subverting credit and abolishing debts, British hostility is insured, British commerce excluded. Besides, French islands in every war are destitute of the protection of a naval force; they ae forced to depend on the resources of their own soil, and on the supplies that the United States will furnish. The neutrality, and still more the friendship and coöperation of the United States, will be sufficient to preserve their colonies, and eventually to turn the scale of power, in the contest for empire, in favor of France. Having no trade of her own, she is our customer, not our rival; her public ships, fugitives on the ocean, are seldom its tyrants. She is interested, and has the opportunity to foment the passions which arise in America from the use, and too frequently from the abuse, of the British dominion of the sea.

Is it then difficult to explain, by this theory, all the conduct of France and her emissaries, and the coöperation of her partisans in America? She has exerted her diplomatic skill to seize Louisiana, Florida, and Canada, and employed her Genets to enlist men in our back country to occupy them. She was, in 1783, averse to our aggrandizement, lest it should make us strong enough to stand alone and to do without her aid.[54] She has opposed every step towards the stability of our government, and for the establishment of its resources and credit. Her emissaries, in 1783, opposed the grant to the army, wishing to foment factions and divisions; in 1787, the Federal Constitution; in 1789, the funding system. She has been leagued with every faction, as Fauchet's intercepted letter shows. There is no doubt that the jacobin gazettes are in her pay. The despatches from Mr. Gerry, Marshall, and Pinckney, show that she relies on her power over the constituted powers of the United States. She has interfered in our elections; and she needs us as instruments of her hatred of England too much to lose a moment, or any practicable means, or to forbear any expense, that will secure the preponderance of her influence in our counsels.

There is foreign influence, and it is French.

THE NEW ROMANS I

The Palladium, APRIL 28, 1801

To RAISE curiosity, wonder, and terror, is the ordinary effect of great political events. All these, but especially wonder, have been produced by the progress of the French Revolution. To wonder is not the way to grow wise; to extract wisdom from experience we must ponder and examine; we must search for the plan which regulates political conduct, and its ultimate design. To know what is done, without knowing why it is done, and with what spirit it was undertaken, is knowing nothing; it is no better than laborious ignorance and

---

[54] *The Treaty of Paris, which ended the revolutionary war in 1783, but which the French wished to have delayed.*

studious error. Such has been the crude mass of newspaper information, the blind and undistinguishing admiration of French victories. It would be difficult to understand all that it is profitable to know in regard to these surprising events, if history did not teach us that like actors and like scenes have been exhibited in ancient days, and that we may, if we will, learn wisdom from the sad experience of the nations which have gone before us.

Since the Romans, no nation has appeared on the stage of human affairs with a character completely military, except the French; and that character was mingled with the commercial until the revolution.

With less than half a million of citizens in her whole territory, according to the census of enumeration preserved by Dionysius of Halicarnassus,[55] Rome, soon after the expulsion of her kings, was ready to commence the conquest of Italy, a country scarcely less populous than France. It was, however, divided into petty states, many of which were as numerous, as brave, and as warlike as the Romans; but there was an immense difference in their national character and maxims of state. The citizens of Rome were all soldiers; they had no pay; all that rewarded their toils in war was pillage. Poor as they were—and bands of robbers are ever poor—the spoils of an enemy's camp, or the division of conquered lands, was ample reward for a fortnight's campaign. Their enemies were near at hand and ever ready for combat; of course, the term of service was short, but the calls for it were frequent. In Rome, therefore, there was but one trade, and that was war; all were soldiers. Accordingly, Rome could array sixty thousand of the firmest infantry in the world, while she had not five hundred thousand citizens. A province in Italy, with a million, did not offer to resist one demi-brigade of French soldiers. What a prodigious difference!

---

[55] *Dionysius of Halicarnassus*, Antiquitates Romanae.

Holland is now kept in subjection by twenty thousand French troops, and its miserable people are ground to powder to pay and clothe these ragged masters for the trouble they take to oppress them.

One eighth of the population of Rome were soldiers, the best in the world; the United States, with not less than five million five hundred thousand people, are pronounced by the democrats to be beggared and ruined to such a degree, that the children in every farm house will go supperless to bed to maintain three thousand; nay, that this standing army of three thousand was raised with the design, and possesses the force and means, as well as disposition, to enslave the people and to set up a monarchy in America. France is exceedingly populous, and cannot need, if she could bear, as great a draft from her numbers as Rome; no modern nation has, however, come so near being, like the Romans, all soldiers, as the French. It is exceedingly difficult to state the proportion of soldiers to other citizens. It has generally been thought that Germany had soldiers in proportion of one to a hundred. The distresses of Austria and the zeal of the Hungarians may have doubled the proportion, during the most trying periods of the war with France. There is, however, reason to believe, that in the energies of Robespierreism, France, with her sixteen armies, arrayed within and without her territory nearly one twelfth of her vast population. Without a merchant ship, her navy hauled up, arts stagnant, capital spent, skill occupied in making arms, Lyons blown up with gunpowder, the only place to find business, to get bread, fame, and promotion, was in the army; no modern state has been so nearly all military. This was not the effect of her momentary distresses; it was the plan of her government, and a consequence of the character of her people. Her government, ever changing hands, was ever the same in spirit. Like Rome, who extended her conquests, while she was convulsed with civil war, every change has breathed new fury into the military enthusiasm of France. One passion, like a tyrant, has banished all others; it is the only one, that has aliment, or finds scope for its exercise. We see how prevalent this passion is in every French bosom; for the emigrants who came here and to England, bespattered with the blood and brains of their fathers, and wives, and kindred, strut on the news of their victories, as if they were an inch taller on the success of their oppressors, and they weep and mourn when their fleets or armies are beaten. In France, the age of chivalry is not gone; a spirit, more ardent than the crusades engendered, glows there, which burns not for liberty, but for conquest. The money-getting and money-loving Dutch and Americans can scarcely credit the influence of this passion. Doubts of this sort are plausible errors; and they oppose metaphysics, as to what ought to govern men, to the confounding and decisive authority of experience, which determines what does govern men.

It might, if it were necessary, be shown, that the chivalry of the military spirit ever was predominant in that country; all that was respected was military. The lower classes were emulous of this spirit, and they allowed that gentility consisted in bearing arms; the common soldiers fought duels, affected to be men of honor, and gloried in the distinction of wearing ragged uniform and eating bad provisions for the grand monarque. All this happened before the revolution. It might be added, that all trades, that merchandise, and a condition of labor were ever held base and degrading. It happened that the merchants, to whom honor was not ascribed, wanted honor and integrity. They were brought down, as might naturally be expected, to the rank in which they were held. There was nothing that ought to rival the splendor of military distinction; there was nothing in the state that did rival it. All other passions were quenched; all the energies of the human character were concentred in the passion for arms. The revolution came and sublimated all the passions to fury and extravagance; it gave an immediate preponderance, nay, a sole dominion to the love of glory. The national guards were formed, and their epaulets and swords were worth more in their eyes than liberty.

The bloody struggle that has buried arts, and institutions, and wealth, and thrones, and churches of God under heaps of cinders, has given that strength to this passion, which might be expected from partial indulgence and strict discipline.

Very early the French perceived the affinity of their national character with that of the Romans; though it is, manifestly, with the Romans after they were corrupted and had lost their liberty. Their vanity instantly prompted them to emulate this model, and to illustrate this resemblance; they have been vain of their consuls and tribunes, and they have adopted the haughty demeanor, as well as the insidious art of the Roman senate. If modern nations are any better than barbarians, they ought to mark the spirit of these new Romans, and exert in self-defence a spirit of intelligence and patriotism, which was wanting to the ancient world, and which might have saved them from bondage. It is much to be desired, that your learned correspondent would pursue his comparison of the French and Roman policy. It is what popular prejudice needs, and I perceive, by the *Aurora*, it is what jacobinism dreads.

THE NEW ROMANS II

The Palladium, MAY 5, 1801

CONQUEST being the object of the Romans, and the spirit of the people being in a high degree martial, the next care was to train up men to be conquering soldiers. They believed

424

that they could, and that they ought to achieve more than other soldiers; and therefore they cheerfully submitted to the augmentation of labor, and self-denial, and danger, that this preëminence of glory and courage were bound to sustain. Their patriotism was little less than self-love; they heard of nothing but what was due to their country; they lived, and acted, and were bound by oath, if necessary, to die for it. The republic was a sort of divinity, which commanded their reverence and affection, and which alone conferred the rewards that were proper for heroes. This sentiment was strengthened by the rigor of the maxims, which then regulated war; to be conquered, or even to be a prisoner, was to be annihilated as a Roman, and for ever deprived of an inheritance of glory more precious than life. Religion added force to these popular sentiments, and a Roman false to them was more abhorred than an Arnold.

Such was the force of this complex and skilful machinery, that the Roman soldiers were heroes; they were all that men could be. Their country was a camp; and peace, a time not of rest but of preparation and exercise. They were taught to carry vast burdens, to march loaded like pack-horses, to take fifteen days' provisions, to transport weapons heavier than their enemies' intrenching tools, and much of the equipage of war, which is now conveyed by thousands of wagons. This habitual endurance of hardship made it familiar, hardened them to the rigor of climates and the most violent efforts; they were seldom sick. Their celerity in marching, their perfect discipline, their promptness to rally after a repulse, their unwearied perseverance in battle, were as extraordinary and as terrible to the foe as their heroic courage. They claimed to be, and their enemies admitted that they were, a superior race of men. This lofty opinion realized itself; they did not rely on numbers, but thought it enough to send a popular general with two legions, (not sixteen thousand men,) to overthrow the empires of Tigranes or

Jugurtha; they expected, and experience justified their expectation, that the terror of the Roman name would be more effectual than legions. Accordingly, the subjects and allies, and even the children of the invaded kings, seldom failed to desert his cause, who was the enemy of Rome, and of course, devoted to ruin.

If this view of the military character of Rome has not led the mind of the reader to mark its resemblance with the French, it is not because the latter have omitted any means in their command to form themselves on the Roman model. As the French soldiers compose a large part of the able-bodied citizens, they are a better sort of men than are found in the ranks of their enemies. In England, for example, a prosperous commerce and vast manufactures leave only refuse and scum for their armies; the French soldiers are really Frenchmen, and animated with a large portion of that fiery impetuous zeal for the glory of the nation, which is so remarkably characteristic. It is a subject on which no Frenchman, however his country may have misused him, can be cold. All that taxes, that confiscation, or that foreign spoil could supply has been promised as reward; and all that art or eloquence could do has been used as incitement. In France too, as in Rome, there is no claim of power and distinction, but what is derived from the sword; the consuls were generals, and all the offices were considered as in a degree military; no man can be great in France unless he is a great general. The Abbé Sieyes has been made a consul, and for wisdom in the cabinet, report assigns him the first place; when Caligula made his horse a consul, he did not make him as able and learned as Sieyes, but he invested him with the exact measure of power that Bonaparte allows to his colleague. The army, conscious of being the fountain of power, would as soon submit to the authority of a woman as of any man eminent in any other art than the military, and ignorant of that. When therefore all glory, all distinction in the state, and the exclusive title to a share in the government of it, are confined to the military, no wonder that art has been carried to a degree of perfection far beyond the attainments of the rival states.

If those states were equally emulous of glory, if their subjects were all soldiers, and if all arts were held in contempt that were not subservient to arms, they would be on a footing with the French. But since the discovery of America, the systems of all the European governments have been commercial; they have patronized the arts that would procure riches, as preferable to those which confer power. The public sentiment of every other nation has been rather that of avarice than of ambition. The military profession has been, in consequence, separated from every other, and in some measure degraded in estimation, as the only one that earns nothing, and that is corrupted by idleness. The rest of the society has become unwarlike, unfit for toil, insensible to glory. The citizen, attached to his ease, his property, and family, considers it as both ruin and disgrace to become a soldier. Is it strange, then, that the entire mass of France should overpower its enemies? From the difference of character and situation, no other decision could have happened, than that which has happened.

France, subject to the most energetic despotism in the world, poured forth her myriads in arms. Formerly, a few strong fortresses, or a ridge of mountains, were called barriers; and to subdue a country these obstacles must be overcome; many campaigns were made by the famous Marlborough to break the line of the iron frontier of France, as the Netherlands have been called. The French have changed this system of war in a very extraordinary manner. By the immensity of the mass of their armies, by their great extent, occupying the whole frontier of an enemy's country, by the astonishingly numerous artillery, the rapid marches, the attacks made in concert in many places at once, from the lower Rhine to the

Mincio and Adige, though at the distance of one hundred and fifty leagues, by the unwearied renewal of those attacks, if the first fails, and by the endless reinforcements of fresh troops, a state is now subdued, as soon as formerly Marlborough could take a town; the field of battle extends over several provinces; the map of a country is not extensive enough for the plan of a camp; all the heights and commanding positions are occupied in such a manner that the two wings of the army are, perhaps, one hundred and fifty miles apart; if one of the enemy's posts can be passed by, or his forces are dislodged from them, he must fall back to take the next best position in his rear, and thus a country falls in a day, and, perhaps, without a battle.

It is evident, that this new method of employing so vast armies, and this wasteful activity of manœuvring and fighting incessantly, by which a campaign has become unusually destructive of human life, will require Europe to be more military than ever; all must be soldiers, or all will be slaves; and this boasted and boastful revolution will tend to hasten and to fix for ages both barbarism and despotism.

THE NEW ROMANS III

The Palladium, MAY 12, 1801

ART cannot soon form the character of a nation, nor can violence soon change it. Of all the barbarous nations, the Franks were the most martial. Fourteen hundred years ago, they formed their petty tribes into a conquering nation. The greatness of the nation early inspired ambition, which several able and warlike princes inflamed into a national enthusiasm.

While most other European states were feeble by their divisions, the French were powerful, and aspired to dominion and influence over other nations. More than a thousand years ago, their kings led armies into Italy, and parcelled out its governments, as Bonaparte has done. The splendor of the reign of Charlemagne fascinated the French, as much as their late victories, and established the pretensions of their vanity to be the great nation, the arbiters of Europe. The compactness, as well as immensity, of their force engaged them in every war that occurred. We know the power that habit has to form the characters of individual men and whole nations; by continual wars, the French lost nothing of the military spirit of their barbarous ancestors. The crusades and the age of chivalry exalted this spirit to its highest degree, and greatly distinguished the French among the crusaders. The Edwards, and still more Henry the Seventh, of England, and afterwards the wise Elizabeth, introduced commerce and the arts, and gave a new turn to the enterprise of the English nation. It may be conjectured, with some appearance of probability, that the insular position of England very early determined the English character towards the arts of peace. As soon as the struggles between the king and the barons, and the rival houses of York and Lancaster, afforded any respite from arms, and any interior order in the kingdom, two consequences resulted: a greater portion of the English inhabited the country, the country being as safe to inhabit as the cities; the yeomanry, or cultivators of land, increased in wealth and influence in the state, and constituted the mass and body of the nation; husbandry forms a class of men, and a determined character for the class, very unlike that of soldiers. A second consequence, and connected with the former, was that the English were afterwards engaged less actively, and indeed less dangerously in wars than their rivals: except the incursions of the Scotch, their wars were abroad, they were only occasional and of short duration.

When the reign of Henry the Seventh, and the discovery of America, awakened the ardor of discovery and commercial enterprise, this new propensity found little rivalship or impediment from the military passion, and as it was fostered afterwards by Elizabeth and the Stuarts, the English soon became a shopkeeping nation, *une nation boutiquiere*, as the French contemptuously denominate them. Hence, the passion to acquire is characteristic of the English; the passion to rule is predominant with the French; the one seeks gain, the other glory.

The causes which have led to this national character, not only lie deep in the most remote antiquity, but events of a more recent date have contributed to decide, and for ever to fix their preponderance.

The ravages of national wars frequently exposed the country people to spoil and violence; but the great lords and feudal chiefs claimed and exercised the right of private vengeance. Hence, animosities and endless civil wars desolated the continental states of Europe. The only places of security were the fortified towns. Thus it happened, that the country was inhabited by a wretched, defenceless peasantry, without character or spirit, and subject to the *corvee* or ruinous slavery of performing certain labor for their lords, and to a whole system of feudal exactions and oppressions so heavy and so dispiriting, as to prevent their having any character of their own, or any influence on that of the nation. Indeed, emulation will be directed towards such qualities as are esteemed; and there was nothing in the condition of the laboring class to gratify pride or to inspire it. The soldiers only were respected or imitated; they gave the tone and the fashion to every thing in France. Cities were not much occupied in arts, and not at all in commerce. They were crowded with retainers to princes and nobles, who even wore their livery and fed at their tables; they followed them in war, and their multitude was the rule by which the magnificence and power of the nobles was measured and displayed.

Thus the taste and manners of the French were not formed, like the English, in solitude and by the occupations of country life. Fashion governed the crowds in cities, and the nobles and their martial followers alone gave law to fashion; arms engrossed all thoughts, the business of war and the conversation of peace.

When Louis the Eleventh humbled the great lords of France, and established a standing army, his sagacity discerned that this leading propensity of the French character was to be used as the instrument to keep the nation in subjection. His successors cherished the military sense of honor as the basis and guardian principle of the monarchy. The *noblesse* despised trade, and an artisan, however ingenious, was one of the *people*, or populace or mob.

From hence it followed, that arms alone were honored; a rich man could not pretend to be a gentleman till he had served a campaign; and the French noblesse preserved, undiminished, the gallantry, the impetuous valor that courted danger, which so much distinguished the age of the crusades and of chivalry: that gallant race was extinct, excepting in France.

The revolution began, and was in a great measure effected, not by quenching this chivalrous spirit, but by awakening it in the rabble. They were sensible to honor and shame, and they claimed to be as brave, and therefore as much gentlemen, as the noblesse. This emulation, the more lively for being newly inspired, animated the attack of the Bastile, arrayed the national guards, and spread the power of enthusiasm, like the electric fluid, over all France. The leaders of the revolution, as skilful to guide as to excite the popular ferment, availed themselves of these new energies to raise armies, and after having subverted the monarchy, to find work for them in a war with Austria. The progress of this war, it was foreseen, would throw all the political and physical power of France into their hands, as the fervor of the revolution had already given them absolute power over opinion. Never, in the history of mankind, did the rulers of a nation possess an influence so combined and so unlimited. Robespierre held all France in his hand as a machine, he wielded it as a weapon, while the emperor and the king of Great Britain, whom the French call despots, could command only the surplus of the revenues, and some fragments of the force of their states.

But the manner in which this gigantic despotism has proceeded, will best illustrate the popular sentiment, from which it sprung, and the end which alone it deems worthy of its ambition and its efforts.

THE NEW ROMANS IV

The Palladium, MAY 26, 1801

It has been attempted to show, that military glory has ever been the first object of desire, the most fascinating claim to superior consideration in France.

Savages take their character from their situation as individuals, from their appetites and their wants, rather than from any sympathy of national sentiment; hunger makes them hunters; fear, and sometimes revenge, makes them warriors. But in polished societies, men derive their national cast from their intercourse with one another. Absolute want is felt by few, and those who feel it are without influence on the society. Man ceases to be merely an individual; he models his desires and his sentiments according to his relation to the national body, of which he is a member. That class in society which is the most respected, is the most imitated. It has been shown, that the class of artisans, or that of merchants, did not hold that envied place in France, but that the men of the sword did.

This being the national sentiment, it is obvious that the government could not disobey, much less offend or shock, that sentiment, without losing in a moment all its hold on the popular affections. A dastardly policy, a dread of war with Austria or England, would have blasted the new leaders with disgrace. Taken, as they were, from the lowest classes of the nation, they would have been charged with having souls as mean as their condition, too mean to govern a republic, all whose citizens claimed an equal rank with their high-spirited nobles, and who required, that the great nation should adopt the lofty pretensions, and display the impetuous courage, of its military class. All the classes of society claimed an equality, and to be at the top, and thus the depression of ranks instantly produced an elevation of national spirit. Believing that they were all sovereign, and that France, by raising its spirit, had raised its power, they were anxious to make such a display of it, as should astonish and confound kings, whom they hated, and the English nation, whom they envied and feared. They considered their new liberty as a new rank, and the highest rank, which of course in their eyes, was military; and that this sudden dignity was neither solidly established, nor sufficiently enjoyed, unless the power of France was displayed in a manner to excite both terror and wonder, to make kings quake and their subjects admire. How dear a triumph for republicanism! How lofty a stage for equality!

Indeed, it is not in the nature of things that any strong popular impulse should be satisfied without action. The more sudden, surprising, and violent the action, the more likely is it to gratify and to prolong this impulse. All democracies are governments by popular passions. These cannot exist and be at rest; they cannot be indulged, and yet kept within the limits of moderation or principle. They sweep like whirlwinds, that are not stopped by desolation, but as they destroy, they level obstacles and are quickened in their progress. They pour like torrents from the mountains, and if they reach the plains in their fulness, they are inundations unconfined by banks; the violence of each soon scoops for itself a narrow channel, and that is a dry one.

One auxiliary cause of the military passion of the French has not been mentioned in its proper place; it must not be omitted in the examination of characters. The English, their great rivals, ever thought themselves entitled to take rank as a free nation. The French could not vie with the English for liberty; but vanity, repelled from one course, sought and found relief in another: "we are the most gallant people of Europe; these islanders, proud of their liberty, shall not be permitted to despise, they shall fear us." Pride, hot in the race of emulation, and smarting with the wound of its imputed degradation by slavery under an absolute monarch, grew prouder, when it wore its armor and surveyed its trophies. In that contemplation, every Frenchman stretched into a giant, and felt persuaded that France alone was peopled by the race of Anak.

All this military fervor, with all its strength and all its blindness, was transferred by the revolution into the people, *la bourgeoisie*, who claimed to be nobles, and who knew no other way to display it, than the usual and acknowledged one for men of rank, by military distinction.

Accordingly, in the first era of the revolution, the formation of the national guards, and the establishment of rank equal to veterans, awakened the sleeping pride of every heart, and mingled the love of liberty with self-love too intimately to allow them afterwards to be dissociated. Pride received a new impulse to its current, but it ran in the old channel.

No sooner had the revolution attracted attention, than each Frenchman felt his individual title to preëminence, as well as that of the nation, to be subjected to a trial. He now claimed to be freer than the free, to be freer than an Englishman or American, as he had ever pretended to be the first among polished and brave men. Their common sentiment was, of course, that the friendship of those who resembled them in liberty was a *debt;* the submission of those who were inferior to them in force and courage was *a decree of fate.* The supposed hatred of kings, because *they* had made a republic, their contempt, because they had made a vile rabble rulers, alike stimulated their national vanity to assert claims that were thus disputed, and if possible, to make them indisputable. They perceived that France was a stage, and that the curiosity of mankind expected something magnificent in the scenes, something preternatural in the actors, something that would dazzle and astonish; that would make criticism distrustful of its rules, and awe contradiction into silence.

The revolution itself was one of those portentous but rare events, which originate from the operation of moral causes, from the intestine agitation of the human mind; a fermentative power, that destroys the forms and the essences of the political body, and yet in its progress separates a larger portion of that pungent spirit, that was formerly the hidden aliment of its life, and is now its preservative from corruption. But while all France was steaming with this pervading heat, and twitching with the spasms of enthusiastic passion, its popular leaders, assuming imposing names, and exercising a despotism that had neither known limits nor definition, suddenly found themselves invested with a power that seemed miraculous. They could lead the nation out like an intoxicated giant; or like a war elephant to tread down an enemy's ranks, and train him rather to be furious than intimidated by his wounds.

The spirit of the revolution, like that of the crusades, is a fierce and troubled spirit; and like that, it may take two centuries to quiet it. The Reformation of Luther, more necessary and more salutary, entailed three ages of war upon Europe. It is a prodigious power, which the monarchy could not resist; but which the chiefs of the military democracy have successively attempted to guide.

It may seem to most readers a paradox that so much weight should be allowed to the popular sentiment, in a country so devoted to despotism as France. It should be remembered that even a despotism has but a limited physical strength: it must depend on other props than mere force; it must make an auxiliary of public opinion. The grand seignior governs Turkey by the aid of superstition more than by his janissaries; and even in France, where the people seem to be annihilated, and are nothing in the subordinate plans of the government, the great objects of policy must be chosen and conducted with no small condescension to their wishes. For instance, a peace that should strip France of her conquests, that should tear the laurels from the army, that should expose the French nation to any loss of the reputation that victory has conferred, would shake the throne of the boldest usurper that has enslaved them. The claims of their vanity have been exorbitant from the first, and every new set of tyrants has promised still further to exalt that vanity. Indeed they have kept their word!

It is probable that sensible Frenchmen have long ago discerned that they did not possess liberty, and that they were not in the road to attain it; but they appeared to be in that road, and that illusion concealed their chains and soothed their sense of disappointment. They could bear it, that they were not freemen, it was what they were used and reconciled to; but they would not bear not to be conquerors. Their love of liberty was tractable; their vanity untractable. Accordingly, they gloried in the enthusiasm of their efforts to expel the Prussians, who, by invading, had profaned the territory of the republic; although no tyranny could be more odious or sanguinary than that for which they fought. They have borne taxes, paper money, famine, tyranny in all its worst forms, not merely with ordinary patience, but with alacrity, because the French nation struck Europe with admiration and terror. While religion and morals took flight, industry starved, and innocence bled, national vanity has had its banquets; its frequent feasts have become its ordinary living, and now it would pine without a profusion of dainties.

THE NEW ROMANS V

The *Palladium*, MAY 29, 1801

A MIDST all the confusion of the changes in the government of France, the rulers have formed their policy on the basis of the vanity of the nation; every new set has promised aggrandizement and glory to France, and the infliction of a signal vengeance on its enemies.

This constancy in adhering to the same maxims of policy, while the men at the head of affairs were kings only for three months, may seem surprising. But Sparta preserved nearly the same character seven hundred years, though many violent revolutions occurred; and Rome acted as long, and even more uniformly, on the strength of the national sentiment, that she could not exist at all unless as a conqueror and mistress of the world; yet Rome changed her consuls yearly.

The diversity of the character of her magistrates was lost in the uniformity and force of her own.

In the very beginning of the French popular government, the national vanity was soothed by the incense of flattery from its own demagogues, and the natural jacobins of every civilized state. Addresses from clubs and from individual incendiaries were multiplied, and graciously received at the bar of the convention. It seemed to be a Roman senate, sitting judicially to hear the grievances of all nations, and to parcel out the world into provinces. Anacharsis Cloots appeared and harangued the assembly, as the orator of the human race.[56] In November, 1792, the safety and independence of all states was formally attacked by the decree that France would assist the rebels of all countries against their governments. The apologists for French extravagances, after some fruitless attempts to justify the principle of this outrage on all mankind, have next endeavored to palliate: they say less was intended than the words of the decree seem to import. When the conduct of France discredited even this palliation, it has been since insisted that the decree was adopted in times of violence and confusion, and that it has been formally annulled. All periods have been violent, and marked with a more than Roman contempt of the rights as well as the opinions of mankind. But Gregorei, in his labored report to the assembly on the laws of nations, in which this monstrous decree is supposed to be annulled, expressly says, that the application of the principles he had exhibited is the right only of the nations whose governments are founded on the rights of man. The best proof, however, that France has not in form renounced the decree, is that she has invariably adhered to it in fact.

It appears, by the publications of Brissot and others, that

---

[56] *Pseudonym of Baron Jean Baptiste Clootz, a Prussian who became a French citizen, advocated extreme revolutionary and aesthetic principles in Paris, and was executed (1794). Ames's spelling, "Cloots," or cloven-hoofed, may be a pun on the name, to say, "Devil."*

the French rulers, like the Roman senate, believed it to be necessary rather to employ the fiery turbulent spirit of the nation in war abroad, than to let it employ itself in sedition at home. It is a general opinion among the democrats of all countries, that France was attacked by a royal coalition, jealous of her republicanism. The fact is, the French began the war in Flanders against the emperor when his towns were without garrisons, the fortifications had been recently pulled down, and the troops ordinarily kept on foot, for their defence, did not amount to half their complement.

With such a spirit as raged in France, and with such interests and means to turn the fury of the popular passions against the emperor and the king of England, peace was not to be maintained. When a whole street is on fire, can a man sit at his ease and say, my house is of brick; let my next neighbor burn; the fire will burn out, and then the bustle and danger will be over. Such are the speeches made, and with great popular effect, to inflame the admirers of democracy with a zeal for injured, invaded France.

———— Jam proximus ardet Ucalegon.[57]

The conflagration of every thing combustible in France rendered it impossible for other powers to be at peace; and as France will not and cannot change her political character, Europe will not be permitted long to enjoy it. So vast a power is a continual incentive to ambition; and such a national military spirit naturally leads to power. There are many states in Europe still that might tempt a conqueror; there is not one except Great Britain that has the spirit and means to resist him.

It has been already shown that the only prevailing popular sentiment was the military one. The excess of that passion has enabled the government to maintain tranquility as profound as if there was no war. The French saw tyranny in

---

[57] *Then next Ucalegon was burned.*

Paris, oppression in the provinces; all commerce, all credit, all manufacture was ruined; but as an offset for want, slavery, and ruin, there was victory, and all France shouted for joy.

The manner in which this Roman power has been used is truly Roman. The neighboring states have been made not merely the objects of conquest, but the instruments of ambition, to effect more conquests. Except Great Britain, Portugal, and Turkey, there is not one enemy left whom France has not made her ally. The emperor and the king of Naples are to be dishonored by a stipulation that their faithful protectors, the English, shall be excluded from their ports. Portugal is supposed, by this time, to be forced to adopt the like measure. To cut up Turkey is said to be the object of a late treaty between Bonaparte and the Emperor Paul of Russia. If this should be effected there will be new struggles and revolution; the established order and balance of Europe will be subverted from their foundations; and happy will it be, if, after thirty years war, it should be settled again as firmly as it was by the peace of Westphalia, in 1648.

It was in like manner the policy of Rome to make use of her feeble enemies to destroy such as were strong. The Ætolians in Greece were first engaged to assist in destroying Philip of Macedon. They, finding themselves duped and enslaved by the Romans, called in Antiochus, King of Syria, to assist them in their defence. The cities of Greece were gained, and dexterously played off to destroy the liberties of Greece. While Rome and Carthage were contending, the great powers, still unconquered, took no part in the contest. Thus Rome not only attacked them one after another, but was always sure to have the assistance of an old enemy, whom she had just conquered into an alliance, to overpower a new one. Hannibal, after his defeat, fled to Antiochus; it was then too late, for Carthage had received the law of the conqueror. Antiochus interfered in the affairs of Greece after Philip of Macedon was humbled, and forced to be the ally of Rome against him. Mithridates, king of Pontus, had no ally till his power was much enfeebled—then Tigranes joined him, in time to be defeated. Greece would have been strong if it had been united; but its numerous governments were jealous of one another, often at war, and ready to call in the Romans to enslave them all. It seems astonishing that neither Macedon, nor Greece, nor Syria, nor Egypt, made treaties of mutual defence, or took any sensible measure to employ all their joint forces in self-preservation. The world would have been saved from slavery.

There is scarcely a single article of Roman policy, in which we do not perceive the servile imitation of the French; and if Great Britain was a republic, as Carthage was, there would be a faction in its bosom, devoted to France, strong enough to ensure her slavery. The fall of Great Britain would quench every hope of the recovery of the independence of Europe; a new Roman servitude would spread over the civilized world. The United States would be exposed to new toils, conflicts, and dangers; faction would raise her snaky head with new audacity, confiding in the support that France would give to her efforts. We might be alarmed in time to see the approach of a foreign tyrant; but we should have to fight for our independence, or to resign it.

THE OBSERVER

———

The Palladium, FEBRUARY 20, 1801

THE FRENCH REVOLUTION is a sort of experimental political philosophy, in which many foolish opinions are tried and found wanting. The jacobins are, however, like quacks who recommend their patent medicines. Experience has no effect

441

on them to cure their delusion. They say their elixir of immortality has not yet been fairly tried, and that some aristocratic patients stopped breathing only to effect the disgrace of their nostrums. They would give a whole nation a quietus at once if they could only persuade them to swallow some liquor of long life, some restorative pill or some powder that is to sweeten the blood. Accordingly, the jacobin papers even yet manifest how little they learn from the direful experience of France; for even yet they dare to call the success of French arms the cause of liberty and republicanism. Whether we have any fools left who still flounder in this confusion of mind is more than I know; but many jacobins, it is certain, still claim credit for their sincerity to that amazing extent of infatuation.

France is the only state in Europe completely military; they are now what the Turks lately were, all soldiers, or all liable to be made soldiers. Their spirits have been wrought up by eight years of war, by revolution, and by the excesses of what our mobocrats call liberty, into a ferment equal to that of the ancient crusaders. No state could be safe while France had the power to disturb them; and every state that thought itself safe in inaction has fallen; the only powers that yet stand are those that resisted with courage. France has not changed; the danger to other nations is not less, and the only path to safety is thorny and perilous; it is to be trodden in arms. Mithridates, Antiochus, Perseus, the Etolian and Achæan leagues were successively lost, either by seeking an alliance with ancient Rome, or by neglecting the obvious policy of confederating with other states in like peril; Perseus allied with Antiochus, or Mithridates with Sertorius, might have saved the world from servitude. France now claims empire, and will not bear rivalship. Austria and England can have no peace; they will fail, unless their arms should so far cripple their foe as to disable him from prosecuting his scheme of universal dominion. France is as revolutionary as ever; Bonaparte keeps down jacobinism at home, but it deeply concerns him to stir it up in every other state where French influence is wanted. Jacobinism is therefore more than ever to be dreaded by England and Austria, because its operations in France are more artfully disguised by the government. It is more than ever to be dreaded in America, because the moment approaches when its success can be turned to immediate account. What event could ever happen more auspicious to her views than to have an administration that would bend the laws and commercial systems of this country to the policy of that? Mr. Madison's famous commercial resolutions were grounded on the idea of making America useful as a colony to France; not how we should make our trade the most useful to ourselves. The New England merchants had sense enough to understand this delusive, this disgraceful policy, and spurned at it. They will do it again if it should be repeated. We are still wanted by France, and to have us she must spread jacobinism. It might and would help her to rule our citizens, though, if suffered to prevail in France, it might hinder Bonaparte from quietly ruling Frenchmen at home.

SKETCHES OF THE STATE OF EUROPE I

The Palladium, MARCH 6, 1801[58]

THE POLICY and conduct of the French, since the commencement of their revolution, exhibit very little of novelty, except in the degrees of political intrigue, and revolutionary

---

[58] *Seth Ames, in the 1854 edition of this work, omitted the present essay, which had been included in the 1809 edition. Ames explained the omission with reference to evidence that the essay was actually "the*

443

cruelty and injustice. Wrought up almost to a state of phrenzy by an unexampled combination of circumstances and events, they have applied principles and adopted practices with a skill and ardour, which have hitherto rendered them the terrour and scourge of Europe. As this revolution has, at different periods, involved the interests, and called forth the exertions of almost all the European powers, it will be necessary to look at their designs and relative positions at its commencement.

A sense of common danger, and those laws, which, in peace and war, have always regulated the great republic of the European states, impelled them to check, by force of arms, the progress of that revolutionary system, which was wasting France and threatening the rest of Europe. Accordingly, Prussia, Austria, Spain, Holland, and England, at an early period, united to repress the spirit of jacobinism, and, by timely and vigorous exertions, hoped to obtain security to themselves, and restore tranquillity to France. But, in spite of all opposition, her armies penetrated into Holland, Germany, and Italy. In the management of this war France has imitated the policy of the Romans, in detaching members of confederacies against them, from their alliance. Sensible that the united exertions of Europe would disable them from propagating their principles and extending their territory, they felt the necessity of separating the allied powers to accomplish their ambitious projects. Of course, jealousies were excited among them, separate interests were brought into view, the blind pursuit of which tended to ruin the common cause by diverting the collected energies of the coalition. The king of Prussia, jealous of the house of Austria,

work of another author." However, inasmuch as he did not share that evidence with us, inasmuch as the essay is the first of a series that bears every indication of proceeding from the same pen, and until we shall be able independently to verify the judgment that it is not Ames's work, we are restoring this essay to the corpus of Fisher Ames's works.

and reluctant to contribute to its aggrandizement, soon entered into negotiations for a separate peace, and, by scrupulously watching the internal state of his dominions, and maintaining a military force ready to act as occasion might require, has ever since been able to support his authority at home, and hold a neutral position in the midst of contending nations. Holland, spiritless and panick-struck at the successes and power of France, yielded, with a feeble struggle, her resources and liberties into the hands of French robbers and tyrants, who have, at length, broken her ancient spirit, and still continue to drill and whip her to the performance of the most humiliating services for the great nation. Spain, paralyzed with fear, and willing to make any sacrifices to preserve life, broke from the confederacy in defiance of the most solemn treaties, and, like Holland, submitted herself to the unqualified disposal of France.

But here it may be asked, why have the French permitted the church and the throne to rest quietly upon their ancient foundations? The destruction of kings and priests, is the first article in the revolutionary code: why then have they not planted the tree of liberty in Madrid, and proclaimed the downfall of civil and ecclesiastical tyranny? Upon the ruin of these, they have founded their claim to superiour light and wisdom. In every other country, where, by arts and arms, they have obtained a permanent footing, existing establishments have been subverted, and constitutions made after the newest fashion imposed upon the people, for which nothing has been demanded but submission, gratitude, and the "simple tithe of all they had." Some powerful reasons, therefore, must have dictated a line of policy so opposite to their professions and feelings, and so different from that, which, in other countries, they have invariably pursued. It is not probable, that the French were, at any time, doubtful of success in an enterprise against Spain and Portugal. An army of thirty thousand men was drawn out, and a general appointed to lead them through Spain to the heart of Portugal; but motives of policy checked the enterprise, and led France to employ her armies, where their successes would not be followed by equal or superiour advantage to her enemies. It was foreseen, that if Spain should be revolutionized, the commerce of her colonies in the West-Indies and upon the continent would greatly increase the power of England, and more than balance the accession of strength which would be gained from the plunder of Portugal. Had the project for breaking up the ancient establishments of Spain, and weakening the allies by the destruction of Portugal, been carried into effect, the Spanish and Portuguese colonies would have thrown off their dependence upon the mother countries, and assumed the station of independent states, or put themselves under the protection of England or the United States. In either case, England would have felt, that her *sinews of war were made stronger*, and her ability of continuing it increased. Such, then, have been the motives, which, while they have deterred the French from adding Spain and Portugal to the list of new republics, have manifested the hollowness of their professions, and their deep-laid schemes of unlimited domination.

While the French were hot in the pursuit of conquest, a grand alliance, in which the Russian emperour was to put forth his energies, was formed for the purpose of driving the French from Italy in a single campaign, and of carrying the war into France. It is probable, that the emperour Paul engaged with as disinterested views, as those of any member of the confederacy, and with a determination to restore the ancient government of France. Suwarrow, a perfect master in all the schemes and artifices of war, who alone knew to lead Russian troops to victory, was entrusted with the chief command. In a few months he broke the force of the French in Italy, and proceeded to the conquest of Switzerland. But here an untoward combination of circumstances defeated his designs, and compelled him to retreat. The Austrians failed in the execution of that part of the plan assigned to them; the army in Switzerland under the command of Hotze had been routed, and Hotze himself killed, by the unexpected descent of the army of Lecourbe and Massena from the Alps; and the troops of Suwarrow, exhausted and without supplies, were obliged to save themselves by flight. Suwarrow was extremely exasperated at the conduct of the Austrians, and, although the Russians cooperated with the English in an unsuccessful expedition to Holland, the retreat of Suwarrow from Switzerland seems to have been the first step towards the secession of Paul from the coalition. Here was given a fair opportunity for court intrigue to interpose, and represent the partiality of the English for the Austrians, the mercenary views of the house of Austria, manifested in a disposition to make no sacrifice of private interests for the sake of the common cause. Paul, naturally capricious, being led to suspect that the allies meant to weaken his power by employing his troops as mercenaries against France, withdrew from the alliance with indignation. At this time, it is probable that his attention was diverted with the idea of extending his dominions in Turkey.

Notwithstanding Austria has been often charged with selfish and mercenary views in the conduct of the war, it may be doubted, whether, previous to the secession of Paul, she acted inconsistent with the best interests of the coalition. Her taking possession of the reconquered places in Italy might have been with the view of throwing into them such forces, as would have formed a barrier to the future progress of the French: in themselves, they were feeble and needed protection, and the interests of the alliance probably demanded, that they should be secured from the grasp of their enemies.

SKETCHES OF
THE STATE OF EUROPE II

The Palladium, MARCH 13, 1801

THE CHANGE of the politics of Russia is one of the chief facts to attract attention. Whether this change originated from mere whim and fickleness of temper of the emperor, or from deep views of future advantage to Russia, we know very little, and the little that we do know affords no very satisfactory ground even for conjecture. Politically speaking, Russia, as a member of the European state, is still an undiscovered country; it is an empire so vast, so new, so motley, and so barbarous; it is such a Babel, whose tongues are yet so confounded; a gigantic infant that changes so often by its growth, and so much oftener by its caprice; time is doing so much, and accident so much more, to give it a determinate impression and character,—that no one has cause to be ashamed of his ignorance of its politics. It is, perhaps, after all, a question whether Paul is not as rash as his father, Peter the Third, in his conduct, and whether a revolution like that which dethroned his father, in 1762, will not soon happen.

Be that as it may, it is impossible to look at the present position of the great European powers without being struck with this contrast: in 1793, all were joined with Great Britain in opposition to France; now all are leagued in opposition to Great Britain. Perhaps it will be seen again that a single power is an overmatch for a confederacy.

The pretexts of Russia to justify this new system are frivolous; for the British dominion of the seas is no grievance to Russia. Sweden and Denmark are mere satellites, and act only as they are acted upon. Russia has no commerce to be cramped by searches. Its industry is little, its trading capital less, and its mercantile navigation nothing. Besides, the very British men-of-war that thus rule the seas are furnished with Russian hemp, and cordage, and iron. The pretext, therefore, amounts to nothing more than that the English are their best customers for naval stores. Lazy and poor nations must depend on such as are industrious and rich; but it is absurd to say that Russia is or can be the rival of England. A man barefoot is no rival of the shoemaker; a naked man in a cold climate must depend on the woollendraper. Russia sells a superfluity that it cannot use nor work up, and that nobody would pay for if England did not. Commercially speaking, therefore, it seems obvious and certain that the interests of Russia are not pursued or regarded by the authors of the war.

But great nations make light of the affair of gain or loss in trade when political considerations intervene; for if England did not rule the ocean Russia could not. It would be France, the little finger of whose despotism would be found thicker than the British loins. Russia must have other motives.

Turkey has been long a defenceless prey to any of the powerful states, and would long ago have been devoured if their mutual jealousy had not delayed her fate. There has been no period since the Turks took Constantinople, in 1453, when it was so easy for Russia to conquer the European provinces of this paralytic empire. The rulers of France, at all other times interested to save Turkey, have now no objects but such as are personal and temporary. Bonaparte would be glad to say to Paul, let me alone; do you conquer on your side; I wish to meet with none of your interruption in conquering on mine. France is at war with Turkey, and eager to establish her colony in Egypt; Austria is beaten, and England has her hands full; it would not be strange, therefore, if Paul should be found to look for the recompense of his war with England in the conquest of the Greek provinces, or in a treaty with the Porte that would assure to him their final subjection. This is but conjecture, perhaps not plausible. The second son of the Emperor Paul is named Constantine, and was taught Greek to gain the affections of his intended subjects. This fact has long been well known. Europe is a gaming table, where the bets are often shifted, and sometimes the players as well as the luck. There is scarcely any thing that we are not to expect to see staked by the gamesters, especially as they make no scruples, as in the case of Venice, to play for what is none of their own.

It is natural to ask whether England can face a world in arms. That armed world is very far from her happy island, and whilst she triumphs on the seas, they must keep their distance. Famine might enrage her laboring people, and convulse her within, but the government is active in its measures to prevent that evil. The contest is therefore left to the trial of her resources. These are wonderful, and the exclusive empire and commerce of the seas will not ultimately lessen them. It is a splendid lesson to America of the energies that industry, and such a government as will protect its earnings, can command. Our free republican government, we trust, is such a government; and we hope our new rulers will not hate commerce as a New England gold-mine, nor check it, lest the moneyed interest, as the democrats call the proceeds of trade and fisheries, should surpass and outweigh the landed interest, as they call the tobacco planters, God's chosen people, if ever he had a chosen people.[59]

Great events are to be looked for, and whatever they may be, it is wise policy and obvious duty for our government to disentangle our politics from France, who wants to use our strength, and to cherish as much as possible the commercial spirit that will make America rich by industry, and thus to gain strength while Europe grows poor by war. Happy shall

---

[59] *Mockery of Jefferson, who referred to farmers as "God's chosen people" in his* Notes on the State of Virginia.

we be if, while we gain riches, we do not lose our spirit, and if peace abroad shall not embitter dissensions at home.

In this momentous contest between Great Britain and the numerous foes who have joined with France against her, it is probable that the profits of our commerce will be enlarged, and the danger of our being forced into the war much lessened. If Britain, however, should be very unsuccessful, we might then expect France would a second time require us, as Genet did before, to vindicate our neutral rights by arms; in other words, to fight her enemy in her cause. It seems to be therefore as clear as the noonday sun, that our interest, our peace, and our commercial liberty require that France should not, by humbling and weakening England, be able to take the high ground to command America to join her. We know that France would do it in a day, if she had, which, thank God, she has not, the means to enforce her commands.

It is a singular proof of the utter want of all patriotism in the violent spirit of jacobinism, that the *Aurora* and *Chronicle* are incessantly exhibiting the triumphs of France as the security of America, and the overthrow of the British dominion of the sea as our triumph and final emancipation. This is senseless and absurd beyond measure. France has no enemy that can face her at land. The British naval power is a counterpoise. Each of these nations is thus a check on the other, and both court friends among the powers who could help or hinder their operations. Some little respect is thus procured for neutrality; whereas, if England were beaten at sea as completely as Austria is at land, France would domineer both on sea and land; the civilized world would be subject instantly to a despotism as arrogant, as rapacious, as unfeeling as that of Rome; her arms would be vigorously employed to spread her power from the Ganges to the Ohio.

The *Aurora* and *Chronicle* are desired to notice these sentiments, and they are invited to represent them as the proofs of partiality for Britain, and of the force of British influence; there are many hundreds of their readers weak enough to accept such proofs as demonstrations. It would be easy to retort on the jacobins that their aversion to admit such ideas is a clear indication that they love France well enough to help her to be the universal despot, and that they love America so little they would rejoice to see her the satellite of that despot. It is obvious that the security of feeble states must depend on the power of the great states being balanced and divided; and those Americans who can deliberately wish to see Britain conquered at sea, must be traitors or fools.

In the course of this great contest facts and principles are established of the most momentous concern to all independent nations. The first leading observation is, that wretched is the condition of subjects when the state itself is small and feeble. Holland had no patriotism, because its strength was little, and division and discord made that little less. It has been a prey, and its wealth has been squeezed out by taxes openly laid to fill the French treasury. A tax of ten per cent. on income, excepting the poorer classes, who were to be used as *sans culottes*, was imposed in the first year of their slavery, six per cent. of which was for France. The rich were declared lawful prize; and France, the captor, divided the spoil like the lion in the fable. Switzerland and the Italian republics and states exibit the wretchedness of the people where the public force is feeble.

Another observation is, that where the executive authority is weak patriotism is extinct. Holland was uneasy because the stadtholder was the first magistrate. But, had the execution of the laws been duly intrusted to him, he would have resisted foreign influence with better success than he did; the Dutch would not have lost their patriotism before they lost their country. Switzerland was more than half conquered before it was invaded. England, on the contrary, has made it dangerous

452

to be a traitor; and neither France nor England allows faction to grow formidable before it is crushed.

Again, we must remark, how much less resistance is made by states that are confederated, or broken up into separate sovereignties, as Germany, Italy, and Switzerland, than by such as, like France and England, are one and indivisible. Every Frenchman in this country has been a stickler for state sovereignty; and in France, every Frenchman has cried, no federalism, the republic one and indivisible. Accordingly France has taken care to make her neighbors weak and dependent by clipping and slicing their territory into petty republics: she will not suffer any body to be great but herself. Germany formerly kept the legions of Rome at bay, and now it is overrun in one campaign; yet Germany is scarcely less populous or warlike than France. Italy has done nothing; but her petty sovereigns have waited the event of battles to see who should be their masters. Switzerland has done nothing worthy of her liberty and ancient glory.

Is it not, therefore, to be hoped, that if great changes must be violently made in Europe, they will be chiefly such as will consolidate the monstrous confederations of many heads without a common body or one soul, and that the smaller powers will be formed into great states, so as to increase the future security for the liberty, and independence, and happiness of their subjects?

We take occasion to declare, however, that we are not desirous to see the American separate state powers attacked. As they are, let them remain, till experience suggests changes, and the people are freely willing to make them. We do not pretend, however, that a discerning patriot ought not to apprehend the ambitious abuse that faction is trying to make of the powers of the great states, Pennsylvania and Virginia, and of the disturbance, foreign influence, and consequent weakness of the national force. This point is of late much better understood in New England.

RUSSIA

The Palladium, JULY, 1801

Few things are worse understood than the condition of the Northern Powers in respect to England, especially Russia. English capital has made their potash first, and then paid for it; it has bought their hempseed, paid for ploughing the land, and then purchased the hemp; advances were made by English merchants of the capital, many months before the product appeared at market. This has been so well understood, that American merchants have sent a purchasing capital, a year beforehand, into Russia to get hemp and cordage. The democrats will cry out, this is colonial dependence; and ring all the changes on their set of bells. It is true, countries half settled and not half civilized are, in fact, dependent on countries that are blessed with good government, and the laying up of industry. Accordingly, the war of Russia against England is the effort of poverty against the very wealth that alone must employ it.

Errors in politics so gross cannot be atoned for by moderate chastisement. It is impossible that Russia should not suffer political evils of magnitude, in consequence of the infatuated counsels of her deceased madman. Ignorance is the proper soil for French principles to sprout in; of course, Russia is in danger of being infected, and after all it cannot be the political interest of Russia to aggrandize France. The naval power of Great Britain is, ever has been, and must be, favorable to Russia; the territorial greatness of France ever will be an impediment. France is interested to keep Turkey from falling; France never wishes to see any power great but herself. Eternal barriers are placed between Russia and France; and no tricks of Bonaparte, no caprices of Paul can

level them. The attempt to disregard the fixed political laws
of her being, will entail incalculable evils on Russia; it is
possible to play the fool in politics as in private life, but
never with impunity.

THE BALANCE OF EUROPE

The Palladium, MAY 28, 1802

TWO HUNDRED and eighty years ago, Francis I. king of
France, and Charles V. emperor of Germany, king of Spain,
possessor of the dominions of the house of Austria in Germany,
Italy, and the Low Countries, began the contests of ambition
which have since regulated the *balance of Europe.*

Russia and Prussia were then nothing; England was not
much, for we are to deduct from its present power Scotland,
which was hostile, Ireland, little better civilized than the six
nations, and the American colonies and India settlements,
neither of which were then begun. England then had the
weight of a feather, but of a feather that could turn the scale.
Henry VIII. had not always the good sense to throw his
weight into the right scale; he acted from passion rather than
from policy. France was greatly overmatched, and should
have had his aid. Afterwards the troubles in France reduced
that country to a state of insignificance, and Philip II. king
of Spain, remained the preponderant power of Europe. After
the middle of the seventeenth century, Louis XIV. advanced
to the front rank, as the leader of the European republic.
Charles II. of England, loved his pleasures too much, and
trusted his parliament too little, to dispute that rank with
him. Accordingly, Louis made great conquests, and annexed

455

Alsace, Lorraine, and a part of the Low Countries, to his vast monarchy.

At that time there were only three powers in the north of Europe: Denmark, Sweden, and Poland. Sweden, especially, was highly military; and the size of her army made amends for the scantiness of her wealth and people. Russia was not born, and Prussia was not then gathered as a nation. England, Holland, and Austria, formed a balance in the beginning of the eighteenth century for the immense power of France. Spain was then nothing; for an Austrian and a Bourbon prince were competitors for its crown.

Something like a balance was, however, actually maintained; for at all times, the ambition to establish a universal monarchy existed; but by great good fortune, sufficient obstacles to its accomplishment also existed. These were found in the combination of the weaker powers.

One reason for the success for this combination may be ascribed to the inferior military establishments of the several European states at that period. A great power found it very difficult to maintain a great army; and a small state with a large army, and especially aided by a confederacy with other weak states, could effectually resist a great conqueror.

Hence we may observe the great change in the face of Europe within a century. Armies are large, and more in proportion to the size of the several states. New combinations of politics are formed, in consequence of the gradual and experienced insignificance of the weak states. New powers, as Russia and Prussia, have arisen; and the independence of all requires that new principles should be adopted to support the balance, without which one nation will be the tyrant, and the rest slaves.

By the treaty of Westphalia, in 1648, Germany was condemned to endless anarchy. Its state sovereignties were scarcely to be counted or controlled.

Whatever is divided is weakened; and in politics, whatever

is weakened is exposed as a prey. Accordingly, in every war, Germany furnished soldiers for France, and her own sons were employed to cut one another's throats.

Holland had some patriotism one hundrd years ago; faction has since extinguished it; and instead of its being the enemy, it proved, in 1794, the auxiliary of French domination.

In weak states fear rules; temporary expedients are sought, and the rulers seldom fail in the end to act for their destroyers, because they are afraid to act against them. Hence it is that the weak states of Europe have lately proved more than passive to France; they have made a merit of devoting themselves to destruction.

In the present position of Europe, it is obvious that France domineers. She has gained positively, by adding territory to her dominions equal in size, wealth, and people, to a second-rate kingdom; she has gained relatively, by removing Austria to a distance, and by weakening that ancient rival to such a degree as to secure her inaction for an age.

Prussia has gained prodigiously by the partition of Poland. It was natural to think that Prussia had become powerful enough to disregard France; but it has unexpectedly happened that Prussia has gained power without gaining entire independence. Austria is weaker, but France is stronger than ever. Besides, Russia is more than ever the preponderating power of the North. Of course it is, that Prussia still leans upon France, is more than ever afraid to provoke her displeasure, and perhaps more than ever really interested in her alliance, to secure herself against Russia.

France then finds no counterpoise in Prussia. Sweden and Denmark are no longer of any consequence. Their armies no longer bear any proportion to their extent of territory, and other powers have augmented their forces in proportion to their number of subjects. Denmark and Sweden have of course declined, both positively and relatively. Poland is annihilated as an independent power. Prussia, instead of

457

balancing the power of France, is her ally, nearly as Latium was the ally of Rome.

Russia is a colossus; but with one foot on the Frozen Ocean, and the other on the Black Sea, she cannot reach her antagonist in the south of Europe.

No foe is near enough, or powerful enough to save Europe from subjection, but Great Britain. Every independent power has therefore a manifest interest in the sufficiency of the British force to balance that of France.

It will be objected that Britain has vastly grown in her naval strength; that if France domineers on the land, Great Britain is the despot of the ocean. Why, therefore, it will be asked by the democrats, shall we view the aggrandizement of France with terror, when her enemy is no less formidable, and much more in our way, sometimes as a competitor, often as a tyrant?

The answer is, that the modern balance of power in Europe is only of the great powers; the minor powers are no more. Switzerland, the Italian princes and states, Holland, even Spain and the Baltic states, excepting Russia, are annihilated. Either there can be no balance, or it must be formed by the counterpoise of great states. When therefore France has grown to such a giant size, no dwarf can be her antagonist. The prodigious increase of the British navy is some counterpoise, but we fear a very insufficient one, for the tremendous means and still more formidable spirit of France.

It is allowed that the British navy, considered in an abstract point, is too large and too superior to that of all other nations, especially of our own. But naval power, it may be said, is rather less fitted for the purposes of national aggrandizement than any other. It is very likely to provoke enemies, and not well adapted to subdue them. It is a glittering defensive armor. And surely all independent nations ought to rejoice that Great Britain wears it. Great as its energy is, it is not too great to defend her from her adversary. If it be an evil for that navy to be so great, it is clearly a less evil than for the French power to be freed from its resistance. Remove that resistance, and France would rule the civilized world.

Turkey was formerly a great power, and a check on Austria and Russia. But as France finds Turkey too weak for that purpose; as she finds that the fall of her old ally is not to be prevented, her policy will be to profit by her fall.

We have seen the eagerness of Bonaparte to possess himself of Egypt; and had it not been for Sir Sidney Smith, perhaps he would have conquered Syria, and marched to Constantinople. As long as France remains inferior at sea, she will desire to use the Turkish dominions as a station to confine the Russians to the Black Sea, and to collect the troops and resources to annoy the English empire in India. France, moreover, will desire to seize a part of Turkey, at least Candia, because if she does not, Russia will. Turkey cannot be long hindered from falling, and cannot fall without producing a scramble for her spoils.

It is hence, on the review of European affairs, obvious to remark, that all the states have become military in some proportion to their wealth and populousness. Hence the weak states, that were of consequence one hundred years ago, have sunk into insignificance since the great powers have armed and taken their natural superiority. Hence also it is apparent, that nothing but military strength is any security for national independence, as all the weak states have become abject, weak, and despised. It is also evident that the great powers have grown in strength, and that France has outgrown them all. Great Britain has, indeed, increased in commerce and wealth, and France has declined in both; but France has despised all occupation but that of the sword; she has destroyed her artisans and multipled her soldiers. This has ensured her poverty and her conquest; it has filled her army and emptied her workshops. England, on the contrary, has found her prosperity an impediment to her warlike operations.

A man's labor is worth much in England, and it is expensive to use it in the field of war; it is of use to France only in that field.

It takes England, therefore, a long period to put on her armor, and it is worn with infinite expense. But after it is adjusted to her limbs she is capable of vast energy, because she gradually adopts a war system, and accommodates her industry to her situation. The war at length creates its own resources; and industry, that is ever found when pressed by necessity, capable of working miracles, is sure to display them in furnishing the resources. Accordingly we conclude that the peace, by disarming England, exposes her to a danger and disadvantage infinitely beyond what she had to apprehend from the continuance of the war.[60]

France experiences no such disadvantage. She will not let her troops be idle. If Touissaint[61] should not find employment for them, she will send them to Louisiana; she will find work or make it.

But England has increased, too, in military strength and spirit. Our democrats are silly enough to think that nation subject to a standing army; the truth is, a militia, an effective militia of the real people, constitutes the force of Great Britain; it is the nation that holds the sword.

Add to this the vast increase of the British power in India. On the whole, we may hope that Great Britain will be able to maintain the post of glory and danger in which she is placed. She cannot defend herself without making other nations secure; nor is it possible that her fall should happen without infinite peril, perhaps utter ruin, to the independence of all other powers. France was formerly emulous of com-

---

[60] *The Peace of Amiens, concluded March, 1802.*

[61] *Toussaint L'Ouverture led slave uprisings on the island of Santo Domingo from 1796 to 1803, following which the slaves were liberated from French dominance by defeating a Napoleonic army.*

mercial greatness; but the spirit that Colbert awakened,[62] and that seemed to balance the spirit of chivalry of the nation, is apparently quenched. France is more military and less commercial than ever she was before; England, on the contrary, is more than ever commercial. The basis of her naval superiority is widened. Hence we may infer that Britain will continue to beat France at sea.

This review also serves to exhibit, in a proper light, the policy, if it be policy, of disarming the United States at a time of unprecedented danger. While all Europe is sliding from its old foundations; while France is pouring myriads of black, white, and ring-streaked banditti into St. Domingo, and is ready to vomit them on our shores, we are boastfully consigning our little army to nothing, and our navy to the worms.

It is in peace only that armies can be trained; it is in peace only that navies can be prepared, and a very long preparation is requisite. We have abolished revenue enough that no poor man felt, the collection of which sent no son of laborious poverty supperless to bed, to build a fleet sufficient for our protection. Coaches, loaf sugar, and whisky, are to go free, and our commerce to wear shackles. Nothing is easier than for the United States to provide thirty ships of the line and sixty frigates. Such a force would protect our rights; and for want of it, France alone has plundered us of more than such a fleet would have cost to build, and equip, and maintain during the late war.

It is childish prattle to inquire, what need have we of force? A nation that neglects its naval and military power, will not preserve its independence; weakness is subjugation. *Si vis pacem para bellum*[63] is a maxim of good sense, but not

---

[62] *Jean Baptiste Colbert, controller general of finances for Louis XIV, 1662–1683.*

[63] *Inasmuch as the strength of peace matches war.*

of the democrats. To be without force or treasure used to be deemed the course for a government to be without consideration; but of late it is deemed to be, though an evil, yet a less evil than another, that those who are dismantling our government like an old ship, that is to be broken up for the old iron, should be without popularity.

How long shall men, whose views are merely party or personal, whose foresight scarcely reaches a week forward, be encouraged by our suffrages to work for our undoing! A system so selfish and so mean, that begins and ends with the individual interests of those who act for us, is too gross to be misunderstood, and too mischievous long to be tolerated. It appears probable, that the *people* will clearly discern how they ought to vote, two years before they will have the opportunity. Federal truth has begun its awful progress, and it will prevail; its sun has set to rise again.

POLITICAL REVIEW I

The Palladium, OCTOBER 1, 1802

THE WAR of arms is at an end; the war of the custom-house is commenced between France and England. More than ever their policy relates to the concerns of other powers; and the consequences of their competition will show that the same act, which has given peace to themselves, has scattered the seeds of discord among their neighbors. To lessen the commerce of England, will lessen her power. Bonaparte will, therefore, try all the means that his policy can employ, to make his rival defenceless, before he forces her to be hostile.

It is not clear, that the people of England were willing any longer to prosecute the war; but it is now unquestionably clear, that it was their great ultimate interest to pursue it. Peace has brought with it no new resources; it has dried up those which spring up with a state of war; for war makes many of its own means. Peace divides the commerce that war gave to her entire; her enemies, who lately did not own a ship, are now England's competitors. Their business was to destroy; now it is to produce and to fabricate. They want less; they supply more. They diminish her means; and they recruit their own. England looks at the peace with mingled shame and dread; shame, because she is already degraded in the eyes of strangers, if not in her own; with dread, for France has gained new power, and shows her old ambition.

It is childish to say, that Mr. Pitt ought to have proceeded with the war, if he understood the position of things. He understood it; but it is alleged, and perhaps it is true, that the British nation preferred present ease, which they expected, and have failed of realizing by peace, to the glory, the burdens, and the distant ultimate security of war. We Americans choose to say, and we are vainglorious enough to believe, that the people are not counted for any thing anywhere, except in America. The truth is, the voice of the nation, when it conveys its wisdom or its deliberate mistakes, is more sure to penetrate audibly, and with effect, the recesses of St. James's, than those of Monticello. The British nation was weary of the war, and therefore it was ended. Peace will present an aspect of danger, which its courage will not be summoned to face. The only question is whether, on viewing its formidable consequences, its policy will be able to surmount or elude them. A nice problem it is. America is infinitely interested in its favorable solution.

When we behold France with a power so vast as to excite and enable her to undertake almost every thing, and a spirit still more romantic and vast, to prompt her to achieve impossibilities, we are led to think of a new Roman empire, under which the civilized world is first to bleed, and then to sweat in chains. We again see Rome, after the first Punic war; and, alas! we see Europe without a Hannibal, unless we look for him in England's Nelson or Smith. The little states are nothing; they are slaves, paid by titles to freedom for hewing wood and drawing water. The king of Prussia, though powerful, is no Philip; he is only an Attalus or Eumenes, under France. Spain has nothing of an independent monarchy but the name. As to Holland, Switzerland, and the Cisalpine or Italian republics, they are republics during pleasure; they are sovereign, as Deiotarus, or Ariarathes, or Prusias were, to tame them for subjection. They are new recruits for the French republic, committed first to the drill-sergeant, before they are turned into the ranks. They will be cudgelled, if they prove refractory. They will be made to obey like slaves, and yet to say and to swear, on occasion, that they are sovereign and independent, as may best suit the ambitious policy of France. Old Rome was too cautious and too much in earnest in her plan, to make a conquered people her subjects at once. She gave them a king, or made a pretty little snug independent republic for them, till every man was dead and gone who was born and educated in independence: her bitter drugs were all given in honey. So it is with France. Europe has no longer any minor powers; they are swallowed up by France. Her establishment in Louisiana, which, though certain, is delayed only to choose the moment when it will be most fatal to us, will convince even America, that distance is no protection; the plagues of Egypt will be in our bosoms, and in our porridge-pots. Our pity or our folly has made us weep or wonder at the events of Europe. We have had our spasms, when we saw distress and disease abroad; we are doomed by fate to scratch with a mortal leprosy of our own; Gehazi, by accepting bribes, is smitten with Naaman's pestilence. Our government has little force, and, since the deplorable fourth of March, 1801,[64] less than ever, to defend Kentucky and Tennessee from the arms of France; soon or late they will fall victims to their arts. In spirit and policy we are Dutchmen; we are to lose our honor and our safety; and the economical statesmen, whom the wrath of heaven has placed at our head, will inquire what are they worth in shillings. Every penny of their folly will cost a pound.

But, say Job's comforters, France is a republic, and, of course, a sister republic will not only find friendship, but security in the aggrandizement of France. Miserable comforters are all these! Before this boasted revolution, Europe had many free republics. Alas! they are no more. France, proclaiming war against palaces, has waged it against commonwealths. Switzerland, Holland, Geneva, Venice, Lucca, Genoa are gone, and the wretched Batavian, Helvetian, and Italian republics, are but the faint images, the spectres, that haunt the sepulchres where they rot. So far has France been from paying exclusive regard to republics, that she has considered them, not as associates, but as victims. Venice she sold to the emperor. Holland she taxed openly for her own wants, till she drove her rich men into banishment. She "ransomed Dutch liberty" with a vengeance "from the hands of the opulent;"—so far she took counsel from the Worcester farmer; or he from her admired example. From Switzerland, she drained her youth to be food for gunpowder. This is not all. But the king of Etruria is tricked out in purple robes, like a playhouse monarch, to tread the stage in mock dignity. The proud Spaniard finds for France gold and dollars, and for that proof of "civism" he is treated as head-servant in

---

[64] *The inauguration of Thomas Jefferson.*

Bonaparte's kitchen. So that to favor kings, and to depress, plunder, and destroy republics, has been the sure and experienced consequence of French domination.

Let the ignorant hirelings of France prattle about the cause of liberty. Let them repeat, the second million of times, the silly lie, that we triumph with France. Her triumphs are terrible. A voice seems to issue from the tombs of the fallen republic for our warning. Our citizens are warned, though our government is not; and they would be armed, if France or fate did not ordain that we should be disarmed and defenceless.

POLITICAL REVIEW II

The Palladium, OCTOBER 5, 1802

ONE of the consequences of the progress of ancient Rome to empire was to lower the spirit of all other nations, while she raised her own. Already Bonaparte talks in the tone of a master; and his rivals and enemies, like slaves. The emperor of Germany has congratulated him in form, because he has elected himself president of the Italian republic. The grand Turk has renewed his old treaties with the man whose expedition to Egypt, in a time of profound peace, showed his absolute contempt of their obligation. Russia smothers her anger on account of Malta and Corfu. All Europe is striving to make its hypocrisy conceal its terror.

After every former war, the question in every state was, how to arrange its concerns so as best to profit by the mutual dread in which every power stood of its neighbor. Since the treaty of Amiens, the little powers are extinct, and the only concern is, how to find defence against France: there is but one leviathan, and half a score of small fish.

But as France emulates old Rome, it is material to note the points of difference and resemblance.

Rome achieved her conquest while she was republican; France is now imperial, precisely in the state in which Rome became pacific and began to feel decline.

France is as corrupt, and has had as much to corrupt her as Rome had, after the horrors of her civil wars. Yet it is probable Bonaparte is less of a politician and more of a warrior, than Augustus, the second Roman Cæsar. The Roman, too, had no foe near him. Parthia lay beyond the Euphrates; and a desert of parching sand, without fountains of water, divided the two great empires of Rome and Parthia from each other. Wars, when they were waged, were therefore produced by vainglory, and very little interested the passions of the people of either of these states. In order to make the comparison fairly, we must suppose that Cornelius Sylla, instead of abdicating the dictatorship, remained at the head of the Roman armies, the Bonaparte of Rome. Even then, we shall scarcely find a formidable enemy left. Gaul and Britain were barbarous; Carthage, Greece, Macedonia, and the Syrian monarchy under Antiochus, were reduced to subjection. Whereas the modern Sylla finds in England, Austria, and Russia, a Hannibal, a Philip, and a Mithridates.

France, then, as military as Rome was under the Cæsars, finds in these obstacles infinitely greater incentives to her ambition than they did. She has enemies near, and in force. Of necessary consequence, her system will not be pacific; to make the power of her enemies less, will be the same thing as to make her own greater. The power of England, depending on her navy, will necessarily engage her active hostility. She will try the utmost efforts of her policy and "diplomatic skill" to detach the United States from being customers of Great Britain; and will, if possible, unite them to herself, as auxiliaries to her scheme of aggrandizement. We have some thousands of jacobins wicked enough, and some tens of thousands of democrats weak enough, to second her plan. They are ready to make the United States the tool of France, and, in that illustrious character, to revive the famous resolutions of Mr. Madison[65] and the report of Mr. Jefferson on the privileges and restrictions of our commerce with foreign nations, so as to render Congress the instrument of their war upon Sheffield, Manchester, and Birmingham, in England. Mr. Madison, who knew a great deal less than nothing at all of his subject, fancied that we could starve these manufacturers; and because we could, he humanely and wisely insisted that we ought, to starve them; and therefore that we ought to frame regulations by which our consumers and the English manufacturers would both suffer, and the French would gain. All this, so worthy of a Frenchman, was to be done to restore to trade its liberty; it was to suffer force, in order to be free. It was to be compelled to do, as it ought to be disposed, but was not disposed to do. Not one merchant supported this scheme; but it will be revived.

France will soon have Louisiana. A formal treaty has already given it to her, and all our papers have published its contents.[66] She only waits for a more convenient season;

---

[65] *Late in 1793, just before retiring from office as Washington's secretary of state, Jefferson sent to Congress a* Report on the Privileges and Restrictions on the Commerce of the United States in Foreign Countries. *The report was intended to prove that France's commercial policy was more friendly to the United States than was Great Britain's. James Madison introduced into Congress in 1794 his commercial resolutions, the purpose of which was to end American dependence on British markets and capital, and to orient American commerce toward France. Madison had actually anticipated his 1794 resolutions in 1789, when he called for a policy of "discrimination" against Britain in the establishment of the first impost bill under the new government.*

[66] *Treaty of Luneville, February 9, 1801, in which Spain ceded Louisiana to France.*

she waits to conquer the islands. She waits to let the true Americans recover from their fears, and have her partisans profit by their superiority in our counsels. She will depend on our fears to do all the mischief she meditates against Great Britain, as a peace-offering, to obtain the delay of that which she meditates against us; but she will not delay it long, even though we should commence a war of acts of congress against British ships and manufactures.

Louisiana will produce as much cotton as Great Britain imports; Georgia already yields two thirds of that amount. France will be in a hurry to send her legions to settle these fertile lands, vast enough in extent for an empire. She will be able to block up the Mississippi. She will be able to make terms for our degradation. She will menace our frontiers, while her faction in our bosom will enfeeble the centre. In a military and financial view we shall become weaker than ever, at the very moment when we shall more than ever have need of force.

Our wealth, supposed by the democratic babblers to be the incentive to war, is the security for our tameness. To get, and to keep, and to enjoy, is the spirit of our nation; but to keep with honor and security is no part of common arithmetic. The world, France excepted, is now peopled with Dutchmen. England is made tame by her banking and funded wealth; she is bound in golden chains. France intends to take them off, and to put on chains of iron. Compared with England, France is now what her own Parisian rabble was in 1790, prone to any change, because there is much wealth to be gained, none to be hazarded. Our half-witted democrats insist that great wealth produces war. So far is this from being true, that the pursuit and the possession of wealth make a nation not less servile than sordid, willing to take kicks for pay, and to prefer gain to honor and security. France has the spirit of a camp; the peace of Amiens shows that England has that of a counting-house.

POLITICAL REVIEW III

The Palladium, OCTOBER 8, 1802

CORRECT VIEWS of European politics lead to sound results of the public judgment on our own. We have been long, too long, amused with the democratic prattle about the love of peace, and the love of our fellow-men, and the millennium, that would begin as soon as all kings were murdered, and all the citizen kings were fairly crammed together, forty deep, into a Philadelphia state-house yard, or a Paris field of Mars, or a London Copenhagen-house, to exercise, as a triumphant mob, their imprescriptible and more than royal rights and functions. On the contrary, instead of perpetual peace among nations, we see a state of things which renders all hope of any long peace ridiculously chimerical. Two mighty champions stand observing each other; and though they have suspended the combat, they have not laid aside their arms; they are furbishing them up, expecting to renew it. England is in dread for her existence; France is full of impatience to effect the consummation of her ambition. Peace will afford neither to the one nor the other an hour of relaxation or repose. It will turn no swords into ploughshares; but it is an awful interval of danger and terror, which requires that England, at least, should beat her ploughshares into swords. Including her militia, her land forces will exceed in the peace establishment, as it is called, the number she had on foot at the end of the American war. A peace that requires more soldiers than such a war is not the beginning of the expected millennium.

How ardent France is to extend her domination, no man of the least sense and observation can need to be told. She has not lost a minute to recover St. Domingo, nor to prepare a great army to take possession of Louisiana, as soon as it will best answer her purpose. Since the preliminaries of peace were signed on the first of October 1801, Bonaparte has appointed himself president of the Italian republic, in other, but not plainer words, king of Italy. She has a treaty with Portugal, which brings her near enough to the mouth of the great river Amazon to secure at a future day her command of the vast territory, bigger than all France, lying on that river. She has prohibited all importation of English manufactures; and has obliged her viceroy, the king of Spain, and her subjects in Holland, to do the like.

With these decisive marks of rooted hostility, with these undisguised preparations of the means to renew the contest, whenever it can be done with the best prospect of subverting the government and independence of Great Britain, with all the parade of equipping new navies in France, and her Spanish and Dutch provinces, and with her legion of honor, the consuls, prætorian guards, and with the draft of twice sixty thousand men, to fill up the ranks of her armies, who will doubt that she is intent on the schemes of her ambition, and will go to war on the first favorable occasion for their accomplishment?

Whether Great Britain is competent to defend herself against a force so vast, and a spirit of hostility so rancorous and ardent, is a question of infinite importance to the whole civilized world, and perhaps of as much to the United States as to any nation in it.

The examination of this subject deserves the best pens. We invite men of ability to favor us with such authentic statements of the commerce, revenue, and forces of the British empire and of France, as will assist us to make conjectures. The world is threatened with subjection to French military despotism. Unless Great Britain can defend herself, we are to look for such another age of iron as passed in the twelfth century, when soldiers were ruffians, and all that were not soldiers were slaves.

In this scene it is some consolation to perceive that Britain at length discerns her danger. The popularity of the peace is greatly impaired; and the aggrandizement of France, since the preliminaries, has awakened the pride and the fears of the nation.

British wealth, commerce, and naval force have greatly increased since the peace of 1783. Her manufactures exported at that period were about nine million and a half of pounds sterling; at the peace of 1801, twenty-four millions. Her whole exports in 1783, fourteen millions; in 1801, thirty-five millions. In 1783, her merchant shipping less than six hundred thousand tons; in 1801, fifteen hundred thousand. In 1783, her armed ships of all sorts in commission, less than four hundred; in 1801, seven hundred.

As this great increase, however, is owing in a great measure to the war, the question returns, will Great Britain be able to keep this superiority over France and her dependencies? During the war the British navy destroyed the commerce and navigation of her enemies. This forced them to make use of American ships and capital to do that for them which Great Britain would not permit them to do for themselves. Hence the vast profits of American ships and merchants; and hence too the absurd clamor of the democrats, who cursed Great Britain as the tyrant of the seas, because she forced our rivals to become our customers. The boasted principle of free ships, free goods,[67] would deprive the United States of

---

[67] *The French-American riposte to English claims that an enemy's goods could find no sanctuary under a neutral flag, upheld during the era of wars from 1756 to 1812. The British position was expressed in the Rule of the War of 1756. The French-American position, in 1793, had taken the form of several European treaties over a hundred and fifty years that sought to fix the rights of neutrals. In the struggle with Republican France the British ultimately extended their view to denominate even food as contraband. The British did allow neutral commerce to continue*

a great part of the fair profits of their neutrality. Belligerent nations could in that case transact their own affairs, and neutrals would have no gains but freight. This observation is a digression, but it was obviously proper to make it, as the democrats have never ceased to misrepresent the subject.

It is little to be expected that America will retain all her navigation and commerce. The nations which the British navy depressed are now making regulations to revive their commerce and their colony monopolies. France, the boasted friend of commercial liberty, is setting the example. Indeed it is clear that the sole object of her policy is to stir up every nation to a contest with England, to break down the English navigation act, and to establish a more rigorous monopoly system of her own.

The vast capital of England, augmented as it is beyond all former times, and beyond all proportion with her rivals, her manufacturing skill, and the excellence and stability of her government, so favorable to property, are advantages which France has little to counterbalance, except the goodness of her soil and climate, and the populousness of her territory. Great Britain has gained much in respect to political strength by her union with Ireland, a measure that will extend her growth for some ages; for Ireland is yet semibarbarous, and the more it civilizes the more it will augment the strength of the empire. The conquest of Tippoo's country, the Mysore, in India, consolidates her valuable dominions in that quarter of the globe. Ceylon is an important acquisition, and we wish it was in our power to state how important to English

---

on the same ground as existed prior to the outbreak of hostilities. The French sought to challenge this decree by excluding the United States from its parallel decrees and insisting on honoring the terms of their treaty of alliance during the revolutionary war, "free ships make free goods." The Americans were divided: the republicans opting for the French claim, the federalists ultimately willing to waive the right of neutrality, as a last resort, "to preserve peace and national credit." See Samuel Bemis, Jay's Treaty.

commerce. In the West Indies, Trinidad is large enough to absorb many millions of British capital, and to become another Jamaica.

On the whole, France has gained power, and has lost nothing of her arrogance; Great Britain sees her danger, and, without having lost any of her strength, has recovered her spirits.

THE WAR IN EUROPE

The Repertory, MAY, 1805

TWELVE YEARS AGO the war that was kindled by the French Revolution was represented to be exclusively worthy of the attention of Americans. While the French were pulling down their government, nothing seemed so fine as their very worst conduct, to the party who were leagued together to pull down our own. They called our eyes to the banks of the Rhine, where the battles of liberty, as they were fools enough to say, were fighting; and we roasted oxen for joy because Pichegru took Amsterdam, and made the Dutch as free as the West India negroes.

This sort of noise is a good deal hushed, for two reasons: one is, the jacobins have got their object, and our government is down; the other is, the mask of French hypocrisy has dropped off, or is so torn in their scuffles that we can plainly see the knaves' faces of their liberty-loving demagogues. French examples are not now quoted, now, when they are most instructive, because they really, in some degree, alarm and deter the dupes whom they lead: asses trot the better in

474

dangerous roads for wearing their blinders. Hence it is that our lords and masters of Virginia affect to dislike all discussions of the political probabilities of the war, and to consider our curiosity as useless and badly directed. Our lazy masters are in fact so engrossed with the care of governing us for their own exclusive benefit, that they have not much relish for any other reflections; and, besides all other considerations, Mr. Jefferson and his cabinet have a mortal dread of the power of Bonaparte, which has not been in the least abated by their experienced necessity since the purchase of Louisiana to court and flatter him. They are quaking with fear that he will require from them more assistance than they dare either to give or refuse him. They have yielded the point with regard to the trade with St. Domingo with as much poverty of spirit as might be expected,[68] and our seamen will be whipped and buried in dungeons, or tucked up at the yard-arm, as the great nation may by its emperor think fit to decree. The trade is not denied to be lawful, yet its interdiction is better, no doubt our patriots will say, than a war.

We have seen, too, how quarrelsome an act Mr. . . . . was disposed to get passed for the protection of our seamen, that is, of British seamen, who were to be forcibly protected when they had deserted to our vessels.

In all this, and in every thing else, the power of Bonaparte crosses the Atlantic. It is childish to inquire, what harm do we suffer by his making himself king of Italy? We answer, by his power he makes himself the king of terrors to Mr. Jefferson; and if we are not embroiled with England to please him, it is because, afraid as our brave rulers are of Bonaparte,

---

[68] *In the course of the quasi-war with France, which occurred during the Adams administration, the United States traded with Santo Domingo, helping Toussaint L'Ouverture consolidate his hold on the island. When the Treaty of 1800 (Morfontaine) was signed with France, ending the conflict, the United States was again bound to treat Santo Domingo as a French colony and to leave Toussaint to his fate.*

they are still more afraid of getting into a war with England that would instantly smash their popularity to atoms.

Let no person that remembers Mr. Madison's famous commercial resolutions, in which he proposed to fight for France by a war of regulations, let no such person deny the effective and dangerous influence of the preponderant power of France on the peace and safety, the honor, and, let us add, the honesty of our government. For be it remembered also, the ever to be abhorred project of confiscating British debts grew out of the same passion for France and hostility to England.

Nor is the loss of that silly fondness a security for spirited and independent counsels in America. Our rulers are of a sort and character to act from their fears; and their fear is a much more steady cause of action than their love. Of course, we are to expect that the vast power of France will not cease to manifest itself, to the injury of our trade, to the oppression of our brave seamen, and to the infinite disgrace of the government that abandons them.

Let us then dare to survey this huge Colossus, about whose legs we have the honor to creep.

There was a time, when the people of France were really infatuated with the notion of republican liberty. They say themselves it was a delusion, and has passed away. But it lasted long enough to break down and destroy every thing in France that was not military, and by its contagion in Germany, Holland, Switzerland, and Italy, to enfeeble and divide all the force that ought to have resisted France. The conquests of France have flattered the national vanity, and by accumulating the spoils of so many nations, have in part filled up the void that was made by the destruction of commercial and manufacturing capital. Instead of the opulence of the crowded mart or busy workshop, the country was filled like the camp of Attila or Tamerlane, with spoils and trophies.

The naval superiority of the British, by destroying their trade, has contributed to decide and prolong this exclusively military character of the French.

We are then to view France as a political phenomenon, not less tremendous by her having renounced every trade but that of a conqueror, than by her colossal size. Like the old Romans, and indeed like every other nation intoxicated with a passion for conquest, the French are completely military, and their ardor is a kind of fanaticism, such as made the successors of Mahomet the monarchs of the East.

The Romans, in like manner, contended for almost five centuries with the petty nations of Italy, their equals in valor, their inferiors only in discipline. In this hardy school they were trained for conquest. But after they had gained the dominion of Italy, they never again contended with their equals. The Carthaginians, though sustained for sixteen years by the transcendent genius of Hannibal, were almost equally enfeebled by their spirit of commerce and their spirit of faction. The Macedonians, like the modern Prussians, had a fine army, a full treasury, and a state of but moderate extent, hemmed in by jealous, hostile neighbors. In conquering them and the rest of Greece, the Romans found the Ætolians and some other states ready to accept chains, and to impose them on their countrymen. The light of Greece, the most refulgent the world ever saw, was quenched with its liberty. Egypt was so sunk in vice, that it fell without a contest. Antiochus the Great, king of Syria, had an infinite number of men, but few soldiers. The glory and the spoils of his conquest were greater than its difficulty. Gaul, the modern France, was filled with barbarians, who had not the sense nor perhaps the power to unite against Cæsar, and they fell in succession. Spain resisted longer and more desperately, but not as a nation combined to resist an invader, but by endless partial insurrections to throw off its chains.

The power of Mithridates was too recently formed, and composed of states too near barbarism, to contend with Rome; yet for many years he proved her most dreaded foe.

Thus it was that the chief difficulties in conquering the old world were really surmounted before Rome was known to have formed the design, or perhaps was conscious she had it to undertake.

France in like manner has been for many centuries exercised in arms. She has had to contend with all her neighbors, her equals in valor, her inferiors in military institutions and spirit. Thus a nation has been educated for the conquest of the world. Spain, once her superior, is now her vassal. Austria, her rival, is chained to a prison floor by her hatred of Prussia, her dread of France, and perhaps her still greater dread of Russia. Fear and policy will both make her subservient to Bonaparte, unless he should prefer the active assistance of Prussia to that of Austria. He seems to have the best grounds to expect that, if Russia should be his enemy, he will have one of the other two for an ally. On this supposition, we can scarcely conceive of an efficient alliance against France on the continent of Europe. While its numerous states were independent, and the safety of each was the care of all, the ambition of France was more troublesome than formidable. In this school of policy and arms, this gymnasium, in which all strenuously contended and in turns excelled, France like a prize-fighter acquired the hardiness, the dexterity, and the force that have made her the victor. The revolution has suddenly opened her eyes to contemplate her situation, and all her ardor is awakened by perceiving, that already more than half her ambitious work is done. Less fighting, less hazard, than her rivalships with the house of Austria have cost the Bourbons, will make her mistress of Europe from the Baltic to the Hellespont. With sixty millions of people in France and its dependencies, half the population of the Roman empire under Trajan, she has twice the force. The Russians, like the ancient Parthians, are her only enemies on land, and they are too distant to be formidable.

The other states of Europe, England excepted, are more than half subdued by their divisions and their fears.

It is absurd to suppose that this power, so tremendous to every lover of his country, will be inert for want of pecuniary resources. The Dutch and Italians sow, and the French reap. *Sic vos non vobis fertis arata boves.*[69] Old Rome, after the conquest of Macedonia, subsisted for more than a hundred years by tributes without taxes. Mahomet, Genghis Khan, and Tamerlane did not stop to ask their collectors of taxes, whether they should conquer Asia.

Nor will the people of France grow weary or ashamed of their yoke, and rise to throw it off; they are nothing, the army is every thing. Besides, they are really proud of the glory of their master, and from their very souls rejoice in the distinction of their chains.

Can it be, some will say, that the man who basely fled from his brave comrades in Egypt, the man red with assassination at Joppa, the obscure Corsican, an emperor only by his crimes, will be preferred to the Bourbons? Yes; the army prefers him. The revolution, like a whirlwind, has swept all the ancient hierarchy, nobility, and land proprietors away, and the new race have an interest to maintain the new establishments of the usurpation. Did the populace of Rome ever shift their government, because an usurper had obtained the people by money or by blood? No; as soon as men perceive that there is a force superior to their own, they desist from making any efforts against it; the proud Romans were as passive in the yoke as the Dutch are now.

The destinies of the civilized world then obviously depend

---

[69] *And so, do you not bring along with you oxen for your plows?*

479

on their ability to resist this new Roman domination. Russia has no fears of being subjugated, and for that very reason, will act with less zeal and less faithfulness in what ought to be the common cause against France. She will pursue the projects of her ambition, which seek aggrandizement in the south of Europe, and as a naval power. Hence, it is to be feared her coalition with England will not be cordial enough to be successful; and the only sort of success that is of any moment in this discussion, is the reduction of the power of France. Russia aspires to an influence in the German empire, which cannot fail to alarm and disgust both Prussia and Austria; and hence it was, that she lately interfered in the affair of the German indemnities. She also seeks a footing in the Mediterranean, preparatory to her designs against the Turks. It was on this account she wished to occupy Malta, and that she now fills Corfu with her troops. These are selfish and dangerous schemes, which England cannot second or approve.

If, nevertheless, Russia should obtain of Prussia and Austria, that the one should be neutral, and the other an associate against France, a continental war is to be expected. In case English money and an English army should aid the allies, Bonaparte would find his supremacy again in hazard.

But England, the great adversary of France, cannot become a military nation, in the sense that the French are, nor it is to be feared, in the degree that the crisis absolutely requires she should. Her commerce binds her in golden fetters. An artisan or a farmer is worth, probably, one hundred pounds sterling to the nation. To make such men soldiers, great bounties must be paid, and great sacrifices suffered. To feed and provide an English army, is also very expensive; want and military fanaticism crowd the ranks of Bonaparte, and their enemies or their allies provide their subsistence. Unfortunately, too, Mr. Pitt yielded to the pressure of the moment, and accepted the delusive services of his half million of volunteers. It is impossible he should think these men of buckram fit to withstand the men of steel, if they should invade the island.

In times of great danger, popular notions are often worse than frivolous. The volunteer force is factious, expensive, and useless, as every soldier knows. But it is worse. It has made the nation unmanageable, puffed them up with a vain dependence on the show of force, a show as empty as that of the army of Crœsus, and has made their rulers afraid to impose, and the people unwilling to bear, the necessary burdens of real soldiership. The strength of a modern state at war consists in its soldiers, not in the trappings of the peaceable apprentices, who are arrayed in scarlet to act the comedy of an army. England consumes its men and means to act this comedy, and is thus chained down to the expense and the despair of a defensive system.

Had she an efficient disposable army of one hundred thousand men, one third of whom could be employed in expeditions, or in coöperation with continental allies, the cause of Europe and of the civilized world would not be quite desperate. If the enslaved nations would exert half as much force to recover their liberty, as the French will make them employ to subjugate the yet unconquered states, the contest against France might be renewed with hopes of advantage.

Let not the men in power in America deceive themselves. If Bonaparte prevails, they will be his vassals, even more signally than they are at present. The trade of this country has already twice been made the spoil of France. The insolent aggressor is obstructed by the British navy, and not by his friendship for us, or respect for our rights, from repeating and extending his rapacity and violence. Least of all is he restrained by any opinion of the force of our nation, or the spirit of our government.

NEW COALITIONS AGAINST FRANCE

The Repertory, OCTOBER, 1805

IT APPEARS PROBABLE, that a new coalition is forming against France, and that Russia, Sweden, and Austria are in alliance with England. We are told that a great body of Russians is moving through Poland, and will be ready to reënforce the Austrians in season to repel any attack, that the French usurper, who is accustomed to strike before he threatens, may be expected to make upon the latter. The struggle for the recovery of Italy from the French is to be renewed; and instead of invading England, Bonaparte will have to contend once more for his crown. The neutrality, if not the coöperation of Prussia and Denmark, is foretold.

It is natural, that the first indications of a powerful confederacy against France should be interpreted to promise every thing to Englishmen, weary of the known weight, and dejected by the prospect of the unknown length of the contest. Coalitions ever promise much in their inception; they usually disappoint all in their progress. A single power has generally proved an overmatch for their arms. The honey-moon may possibly last till the allies have taken the field and fought the first battle; but the good or bad fortune of that battle is almost sure to dissolve the ties of their mutual confidence, if not the bands of that alliance. If defeated, they throw the blame on one another; if victorious, they are made envious and jealous by the allotment of the spoil.

No doubt Austria will be hearty in the cause, for she will fight for her life; but her very fears may be skilfully used by Bonaparte to detach her from the confederacy. He may offer her some Turkish provinces; he may yield other points of real magnitude, that will give her a temporary security, or the show of it, which she may deem preferable to a more hazardous obstinacy in the contest.

This Austria may deem herself almost compelled to prefer, by an early discovery of the tardiness of the disposition of the Russian cabinet, and perhaps still more emphatically, by the detection of its immeasurable ambition.

Russia has probably no fears of the French, and can have no hopes of aggrandizement by wresting any thing from them. Russia will enter the lists, therefore, with very different views, and infinitely less ardor than Austria; she must engage in the war from calculation. It may offend her pride, that the French emperor plays the first part in Europe; she may dread a great loss of consideration and political influence, unless she contends with him; but her means for a long war are not considerable. It may be said that England is rich, and will supply the primary means. Large subsidies will no doubt invigorate and hasten the military operations of this power; it is nevertheless a great mistake to suppose that a prodigious expense will not be left, after all the English guineas are counted in St. Petersburg, to be defrayed by the Russian government. These are reasons, therefore, for a natural apprehension that the efforts of the Russians will be made upon a less scale, and with less energy, and continued for a much shorter time, than any man will prescribe for effecting the only rational object of a continental war, a reduction of the colossal power of France. All independent nations must quake within sight and almost within touch of their fetters, till this is done.

And to do it surely, more than one campaign is necessary. France will assuredly set her foot on the world's neck, if the force and the spirit do not exist somewhere, to face her in arms with a steadiness equal to her own ambition. England alone has that force and spirit; a confederacy is a rope of sand, and will break to pieces, or at least manifest its total inefficiency, in a year. But as soon as the English nation can be made to view the contest in its true light, and what is ten times as much to the purpose, to feel it as they see it, they will boldly rely on themselves, and cautiously ask or take assistance from their allies. For these allies, the Russians especially, may claim the partition of Turkey, in recompense of a longer perseverance. A dismembering ambition would quench all hope of tranquillity in Europe. It would also inevitably dissolve any coalition that could be formed. Neither Austria nor England would assent, much less assist, to confer universal empire on Russia.

France has had time to consolidate her new empire. All that policy and violence can do has been done, and all that arms can do will be done to maintain her acquisitions. To maintain them, is probably as much a national cause with the French, as it was with the Romans, to keep Hannibal out of Rome after the battle of Cannæ. French vanity will not therefore be subdued, it will be irritated and roused by national losses and by the disgrace of their arms. Bonaparte's own vanity, and that of his nation, would probably require that England should be invaded, if the ripening of the expected coalition should not furnish, perhaps the occasion, and certainly the excuse, for the abandonment of that extravagant project. In this view of the matter, the coalition will prevent more good than we can imagine it will ever achieve; for of all the possibilities of a speedy remedy of the present enormous evils of Europe, by the reduction of the preponderant power of France, the only one that holds out any rational promise, is that of the invasion. Two hundred thousand men landed in England, and the winners of the first three or four battles, would certainly fall at last, and involve the imperial usurper in their fall. His boasted glory would sink even faster than his power. The enslaved nations would then make haste to break their chains.

But supposing no invasion, which in the event of a new coalition is no longer to be supposed, it then becomes impossible even to conceive of any remedy, but a late and exceedingly gradual one.

To fight down gigantic France to her former size, so that other nations may again breathe in safety and independence, can scarcely take less than a half a century of prosperous warfare. These mushroom products of accident, money, or intrigue; these brittle, ephemeral coalitions, are quite inadequate to the end. While they last they will cherish false hopes; and when they fail they will engender groundless fears; and for the next seven years may prevent the discovery, and delay the resort to the only effective resources of safety. For England alone, we repeat it, is pledged, is pinned, and nailed down to the combat. To sit and take blows is hard, but she still has the privilege, the precious, glorious privilege the Dutch, Swiss, and Italians have lost, of returning them. Every war brings its burdens and losses, but this war brings its terrors too, for it hazards, and will decide upon her life and honor. The decision cannot be evaded, the contest cannot even be intermitted, without her ruin. By eighteen months of treacherous peace she suffered a greater reduction of comparative strength than by eight years of war. Her warlike efforts for this whole century would not impoverish her; a delusive calm, called peace, for three years, would put an end to her efforts forever. She has men, she has courage, she has all the means of self-defence; she wants only that overpowering impression upon her people that time will make, though it is not yet made, to have the command of those means. She must rouse as Carthage did in the third Punic war, but not so late. Her Foxes and her Burdetts will be silent when the very rabble are convinced that England cannot exist at all unless the power of France be reduced; that as long as she contends for the reduction of that power she enjoys both existence and glory. She is therefore to choose war, not as a state preferable to peace, but preferable to the ignominy of wearing French chains. When these ideas, unfortunately so well vouched by her situation, are admitted by all men in the nation, (and the time is coming when they will be irresistible,) every thing in England will become a weapon of war, and every man a soldier or sailor to wield it. The minister will have reason to rely on the abundance of resources, and what is more to the purpose of the war, on the perseverance and patience of the public. English spirit, thus roused, might laugh at mercenary coalitions and French menaces. France can have no commerce; and a nation of soldiers must thrive by spoil, and not by manufactures. If, to get fresh spoil, they enlarge the circle of their depredations they rouse new enemies, and create more zealous coalitions, than English guineas can buy.

These opinions will, no doubt, seem extravagant to many persons; but the evil of French domination is now of many years standing; it is not very rational to suppose that a battle or a campaign is to cure it. There are many evils which attend human life through the entire course of it. Perhaps it is made in wisdom, and in mercy, too, by the great Ruler of the universe, the condition of an Englishman's life, that he shall spend the whole of it in fighting the French; and if his sons and his grandsons should think liberty and independence intolerable on these terms, let them lie down in the dust, in the peace of slavery, and try to forget their honors and their ancestors.

THE COMBINED POWERS AND FRANCE

The Repertory, DECEMBER, 1805

THE POWER of France is so tremendously preponderant that every friend to the liberty and independence of nations must wish to see it reduced. If the people of the United States deserve one half the praise they take to themselves for good sense, such must be their wish. Men's heads and hearts must be indeed strangely perverted, if they could have a speculative liking to behold one great tyrant set up over all other nations. To put it to the test, let them ask themselves how they would incline, if the question now was, to set up a domestic tyrant over our own. Every lover of liberty and independence must therefore, of necessity, be the enemy, as far as wishing goes, of the French arms in the present great contest. He will anxiously inquire, is the new coalition likely to reduce the French power?

When he reads of three hundred thousand Austrians, two hundred thousand Russians, and perhaps fifty thousand Hessians, assembling and marching against Bonaparte, he will be ready to exclaim, France cannot withstand such a force. For the first time, the odds of numbers is against her. To this array of armies we add the Swedes, the English, who are embarking, it is said, fifty thousand, the Austrians and Hungarians, who may yet rise *en masse* to reënforce their emperor, and the immense body of Russians, who are kept ready to enter Germany and Italy. We very soon count up a million of men on paper, and we feel the inspirations of the English printers' valor, who already consider Bonaparte as dethroned.

Men's wishes are great deceivers. France contains more millions of men than Bonaparte can ever think fit to array in arms, and he can array as many of them as he may want; and as he allows no trade, commerce, or profession, to impede, or for one hour to delay his requisitions; as France is nothing but military, and every man a soldier, whenever Bonaparte has occasion to call and make him such, it is the easiest thing in the world for the French to outnumber their enemies in the field. Add to this, France is as near to Germany as the greater part of the subjects of Austria, and more Germans will assist the French armies than the armies of Austria. If distance only be considered, more Frenchmen

487

can be brought to act in the field than Austrians, Swedes, or Russians.

Another consideration of no little moment is, that France is surrounded by states newly conquered from her enemies, whom she can squeeze, and even crush, without any danger of resistance. The weight of the war may be thrown upon the German circles on the left bank of the Rhine, newly annexed to France, upon Hanover and the German neutral electorates, upon Spain, Holland, Portugal, and Italy. It will be asked, will not this mode of overburdening the people, who are told of their honor and happiness in being annexed to France, render the French odious, unpopular, and weak, in those countries? The answer is, the French people will see that their own burdens are the lighter for their excessive weight on those wretched vassals. In the war that ended in 1763, the great king of Prussia exacted every thing from conquered Saxony; he would not spare his enemies, because he wished to spare his subjects. In like manner the French will use the blood, and sinews, and marrow of the Dutch, Hanoverians, and Italians, as if they were oxen; nor will they provoke resistance from those wretches, for two reasons; they will be watchfully kept down by French soldiers; and again, be it noted well, the French have not conquered any country without raising to power the base and desperately wicked among the conquered people, who of course are interested and disposed to keep their fellow countrymen under the yoke of servitude.

Thus, over and above the gigantic force of France itself, it is evident the French can command prodigious resources of men, money, and every article of use in war, from the late subjects of her enemies. She no sooner overpowers one enemy than she uses and consumes his force in conquering another.

If we consider the vast extent and unexhausted fertility of the French territory, including the dependencies of France, we cannot doubt that means enough of every sort exist; and moreover, we can doubt as little, that the government is the most formidable despotism existing on the face of the earth, and can draw forth those means. Of men and warlike resources, then, France has enough.

It is, perhaps, of the nature of despotism, to contract early infirmities. It is a giant, whose first energies are augmented, yet wasted by frenzy. It is a torrent from the hills that nothing can resist; yet it soon scoops for itself a channel, wide enough, indeed, to display its ravages, but deep enough to confine them. A tyrant cannot reign and oppress by his single force; he must really interest, and interest prodigiously, a sufficient number of subordinate tyrants in the duration of his power. As he will select these because he knows them to possess an extraordinary share of ability to serve him, these first appointments will give all imaginable efficacy to his authority. In reward for serving him, he must allow them to serve themselves; he must wink at their abuses and exactions. But after the lapse of one generation, these abuses become the inheritable rights of the first set of subordinate agents or their descendants; the state is exhausted and consumed by abuses, which time has made inveterate, and which the new-made great have an interest in aggravating. The monster, despotism, whose youth was passed in riot, is then crippled by the gout, and is equally disabled from enduring either labors or remedies. Nothing can be more certain than that free states are the most capable of energy.

But a youthful tyrant has a sort of preternatural strength that is truly formidable; such is Bonaparte's. France has thrown off the encumbrances of ranks and orders, of laws and religion, and seemed to awake at once from the sleep of ages. Every thing that is genius has been roused by seeing all that is alluring in power and wealth brought within its reach. All France has teemed with ambition, like the earth in seed-time. These circumstances have imparted to the

French character, always highly susceptible, a most extraordinary energy. And if any persons, wedded to a favorite system, shall please to say, that as the hope of liberty is now extinguished, the French are no longer ardent enthusiasts, but reluctant slaves, let them be told that the ardor for glory remains though the passion for liberty is no more. The people are now engaged in a more intelligible, and be it added, a more enchanted pursuit. They believe that they know how to beat their enemies; and that they do not know how to prevent or remedy the oppressions of their rulers. It will be conceded, also, that the revolution has brought forward the ablest generals, and that Bonaparte has employed them.

Admitting, then, that the French armies are numerous enough, that they are well commanded, and that the soldiers have the double advantage of strict discipline and actual service, it is not easy to discern the grounds, on which the English seem so confidently to rely, that the French will be beaten. The Austrians and Russians are, no doubt, good soldiers; not better however than the French. It is to be feared the coalition will be defeated in its first attempts.[70] The great distance of the Russian dominions, and the deficiency of pecuniary means scarcely allow us to expect that Russia will persevere long in a very unhopeful contest. Austria, without Russia, is certainly unequal to the contest. It is probable that much is expected from the first impression of the arms of the coalesced powers; if that expectation should fail, we cannot see any motives Russia has for fighting on, campaign after campaign, in case France should hold out to resist.

And is there the least reason to suppose France will not hold out to resist many years? The glory of France is the cause of all Frenchmen; pity it is we pence-saving Americans had not a small spice of their character. They will suffer

---

[70] *In justice to the writer of these speculations, it must be remarked, that they were penned at least ten days before the report arrived of the capture of thirty thousand Austrians.* Note of the Newspaper Editor.

much, and attempt every thing, sooner than permit their enemies to triumph over them; defeats, by irritating their vanity, will rouse their spirit.

We shall be told, in reply, it is only the splendor of success that attaches the French to the fortune of Bonaparte. But they are really, in their inmost souls, proud of that success. Besides, let it be remembered, every thing that is now exalted in France would be brought low again by the return of the Bourbons: there is nothing left in church or state that is not the work of the revolution. The Bourbons might pardon rebels and usurpers; but could they employ them all, or trust any of them? Could they refuse to employ or trust the emigrant nobility, who have borne exile and poverty with them? Yet this must be refused, or the nobles and princes of the new order of things must step down again to the democratic floor. Probably a million of active, high-spirited men in France, now in some office, would hazard life, and perhaps scorn it as a condition of disgrace, sooner than restore the Bourbons.

Where, then, is the reason to suppose that France will not make efforts, endure reverses, and even create another tyrant, in case Bonaparte should fall in battle, or die in his bed? Where is the country in Europe that has so little to fear from division within as France? as France we say, still smarting with the sense, and in case of Bonaparte's death, ready to quake with the dread, of the curse of civil war?

The French despotism, we greatly fear, will prove a colossus of iron, which this coalition will be unable to hew down with the sword, or to lift from its place. Another revolution, like an earthquake, might break its limbs; and time will slowly corrode it with rust: in fifty years it may be still hateful to its neighbors, and dreadful only to Frenchmen. We have not the most to hope from the powers that are nearest its own size; but from that which has the capacity to maintain the longest resistance; we mean England. For the reasons we have before assigned, it is our belief the French despotism will never be more formidable than it is now: if it should not finish its conquering work while Bonaparte lives, it will never be finished. This is clear, if it cannot conquer England it will not conquer the world. Thus we are brought to the question, so perpetually recurring to our anxiety, so awfully interesting to every civilized nation in the world, will France be able to conquer England?

It is commonly said, if the British navy did not protect that island, it would be certainly conquered. This is no part of our creed. A state containing fifteen or sixteen millions of souls is not to be conquered, unless the government is of a sort to breed factions, and one of them joins the foreign enemy to enslave the state. There is every appearance that the French faction in England, which in the beginning of the revolution was so clamorous and formidable, is now equally destitute of pretext, and of means of mischief. If the British channel should be filled with gravel, and raked and hardened like a turnpike, the English would become more military, and have to fight many desperate battles for their liberty, which, though they should lose those battles, they would ultimately preserve. Certainly there is no want of physical force, no deficiency of courage to maintain it, even if the coast of Brittany touched the coast of Essex.

With these opinions, it follows that the threatened invasion was one of the most desirable events; it afforded the only certain and near prospect of the disgrace and overthrow of the French power. If the coalition really hindered the invasion, it has done England an injury which it will never repair. But as the attempt was long delayed, and the conduct of Austria and Russia was so ostentatiously complained of for hindering its execution, there is great reason to believe there was no serious intention to make it.

Great Britain now can expect no such hopeful opportunity to cripple her adversary as long as the coalition lasts; her hopes are rested on the military operations of the coalesced powers. This is one of the serious evils of that coalition. Englishmen are unhappily made to depend on the efforts of Russians and Austrians, which we apprehend (and we have taken some pains to explain the grounds of our apprehensions) will ultimately fail of their object. They depend too much on others, too little on themselves. Should Russia find some ambitious reasons for deserting the alliance, Austria must become a vassal of France. England must then face her adversary alone, with his insolence and means augmented, and weariness and despair pervading every English heart. Then perhaps she would think herself obliged to make peace. Thus the tired traveller, benumbed with cold, grows drowsy and sits down to rest—he sleeps, to wake no more. England would be more certainly ruined by peace than Bonaparte by the invasion. If, instead of using her arms, she trusts a second time to her enemy's moderation, he will never permit her to resume them. A peace by England, after the defeat of the new coalition, will give to France an unlimited command of means of every sort. The Persian kings did not encourage commerce, but the Phœnicians, Rhodians, and people of Cyprus did, and of course the king of Persia could command the sea. Tributary Europe would furnish treasure to build fleets; and the whole coast from the Baltic to the Adriatic would supply seamen. We Americans are already advised to interdict the manufactures of England; and France will oblige every other country to do it. While the war lasts, necessity is stronger than even French despotism; all Europe, and even France herself, consumes British goods; but peace would restore to Bonaparte the power to shut all the ports of Europe against England.

What then are we to think of the coalition, as it affects England, but that it will deceive her hopes and aggravate her embarrassments? Standing alone, and depending solely on herself, she is invincible. It is in her power, without any material diminution of her wealth, and with a diminished hazard of her safety, to fight France, till French despotism becomes wasted with its vices and decrepid with age, till it loses much of its impetuosity, and employs half its force in quelling insurrections; till the legion of honor shall create one emperor, the army of the Rhine a second, and the army of Italy a third.

THE SUCCESSES OF BONAPARTE

The Repertory, MARCH, 1806

THE RAPID and decisive successes of Bonaparte have inflated the ignorant rabble of our democrats with admiration, and filled every reflecting mind with astonishment and terror. The means that most men deemed adequate to the reduction of his power have failed of their effect, and have gone to swell the colossal mass that oppresses Europe; his foes are become his satellites. Austria, the German states, Prussia, Naples, and perhaps Sweden, seem to have been fated, like comets, to a shock with the sun, not to thrust him from his orb, but to supply his waste of elemental fire. Bonaparte not only sees the prowess of Europe at his feet, but all its force and treasure in his hands. We except Russia and England. But Russia is one of those comets on its excursion into the void regions of space, and is already dim in the political sky; England passes, like Mercury, a dark spot over the sun's disk; and to Bonaparte himself she seems, like the moon, to intercept his rays. He cannot endure to see her so near his splendor, without being dazzled or consumed by it.

He wants nothing but the British navy to realize the most extravagant schemes of his ambition. A war that should give him possession of it, or a peace, like the last, that should humble England, and withdraw her navy from any further opposition to his arms, would give the civilized world a master. All the French, and of course all our loyal democrats, have affected to treat that apprehension as chimerical. Yet who, even among those whom faction has made blind, could refuse to see that the transfer of the British navy to France would irreversibly fix the long-depending destiny of mankind, to bear the weight and ignominy of a new Roman domination.

We may say the aggravated weight, for Rome preserved her morals till she had achieved her conquests; France begins her career as deeply corrupt as Rome ended it. The Roman republic, after having grown to a gigantic stature from its soundness, rotted when it died; but that of France, surviving the principles, and at length the name of a republic, has drawn aliment from disease, and we of this generation have seen it crawl, like some portentous serpent from a tomb, glistening and bloated with venom from its loathsome banquet. France has owed the progress of her arms to the prevalence of her vices. These were the causes of the revolution; and the revolution has in turn made these the instruments of French aggrandizement. By the persecution of all that was virtue, the leaders gave encouragement to all that was vice; and thus they not only acquired the power to spend the nation's last shilling, but imparted to the rabble all the ardor of enthusiasm, and all the energies that the love of novelty, of plunder, and of vengeance could inspire. The means they commanded were not such as arise from the just and orderly government of a state, but from its dissolution. The priests, the rich, and the nobles, were offered as human sacrifices on the altar of the revolution, and still more emphatically of French ambition.

Thus France, like Polypheme in his cave, grew fat with carnage.[71] Other states could not, without submitting to a

---

[71] *Polyphemos, the cyclops, son of Poseidon, trapped Odysseus and his men within his cave and ate them one by one, until Odysseus, through a ruse, expunged his single eye and escaped with the remnant of his forces. Homer's* Odyssey, book IX.

like revolution, oppose her with equal arms. So far from it, they found that all those whom vice and want had made the enemies of the laws of their country, were banded together as the friends of France.

Thus it was that the French armies no sooner entered Italy than they arrayed in arms an Italian rabble, to hold all those who had any thing to lose, in fear and inactivity, till they could be regularly plundered. The leaders of this rabble were invested with the mock dignities of the Cisalpine government. The like was done in Holland and Switzerland.

The new yoke, therefore, which the abject nations are so near taking on their necks, cannot be light. That France may rule everywhere, the worst of men must be permitted everywhere to rule in the worst of ways. The Roman yoke was iron, and it crushed as well as wearied the provinces; but the domination of culprits and outlaws, claiming much for themselves, and exacting more for their masters in France, will place the people between the upper and the nether millstone.

If the miserable dupes of France, so loyal to the commands of her envoy, can wish destruction to the British navy, and can really think American liberty the safer for its future tenure by the good pleasure of Bonaparte, such men are certainly fitter subjects for medicine than argument; where such sentiments do not spring from the rottenness of the heart, they must escape through some crack in the brain.

There was a time when the infatuation in favor of France was a popular malady. If that time has so far passed over that men can either think or feel as Americans ought, it must be apparent that Bonaparte wants but little, and is enraged that he so long wants that little, to be the world's master. Yet at this awful crisis, when the British navy alone prevents his final success, we of the United States come forward, with an ostentation of hostility to England, to annoy her with non-intercourse laws. Are we determined to leave nothing to chance, but to volunteer our industry in forging our chains?

THE DURATION OF FRENCH DESPOTISM

The Repertory, FEBRUARY, 1807

THE ATTEMPT has been repeatedly made, in former communications, to show that the establishment of a universal French monarchy has become an exceedingly probable event; and, moreover, that if the resistance of the British navy should, from any cause whatever, be withdrawn, the United States will become, in effect, a province or department of France. As, from the nature of our government, and the temper and views of the parties that engross its powers, it is a thing ascertained that we must quietly submit to the domination of a master, it is a subject of natural, yet painful curiosity, to inquire, how long will this dominion last?

The answer to this question is, we confess, concealed among the impenetrable secrets of that Providence which disposes of human affairs. Nevertheless, it would belong to the prudent foresight of our rulers, if our rulers were wise, to discern evils in their causes, to retard their progress, and to alleviate their pressure. And since those to whom we have confided the safe keeping of our liberties seem resolved to renounce all dependence on ourselves, and to abandon the ultimate disposal of them to chance and to Bonaparte, it may be of some assistance to our spirit of passive resignation, the only sort of spirit that our fall is likely to rouse, to create, if we can, a hope that a destiny so near its fulfilment, so intolerable in degree, will be transient in duration. If, after only half a century of subjugation by France, the empire of the modern Tamerlane should fall to pieces, the successors of Jefferson (and fifty years of slavery might qualify some of our posterity to be his successors) would no doubt exult that we had recovered our liberty, as we lost it, without effort;

that we had outlived our conqueror; that instead of irritating his resentment, we had prudently endeavored to conciliate his favor by the alacrity of our submission and the largeness of the tribute, which no expensive hostile prepartions had been permitted to impair; that like the flexible willows, we had lain flat to the earth, till the storm had passed over our heads; whereas, if we had stiffened ourselves against its violence, we might have been uprooted like the oaks. And here our rulers may hope to dig from the mire of our public degradation an impure but copious treasure of future popularity for their wisdom and firmness. They have already extracted it from materials scarcely less unpromising and foul.

In political conjectures no guide is in the least a safe one, but experience; and each event is so much determined by its own peculiar circumstances, that analogy often fails, where, it would seem, on first inspection, similitude does not. The Roman empire had its origin about seven hundred and fifty years before Christ; and lasted almost four hundred and eighty years after Christ. This long period of twelve hundred and thirty years, that the Roman state endured, may be called political longevity; and as the French imitate the Romans, we naturally inquire, whether we are to expect to have the yoke of France so long, or half so long, upon our necks. There was scarcely one of the twelve hundred years tht Rome subsisted, that her dominion was not odious or dangerous, and the greater part of the time both odious and dangerous to her neighbors. The weight of her yoke was aggravated by the arrogance of her spirit. She not only chained conquered kings to her car of triumph, but as her proconsuls had to practise oppression in the provinces, that they might be able to practise bribery at Rome, she trod with the weight of a war elephant, having a castle on his back, on the necks of her subjects.

Imagine not, my countrymen, a French conqueror will tread lightly, when you are prostrate. Woe to the vanquished, is ever his maxim. There was no measure, there was no end to the Roman exactions. There is only a small part of the surplus wealth of a state, that a lawful government will touch; and even a usurper will have an interest in sparing more than he takes; but the rapacity of a conqueror is pitiless and insatiable. The populace of Rome voted the confiscation of the wealth of the king of Cyprus; and if a patriot could have proved to them, that with more regard to justice, there would have been less booty, would such considerations have produced a mitigation of the rigor of their decree? A conqueror can take all; and what he leaves he thinks mercy.

It is far from being certain that we know any thing of the foundation of Rome. But however obscure we may deem its origin, there can be no doubt that for several hundred years its territory was small, and the number of its subjects less than half a million. Nevertheless, there can be no stronger proof of the force of her institutions, than that Rome, even in her infancy, and with fewer people than Massachusetts contains, had cherished pretentions of superiority and formed plans of aggrandizement, that seem scarcely credible, even after they have been accomplished. They considered the capital not merely as a fortress, but it was the *"immobile saxum,"*[72] the eminence on which Jupiter had commanded his temple to be built, in token of his protection of his favorite people. Even then they called Rome the eternal city, the metropolis of nations. After the burning of Rome by the Gauls, the removal of the citizens to Veii was opposed, on the ground that the gods had promised the dominion of the world to the inhabitants of that spot. The people, who reverenced the gods, submitted, and proceeded to rebuild their houses, instead of occupying much better houses at Veii.

France, on the contrary, from the first union of the tribes of the Franks under Clovis, has been a powerful state. It is

---

[72] *The immovable rock.*

true, the national character has been ever in a high degree warlike; but the individual character of the Roman citizens was infinitely more so. Modern armies, the French as well as the rest, are formed of the lowest of the populace—the Romans excluded all such from the honor of bearing arms. In the early ages of the republic, and indeed till the time of Marius, the Roman soldiers were the proprietors of the land. The prodigious force of a state, though small in territory and number of people, whose citizens were all soldiers, will appear from this fact. Not long after Rome was taken by the Gauls, and had seemed to be ruined, the little state of Latium revolted and took arms against the republic. Rome instantly arrayed ten legions of citizens, an army scarcely less in numbers, and superior in force and discipline to that which a confederacy of half Europe was able to furnish under king William against Louis XIV. At the present day, such a city and territory as then formed the Roman republic, nay, modern Rome itself and the very same territory would be awed into submission and kept in fear by a regiment of foot and two or three squadrons of horse. There can be no doubt, that ten such legions composed a more powerful army than the million with which Xerxes invaded Greece, or than all the forces Darius could oppose to Alexander the Great. It is far from certain that Alexander's own army would have proved a match for the Romans.

If, then, we make the comparison, which the vanity of the great nation ardently desires to exhibit, we must not compare Frenchmen and Romans, but the modern empire of France with the old Roman empire, after the subversion of the republic. There may be some resemblance between the means and policy of the two states, though there is none in the character of the individuals. It is true, that the French recruit their army by conscriptions; but it is also true, that the men, who are not thus drafted into the army, are mere unwarlike citizens. It was otherwise in Rome. The nobles were all generals, and the common people the best soldiers in the world.

But after the civil wars of Marius and Sylla, the refuse of the city of Rome were admitted into the armies, and the owners of land in Italy were expelled by force, to make donations of farms to the conquering soldiers. After these events, Rome was filled with a spiritless and abject multitude. Instead of the people, who had looked with defiance upon the triumphant banners of Hannibal waving in sight of their walls, like every other overgrown city, it trembled and submitted on every hostile summons.

Rome acquired her conquests not only by the superiority of her institutions, but because those institutions had made the individual Romans superior to their enemies; but when all the nations around the Mediterranean had submitted to her sway, this personal superiority was no longer to be seen anywhere, except in the Roman armies. They long excelled all rivals and enemies in every soldierly qualification; and here, perhaps, the similitude between Rome and France begins.

The French armies are no doubt, superior in Europe; whether they outnumber their enemies, or place a much larger proportion of cavalry in every field of battle, or bring with them more field pieces and serve them more skilfully than their enemies. Whatever may be the cause of this superiority, the fact is indisputable, that the French are at least as much superior to the Prussians, as the Romans were to the Macedonians.

Our principal question, then, recurs, assuming it for certain that the French will establish a universal empire, how long will it last? In a battle, the best of the two armies will win the victory; but though conquests may be won by victories, it is extremely difficult to conceive what means any conqueror can possess long to maintain them. The petty states bordering on Rome were gradually, in a course of four hundred years, subdued by her arms; nor was the final conquest achieved without admitting them as allies, to be partners of her dominion and the associates of her glory. At length their union with the state was as perfect as that of Normandy, once a hostile province, now is with the rest of France. But the Samnites had more power, and more implacable hatred to Rome than her other foes; and therefore they were nearly exterminated, like the insurgents of La Vendee.

Thus Italy was moulded into one state, before Pyrrhus, and after him the Carthaginians, contended with Rome. Macedonia was not a great state, but Philip and Perseus had fine armies. When these were routed, Macedonia was what Prussia is now. Greece, like the German empire, was an anarchy of republics, which, because it was easy to divide, it cost no trouble to subdue, or to keep in subjection. Egypt, under the Ptolemies, was as despicable as the French found it lately under the Mamelukes. The Romans overthrew Antiochus the great, and seized all the provinces of Asia more easily than their best general could take the single cities of Carthage or Numantia.

To preserve her conquests, Rome built no fortresses, and resorted to no other means than armies and colonies. Her empire contained, Mr. Gibbon computes, about one hundred and twenty millions of souls; yet her army did not exceed sixty legions, being less than four hundred thousand men.

The French keep on foot more soldiers; but it is to be considered, their career of conquest was begun only ten years ago. They have imposed their yoke on nations, not divided into a hundred independent tribes, like the Gauls and Spaniards, not barbarians, like the Germans, not effeminate, like the Asiatics, but on nations, who confided so entirely on their union, resources, and spirit, that they supposed it impossible they should be conquered. The states now subject to France exceed her in the number of soldiers, they still exceed her in the number of people. Their fall has roused every passion of pride, fear, and vengence; and there is not the least reason to suppose, that the insolence and rapacity of the conqueror will suffer them to subside. The difference of language, character, and condition will prevent their assimilation into one people for many years.

Long before such an assimilation could take place, the military despotism of France will be weakened by its own intemperance and excess. As Bonaparte reigns by uniting in himself the command of all the armies, whenever his death, infirmity, or adversity shall afford the opportunity, may we not expect that the command of a great separate army will inspire into its chief the design of independence? For instance, Poland and the north of Germany, which, let it be observed, the Romans could never subdue, could not be holden without a large French army; nor would that army, stationed for many years in the same quarters, lose the occasion of a vacancy in the government, to consider their general as their emperor or king, and to place him on the throne of the country subject to their military jurisdiction. It is in vain for Bonaparte to multiply decrees of his senate, declaring his empire indivisible and hereditary. It is possible, and indeed probable, that the government of France itself may, after many years of convulsion, become so.

But the vast countries overrun by the French will not lose their ancient honors and their recent shame; and if the descendants of their expelled princes should not recover their thrones, if their former subjects should not resume their arms, and chase the French out of their territories, yet the ambition of the French generals will divide the empire. The conquests of Charlemagne were sudden; but the nations, who were rather confounded than subdued, resumed their independence under his feeble successors.

The wars of the ancients were marked with a peculiar animation and even ferocity. The weaker always dreaded, and generally suffered every extremity from the fury of the victor. The people were slaves, and all their property, including lands and houses, was booty. Such contests could not be maintained with the half hostile, half traitorous languor of the modern wars against France. They needed, and they roused all the energies of all the citizens. But when the war was over, the conqueror stripped his captives as naked of power as of all other possessions. Hence it was that the Romans found it so extremely difficult to subdue enemies, who fought to the last with all the energy of despair; and hence too it was, that when once effectually conquered, we hear no more of their resistance. The Romans were not greatly troubled with insurrections, except of their armies.

It is however the law, as well as the motive of modern conquests, to preserve rather than to destroy. The subjects change masters; they are oppressed by military contributions, but they are not wholly stripped. It is scarcely possible that the mildest exercise of a conqueror's rights should not enrage them, or that any modern mitigation of them should wholly disarm their vengeance.

It ought to be observed, too, as a consequence of the last remark, that in the times of the Roman emperors, the population of every country was in a great measure composed of slaves; that of Europe, which France has overrun, is much sounder. Rome, soon after the expulsion of the kings, was filled with citizens, who were all soldiers; but in the time of the emperors its vast walls were crowded with perhaps a million of slaves, who were all abject and base. As this was the case in Rome, it was still worse in Alexandria, Antioch, Nicomedia, Carthage, Sirmium, Aquileia, Ravenna, and Naples. A degenerate race of conquerors could keep slaves in subjection.

But the people of Germany are at least as warlike as those of France. It is therefore extremely difficult to conceive what means the conqueror possesses, or can employ always to keep his equals in his chains. Their princes may lose their thrones; but we cannot resist the opinion, that, ultimately, the nations will recover their independence.

Supposing, then, that the French empire is, in its very structure and principles, a temporary sway, that the causes, whatever they may be, which have made its action irresistible, produce and prolong a reaction sufficient in the end to counteract their impulse, ought we not, as men, as patriots, to hope that Great Britain may be able to protract her resistance till that reaction shall be manifested? And as mere idle wishes are unbecoming the wise and the brave, ought not the American nation to make haste to establish such a navy as will limit the conqueror's ravages to the dry land of Europe? We have more than a million tons of merchant shipping; more, much more, than Queen Elizabeth of England, and Philip II. of Spain, both possessed in the time of the famous armada. We may be slaves in soul, and possess the means of defence, without daring to use them. We do possess them, and if our spirit bore proportion to those means, in a very few years our ships could stretch a ribbon across every harbor of France, and say with authority to the world's master, stop; here thy proud course is stayed.

X.

EULOGIES

====

THE CHARACTER OF BRUTUS

The Repertory, AUGUST, 1805

Brutus killed his benefactor and friend, Cæsar, because Cæsar had usurped the sovereign power; therefore, Brutus was a patriot, whose character is to be admired, and whose example should be imitated, as long as republican liberty shall have a friend or an enemy in the world.

This short argument seems to have hitherto vindicated the fame of Brutus from reproach, and even from scrutiny; yet perhaps no character has been more overrated, and no example worse applied. He was no doubt an excellent scholar and a complete master, as well as faithful votary of philosophy; but in action the impetuous Cassius greatly excelled him. Cassius alone, of all the conspirators, acted with promptness and energy, in providing for the war which he foresaw the death of Cæsar would kindle; Brutus spent his time in indolence and repining, the dupe of Anthony's arts, or of his own false estimate of Roman spirit and virtue. The people had lost a kind master, and they lamented him. Brutus summoned them to make efforts and sacrifices, and they viewed his cause with apathy, his crime with abhorrence.

Before the decisive battle of Philippi, Brutus seems, after the death of Cassius, to have sunk under the weight of the sole command. He still had many able officers left, and among them Messala, one of the first men of that age, so fruitful of great men; but Brutus no longer maintained that ascendant over his army, which talents of the first order maintain everywhere, and most signally in the camp and field of battle. It is fairly then to be presumed, that his troops had discovered that Brutus, whom they loved and esteemed, was destitute of those talents; for he was soon obliged by their clamors, much against his judgment, and against all prudence and good sense, to give battle. Thus ended the life of Brutus, and the existence of the republic.

Whatever doubt there may be of the political and military capacity of Brutus, there is none concerning his virtue; his principles of action were the noblest that ancient philosophy had taught, and his actions were conformed to his principles. Nevertheless, our admiration of the man ought not to blind our judgment of the deed, which, though it was the blemish of his virtue, has shed an unfading splendor on his name.

For though the multitude to the end of time will be open to flattery, and will joyfully assist their flatterers to become their tyrants, yet they will never cease to hate tyrants and tyranny with equal sincerity and vehemence. Hence it is, that the memory of Brutus, who slew a tyrant, is consecrated as the champion and martyr of liberty, and will flourish and look green in declamation, as long as the people are prone to believe that those are their best friends, who have proved themselves the greatest enemies of their enemies.

Ask any one man of morals, whether he approves of

assassination; he will answer, no. Would you kill your friend and benefactor? No. The question is a horrible insult. Would you practise hypocrisy and smile in his face, while your conspiracy is ripening, to gain his confidence and to lull him into security, in order to take away his life? Every honest man, on the bare suggestion, feels his blood thicken and stagnate at his heart. Yet in this picture we see Brutus. It would perhaps be scarcely just to hold him up to abhorrence; it is certainly monstrous and absurd to exhibit his conduct to admiration.

He did not strike the tyrant from hatred or ambition; his motives are admitted to be good; but was not the action nevertheless bad?

To kill a tyrant is as much murder as to kill any other man. Besides, Brutus, to extenuate the crime, could have had no rational hope of putting an end to the tyranny; he had foreseen and provided nothing to realize it. The conspirators relied, foolishly enough, on the love of the multitude for liberty—they loved their safety, their ease, their sports, and their demagogue favorites a great deal better. They quietly looked on as spectators, and left it to the legions of Anthony, and Octavius, and to those of Syria, Macedonia, and Greece, to decide in the field of Philippi, whether there should be a republic or not. It was accordingly decided in favor of an emperor; and the people sincerely rejoiced in the political calm, that restored the games of the circus, and the plenty of bread.

Those who cannot bring their judgments to condemn the killing of a tyrant, must nevertheless agree that the blood of Cæsar was unprofitably shed. Liberty gained nothing by it, and humanity lost a great deal; for it cost eighteen years of agitation and civil war, before the ambition of the military and popular chieftains had expended its means, and the power was concentrated in one man's hands.

We shall be told the example of Brutus is a good one, because it will never cease to animate the race of tyrant-killers. But will the fancied usefulness of assassination overcome our instinctive sense of its horror? Is it to become a part of our political morals, that the chief of a state is to be stabbed or poisoned, whenever a fanatic, a malcontent, or a reformer shall rise and call him a tyrant? Then there would be as little calm in despotism as in liberty.

But when has it happened that the death of a usurper has restored to the public liberty its departed life? Every successful usurpation creates many competitors for power, and they successively fall in the struggle. In all this agitation, liberty is without friends, without resources, and without hope. Blood enough, and the blood of tyrants too, was shed between the time of the wars of Marius and the death of Anthony, a period of about sixty years, to turn a common grist-mill; yet the cause of the public liberty continually grew more and more desperate. It is not by destroying tyrants that we are to extinguish tyranny; nature is not thus to be exhausted of her power to produce them. The soil of a republic sprouts with the rankest fertility; it has been sown with dragon's teeth. To lessen the hopes of usurping demagogues, we must enlighten, animate, and combine the spirit of freedom; we must fortify and guard the constitutional ramparts about liberty. When its friends become indolent or disheartened, it is no longer of any importance how long-lived are its enemies; they will prove immortal.

Nor will it avail to say, that the famous deed of Brutus will forever check the audacity of tyrants. Of all passions fear is the most cruel. If new tyrants dread other Bruti, they will more naturally soothe their jealousy by persecutions, than by the practice of clemency or justice. They will say the clemency of Cæsar proved fatal to him. They will augment their force and multiply their precautions; and their habitual dread will degenerate into habitual cruelty.

Have we not then a right to conclude, that the character of Brutus is greatly overrated, and the fashionable approbation of his example horribly corrupting and pernicious?

A SKETCH OF THE CHARACTER
OF ALEXANDER HAMILTON

*The following sketch, written immediately after the
death of the ever to be lamented Hamilton, was read
to a select company of friends, and at their desire
it first appeared in the Repertory, July, 1804.*

It is with really great men as with great literary works, the
excellence of both is best tested by the extent and durableness
of their impression. The public has not suddenly, but after
an experience of five-and-twenty years, taken that impression
of the just celebrity of Alexander Hamilton, that nothing but
his extraordinary intrinsic merit could have made, and still
less could have made so deep and maintained so long. In
this case, it is safe and correct to judge by effects; we
sometimes calculate the height of a mountain, by measuring
the length of its shadow.

It is not a party, for party distinctions, to the honor of our
citizens be it said, are confounded by the event; it is a nation
that weeps for its bereavement. We weep, as the Romans
did over the ashes of Germanicus. It is a thoughtful, foreboding
sorrow, that takes possession of the heart, and sinks it with
no counterfeited heaviness.

It is here proper and not invidious to remark, that as the
emulation excited by conducting great affairs commonly trains
and exhibits great talents, it is seldom the case that the
fairest and soundest judgment of a great man's merit is to be
gained, exclusively, from his associates in counsel or in
action. Persons of conspicuous merit themselves are, not
unfrequently, bad judges and still worse witnesses on this
point; often rivals, sometimes enemies; almost always unjust,
and still oftener envious or cold. The opinions they give to

the public, as well as those they privately formed for themselves, are of course discolored with the hue of their prejudices and resentments.

But the body of the people, who cannot feel a spirit of rivalship towards those whom they see elevated by nature and education so far above their heads, are more equitable, and, supposing a competent time and opportunity for information on the subject, more intelligent judges. Even party rancor, eager to maim the living, scorns to strip the slain. The most hostile passions are soothed or baffled by the fall of their antagonist. Then, if not sooner, the very multitude will fairly decide on character, according to their experience of its impression; and as long as virtue, not unfrequently for a time obscured, is ever respectable when distinctly seen, they cannot withhold, and they will not stint their admiration.

If, then, the popular estimation is ever to be taken for the true one, the uncommonly profound public sorrow for the death of Alexander Hamilton sufficiently explains and vindicates itself. He had not made himself dear to the passions of the multitude by condescending, in defiance of his honor and conscience, to become their instrument; he is not lamented, because a skilful flatterer is now mute for ever. It was by the practice of no art, by wearing no disguise; it was not by accident, or by the levity or profligacy of party, but in despite of its malignant misrepresentation; it was by bold and inflexible adherence to truth, by loving his country better than himself, preferring its interest to its favor, and serving it when it was unwilling and unthankful, in a manner that no other person could, that he rose; and the true popularity, the homage that is paid to virtue, followed him. It was not in the power of party or envy to pull him down; but he rose with the refulgence of a star, till the very prejudice that could not reach, was at length almost ready to adore him.

It is indeed no imagined wound that inflicts so keen an anguish. Since the news of his death, the novel and strange events of Europe have succeeded each other unregarded; the nation has been enchained to its subject, and broods over its grief, which is more deep than eloquent, which though dumb, can make itself felt without utterance, and which does not merely pass, but like an electrical shock, at the same instant smites and astonishes, as it passes from Georgia to New Hampshire.

There is a kind of force put upon our thoughts by this disaster, which detains and rivets them to a closer contemplation of those resplendent virtues, that are now lost, except to memory, and there they will dwell for ever.

That writer would deserve the fame of a public benefactor who could exhibit the character of Hamilton, with the truth and force that all who intimately knew him conceived it; his example would then take the same ascendant as his talents. The portrait alone, however, exquisitely finished, could not inspire genius where it is not; but if the world should again have possession of so rare a gift, it might awaken it where it sleeps, as by a spark from heaven's own altar; for surely if there is any thing like divinity in man, it is in his admiration of virtue.

But who alive can exhibit this portrait? If our age, on that supposition more fruitful than any other, had produced two Hamiltons, one of them might then have depicted the other. To delineate genius one must feel its power; Hamilton, and he alone, with all its inspirations, could have transfused its whole fervid soul into the picture, and swelled its lineaments into life. The writer's mind, expanding with his own peculiar enthusiasm, and glowing with kindred fires, would then have stretched to the dimensions of his subject.

Such is the infirmity of human nature, it is very difficult for a man who is greatly the superior of his associates, to preserve their friendship without abatement; yet, though he could not possibly conceal his superiority, he was so little inclined to display it, he was so much at ease in its possession, that no jealousy or envy chilled his bosom, when his friends obtained praise. He was indeed so entirely the friend of his friends, so magnanimous, so superior, or more properly so insensible to all exclusive selfishness of spirit, so frank, so ardent, yet so little overbearing, so much trusted, admired, beloved, almost adored, that his power over their affections was entire, and lasted through his life. We do not believe that he left any worthy man his foe who had ever been his friend.

Men of the most elevated minds have not always the readiest discernment of character. Perhaps he was sometimes too sudden and too lavish in bestowing his confidence; his manly spirit, disdaining artifice, suspected none. But while the power of his friends over him seemed to have no limits, and really had none, in respect to those things which were of a nature to be yielded, no man, not the Roman Cato himself, was more inflexible on every point that touched, or only seemed to touch, integrity and honor. With him, it was not enough to be unsuspected; his bosom would have glowed, like a furnace, at its own whispers of reproach. Mere purity would have seemed to him below praise; and such were his habits, and such his nature, that the pecuniary temptations, which many others can only with great exertion and self-denial resist, had no attractions for him. He was very far from obstinate; yet, as his friends assailed his opinions with less profound thought than he had devoted to them, they were seldom shaken by discussion. He defended them, however, with as much mildness as force, and evinced, that if he did not yield, it was not for want of gentleness or modesty.

The tears that flow on this fond recital will never dry up. My heart, penetrated with the remembrance of the man, grows liquid as I write, and I could pour it out like water. I could weep too for my country, which, mournful as it is, does not know the half of its loss. It deeply laments, when it turns its eyes back, and sees what Hamilton was; but my soul stiffens with despair when I think what Hamilton would have been.

His social affections and his private virtues are not, however, so properly the object of public attention, as the conspicuous and commanding qualities that gave him his fame and influence in the world. It is not as Apollo, enchanting the shepherds with his lyre, that we deplore him; it is as Hercules, treacherously slain in the midst of his unfinished labors, leaving the world overrun with monsters.

His early life we pass over; though his heroic spirit in the army has furnished a theme that is dear to patriotism and will be sacred to glory.

In all the different stations in which a life of active usefulness has placed him, we find him not more remarkably distinguished by the extent, than by the variety and versatility of his talents. In every place he made it apparent, that no other man could have filled it so well; and in times of critical importance, in which alone he desired employment, his services were justly deemed absolutely indispensable. As secretary of the treasury, his was the powerful spirit that presided over the chaos:

> Confusion heard his voice, and wild uproar
> Stood ruled. . . . .

Indeed, in organizing the federal government in 1789, every man of either sense or candor will allow, the difficulty seemed greater than the first-rate abilities could surmount. The event has shown that his abilities were greater than those difficulties. He surmounted them—and Washington's administration was the most wise and beneficent, the most prosperous, and ought to be the most popular, that ever was intrusted with the affairs of a nation. Great as was Washington's merit, much of it in plan, much in execution, will of course devolve upon his minister.

As a lawyer, his comprehensive genius reached the principles of his profession; he compassed its extent, he fathomed its profound, perhaps even more familiarly and easily, than the ordinary rules of its practice. With most men law is a trade; with him it was a science.

As a statesman, he was not more distinguished by the great extent of his views, than by the caution with which he provided against impediments, and the watchfulness of his care over right and the liberty of the subject. In none of the many revenue bills which he framed, though committees reported them, is there to be found a single clause that savors of despotic power; not one that the sagest champions of law and liberty would, on that ground, hesitate to approve and adopt.

It is rare that a man, who owes so much to nature, descends to seek more from industry; but he seemed to depend on industry, as if nature had done nothing for him. His habits of investigation were very remarkable; his mind seemed to cling to his subject till he had exhausted it. Hence the uncommon superiority of his reasoning powers, a superiority that seemed to be augmented from every source, and to be fortified by every auxiliary, learning, taste, wit, imagination, and eloquence. These were embellished and enforced by his temper and manners, by his fame and his virtues. It is difficult, in the midst of such various excellence, to say in what particular the effect of his greatness was most manifest. No man more promptly discerned truth; no man more clearly displayed it; it was not merely made visible, it seemed to come bright with illumination from his lips. But prompt and clear as he was, fervid as Demosthenes, like Cicero full of resource, he was not less remarkable for the copiousness and completeness of his argument, that left little for cavil, and nothing for doubt. Some men take their strongest argument as a weapon, and use no other; but he left nothing to be inquired for more, nothing to be answered. He not only disarmed his adversaries of their pretexts and objections, but he stripped them of all excuse for having urged them; he confounded and subdued as well as convinced. He indemnified them, however, by making his discussion a complete map of his subject, so that his opponents might, indeed, feel ashamed of their mistakes, but they could not repeat them. In fact, it was no common effort that could preserve a really able antagonist from becoming his convert; for the truth, which his researches so distinctly presented to the understanding of others, was rendered almost irresistibly commanding and impressive by the love and reverence which, it was ever apparent, he profoundly cherished for it in his own. While patriotism glowed in his heart, wisdom blended in his speech her authority with her charms.

Such, also, is the character of his writings. Judiciously collected, they will be a public treasure.

No man ever more disdained duplicity or carried frankness further than he. This gave to his political opponents some temporary advantages, and currency to some popular prejudices, which he would have lived down if his death had not prematurely dispelled them. He knew that factions have ever in the end prevailed in free states; and, as he saw no security (and who living can see any adequate?) against the destruction of that liberty which he loved, and for which he was ever ready to devote his life, he spoke at all times according to his anxious forebodings; and his enemies interpreted all that he said according to the supposed interest of their party.

But he ever extorted confidence, even when he most provoked opposition. It was impossible to deny that he was a patriot, and such a patriot as, seeking neither popularity nor office, without artifice, without meanness, the best Romans in their best days would have admitted to citizenship and to the consulate. Virtue so rare, so pure, so bold, by its very purity and excellence inspired suspicion as a prodigy. His enemies judged of him by themselves; so splendid and arduous were his services, they could not find it in their hearts to believe that they were disinterested.

Unparalleled as they were, they were nevertheless no

otherwise requited than by the applause of all good men, and by his own enjoyment of the spectacle of that national prosperity and honor which was the effect of them. After facing calumny, and triumphantly surmounting an unrelenting persecution, he retired from office with clean, though empty hands, as rich as reputation and an unblemished integrity could make him.

Some have plausibly, though erroneously inferred, from the great extent of his abilities, that his ambition was inordinate. This is a mistake. Such men as have a painful consciousness that their stations happen to be far more exalted than their talents, are generally the most ambitious. Hamilton, on the contrary, though he had many competitors, had no rivals; for he did not thirst for power, nor would he, as it was well known, descend to office. Of course he suffered no pain from envy when bad men rose, though he felt anxiety for the public. He was perfectly content and at ease in private life. Of what was he ambitious? Not of wealth; no man held it cheaper. Was it of popularity? That weed of the dunghill he knew, when rankest, was nearest to withering. There is no doubt that he desired glory, which to most men is too inaccessible to be an object of desire; but feeling his own force, and that he was tall enough to reach the top of Pindus or of Helicon, he longed to deck his brow with the wreath of immortality. A vulgar ambition could as little comprehend as satisfy his views; he thirsted only for that fame, which virtue would not blush to confer, nor time to convey to the end of his course.

The only ordinary distinction, to which we confess he did aspire, was military; and for that, in the event of a foreign war, he would have been solicitous. He undoubtedly discovered the predominance of a soldier's feelings; and all that is honor in the character of a soldier was at home in his heart. His early education was in the camp; there the first fervors of his genius were poured forth, and his earliest and most cordial friendships formed; there he became enamored of glory, and was admitted to her embrace.

Those who knew him best, and especially in the army, will believe, that if occasions had called him forth, he was qualified, beyond any man of the age, to display the talents of a great general.

It may be very long before our country will want such military talents; it will probably be much longer before it will again possess them.

Alas! the great man who was at all times so much the ornament of our country, and so exclusively fitted in its extremity to be its champion, is withdrawn to a purer and more tranquil region. We are left to endless labors and unavailing regrets.

Such honors Ilion to her hero paid,
And peaceful slept the mighty Hector's shade.[73]

The most substantial glory of a country is in its virtuous great men; its prosperity will depend on its docility to learn from their example. That nation is fated to ignominy and servitude, for which such men have lived in vain. Power may be seized by a nation that is yet barbarous; and wealth may be enjoyed by one that it finds or renders sordid; the one is the gift and the sport of accident, and the other is the sport of power. Both are mutable, and have passed away without leaving behind them any other memorial than ruins that offend taste, and traditions that battle conjecture. But the glory of Greece is imperishable, or will last as long as learning itself, which is its monument; it strikes an everlasting root, and bears perennial blossoms on its grave. The name of Hamilton would have honored Greece in the age of

---

[73] *Homer's* Iliad, *book XXIV, l. 805.*

518

Aristides. May heaven, the guardian of our liberty, grant that our country may be fruitful of Hamiltons, and faithful to their glory!

EULOGY OF WASHINGTON

Delivered at the Request of the Legislature of
Massachusetts, FEBRUARY 8, 1800

IT IS NATURAL that the gratitude of mankind should be drawn to their benefactors. A number of these have successively arisen, who were no less distinguished for the elevation of their virtues than the lustre of their talents. Of those, however, who were born, and who acted through life as if they were born, not for themselves, but for their country and the whole human race, how few, alas, are recorded in the long annals of ages, and how wide the intervals of time and space that divide them! In all this dreary length of way, they appear like five or six light-houses on as many thousand miles of coast; they gleam upon the surrounding darkness with an inextinguishable splendor, like stars seen through a mist; but they are seen like stars, to cheer, to guide, and to save. Washington is now added to that small number. Already he attracts curiosity, like a newly-discovered star, whose benignant light will travel on to the world's and time's farthest bounds. Already his name is hung up by history as conspicuously as if it sparkled in one of the constellations of the sky.

By commemorating his death, we are called this day to yield the homage that is due to virtue; to confess the common debt of mankind as well as our own; and to pronounce for posterity, now dumb, that eulogium, which they will delight to echo ten ages hence, when we are dumb.

I consider myself not merely in the midst of the citizens of this town, or even of the state. In idea I gather round me the nation. In the vast and venerable congregation of the patriots of all countries and of all enlightened men, I would, if I could, raise my voice, and speak to mankind in a strain worthy of my audience, and as elevated as my subject. But you have assigned me a task that is impossible.

O if I could perform it, if I could illustrate his principles in my discourse as he displayed them in his life, if I could paint his virtues as he practised them, if I could convert the fervid enthusiasm of my heart into the talent to transmit his fame as it ought to pass to posterity,—I should be the successful organ of your will, the minister of his virtues, and, may I dare to say, the humble partaker of his immortal glory. These are ambitious, deceiving hopes, and I reject them; for it is, perhaps, almost as difficult, at once with judgment and feeling, to praise great actions as to perform them. A lavish and undistinguishing eulogium is not praise; and to discriminate such excellent qualities as were characteristic and peculiar to him would be to raise a name, as he raised it, above envy, above parallel, perhaps, for that very reason, above emulation.

Such a portraying of character, however, must be addressed to the understanding, and therefore, even if it were well executed, would seem to be rather an analysis of moral principles than the recital of a hero's exploits.

With whatever fidelity I might execute this task, I know that some would prefer a picture drawn to the imagination. They would have our Washington represented of a giant's size, and in the character of a hero of romance. They who love to wonder better than to reason, would not be satisfied with the contemplation of a great example, unless, in the exhibition, it should be so distorted into prodigy as to be both incredible and useless. Others, I hope but few, who think meanly of human nature, will deem it incredible that even Washington should think with as much dignity and elevation as he acted; and they will grovel in vain in the search for mean and selfish motives that could incite and sustain him to devote his life to his country.

Do not these suggestions sound in your ears like a profanation of virtue? and while I pronounce them, do you not feel a thrill of indignation at your hearts? Forbear. Time never fails to bring every exalted reputation to a strict scrutiny: the world, in passing the judgment that is never to be reversed, will deny all partiality even to the name of Washington. Let it be denied, for its justice will confer glory.

Such a life as Washington's cannot derive honor from the circumstances of birth and education, though it throws back a lustre upon both. With an inquisitive mind, that always profited by the lights of others, and was unclouded by passions of its own, he acquired a maturity of judgment, rare in age, unparalleled in youth. Perhaps no young man had so early laid up a life's stock of materials for solid reflection, or settled so soon the principles and habits of his conduct. Gray experience listened to his counsels with respect, and at a time when youth is almost privileged to be rash, Virginia committed the safety of her frontier, and ultimately the safety of America, not merely to his valor, for that would be scarcely praise, but to his prudence.

It is not in Indian wars that heroes are celebrated; but it is there they are formed. No enemy can be more formidable, by the craft of his ambushes, the suddenness of his onset, or the ferocity of his vengeance. The soul of Washington was thus exercised to danger; and on the first trial, as on every other, it appeared firm in adversity, cool in action, undaunted, self-possessed. His spirit, and still more his prudence, on

the occasion of Braddock's defeat, diffused his name throughout America, and across the Atlantic. Even then his country
viewed him with complacency, as her most hopeful son.

At the peace of 1763, Great Britain, in consequence of
her victories, stood in a position to prescribe her own terms.
She chose perhaps better for us than for herself; for by
expelling the French from Canada we no longer feared hostile
neighbors; and we soon found just cause to be afraid of our
protectors. We discerned even then a truth, which the conduct
of France has since so strongly confirmed, that there is
nothing which the gratitude of weak states can give that will
satisfy strong allies for their aid, but authority; nations that
want protectors will have masters. Our settlements, no longer
checked by enemies on the frontier, rapidly increased; and
it was discovered that America was growing to a size that
could defend itself.

In this perhaps unforeseen, but at length obvious state of
things, the British government conceived a jealousy of the
colonies, of which, and of their intended measures of
precaution, they made no secret.

Our nation, like its great leader, had only to take counsel
from its courage. When Washington heard the voice of his
country in distress, his obedience was prompt; and though
his sacrifices were great, they cost him no effort. Neither the
object nor the limits of my plan permit me to dilate on the
military events of the revolutionary war. Our history is but a
transcript of his claims on our gratitude: our hearts bear
testimony, that they are claims not to be satisfied. When
overmatched by numbers, a fugitive with a little band of
faithful soldiers, the States as much exhausted as dismayed,
he explored his own undaunted heart, and found there
resources to retrieve our affairs. We have seen him display
as much valor as gives fame to heroes, and as consummate
prudence as insures success to valor; fearless of dangers that
were personal to him, hesitating and cautious when they

affected his country; preferring fame before safety or repose, and duty before fame.

Rome did not owe more to Fabius than America to Washington. Our nation shares with him the singular glory of having conducted a civil war with mildness, and a revolution with order.

The event of that war seemed to crown the felicity and glory both of America and its chief. Until that contest, a great part of the civilized word had been surprisingly ignorant of the force and character, and almost of the existence, of the British colonies. They had not retained what they knew, nor felt curiosity to know the state of thirteen wretched settlements, which vast woods inclosed, and still vaster woods divided from each other. They did not view the colonists so much a people as a race of fugitives, whom want, and solitude, and intermixture with the savages, had made barbarians.

At this time, while Great Britain wielded a force truly formidable to the most powerful states, suddenly, astonished Europe beheld a feeble people, till then unknown, stand forth, and defy this giant to the combat. It was so unequal, all expected it would be short. Our final success exalted their admiration to its highest point: they allowed to Washington all that is due to transcendent virtue, and to the Americans more than is due to human nature. They considered us a race of Washingtons, and admitted that nature in America was fruitful only in prodigies. Their books and their travellers, exaggerating and distorting all their representations, assisted to establish the opinion, that this is a new world, with a new order of men and things adapted to it; that here we practise industry, amidst the abundance that requires none; that we have morals so refined, that we do not need laws; and though we have them, yet we ought to consider their execution as an insult and a wrong; that we have virtue without weaknesses, sentiment without passions, and liberty without factions.

These illusions, in spite of their absurdity, and perhaps because they are absurd enough to have domination over the imagination only, have been received by many of the malcontents against the governments of Europe, and induced them to emigrate. Such allusions are too soothing to vanity to be entirely checked in their currency among Americans.

They have been pernicious, as they cherish false ideas of the rights of men and the duties of rulers. They have led the citizens to look for liberty, where it is not; and to consider the government, which is its castle, as its prison.

Washington retired to Mount Vernon, and the eyes of the world followed him. He left his countrymen to their simplicity and their passions, and their glory soon departed. Europe began to be undeceived, and it seemed for a time, as if, by the acquisition of independence, our citizens were dispointed. The confederation was then the only compact made "to form a perfect union of the states, to establish justice, to insure the tranquillity, and provide for the security of the nation;" and accordingly, union was a name that still commanded reverence, though not obedience. The system called justice, was, in some of the states, iniquity reduced to elementary principles; and the public tranquillity was such a portentous calm, as rings in deep caverns before the explosion of an earthquake. Most of the states then were in fact, though not in form, unbalanced democracies. Reason, it is true, spoke audibly in their constitutions; passion and prejudice louder in their laws. It is to the honor of Massachusetts, that it is chargeable with little deviation from principles; its adherence to them was one of the causes of a dangerous rebellion. It was scarcely possible that such governments should not be agitated by parties, and that prevailing parties should not be vindictive and unjust. Accordingly, in some of the states, creditors were treated as outlaws; bankrupts were armed with legal authority to be persecutors; and by the shock of all confidence and faith, society was shaken to its foundations.

Liberty we had, but we dreaded its abuse almost as much as its loss; and the wise, who deplored the one, clearly foresaw the other.

The peace of America hung by a thread, and factions were already sharpening their weapons to cut it. The project of three separate empires in America was beginning to be broached, and the progress of licentiousness would have soon rendered her citizens unfit for liberty in either of them. An age of blood and misery would have punished our disunion; but these were not the considerations to deter ambition from its purpose, while there were so many circumstances in our political situation to favor it.

At this awful crisis, which all the wise so much dreaded at the time, yet which appears, on a retrospect, so much more dreadful than their fears; some man was wanting who possessed a commanding power over the popular passions, but over whom those passions had no power. That man was Washington.

His name, at the head of such a list of worthies as would reflect honor on any country, had its proper weight with all the enlightened, and with almost all the well-disposed among the less informed citizens, and, blessed be God! the Constitution was adopted. Yes, to the eternal honor of America among the nations of the earth, it was adopted, in spite of the obstacles, which in any other country, and perhaps in any other age of *this*, would have been insurmountable; in spite of the doubts and fears, which well-meaning prejudice creates for itself, and which party so artfully inflames into stubbornness; in spite of the vice, which it has subjected to restraint, and which is therefore its immortal and implacable foe; in spite of the oligarchies in some of the States, from whom it snatched dominion;—it was adopted, and our country enjoys one more invaluable chance for its union and happiness: invaluable! if the retrospect of the dangers we have escaped shall sufficiently inculcate the principles we have so tardily established. Perhaps multitudes are not to be taught by their fears only, without suffering much to deepen the impression; for experience brandishes in her school a whip of scorpions, and teaches nations her summary lessons of wisdom by the scars and wounds of their adversity.

The amendments which have been projected in some of the states show, that in them, at least, these lessons are not well remembered. In a confederacy of states, some powerful, others weak, the weakness of the federal union will sooner or later encourage, and will not restrain, the ambition and injustice of the members: the weak can no otherwise be strong or safe, but in the energy of the national government. It is this defect, which the blind jealousy of the weak states not unfrequently contributes to prolong, that has proved fatal to all the confederations that ever existed.

Although it was impossible that such merit as Washington's should not produce envy, it was scarcely possible that, with such a transcendent reputation, he should have rivals. Accordingly, he was unanimously chosen President of the United States.

As a general and a patriot, the measure of his glory was already full; there was no fame left for him to excel but his own; and even that task, the mightiest of all his labors, his civil magistracy has accomplished.

No sooner did the new government begin its auspicious course, than order seemed to arise out of confusion. Commerce and industry awoke, and were cheerful at their labors; for credit and confidence awoke with them. Everywhere was the appearance of prosperity; and the only fear was, that its progress was too rapid to consist with the purity and simplicity of ancient manners. The cares and labors of the president were incessant; his exhortations, example, and authority, were employed to excite zeal and activity for the public service; able officers were selected, only for their merits; and some of them remarkably distinguished themselves by their successful management of the public business. Government was administered with such integrity, without mystery, and in so prosperous a course, that it seemed to be wholly employed in acts of beneficence. Though it has made many thousand malcontents, it has never, by its rigor or injustice, made one man wretched.

Such was the state of public affairs; and did it not seem perfectly to ensure uninterrupted harmony to the citizens? Did they not, in respect to their government and its administration, possess their whole heart's desire? They had seen and suffered long the want of an efficient constitution; they had freely ratified it; they saw Washington, their tried friend, the father of his country, invested with its powers; they knew that he could not exceed or betray them, without forfeiting his own reputation. Consider, for a moment, what a reputation it was; such as no man ever before possessed by so clear a title, and in so high a degree. His fame seemed in its purity to exceed even its brightness. Office took honor from his acceptance, but conferred none. Ambition stood awed and darkened by his shadow. For where, through the wide earth, was the man so vain as to dispute precedence with him; or what were the honors that could make the possessor Washington's superior? Refined and complex as the ideas of virtue are, even the gross could discern in his life the infinite superiority of her rewards. Mankind perceived some change in their ideas of greatness; the splendor of power, and even of the name of conqueror, had grown dim in their eyes. They did not know that Washington could augment his fame; but they knew and felt, that the world's wealth, and its empire too, would be a bribe far beneath his acceptance.

This is not exaggeration; never was confidence in a man and a chief magistrate more widely diffused, or more solidly established.

If it had been in the nature of man, that we should enjoy liberty, without the agitations of party, the United States had a right, under these circumstances, to expect it; but it was impossible. Where there is no liberty, they may be exempt from party. It will seem strange, but it scarcely admits a doubt, that there are fewer malcontents in Turkey than in any free state in the world. Where the people have no power, they enter into no contests, and are not anxious to know how they shall use it. The spirit of discontent becomes torpid for want of employment, and sighs itself to rest. The people sleep soundly in their chains, and do not even dream of their weight. They lose their turbulence with their energy, and become as tractable as any other animals; a state of degradation, in which they extort our scorn, and engage our pity, for the misery they do not feel. Yet that heart is a base one, and fit only for a slave's bosom, that would not bleed freely, rather than submit to such a condition; for liberty, with all its parties and agitations, is more desirable than slavery. Who would not prefer the republics of ancient Greece, where liberty once subsisted in its excess, its delirium, terrible in its charms, and glistening to the last with the blaze of the very fire that consumed it?

I do not know that I ought, but I am sure that I do, prefer those republics to the dozing slavery of the modern Greece, where the degraded wretches have suffered scorn till they merit it, where they tread on classic ground, on the ashes of heroes and patriots, unconscious of their ancestry, ignorant of the nature and almost of the name of liberty and insensible even to the passion for it. Who, on this contrast, can forbear to say, it is the modern Greece that lies buried, that sleeps forgotten in the caves of Turkish darkness? It is the ancient Greece that lives in remembrance, that is still bright with glory, still fresh in immortal youth. They are unworthy of liberty who entertain a less exalted idea of its excellence. The misfortune is, that those who profess to be its most passionate admirers have, generally, the least comprehension of its hazards and impediments; they expect that an enthu-

siastic admiration of its nature will reconcile the multitude
to the irksomeness of its restraints. Delusive expectation!
Washington was not thus deluded. We have his solemn
warning against the often fatal propensities of liberty. He
had reflected, that men are often false to their country and
their honor, false to duty and even to their interest, but
multitudes of men are never long false or deaf to their
passions; these will find obstacles in the laws, associates in
party. The fellowships thus formed are more intimate, and
impose commands more imperious, than those of society.

Thus party forms a state within the state, and is animated
by a rivalship, fear, and hatred, of its superior. When this
happens, the merits of the government will become fresh
provocations and offences, for they are the merits of an
enemy. No wonder then, that as soon as party found the
virtue and glory of Washington were obstacles, the attempt
was made, by calumny, to surmount them both. For this, the
greatest of all his trials, we know that he was prepared. He
knew that the government must possess sufficient strength
from within or without, or fall a victim to faction. This *interior*
strength was plainly inadequate to its defence, unless it could
be reinforced from *without* by the zeal and patriotism of the
citizens; and this latter resource was certainly as accessible
to President Washington as to any chief magistrate that ever
lived. The life of the federal government, he considered, was
in the breath of the people's nostrils; whenever they should
happen to be so infatuated or inflamed as to abandon its
defence, its end must be as speedy, and might be as tragical,
as a constitution for France.

While the president was thus administering the government
in so wise and just a manner, as to engage the great majority
of the enlightened and virtuous citizens to coöperate with
him for its support, and while he indulged the hope that time
and habit were confirming their attachment, the French
Revolution had reached that point in its progress, when its

terrible principles began to agitate all civilized nations. I will not, on this occasion, detain you to express, though my thoughts teem with it, my deep abhorrence of that revolution; its despotism by the mob or the military from the first, and its hypocrisy of morals to the last. Scenes have passed there which exceed description, and which, for other reasons, I will not attempt to describe; for it would not be possible, even at this distance of time, and with the sea between us and France, to go through with the recital of them without perceiving horror gather, like a frost, about the heart and almost stop its pulse. That revolution has been constant in nothing but its vicissitudes and its promises; always delusive, but always renewed to establish philosophy by crimes and liberty by the sword. The people of France, if they are not like the modern Greeks, find their cap of liberty is a soldier's helmet; and with all their imitation of dictators and consuls, their exactest similitude to these Roman ornaments is in their chains. The nations of Europe perceive another resemblance in their all-conquering ambition.

But it is only the influence of that event on America, and on the measures of the president that belongs to my subject. It would be ungratefully wrong to his character, to be silent in respect to a part of it, which has the most signally illustrated his virtues.

The genuine character of that revolution is not even yet so well understood as the dictates of self-preservation require it should be. The chief duty and care of all governments is to protect the rights of property, and the tranquillity of society. The leaders of the French revolution from the beginning excited the poor against the rich. This has made the rich poor, but it will never make the poor rich. On the contrary, they were used only as blind instruments to make those leaders masters, first of the adverse party, and then of the state. Thus the powers of the state were turned round into a direction exactly contrary to the proper one, not to preserve tranquillity and restrain violence, but to excite violence by the lure of power and plunder and vengeance. Thus all France has been, and still is, as much the prize of the ruling party as a captured ship, and if any right or possession has escaped confiscation, there is none that has not been liable to it.

Thus it clearly appears, that in its origin, its character, and its means, the government of that country is revolutionary; that is, not only different from, but directly contrary to, every regular and well-ordered society. It is a danger, similar in its kind, and at least equal in degree, to that with which ancient Rome menaced her enemies. The allies of Rome were slaves; and it cost some hundred years' efforts of her policy and arms to make her enemies her allies. Nations at this day can trust no better to treaties; they cannot even trust to arms unless they are used with a spirit and perseverance becoming the magnitude of their danger. For the French Revolution has been from the first hostile to all right and justice, to all peace and order in society; and therefore its very existence has been a state of warfare against the civilized world, and most of all against free and orderly republics, for such are never without factions, ready to be the allies of France, and to aid her in the work of destruction. Accordingly, scarcely any but republics have they subverted. Such governments, by showing in practice what republican liberty is, detect French imposture, and show what their pretexts are not.

To subvert them, therefore, they had, besides the facility that faction affords, the double excitement of removing a reproach, and converting their greatest obstacles into their most efficient auxiliaries.

Who, then, on careful reflection, will be surprised that the French and their partisans instantly conceived the desire, and made the most powerful attempts, to revolutionize the American government? But it will hereafter seem strange that their excesses should be excused as the effects of a struggle for liberty; and that so many of our citizens should be flattered, while they were insulted with the idea that our example was copied and our principles pursued. Nothing was ever more false or more fascinating. Our liberty depends on our education, our laws and habits, to which even prejudices yield; on the dispersion of our people on farms, and on the almost equal diffusion of property; it is founded on morals and religion, whose authority reigns in the heart; and on the influence all these produce on public opinion, before that opinion governs rulers. Here liberty is restraint; there it is violence; here it is mild and cheering, like the morning sun of our summer, brightening the hills and making the valleys green; there it is like the sun, when his rays dart pestilence on the sands of Africa. American liberty calms and restrains the licentious passions, like an angel, that says to the winds and troubled seas, be still; but how has French licentiousness appeared to the wretched citizens of Switzerland and Venice? Do not their haunted imaginations, even when they wake, represent her as a monster, with eyes that flash wildfire, hands that hurl thunderbolts, a voice that shakes the foundation of the hills? She stands, and her ambition measures the earth; she speaks, and an epidemic fury seizes the nations.

Experience is lost upon us if we deny that it had seized a large part of the American nation. It is as sober and intelligent, as free and as worthy to be free as any in the world; yet like all other people we have passions and prejudices, and they had received a violent impulse, which for a time misled us.

Jacobinism had become here, as in France, rather a sect than a party, inspiring a fanaticism that was equally intolerant and contagious. The delusion was general enough to be thought the voice of the people, therefore claiming authority without proof, and jealous enough to exact acquiescence without a murmur of contradiction. Some progress was made in training multitudes to be vindictive and ferocious. To them nothing seemed amiable but the revolutionary justice of Paris; nothing terrible but the government and justice of America. The very name of *patriots* was claimed and applied in proportion as the citizens had alienated their hearts from America, and transferred their affections to their foreign corrupter. Party discerned its intimate connection of interest with France, and consummated its profligacy by yielding to foreign influence.

The views of these allies required that this country should engage in war with Great Britain. Nothing less would give to France all the means of annoying this dreaded rival; nothing less would ensure the subjection of America, as a satellite to the ambition of France; nothing else could make a revolution here perfectly inevitable.

For this end the minds of the citizens were artfully inflamed, and the moment was watched and impatiently waited for, when their long-heated passions should be in fusion to pour them forth, like the lava of a volcano, to blacken and consume the peace and government of our country.

The systematic operations of a faction, under foreign influence, had begun to appear, and were successively pursued, in a manner too deeply alarming to be soon forgotten. Who of us does not remember this worst of evils in this worst of ways? Shame would forget, if it could, that in one of the states amendments were proposed to break down the federal Senate, which, as in the state governments, is a great bulwark of the public order. To break down another, an extravagant judiciary power was claimed for states. In another state a rebellion was fomented by the agent of France; and who, without fresh indignation, can remember that the powers of government were openly usurped, troops levied, and ships fitted out to fight for her? Nor can any true friend to our government consider, without dread, that soon afterwards, the treaty-making power was boldly challenged for a branch of the government, from which the Constitution has wisely withholden it.

I am oppressed, and know not how to proceed with my subject. Washington, blessed be God! who endued him with wisdom and clothed him with power; Washington issued his proclamation of neutrality, and at an early period arrested the intrigues of France and the passions of his countrymen, on the very edge of the precipice of war and revolution.

This act of firmness, at the hazard of his reputation and peace, entitles him to the name of the first of patriots. Time was gained for the citizens to recover their virtue and good sense, and they soon recovered them. The crisis was passed and America was saved.

You and I, most respected fellow-citizens, should be sooner tired than satisfied in recounting the particulars of this illustrious man's life.

How great he appeared while he administered the government, how much greater when he retired from it, how he accepted the chief military command under his wise and upright successor, how his life was unspotted like his fame, and how his death was worthy of his life, are so many distinct subjects of instruction, and each of them singly more than enough for an elogium. I leave the task, however, to history and to posterity; they will be faithful to it.

It is not impossible that some will affect to consider the honors paid to this great patriot by the nation as excessive, idolatrous, and degrading to freemen, who are all equal. I answer, that refusing to virtue its legitimate honors would not prevent their being lavished in future, on any worthless and ambitious favorite. If this day's example should have its natural effect, it will be salutary. Let such honors be so conferred only when, in future, they shall be so merited; then the public sentiment will not be misled, nor the principles of a just equality corrupted. The best evidence of reputation is a man's whole life. We have now, alas! all Washington's before us. There has scarcely appeared a really great man whose character has been more admired in his lifetime, or less correctly understood by his admirers. When it is comprehended, it is no easy task to delineate its excellences in such a manner as to give to the portrait both interest and resemblance; for it requires thought and study to understand the true ground of the superiority of his character over many others, whom he resembled in the principles of action, and even in the manner of acting. But perhaps he excels all the great men that ever lived, in the steadiness of his adherence to his maxims of life, and in the uniformity of all his conduct to the same maxims. These maxims, though wise, were yet not so remarkable for their wisdom as for their authority over his life; for if there were any errors in his judgment, (and he discovered as few as any man,) we know of no blemishes in his virtue. He was the patriot without reproach; he loved his country well enough to hold his success in serving it an ample recompense. Thus far self-love and love of country coincided; but when his country needed sacrifices that no other man could or perhaps would be willing to make, he did not even hesitate. This was virtue in its most exalted character. More than once he put his fame at hazard, when he had reason to think it would be sacrificed, at least in this age. Two instances cannot be denied; when the army was disbanded; and again, when he stood, like Leonidas at the pass of Thermopylæ, to defend our independence against France.

It is indeed almost as difficult to draw his character as the portrait of virtue. The reasons are similar; our ideas of moral excellence are obscure, because they are complex, and we are obliged to resort to illustrations. Washington's example is the happiest to show what virtue is; and to delineate his character we naturally expatiate on the beauty of virtue; much must be felt and much imagined. His preëminence is not so much to be seen in the display of any one virtue as in the possession of them all, and in the practice of the most difficult. Hereafter, therefore, his character must be studied before it will be striking; and then it will be admitted as a model, a precious one to a free republic.

It is no less difficult to speak of his talents. They were adapted to lead, without dazzling mankind; and to draw forth and employ the talents of others, without being misled by them. In this he was certainly superior, that he neither mistook nor misapplied his own. His great modesty and reserve would have concealed them, if great occasions had not called them forth; and then, as he never spoke from the affectation to shine, nor acted from any sinister motives, it is from their effects only that we are to judge of their greatness and extent. In public trusts, where men, acting conspicuously, are cautious, and in those private concerns, where few conceal or resist their weaknesses, Washington was uniformly great, pursuing right conduct from right maxims. His talents were such as assist a sound judgment, and ripen with it. His prudence was consummate, and seemed to take the direction of his powers and passions; for as a soldier, he was more solicitous to avoid mistakes that might be fatal, than to perform exploits that are brilliant; and as a statesman, to adhere to just principles, however old, than to pursue novelties; and therefore, in both characters, his qualities were singularly adapted to the interest, and were tried in the greatest perils, of the country. His habits of inquiry were so far remarkable, that he was never satisfied with investigating, nor desisted from it, so long as he had less than all the light that he could obtain upon a subject, and then he made his decision without bias.

This command over the partialities that so generally stop men short, or turn them aside in their pursuit of truth, is one of the chief causes of his unvaried course of right conduct in so many difficult scenes, where every human actor must be presumed to err. If he had strong passions, he had learned to subdue them, and to be moderate and mild. If he had weaknesses, he concealed them, which is rare, and excluded them from the government of his temper and conduct, which is still more rare. If he loved fame, he never made improper compliances for what is called popularity. The fame he enjoyed is of the kind that will last forever; yet it was rather the effect, than the motive, of his conduct. Some future Plutarch will search for a parallel to his character. Epaminondas is perhaps the brightest name of all antiquity. Our Washington resembled him in the purity and ardor of his patriotism; and like him, he first exalted the glory of his country. There it is to be hoped the parallel ends; for Thebes fell with Epaminondas. But such comparisons cannot be pursued far, without departing from the similitude. For we shall find it as difficult to compare great men as great rivers; some we admire for the length and rapidity of their current, and the grandeur of their cataracts; others, for the majestic silence and fulness of their streams: we cannot bring them together to measure the difference of their waters. The unambitious life of Washington, declining fame, yet courted by it, seemed, like the Ohio, to choose its long way through solitudes, diffusing fertility; or, like his own Potomac, widening and deeping his channel, as he approaches the sea, and displaying most the usefulness and serenity of his greatness towards the end of his course. Such a citizen would do honor to any country. The constant veneration and affection of his country will show, that it was worthy of such a citizen.

However his military fame may excite the wonder of mankind, it is chiefly by his civil magistracy, that his example will instruct them. Great generals have arisen in all ages of the world, and perhaps most in those of despotism and darkness. In times of violence and convulsion, they rise by the force of the whirlwind, high enough to ride in it, and direct the storm. Like meteors, they glare on the black clouds with a splendor that, while it dazzles and terrifies, makes

537

nothing visible but the darkness. The fame of heroes is indeed growing vulgar; they multiply in every long war; they stand in history, and thicken in their ranks, almost as undistinguished as their own soldiers.

But such a chief magistrate as Washington, appears like the polestar in a clear sky, to direct the skilful statesman. His presidency will form an epoch, and be distinguished as the age of Washington. Already it assumes its high place in the political region. Like the milky way, it whitens along its allotted portion of the hemisphere. The latest generations of men will survey, through the telescope of history, the space where so many virtues blend their rays, and delight to separate them into groups and distinct virtues. As the best illustration of them, the living monument, to which the first of patriots would have chosen to consign his fame, it is my earnest prayer to heaven, that our country may subsist, even to that late day, in the plenitude of its liberty and happiness, and mingle its mild glory with Washington's.

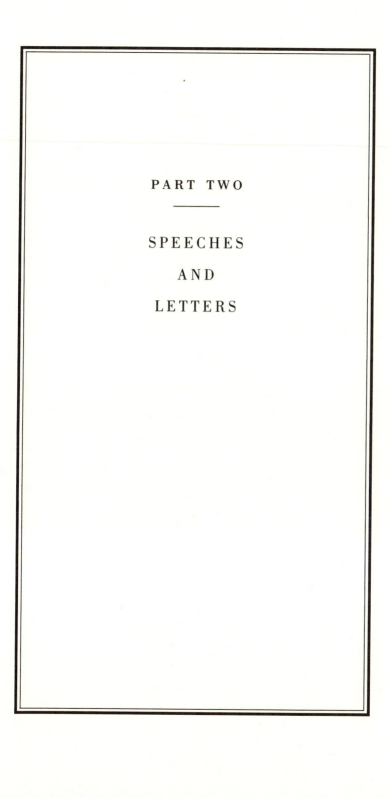

PART TWO

———

SPEECHES

AND

LETTERS

1788

SPEECHES IN THE CONVENTION

OF MASSACHUSETTS

JANUARY 15, 1788

(Art. 1, sec. 2, On constituting the House of Representatives; the Propriety of Biennial elections.)

I DO NOT REGRET, Mr. President, that we are not unanimous upon this question. I do not consider the diversity of sentiment which prevails, as an impediment in our way to the discovery of truth. In order that we may think alike upon this subject at last, we shall be compelled to discuss it by ascending to the principles upon which the doctrine of representation is grounded.

Without premeditation, in a situation so novel, and awed by the respect which I feel for this venerable assembly, I distrust extremely my own feelings, as well as my competency

541

to prosecute this inquiry.[1] With the hope of an indulgent hearing, I will attempt to proceed. I am sensible, sir, that the doctrine of frequent elections has been sanctified by antiquity; and it is still more endeared to us by our recent experience, and uniform habits of thinking. Gentlemen have expressed their zealous partiality for it. They consider this as a leading question in the debate, and that the merits of many other parts of the constitution are involved in the decision. I confess, sir, and I declare, that my zeal for frequent elections is not inferior to their own. I consider it as one of the first securities for popular liberty, in which its very essence may be supposed to reside. But how shall we make the best use of this pledge and instrument of our safety?

A right principle, carried to an extreme, becomes useless. It is apparent that a declaration for a very short term, as for a single day, would defeat the design of representation. The election in that case would not seem to the people to be of any importance, and the person elected would think as lightly of his appointment. The other extreme is equally to be avoided. An election for a very long term of years, or for life, would remove the member too far from the control of the people, would be dangerous to liberty, and, in fact, repugnant to the purposes of the delegation. The truth, as usual, is placed somewhere between the extremes, and, I believe, is included in the proposition: the terms of election must be so long that the representative may understand the interests of the people, and yet so limited, that his fidelity may be secured by a dependence upon their approbation.

Before I proceed to the application of this rule, I cannot forbear to premise some remarks upon two opinions which have been suggested.

Much has been said about the people's divesting themselves of power, when they delegate it to representatives; and that

---

[1] *This was Mr. Ames's first speech in a state assembly.* [S. AMES]

all representation is to their disadvantage, because it is but an image, a copy, fainter and more imperfect than the original, the people, in whom the light of power is primary and unborrowed, which is only reflected by their delegates. I cannot agree to either of these opinions. The representation of the people is something more than the people. I know, sir, but one purpose which the people can effect without delegation, and that is, to destroy a government. That they cannot erect a government, is evinced by our being thus assembled on their behalf. The poeple must govern by a majority, with whom all power resides. But how is the sense of this majority to be obtained? It has been said that a pure democracy is the best government for a small people who assemble in person. It is of small consequence to discuss it, as it would be inapplicable to the great country we inhabit. It may be of some use in this argument, however, to consider that it would be very burdensome, subject to faction and violence; decisions would often be made by surprise, in the precipitancy of passion, by men who either understand nothing, or care nothing about the subject; or by interested men, or those who vote for their own indemnity. It would be a government not by laws, but by men.

Such were the paltry democracies of Greece and Asia Minor, so much extolled, and so often proposed as a model for our imitation. I desire to be thankful, (said Mr. Ames) that our people are not under any temptation to adopt the advice. I think it will not be denied that the people are gainers by the election of representatives. They may destroy, but they cannot exercise, the powers of government in person; but by their servants *they* govern; they do not renounce their power; they do not sacrifice their rights; they become the true sovereigns of the country when they delegate that power, which they cannot use themselves, to their trustees.

I know, sir, that the people talk about the liberty of nature, and assert that we divest ourselves of a portion of it when

543

we enter into society. This is declamation against matter of fact. We cannot live without society; and as to liberty, how can I be said to enjoy that which another may take from me when he pleases? The liberty of one depends not so much on the removal of all restraint from him, as on the due restraint upon the liberty of others. Without such restraint, there can be no liberty. Liberty is so far from being endangered or destroyed by this, that it is extended and secured. For I said that we do not enjoy that which another may take from us. But civil liberty cannot be taken from us, when any one may please to invade it; for we have the strength of the society on our side.

I hope, sir, that these reflections will have some tendency to remove the ill impressions which are made by proposing to divest the people of their power.

That they may never be divested of it, I repeat, that I am in favor of frequent elections. They who commend annual elections are desired to consider, that the question is, whether biennial elections are a defect in the Constitution; for it does not follow, because annual elections are safe, that biennial are dangerous; for both may be good. Nor is there any foundation for the fears of those, who say that if we, who have been accustomed to choose for one year only, now extend it to two, the next stride will be to five or seven years, and the next for term of life; for this article, with all its supposed defects, is in favor of liberty. Being inserted in the Constitution, it is not subject to be repealed by law. We are sure that it is the worst of the case. It is a fence against ambitious encroachments, too high and too strong to be passed; in this respect, we have greatly the advantage of the people of England, and of all the world. The law which limits their Parliaments is liable to be repealed.

I will not defend this article by saying, that it was a matter of compromise in the federal Convention; it has my entire approbation as it stands. I think that we ought to prefer, in this article, biennial elections to annual; and my reasons for this opinion are drawn from these sources:

From the extent of the country to be governed;

The objects of their legislation;

And the more perfect security of our liberty.

It seems obvious that men who are to collect in Congress from this great territory, perhaps from the Bay of Fundy, or from the banks of the Ohio, and the shore of Lake Superior, ought to have a longer term in office than the delegates of a single state, in their own legislature. It is not by riding post to and from Congress, that a man can acquire a just knowledge of the true interests of the Union. This term of election is inapplicable to the state of a country as large as Germany, or as the Roman empire in the zenith of its power.

If we consider the objects of their delegation, little doubt will remain. It is admitted that annual elections may be highly fit for the state legislature. Every citizen grows up with a knowledge of the local circumstances of the state. But the business of the federal government will be very different. The objects of their power are few and national. At least two years in office will be necessary to enable a man to judge of the trade and interests of the state which he never saw. The time, I hope, will come, when this excellent country will furnish food, and freedom (which is better than food, which is the food of the soul) for fifty millions of happy people. Will any man say, that the national business can be understood in one year?

Biennial elections appear to me, sir, an essential security to liberty. These are my reasons:

Faction and enthusiasm are the instruments by which popular governments are destroyed. We need not talk of the power of an aristocracy. The people, when they lose their liberties, are cheated out of them. They nourish factions in their bosoms, which will subsist so long as abusing their honest credulity shall be the means of acquiring power. A democracy is a volcano, which conceals the fiery materials of its own destruction. These will produce an eruption, and carry desolation in their way. The people always mean right, and, if time is allowed for reflection and information, they will do right. I would not have the first wish, the momentary impulse of the public mind, become law; for it is not always the sense of the people, with whom I admit that all power resides. On great questions, we first hear the loud clamors of passion, artifice, and faction. I consider biennial elections as a security that the sober, second thought of the people shall be law. There is a calm review of public transactions, which is made by the citizens, who have families and children, the pledges of their fidelity. To provide for popular liberty, we must take care that measures shall not be adopted without due deliberation. The member chosen for two years will feel some independence in his seat. The factions of the day will expire before the end of his term.

The people will be proportionably attentive to the merits of a candidate. Two years will afford opportunity to the member to deserve well of them, and they will require evidence that he has done it.

But, sir, the representatives are the grand inquisition of the Union. They are, by impeachment, to bring great offenders to justice. One year will not suffice to detect guilt, and to pursue it to conviction; therefore, they will escape, and the balance of the two branches will be destroyed, and the people oppressed with impunity. The senators will represent the sovereignty of the States. The representatives are to represent the people. The offices ought to bear some proportion in point of importance. This will be impossible if they are chosen for one year only.

Will the people then blind the eyes of their own watchmen? Will they bind the hands which are to hold the sword for the defence? Will they impair their own power by an unreasonable jealousy of themselves?

For these reasons, I am clearly of opinion that the article is entitled to our approbation as it stands; and as it has been demanded, why annual elections were not preferred to biennial, permit me to retort the question, and to inquire, in my turn, what reason can be given, why, if annual elections are good, biennial elections are not better?

The inquiry in the latter part of Mr. Ames's speech being directed to the Hon. Mr. Adams, that gentleman said, he only *made the* inquiry for information, and that he had heard sufficient to satisfy himself of its propriety.

SATURDAY, JANUARY 19, 1788, A.M.

(Art. 1, sec. 3, On constituting the Senate;
the Propriety of a six-year term of office.)

MR. AMES observed, that an objection was made against the Constitution, because the senators are to be chosen for *six years*. It has been said, that they will be removed too far from the control of the people, and that, to keep them in proper dependence, they should be chosen annually. It is necessary to premise, that no argument against the new plan has made a deeper impression than this, that it will produce a consolidation of the states. This is an effect which all good men will deprecate. For it is obvious, that, if the state powers are to be destroyed, the representation is too small. The trust, in that case, would be too great to be confided to so few persons. The objects of legislation would be so multiplied and complicated, that the government would be unwieldy and impracticable. The state governments are essential parts of the system, and the defence of this article is drawn from its tendency to their preservation. The *senators* represent the *sovereignty of the states;* in the other house, individuals are represented. The Senate may not originate bills. It need not be said that they are principally to direct the affairs of wars and treaties. They are in the quality of ambassadors of the states, and it will not be denied that some permanency in their office is necessary to a discharge of their duty. Now, if they were chosen yearly, how could they perform their trust? If they would be brought by that means more immediately under the influence of the people, then they will represent the state legislatures less, and become the representatives of individuals. This belongs to the other house. The absurdity of this, and its repugnancy to the federal principles of the Constitution, will appear more fully, by supposing that they are to be chosen by the people at large. If there is any force in the objection to this article, this would be proper. But whom, in that case, would they represent?—Not the legislatures of the states, but the people. This would totally obliterate the federal features of the Constitution. What would become of the state governments, and on whom would devolve the duty of defending them against the encroachments of the federal government? A consolidation of the states would ensue, which, it is conceded, would subvert the new Constitution, and against which this very article, so much condemned, is our best security. Too much provision cannot be made against a consolidation. The state governments represent the wishes, and feelings, and local interests, of the people. They are the safeguard and ornament of the Constitution; they will protract the period of our liberties; they will afford a shelter against the abuse of power, and will be the natural avengers of our violated rights.

A very effectual *check* upon the power of the Senate is provided. A third part is to retire from office every two years. By this means, while the senators are seated for six years, they are admonished of their responsibility to the state legislatures. If one third new members are introduced, who feel the sentiments of their states, they will awe that third whose term will be near expiring. This article seems to be an excellence of the Constitution, and affords just ground to believe that it will be, in practice as in theory, a *federal republic.*

JUNE 21, 1788

*(Commenting on Art. 1, sec. 4, providing for
Congress' control over election of representatives.)*

MR. AMES rose to answer several *objections.* He would forbear, if possible, to go over the ground which had been already well trodden. The fourth section had been, he said, well discussed, and he did not mean to offer any formal argument or new observations upon it. It had been said, the power of regulating *elections* was given to Congress. He asked, if a motion was brought forward in Congress, on that particular, subjecting the states to any inconvenience, whether it was probable such a motion could obtain. It has been also said, that our federal legislature would endeavor to perpetuate themselves in office; and that the love of power was predominant. Mr. Ames asked how the gentlemen prevailed on themselves to trust the state legislature? He thought it was from a degree of confidence that was placed in them. At present we trust Congress with power; nay, we trust the representatives of Rhode Island and Georgia. He thought it was better to trust the general government than a foreign state. Mr. A. acknowledged he came with doubts of the fourth section. Had his objections remained, he would have been obliged to vote against the Constitution; but now he thought, if all the Constitution was as clear as this section, it would meet with little opposition.

JUNE 25, 1788

*(Debating Art. 1, sec. 8, the "powers
to be granted to Congress.")*

MR. AMES, in a short discourse, called on those who stood forth in 1775 to stand forth now; to throw aside all interested and party views; to have one purse and one heart for the whole; and to consider that, as it was necessary then, so was it necessary now, to unite,—or die we must.

Hon. Mr. SINGLETARY. Mr. President, I should not have troubled the Convention again, if some gentlemen had not called on them that were on the stage in the beginning of our troubles, in the year 1775. I was one of them. I have had the honor to be a member of the court all the time, Mr. President, and I say that, if any body had proposed such a constitution as this in that day, it would have been thrown away at once. It would not have been looked at. We contended with Great Britain, some said for a threepenny duty on tea; but it was not that; it was because they claimed a right to tax us and bind us in all cases whatever. And does not this Constitution do the same? Does it not take away all we have—all our property? . . .

Mr. AMES said, that, in the course of the debates, gentlemen had justified the Confederation; but he wished to ask whether there was any danger in this Constitution which is not in the Confederation. If gentlemen are willing to confederate, why, he asked, ought not Congress to have the powers granted by this section? In the Confederation, said Mr. A., the checks are wanting which are to be found in this Constitution. And the fears of gentlemen that this Constitution will provide for a permanent aristocracy are therefore ill-founded; for the rulers will always be dependent on the people, like the insects of a sunshiny day, and may, by the breath of their displeasure, be annihilated.

TUESDAY, FEBRUARY 5, 1788

(On proposals for ratification of the Constitution to be accompanied by proposed amendments rather than conditioned on adoption of a bill of rights.)

Mr. AMES observed that, at length, it is admitted that the Constitution, connected with the amendments, is good. Almost every one, who has appeared against the Constitution, has declared that he approves it, with the *amendments.* One gentleman, who has been distinguished by his zealous opposition, has declared that he would hold up both hands for it, if they could be adopted. I admire this candid manner of discussing the subject, and will endeavor to treat it myself with equal care and fairness. The only question which seems to labor is this: the amendments are not a part of the Constitution, and there is nothing better than a probability to trust to, that they will ever be adopted. The nature of the debate is totally shifted, and the inquiry is now, not what the Constitution is, but what degree of probability there is that the amendments will hereafter be incorporated into it.

Before he proceeded to discuss this question, he wished to notice two objections, which had been urged against his excellency's proposition—that this Convention, being confined in their powers to reject or ratify the Constitution as it is, have no right to propose amendments; and that the very propositions imply the Constitution is not perfect, and amount to a confession that it ought to be rejected. It is well that these objections were not made by a lawyer: they would have been called quibbles, and he would have been accused of having learned them at the bar. Have we no right to propose amendments? This is the fullest representation of the people ever known, and if we may not declare their opinion, and upon a point for which we have been elected, how shall it ever be known? A majority may not fully approve the Constitution, and yet they may think it unsafe to reject it; and they may fully approve his excellency's propositions. What shall they say? That they accept, or reject, and no more?—that they be embarrassed, perhaps, to do either. But let them say the truth, that they accept it, in the hope that amendments will obtain. We are chosen to consider the Constitution, and it is clearly incident to our appointment to declare the result of our deliberations. This very mode of obtaining amendments is pointed out in the Constitution inself. How can it be said that we have no right to propose them? If, however, there was any irregularity in this proceeding, the General Court would not delay to conform it.

If it is insisted that the Constitution is admitted to be imperfect, let those objectors consider the nature of their own argument. Do they expect a perfect constitution? Do they expect to find that perfection in government which they well know is not to be found in nature? There is not a man who is not more or less discontented with his condition in life, and who does not experience a mixture of good and evil; and will he expect that a whole society of men can exclude that imperfection which is the lot of every individual in it? The truth is, we call that condition good and happy, which is so upon the whole. But this Constitution may be good without any amendments, and yet the amendments may be good; for they are not repugnant to the Constitution. It is a gratification to observe how little we disagree in our sentiments; but it is not my purpose to compare the amendments with the Constitution. Whatever opinion may be formed of it by others, Mr. Ames professed to think it comparatively perfect. There was not any government which he knew to subsist, or which he had ever heard of, that would bear a comparison with the new Constitution. Considered merely as a literary performance, it was an honor to our country: legislators have at length condescended to speak the language of philosophy; and if we adopt it, we shall demonstrate to the sneering world, who deride liberty because they have lost it, that the principles of our government are as free as the spirit of our people.

I repeat it, our debates have been profitable, because, upon every leading point, we are at last agreed. Very few among us now deny that a federal government is necessary to save us from ruin; that the Confederation is not that government; and that the proposed Constitution, connected with the amendments, is worthy of being adopted. The question recurs, Will the amendments prevail, and become part of the system? In order to obtain such a system as the Constitution and the amendments, there are but three ways of proceeding—to reject the whole, and begin anew; to adopt this plan upon condition that the amendments be inserted into it; or to adopt his excellency's proposition.

Those who propose to reject the whole, are bound to show that we shall possess some advantage in forming a system which we do not enjoy at present, or that some obstacles will be removed which impede us now. But will that be the case? Shall we adopt another constitution with more unanimity than we expect to find in this Convention? Do gentlemen so soon forget their own arguments? We have been told that the new Constitution will be rebellion against the Confederation; that the interests of the states are too dissimilar for a union; and that Massachusetts can do without the union, and is a match for all the world. We have been warned of the tendency of all power towards tyranny, and of the danger of trusting Congress with the power of the purse and of the sword; that the system is not perfect; there is no religious test, and slavery is not abolished. Now, sir, if we reject the Constitution, and, after two or three years' exertion, another constitution should be submitted to another convention of Massachusetts, shall we escape the opposition which is made in this assembly? Will not the same objections then apply with equal force to another system? Or do gentlemen expect that a constitution may be formed which will not be liable to those objections? Do they expect one which will not annul the Confederation, or that the persons and properties of the people shall not be included in the compact, and that we shall hear no more about armies and taxes? But suppose that it was so framed, who is there, even amongst the objectors, who would give his vote for so paltry a system? If we reject, we are exposed to the risk of having no constitution, of being torn with factions, and at last divided into distinct confederacies.

If we accept *upon condition*, shall we have a right to send members to the new Congress? We shall not; and, of course, this state would lose its voice and influence in obtaining the adoption of the amendments. This is too absurd to need any further discussion.

But, in objection to your excellency's propositions, it is said that it is no more than probable that they will be agreed to by the other states. I ask, What is any future thing that we devise more than probable? What more is another constitution? All agree that we must have one; and it is easy to perceive that such a one as the majority of the people approve *must* be submitted to by this state; for what right have an eighth or tenth part of the people to dictate a government for the whole? It comes to this point, therefore:

Is any method more likely to induce the people of the United States to concur with Massachusetts, than that proposed by your excellency? If it is answered that there is none, as I think it must be, then the objection, that the chance of obtaining the amendments is no more than probable, will come to the ground, and it will appear that, of all chances, we depend upon that which is the safest. For when will the voice of Massachusetts have so powerful an influence as at present? There is not any government now to counteract or awe the people. The attention of the people is excited from one end of the state to the other, and they will watch and control the conduct of their members in Congress. Such amendments as afford better security to liberty will be supported by the people. There will be a Congress in existence to collect their sentiments, and to pursue the objects of their wishes. Nine states may insert amendments into the Constitution; but if we reject it, the vote must be unanimous. Our state, in that case, would lose the advantage of having representatives according to numbers, which is allowed by the Constitution. Upon a few points, and those not of a local nature, unanimity may be expected; but, in discussing a whole Constitution, in which the very amendments, that, it is said, will not be agreed to by the states, are to be inserted, unanimity will be almost a miracle. Either the amendments will be agreed to by the Union, or they will not. If it is admitted that they will be agreed to, there is an end of the objection to your excellency's propositions, and we ought to be unanimous for the Constitution. If it is said that they will not be agreed to, then it must be because they are not approved by the United States, or at least nine of them. Why shall we reject the Constitution, then, for the sole purpose of obtaining that unanimous vote of thirteen states, which it is confidently said, it is impossible we ever shall obtain from nine only? An object which is impossible is out of the question. The argument that the amendments will not prevail, is not only without force, but directly against those who use it, unless they admit that we have no need of a government, or assert that, by ripping up the foundations of the compact, upon which we now stand, and setting the whole Constitution afloat, and introducing an infinity of new subjects of controversy, we pursue the best method to secure the entire unanimity of thirteen states.

But shall we put every thing that we hold precious to the hazard by rejecting this Constitution? We have great advantages by it in respect of navigation; and it is the general interest of the states that we should have them. But if we reject it, what security have we that we shall obtain them a second time, against the local interests and prejudices of the other states? (Who is there, that really loves liberty, that will not tremble for its safety, if the federal government should be dissolved. Can liberty be safe without government?

The period of our political dissolution is approaching. Anarchy and uncertainty attend our future state. But this we know—that Liberty, which is the soul of our existence, once fled, can return no more.)

The Union is essential to our being as a nation. The pillars that prop it are crumbling to powder. The Union is the vital sap that nourishes the tree. If we reject the Constitution,— to use the language of the country,—we girdle the tree, its leaves will wither, its branches drop off, and the mouldering trunk will be torn down by the tempest. What security has this single state against foreign enemies? Could we defend the mast country, which the Britons so much desire? Can we protect our fisheries, or secure by treaties a sale for the produce of our lands in foreign markets? Is there no loss, no danger, by delay? In spite of our negligence and perverseness, are we to enjoy, at all times, the privilege of forming a constitution, which no other nation has ever enjoyed at all? We approve our own form of state government, and seem to think ourselves in safety under its protection. We talk as if there was no danger in deciding wrong. But when the inundation comes, shall we stand on dry land? The state government is a beautiful structure. It is situated, however, upon the naked beach. The Union is the dike to fence out the flood. That dike is broken and decayed; and, if we do not repair it, when the next spring tide comes, we shall be buried in one common destruction.

TO THEOPHILUS PARSONS

BOSTON, JANUARY 8, 1788

MY DEAR SIR:

IT SEEMS to your friends that you, who are our Ajax, are deserting the common cause by your absence from the General Court. Surely, the last session did not inspire you with so much esteem for the present assembly as to induce you to think it safe to leave us alone. For two things we need you to extremity,—*the Lieutenant-Governor*, and a very extraordinary message from the Governor. He has come out, and tells us, that two very respectable States, Virginia and New York, propose a convention to consider amendments. But he is of opinion that a convention is improper. However, he declares openly for the amendments, and a great deal more of the same stuff. The judiciary sytem is in jeopardy.

Can you resist these reasons for coming here? Accept this letter as the effect of the combined wishes of the Federalists, who need your aid, and have long been in the habit of trusting to it. We conceive hopes of taking the ascendency in these transactions; but our hopes rest on *you*. If possible, be here on Tuesday.

I am, my dear Sir, with perfect esteem,
Your most obedient servant,

FISHER AMES

P.S. You are desired to alarm the Cape Ann and Marblehead and other good folks, and bring them with you. We stand in extreme need of all our strength.

1789

===

TO JOHN LOWELL?

NEW YORK, MARCH 15, 1789

DEAR SIR:

YESTERDAY Mr. Madison, Col. or Mr. Page and Mr. Richard B. Lee arrived from Virginia, which makes the House 21 strong. The Senate is still at 8. Mr. R. H. Lee and Mr. Grayson have been, and the latter still is, confined by the gout. The Jersey and Delaware Senators would make a quorum. Many seem to be confident that both houses will be formed this week. I do not expect it so soon. I hope business will be transacted with more alacrity than this delay indicates.

A revenue act will probably be the first business. A judicial system must go out with it. This will be a great work. Where so much is to be done by so few, and those few are not *all* competent to it, it seems very proper to seek aid from those who can give it. I enclose you a sketch (and it is a first imperfect sketch) of a judicial system, which has been proposed and is the subject of conversation of three or four persons only. It has been proposed to exclude from the jurisdication of the federal judicial actions of less value than —————say 300 dollars—arising between a foreigner and a citizen and between citizens of different states. But

559

where the foreigner or citizen of another state is defendant, the action *must* be in the Federal Court, provided the value in dispute be 300 dollars.

These are the outlines. We do not begin to be dogmatical yet, and it is the earnest wish of your friends that you would communicate such reflections upon this, or any other systems as may occur to you. If you think fit to converse with the judges, and such of our brethren of the bar as you may meet with, you will gratify me by doing it. Judge Sullivan and Mr. Parsons ought to think of this subject and will be useful. To prevent expense is one object, and to allay jealousy another. By narrowing rather than extending jurisdiction, perhaps something may be done towards effecting both.

I shall be very much gratified by a letter from you, and am, with great respect,

Your most obedient and humble servant,

FISHER AMES

TO GEORGE RICHARDS MINOT,[2] BOSTON

NEW YORK, MARCH 25TH, 1789

DEAR SIR,

THIS MORNING we have twenty-six representatives; and as thirty are necessary to make a quorum, we are still in a state of inaction. This is a very mortifying situation. Mr. Coles,

---

[2] *Mr. Minot and Mr. Ames were fellow-students, and intimate friends. They were admitted to the bar together, in Boston, in November, 1781. Mr. Minot soon became eminent in his profession, and received many tokens of the public confidence. Their written correspondence appears to have ceased, at the termination of Mr. Ames's service in Congress; probably because they had frequent and more direct personal intercourse. Their friendship continued uninterrupted until Mr. Minot's death, which took place in 1802.* [S. AMES]

of Virginia, is at Philadelphia, detained by a slight indisposition, but is to set off to-day. Two members will be here from Jersey this evening, and if Messrs. Fitzsimmons and Clymer of Philadelphia come in, as we expect, we shall make an house on Friday. Mr. Elmer is expected to join the Senate this evening, which will make the Senate eleven strong. Therefore, we cannot hope for a Congress of both houses this week.

I am inclined to believe that the languor of the old Confederation is transfused into the members of the new Congress. This city has not caught the spirit, or rather the want of spirit, I am vexing myself to express to you. Their hall will cost £20,000 York money. They are preparing fireworks, and a splendid barge for the President, which last will cost £200 or £300.[3]

This State is snarling about elections. But Massachusetts distances all the world. How will it be decided there? Write me. How can you preserve such an obstinate silence? If you knew how fast I am obliged to write this nonsense, you would forgive me for making it such.

We lose £1,000 a day revenue. We lose credit, spirit, every thing. The public will forget the government before it is born. The resurrection of the infant will come before its birth. Happily, however, the federal interest is strong in Congress. The old Congress still continues to meet, and it seems to be doubtful whether the old government is dead, or the new one alive. God deliver us speedily from this puzzling state, or prepare my will, if it subsists much longer, for I am in a fever to think of it. Write me long letters often. Your brother Clark's letter will not be forgotten.

My dear friend, yours affectionately.

---

[3] *A Philadelphia newspaper of April 22d, 1789, informs its readers that "an elegant barge is now building in New York to waft the great Washington across the Hudson, to be rowed by ten sea captains, and one to act as cockswain,"* [S. AMES]

TO WILLIAM TUDOR

NEW YORK, APRIL 1, 1789

DEAR SIR,

I WILL NOT PRETEND that I had any right to expect a letter from you, till I had first written to you. Therefore I will not delay to establish my title to that pleasure. For I must take leave to assure you, that I shall feel very happy in your correspondence.

I have the satisfaction to acquaint you, that a quorum of thirty representatives attended this morning, who proceeded to choose Frederic Augustus Muhlenburg, of Pennsylvania, speaker, and John Beckley, of Virginia, clerk. Mr. Otis confines his pretensions to the clerkship of the Senate. The House adjourned till to-morrow, and will then proceed to organize, &c.

The Senate have eleven only; Mr. Reed of Delaware is expected daily, for the twelfth. It is not clear that they will form this week; but it is very confidently affirmed and expected; of course the business of counting the votes must be delayed, and their majesties elect, (their town meeting majesties, as Hughes calls them) must remain several weeks longer on a footing with their fellow citizens. However, before their arrival, we trust we shall be engaged in business, and be ready with some very necessary acts. The revenue and judiciary cannot be postponed. They are the law and the prophets of our government, and perhaps of every government. The judiciary will be an arduous business. Men of inquiry must turn their thoughts to it, and furnish all the hints which may occur to them.

A great majority of the members of both Houses are federal. A right and temperate administration of government is now the only desideratum. The feds have too much faith in its *good*, and the anti's too much forecast of its *ill* tendencies. Both will be baulked probably.

The Federal Hall is spacious and noble, and so nearly finished, that we shall sit in it to-morrow; we met in a smaller apartment to-day. The people of this city are very zealously federal, and have paid a great sum of money for the building. Their zeal will probably make brother King their representative for the state legislature. He is nominated. This state is on fire about governour—but the fuel does not seem so dry as it is in Massachusetts. I wish to be informed about the politics and events of the day.

FISHER AMES

TO GEORGE RICHARDS MINOT

NEW YORK, APRIL 4, 1789

DEAR SIR,

I PRESUME that you have heard that the House of Representatives met on Wednesday, the 1st, a quorum of thirty attending. They have met daily, and are still occupied in the little business of making arrangements. A committee is employed to form rules and orders. Slower progress will be made in this, by reason of the Senate not having yet a quorum to act upon any bill, in case the House should prepare one. Besides, I am inclined to believe, that there is in every popular assembly a strong resemblance of character—the same refining, quiddling scepticism. The House is composed of sober, solid, old-charter folks, as we often say. At least, I am sure that there are many such. They have been in government before, and they are not disposed to embarrass business, nor are they, for the most part, men of intrigue.

Yet, my friend, I foresee our General Court nicely. I think the debates upon questions of order will be frequent and animated. It may become necessary to consult the Aruspices, whether a man shall be called doorkeeper or sergeant-at-arms. I have given a reason why the delay arising from this source is not to be regretted, the Senate not having formed. Indeed, the little passions which occasion it will be speedily satiated or wearied, and the great business before us will soon make us sufficiently serious. This in confidence, my friend. However, though I am rather less awed and terrified at the sight of the members than I expected to be, I assure you I like them very well. There are few shining geniuses; there are many who have experience, the virtues of the heart, and the habits of business. It will be quite a republican assembly. It looks like one. Many who expected a Roman senate, when the doors shall be opened, will be disappointed. Admiration will lose its feast. In return for this breach of the rules of poetry, I presume the *antis* will laugh at their own fears. They will see that the aristocracy may be kept down some years longer. My dear friend, by these hasty hints I have tried to give my ideas of the character of the House. You will be better satisfied with it than with newspaper stuff. The Senate will be a very respectable body. Heaven knows when they will act. Report is (and has been so these three weeks,) that several senators are just at hand. Let me hear from you frequently. I am rather more happy in your friendship for being vain of it. Your letters will gratify my vanity and comfort my heart; your neglect would make it ache.

I am, dear sir, your friend and humble servant.

SUNDAY, 5TH APRIL

I am this moment informed that Mr. R. H. Lee is arrived, and so the Senate has a quorum.

TO SAMUEL HENSHAW

DEDHAM, MASS., APRIL 22, 1789

DEAR SIR,

YOUR OBLIGING LETTER requires some evidence of the gratitude it produced—I find you had not forgotten me—[O]ther friends have needed my constant teasing to keep alive the recollection of my existence—You thought of me without such a hint—I wish I could amuse you by any information from this place[.] Mr. Strong will enclose the newspapers in which you will find all that is worth knowing—The vice p. is here[.] Tomorrow the pres. will come. Nothing is wanting but spirit & [prudence?] in the administration of the gov't. to produce some of the good effects which are expected from [it.] However, they will come slowly—The antis are few & not violent in Congress. We are busy in contriving an act to get your money. I fear that by straining duties too high, we shall find that you have tied hard knots in the purse strings[.] We hear something of the murmurs of local and state prejudices–but the general wish seems to be to favor the agriculture trade & arts of the country by moderate duties on foreign ships and goods—Indeed, sir, the members are principally solid moderate men, who, without shining talents, have considerable experience and honest intentions[.] Dear Sir, write me again if you wd. gratify me highly, and be assured that I am with esteem.

Dear Sir
Your very humble servant

FISHER AMES

TO WILLIAM TUDOR

NEW YORK, APRIL 25, 1789

DEAR SIR,

I THANK YOU for your favour per mail, and I assure you that I shall be happy to procure that sort of gratification, from time to time, upon the terms of communicating any thing from this quarter, which may be worth your notice.

I cannot act the philosopher, with regard to the intemperate party spirit of our state. The power of the State Legislature extends to the greater part of the objects of government. This fiery zeal will not only disturb the tranquility, but endanger the rights of the citizens, and we shall feel the difference between good and bad government in a multitude of cases, in which the Congress cannot or will not interpose. The federal government is not an Hercules, and if it was, it is yet in the cradle, and might come off second best in a struggle with the serpent. The House of Representatives is composed of men of experience and good intentions, but we have no Foxes nor Burkes. They will be inclined to a temperate, guarded policy. In the present situation of America, and perhaps in almost every possible situation, *it will be necessary for the government to follow, rather than to controul the general sentiment. The dissemination of just sentiments is not very difficult.* The struggle to procure the adoption of the Constitution, has sufficiently disposed the most influential men to the belief and propagation of the opinions most favourable to government. If the imprudence of the government should not hurry them, by measures repugnant to these prepossessions, into the opposite system, I am in hopes that we shall think and act as a nation, and in proportion as state prejudices and preferences shall subside, the federal government will gain strength. For some time the latter will act a temporizing part, though I am not certain that it is ever the safer.—We are a little afraid to direct that all officers, *state* as well as federal, shall be bound by oath, &c. It is said that the states will make proper provision, and it will discover a jealousy of their good intentions, to direct them to do what the Constitution, which is already law, prescribes. We are voting duties with less circumspection. For the sake of a great revenue we impose high duties. An high profit to the smuggler will defeat their efficacy.

Sunday afternoon, 26.—The papers will inform you of all the nothings in regard to the arrival of the President and Vice President. The people were disposed to pay all possible respect to them. When I saw Washington I felt very strong emotions. I believe that no man *ever* had so fair a claim to veneration as he. Next Thursday he is to be received in form by the two Houses, and to take the oath in public. This will impede business a good deal till it shall be over. Fireworks are prepared, which I hope will have a better effect than the illumination. This was done suddenly, it having been countermanded. A violent rain at the time, and the lower windows and upper windows of four story houses being, for the most part, dark, these circumstances took off much of the brilliancy of the spectacle.

FISHER AMES

TO GEORGE RICHARDS MINOT

NEW YORK, MAY 3, 1789, SUNDAY

(Confidential.)

DEAR GEORGE,

I WOULD very cheerfully comply with the wishes expressed in your last, and pursue my sour commentary upon great folks and public bodies, but haste will not permit. I was present in the pew with the President, and must assure you that, after making all deductions for the delusion of one's fancy in regard to characters, I still think of him with more veneration than for any other person. Time has made havoc upon his face. That, and many other circumstances not to be reasoned about, conspire to keep up the awe which I brought with me. He addressed the two Houses in the Senate chamber; it was a very touching scene, and quite of the solemn kind. His aspect grave, almost to sadness; his modesty, actually shaking; his voice deep, a little tremulous, and so low as to call for close attention; added to the series of objects presented to the mind, and overwhelming it, produced emotions of the most affecting kind upon the members. I, Pilgarlic, sat entranced. It seemed to me an allegory in which virtue was personified, and addressing those whom she would make her votaries. Her power over the heart was never greater, and the illustration of her doctrine by her own example was never more perfect.

Inclosed, you have my speech, taken after the debate, while the ideas were so fresh as to make it a very just transcript of my argument. More was said, but what is said in the inclosed was actually delivered. A speech *made afterwards* would not amuse you. My friend, listen. Fenno published the speeches. *Inter nos*, I suppose Goodhue and Gerry wrote theirs, and gave to him. Mine is not flattered by the publication. Suppose it published in the Boston papers as the speech of an anonymous person, or as mine; and if it should be asked how it came to differ from Fenno's, would it do to say, that many other papers take the debates from shorthand writers? I submit it to your friendship to judge whether it will tend to create invidious observations against me, or be a prudent thing. Do you suppress it, or show it to Mr. William Smith at the club, as you please, for the Gazette will not very clearly evince my attention to the business.

Let me beg you to prevent any Centinel, or other, encomiums upon me. They lower a man very much.

I have talked with Thacher about your book.[4] We thought of a list of persons to present a book to, and proposed to ask your choice of twelve out of a larger number. Pray continue your letters, and be assured that I shall not esteem myself when I cease to be, with affection,

Your friend and very humble servant.

I made two speeches, the latter in reply to Madison, who is a man of sense, reading, address, and integrity, as 'tis allowed. Very much Frenchified in his politics. He speaks low, his person is little and ordinary. He speaks decently, as to manner, and no more. His language is very pure, perspicuous, and to the point. Pardon me, if I add, that I think him a little too much of a book politician, and too timid in his politics, for prudence and caution are opposites of timidity. He is not a little of a Virginian, and thinks that state the land of promise, but is afraid of their state politics, and of his popularity there, more than I think he should be. His manner is *something* like John Choate's.[5] He is our first man.

Suppose the list to be

New York—Governor Clinton, the Chancellor Livingston, Col. Hamilton, or Publius.

Jersey—Governor Livingston, Mr. Boudinot.

Pennsylvania—Tench Coxe, Speaker Muhlenburg.

Virginia—Madison, the late President of Congress, Cyrus Griffin.

Carolina—Judge Burke.

---

[4] *History of the Insurrection in Massachusetts.* [S. AMES]

[5] *John Choate, of Ipswich, a member of the Convention of 1788, at which the Federal Constitution was acceded to on the part of the State of Massachusetts.* [S. AMES]

TO [UNKNOWN]

———

NEW YORK, MAY 11, 1789, MONDAY MORNING

DEAR SIR,

I ENCLOSE a bill for the temporary collection of duties, which will not need any commentary of mine to present to your mind the nature and tendency of it. It has not been debated but we have many who think blindness in a temporary matter of no consequence. Some time past I wrote to Mr. Russell requesting his opinion in regard to the rate of duties. I have not received any communication from him, and I have been led to reflect upon the multitude of his engagements, and have felt some apprehension that my letter was thought intrusive, and not warranted by my acquaintance with him. I am not satisfied myself with having troubled him. But I will thank you sir, to converse with him, and to write me his and your opinion on the rate of duties, and whether five per cent *ad valorem* is too high to be punctually collected. It is not complained of. But may be found in practice injurious to the revenue. I would tread on safe ground and evince the moderation, wisdom, and system of government by asking what may be expected to be obtained. The duty on cordage is imposed but I have doubts of its policy. *That* on pickled fish imported is in the same predicament. These are small objects however. But if the duties are considered as immoderate, if they are productive of smuggling, every act of law enforcing the collection will produce hatred and disaffection. A little tendency to fermentation in the states would probably retard the accession of Rhode Island and North Carolina and perhaps prevent it altogether. It seems to me to be risking too much and for too little. It is staking power against cash.

I am obliged to write very hastily and must close. (At the moment they are talking in our house about titles. Nothing said *for* them, but much against. The Senate is in favor of calling the President His Highness the President and Protector of the Liberties of America, or nearly that. The Senate has not actually voted so much, but only non-concurred a vote of the house, which was that it is not proper to give any title. The house, I believe will adhere to their first vote.) The Judiciary system has not lately been talked about. But Mr. Strong tells me that the principles of the system are in some forwardness in the Committee of [the] Senate. The jurisdiction is to be narrowed, so as to avoid the burden of providing for the trial of causes of a small amount and of the ordinary kind. I trust that you have been informed of the nature of it, as I think he has sent it to the judges.

(I shall send you any information from this quarter in my power with great pleasure), and shall think my[self] honored by the continuance of your correspondence. Pray excuse the errors of haste.

I am, Sir, with great respect
Your most obedient and very humble servant

FISHER AMES

DEBATES ON THE RIGHT TO PETITION THE CONGRESS

More than once Ames defended on the floor of the House the propriety of giving a fair hearing to petitions from citizens (even when he disagrees with the petitioner's claims). The following speeches reveal his principles.

———

MAY 13, 1789

POWER OVER SLAVERY

Mr. Parker had ventured to introduce the subject after full deliberation, and did not like to withdraw it. Although the gentleman from Connecticut (Mr. Sherman) had said, that they ought not to be enumerated with goods, wares, and merchandise, he believed they were looked upon by the African traders in this light. He knew it was degrading the human species to annex that character to them; but he would rather do this than continue the actual evil of importing slaves a moment longer. He hoped Congress would do all that lay in their power to restore to human nature its inherent privileges, and, if possible, wipe off the stigma under which America labored. The inconsistency in our principles, with which we are justly charged, should be done away, that we may show, by our actions, the pure beneficence of the doctrine we hold out to the world in our Declaration of Independence.

Mr. Sherman thought the principles of the motion, and the principles of the bill, were inconsistent; the principle of the bill was to raise revenue, the principle of the motion to correct a moral evil.

.   .   .   .

Mr. AMES joined the gentleman last up; no one could suppose him favorable to slavery; he detested it from his soul; but he had some doubts whether imposing a duty on the importation would not have the appearance of countenancing the practice; it was certainly a subject of some delicacy, and no one appeared to be prepared for the discussion. He therefore hoped the motion would be withdrawn.

.   .   .   .

Mr. Madison.—I cannot concur with gentlemen who think the present an improper time or place to enter into a discussion of the proposed motion. If it is taken up in a separate view, we shall do the same thing at a greater expense of time. But gentlemen say that it is improper to connect the two objects, because they do not come within the title of the bill; but this objection may be obviated by accommodating the title to the contents. There may be some inconsistency in combining the ideas which gentlemen have expressed, that is, considering the human race as a species of property; but the evil does not arise from adopting the clause now proposed; it is from the importation to which it relates. Our object in enumerating persons on paper with merchandise, is to prevent the practice of actually treating them as such, by having them in future forming part of the cargoes of goods, wares, and merchandise to be imported into the United States. The motion is calculated to avoid the very evil intimated by the gentleman.

.   .   .   .

The dictates of humanity, the principles of the people, the national safety and happiness, and prudent policy, require it of us. The Constitution has particularly called our attention to it; and of all the articles contained in the bill before us, this is one of the last I should be willing to make a concession upon, so far as I am at liberty to go, according to the terms of the Constitution or principles of justice.

.   .   .   .

I conceive the Constitution, in this particular, was formed in order that the Government, whilst it was restrained from laying a total prohibition, might be able to give some testimony of the sense of America with respect to the African trade. We have liberty to impose a tax or duty upon the importation of such persons, as any of the States now existing shall think proper to admit; and this liberty was granted, I presume, upon two considerations: The first was, that until the time arrived when they might abolish the importation of slaves, they might have an opportunity of evidencing their sentiments on the policy and humanity of such a trade. The other was, that they might be taxed in due proportion with other articles imported;

.   .   .   .

If gentlemen are apprehensive of oppression from the weight

of the tax, let them make an estimate of its proportion, and they will find that it very little exceeds five per cent, ad valorem; so that they will gain very little by having them thrown into that mass of articles; whilst, by selecting them in the manner proposed, we shall fulfil the prevailing expectations of our fellow citizens, and perform our duty in executing the purposes of the Constitution. It is to be hoped, that by expressing a national disapprobation of this trade, we may destroy it, and save ourselves from reproaches, and our posterity the imbecility ever attendant on a country filled with slaves.

I do not wish to say any thing harsh to the hearing of gentlemen who entertain different sentiments from me, or different sentiments from those I represent; but if there is any one point in which it is clearly the policy of this nation, so far as we constitutionally can, to vary the practice obtaining under some of the state governments, it is this.

TUESDAY, NOVEMBER 8, 1791

JOHN TORREY

THE HOUSE resolved itself into a Committee of the Whole House on the Report of the Secretary of War on the petition of John Torrey, administrator of Major Joseph Torrey, deceased.

Mr. AMES objected to the motion for accepting the Report of the Secretary of War. He said, it must be apparent that he was placed by accident in a relation to the subject in debate, which he should not have adopted of choice. With very little knowledge of the parties and their connexions, and the interests that would be involved by the decision, he seemed to be considered as standing sponsor for the petitioner. He might justify this active support of the petition, by assigning motives which were common to other gentlemen;

but as they have continued silent, I will assign a reason for speaking, which is peculiar to myself. Nothing excites a person to a more fervid defence of his opinions, than the supposed discovery that they are misunderstood, and the force of the reasons on which he had formed them, unduly estimated.

Congress promised half-pay to the officers who should continue in service *to the end of the war*—This was afterwards made a commutation for half-pay. Major Torrey continued in service till September, 1783, when he died. The question is, did he continue in service to the end of the war? The provisional articles of peace were signed on the 30th November, 1782; but they were to remain without force till terms of peace should be agreed upon between Great Britain and France. This took place on the 30th January, 1783, and the ratifications were exchanged on the 3d February, 1783, at Paris. The provisional treaty between Great Britain and America was then *a treaty of peace*, and according to the words of that treaty was *concluded*. Accordingly, on the 11th April, 1783, Congress by a proclamation made known those facts, and the stipulations made, in regard to the periods when hostilities should cease, by the contracting parties to the treaty. Hostilities did cease, and before the end of April, 1783, all America was in perfect peace. The late hostile nations shook hands, our vessels sailed in safety, and by sea and land reconciliation succeeded to hostility.

But did all this put an end to the war? The children in the street would answer this question: They would say, it is peace when it is not war. Of all facts, the most notorious seems to be the state of war; and it is the fact that the war was at an end, (and not any after resolve of Congress) that the commutation of Major Torrey was made to hinge upon. When the meaning of a bargain is disputed, it is usual to search out the intention of the contracting parties when it was made. Supposing, instead of interpreting a resolve of

Congress, any twelve of this body had to try a case between two private persons; suppose that a man had given his note of hand for a sum to be paid at the *end of the war*. Would twelve of this House, or would any jury in the country say that the war continued longer than hostilities? In private life, a man would think it touched his character to refuse paying his note in such case. Surely a Government ought to perform its promise with as much delicacy and exactness. Congress did not promise the half-pay, and afterward the commutation on the condition that a man should serve till they should think proper to say the war was at an end. He depended on the stubborn *fact* that it did end, which no resolution of Congress could change; and not on the refining opinion when the officers might safely be discharged—for that we see might be differently formed, according to the different views of policy and safety at the time. An officer having this promise of Congress, has a right to this commutation on the cessation of hostilities, in pursuance of the treaty. If this is disputed, the meaning of the words *"the end of the war,"* should be decided as it was understood at the time of the promise. Will any one believe that the 3d November, 1783, was the term, after the state of war and all the treaties which put an end to it, had been long passed? If any doubt still remains, writers on the law of nations should be consulted. For the officer may justly claim an execution of the promise according to law; that is the umpire between Government and the people. On appealing to the law of nations, we find that war is defined to be "the state in which a nation prosecutes its right by force." "Peace is opposed to the state of war—an accommodation is proposed and conditions agreed on, and thus peace puts an end to war." "When the Powers at war agree to lay down their arms, the agreement is the treaty of peace." "The general and necessary effects of peace, are the reconciliation of enemies and the cessation of hostilities; it restores the two nations to their natural state." Would any jury in this country say, that the matter of fact and the principles of law were not in favor of the petition? Apply these maxims of law to the case. The provisional articles of November, 1782, were of themselves nothing, it is true, but they were to constitute the treaty of peace, whenever Great Britain and France had agreed on the terms of peace. As these two Powers did agree on the 30th January, and ratified the terms on the 3d February, 1783, *then* the provisional articles, to use the very words of the preamble, did *constitute the treaty of peace;* it was *then* a *concluded* thing; and peace in fact took place in the several parts of the world on the appointed days.

It has been said, that the preliminaries were no more than a suspension of arms—that the state of war still continued, until a *definitive* treaty. To this it is answered, that preliminaries bind the national faith, if violated, the perjured faithless nation would kindle a new war. By the law of nations there is not such a distinction as that which is alleged, between preliminary and definitive treaties. Let the authorities for such a distinction be produced by those who make it. But they do not exist—a truce does not put an end to a war—a truce is, however, a suspension of war for a specified term. At the end of this term, the war begins again, of course, without any fresh declaration. But a suspension of hostilities for an indefinite period, is not a truce, but a peace; especially if it is added, that it is agreed upon by the belligerent nations in consequence of a settlement of their disputes, and if it happens in fact that the war is not revived. Those who make so much of a definitive treaty, and so light of preliminaries, should consider that, on their own system, the former is a kind of defeasance which annuls the latter. But when the definitive treaty is signed, the preliminaries, which before were liable to be annulled, now become of force, and the treaty, now become indefeasible, takes its date from the preliminaries. Though this mode of reasoning has not much weight on my mind, it ought to have some with those who have set up the distinction which it is adduced to overthrow.

These are the reasons on which I have formed my opinion that the war ended in fact in April, 1783, when hostilities ceased by mutual agreement of the Powers at war. My opinion is supported by authority much more reputable than any I can give to it. The law courts in this country have decided it judicially; cases of captured vessels, and the question of interest on British debts, have produced decisions in every state of the Union, unless I am misinformed, that the war ended in March or April, 1783. The courts in England, and in every country where the war spread, on trials of property, have made similar decisions. Major Torrey died in September, 1783; shall this body decide against the settled rule of all the law courts?

It remains to remove some objections:

It is alleged, that Congress have by various resolves fixed the period of the war, and have declared that the 3d November, 1783, is the term. If they had declared that it should be computed from the end of the world, it would not alter the truth of the fact. *After* declarations ought not to be received to change their own promises. But a declaration, or a dozen of them, made for another purpose, and not to declare the meaning of the contract, cannot on any principle be received to interpret it. It is not necessary, however, to contend against those resolves of Congress. They are irreconcilable with the former engagement to Major Torrey. In undertaking to reconcile them. I feel that I impose a task on myself, which is made heavy by the prepossessions of many of my friends; I believe the minds of gentlemen are perfectly fair, and well-disposed to doing the petitioner justice. But I hope I shall not be thought to intend any offence, when I remark that certain ideas, such as that this claim is cut off by resolves of Congress, and that on allowing it, confusion would take place in the business of the public offices, were started with the discussion, and they have remained so woven into the texture of the debate, that I think it hard to unravel them. It was soon manifest that there was a general disposition to vote against the petition. This opportunity for debate seems to have been accorded as of grace, rather than as a means of removing any existing doubts of their own. Having adopted these opinions, this is rather a form of refusal than a mode of inquiring; and it seems to have been chosen with every circumstance of decency, and with all possible steadfastness of purpose. Yet I will proceed to state, that the point whether the war was at end when hostilities ended in April, 1783, being already considered fully, we are to look for other reasons than such as relate to the commutation, to explain the resolves of Congress which continued the service of the officers beyond the end of the war, and as late as November, 1783. A mistake seems to have crept in here. It seems to be supposed that the officers were engaged to serve to the end of the war, just long enough to secure their commutation. But the commutation depended on one thing—the term of their service on another. The former was their right at the end of the war; but they were to remain in service till dismissed, unless they should think fit sooner to resign. They held their commissions during the pleasure of Congress. Though when the war ended they had a right to the commutation, they had no right to say their service was at an end. They did not choose to resign: Congress, for wise reasons, did not choose to dismiss them. A foreign army was still in New York. They were sent home on furlough, but drawing pay, and liable to be called into the field. Congress, in their resolves, did not say that it was not peace, but in effect that it was unsafe to disarm. Gentlemen are not well agreed among themselves as to the end of the war. Some fix it at the definitive treaty of September 3, 1783; others at November 3. Their conclusions agree as illy with their principles; for if the definitive treaty put an end to the war,

579

how can the same gentlemen say that the war was kept alive, on the journals of Congress, till November, 1783? Here, then, were Peace and War subsisting quietly together during two months.

The fears of making confusion by opening a door to many applications, seem to be groundless. A man must have died between the end of hostilities and November, 1783, to place a claim on the like footing. The living have had their commutations; they cannot come: and no other officer died in that period, as far as I can learn. I have inquired and cannot find at the office of the Secretary of War any precedent which militates with this claim, nor any reason to suppose that any similar one will be offered. The case is a new one; it stands alone, and probably ever will, and it must be decided on its own merits. Believing the fact to be indisputable that Major Torrey served to the end of the war, confiding in the principles of the law of nations, and the settled decisions of the Judicial Courts, I have endeavored to explain my ideas with perspicuity, and to impress them with force. I have said more than questions touching an individual will often be found to merit; but when public principles are construed to the prejudice of private rights, the debate cannot be treated too seriously.

NOVEMBER 28, 1792

WARNER MIFFLIN'S PETITION

Mr. Steele called the attention of the House to the memorial and representation of Warner Mifflin on the subject of Negro slavery. He had hoped the House would have heard no more of it; but, to his surprise, he found the subject was started anew, and had been introduced by a fanatic, who, not content with keeping his own conscience, undertook to become the keeper of the consciences of other men. Gentlemen in the northern states do not realize the mischievous consequences which have already resulted from measures of this kind, and if a stop were not put to such proceedings, the southern states would be compelled to apply to the general government for their interference.

Mr. AMES rose to explain his motives in presenting the petition. He said it was his opinion, which he had expressed to the House long ago, that this government could not, with propriety, take any steps in the matter referred to in this petition; but, on the general principle, that every citizen has a right to petition the Legislature, and to apply to any member to present his request to the House, he had handed it in. The petitioner is a citizen of Delaware; and had the member from that state been in the House, he should not have thought himself obliged to have introduced it; but that gentleman being absent, the petitioner had a right to apply to a member from any other state. He had no idea of supporting the prayer of the petition, his mind having been long made up on the subject. He considered it as totally inexpedient to interfere with the subject, and had uniformly opposed the applications made at a former session of Congress.

TO GEORGE RICHARDS MINOT

NEW YORK, MAY 14, 1789, THURSDAY EVENING

DEAR FRIEND,

I HAVE just left a letter for you in the post-office, where I received yours, and saw Mr. Geyer, Junior, who is going to Boston, by way of Providence. I will not hesitate to write again, because my letter, per post, will be found very empty, and will not reach you so soon as this. It is not easy to write the transactions of the House, because I forget the topics which do not reach you by the newspaper. A committee of both Houses had reported that it is not proper to address the President by any other title than that in the Constitution. The House agreed to the report, without debate. But the Senate rejected it, and notified the House that they had nonconcurred. The House was soon in a ferment. The antispeakers edified all aristocratic hearts by their zeal against titles. They were not warranted by the Constitution; repugnant to republican principles; dangerous, vain, ridiculous, arrogant, and damnable. Not a soul said a word *for* titles. But the zeal of these folks could not have risen higher in case of contradiction. Whether the arguments were addressed to the galleries, or intended to hurry the House to a resolve censuring the Senate, so as to set the two Houses at odds, and to nettle the Senate to bestow a title in *their* address, is not clear. The latter was supposed, and a great majority agreed to appoint a committee of conference. The business will end here. Prudence will restrain the Senate from doing any thing at present, and they will call him President, &c., simply.

Another molasses battle has been fought. Like modern victories, it was incomplete, but we got off one cent. Two or three of our side happened to be out when the last and deciding vote passed, otherwise we should have reduced it to four cents, the *ne plus ultra*. A very important vote passed to-day, allowing ten per cent. discount on the duties of goods in American bottoms, which will be half a cent on molasses. The Senate will, I trust, revise our doings with a temperate spirit. The Senate is a very respectable body. An excise is a topic on which my zeal is beginning to kindle. I see, or think I see, the most evident necessity for drawing from that resource some part of the revenues. The southern people dread it, and say that the excise is an odious, unpopular tax, and will fall unequally on them. They are afraid for their

582

whiskey. Madison will oppose this, and it will be a work of labor and some responsibility. But I dread the consequence of leaving it untouched, and at the mercy of the state governments, who can, by that measure, defeat the operation of our protecting duties, and excise our manufactures at their markets. Other ill effects may, and many will inevitably, flow from the neglect of this resource.

Tell Dexter that five cents per quintal is allowed on the export of fish. Salted provisions in a proper degree, I forget what. I think the same per barrel.

Your, I mean our, Wednesday night club is very censorious, and I suppose my hypercriticism on their criticism will not be spared. I thank Mr. Eliot and Mr. Minot for their loyalty and taste. The sentences are rather long, and not so simply constructed as Blair would have them, but may not the meaning be readily known? Is not a very considerable degree of beauty and elegance consistent with a small degree of obscurity? I admire the sentiments. The writer seems to have *thought* and *felt* when he wrote. Addresses are commonly made by turning a crank of Swift's essay-mill. This is the work of the head and the heart, and, I will maintain, in spite of the club, is evidence of the superior excellence of both. Had the club attended the delivery of it, I think their censure would have been spared.[6] My compliments to them, and let them know that I am ready to obey their instructions, like a good man and true.

Your late kind attentions have led me to consider whether my esteem and value for your friendship can be heightened. I am, dear George, yours affectionately.

Will you desire Adams and Nourse[7] to send me the Excise Acts of Massachusetts?

---

[6] *He is supposed to refer to Washington's Inaugural Address.* [S. AMES]

[7] *Printers of the Independent Chronicle* [S. AMES]

DEBATES ON IMPOSTS AND PROVISIONS
FOR THE PUBLIC CREDIT

Money bills were the most important measures raised for discussion in the House from first to last. Ames played a major role in all of them. On April 8, 1789, James Madison introduced into the House of Representatives, in Committee of the Whole, a plan for raising revenue through tariff and tonnage duties. According to the tariff bill, most imported goods, would be taxed at a flat rate ad valorem, *while certain enumerated goods which were capable of bearing higher duties would be taxed at various rates.*

When Madison proposed a duty of eight cents per gallon on molasses—a tax of about fifty per cent of its values—Ames quickly objected. Since molasses was imported principally in Massachusetts, the importance of the subject was acutely felt by that state's representatives. In his first speech in Congress, on April 14, he helped to persuade the committee to reduce the tax to six cents. He stressed both the importance of the molasses trade to the fishing, manufacturing, and trading interests of his state, and the fact that molasses was a staple in the diet of his constituents. As such, he believed that to tax it at a rate that was generally reserved for luxury items was not proper. On May 9, the duty on molasses was again the subject of debate. Ames rose twice on that day, and yet again on May 11, to plead for moderate duties. His arguments, along with those of other New England representatives, induced the House to lower the duty to five cents. The duty was eventually lowered to two and one half cents by the Senate, where it remained when the bill became law on July 4.

Just before the House sent the tariff bill up to the Senate, Madison made a motion to amend it by adding a clause for limiting its duration. Ames expressed his doubts as to the propriety of the motion. After hearing arguments on both sides of the question, he delivered a speech on May 15, in which he argued that the government must do everything in its power to provide permanent funds for paying off the national debt. Only then, he thought, would the public credit be established on the most secure foundation possible.

Mr. AMES considered this as a very important question, and in order that his own mind might be fully enlightened, he had listened with the most unwearied attention to the arguments urged on both sides; but he was far from being satisfied that the motion was necessary or proper for the House to adopt. The principal reason offered in its support was, that the revenue is not specially appropriated; but he could not perceive that this furnished a reason why the clause should be introduced; either gentlemen are afraid that the Senate will not agree to the appropriation, or they will agree. If they will agree, there is no reason for distrust; if they will not agree with the House, then we ought not to trust them with this bill, until we bring forward a clause for the purpose of appropriating the fund it is intended to raise. Gentlemen tell us the act is imperfect, and therefore ought to be limited; if this be the case, it may be a good reason for recommitting the bill, but can be none for adopting the clause. If we have not taken up time enough in adjusting and considering the several parts of this law, let it be readjusted and reconsidered in a committee of the whole, until gentlemen are satisfied as to its perfection.

Gentlemen tell us they are willing to make the revenue commensurate with the debt. If they do this, all the inconveniences resulting from the imperfection of the system will be entailed upon us for a number of years. Other gentlemen mention a year or two for its limitation. Can the House listen seriously to such a proposition? If we were to tell our creditors that we are making provision for them for one year, would it tend to inspire them with confidence in our wisdom or justice? Would our foreign creditors believe we were scrupulously fulfilling our engagements with them? No: nothing less than a fixed, permanent system, can beget confidence or give security. An illusory system of one or two years duration would engender distrust; its very visage would make the public suspect deception. If we do not mean to deceive, why not make the provision commensurate to the occasion? His idea of a temporary act was *pro hac vice*, by way of experiment; but he thought the House could not make the experiment with this bill, because the public credit would not admit it. If this act be made for one year, will it not be a considerable expense to the public by going over all the ground again, which had taken the house such a length of time to discuss?

Gentlemen have insisted upon the necessity of keeping the purse-strings in their hands. What do they mean by this? What power have the House over the money that comes into the treasury? Are they at liberty to apply it to their own use? Do not Congress declare the revenue to be the property of the public creditors, when they appropriate it to their use? Shall we say the people, then, keep the purse-strings in their hands? For what honest purpose shall they keep them? Why shall we, the House of Representatives, detain the money of foreigners? Does it not seem to carry fraud on the face of it? One gentleman says that he is unwilling to trust a future Senate; but if it shall be of equal integrity with the present, why should he hesitate? The state will be equally careful of obtaining a good representation, for their own sakes. But suppose the reverse should happen, do we not act wisely in making a provision for the security of our honor and the public welfare, which cannot be destroyed by one misguided branch of the Legislature? Now, suppose this law to expire, and the Senate should be unwilling to provide for the objects

we have in contemplation, will this not prevent the representatives of the people from carrying their wishes into
execution? But if the Senate be willing to co-operate with
the House, for what honest reason do we endeavor to retain
this power? Besides, if the act is imperfect, will it not be
easier to correct the imperfect part than to frame a new
system? Surely gentlemen are under a great mistake when
they suspect danger to arise from the revenue continuing to
flow into the public treasury. Have not the House a complete
command over it? No money can be drawn out but by
appropriations by law. The President cannot touch it. Does
it increase the power of the Senate? The Senate have no
command over it, unless authorized by law. Can the House
of Representatives make any use of it? They cannot get a
farthing, because the consent of the Senate is required to
enable them to draw for it.

What has been the conduct of Great Britain, in relation
to her funds? What has carried the credit of that kingdom to
a superior eminence, but the attention she has paid to public
credit? He considered these advantages as having made that
nation rich and powerful. He believed a like conduct on our
part would produce the same consequences, because our
Government is of such a nature as to give the public creditors
the greatest security they could wish. If the revenue is
appropriated, and the law for collecting it is without any
limitation, the funds cannot be taken away without a positive
act of injustice, to which both Houses of the Legislature must
assent by a majority of two-thirds, or three independent
parties must unite. It was therefore three to one in favor of
the public creditor, that the funds appropriated to his use
would not be annihilated. Under these circumstances, Government might more safely be trusted. This, he observed,
was not the case under despotic princes; their will alone
could tear away the security of the subject. Under a pure

democracy, the case was almost as bad; no confidence could be placed, because the caprice and whim of one body could dictate a change.

Now an act that expires at a limited period revives the topics of partial politics and opposing interests, which involves expense; besides, it affords less confidence, because a variety of circumstances may occur to prevent a continuation of the necessary provision to establish the foundation of credit. It may be prevented by the mere disagreement of the two Houses. This uncertain situation of the public credit will prevent the government from re-loaning their foreign and domestic debt, which might otherwise be done to very great advantage at a reduced interest. Viewing the subject in all these points of light, he could not help being opposed to the motion.

.   .   .   .

Mr. AMES could not bear to lie under the imputation of inconsistency, with which he was charged, inasmuch as he contended against the limitation of a bill he had opposed as oppressive in some of its parts. He believed the amendment now offered was new to almost every gentleman. For his part, he had always supposed it was intended as a permanent system. He remembered many gentlemen made use of this expression, through the various debates which had taken place in the several stages of the bill. He had understood it in this light, and had therefore combated, with some degree of energy, such parts as appeared to him impolitic or unjust. He imagined the gentlemen on both sides had labored to make the bill as perfect as possible, with a view of making an equitable provision for the public exigencies, which should affect all parts of the Union with the greatest degree of impartiality.

.   .   .   .

Mr. AMES.—I have not had the advantage of hearing all the arguments in support of the eight cents proposed; but those I have heard I am not satisfied with. The principles on which this tax is founded, I understand to be this: that it is an article of luxury, and of pretty general consumption, so that the duty is expected to fall equally upon all; but that it will not operate in this manner, I think is easily demonstrable. Can a duty of fifty per cent. ad valorem, paid, as it were, in an exclusive manner, by the State of Massachusetts, be equal? No, sir. But taking it as a part of the general system, can it be equal unless a proportionable duty, equal to fifty per cent. is laid upon articles consumed in other parts of the Union? No, sir; and is it in the contemplation of gentlemen to lay duties so high as to produce this equality? I trust it is not; because such duties could never be collected. Is not, therefore, eight cents disproportioned to the rates fixed, or intended to be imposed on other articles? I think it is; and, if to these considerations we add what has been said before, relative to its being a raw material important to a considerable manufacture, we cannot hesitate to reject it.

The people will indubitably continue to use ardent spirits, until the slow operation of the law shall produce other habits; and while they continue to use them, it is better for this country that they use the kind which is wished to be indirectly taxed. It must be better, because it is manufactured within ourselves, and gives useful employment to a considerable number of our fellow citizens. It must be better because the goods which we export for the raw materials, are drugs upon our hands. Certainly the trade is mutually beneficial to the parties concerned; but it is so in a greater degree to us than to them. We exchange for molasses, those fish that it is impossible to dispose of any where else; we have no market within our reach, but the islands from whence we get molasses in return, which again we manufacture into rum. These circumstances form a material link in our chain of navigation, and upon our success in navigation the most important interests of the United States depend. It is scarcely possible to maintain our fisheries with advantage, if the commerce for summer fish is injured, which I conceive it would be very materially, if a high duty is imposed upon this article; nay it would carry devastation throughout all the New England states, it would ultimately affect all throughout the Union. Will gentlemen, who declare themselves the friends of manufactures, support the opinion, that a raw material ought to be saddled with an excessive duty, that the imposition should be at a higher rate than what is laid upon manufactured articles; at a time too when the price is such that the home manufacture cannot support a successful competition with the other, even in our own markets? No, gentlemen will not be so inconsistent: they know and advocate the policy of supporting the manufactures of our country, by giving them such advantages as are consistent with the general good.

I shall proceed to show the importance of the present subject, in another point of light. The taking of fish on the banks is a very momentous concern, it forms a nursery for seamen, and this will be the source from which we are to derive maritime importance. It is the policy of some nations to drive us from this prolific source of wealth and strength; but what their detestable efforts have in vain endeavored to do, you will accomplish by a high duty on this article. Our situation with respect to the fishing banks, and our vicinity to the West India islands, are natural advantages, which all the machinations of jealousy cannot prevent us the enjoyment of. The habits of our fishermen are well calculated to improve these advantages to perfection, and no nation can carry on the business at so small an expense; it is these circumstances that render our fish cheap while this cheapness insures us a sale, and enables us to be successful competitors in every port that will receive us. Our best fish will find its way to the best markets, while the slaves in the West Indies will consume the refuse. If we can exchange that part, therefore, which would be otherwise thrown away, it is so much clear gain to the community. Hence, this country by increasing the demand of our fish increases the navigation; gentlemen will therefore be cautious how they adopt a measure that affects, or only seems to affect, one of the most important interests of the United States.

However gentlemen may think the use of this article dangerous to the health and morals of our fellow citizens—I would also beg them to consider, that it is no more so than every other kind of spirituous liquors; that it will grow into an article for exportation; and although I admit we could export it even encumbered with the duty proposed, yet by it we run the risk of having the manufacture totally ruined, for it can hardly now stand a competition at home with the West India rum, much less can it do so abroad. If the manufacturers of country rum are to be devoted to certain ruin, to mend the morals of others, let them be admonished that they prepare themselves for the event: but in the way we are about to take, destruction comes on a sudden, they have not time to seek refuge in any other employment whatsoever. If their situation will not operate to restrain the hand of iron policy, consider how immediately they are connected with the most essential interests of the union, and then let me ask if it is wise, if it is reconcilable to national prudence, to take measures subversive of your very existence? For I do contend, that the very existence of the eastern states depends upon the encouragement of their navigation and fishery, which receive a deadly wound by an excessive impost on the article before us.

I would concur in any measure calculated to exterminate the poison covered under the form of ardent spirits, from our country; but it should be without violence. I approve as much as any gentleman the introduction of malt liquors, believing them not so pernicious as the one in common use; but before we restrain ourselves to the use of them, we ought to be certain that we have malt and hops, as well as brew-houses for the manufacture. Now I deny that we have these in sufficient abundance to the eastward; but if we had, they are not taxed. Then why should the poor of Massachusetts be taxed for the beverage they use of spruce, molasses, and water—it surely is unreasonable. I hope gentlemen will not adopt the motion for eight cents until they are furnished with some better evidence of its propriety and policy than any that has yet been given, or as I suspect that can be given.

APRIL 16, 1789

ON MOTION of Mr. AMES, barley was taxed six cents, and lime one hundred cents. He just stated that these articles were imported in considerable quantities from a neighboring state that had not yet adopted the constitution; and, perhaps, said he, our political situation is such as to make some regulation on this head necessary.

. . . .

Mr. AMES thought this a useful and accommodating manufacture, which yielded a clear gain of all it sold for, but the cost of the material; the labor employed in it would be thrown away, probably, in many instances. It could not be said that it required a large capital, or extraordinary abilities, to acquire a knowledge of the art. It has grown up, with little encouragement, to an astonishing degree of perfection; it has become usual for the country people in this State to erect small forges in their chimney corners, and in winter, and on evenings when little other work could be done, great quantities of nails were made even by children; perhaps enough might be manufactured in this way to supply the continent. These people take the rod iron of the merchant, and return him nails; in consequence of this easy mode of barter, the manufacture is prodigiously great. But these advantages are not exclusively in the hands of the people of Massachusetts;

the business can be prosecuted in a similar manner in every State exerting equal industry. He hoped the article would remain in the bill.

APRIL 28, 1789

Mr. AMES.—I appeal, Mr. SPEAKER, with confidence, to the justice of this House, though I am far from being convinced that any liberality has been shown in fixing the duty on molasses; but I am persuaded that Congress will adopt no measures but those they can justify on principle to their constituents.

I conceive, sir, that the present Constitution was dictated by commercial necessity more than any other cause. The want of an efficient government to secure the manufacturing interests, and to advance our commerce, was long seen by men of judgment, and pointed out by patriots solicitous to promote our general welfare. If the duty which we contend against is found to defeat these objects, I am convinced the representatives of the people will give it up. I trust that gentlemen are well satisfied, that the support of our agriculture, manufactures, navigation, and fisheries, are objects of very great moment. When gentlemen contemplate the fishery, they admit its importance, and the necessity we are under of encouraging and protecting it, especially if they consider its declining situation; that it is excluded from those advantages which it formerly obtained in British ports, and participates but in a small degree of the benefits arising from our European allies, whose markets are visited under severe restrictions; yet, with all these discouragements, it maintains an extent which entitles it to the fostering care of Government. There are taken upon an average, 400,000 quintals of fish;

in this branch of business, as was stated by my colleague, there are employed 24,000 tons of shipping in the transportation of the fish to market, and, in the returns of molasses, near an equal tonnage is employed. The building of these vessels furnishes no inconsiderable employment to another important interest; the vessels, it is true, are but small, yet, after every deduction on this account, the concern will be found interesting to the public welfare. If it is true, and I believe it is, that agriculture and commerce are mutually dependent upon each other, and there is a probability that the additional burthen we have imposed will injure the latter, gentlemen ought to be cautious how they persist. If they even doubt of its effects being hurtful, they ought not to vote for its continuance; now, I think I can raise such doubts in gentlemen's minds, and dare commit myself to their candor for the consequences. Notwithstanding gentlemen have expressed a uniform desire to encourage manufactures, (and I have been with them in accomplishing this object,) they now desert their principles. When it has been contended that the duty ought to be low, inasmuch as molasses is a raw material, it has been replied, that the manufacture is pernicious. It has been said, that promoting our own distillation will exclude foreign rum, and consequently affect the revenue; but does not the same argument apply to every article of domestic manufacture? Has it not all along been contended, that it is proper in the general government to nurture those interests which have had the particular regard of the individual states, upon the principle that the state legislatures knew feelingly what were the best means to advance their interest? Has not the position been fully established, that promoting the interests of particular states increases the general welfare? After this, can gentlemen tell us we are advocating a local policy? That we are sacrificing the interest of 3,000,000 people to the establishment of a few New England distilleries? For my part, I ground my opinion upon national principles;

and from these I conclude, that molasses ought not to be taxed, or taxed but very lightly.

The gentleman from Virginia fears the loss of revenue from the success of this manufacture. To quiet his apprehensions, it will be only necessary for me to remind him of what he ingeniously urged a few days ago on this point, in order to obtain a discrimination in favor of the brandy of France. He told us, that, although the State of Virginia had imposed no duty on brandy, but a heavy one on West India rum, that under this encouragement there were not more than 10,000 gallons of brandy imported, while there were 600,000 gallons of rum; inferring from this fact, that there was no probable ground for suspecting the consumption to change from the one to the other article. If no danger is to be apprehended from brandy, much less can New England rum stand a competition with Jamaica spirit; the force of habit will not be more easily overcome in this case than the other. Besides, it is well known that a great proportion of the people will not drink it at all; it is a kind of genteel thing to affect disgust and loathing at the very name, much less will they suffer the despised liquor to pollute their mouths. So far are we from having ground to dread the effect of a competition on this side, that the contrary may be justly apprehended. The custom and fashion of the times countenance the consumption of West India rum. I consider it good policy to avail ourselves of this means to procure a revenue; but I treat as idle the visionary notion of reforming the morals of the people by a duty on molasses. We are not to consider ourselves, while here, as at church or school, to listen to the harangues of speculative piety; we are to talk of the political interests committed to our charge. When we take up the subject of morality, let our system look towards that object, and not confound itself with revenue and protection of manufactures. If gentlemen conceive that a law will direct the taste of the people from spirituous to malt liquors, they must have more romantic notions of legislative influence than experience justifies.

When it was asked, what is the occasion of a high duty? It was answered, that it is necessary in order to come at the proper tax on rum; but I insist, that there is no such necessity while an excise is within our reach, and it is in this mode only that you can obtain any considerable revenue. The gentleman from Virginia has said, that the manufacture of country rum is in no kind of danger of destruction from the duty on molasses. He has stated to the House the quantity made before the revolution, and goes on to argue, that as West India rum paid no duty, and molasses paid some, if the manufacture thrived under these disadvantages, why should it not continue to support itself in future? I believe this matter easy to be accounted for, though I fear it will not be in my power to make a proselyte on the occasion. I should be vain of such success, and therefore I shall proceed. There were many very considerable markets for New England rum cut off entirely by the revolution; even those that remain we have to encounter with rivals, who successfully contend for a preference. Previous to the late war, we had a market in Nova Scotia, Newfoundland, and Canada, all the Southern colonies, Europe, and Africa. We are now obstructed from going to many of those, to Quebec, and Newfoundland; and our trade gains no ground in others to make up the difference. Consider the state of the fisheries. At that time we possessed them unrivalled; it was the policy of Britain to favor our efforts; believing that our success tended to increase her maritime strength, she dealt out to us an annual bounty equal to £20,000 sterling, for the fish we took. All her ports were open to us; we could carry it to what market we pleased, and obtain molasses at a low price for the distilleries. But the present state of the business bears no comparison with its former situation; the trade is confined to a less channel, in which, instead of bounties, we meet with restrictions. Our fish pay a duty of twelve dollars a quintal, which is given by government as a premium in favor of their own fisheries. This imposition amounts to more than the value of the article; yet, even under all these discouragements, there are but six ports in the West Indies that we can go to: St. Lucia, three in Hispaniola, one in Guadaloupe, and one in Martinico. This being the case, the duties are rigidly exacted of us, and we have no other means of vending it but by the exchange of molasses. Nor is this the end of the evil; I fear it is seriously to be apprehended that we may shortly be deprived of this market also. The merchants of L'Orient have represented to the King, that it would be for the interest of their colonies to distil the molasses in the islands. Upon the strength of this idea, distil-houses are erected there, and bid fair to rival us in the business of supplying not only Europe and Africa, but even our own country. Now, from this view of the ground on which we stand, will gentlemen say, we can maintain and defend ourselves as well as we did before the war? If we even had the same advantages in vending the rum, the business would not be equally profitable, as the price of molasses has increased, and our fish has fallen. In short, unless some extraordinary measures are taken to support our fisheries, I do not see what is to prevent their inevitable ruin. It is a fact, that near one-third of our fishermen are taken from their profession—not for want of skill and abilities in the art, for here they take the rank of every nation on earth—but from the local, chilling policy of foreign nations, who shut us out from the avenues to our market. If, instead of protection from the Government, we extend to them oppression, I shudder for the consequences. But I will not enlarge on this head, trusting that gentlemen are convinced of the importance of the interest, and do not mean to destroy it.

Mr. SPEAKER, we are not to consider molasses in the same light as if it was in the form of rum. We are not to tax a necessary of life in the same manner as we do a pernicious luxury. I am sensible an attempt to draw a critical line of distinction in this case, between what is necessary and what is a luxury, will be attended with some difficulty; but I conceive the distinction sufficient for our present purpose, if it prove molasses to be necessary for the subsistence of the people. No decent family can do without something by way of sweetening; whether this arises from custom, or necessity of nature, is not worth the inquiry; if it is admitted to be a requisite for the support of life, a tax on it will be the same as a tax on bread; it is repugnant to the first principles of policy to lay taxes of this nature in America. What is it that entitles the United States to take rank of all the nations of Europe, but because it is the best country for the poor to live in? If we go on taxing such articles as salt and molasses, these advantages will not long continue to be ours. It may be said, that sugar is also a necessary of life—true; but molasses, inasmuch as it is cheaper, can be more easily obtained, and enters more into the consumption, at least of the poor. They apply it to various uses; it is a substitute for malt, in making beer; and shall it be said that the general government descends to small beer for its revenue, while strong beer remains duty free? Why shall this difference be made between the common drink of one part of the continent and the other, unless it be with a view to drive the people to drinking simple water? The gentleman from Virginia contends, that the consumers of eight pounds of sugar pay more than those who use eight pounds of molasses; this may be true, but from the variety of ways in which molasses is used, eight pounds is sooner consumed than six or four pounds of sugar, which makes up the difference. But do gentlemen mean that the poorest and weakest part of the community shall pay as much for what they use as the richer classes? Is this the reward of their toil and industry?

It has been stated as a fact by my colleague, (Mr.

GOODHUE,) that Massachusetts will pay more by the impost on molasses than Pennsylvania will on both rum and sugar. The population and strength of these two states are nearly equal; then why should this disproportion be contended for? Is it supposed that Massachusetts will not contribute her proportion on other articles? This, on examination, will be found not to be the case. Gentlemen say the state that exports least, imports least; but, does it not follow, that this state pays according to her ability to pay? If the products of Massachusetts are neither so rich or valuable as those of the southern states, ought she to pay the impost in the same proportion?

The question is plainly reducible to this: shall we tax a necessary of life in the same proportion as a luxury? Gentlemen will not contend for either the justice or policy of such a measure; but they say the necessity of the case obliges them; they cannot come at the luxury but through the raw material. They say they cannot lay an excise. I ask why not? People may justly think it burthensome to raise all our supplies from impost. Much can be obtained from this source, to be sure, by touching every thing; but I would recommend touching such things as are essential to subsistence lightly, and bring in the excise as a means of obtaining the deficiency; it will be the more certain way of making country rum contribute its proportion. I am not against a duty in this shape; but if the hand of government is stretched out to oppress the various interests I have enumerated, by an unequal and oppressive tax on the necessaries of life, I fear we shall destroy the fond hopes entertained by our constituents, that this government would ensure their rights, extend their commerce, and protect their manufactures. Mothers will tell their children, when they solicit their daily and accustomed nutriment, that the new laws forbid them the use of it, and they will grow up in a detestation of the hand which proscribes their innocent food and the occupation of their fathers; the language of complaint will circulate universally, and change the favorable opinion now entertained to dislike and clamor.

The House will not suppose we are actuated by local interests in opposing a measure big with such dangerous consequences to the existence of the Union. They will admit we have reason for persisting in our opposition to a high duty, and may be inclined to join us in reducing it either to five per cent. or at most to one cent per gallon. If the apprehensions we have expressed shall be realized, let it rest upon the advocates of the present measure; we have done our duty, and it only remains for us to submit to that ruin in which the whole may be involved.

. . . .

MR. AMES said, he should be sorry if he had made use of any language to injure any gentleman's feelings. He did not mean to infer that the people of Massachusetts possessed any excellence over their southern brethren; far from it. He was satisfied that their hearts beat with equal warmth, and their minds contemplated with equal precision; he believed that the most cordial regard subsisted on the part of the citizens of Massachusetts toward their fellow-citizens in other states; he therefore hoped that nothing local would be attributed to him on the occasion.

Was the language of gentlemen to be, let us lay a poll-tax of three-fourths of a dollar on the fishermen, I ask, would the House sit quiet even to hear the proposition? It is not because a tax is light that it is proper. It is supposed that the fishermen must be poor if they are not able to pay this. I contend they are very poor, they are in a sinking state, they carry on their business in despair; but gentlemen will ask us, why then do they not quit the profession? I answer, in the words that are often used in the eastern country respecting the inhabitants of Cape Cod, they are too poor to live there, and they are too poor to remove. With respect to our distilleries, the gentleman assumes as a fact that they have not declined; but the contrary is true—there is not more than three-fourths of the business done now that used to be, beside the quantity is not only lessened, but the profit on what is sold is also less. Those nations that used to supply us with the raw material are becoming our rivals; even our home market is not secured to us.

Gentlemen who contend for the encouragement of agriculture, should recollect that nature has denied us fertility, but she has placed along our shores an inexhaustible store. To labor on our land seems to be exerting ourselves against nature; our industry is therefore directed to a more productive business, and ought not this to be entitled to equal encouragement with any other. A tax upon molasses has been sufficiently demonstrated to be a tax upon the fisheries; and will gentlemen continue this burthen upon Massachusetts alone, when she pays her full proportion on all other articles, according to her abilities to consume them? Oppression will lead to smuggling, and when once a system of this kind is formed, the persons engaged in it will not stop at molasses alone, they will include every other article in an illicit trade, so that it is impossible to know the extent of the evil, or provide a remedy. If these facts and arguments are sufficient to produce doubts in gentlemen's minds, they will hesitate in concurring with the committee in this article of the report; for, in cases of uncertainty, I take it to be the wisest way not to proceed in a dubious track.

MAY 5, 1789

MR. AMES .—I hope the reduction moved for by the gentleman who has just sat down will not be agreed to; for I trust the House is not satisfied with the reasons offered in its support. A great deal has been now said respecting the jealousy entertained of the advantages given by this preference to some states; a great deal was also said before the committee adopted the measure. I do not think this doctrine of jealousy is natural to us. I know it has been cultivated by the British, and disseminated through the United States; they had their particular views in exciting such ideas; but I do not believe, that because we have various we have opposite interests. Upon examination there will be found but few of our interests that clash with each other so much as to admit a well grounded jealousy. Nature has so arranged our circumstances, that the people of the several states pursue various employments which support each other. If one end of the continent is employed in manufactures and commerce, the other is attentive to agriculture; so far are they, therefore, from being rivals, that, both in a natural and political sense, they mutually are necessary and beneficial to each other's interests. I wish gentlemen, before they insist upon this jealousy, would point out the causes of its existence. So far from this being the case, I believe the individual interest of each part is compatible with the general interest; and that the public opinion is the same, is clearly demonstrated by the attachment professed by every part to remain in union—it is acknowledged, that on this principle our existence as a nation depends.

This being the case, I do not listen with any great degree of concern to arguments founded on that cause. So far from surveying the affluence or ease of my southern brethren with the jaundiced eye of jealousy, I contemplate their prosperity with ineffable satisfaction. I look with an equal eye upon the success of every state through the whole extent of United America. I wish their interests to be equally consulted; and, if I may judge of the feelings of the people, by those of their representatives on this floor, I may venture to say, there was never less reason to apprehend discord or envy than at this time. I believe the fact is so, because I feel it. I appeal with confidence to the gentlemen round me, whether they have not found the disposition of those who were suspected most to favor navigation, ready to concede what was asked for the encouragement of every other interest? Whether a like conciliatory conduct has not been observed by the advocates of manufactures? I ask gentlemen, whether the language they have heard from the several parts of this House has not been much more congenial to their sentiments than they expected, and the measures pursued more coincident to their feelings than what they looked for? I believe, at the moment I am making this observation, the breasts of gentlemen beat in concert with it; I am sure my feelings accord most cordially in the sentiment.

I believe the encouragement of our navigation is looked upon to be indispensably necessary; its importance has never been denied. Now, I ask if gentlemen are inclined to support and extend our navigation, whether they are not willing to proportion the mean to the end, and adopt measures tending to increase the quantity of American shipping? It has been often justly remarked, that the Constitution, under which we deliberate, originated in commercial necessity. The mercantile part of our fellow citizens, who are the firm friends to an equal and energetic government, hope the improvement of our navigation may obtain the attention of Congress; it is but justice that it be early attended to, and it will give general satisfaction to find it considered as an important object by the general government. The most liberal of the friends of American commerce only wish for such regulations as may put our navigation on a footing with foreigners. If other nations have restricted our navigation by regulations or charges, we must restrict them by a tonnage, or some other duty, so as to restore an equality; but this will not be found to be the case in the present instance. The moderate and inconsiderable duty of thirty cents on foreigners in treaty, and fifty cents on others not in treaty, will not enable our vessels to go abroad with as much advantage as foreigners can come here; so that the proposed encouragement may perhaps fall short of procuring us a maritime strength equal to our national security.

The gentleman from Georgia (Mr. JACKSON) says, that five thousand hogsheads of tobacco are now rotting in the warehouses for want of ships to carry them to market. If this is the case, it proves we have depended long enough upon foreigners to supply us with the means of transportation; let us now make some provision that will prevent the like taking place again. If proper encouragement is now given, we may perhaps in a short time have enough of shipping to supply all the states. If the productions of another year must lie in the planters' hands, they will feel a greater loss and inconvenience than the payment of half a dollar additional freight per ton, if it was certain that they would be subjected to such a burthen:—judge from this circumstance, whether there is a competition of interests in the United States. Does not the contrary appear to be the fact? Gentlemen will please to consider how unfavorable it is to commerce, to have the success of their business depend upon the caprice or mercy of any foreign nation. If your produce is to lie till they come to carry it away, you cannot be said to have the command of your property, or possess those advantages which the bounty of nature has given you. How much better is it to go with vessels of our own in search of a market, than to wait for others to take our produce away until it perishes on our hands? Let me ask gentlemen, if they think the produce of Massachusetts would be sold if we were unable to seek a market for ourselves? Would foreigners come to New England in search of our whale oil and fish? No; foreigners are hostile to our fisheries; so far from encouraging us, by buying what we have for sale, they wish and labor to destroy our trade; their attempts are defeated by our ability to go abroad and seek a market for ourselves. This demonstrates clearly, that, in order to extend the sale of our productions, we must have vessels of our own to find out a market, and be guided by actual experience to that which is best.

The observations of gentlemen tending to show that one end of the continent will suffer more by the regulation contemplated by the House than the other, are, I conceive, not well founded. The price of freight will equalize itself. If the people of Carolina or Georgia pay a high freight in consequence of the tonnage duty, the State of Massachusetts must pay the same, or her vessels will go to the southward in search of freight, so that the eastern states have no peculiar interest in the measure. It has been suggested, that because Massachusetts has foreign vessels in her employ, she cannot transport produce for others—Massachusetts, by reason of that influence which Britain has, is obliged to receive some of her supplies in foreign bottoms, but this is only a proof that the evil requires a remedy. I might here easily draw a picture of the distress to which the eastern country is subjected for want of a protecting hand; her shipwrights are glad to work for two shillings and six pence a day, or less, and less will not maintain them and their families. Their lumber is of no value, it lies rotting in the forests, for want of encouragement to frame it into ships; the other artisans are clamorous for employment, and without a speedy relief they will have to desert the country. I believe if this relief is extended to them, it will give a spring to their industry, and a little time will render them serviceable to their fellow citizens in the South. They will find markets for their tobacco which is now rotting, and their valuable productions will be transported to all parts of the globe. From these circumstances, I am led to beg gentlemen to consider, that the improvement and extension of our navigation is one of the most important objects that can come before the Legislature; that there are abundant proofs that a regulation in favor of American shipping is absolutely necessary to restore them to an equality with foreigners; and if they are convinced with me of its importance and necessity, they will not think the sums agreed to in committee too high for the purpose of protecting the navigation of the United States.

MAY 11 AND MAY 12, 1789

Mr. AMES thought the gentleman from Pennsylvania (Mr. FITZSIMMONS) had misunderstood the gentleman from South Carolina (Mr. TUCKER) respecting his pledging himself to vote in favor of molasses. He believed the gentleman from South Carolina incapable of making any improper accommodation either on this or any other occasion; the subject had never been mentioned to him, nor he believed to any body else, much less could the gentleman's intention be the result of bargain or compromise. For his own part, he would never consent to such a degradation of his rights as a member of the House, as to stipulate for the exercise of his opinion.

. . . .

Mr. AMES was willing to proceed to the consideration of that subject; he did not wish it deferred to the end of the list, that it might be held over them *in terrorem;* there were several articles in the list, which he did not conceive to be taxed too high for collection, or out of proportion with others, therefore it was likely they would not be reduced. If this was the case, the reduction would not be general, and the gentleman from South Carolina might not think it his duty to favor the reduction of molasses. He wished every article to stand upon its own bottom. If molasses was too high, the committee would lower it; if not, they will continue it at the rate it is, and the business would be done with. If the committee were disposed to proceed, he was ready to take up the subject.

. . . .

Mr. AMES was sensible that any further discussion of the present subject was unpleasant, nay, it was painful to the committee; but he had such impressions on his mind with regard to its importance, that he must trespass on them again. On all subjects demonstration is desirable, but there is only one science capable of complete demonstration. Many other sciences admit of different degrees of demonstration; but of all the sciences on earth, the science of politics is the least capable of affording satisfactory conclusions, while it is the one that, from its importance, requires the greatest degree of certainty; because when we are to consider those things which relate to the welfare of nations, it is of consequence, and nothing can be more desirable than that we adopt just principles in order to come at proper conclusions. In this science it is dangerous to adopt the visionary projects of speculators, instead of principle. We ought to be cautious, therefore, in selecting the information upon which we form our system.

He trusted to make it appear in the course of his arguments, that the propriety of the particular measure under discussion depended upon local knowledge, and yet it would be found of national concern. He believed it could be clearly proved to be as much the interest of one part as of another to have the duty reduced.

It was laid down as a principle, that all duties ought to be equal. He believed, if gentlemen gave themselves time for consideration, they would not contend this duty was equal. He said he had made some calculations, which demonstrated the inequality to a very surprising degree. The tax operated in two ways: first, as a tax on a raw material, which increased the price of stock and narrowed the sale; and second, as a tax on an article of consumption. It required the distillation and the consumption to be equal in every part of the Union to render the duty equal in its operation; but no gentleman contended that the consumption or distillation was equal. The gentleman from Virginia said, on a former occasion, that Massachusetts would not contribute her proportion of the national revenue, because her exports were not equal to the southern states, and of consequence her imports are less; but if this fact is examined, it will be found that she does export in full proportion with the southern states. Examine her custom-house books and you will find it; but Massachusetts is greatly concerned in navigation, and the wages of her seamen ought to be added to the amount of the profits of her industry. Then if we consider her consumption, we shall find it in proportion also. Admitting the people of New England to live more moderate than the opulent citizens of Virginia or Carolina, yet they have not such a number of blacks among them, whose living is wretched, consequently the average consumption per head will be nearly the same. The fact is, that all taxes of this nature will fall generally in proportion to the ability to pay.

Laying a heavy duty on molasses incurs the necessity of allowing a drawback on country rum. By this system we may lose more revenue than we gain; any how, it will render it very uncertain. It is a question of some importance, whether it would not be beneficial to the United States to establish a manufacture, which would be very lucrative. But waiving that consideration, he would ask gentlemen, if there was any propriety in taxing molasses in its raw state with a duty intended to be laid on rum? Certainly this had better be by way of excise. In this mode the revenue would escape fraud by smuggling, which would otherwise be unavoidable. The tax was such a temptation, being thirty per cent. upon its value, that no checks could prevent a clandestine trade being carried on.

Without the molasses trade is continued, the fishery cannot be carried on. They are so intimately connected, that the weapon which wounds the one will stab the other. If by such measures as these we ruin one of the most valuable interests of the United States, will not the people have a right to complain, that, instead of protecting, you injure and destroy their pursuits? He did not mean to say that the people would form unwarrantable combinations; but their exertions to support the government will be damped; they will look with chagrin on the disappointment of their hopes; and it will add to their vexation, that they have been deceived under the most flattering appearances; for who could conceive that a government, constructed and adopted in the manner this has been, could ever be administered to the destruction of that welfare which it was formed to support?

He recommended experience as the best guide, and said, that it was decidedly against high duties, particularly on molasses; and concluded with appealing to the justice and wisdom of the committee for a determination on this subject.

MAY 12, 1789

MR. AMES wished to reply to the observation made yesterday by the gentleman from Virginia. Does that gentleman, said he, recollect, if we lay an excise, we prevent the burthen from being imposed upon the poor for their subsistence, as molasses, in the raw state, will be lightly taxed? In the next place, it is more favorable to the importers of that article than the impost; it does not require so large a proportion of their capital to be advanced in payment of duties, nor do they run the risk of bad debts, because it may be so regulated that the retailer shall secure the duty. Another reason is, it will save the expense of a numerous host of custom-house officers, tide-waiters, &c. These considerations proved, that if the excise was no better than an impost, it was no worse; and as the duty would be better collected, and give less reason for smuggling, which, above all things was dangerous to the revenue, it was sufficient to warrant the committee in giving the excise duty a preference.

MARITIME DUTIES

MAY 5, 1789

Mr. AMES was obliged to the gentleman for his offer to exclude foreigners, but he did not wish to go so far. He had hopes that a shorter period than gentlemen seemed to contemplate, would be sufficient to improve the navigation of the United States, and expected every state as well as Massachusetts would be able to transport a great part of its own productions.

MAY 6, 1789

Mr. AMES—It has been said, that the duty on foreigners ought not to exceed more than two or three times what has been laid upon our own tonnage. I beg to remind gentlemen, it never was the intention of the House to impose any duty whatever on American shipping: the six cents that were laid was upon a different principle. This being the case, gentlemen will not draw any inference from what was done, to favor what is yet to be done; where the principles are inconsistent, the comparison does not hold good.

.   .   .   .

MR. MADISON.—I do not differ with my colleague, (Mr. BLAND,) when he says that the agricultural interest ought not to be sacrificed. I consider every other interest as secondary; but yet some concessions ought to be made, in order to prevent the ruin of a very important concern. If the question was, which of the two should be destroyed by the preference we give, I should have no hesitation;—but I believe both interests are compatible and consistent with each other. I do not consider this subject as it respects revenue: my great object is to provide a maritime defence against a maritime danger. I wish, in doing this, that the burthen should be equally borne; but I do not think a small disproportion is a sufficient reason for rejecting the measure. The expedient I proposed will tend to lessen the inequality, and therefore I hope it will be agreed to. I shall move it, if the question for reducing now before the House is agreed to.

Mr. AMES declared himself against reducing the duty so low, and asked the gentleman what he meant to propose, for the present, on the vessels of nations not in treaty?

Mr. MADISON replied, that he would move to reduce it from fifty to forty; but then he would make it sixty cents per ton, after December, 1790.

MAY 7, 1789

MR. AMES—The gentlemen from the southward, who suppose their states most likely to be affected by a discrimination in the tonnage duty, have concluded their arguments with a candor, which I conceive does honor to their patriotism. They declare themselves willing to encourage American shipping and commerce, though they do not join with us in the sum we think necessary to be laid on foreign tonnage to accomplish so important an object. If sufficient encouragement is given, and by our regulation American vesssels are put on a footing with foreigners, I think we may flatter ourselves with the prospect of seeing our navigation immediately flourish. We have reason to expect a very considerable addition to our shipping in the course of one year. Experience has convinced us, that 25,000 tons can be built within double that period, by the town of Boston alone. The other ports in Massachusetts can furnish 37,000 tons, New Hampshire a considerable quantity, and if the other states furnish their proportion, we shall soon find ourselves independent of European nations for the transportation of our products. If forty cents at present, and the seventy-five cents in expectation, are thought a sufficient encouragement for the purpose, I shall not object to the motion.

MAY 13, 1789

Mr. AMES.—in opposition to the motion, observed that, from the introductory observations of the gentleman, he anticipated something which would conduce much to the advantage of our allies: but it had terminated in a proposition to testify our gratitude to that nation, which, in any event, cannot be much benefited by the discrimination proposed, if it should be adopted. Adverting to what had been said upon treaties, he doubted whether any treaties were of any advantage to us, and therefore he was not solicitous to have them increased. Our ships are at present, notwithstanding the treaty, admitted with almost as much facility into the British as into the French islands. The great design in the increase of tonnage is to increase our own navigation; but the gentleman's plan is to testify our gratitude to our allies by waging a commercial war with nations not in treaty. The question the last session was thoroughly discussed, and he hoped that it would not be renewed the present, especially when it is considered that the other House was so strongly against it. If we make a distinction here, we ought to carry it through, and lessen the duties in other instances.

The question being put, it was carried in the affirmative, ayes 32, nays 19. The resolution as amended was then agreed to by the committee, and stands thus:

> "That the tonnage on all foreign-built bottoms belonging to nations not in commercial treaty with the United States, be raised to the sum of one dollar per ton, from and after the first day of January next."

MAY 9, 1789

MR. AMES.—I wish the committee may consider, with the attention the subject demands, whether the duties are too high or not? It is hardly possible, I own, to contemplate this subject as a practical question. We shall find it necessary to consider attentively, before we proceed any further, what the objects of our government are; and, having discovered them, we are to consider whether the proposed measure will answer the purposes intended. I believe, in every point of view that we can possibly consider it, the subject of revenue will be thought to be one of the primary objects to which the power of government extends. It has long been apprehended, that an ill administration of the new Constitution was more to be feared, as inimical to the liberties of the people, than any hostility from the principles of the Constitution. Of all the operations of government, those which concern taxation are the most delicate as well as the most important. This observation applies to all governments. Revenue is the soul of government, and if such a soul had not been breathed into our body politic, it would have been a lifeless carcass, fit only to be buried. I would wish this soul might be actuated by rational principles, that, in establishing a revenue system, we might go on a superior principle to that which has heretofore been the governing principle in the United States; that we might consider what was most adequate to the object. The nature of the revenue system in this government is to the last degree important; for want of the soul, the late government was found utterly incapable of invigorating and protecting industry, or securing the Union; therefore these seem to be the great objects which we are to accomplish. I consider the present question as a direct application to the principles of the constitution; it will either support or destroy them. If the revenue system should fall with oppressive weight on the people, if it shall injure some in their dearest interests, it will shake the foundation of the government. However the newspapers may stand your friends, and trumpet forth panegyrics on the new constitution, if your administration does not give satisfaction, you will find all ineffectual that they can do, whilst the people are against you. This being admitted, the government will not push their regulations too far; they will consider the weaknesses and prejudices of the individual members of the Union. When they lay a tax, they will consider how far it is agreeable to them, and how far the measure is wise in itself. If it is said the article to be taxed is a luxury, and the government is zealous to correct the vice, they will be careful they do not do it in too severe a manner; the principle would be capable of great expansion:

all the enjoyments of social life are luxuries, and, as objects of revenue, we ought to set a price on the enjoyment, without suppressing their use altogether. Neither ought we to consider what the article in this point of view is able to pay, so much as what we may reasonably expect to collect from it.

I believe various opinions are entertained on this subject. I have been told, the sentiments of some respectable merchants favor high duties, but I know there are as respectable gentlemen, whose judgment and information are much to be relied upon, decidedly of the contrary opinion, who think that we are treading upon ice; that if we impose these high duties at this time, we are doing an irreparable injury to our country: to that opinion I am myself inclined. I do apprehend very great inconveniences will result from pursuing these measures. I fear the collection will be insecure, your laws not be executed, and, of consequence, your government fall into contempt. In collecting a revenue, I would determine with accuracy what might be expected; but in case of high duties, no calculation can be made; it rests with the self-interest of individuals to determine what shall be paid. Notwithstanding all the observations which gentlemen have made, to show the probability of collecting the duties with certainty, I have still very serious doubts, and if the government cannot collect the revenue, the system is not worth supporting. Government is founded in necessity, its powers are to check the unruly sallies of self-interest; to restrain which requires an unwearied attention in every department of government. It can hardly be thought good policy, therefore, to incite them, by great allurements, to violate the laws, to which mankind are naturally too prone. Now, we know that there are but two ways to prevent the perpetration of fraud upon the revenue, arising from an impost upon the importation of merchandise; one is, to lay the duties so low as not to offer an inducement to smuggling; the other is, by increasing the impediments and risk, so as to counterbalance the temptation. The checks and precautions ought to amount to a complete evidence that the law cannot be evaded, otherwise we not only suffer a loss of money but of reputation also. Taking it upon this principle, I am at a loss to imagine how gentlemen can suppose they can collect thirty or forty per cent. on the value of goods imported, unless our laws are better constructed than the laws of other nations. In those countries, where the best regulations have been adopted upon the experience of ages, it is found impossible, in cases of high duties, to prevent illicit trade; how can we, then, who have not that experience, nor a more nervous executive, expect to raise forty per cent. in the first instance? For my part, I despair of it. What grounds have gentlemen for entertaining such ideas? Do they think, there is any thing in our local situation to enable them to make sure work of it? They have told us, that the governments of the southern and middle states heretofore collected the duties with tolerable certainty. I admit it, because there are natural causes existing there rendering the collection practicable; but there are no such causes to the eastward. The Chesapeake and Delaware are the two great avenues through which the navigation must enter into those countries; the other avenues are few, and may be easily guarded. Add to this another consideration, that their trade is principally carried on in large vesssels, and by foreigners; their citizens are generally concerned in agriculture. These circumstances compounded operate thus. If they are subjected to high duties, strangers have less knowledge of the country, and are without the connexion necessary to ensure success to smuggling; besides, the people, considering the money as coming out of the pockets of foreigners, are more desirous of having it paid with certainty, than they would probably be if it was demanded of their friend and neighbor. But let us consider the situation of Massachusetts and New Hampshire. The foreign shipping employed in their trade is very inconsiderable, consequently the motive which operates in Virginia will be insensibly felt in those states; but the citizens of Massachusetts are generally a commercial people, the greater proportion along the coast are engaged in commerce. Perhaps, if I thought so highly of state honors as the subject demands, I might be concerned at being obliged to speak the truth; but the duty I owe to the Union induces me to forego every consideration of that nature. If I am under an impression that your laws will be unpopular, and left without that support from the people necessary for their due execution, I must come forward and warn you of the danger. From the experience we have had of the opposition of our people to the British acts of Parliament, because they were either unjust or unpopular, I am led to fear, if the same opinion is entertained with respect to our ordinances, that they will be defeated in a similar manner. The habit of smuggling pervades our counry. We were taught it when it was considered rather as meritorious than criminal; therefore we have just reason to apprehend their success in evading the public impositions, although the temptations should be small.

The State of Massachusetts has a prodigious extent of seacoast, of near one thousand miles in length, indented with innumerable bays and rivers, forming the finest, most accessible, and securest harbors in the world. It must be impossible to guard them all, even if our population was crowded; add to this, that there are two thousand sail of vessels, large and small, coming in and going out constantly. If this statement is true, I ask gentlemen whether a law can be enforced that is repugnant to the judgment, feelings, and interests of so large a proportion of the people, possessing every possible advantage to elude your grasp? The former government, with a wakeful vigilance and anxious desire, endeavored in vain to seize this object. The state governments, instituted by the people themselves for their particular benefit, have hitherto been unable to execute laws of this nature. If the same cause for evasion exists under the general government, will it not produce the same effect? I know of no peculiar power residing in us that the state governments were not in the possession of at the time they made unsuccessful efforts to obtain revenue by a system of high duties: what, then, do we expect? The merchants are to associate, and form a phalanx in our support; private honor is to be called in aid of public measures. If this is done, what then? I have no doubt of the virtue and patriotism of many of these gentlemen; the most respectable merchants will disdain to smuggle; but there will ever be found a band of inferior characters, I care not what you call them, infamous parricides, ready to defraud your revenue by evasion, or any other means in their power. These men will get the business into their hands, and being under no restraint of honor or virtue, rob you by secret means of the great essential to the well-being of the government. It will become impracticable to support it by other means, and we shall stand a monument of imbecility to future ages.

If gentlemen will consider how large a revenue may be drawn from the commerce of this extensive and fertile country, they will know the value of the stake they play for, and not risk it at a single cast. If we begin with laying moderate duties, it will redound to our honor, and give our constituents a confidence in the government. When this shall be well established, and when they find themselves happy under its benign influence, they will be bound by an interest arising from experience, as well as by principle, to support you. Under these manifestations of mutual regard, the duties may increase as the wants of government demand, without exciting clamor or complaint. If my principles are right, and they rest upon the sure basis of experience, it will not be enough that gentlemen say our duties will probably be collected; they must go farther, and demonstrate that there cannot be a reasonable doubt entertained of our success. The magnitude of the object we risk demands as great a degree of certainty as to its effects as the nature of the case will admit. If a heavy impost is the least beyond what the powers of government can reach, a punctual collection of the difference in the duties will not compensate for the hazard we engage in.

I submit it to gentlemen to say, whether there is any other reason for laying high duties but what arises from pecuniary considerations? If there be not, and it is well known that a moderate duty realizes as much revenue as a high one, gentlemen will concur in the reduction. It is easy to determine by experience, that it will be agreeable to the citizens; if so, it will bring them in individually to the aid of the government, which they will learn to venerate and obey. How much better is this than holding out temptations for men to enrich themselves and beggar your treasury, to trample on your laws, and despise the government itself?

.   .   .   .

Mr. AMES.—The gentleman from Pennsylvania set out with informing us that nothing new had or could be offered on the subject, yet you found, Mr. Chairman, the gentleman had a good deal to say, which I thought new and much to the purpose. As to applying the observation to myself, in common with the advocates for low duties, I shall decline it, only noting that the long discussion which the subject has had, would restrain me from rising on this occasion, more than any remarks of the nature made by the gentlemen from Pennsylvania and Connecticut; but I am actuated by higher motives than a regard to my own feelings, otherwise I should come reluctantly forward to press arguments which the committee may be fatigued with listening to. But I feel such strong impressions on my mind, with regard to the effects our impost law is likely to produce, that I cannot pass it over with a silent vote. I must admonish gentlemen, that the events which may result from our present measures are of the most alarming nature. When I was up before, I endeavored to show the degree of power the government could exercise without being charged with an ill administration. I shall now proceed briefly to consider the arguments used in reply to what has been advanced by the advocates for moderate duties. I believe it is a good rule to judge of the strength of a cause by the arguments used to defend it; and here I must take the liberty of saying, that the gentlemen on the other side of the question have adduced not one to support their opinion that has carried conviction to my mind. I consider that, by a decision of this question, the good which the new government is expected to produce may be rendered problematical. Though I am fully impressed with the necessity there is for revenue to supply the public expenses, yet I cannot believe we are likely to obtain more by heavy duties than by temperate ones, and it is to this point which my arguments tend. I do not believe that in either case we shall procure fully sufficient to supply the public demands. If we have to procure 8,000,000 dollars, I venture to say, not near the half could be raised by an impost system; but admitting that it could by a high scale of duties for the first year, it could not be done in the subsequent ones. Now, I regard this as a permanent system of revenue, rather than a productive one; if it is laid high, you will find your collection annually diminish. Now, will any government take such measures in gathering in its harvest, as to ruin the soil? Will they rack-rent their tenants in such a manner as to deprive them of the means of improving the estate? Such can never be the policy of this enlightened country. We know, from the fundamental principles of republics, that public opinion gives the tone to every action of the government—the laws ought to correspond with the habits and manners, nay, I may almost add, wishes of the people. Well, Mr. Chairman, we are told a tax upon rum is popular; I will agree with the gentlemen; but still a high duty will induce people to run it, and though the consumer may pay the tax without complaining, yet it will go into the pockets of individuals who defraud your revenue. Gentlemen have complained that we do not offer a substitute for what we find fault with. I will endeavor to explain a system I would place in the room of this. I would reduce the duties generally so low as to hold out no encouragement to smuggling; in this case, it is more than probable, the amount of the impost, at the end of one year, would exceed the collection under the present rate. By giving this proof of moderation and wisdom, we should obtain the public favor and confidence; the government would be acquiring strength, its movements would be more certain, and we could in every subsequent year extend the system, and make the whole productive; then it would be in the power of government, by aids, to improve our agriculture, manufactures, and commerce. Our imports are now very great; by the increase of our commerce, we shall probably find our revenue produce twice as much seven years hence as it can be expected to do at present.

The duty on West India rum is moderate and popular, say gentlemen; it is not the interest of Massachusetts that it should be reduced; so I am arguing against the interest of the State I have the honor to represent. The higher the duty on West India rum, the more country rum will be used; but I should sacrifice the sacred trust deposited in my hands, if I were to be actuated by a local motive of this nature. The higher the duty, the more officers must be multiplied, the more guards must be employed, the more troops must be kept in pay, for the suppression of clandestine trade. Under high duties, the people will pay much, the Government receive little. Will they not, then, justly complain of the useless burthens you have imposed? Useless I call them, unless government have in contemplation to make them conducive to oppress and injure their constituents. If you punish severely the breach of your laws, will not the people combine against them? Will it not be an additional source of dissatisfaction, that the attempts to relieve them are unsuccessful? If gentlemen consider this subject seriously, they will see cause to be alarmed. Who, in this case, can you apply to for support? Not to the people, they want an alleviation of their miseries; you have, then, nothing left but the impotency of a government not sufficiently matured to support itself.

Gentlemen say that the funds to be produced by the proposed impost are insufficient for the public demands: if so, why not stop somewhat shorter? If we must have recourse to some other mode of obtaining revenue, let us divide the burthen, and not destroy one means by loading it too heavily; if we do, the other means will not only have its own proportion to sustain, but the accumulation of its weakened fellow. Or, do gentlemen suppose they will clear the United States of incumbrances by one effort? They do not. Why are we to grasp at so much in this way? It would be much better to call in the aid of other taxes and excises, than, by overloading, depress one of the most capable and valuable funds in our possession. Under the British government, they have excise, stamp duties, impost, malt, and land-tax, from which to defray their expenses; why should we endeavor to do that with a single fund, when we have more in our power?

The gentleman from Pennsylvania (Mr. FITZSIMMONS) has mentioned the great probability there is of getting a great duty from this article, because the consumption is more extensive in the United States than in any other part of the world; but this circumstance will furnish a strong inducement to smuggle. He says there is but a small quantity of rum smuggled into England. Gentlemen no doubt consider, that Great Britain is an island well watched; her cutters and custom-house boats are ever on the look-out; but, with all these guards, and the advantage of her insular situation, she is unable to prevent smuggling.

It has been remarked, that under the state laws, experience has taught us that such duties as the bill has in contemplation can be collected; and the gentleman says, if they be collected under the state laws, they can be collected under this government. If they have been able to collect high duties in Virginia, it is because their trade is confined to enter at one channel. But it is not so with the eastern states; there every attempt to raise high duties has proved ineffectual; and the universal opinion there is, that five per cent. would be more productive of revenue than fifty. This is not mere matter of opinion, as has been said, but is demonstrable from facts.

The principle of taxation is to produce the greatest sum of money with the greatest ease to the community. If a gentleman in trade has on hand a cargo of rum, he is able to afford it at a less price than the person who imports it subject to these duties; therefore, the latter will be under the necessity of smuggling, or storing his commodities, for he cannot afford to sell at a loss. A gentleman has mentioned, that if we do not succeed in the collection of these duties, we may lower them. But will any gentleman say, that if we lose our duty by the establishment of a system of smuggling, we shall not continue to lose after the law shall be repealed, and a lower rate of duties is imposed? If gentlemen depend upon this fund alone, I think they ought not to strain it too much; though I do not know why we should not take to our aid an excise duty; it certainly is not unpopular as it respects the distillation of spirits. If I were an enemy to the Constitution, I should be an advocate for high duties; because it would disgust the people, and render the government unpopular; but, as I am a sincere friend to the government now established, and desire its perpetuity, I am against any measure which I think will endanger its existence.

TO GEORGE RICHARDS MINOT

NEW YORK, MAY 16TH, 1789 SATURDAY EVENING

(Confidential so far as you think it may be needful.)

DEAR FRIEND,

I AM TIRED, lazy, have written twice before by the late post and by this conveyance, and therefore think I shall write little now. Gore not chosen; Jarvis, Dawes, Russell resigned; Boston topsy-turvy. Public life is very subject to mortality, as well as sin and sorrow. I do not admire every thing here. Lately it was debated whether the ships of nations in treaty should pay less tonnage than other foreigners. It passed in the affirmative. I was silent, but voted with the minority. The New England representatives, I believe, thought as I did, but voted for it, because a higher tonnage was imposed on the shipping of nations not in alliance, (say British,) than would have been voted otherwise. So that our shipping has the more advantage. Is that a just principle of action? It is little and mean, as well as unwise and unsafe, to discriminate. I wish I may never sacrifice national principles to local interests.

Yesterday it was moved by Madison to make the Impost Bill temporary. This, at the close of the business, without notice, astonished me. I opposed it instanter. He supported it by reasons which I despise. It was, he said, anti-republican to grant a perpetual revenue, unappropriated; it was unwise to part with the power; and the Senate, or a third of the Senate, could prevent a repeal or amendment of the act, though it was already said to be imperfect, and might prove oppressive; the act was perpetual, and the debt might be paid in a few years. Why should the people pay longer than the occasion required? The Senate and President might not agree to repeal the law, though the debt might be paid, unless their terms were agreed to; that it was an experiment, and it would be a thing unprecedented to establish a perpetual tax. You will think this resembles the cant of our Nassons.[8]

I retorted that he and Fitzsimmons had spoken with scorn of a temporary system, but now their consistency had yielded to their republicanism; they would not trust the Senate nor even themselves, with the power of appropriating the money, though if a surplus should arise, not a farthing could be touched without. But was the power of imposing new taxes less than that of appropriations? They had reckoned their wealth on paper, and were concerned at the excess of it. They were afraid of its producing another evil, an excess of credit. But the rate of duties was so high as to relieve me from the fear of the first, and the limiting the act would repel the other evil. That money is power, a permanent revenue is permanent power, and the credit which it would give was a safeguard to the government. With all the powers which we had, and the most prudent exercise of them, it was not to be imagined that the government was too strong, or too competent to preserve its being; it was weak, young, and counteracted. Instead of immortality, we took a lease for years. Necessity forced us upon a revenue system now. A few years hence would the zeal for government be so warm? would not factions arise? should not we hear again of state interests, and the threats of those who will complain of actual

---

[8] *Major Samuel Nason, (or Nasson, as his name was sometimes spelt,) of Sanford, York county, Maine, was a member of the Massachusetts Convention, held in 1788, for the adoption of the Federal Constitution. He appears to have somewhat affected the heroic and ornate style of eloquence, and voted in the negative on the general question of the adoption.* [S. AMES]

oppression? The system was not liked now; half the opposition to another act would destroy all credit. We might have occasion to pledge our funds. Why make our own terms with our creditors bad? If the bill is bad, mend it. It was strange that men, who so lately defended the bill as a good one, should now admit the truth of our objections, and try to reconcile us to the blunders of it, by the hope that we should not have long to endure them. A *perpetual* act might be repealed or amended. It was a play on words. But the funds, if pledged, could not be taken away without an *act*. A temporary act might expire, and it was a mere non-feasance not to renew it. The papers will give you some further state of the debate, though nothing of it is yet published, that I know. I supposed it might amuse you to state a little of it as it came into my head. The yeas and nays were called for to-day; eight against limiting, forty-one for it. My friends voted against me, I suppose, on the principle that the molasses duty five cents, and some other points, are wrong, and the sooner the act expires the better. But, is it not a risk, to trust the revenue in future to the caprice of the antifederalism, the state politics, or the knavery of these folks? No revenue, no government, is a truth, and may you not be forced to buy their consent to a revenue to keep life in the government, either by amendments, by renouncing protecting and navigation duties, or by damning the debt? On the other hand, is there any color of reason for a temporary regulation? I am sick of fluctuating counsels, of governing by expedients. Let us have stability and system. I glory in my side of the question. I think Mr. Madison was chagrined. Spleen at reducing molasses was a part of his motive. He talked very differently of the Senate lately. Fitzsimmons is very like our . . . . He said to me in private, formerly, that a temporary system was despicable and ruinous. Publicly, he called it, in a former speech, a paltry one. I reproached him with the last term in my speech. He felt it very sensibly. The bill is gone to the Senate with all its imperfections. I wish to serve your brother, and speak of him to Mr. Strong, but cannot give a word of information what, or when, any thing will be done.

Yours, &c.

P.S. I break off short, for it grows late. Write me when the House get together, how they look, &c. The bill passed for seven years. Madison was for twenty-five, which was a very ridiculous comment on his own principles.

TO GEORGE RICHARDS MINOT

MONDAY, MAY 18, 1789

DEAR FRIEND,

I AM sitting very lazily in the House, who are debating about the manner of enrolling the acts of Congress, which I care little about. I suppose the object is to have a clerk of enrolments, with a view of providing a good warm office for . . . . . Fame is as flattering as other painters, and as seldom draws likenesses. I thought . . . . . another Seneca or Plato, before I saw him. Now, I think him an *old woman*. He is a smooth, plausible Irishman, but superficial, arrogant, and rapacious. Whether I know enough of him to support this opinion, is of little consequence, for I write to you only.

I enclose a part of the Journal; as much as I could get at. I will send you more with pleasure.

Pray let me know how the General Court looks and acts.

Fitzsimmons, of Philadelphia, is supposed to understand trade, and he assumes some weight in such matters. He is plausible, though not over civil; is artful, has a glaring eye, a down look, speaks low, and with apparent candor and coolness. I have heard him compared to . . . . . The similitude is not unapt. He is one of those people, whose face, manner, and sentiments concur to produce caution, if not apprehension and disgust. Madison is cool, and has an air of reflection, which is not very distant from gravity and self-sufficiency. In speaking, he never relaxes into pleasantry, and discovers little of that warmth of heart, which gives efficacy to George Cabot's reasoning, and to Lowell's. His printed speeches are more faithful than any other person's, because he speaks very slow, and his discourse is strongly marked. He states a principle and deduces consequences, with clearness and simplicity. Sometimes declamation is mingled with argument, and he appears very anxious to carry a point by other means than addressing their understandings. He appeals to popular topics, and to the pride of the House, such as that they have voted before, and will be inconsistent. I think him a good man and an able man, but he has rather too much theory, and wants that discretion which men of business commonly have. He is also very timid, and seems evidently to want manly firmness and energy of character.

FISHER AMES

TO UNKNOWN

NEW YORK, MAY 19, 1789

DEAR SIR,

YESTERDAY a bill was debated providing for the collection of the duties. It proposed to adopt the state laws, which would operate unquestionably in favor of the state officers, though the appointment of all officers was to be with the

President and Senate. So many difficulties occurred, and some of them related to the mode of recovering forfeitures and penalties, that the bill was ordered, with the general consent, to lie on the table.

The impost bill is gone to the Senate and is to be debated there on Thursday. It is supposed that some amendments will be proposed. This house have a Committee for reporting a bill for the collection of the duties. Probably, it will be reported this week—and will be attended with many real difficulties, which as is assured in public bodies, will not be lessened by the scrutiny that will be made.

I understand that the President expects a formal application to be made to him for an office by petition. Major Rice will act accordingly. I esteem him, and believe him capable of serving the public will, and disposed to do it. I delivered your letter to the President.

I am, dear Sir, with respectful esteem,
your most humble servant,

FISHER AMES

P.S. The House are now about settling the civil department and are beginning with the Treasury and the Department of foreign affairs.

TO GEORGE RICHARDS MINOT

———

NEW YORK, MAY 19, 1789

MY DEAR FRIEND,

YOU WILL SEE, by the papers, that your friend was left in a small minority, on the late question whether the Impost Bill should be limited. We shall not adopt the State laws for the purpose of collecting the duties. A bill for that purpose was ordered to lie on the table. It would have been a very proper completion of the temporary system.

We are about forming the civil departments. I cannot give you any information on the subject yet. Dr. Appleton wrote me a very judicious, friendly letter, some days ago. Pray thank him, and say to my friends how much I think of them. I must conclude.

Your friend.

P.S. Our House have been voting to vest the power of removing certain officers, say the Minister of Foreign Affairs, in the President only, without the concurrence of the Senate. The idea was to give him this power, and consider him as responsible for the use of it. To-morrow it will be debated whether the Treasury shall be directed by a board or by one person.

TO NATHANIEL BISHOP

RICHMOND, MAY, 1789

MY DEAR SIR,

You WILL do me but justice to believe that I received your favor of the 13th with real satisfaction. It is impossible I should forget how much confidence and esteem your conduct in the General Court procured you—and till I do, I shall be happy to preserve a place in your remembrance. My heart will not suffer me to be indifferent to the approbation of men whose own hearts bestow it on themselves—

I saw and listened to Washington with as much emotion as you have supposed—It seemed to be a deception—a kind of allegorical vision, which overwhelmed the senses with vast objects, and the mind with vast reflections. The crowd was great—but not a stupid one—each expressing as much admiration and joy as a painter would have on his canvas. The modesty, benevolence and dignity of the President cannot be described—your own feeling heart must finish the picture—

I most sincerely wish the aid of our friend. With so good an head and heart, and such a spirit of perseverance and decision, I should think him inestimable. The love of ease prevents most men from doing so much, or resisting so long as they would wish, and are in fact able to do. I look round our house almost daily, and calculate the impression his abilities and determined character would make in it. I thank you for your list of votes.

I join with you in regretting that Masstts. has treated with so much neglect one of her best citizens. I think Gen. Lincoln one of the best and more useful our state ever bred.

Our impost bill is gone to the Senate. There, I trust it will be amended. The duties appear to me too high. Prudence seems to direct that we should begin with moderate duties, make the collection strict, and, if necessary, raise them gradually—Indeed, as luxury and population increase the revenue would augment. But high duties, I fear will produce smuggling, discontent, and an empty treasury. Indeed, great objects will be risked—and not *for* great ones.

I hope you will attend the General Court again—Some people have been busy to furnish reasons for good men to watch them another year—The general gov't will not be supported by the concurrence of some leading men. I hope the representation of your county is well disposed—

You will gratify me by any communications from your quarter, or from the Gen. Court.

I am, my dear sir, with sincere esteem
your most obt. humble ser.

FISHER AMES

TO GEORGE RICHARDS MINOT

MAY 27, 1789, ELECTION DAY IN MASSACHUSETTS

DEAR FRIEND,

You GIVE yourself unnecessary trouble to make apologies in regard to your not having sooner noticed my information respecting your books. For I take pleasure in thinking that I can be of any use to you, and you oblige me by putting my disposition to the trial. I am a cordial wellwisher to your brother Clarke, for his sake as well as yours, and I am not troubled or teased with his application. I have seemed a little negligent, I am sensible, but haste and the present undecided state of appointments prevented my writing particularly about it. I am totally uncertain what offices will be created, and how appointments will be made. I will not forget nor neglect him.

Your letter is dated *June 20*, by a kind of anticipation. I understood the date, and am not disposed to be witty, in a captious way. I am gratified by your correspondence, only let me beg that you will not consider it as a duty, or that I claim it. I will not complain if you should not write once a month, though I shall be pleased to read your letters at all times. When you feel disposed, write. Let the pen go freely. I will do the like. To people whom I do not so much esteem, I will write punctually and in form. You will have such claims on your time, that I should be cruel to require more labor of you.

You call my letter a desponding one. I had forgot every syllable of it. Before yours came, the weather had become fair, and my memory had lost the traces of the ideas which

632

it seems *that* had conveyed to you. A man who feels too much, which you justly observe, a public man should not, will represent things in a stronger manner than he feels them. The habit of feeling strongly produces that of expressing strongly, and I am not sure that strong expressions, *e converso*, do not produce strong feelings. All this is my case. With a warm heart, and an hot head, I often dupe my friends and myself. I felt chagrined at the yawning listlessness of many here, in regard to the great objects of the government; their liableness to the impression of arguments *ad populum*; their state prejudices; their overrefining spirit in relation to trifles; their attachment to some very distressing formalities in doing business, and which will be a curse to all despatch and spirit in transacting it. I compared these with the idea I had brought here, of demi-gods and Roman senators, or at least, of the first Congress. The objects now before us require more information, though less of the heroic qualities, than those of the first Congress. I was sorry to see that the picture I had drawn was so much bigger and fairer than the life. Add to this, that the rashness and madness of the rate of duties justified my fears, and my judgment converted my chagrin into terror approaching to despair. (In this particular *note* the language is too strong for the occasion.) But since, I have reflected coolly, that in all public bodies, the majority will be such as I have described—I may add, ought to be such; and if a few understand business, and have, as they will, the confidence of those who do not, it is better than for all to be such knowing ones; for they would contend for supremacy; there would not be a sufficient principle of cohesion. The love of ease makes many, who are knowing, submit to the judgment of others, more industrious, though not more knowing, than themselves, and this cements the mass. It produces artificial ignorance, which, joined with real ignorance, has been found, in fact, to furnish mortar enough for all public assemblies. The House is composed of very good men, not shining, but honest and reasonably well-informed, and in time they will be found to improve, and not to be much inferior in eloquence, science, and dignity, to the British Commons. They are patriotic enough, and I believe there are more stupid (as well as more shining) people in the latter, in proportion.

The Senate has begun to reduce the rate of duties. Rum is reduced one third. Jamaica ten cents, common, eight. Molasses from five to four. This is not proportionally lowered. I feel as Enceladus would if Etna was removed. The Senate, God bless them, as if designated by Providence to keep rash and frolicsome brats out of the fire, have demolished the absurd, impolitic, mad discrimination of foreigners in alliance from other foreigners.

The business of titles sleeps. It is a very foolish thing to risk much to secure; and I wish Mr. Adams had been less undisguised.[9] I do not fear tyranny from giving, nor contempt from refusing, a title. Mr. Adams is greatly respected, and I have no doubt will be eminently useful, and enough on his guard in relation to delicate points. He has been long absent, and at first he had not so clear an idea of the temper of the people as others who had not half his knowledge in other matters.

You give me excellent advice in regard to Dwight's good example. I never think of that fascinating subject without trying to unbewitch myself by the school-boy trash about one, who "all the bread and cheese he got, he laid upon a shelf," and when the quantity was sufficient, the story proceeds, that he got a wife. You are sensible that I am not in the land of bread and cheese. I know not what I am here for. I was satisfied with my former condition, and was looking forward to a better. Now my future state seems to be receding.

---

[9] *This remark is supposed to refer to Mr. Adams's work, entitled "Discourses on Davila."* [S. AMES]

Is this enigmatical? I believe what I write often seems to be nonsense, for want of an interpretation.

George Cabot is coming here in two or three weeks with his wife, on a journey for her health. I shall see him with a great deal of pleasure. I see a Massachusetts man with pleasure; but Dawes,[10] whom I could ask a million questions, seemed to be worth his weight in money. He has done right in declining his seat. I must finish.

Your affectionate friend.

TO GEORGE RICHARDS MINOT

NEW YORK, MAY 29, 1789, FRIDAY MORNING

*(This letter is a piece of egotism. You may read
as little as you think fit.)*

DEAR MINOT,

YOURS by the post reached me last evening. You give me your advice with a delicacy which evinces your discernment of the frailty of the human heart. In general, advice procures little thanks, and does little good. Those who need, will seldom bear it, and those who can best give, will seldom risk giving it. Your giving it is very far from hurting my pride. If I had not in some degree your good opinion, and to a very great degree your good wishes, you would not have done the act of kindness which calls for all my gratitude. I am proud that you think my temper will bear it, and I submit

---

[10] *Thomas Dawes, a member of the club, and well known afterwards as Judge of the Municipal Court in Boston.* [S. AMES]

to your friendly discipline with cheerfulness. Submit, did I say? I ask, I entreat it. Your friendship will be as useful, as it has ever been agreeable. Your office will not be a sinecure.

My letter by this day's post was sent to the office before yours came. It will serve as an answer to yours, however, for I enlarge, in that, upon my proneness to represent things too strongly. But did I express any contempt for Madison? Upon my word, I do not recollect a word of it, and there is not in my heart a symptom of its having ever been there. Before I came, I was cautioned against pinning my faith on any man's sleeve. I was afraid of it, for I think I am not apt to resist the influence of those whom I esteem. But I see in Madison, with his great knowledge and merit, so much error, and some of it so very unaccountable, and tending to so much mischief, that my impatience may have tinctured my letter with more gall than I remember. Why I disapprove the limitation of the revenue act, I have told you. I will add, this is a government over governments. We may find it as hard to get a revenue bill reënacted, as the kings of England used to find money-bills, and for the same, or even stronger, reasons. It may be used as a means of starving the government into concessions and sacrifices. A million of popular objections will furnish additional motives and a safe pretext. If I am in the wrong on this point, I am very much in the wrong. If accident or mistake made me warm at first, reflection has made me obstinate. I believe that Madison is not at ease on this point, and I think I have seen him struggling to disentangle himself from his own web. He was decided for the tonnage acts being *un*limited. His former friends could not see the difference of the cases, and were refractory. I will not say another word about it. But do you think me in the wrong? Take the pains to point out my error.

You may be assured that I was not betrayed into any warmth in the argument in the House, that I know of. There are certain bounds which my zeal arrives at, almost instantly.

The habit of being in public assemblies has imposed sufficient restraint on my mind, and I seldom pass those bounds. You know what they are. You know my manner of reasoning in public, and I am sensible that the excess of that zeal would very much lessen me. Your caution is very necessary, however; for if I do not offend, it is a frailty to which I am constantly liable. I say many words, you see, about it.

I do not remember any thing relating to shipping or navigation in which I took an opposite side to Madison, in the public debates. The discrimination seems to me undignified and impolitic. I voted against it silently. The States not in alliance allow us as good terms of admission into their ports, as we get from our allies, and probably better than we could get by treaty. I am now unable to account for Madison's passionate attachment to the discrimination. It is a favorite point with the Frenchmen in town. Yet it is admitted, that it will not benefit France. Why then urge it? Is it to affront the English, and to create a closer connection with her enemy? He is very much devoted to the French, it is said, and his reasonings were not very logical, nor much to the credit of his political character. That you may be less liable to misunderstand my idea of him in future, take this explication of it. He is probably deficient in that fervor and vigor of character which you will expect in a great man. He is not likely to risk bold measures, like Charles Fox, nor even to persevere in any measures against a firm opposition, like the first Pitt. He derives from nature an excellent understanding, however, but I think he excels in the quality of judgment. He is possessed of a sound judgment, which perceives truth with great clearness, and can trace it through the mazes of debate, without losing it. He is admirable for this inestimable talent. As a reasoner, he is remarkably perspicuous and methodical. He is a studious man, devoted to public business, and a thorough master of almost every public question that can arise, or he will spare no pains to become so, if he happens to be in want of information. What a man understands clearly, and has viewed in every different point of light, he will explain to the admiration of others, who have not thought of it at all, or but little, and who will pay in praise for the pains he saves them. His clear perception of an argument makes him impressive, and persuasive sometimes. It is not his *forte*, however. Upon the whole, he is an useful, respectable, worthy man, in a degree so eminent, that his character will not sink. He will continue to be a very influential man in our country. Let me add, without meaning to detract, that he is too much attached to his theories, for a politician. He is well versed in public life, was bred to it, and has no other profession. Yet, may I say it, it is rather a science, than a business, with him. He adopts his maxims as he finds them in books, and with too little regard to the actual state of things. One of his first speeches in regard to protecting commerce, was taken out of Smith's *Wealth of Nations*. The principles of the book are excellent, but the application of them to America requires caution. I am satisfied, and could state some reasons to evince, that commerce and manufactures merit legislative interference in this country, much more than would be proper in England. The drain that is making of our people beyond the mountains, and the want of sufficient intercourse between the manufacturing and staple states, the British credit, British agents, &c., are among the circumstances which furnish those reasons. I say again, that he is afraid, even to timidity, of his state, and has reasoned, to my disgust and surprise, about the topics I have mentioned so strongly. I am less ambitious, and, upon my word, less distinguished than you think me. I am as silent as I can possibly be, and am not in a hurry to take consequence. I shall certainly have as much as I deserve, and if I should get more, I should soon lose it. I am resolved to apply closely to the necessary means of knowledge, as I well know it is the only means of acquiring reputation. I have scarcely opened my mouth in the House these ten days, and if my restraining grace should hold out against the temptations I am exposed to, my judgment will lead me to decline any part in the tedious frivolity of the daily business. We are not in haste, or at least, have not learned to be in a hurry to advantage. I think it is the most dilatory assembly in the universe. Which do you most admire at this moment, my candor or my prudence? The latter is not offended by confiding the remark to you, and truth will prove the former clear. Thus endeth the first lesson. Amen.

TO GEORGE RICHARDS MINOT

NEW YORK, MAY 31, 1789

DEAR FRIEND,

YOURS of the 24th is before me. You propose a weekly exchange of letters. You call yourself the *Father Carnes* of the Club. You will not pretend to be of so much importance to a member of the Federal House as that gentleman would be.

I do not believe you will read, or that you have ever read, one of my public-spirited letters on the floor of the house.

The club are, however, my constituents, as Major Reed says; and I cannot disobey the *instructions of my constituents.*

I am already remarkable for my scribbling. My fellow-lodgers call me the Secretary of State. I will not promise punctuality, but if I may calculate upon the future by the past, I shall write twice a week. I leave it to the clerical members of the club to decide whether my letters would not read better if they were not so long and so frequent.

The Senate are reducing the rate of duties: Jamaica spirits to ten cents; other spirits to eight; Madeira eighteen; other wines ten; molasses will probably be reduced to three. If so reduced, I am afraid the drawback will be refused. The House will submit to the amendments reluctantly. I think they will pass.

The collection bill is reported. It is longer, and has more checks than the Massachusetts impost. It will be debated this week. Mr. Dawes will inform you more fully about the state of our politics than I can do. I wish most earnestly that Congress would despatch the civil departments, the necessary revenue acts, say impost and excise, the judiciary, and have a recess of a few months, leaving the business of appropriating the revenue, till we have one,—say next session. It would be well to see the people who sent us, and to hear what they have to say. If we keep shut up here, we shall forget their sentiments, and lay such duties as they will disapprove. Is not this a very republican sentiment? It will do to read, in the character of Mr. Carnes. There is much to do, but I think we should do wisely to postpone all the subjects of legislation, which will admit of it. The prospect of a recess would produce despatch.

What shall we do with Rhode Island? Would it be too condescending to send a recommendation to their Assembly to call a convention, in the words of the former Congress? Would it be proper to make their produce liable to the same duties as foreign produce, after the 1st of December next, when North Carolina may perhaps accede, so as to allow time for the Rhode Island folks to adopt it? Would it——(At this place I was called down to see company, and I do not know what should fill up the blank.) I understand that the House in Massachusetts is likely to be well disposed, and less numerous than the last. I wish they may pass the School Bill as it was sent up to the Senate. I would have our state first for knowledge, in the Union. Some are of opinion that ignorance produces loyalty. In 1786 it was otherwise, and I believe it will ever be found, that the best informed among the people are the most governable. You dislike the responsibility of the President in the case of the Minister of Foreign Affairs. I would have the President responsible for his appointments; and if those whom he puts in are unfit, they may be impeached, on misconduct, or he may remove them, when he finds them obnoxious. It would be easier for a minister to secure a faction in the Senate, or get the protection of the senators of his own state, than to secure the protection of the President, whose character would suffer by it. The number of the senators, the secrecy of their doings, would shelter *them*, and a corrupt connection between those who appoint *to* office, and who also maintain *in* office, and the officers themselves would be created. The meddling of the Senate in appointments is one of the least defensible parts of the Constitution. I would not extend their power any further. I must finish.

Yours, affectionately.

TO THOMAS DWIGHT

NEW YORK, JUNE 11, 1789

DEAR SIR,

I BEGIN to wish you would break silence. I hear, by Mr. Cabot, of the return or arrival of the new married pair, whom God bless, to Springfield.

.   .   .   .

I write in a violent hurry. Company interrupted my writing, and the post-office is near closing.

641

The Senate has finished the impost bill. It is not sent down yet. Molasses at two and a half cents, and no drawback on exportation. I hope the House, proud and stubborn as they are, will comply with the amendments, and pass the bill as speedily as possible.

The bill for the collection of the duties produces much debate, as indeed every thing does. Our House is a kind of Robin Hood society, where every thing is debated. The judicial business is maturing fast in the committee of the Senate.

Mr. Madison has introduced his long expected amendments.[11] They are the fruit of much labor and research. He has hunted up all the grievances and complaints of newspapers, all the articles of conventions, and the small talk of their debates. It contains a bill of rights, the right of enjoying property, of changing the government at pleasure, freedom of the press, of conscience, of juries, exemption from general warrants, gradual increase of representatives, till the whole number, at the rate of one to every thirty thousand, shall amount to   , and allowing two to every State, at least. This is the substance. There is too much of it. Oh! I had forgot, the right of the people to bear arms.

Risum teneatis amici?

Upon the whole, it may do some good towards quieting men, who attend to sounds only, and may get the mover some popularity, which he wishes.

It grows dark, and I must finish.

Yours, affectionately.

---

[11] *A proposition to amend the Constitution, in compliance with the expressed wishes of most of the States, was early introduced by Mr. Madison. Seventeen amendments were agreed upon in the House, which were reduced by the Senate (partly by compression of two or three into one) to twelve. Ten were ultimately adopted by the people.* [S. AMES]

TO GEORGE RICHARDS MINOT

NEW YORK, JUNE 12, 1789, FRIDAY

DEAR MINOT,

I INCLOSE, for Mr. Benjamin Russell, some of the amendments of the impost bill in Senate. Please to hand it to him. He has been very civil in sending me papers.

Your brother, Clarke Minot, wrote me by the last post. The appointments seem to be almost as far off and uncertain as ever. There is proposed a collector and naval officer to each port. But the nature and number of offices is totally uncertain in this state of the bill. It is daily debated. With tolerable diligence, and good temper, which has not been wanting hitherto, it will be finished next week, and sent to the Senate. The civil departments will employ us next, and the judiciary the Senate. They will finish their stint, as the boys say, before the House has done. Their number is less, and they have matured the business in committee. Yet Mr. Madison has inserted, in his amendments, the increase of representatives, each State having two at least. The rights of conscience, of bearing arms, of changing the government, are declared to be inherent in the people. Freedom of the press, too. There is a prodigious great dose for a medicine. But it will stimulate the stomach as little as hasty-pudding. It is rather food than physic. An immense mass of sweet and other herbs and roots for a diet drink.

Mr. Barrett will wait, and I must finish. But be assured that I am, affectionately.

Your friend.

[P.S.] The judiciary bill is reported in Senate, ordered to be printed, and to have a second reading next Monday week.

SPEECHES ON THE PRESIDENT'S POWER
TO REMOVE EXECUTIVE OFFICERS

*James Madison's motion for establishing the departments con-
tained a clause to the effect that the department heads should
"be removable by the President." Since the Constitution was
silent as to the removal of executive officers, save for impeachment,
the clause provoked a spirited debate. Those opposed to the clause,
on the one hand, differed among themselves as to the power of
removal. Some thought that executive officers could be removed
only by impeachment, while others thought that the power simply
to dismiss officers resided* somewhere *in the government. Most of
the latter believed that, since the department heads were appointed
by the President with the advice and consent of the Senate, both
authorities must have a part in the removal. Those in favor of
the clause, on the other hand, agreed that the power to remove
executive officers was inherently an executive power. As the
Constitution vested the executive power in the president, they
reasoned, the power of removal must be his alone. In this debate,
Ames and Madison worked as a tandem.*

*After the question of removal was settled, another difficulty
arose over the provision making it the duty of the Secretary of
the Treasury to "digest and report plans" to the House on financial
matters. Members argued that the clause would give the Secretary
undue influence over Congress, dangerously intermingling executive and legislative powers. Fisher Ames expressed his opinion
that the "deep, dark, and dreary chaos" of the nation's finances
enjoined Congress to accept whatever aid the Secretary could
give. Again, Ames worked with Madison to construct the Federalist
edifice. It is not known, however, whether he knew, as other
representatives did not, that Madison was counselling Washington
already to appoint Hamilton treasury secretary.*

*The latter question frequently troubled the House, above all
during Hamilton's tenure as Secretary of the Treasury. In his*

speech to the second session of the Second Congress, President Washington urged that the public debt be discharged as speedily as possible. On November 19, 1792, Thomas Fitzsimmons moved that the Secretary of the Treasury be directed to prepare a plan for that purpose. The motion immediately renewed the controversy over the Secretary's duty to "digest and report plans" to Congress, which had agitated the House in 1789.

Later, in 1793, Virginia's William Branch Giles filed a series of charges against the Secretary of the Treasury. Giles' resolutions demanded that certain records related to the charges be reported to Congress. In that debate Ames defended the original statement of "Executive Privilege."

JUNE 18, 1789

MR. AMES.—I believe there are very few gentlemen on this floor who have not made up their opinions; therefore it is particularly disagreeable to solicit their attention, especially when their patience is already exhausted, and their curiosity sated; but still I hope to be of some use in collecting the various arguments, and bringing them to a point. I shall rather confine myself to this task, than attempt to offer any thing that is new. I shall just observe, that the arguments of the gentleman from Pennsylvania, (Mr. SCOTT), which are complained of as being ridiculous, were arguments addressed to the understandings of the committee; my own understanding was enlightened by them, although they wore the garb of pleasantry. But to proceed to my main object.

The question, so far as it relates to the Constitution, is this: whether it has vested the sole power of removing in the President alone, or whether it is to take place by and with the advice and consent of the Senate? If the question of constitutionality was once despatched, we should be left to consider of the expediency of the measure. I take it to be admitted on all hands, though it was at first objected to by a worthy gentleman from South Carolina, that the power of removal from office, at pleasure, resides somewhere in the government. If it does not reside in the President, or the President and Senate, or if the Constitution has not vested it in any particular body, it must be in the legislature; for it is absurd to suppose that officers once appointed cannot be removed. The argument tending to prove that the power is in the President alone, by an express declaration, may not be satisfactory to the minds of those gentlemen who deem the Constitution to be silent on that head. But let those gentlemen revert to the principles, spirit, and tendency of the Constitution, and they will be compelled to acknowledge that there is the highest degree of probability that the power does vest in the President of the United States. I shall not undertake to say that the arguments are conclusive on this point. I do not suppose it is necessary that they should be so; for I believe nearly as good conclusions may be drawn from the refutations of an argument as from any other proof. For it is well said, that *destructio unius est generatio atterius.*

It has been said, and addressed with solemnity to our consciences, that we ought not to destroy the Constitution, to change or modify it; nay, it has been inferred that it is unnecessary and dangerous for us to proceed in this inquiry. It is true we may decide wrong, and therefore there may be danger; but it is not unnecessary. We have entered too far in the discussion to retreat with honor to ourselves, or security to our country. We are sworn as much to exercise constitutional authority, for the general good, as to refrain from assuming powers that are not given to us. We are as responsible for forbearing to act, as we are for acting. Are we to leave this question undetermined, to be contended for between the President and the Senate? Are we to say, that the question to us is indissoluble, and we therefore throw it upon the shoulders of the President to determine? If it is complex and difficult, it is certainly disingenuous in us to throw off the decision; besides, after so long a debate has been had, a decision must be made, for it never would do to strike out the words; as that would be deciding, and deciding against the power of the President.

It must be admitted that the Constitution is not explicit on the point in contest; yet the Constitution strongly infers that the power is in the President alone. It is declared that the executive power shall be vested in the President. Under these terms all the powers properly belonging to the executive department of the government are given, and such only taken away as are expressly excepted. If the Constitution had stopped here, and the duties had not been defined, either the President had had no powers at all, or he would acquire from that general expression all the powers properly belonging to the executive department. In the Constitution the President is required to see the laws faithfully executed. He cannot do this without he has a control over officers appointed to aid him in the performance of his duty. Take this power out of his hands, and you virtually strip him of his authority; you virtually destroy his responsibility—the great security which this Constitution holds out to the people of America.

Gentlemen will say, that, as the Constitution is not explicit, it must be matter of doubt where the power vests. If gentlemen's consciences will not let them agree with us, they ought to permit us to exercise the like liberty on our part. But they tell us we must meet them on the ground of accommodation, and give up a declaration that the power of removal is in the President, and they will acquiesce in declaring him to have the power of suspension; but they should recollect, that in so doing we sacrifice the principles of the Constitution.

It has been frequently said, that the power of removing is incidental to the power of appointing: as the Constitution implies that all officers, except the judges, are appointed during pleasure, so the power of removal may, in all cases, be exercised. But suppose this general principle true; yet it is an arbitrary principle, I take it, and one that cannot be proved. If it were denied, it could not be established; and if it were established, it is still doubtful whether it would make for the adverse side of this question or not; because it is doubted whether the Senate do actually appoint or not. It is admitted that they may check and regulate the appointment by the President, but they can do nothing more; they are merely an advisory body, and do not secure any degree of responsibility, which is one great object of the present Constitution. They are not answerable for their secret advice; but if they were, the blame divided among so many would fall upon none.

Certainly this assumed principle is very often untrue; but if it is true, it is not favorable to the gentlemen's doctrine. The President, I contend, has expressly the power of nominating and appointing, though he must obtain the consent of the Senate. He is the agent; the Senate may prevent his acting, but cannot act themselves. It may be difficult to illustrate this point by examples which will exactly correspond. But suppose the case of an executor, to whom is devised land, to be sold with the advice of a certain person, on certain conditions; the executor sells, with the consent and upon the conditions required in the will; the conditions are broken;—may the executor re-enter for the breach of them? Or has the person, with whom he was obliged to consult in the sale, any power to restrain him? The executor may remove the wrongful possessor from the land, though perhaps by the will, he may hold it in trust for another person's benefit. In this manner the President may remove from office, though, when vacant, he cannot fill it without the advice of the Senate. We are told it is dangerous to adopt constructions, and that what is not expressly given, is retained. Surely it is as improper in this way to confer power upon the Senate as upon the President; for if the power is not in the President solely by the Constitution, it never can be in the President and Senate by any grant of that instrument. Any arguments, therefore, that tend to make the first doubtful, operate against the other, and make it absurd. If gentlemen, then, doubt with respect to the first point, they will certainly hesitate with respect to the other. If the Senate have not the power, and it is proved that they have it not, by the arguments on both sides, the power either vests with the President or the Legislature; if it is at the disposal of the latter, and merely a matter of choice with us, clearly we ought not to bestow it on the Senate; for the doubt, whether the President is not already entitled to it, is an argument against placing it in other hands. Besides, the exercise of it by the Senate would be inconvenient; they are not always sitting; it would be insecure, because they are not responsible; it would be subversive of the great principles of the Constitution, and destructive to liberty, because it tends to intermingle executive and legislative powers in one body of men; and this blending of powers ever forms a tyranny. The Senate are not to accuse offenders; they are to try them; they are not to give orders, but, on complaint, to judge of the breach of them. We are warned against betraying the liberties of our country; we are told that all power tends to abuse; it is our duty, therefore, to keep them single and distinct. Where the executive swallows up the legislature, it becomes a despotism; where the legislature trenches upon the executive, it approaches towards despotism; and where they have less power than is necessary, it approximates towards anarchy. We should be careful, therefore, to preserve the limits of each authority in the present question. As it respects the power of the people, it is but of little importance. It is not pretended that the people have reserved the power of removing bad officers. It is admitted on all hands, that the government is possessed of such power; consequently, the people can neither lose nor gain power by it. We are the servants of the people; we are the watchmen, and we should be unfaithful in both characters, if we should so administer the government as to destroy its great principles and most essential advantages. The question now among us is, which of these servants shall exercise a power already granted? Wise and virtuous as the Senate may be, such a power lodged in their hands will not only tend to abuse, but cannot tend to any thing else. Need I repeat the inconveniences which will result from vesting it in the Senate? No, I appeal to that maxim which has the sanction of experience, and is authorized by the decision of the wisest men; to prevent an abuse of power, it must be distributed into three branches, who must be made independent, to watch and check each other. The people are to watch them all. While these maxims are pursued, our liberties will be preserved. It was from neglecting or despising these maxims, that the ancient commonwealths were destroyed. A voice issues from the earth which covers their ruins, and proclaims to mankind the sacredness of the truths that are at this moment in controversy. It is said that the Constitution has blended these powers which we advise to keep separate, and therefore we ought to follow in completing similar regulations. But gentlemen ought to recollect that that has been an objection against the Constitution; and if it is a well founded one, we ought to endeavor, by all that is in our power, to restrain the evil rather than to increase it. But perhaps, with the sole power of removal in the President, the check of the Senate in appointments may have a salutary tendency. In removing from office, their advice and consent is liable to all the objections which have been stated. It is very proper to guard the introduction of a man into office by every check that can properly be applied; but after he is appointed, there can be no use in exercising a judgment upon events which have heretofore taken place. If the Senate are to possess the power of removal, they will be enabled to hold the person in office, let the circumstances be what they may that point out the necessity or propriety of his removal. It creates a permanent connexion; it will nurse faction; it will promote intrigue to obtain protectors and to shelter tools. Sir, it is infusing poison into the Constitution; it is an impure and unchaste connexion; there is ruin in it; it is tempting the Senate with forbidden fruit; it ought not to be possible for a branch of the legislature even to hope for a share of the executive power; for they may be tempted to increase it, by a hope to share the exercise of it. People are seldom jealous of their own power; and if the Senate become part of the executive, they will be very improper persons to watch that department; so far from being champions for liberty, they will become conspirators against it.

The executive department should ever be independent, and sufficiently energetic to defeat the attempts of either branch of the legislature to usurp its prerogative. But the proposed control of the Senate is setting that body above the President; it tends to establish an aristocracy. And at the moment we are endangering the principles of our free and excellent Constitution, gentlemen are undertaking to amuse the people with the sound of liberty. If their ideas should succeed, a principle of mortality will be infused into a government, which the lovers of mankind have wished might last to the end of the world. With a mixture of the executive and legislative powers in one body, no government can long remain uncorrupt. With a corrupt executive, liberty may long retain a trembling existence. With a corrupt legislature, it is impossible; the vitals of the Constitution would be mortified, and death must follow on every step. A government thus formed would be the most formidable curse that could befall this country. Perhaps an enlightened people might timely foresee and correct the error; but if a season were allowed for such a compound to grow and produce its natural fruit, it would either banish liberty, or the people would be driven to exercise their unalienable right, the right of uncivilized nature, and destroy a monster whose voracious and capacious jaws would crush and swallow up themselves and their posterity.

The principles of this Constitution, while they are adhered to, will perpetuate that liberty which it is the honor of Americans to have well contended for. The clause in the bill is calculated to support those principles; and for this, if there was no other reason, I should be inclined to give it my support.

JUNE 16, 1789

MR. AMES.—When this question was agitated at a former period, I took no part in the debate. I believe it was then proposed, without any idea or intention of drawing on a lengthy discussion, and to me it appeared to be well understood and settled by the House; but since it has been reiterated and contested again, I feel it my bounden duty to deliver the reasons for voting in the manner I then did, and shall now do. Mr. Chairman, I look upon every question which touches the Constitution as serious and important, and therefore worthy of the fullest discussion, and the most solemn decision. I believe, on the present occasion, we may come to something near certainty, by attending to the leading principles of the Constitution. In order that the good purposes of a federal government should be answered, it was necessary to delegate considerable powers; and the principle upon which the grant was made, intended to give sufficient power to do all possible good, but to restrain the rulers from doing mischief.

The Constitution places all executive power in the hands of the President, and could he personally execute all the laws, there would be no occasion for establishing auxiliaries; but the circumscribed powers of human nature in one man, demand the aid of others. When the objects are widely stretched out, or greatly diversified, meandering through such an extent of territory as that the United States possess, a minister cannot see with his own eyes every transaction, or feel with his hands the minutiæ that pass through his department. He must therefore have assistants. But in order that he may be responsible to his country, he must have a choice in selecting his assistants, a control over them, with power to remove them when he finds the qualifications which induced their appointment cease to exist. There are officers under the Constitution who hold their office by a different tenure —your judges are appointed during good behavior; and from the delicacy and peculiar nature of their trust, it is right it should be so, in order that they may be independent and impartial in administering justice between the government and its citizens. But the removability of the one class, or immovability of the other, is founded on the same principle, the security of the people against the abuse of power. Does any gentleman imagine that an officer is entitled to his office as to an estate? Or does the legislature establish them for the convenience of an individual? For my part, I conceive it intended to carry into effect the purposes for which the Constitution was intended.

The executive powers are delegated to the President, with a view to have a responsible officer to superintend, control, inspect, and check the officers necessarily employed in administering the laws. The only bond between him and those he employs, is the confidence he has in their integrity and talents; when that confidence ceases, the principal ought to have power to remove those whom he can no longer trust with safety. If an officer shall be guilty of neglect or infidelity, there can be no doubt but he ought to be removed; yet there may be numerous causes for removal which do not amount to a crime. He may propose to do a mischief; but I believe the mere intention would not be cause of impeachment. He may lose the confidence of the people upon suspicion, in which case it would be improper to retain him in service; he ought to be removed at any time, when, instead of doing the greatest possible good, he is likely to do an injury to the public interest by being continued in the administration.

I presume gentlemen will generally admit that officers ought to be removed when they become obnoxious; but the question is, how shall this power be exercised? It will not I apprehend be contended, that all officers hold their offices during good behavior. If this be the case, it is a most singular government. I believe there is not another in the universe that bears the least semblance to it in this particular; such a principle, I take it, is contrary to the nature of things. But the manner how to remove is the question. If the officer misbehaves, he can be removed by impeachment; but in this case is impeachment the only mode of removal? It would be found very inconvenient to have a man continued in office after being impeached, and when all confidence in him was suspended or lost. Would not the end of impeachment be defeated by this means? If Mr. Hastings, who was mentioned by the gentleman from Delaware (Mr. VINING) preserved his command in India, could he not defeat the impeachment now pending in Great Britain? If that doctrine obtains in America, we shall find impeachments come too late; while we are preparing the process, the mischief will be perpetrated, and the offender will escape. I apprehend it will be as frequently necessary to prevent crimes as to punish them; and it may often happen that the only prevention is by removal. The

superintending power possessed by the President, will perhaps enable him to discover a base intention before it is ripe
for execution. It may happen that the Treasurer may be
disposed to betray the public chest to the enemy, and so
injure the government beyond the possibility of reparation;
should the President be restrained from removing so dangerous
on officer, until the slow formality of an impeachment was
complied with, when the nature of the case rendered the
application of a sudden and decisive remedy indispensable?
But it will, I say, be admitted, that an officer may be
removed. The question then is, by whom? Some gentlemen
say by the President alone; and others, by the President, by
and with the advice of the Senate. By the advocates of the
latter mode, it is alleged, that the Constitution is in the way
of the power of removal being by the President alone. If this
is absolutely the case, there is an end to all further inquiry.
But before we suffer this to be considered as an insuperable
impediment, we ought to be clear that the Constitution
prohibits him the exercise of what, on a first view, appears
to be a power incident to the executive branch of the
Government. The gentleman from Virginia (Mr. MADISON)
has made so many observations to evince the constitutionality
of the clause, that it is unnecessary to go over the ground
again. I shall therefore confine myself to answer only some
remarks made by the gentleman from South Carolina, (Mr.
SMITH.) The powers of the President are defined in the
Constitution; but it is said, that he is not expressly authorized
to remove from office. If the Constitution is silent also with
respect to the Senate, the argument may be retorted. If this
silence proves that the power cannot be exercised by the
President, it certainly proves that it cannot be exercised by
the President, by and with the advice and consent of the
Senate. The power of removal is incident to government; but
not being distributed by the Constitution, it will come before
the legislature, and, like every other omitted case, must be
supplied by law.

Gentlemen have said, when the question was formerly before us, that all powers not intended to be given up to the general government were retained. I beg gentlemen, when they undertake to argue from implication, to be consistent, and admit the force of other arguments drawn from the same source. It is a leading principle in every free government, it is a prominent feature in this, that the legislative and executive powers should be kept distinct; yet the attempt to blend the executive and legislative departments in exercising the power of removal, is such a mixing as ought not to be carried into practice on arguments grounded on implication. And the gentleman from Virginia, (Mr. WHITE's,) reasoning is wholly drawn from implication. He supposes, as the Constitution qualifies the President's power of appointing to office, by subjecting his nomination to the concurrence of the Senate, that the qualification follows of course in the removal.

If this is to be considered as a question undecided by the Constitution, and submitted on the footing of expediency, it will be well to consider where the power can be most usefully deposited for the security and benefit of the people. It has been said, by the gentleman on the other side of the House, (Mr. SMITH,) that there is an impropriety in allowing the exercise of this power; that it is a dangerous authority, and much evil may result to the liberty and property of the officer, who may be turned out of business without a moment's warning. I take it, the question is not whether such power shall be given or retained; because it is admitted on all hands, that the officer may be removed; so that it is no grant of power; it raises no new danger. If we strike out the clause, we do not keep the power, nor prevent the exercise of it; so that the gentleman will derive none of the security he contemplates by agreeing to the motion for striking out. It will be found, that the nature of the business requires it to be conducted by the head of the executive; and I believe it will be found even there, that more injury will arise from not removing improper officers, than from displacing good ones. I believe experience has convinced us that it is an irksome business; and officers are more frequently continued in place after they become unfit to perform their duties, than turned out while their talents and integrity are useful. But advantages may result from keeping the power of removal *in terrorem* over the heads of the officers; they will be stimulated to do their duty to the satisfaction of the principal, who is to be responsible for the whole executive department.

The gentleman has supposed there will be great difficulty in getting officers of abilities to engage in the service of their country upon such terms. There has never yet been any scarcity of proper officers in any department of the government of the United States, even during the war; when men risked their lives and property by engaging in such service, there were candidates enough. But why should we connect the Senate in the removal? Their attention is taken up with other important business, and they have no constitutional authority to watch the conduct of the executive officers; and therefore, cannot use such authority with advantage. If the President is inclined to shelter himself behind the Senate, with respect to having continued an improper person in office, we lose the responsibility, which is our greatest security; the blame among so many will be lost. Another reason occurs to me against blending these powers. An officer who superintends the public revenue will naturally acquire a great influence. If he obtains support in the Senate, upon an attempt of the President to remove him, it will be out of the power of the House, when applied to by the First Magistrate, to impeach him with success; for the very means of proving charges of mal-conduct against him, will be under the power of the officer; all the papers necessary to convict him may be withheld while the person continues in his office. Protection may be rendered for protection; and as this officer has such extensive influence, it may be exerted to procure the re-election of his friends. These circumstances, in addition to those stated by the gentleman from Jersey, (Mr. BOUDINOT,) must clearly evince to every gentleman the impropriety of connecting the Senate with the President in removing from office.

I do not say these things will take effect now, and if the question only related to what might take place in a few years, I should not be uneasy on this point, because I am sensible the gentlemen who form the present Senate are above corruption; but in future ages, (and I hope this government may be perpetuated to the end of time,) such things may take place, and it is our duty to provide against evils which may be foreseen, but, if now neglected, will be irremediable.

I beg leave to observe further, that there are three opinions entertained by gentlemen on this subject. One is, that the power of removal is prohibited by the Constitution; the next is, that it requires it by the President; and the other is, that the Constitution is totally silent. It therefore appears to me proper for the House to declare what is their sense of the Constitution. If we declare justly on this point, it will serve for a rule of conduct to the executive magistrate; if we declare improperly, the judiciary will revise our decision; so that at all events I think we ought to make the declaration.

JUNE 18, 1789

MR. LIVERMORE .—If the consent of the Senate be absolutely requisite with respect to appointments, it is one thing; but if the President has no more to do than to ask their opinion, or to receive their advice, it is another thing. The latter appeared to him to be the sentiment of another gentleman from Massachusetts, (Mr. AMES.)

[Mr. AMES rose and denied such an opinion. His idea was that the President was the agent, and the Senate a check to regulate his agency.]

JANUARY 9, 1790

REPORT OF THE SECRETARY
OF THE TREASURY

MR. AMES conceived it to be the duty of the House to obtain the best information on any subject; but on this very important one they ought to be particularly careful to get it from the highest source. The Secretary of the Treasury is a most important and responsible officer; the delicacy of his situation required every indulgence to be extended to him, that had a tendency to enable him to complete the arduous undertaking in which he was engaged. It would be a real misfortune that a salutary measure should be defeated for want of being understood; yet the most advantageous plans may miscarry in their passage through this House, by reason of their not being clearly comprehended. He hoped, therefore, that the financier would be authorized to make such communications and illustrations as he judged necessary; but he wished these communications to be in writing; in this shape they would obtain a degree of permanency favorable to the responsibility of the officer, while, at the same time, they would be less liable to be misunderstood.

JANUARY 28, 1790

REPORT OF THE SECRETARY
OF THE TREASURY

Mr. AMES observed, that the subject of the Secretary's report, on the means of promoting public credit, is the order for this day; but when I consider the circumstances under which this order was entered into, I am inclined to wish for an extension of the time. It will be recollected that this report was ordered to be printed, in order that the members might have it in their hands for consideration; when this was done, it was expected that the printing would be more expeditiously executed than the event has demonstrated it could be, of consequence our time for deliberation has been curtailed; and those gentlemen who were against so early a day before, will think the present rather premature. In order to accommodate them, I shall move you a longer day than otherwise I might be disposed to do; and if I am seconded, I move that the order of the day be postponed till next Monday week.

JUNE 25, 1789

Mr. AMES hoped the subject might be treated with candor and liberality; he supposed the objections were made on those principles, and therefore required a serious answer. The worthy gentleman who first expressed his aversion to the clause seemed to be apprehensive that the power of reporting plans by the Secretary would be improper, because it appeared to him to interfere with the legislative duty of the House, which the House ought not to relinquish.

Whenever it is a question, Mr. Speaker, said he, whether this House ought, or ought not, to establish offices to exercise a part of the power of either branch of the government, there are two points which I take into consideration, in order to lead my mind to a just decision; first, whether the proposed disposition is useful; and, second, whether it can be safely guarded from abuse. Now I take it, sir, that the House, by their order for bringing in a bill to establish the Treasury Department in this way, have determined the point of utility; or, have they erred in adopting that opinion, I will slightly make an inquiry. How does it tend to general utility? The Secretary is presumed to acquire the best knowledge of the subject of finance of any member of the community. Now, if this House is to act on the best knowledge of circumstances, it seems to follow logically, that the House must obtain evidence from that officer; the best way of doing this will be publicly from the officer himself, by making it his duty to furnish us with it. It will not be denied, sir, that this officer will be better acquainted with his business than other people can be. It lies within his department, to have a comprehensive view of the state of the public revenues and expenditures. He will, by his superintending power over the collection, be able to discover abuses, if any, in that department, and to form the most eligible plan to remedy or prevent the evil. From his information respecting money transactions, he may be able to point out the best mode for supporting the public credit; indeed, these seem to me to be the great objects of his appointment.

It is, perhaps, a misfortune incident to public assemblies, that from their nature they are more incompetent to a complete investigation of accounts than a few individuals; perhaps in a government so extended, and replete with variety in its mode of expenditure as this, the subject may be more perplexing than in countries of smaller extent, and less variety of objects to guard. The science of accounts is at best but an abstruse and dry study; it is scarcely to be understood but by an unwearied assiduity for a long time; how then can a public body, elected annually, and in session for a few months, undertake the arduous task with a full prospect of success? If our plans are formed upon these incomplete investigations, we can expect little improvement; for I venture to say, that our knowledge will be far inferior to that of an individual, like the present officer. Hence I contend, sir, that the Secretary is a useful and invaluable part of the government.

I would not have it understood that I am against an inquiry being made into this subject at every session of the legislature. I think such a practice highly salutary, but I would not trust to a hasty, or perhaps injudicious examination of a business of this magnitude; on the contrary, I would take every precaution in ascertaining the foundation upon which our revenues are to stand.

If we consider the present situation of our finances, owing to a variety of causes, we shall no doubt perceive a great, although unavoidable confusion throughout the whole scene; it presents to the imagination a deep, dark, and dreary chaos; impossible to be reduced to order without the mind of the architect is clear and capacious, and his power commensurate to the occasion; he must not be the flitting creature of a day, he must have time given him competent for the successful exercise of his authority. It is with an intention to let a little sunshine into the business that the present arrangement is proposed; I hope it may be successful, nor do I doubt the event. I am confident our funds are equal to the demand, if they are properly brought into operation; but a bad administration of the finances will prove our greatest evil.

But is our proposed arrangement safe? Are the guards

sufficient to prevent abuse? I am perfectly satisfied it can be made so, and hope the united exertions of both Houses will effect it. How is the power complained of by the honorable gentlemen over the way (Mr. PAGE and Mr. TUCKER) unsafe? We are told, the plans reported may have an undue influence. Upon what ground is this opinion rested? Do the gentlemen apprehead the facts will be fallaciously stated? If so, I would ask, cannot they be detected? If facts are faithfully stated, and the deductions are fair, no doubt the plan will be patronized; and will gentlemen say that it ought not? I believe there is little danger of imposition, for a person in this situation would hardly run the risk of detection, in a case where detection might be easy by an examination of the books and vouchers, and his reputation be destroyed.

What improper influence could a plan reported openly and officially have on the mind of any member, more than if the scheme and information were given privately at the Secretary's office?

Nor, Mr. Chairman, do I approve what the gentlemen say with respect to calling on the Secretary for information; it will be no mark of inattention or neglect, if he take time to consider the questions you propound; but if you make it his duty to furnish you plans of information on the improvement of the revenue and support of public credit, and he neglect to perform it, his conduct or capacity is virtually impeached. This will be furnishing an additional check.

It has been complained of as a novelty; but, let me ask gentlemen, if it is not to an institution of a similar kind that the management of the finances of Britain is the envy of the world? It is true, the Chancellor of the Exchequer is a member of the House that has the sole right of originating money bills; but is that a reason why we should not have the information which can be obtained from our officer, who possesses the means of acquiring equally important and useful knowledge? The nation, as well as the Parliament of

Britain, holds a check over the Chancellor: if his budget contains false calculations, they are corrected; if he attempts impositions, or even unpopular measures, his administration becomes odious, and he is removed. Have we more reason to fear than they? Have we less responsibility or security in our arrangement of the Treasury department? If we have, let us improve it, but not abridge it of its safest and most useful power. I hope the committee will refuse their approbation of the present motion.

NOVEMBER 21, 1792

Mr. AMES rose at a late hour in the debate, but before he would pretend to intrude upon the patience of the House, (a motion for taking the question being then under consideration,) he requested to know whether it was most agreeable to put the question? A general desire to hear his arguments, however, prevailed, and he proceeded nearly in substance as follows:

It is so fashionable to introduce the Funding System upon every occasion, it would perhaps appear strange to say that it is out of order upon any. To my mind, and probably to most gentlemen present, it will be difficult to perceive that the question before us bears any relation to that subject, or to the frontier bill, the excise, the perpetual taxes, the encouragement of manufactures, and many other topics, which, somehow or other, have been interwoven with the debate. At this late hour of the day, and in so wearisome a stage of the question, I may be permitted to decline any further notice of these auxiliary subjects.

The great end we have in view is the paying off the public debt. This object, truly important in itself, unites the best sense and strongest wishes of the country. It is our duty to provide means for the accomplishment of this end. All agree that a plan is necessary. It must be framed with wisdom and digested with care, so as to operate with the greatest effect, till the whole debt shall be extinguished. The true question is, Which is the best mode of framing this system? Several modes have been preferred by different persons. Some advocate the appointment of a select committee of this House; others insist that the House in Committee of the Whole is the only proper mode; while others, who defend the original motion, desire to have a plan prepared and submitted by the Secretary of the Treasury. It may obviate the force of many of the arguments we have heard to remark, that it is not asserted that either of the several modes is intrinsically incapable of effecting the purpose. It would be improper to say that a select committee could not be formed who would be able to collect the materials for an exact knowledge of the subject, and who, after acquiring that knowledge, would be able to form a sound judgment. Neither would it be just nor respectful to deny, in the abstract, the capability of the House in Committee to digest such a plan. But the question still returns, Which of the three methods is the best to begin with? Neither this House nor a select committee are pretended to be already possessed of the knowledge which is requisite to the framing a system for a sinking fund. The very materials from which this knowledge is to be gleaned are not in the possession of this House—they are in the Treasury Department. Neither the curiosity nor the legislative duty of members lead them to resort daily to the Treasury to investigate official details; and even if it were so, the officer at the head of the department, having his mind incessantly occupied with his official business, must be admitted to possess a more familiar and ready, if not a more ample, knowledge of the subject. Indeed, the situation of the Secretary of the Treasury is so evidently favorable to his digesting the plan of a sinking fund, that it seems unnecessary to urge it even to those who are opposed to the reference. For their objections imply the preference of the mode, in point of expediency, as strongly as those who explicitly recommend it. They say the plan of the Secretary will come forward with too much advantage. Members, say they, not having the aid of these means of information which the Secretary possesses, will not be able to resist the train of reasoning with which he will introduce his plan. It is even expressly admitted that the information of the Treasury Department is necessary, and must be called for; but they would not receive it with the reasoning of the Secretary. Without wasting time to prove this point, common sense will decide instantly that the knowledge of our financial affairs, and of the means of improving them, is to be obtained the most accurately from the officer whose duty it is made, by our own law, to understand them; who is appointed and commissioned for that very purpose; and to whom every day's practice in his office must afford some additional information of official details, as well as of the operation of the laws. The arguments on both sides end in the same point, that the information of the Secretary would be useful. Our object being to prefer that mode of preparing a plan which is adapted to present us the best, the argument might end here, if it were not that the Constitution is alleged to forbid our resorting to the Secretary. I reverence the Constitution, and I readily admit that the frequent appeal to that as a standard proceeds from a respectful attachment to it. So far it is a source of agreeable reflection. But I feel very different emotions when I find it almost daily resorted to on questions of little importance, when, by strained and fanciful constructions, it is made an instrument of casuistry. It is to be feared it may lose something in our minds in point of certainty, and more in point of dignity.

And what is the clause of the Constitution opposed to the

receiving a plan of a sinking fund from the Secretary? Bills for raising revenue shall originate in this House. I verily believe the members of this House, and the citizens at large, would be very much surprised to hear this clause of the Constitution formally and gravely stated as repugnant to the reference to the Treasury Department for a plan, if they and we had not been long used to hear it.

To determine the force of this amazing constitutional objection, it will be sufficient to define terms. What is a bill? It is a term of technical import, and surely it cannot need a definition; it is an act in an inchoate state, having the form but not the authority of a law. What is originating a bill? Our rules decide it. Every bill shall be introduced by a motion for leave, or by a committee.

It may be said the plan of a sinking fund, reported by the Secretary, is not in technical, or even in popular language, a bill—not by the rules of the House or those of common sense is this motion the originating a bill. By resorting to the spirit of the Constitution, or by adopting any reasonable construction of the clause, is it posssible to make it appear repugnant to the proposition for referring to the Secretary? The opposers of this proposition surely will not adopt a contruction of the Constitution. They have often told us we are to be guided by a strict adherence to the letter; that there is no end to the danger of constructions. The letter is not repugnant; and will it be seriously affirmed that, according to the spirit and natural meaning of the Constitution, the report of the Secretary will be a revenue bill, or any other bill, and that this proposition is originating such a bill? If it be, where shall we stop? If the idea of a measure which first passes through the mind be confounded with the measure subsequent to it, what confusion will ensue! The President, by suggesting the proposition, may as well be pretended to originate a revenue bill; even a newspaper plan would be a breach of the exclusive privilege of this House; and the liberty of the press, so justly dear to us, would be found unconstitutional. Yet, if, without any order of the House, the draft of an act were printed, and a copy laid before every member in his seat, no person will venture to say that it is a bill, that it is originated, or can be brought under the cognizance of the House, unless by a motion in conformity to the rules and orders. The report of the Secretary in regard to manufactures, so often adverted to, has not yet been acted upon; does that appear on our Journals as a bill? Language has not yet been perverted to such a degree as to assert any such thing; and yet the constitutional objection implies opinions no less. I rely upon it, that neither the letter of the Constitution, nor any meaning that it can be tortured into, will support the objection which has been so often urged with solemn emphasis and persevering zeal.

If the Constitution be admitted, therefore, to authorize the reference to the Secretary, why should not the mode which is proved to be the most expedient be immediately adopted? Here we meet another objection. It is said, that the legislative and executive branches of government are to be kept distinct, and this reference will produce an improper blending of them. It is a truth that these departments are to be kept distinct; but the conclusion drawn from it is altogether vague. The execution of every trust requires some deliberation, and many of them call into action the highest powers of the human mind, and the most intense and persevering application of them; yet these trusts are to be executively performed, and it by no means follows, that the officer charged with them invades the deliberative functions of Congress. On the other hand, many laws are the result of plain principles or parts of the Constitution, and Congress, by enacting them, only executes the Constitution. Yet, here is no encroachment upon the executive branch. The truth is, the Constitution has allotted powers to the several branches of the government, and by that rule we are to judge of their several limits. The PRESIDENT proposes measures to the legislature, in conformity to the Constitution; yet no one ever supposed that his doing so is a departure from a just theory; nor has it, as far as I know, been ever insinuated till of late, in this or any other country, that the calling for information from officers, any more than the calling for testimony from witnesses, amounts to a transfer of our legislative duty. It is very easy to conceive how much increased information may aid us in deliberating, but it is hard to discern how we are to profit by the want of it. It is true it is our peculiar province to deliberate, but neither the letter of the Constitution, nor the law establishing the Treasury Department, nor the reason of the case, have restrained us from calling for official information. It is not true in fact, that the deliberative and executive departments are blended by referring to the Secretary. Any objections deduced from an over-refining theory, and not warranted by the Constitution, might need an answer if we were now framing a government, but can have no force in the administration of one. Indeed, it is a very scholastic, and very imposing mistake, to abandon the letter and meaning of the plan of government we act under, and to undertake to reason independently, as if we were now settling the institutes of a political treatise.

The expediency of this question of referring to the Secretary, which is brought into dispute, involves many others which will admit of none. In framing the plan of a sinking fund is the officer at the head of our finances to have any agency? If it be said he is not, then, it may be demanded, why is an idle officer and an useless office kept up? The sense of mankind as well as the practice of nations, seems to show that where there are finances there should be a financier; that he should possess at least common talents, and more than common industry in the application of them to his duty.

This is not a point to be proved now for the first time. The law of the old Congress and their practice were conformable to this motion. We hear often of the people being opposed to these references. So far as I have been informed the opposition is a novelty. The law establishing the Treasury Department, passed by a great majority, expressly makes it the duty of the Secretary to prepare and report plans of finance. Scarce a whisper of objection was then heard in the House, and not one, I believe, in the country. Our own practice of referring has passed unresisted till of late. Gentlemen now opposed to this reference, in one instance, if I recollect rightly, referred to the Attorney General to revise a plan of the judicial department, and on another to require the Secretary of State to report on the means for improving our trade and navigation. These objects partake as much of legislation, and are as incommunicable as the subject of discussion. The former votes and arguments of gentlemen opposed to the present reference afford some proof of its fitness as well as constitutionality.

The intrinsic reasonableness of this practice is not less than its authority from law and precedent, and what is more, the precedent of its opposers.

Private affairs prosper by skill, economy, and industry, in the management of them. The finances of a nation, though infinitely more important, require nothing more than economy upon a great scale. Let the moneyed affairs of a country be made everybody's business, and nobody will do it. Would you have them prosper, let them be confided to one man, who, however, shall be under the strict control of the law, and rigidly responsible for his doings. That man, if he loves an honest reputation as much as a man of common sense and feeling may be expected to do, will make the public business his own; he will put his character at risk: his time and all his talents will be devoted to the public. Such will be his dispositions; now what will be his opportunities to render service? He will have, at one view before him, the whole arrangements of finance: the imports and exports, the receipts and expenditures, the operation of the law, the means of improving it; the frauds committed or attempted on the revenue, and the checks to guard it; the well founded objections against the law and the prejudices which time or conciliatory conduct may efface, the appropriations of the revenue—the places where and terms on which loans may be obtained, as well as the state of foreign trade; the regulations of foreign nations, and perhaps it may be added, in subordination to the Chief Magistrate, the state of treaties and negotiations. It will be seen that the ordinary discharge of his duty, as well as that which will oblige him sometimes to conflict against prejudices, and sometimes against fraud, will render the details of finance familiar to him, and will almost force him to adopt plans for reducing this great mass into system and order.

Is it to be denied that in consequence he will possess some means of information which this House or a committee must acquire only by slow and laborious investigation? In pursuing it the time might fail, and the materials get confused. Yet, allowing it effected, they have gained no more than it is his duty to furnish on the order of this House, and this is what we are contending for. If we call for it and he is not able to give it, we shall thus expose his incapacity or negligence. The public opinion, thus enlightened, will soon displace the officer, and a fitter man will succeed him. In this way, the people will exercise an effective control over their servants.

Be the information given by the officer what it may, the sources from which his inferences are drawn, his facts and reasonings, are publicly exposed. They are equally in possession of every member, who is thus placed on an equal, and on the best footing to attack or defend the report. As much cannot be said of the report of a select committee or a Committee of the Whole. It has been intimated, that in framing a report, the Secretary would be liable to misinformation, to some local or other attachments. This is possible for he is a man; but will the Committee be free from it? The Secretary is answerable for his conduct to the nation, and certainly he is not more subject to local partialities than members are to their respective districts. The advantage of impartiality in the first concoction of a report seems to be evidently in favor of a reference.

It has been said, on the other side, information may be wanted, it is true, from the Secretary; but let the House first make progress in the business, and then receive it by a committee advising with the Secretary. If this may be done, what becomes of the constitutional difficulties and all we have heard of the transfer of our deliberative power?

But, if we are to have the official information, why should we set out without it? why should it not be given openly, so as to put all the members on an equality, and before prepossessions are formed with regard to plans, which might make a late report from the Treasury appear to come in aid of one party or another? Would the style of declamation be less vehement against the secret communications of a Secretary with the Committee, than against a report made in the face of day, and subject to the criticism not only of this House, but of an enlightened nation?

It is not my present design to ask for what purpose of argument or of candor it is so often insinuated, that the question really is, whether this House shall legislate, or whether it shall transfer the power of making laws to the Secretary of the Treasury?

With all this official information previously before us, are we less qualified or worse disposed to deliberate? It would be extravagant to affirm that, in proportion as our means of information are made complete, we are worse situated to legislate; and, as to the spirit of inquiry, I do not remember that the reports of the Secretary have blunted it. From the manner in which they have been discussed heretofore, those gentlemen will confide in the assurance I venture to give them, that they will be thoroughly sifted. They have not always passed unaltered, and never without passing through the fire of a debate.

We may repeat it, therefore, what color is there for saying that the Secretary legislates? Neither my memory nor my understanding can discern any. I am well aware that no topic is better calculated to make popular impressions; but I cannot persuade myself that the people will charge us with neglect or violation of duty, for putting ourselves into a situation to discharge it in the best and most circumspect manner.

There is another ground of objection, which is urged against the reference. It is said, it gives undue influence to the Treasury. The reasonings of the Secretary, which accompany his reports, are alleged to excite an influence which cannot be resisted. There are two sorts of influence: one, which arises from weight of reason and the intrinsic merit of a proposition; the other, personal influence. As to the former, it is hard to conceive of the influence of reasoning which cannot be analyzed and made capable of exact estimation by the reasoning faculties of those to whom it is submitted; and that estimation, be it what it may, ought to obtain. No one can wish to see it underrated.

But we are told by the opposers of a reference, that it is incredible that one man, be his official opportunities what they may, should possess more information than the members of this House, collected from every district of the country. Then I answer, with inferior information, it would be impossible his reasoning should overpower and confound the superior information of the House. The members will be in the less danger from this officer, if, as we are told, he is misinformed by correspondents, and has repeatedly discovered on subjects of revenue and finance, a princely ignorance. This, we are told, however, by gentlemen who urge the danger of losing our independence and our faculties of discernment, as soon as we suffer a report, with its reasonings, to be made to the House.

If it be personal influence, independently of reason and evidence, which is apprehended by gentlemen opposed to the reference, for whom do they apprehend it? For themselves, or for us who advocate the motion? Surely, if they do not feel, we do not fear it; we know how to respect their independence of spirit; they would disdain an imputation of the sort; their candor will permit us to say, if it be a neighborly concern they feel for us, there is no occasion for it.

On the whole, if we regard the Constitution, we find not the least color for bringing it into question on this debate. The law and usage of the old Congress corresponded with this motion. Our own Treasury law expressly makes it the duty of the Secretary to prepare and report plans; and shall the practice of one branch run counter to that which is made the course of his duty by the law of the land? It would be an uncommon and very irregular mode of repealing a law. The advantages of this practice of referring, are manifest and great: more information is obtained, and more order, intelligence, and system, are preserved in the administration of the finances. The old Congress and the several states have exhibited expensive and deplorable proofs of the evils incident to want of order, as well as to the number of systems of finance and financiers. With this mass of evidence before your eyes, it cannot be believed that we shall take any step which will tend to introduce disorder and inefficiency into our finances.

MARCH 1, 1793

GILES RESOLUTIONS

[MADISON] . . . If anything could heighten astonishment on this occasion it must be the reason assigned by the Secretary for any obscurity that might have hung over our finances—"that, till the last resolutions, no call had been made on the

674

department which rendered it proper to exhibit a general view of the public moneys and funds, or to show the amount and situation of such as were unapplied." Mr. M. would not decide that the legislature was free from blame in not using more full and efficacious means of obtaining such information as would have removed all obscurity. But, whatever degree of blame might fall on them, it never could be admitted that their calls on the department had furnished no proper occasion for exhibiting a full view of the public finances.

Mr. AMES prefaced his remarks on the subject before the Committee by some observations on the nature of the charges brought forward. He was happy that they were determinate, and conceived that the defence could be crowded in a nutshell. As to the first charge in the resolution immediately before the Committee, he had seen no proof in support of it brought forward. It is founded only on assertion, and he conceived that contra-assertion was sufficient to meet it. No authority, it was said, was given to the Secretary to obtain the loan under the blended authority of both acts. This is not one of the charges included in the resolutions before the Committee, and therefore this is not the time to answer it. However, if this were fact, nothing criminal could in consequence be imputed; and, since the purposes of both laws were carried into execution, there could be no ground for saying that either was violated. He said much on the impracticability of the line of conduct which some gentlemen appeared to think ought to have been followed by the Secretary. It was impossible to keep different funds, differently appropriated, so inviolably separate as that one might not be used for the object of the other; all was right, he conceived, provided what was taken was to be replaced. He was also of opinion that the overflowing of one fund could be applied to make up the deficiency of another; and that all that is necessary is to give priority to the appropriation. The money paid in Europe for interest on the loan was said to have been improperly applied, because the fund appropriated for the purpose was here. He insisted that that money was absolutely represented here by an equal sum: and he contended that, though the interest was not paid in the identical coin appropriated, yet, by allowing a very reasonable latitude of expression, it could be said that the interest was paid with the money appropriated, for the applicability of the sums there depended on the existence of the fund here. He next turned to the second charge in the resolution; and, after showing that the natural presumption was, that the Secretary either was instructed or had a discretionary power, he then vindicated his conduct in respect to the drafts of money to this country. He did honor to the motives of the gentlemen who had instituted the inquiry, and concluded an elegant speech, by a contrasted picture of our former and present situation as a country, dwelling upon the importance of preserving harmony, and insisting on the danger of giving rise to suspicions against a highly responsible officer, and of bringing forward charges not to be supported by proof.

TO GEORGE RICHARDS MINOT

NEW YORK, JUNE 23, 1789

DEAR FRIEND,

I HAVE written so often, that my conscience did not reproach me with any neglect of duty to you, or to our good friends in the club. I am not able to write fine-spun sentiments and grave remarks, and to give my letter the ease of epistolary writing. I would write, as I am used to converse with you; and as to matter of fact, the newspapers take the advantage of me, and possess themselves of every novelty, before I could send it. You will see of course how slender materials are left me, to gratify the curiosity of our friends. The debate in relation to the President's power of removal from office, is an instance. Four days' unceasing speechifying has furnished you with the merits of the question. The transaction of yesterday may need some elucidation. In the committee of the whole, it was moved to strike out the words "to be removable by the President," &c. This did not pass, and the words were retained. The bill was reported to the house, and a motion made to insert in the second clause, "whenever an officer shall be removed by the President, or a vacancy shall happen in any other way," to the intent to strike out the first words. The first words, "to be removable," &c., were supposed to amount to a legislative disposal of the power of removal. If the Constitution had vested it in the President, it was improper to use such words as would imply that the power was to be exercised by him in virtue of this act. The mover and supporters of the amendment supposed that a grant by the legislature might be resumed, and that as the Constitution had already given it to the President, it was putting it on better ground, and, if once gained by the declaration of both houses, would be a construction of the Constitution, and not liable to future encroachments. Others, who contended against the advisory power of the Senate in removals, supposed the first ground the most tenable, that it would include the latter, and operate as a declaration of the Constitution, and at the same (time) expressly dispose of the power. They further apprehended that any change of position would divide the victors, and endanger the final decision in both houses. There was certainly weight in this last opinion. Yet the amendment being actually proposed, it remained only to choose between the two clauses. I think the latter, which passed, and which seems to imply the legal (rather constitutional) power of the President, is the safest doctrine. This prevailed, and the first words were expunged. This has produced discontent, and possibly in the event it will be found disagreement, among those who voted with the majority.

This is in fact a great question, and I feel perfectly satisfied with the President's right to exercise the power, either by the Constitution or the authority of an act. The arguments in favor of the former fall short of full proof, but in my mind they greatly preponderate.

You will say that I have expressed my sentiments with some moderation. You will be deceived, for my whole heart has been engaged in this debate. Indeed it has ached. It has kept me agitated, and in no small degree unhappy. I am commonly opposed to those who modestly assume the rank of champions of liberty, and make a very patriotic noise about the people. It is the stale artifice which has duped the world a thousand times, and yet, though detected, it is still successful. I love liberty as well as anybody. I am proud of it, as the true title of our people to distinction above others; but so are others, for they have an interest and a pride in the same thing. But I would guard it by making the laws strong enough to protect it. In this debate a stroke was aimed at the vitals of the government, perhaps with the best intentions, but I have no doubt of the tendency to a true aristocracy.

FISHER AMES

TO GEORGE RICHARDS MINOT

NEW YORK, JULY 2, 1789

DEAR FRIEND,

You SEEM to consider me as a kind of traitor to your expectations of a weekly letter. In sober truth, I set out better than I can hold out. While I scribbled the hasty reflections which occurred to me, and which came in more plenty because the novelty of my situation supplied them, I imposed no guard upon my prudence, and felt little reserve. But inasmuch as your club expects my communications, I begin to put on a wise face, and to calculate how very profound the remarks must be, which will be worthy of the attention of those gentlemen. Mr. . . . . may be assured, that I am not hardy enough to expose any undigested, crude opinions, to the censure of so redoubted a critic. Nor would it be safe to lay aside my caution, if any thing should occur which might affect the interests and feelings of the harmless flock under his pastoral charge.

Yesterday, for instance, the tonnage bill came upon the *tapis*. The discrimination in favor of nations in treaty with us, would not go down in the Senate. They expunged the clause which creates it. The House non-concurred. The Senate adhered, and sent back the bill. Mr. Madison, who patronized it, urged the House to adhere to their vote allowing the discrimination. He said it was a point not to be given up. On the other side, it was said to be a mark of obstinacy and ill-temper, thus repeatedly to disagree;—harmony between the two Houses was to be cultivated;—the loss of the bill would ensue, as the Senate was nearly unanimous, and inflexible;—that the loss of revenue, and the injury to the navigation of the Union, which this bill would favor, were weighty considerations. The ayes and noes were demanded by Mr. Page;—the bill passed, thirty-one against nineteen; and so the discrimination is expunged. Whether Mr. Madison's conduct were not a little intemperate; whether there is any reason *for* his principles, which would not operate *against* the loss of the bill, the whole merits of the question of discrimination, that is to say, of favoring the French and restricting the English, will not be clearly understood by the papers. It is proposed to wage a commercial war with England. The proposed measure would not injure, though it would irritate, England. It would not benefit France, though every Frenchman seemed to wish it. And it would deprive our treasury of some revenue, and give less encouragement to our own shipping than it merits. However, the Britons have so large a proportion of the shipping employed in our country, that it would have little effect in the two latter ways. If so, it would be a wanton insult upon one nation, and an empty compliment to the other. Why, then, was it wished and pushed so very zealously? Its commercial effects would be little. Was it for the sake of its political effects? Was it to prolong in America the expiring spirit of alienation and hatred, which the war had fostered against England? The Constitution was supported by arguments tending to prove that general laws of trade were necessary to exclude the Britons from our trade, and great effects were promised, more than can ever be verified. Part is certainly true, and I am clearly of opinion that the navigation and manufactures of America cannot well be too much encouraged. But the people have been led to expect an exclusion of the British rivalry, that we may force or frighten them into an allowance of a free trade to the West Indies, &c.; and the people of Virginia (whose murmurs, if louder than a whisper, make Mr. Madison's heart quake) are said to be very strenuous for a law to restrict the British trade. They owe them money, perhaps would be glad to quarrel with their creditors. Their tobacco will sell in all events. But are we Yankees invulnerable, if a war of regulations should be waged with Britain? Are they not able to retaliate? are they not rich enough to bear some loss and inconvenience? would not their pride spurn at the idea of being forced into a treaty? would not their politics be offended at the partial fondness for France? would not they exclude our potash, flaxseed, &c., and shut us out from their India factories?—perhaps foment the discontents of the Western people, and protect them against the government, and eventually supply their West Indies from the Mississippi. Is it not more prudent to maintain a good understanding with Great Britain, and to preserve a dignified neutrality and moderation of conduct towards all nations? It is said the Senate are willing to put all foreign nations trading here upon the footing of our people in their ports. But is it not a risky measure, exposing a feeble trade, as the American is, to the shock of experiment? Will the people forbear murmuring, if the West India trade should be cut off? Will it not affect our own government? Had we not better wait till government has gained strength? And then, if we can extend our own trade, by retaliating upon foreign nations their own restrictions, I would do it; but I am afraid of taking an intemperate zeal for reformation of commerce for my guide. Some say, let us interdict all trade with the British Islands, unless in our own vessels. Whether we could carry such a law into effect, I doubt. I think we could not. If we could, what effect would it produce? By the neutral ports, from Hamburg, the Baltic, and the British colonies, they would still be supplied with provisions and lumber. But they would be supplied at a dearer rate. Britain could well bear the loss of forty or fifty thousand pounds sterling. But would not a part of that loss fall upon us? Lumber is worth nothing but the labor of getting it to market. We should lose the employment, and our people would make loud complaints, and would smuggle their articles to the British market at a less net price than they get at present. Our restrictions would operate as a bounty upon the produce of the British colonies on the continent.

What an immeasurable length I have spun out my letter to, without intending it.

Perhaps our friends will think me whimsical in these remarks. A vindictive policy, if it merits the name, would be more grateful to the people. I freely declare, that I apprehend the Eastern interest would suffer greatly by any such measures, if taken speedily. The encouragement of our own shipping, though too moderate, will do something, and I trust will be increased from time to time. The duties will protect manufactures tolerably well, and the Southern market for them will be a growing one.[12] Their pay is bad, but they have rich staples. A foundation is laid for the prosperity of the interests, which ought to be dear to us;—perhaps the attempt to do more would be found as pernicious to them in practice, as it is repugnant in theory to the sober dictates of prudence. Our friends will judge with candor, whether my ideas are just. I have not written a word that I intended to write, but I have been so lengthy, that I can only say that I am

Your affectionate friend.

P.S. Though the tonnage bill has passed without the discrimination, I am afraid that there is a strong disposition in both Houses to restrict the trade of foreign nations, especially to the British West Indies, unless carried on in our own vessels. It is principally for that reason, I have dilated upon the subject. Notwithstanding my scruples, such a measure would pass, if set a-going. I think so, because many opposed the discrimination because it did not go far enough.

---

[12] *A few indications of the existence of the cotton manufacture appear in the newspapers at this early date. The Gazette of the United States has an item headed, "Petersburg, Va., July 9, 1789," in the following terms:—"Virginia cloth, of excellent quality and very cheap, may be purchased almost every day of the country people, who come to town for the purpose of making sale of it. It is made of cotton, and several gentlemen have bought full suits of it." Very possibly Virginia may have been the first cotton-manufacturing state.*

The same paper, under date Aug. 15, 1789, says:—"The cotton manufacture is established at Philadelphia and at Beverly. The Boston Assembly have granted 500l. to have at Beverly, as a gratuity for its advancement. It is carried on with Arkwright's machines." [S. AMES]

TO GEORGE RICHARDS MINOT

NO. 1 NEW YORK, JULY 8, 1789

DEAR FRIEND,

WE ARE going on a slow trot, on our journey to the completion of the revenue system. The collection bill is advancing, and as the first of August is the term for the impost to commence, we have agreed to meet at ten in the morning. But though we have so many spurs to expedition, and we seem to feel some of them, yet our progress is very tedious. The bill was at first very imperfect. We labored upon it for some time, settled some principles, and referred it to a large and very good committee. They met, agreed upon principles, and the clerk drew the bill which they reported. We consider it in committee of the whole, and we indulge a very minute criticism upon its style. We correct spelling, or erase *may* and insert *shall*, and quiddle in a manner which provokes me. A select committee would soon correct little improprieties. Our great committee is too unwieldy for this operation. A great, clumsy machine is applied to the slightest and most delicate operations—the hoof of an elephant to the strokes of mezzotinto. I dislike the committee of the whole more than ever. We could not be so long doing so little, by any other expedient. In spite of it, however, I begin to flatter myself with the hope of an adjournment towards the end of August, which heaven grant. I shall take my friend by the hand with new satisfaction.

I have expressed myself so peevishly in regard to the committee of the whole, that common justice will demand a further account of the House. There is the most punctual attendance of the members at the hour of meeting. Three or four have had leave of absence, but every other member actually attends daily, till the hour of adjourning. There is less party spirit, less of the acrimony of pride when disappointed of success, less personality, less intrigue, cabal, management, or cunning than I ever saw in a public assembly. The question of the President's power of removal seemed to kindle some sparks of faction, but they went out for want of tinder. Measures are so far from being the product of caucusing and cabal, that they are not sufficiently preconcerted. Mr. Brown's amendment was such, and it had some effect to divide those whom zeal for the right interpretation of the Constitution had united into a corps. It was a good amendment. Some voted against it from the vexation they felt in having the ground changed.

I am in the House, and, finding this short piece of paper before me, I begun to write, almost by instinct, to you. When I can get another piece, I will write more. I attend at the same time to the debates, which are not of a nature to require a very strict attention.

CONTINUED

A LITTLE of the sourness of party has been produced by the great debate, respecting the President's power of removal. I cannot, with any prudence or propriety, become a critical reviewer of the characters of the leading men. There seemed to be, on both sides, a most sanguine belief of their creed. The talk was to the public rather than to each other. The public will probably think that the quantity is too great for curiosity, and too intricate and fine-spun for conviction. They will, as usual, lump the matter, and decide according to their feelings.

The House has again disagreed to the amendments to the impost bill, and chose a committee of conference. The tonnage bill is in the like state of conference. The favor to nations in treaty, which the Senate are inflexibly opposed to, is the only bone of contention which will delay the passage of the bills. I do not apprehend any more debate, and little delay of either of them.

Now, my dear friend, I have said so much of the bills in detail, you would wish some remarks upon the nature of our transactions, &c., in the general.

There is certainly a bad method of doing business. Too little use is made of special committees. Virginia is stiff and touchy against any change of the committee of the whole. The language of the House is not very unlike that of the General Court, and the repugnance to principles, which our government people would support, is equally invincible. They are for watching and checking power; they see evils in embryo; are terrified with possibilities, and are eager to establish rights, and to explain principles, to such a degree, that you would think them enthusiasts and triflers. Yet there is not a deficiency of good sense and political experience; and I verily believe that almost every man, who impedes the movement of the government by these principles, is guided by pure motives. I have never seen an assembly where so little art was used. If they wish to carry a point, it is directly declared, and justified. Its merits and defects are plainly stated, not without sophistry and prejudice, but without management. I thought the manner of opposing the President's power of removal was artful, two or three days ago, but I now think that the very best method of trying their strength was blundered upon, and finally not perceived to be the best.

685

There is no intrigue, no caucusing, little of clanning together, little asperity in debate, or personal bitterness out of the House. And yet it is very far from being a Roman Senate.[13] I must finish.

Yours, once more.

NO. 2 THURSDAY EVENING, JULY 9

I SHALL not be able to pursue my scribbling much further. The mail is just closing.

You may judge of the character of the House by knowing the classes, into which they may be divided.

Three sorts of people are often troublesome. The antifederals, who alone are weak, and some of them well disposed. The dupes of local prejudices, who fear eastern influence, monopolies, and navigation acts. And lastly, the violent republicans, as they think fit to style themselves, who are new lights in politics; who would not make the law, but the people, king; who would have a government all checks; who are more solicitous to establish, or rather to expatiate upon, some high-sounding principle of republicanism, than to protect property, cement the union, and perpetuate liberty. "This new Constitution," said one Abner Fowler, in 1787, "will destroy our liberties. We shall never have another mob in the world." This is the republicanism of the aristocracy of the southern nabobs. It breaks out daily, tinctures the debates with the hue of compromise, makes bold, manly,

---

[13] *This may be a proper place to mention, that among the questions debated was a proposition that the bill for a department of foreign affairs should be limited to a few years. This proposition was advocated seriously, on the ground that all our intercourse with Europe would gradually be withdrawn, and in a few years there would be no occasion for any such department.* [S. AMES]

686

energetic measures very difficult. The spectre of Patrick Henry haunts their dreams. They accuse the eastern people with despotic principles, and take no small consequence to themselves as the defenders of liberty. Now, my dear friend, you well know that I represent things rather too strongly. In fact, there is perfect good humor. Allow for my overdoing manner, and you will not be deceived by taking the substance of my account for fact.

Yours, affectionately.

NO. 2 CONTINUED

A LITTLE time remains and I proceed. The three classes I have described are strong when united. This does not happen frequently. In all assemblies, the indolent class is numerous, though seldom strong. All these are combined and divided by chance, and seldom move in phalanx. It is pleasant to notice that the division is seldom by states. A large body is capable of a strong impulse, thinks less, and is more guided by its feelings, than a smaller. No *body* can think much, but our body thinks enough, or is in such a position as to be little susceptible of those strong impulses which carry most popular assemblies a great way, without stopping, in a right or wrong direction, as chance or party may happen to direct. We are more likely to hesitate, to temporize, to forbear doing what is right, or to do less than is right, than to usurp power, and to run riot. Our body is so small, as to partake of the senatorial caution and phlegm.

We are not in a hurry to act upon the case of Rhode Island and Vermont. It is not easy to say what is best, but if we knew, we should not readily act with decision. In addition to the obstacles which any measures, positively good or bad, would have to encounter, this would be retarded by the jealousy of a few, who consider those states as unfriendly to the removal to Philadelphia, and an accession to the eastern interest. Now I must finish.

Yours, once more.

TO WILLIAM TUDOR

NEW YORK, JULY 12, 1789

DEAR SIR,

I AM happy to find that you approve the decision of the House upon the question of the President's power of removal from office. The men of information and property, who are stigmatized as aristocrats, appear to me more solicitous to secure liberty than the loudest champions of democracy. They not only wish to enjoy, but to perpetuate liberty, by giving energy enough to government to preserve its own being, when endangered by tumult and faction. A mob is despotic *per se*, and it tends to destroy all liberty. One Abner Fowler, it is said, in 1787, would have the town instruct their members against the constitution—for, he observed, it would destroy their liberties, they could never have another mob. I wish that his judgment may be verified. The executive branch of our government is not strong. I am sure the people cannot be interested on the side of depriving him of any part of his constitutional powers. Those who argued on that side, seemed to consider themselves as the defenders of liberty—

pointed out the danger to the people, and the shameful usurpation of power, in deciding as it was decided. They said the Constitution was not express in giving the power to the President—constructions were, they said, replete with danger, and then they proceeded, upon the strength of construction, to prove that the Senate has the power of advice in removals. This opinion seemed to nourish their zeal, and made them inflexible in their opposition to any infringement of the Constitution. This will appear to the world a serious proof of the degree, in which the understandings of men may be misled, when their passions are heated. This debate seemed to menace faction, but the good humor of the House has returned, and business goes on again as agreeably as formerly. To whatever cause it may be owing, the fact is certain, that there is very little of party spirit in our House, and less seeming intrigue and cabal than I have ever seen in any public body.

Our progress has been slow. There seems in the public to be a general disposition to excuse it, to bring into view the complex nature of the business, and to call it by the name of wisdom and prudent caution. We have certainly proceeded more tardily than I expected, or will affect to approve. But the application to business has been unexceptionable. The whole body actually attends. Not a member absent, except four or five with leave. Punctual attendance of the whole, and at the hour, is given; and very few retire, unless to drink water in the committee room during the five hours' attendance. Our collection bill has been pushed as diligently as I ever knew business prosecuted. It is reported by the committee of the whole to the House, and will be sent in a few days to the Senate. The judicial is before the Senate still. They have laboured upon it as hard as so many schoolmasters or merchants' clerks. I expect it in our House in six or eight days. It will be debated warmly, and I am afraid will not be treated as a system, but made patch work by fanciful amendments. We begin to talk of a recess in August. I wish it most ardently, but am afraid it will not take place till September.

FISHER AMES

CONSIDERING PROPOSALS FOR A BILL OF RIGHTS

On August 21, 1789, the debate on the amendments well under way, Ames contributed to the definitive formulation of the important first amendment to the Constitution. It was then still the fourth resolution:

That in Article 1st, section 9, between clauses 3 and 4, be inserted these clauses, to wit: The civil rights of none shall be abridged on account of religious belief or worship, *nor shall any national religion be established,* nor shall the full and equal rights of conscience in any manner, or on any pretext, be infringed.

The record of the debate reveals Ames' contribution:

On motion of Mr. Ames, the fourth amendment was altered so as to read, "Congress shall make no law establishing religion, or to prevent the free exercise thereof, or to infringe the rights of conscience." This being adopted, the first proposition was agreed to.

———

JULY 21–AUGUST 21, 1789

Mr. AMES hoped that the House would be induced, on mature reflection, to rescind their vote of going into a committee on the business, and refer it to a select committee.

It would certainly tend to facilitate the business. If they had the subject at large before a Committee of the whole, he could not see where the business was likely to end. The amendments proposed were so various, that their discussion must inevitably occupy many days, and that at a time when they can be ill spared; whereas a select committee could go through and cull out those of the most material kind, without interrupting the principal business of the House. He therefore moved, that the Committee of the whole be discharged, and the subject referred to a select committee.

．　　　．　　　．　　　．　　　．　　　．　　　．　　　．　　　．

Mr. AMES declared to the House, that he was no enemy to the consideration of amendments; but he had moved to rescind their former vote, in order to save time, which he was confident would be the consequence of referring it to a select committee.

He was sorry to hear an intention avowed by his colleague, of considering every part of the frame of this Constitution. It was the same as forming themselves into a convention of the United States. He did not stand for words, the thing would be the same in fact. He could not but express a degree of anxiety at seeing the system of government encounter another ordeal, when it ought to be extending itself to furnish security to others. He apprehended, if the zeal of some gentlemen broke out on this occasion, that there would be no limits to the time necessary to discuss the subject; he was certain the session would not be long enough; perhaps they might be bounded by the period of their appointment, but he questioned it.

When gentlemen suppose themselves called upon to vent their ardor in some favorite pursuit, in securing to themselves and their posterity the inestimable rights and liberties they have just snatched from the hand of despotism, they are apt to carry their exertions to an extreme; but he hoped the subject itself would be limited; not that he objected to the consideration of the amendments proposed, indeed he should move himself for the consideration, by the committee, of those recommended by Massachusetts, if his colleagues omitted to do it; but he hoped gentlemen would not think of bringing in new amendments, such as were not recommended, but went to tear the frame of government into pieces.

He had considered a select committee much better calculated to consider and arrange a complex business, than a Committee of the whole; he thought they were like the senses to the soul, and on an occasion like the present, could be made equally useful.

If he recollected rightly the decision made by the House on the 8th of June, it was that certain specific amendments be referred to the Committee of the whole; not that the subject generally be referred, and that amendments be made in the committee that were not contemplated, before. This public discussion would be like a dissection of the Constitution, it would be defacing its symmetry, laying bare its sinews and tendons, ripping up the whole form, and tearing out its vitals; but is it presumable that such conduct would be attended with success? Two thirds of both Houses must agree in all these operations, before they can have effect. His opposition to going into a Committee of the whole, did not arise from any fear that the Constitution would suffer by a fair discussion in this, or any other House; but while such business was going on, the government was laid prostrate, and every artery ceased to beat. The unfair advantages that might be taken in such a situation, were easier apprehended than resisted. Wherefore, he wished to avoid the danger, by a more prudent line of conduct.

AUGUST 15

MR. AMES moved the committee to rise and report progress; which being agreed to,

Mr. SPEAKER having resumed the chair,

Mr. AMES moved to discharge the committee from any further proceeding. He was led to make the motion from two considerations: first, that as the committee were not restrained in their discussions, a great deal of time was consumed in unnecessary debate; and, second, that as the Constitution required two-thirds of the House to acquiesce in amendments, the decisions of the committee, by a simple majority, might be set aside for the want of the constitutional number to support them in the House. He further observed, that it might have an evil influence if alterations agreed to in committee were not adopted by the House.

.   .   .   .

Mr. AMES withdrew his motion, and laid another on the table, requiring two-thirds of the committee to carry a question; and, after some desultory conversation, the House adjourned.

AUGUST 21

Mr. SEDGWICK moved to amend the motion, by giving the power to Congress to alter the times, manner, and places of holding elections, provided the states made improper ones; for as much injury might result to the Union from improper regulations, as from a neglect or refusal to make any. It is as much to be apprehended that the states may abuse their powers, as that the United States may make an improper use of theirs.

Mr. AMES said, that inadequate regulations were equally injurious as having none, and that such an amendment as was now proposed would alter the Constitution; it would vest the supreme authority in places where it was never contemplated.

TO GEORGE RICHARDS MINOT

NEW YORK, JULY 23, 1789

DEAR SIR,

I BEGIN to feel some confidence in the approbation of our progress in business. It seems to have moved with more velocity than formerly. The judicial bill is to be taken up next Monday. If that should not occupy us longer than the spirit of fair inquiry may demand, we shall adjourn in six weeks. I dare not indulge the hope of it. We have had the amendments on the *tapis*, and referred them to a committee of one from a state. I hope much debate will be avoided by this mode, and that the amendments will be more rational, and less *ad populum*, than Madison's. It is necessary to conciliate, and I would have amendments. But they should not be trash, such as would dishonor the Constitution, without pleasing its enemies. Should we propose them, North Carolina would accede. It is doubtful, in case we should not. The agents of Vermont arrived here yesterday. New York has appointed commissioners to treat with them on that subject, which is right, but they erased a clause empowering them to quiet their possessions, which is wrong, and perhaps worse than doing nothing. *That* is the very difficulty with Vermont. A whole people cannot be dispossessed,—and as the land was actually bought, and by labor has become their own, it is not to be expected that they will suffer it to be taken away, or contested. I wish most earnestly to see Rhode Island federal, to finish the circle of union, and to dig for the foundations of the government below the frost.[14] If I did not

---

[14] *The accession of Rhode Island to the Union was thus announced in the "Gazette of the United States," (a Philadelphia Newspaper,) of Wednesday, June 2d, 1790.*

check this emotion, I should tire you with rant. I am displeased to hear people speak of a state out of the union. I wish it was a part of the catechism to teach youth that it cannot be. An Englishman thinks he can beat two Frenchmen. I wish to have every American think the union so indissoluble and integral, that the corn would not grow, nor the pot boil, if it should be broken. I flatter myself that this country *will be* what China *is*, with this difference, that freedom and science shall do here, what bigotry and prejudice do there, to secure the government. For I believe that ignorance is unfavorable to government, and that personal freedom is useful to government, and government (and a braced one too) indispensable to freedom.

Sedgwick has come in, and orders me to quit writing. You know his arbitrary principles,—a spoiled child in the rebellion. So I must obey. But God bless you, King is Senator.

Your friend.

TO THEOPHILUS PARSONS

———

NEW YORK, AUGUST 3, 1789

DEAR SIR:

I THINK it will not be unacceptable to you to peruse the bill reported in the Senate for the punishment of crimes; and therefore I enclose it. You will be gratified to hear that our

---

"*New York. Monday afternoon arrived Sloop Rambler, Capt. Casey, from Newport, Rhode Island, who left that place on Sunday morning last.*

"*By the arrival of Capt. Casey, we have received the authentic information that the Convention of Rhode Island did, on Saturday last, adopt the Constitution of the United States by a majority of two. The yeas were thirty-four—the nays, thirty-two.*" [S. AMES]

excellent friend, General Lincoln, is nominated to the Collector's office in Boston. Every good man in Massachusetts will be gratified.

The Judiciary Bill has not been debated in the House. It is proposed to clear the table of some other business that is unfinished, in order to pay uninterrupted attention to that great subject. The District Judge should be a very respectable man. In order to make his office respectable, and to bring justice as much as possible to men's doors, would it not be proper to empower him to hold two of his four stated courts where he may think proper, and to extend his jurisdiction to all cases not capital, and to give the Circuit Court a concurrent original jurisdiction? Narrowing his jurisdiction will tend to degrade him. Haste will not allow me to enlarge; it is unnecessary to you, for I think your inquiring mind has long ago suggested every idea that I could present. It will be attempted to exclude the federal courts from original jurisdiction, and to restrain them to the cognizance of appeals from the state courts. I think the attempt will fail.

I am, Sir, with sentiments of the truest
esteem, Your very humble servant,

FISHER AMES.

TO GEORGE RICHARDS MINOT

———

NEW YORK, AUGUST 12, 1789.—THURSDAY.

MY DEAR FRIEND,

WE ARE beginning the amendments in a committee of the whole. We have voted to take up the subject, in preference to the judiciary, to incorporate them into the Constitution, and not to require, in committee, two thirds to a vote. This cost us the day. To-morrow we shall proceed. Some general, before engaging, said to his soldiers, "Think of your ancestors, and think of your posterity." We shall make a dozen or two of rights and privileges for our posterity. If I am to be guided by your advice, to marry and live in Boston, it behooves me to interest myself in the affair. It will consume a good deal of time, and renew the party struggles of the states. It will set Deacon Smead and many others to constitution-making, a trade which requires little stock, and often thrives without much custom. The workman is often satisfied to be the sole consumer. Our state is remarkable for it. We made several frames of government, which did not pass. The timber was so green, the vessels rotted on the stocks. However, I am persuaded it is proper to propose amendments, without delay, and if the *antis* affect to say that they are of no consequence, they may be reproached with their opposition to the government, because they protested that the principles were important.

Our friend, Dr. Dexter, may be assured, that the collection law is considered as imperfect. Probably it will need some amendments, every session, these ten years, till experience has taught us how to guard, in the best possible manner, against the infinity of frauds which will be practised. Time at last pressed, and it was necessary to let the law take place with all its imperfections on its head.

A recess is proposed, and ardently desired. I think it a proper thing in itself, and expedient at this juncture. Deacon Smead will be pleased with the intermission of the members' pay.

I never said that I thought Mr. L.[15] should not accept as District Judge. I say he ought. I have my fears whether he

---

[15] Hon. John Lowell, *whose appointment as Judge of the United States Court for the district of Massachusetts, was announced September 4, of this year.* [S. AMES]

will be asked to do it. If the Chief Justice should be Associate Judge, possibly Dana may be District Judge. Our excellent friend, Mr. L. merits every thing in that line. He has my fervent wishes in his favor. If any thing here looks inviting, I should wish to know your pleasure, and aid you in the attainment. Your brother Clarke perhaps would accept a clerkship in one of the great departments. If so, he had better write to General Knox, and to Mr. Jay, and to the Secretary of the Treasury, when known. I will aid him with alacrity and zeal.

The mail is closing, and I must abruptly assure you that I am, affectionately,

Yours, &c.

SPEECHES ON ESTABLISHING A NATIONAL CAPITOL

On August 27, 1789, Thomas Scott of Pennsylvania moved that a permanent residence for the government be established at some central and convenient spot in the nation. This motion caused the House to divide between Southern members who favored a site on the Potomac and Eastern members who favored a site on the Susquehanna.

Each side urged convenience and centrality, attempting to show the superiority of its respective site. Madison argued that the Potomac site would be closer than the Susquehanna to the inhabitants of Pittsburg and the western lands. Ames answered Madison's argument, cleverly quoting from Notes on the State of Virginia *(by Virginia's former Governor, Thomas Jefferson) to substantiate his calculation that the Susquehanna site was in fact nearer to Pittsburg.*

―――――

AUGUST 27–SEPTEMBER 4, 1789

AUGUST 27

MR. SPEAKER being about to put the question on the second Monday in December,

Mr. AMES inquired if the motion to adjourn on the twenty-second of September was not inconsistent with the resolution now offered to the House? A committee had been appointed to report the business of the present session. The committee reported, and so much of that report was accepted as related to the time of adjournment. It therefore appeared to him, that the proposition to take up this subject at the present time was superseded. He was confident it was inconsistent with that determination. It would become necessary to rescind the determination; but whether that would be done or not, depended on the disposition of the Senate. Should they not concur, the House would waste their time, and be obliged to leave the most important business unfinished.

He said he could not suppress some emotions of surprise that gentlemen should propound questions which had not for their object the complete organization of the government. It lies, as yet, prostrate and inanimate; and instead of infusing life into it, and giving motion to the machine, we have been altering our Constitution, and are now entering into a lengthy discussion to determine where we shall sit.

If the gentleman's motion only involved a few abstract propositions in it, it would not be of much importance: but he saw how difficult their decision would be. Were I a stranger, I should apprehend, from the manner in which the motion had been introduced, that it would be a question agitated with as much acrimony as any whatever.

I ever found it a difficult task, on the most trivial occasions, to obtain unanimity. What, then, must be the division on a question, which some gentlemen have said the very existence and peace of the Union depends upon? I believe it will involve as many passions as the human heart can display. Every principle of local interest, of pride and honor, and even of patriotism, are engaged. If the good of the Union requires that the seat of government should be fixed at Pittsburg, I am willing to pledge myself to the honorable gentleman I will vote for it: but I must now vote for postponing the business. It is not sufficient to determine where the seat of government ought to be, but it is necessary the public mind should be prepared to concur with ours. In the decision of questions of this magnitude, where our interests are so materially concerned, the reasons ought to be made public, and they ought to correspond with those of the people.

When I left my constituents, I had no conception of proceedings like this; neither have I as yet formed my opinion; when I do, I pledge myself that it shall not spring from local or selfish principles.

The honorable gentleman has introduced this subject as a very important one: we will consider it as such. If only the centre was to be determined, it might be settled in a very short time. If the oaks and the mountains are to be numbered; if the acres in the United States are also to be the ground of our decision, perhaps a few days' calculation may settle the business.

My opinion is, that the centre of government ought to be a centre of convenience and utility; that the heart should be so placed as to propel the blood to the extremities, with the most equable and gentle motion. I would place the government where it might most effectually guard the extremes, and protect the weak parts. I sincerely wish that the territory now subject to the laws of the Union may continue so, and that government may be so situated as to be enabled to exert its force with the best advantage to ensure the preservation of the Union, and compel obedience to its laws.

The gentleman from Connecticut (Mr. SHERMAN) has justly said that North Carolina and Rhode Island should have a voice in this business.

He said he would not impute unworthy motives to the gentleman who introduced the motion, but would ask him whether the people at large ought not to be equally convinced of their purity? whether, in justice to himself, and to the subject generally, the public mind ought to be better prepared for the occasion? He was not convinced that the government, ill cemented and feeble as it is, could stand the shock of such a measure; and therefore he most earnestly deprecated the event.

SEPTEMBER 3

MR. AMES—I am at a loss to conceive why the gentlemen from Virginia are so agitated and anxious to press the subject of this resolution. One gentleman has asked, is there any thing contained in the proposition which is not true. Is there any thing which is not applicable to the subject? And, by way of conclusion asks, whether the resolution shall not pass? But is such a conclusion necessary to these premises? If they are true, why be so solicitous? Does truth acquire any additional authority from being frequently voted? If they are truths, will not those truths guide us? But I have, sir, another difficulty. If the committee shall vote for these propositions, the gentleman may exhibit other abstract questions for our consideration without limitation, and support them by the same argument. He may ask you, are not these things true? Are they not applicable? And, in this way, we

may encumber our journals with all the multifarious propositions which arise out of this fertile subject. But is there
any necessity for it? Will it not embarrass the committee?
Sir, it is not our business to syllogize upon abstract principles,
like school logicians, but to settle facts. I contend, if the
principles dilated in the motion are incontrovertibly true
there is no use in inserting them.

. . . .

Mr. MADISON.—I hope the committee will not rise for the
purpose mentioned by my colleague; but that they do it in
order to give gentlemen time to consider the facts that have
been brought into view, and with which it will be necessary
to contrast other facts, yet to be mentioned, by those who
wish to bring forward all the truths relative to the great
question now under consideration. I hope there is no desire
among the gentlemen who have made up their minds on this
subject, a subject admitting as great a variety of considerations
as any subject that has or can come before us, to bring it to
a decision in a few hours after it has been disclosed. This
would be so different from their usual candor, that I cannot
suspect any serious opposition will be made to the rising of
the committee.

. . . .

Mr. AMES flattered himself the committee would not rise,
as there could be no doubt but gentlemen were prepared to
decide the question; it had been brought into view a
considerable time since, and the gentleman who now wished
for delay, had been pressing to have it determined. It was
urged, that the public anxiously expected the measure; and
though many wished it suspended, yet the major voice was
in favor of expedition. He conceived that all the facts
necessary to be known were within the reach of the committee,
and that it was not necessary to postpone, in order to
introduce any evidence to establish them. He apprehended
nothing was intended by the rising of the committee but

delay, and then the subject would come forward again, with all the unfortunate circumstances of local attachments. He hoped, as the committee had proceeded so far as to adopt the general principles, they would go on, and agree to the subsequent resolution which was proposed by his colleague.

. . . .

Mr. AMES said he remembered, when this subject came before the House the other day, when we solicited for delay, it was observed, that the necessities of the Union required an immediate decision; that it would take up but little time; that the proper centre might be easily ascertained; that it would depend upon geographical calculation, and that little discussion would be necessary. Now, when circumstances appear to be changed, when the calculation is made, when the House are ready to vote, gentlemen come forward and pretend that they want time. He hoped the question would be now decided. While he was up, he would observe that he did not entertain a doubt of the patriotism and good intentions of the gentlemen from Virginia. He believed, however, that their judgments were influenced by their wishes, for they seemed to be engaged with a degree of eagerness, which none else appeared to feel; the very language of their motion declares this. They seem to think the banks of the Potomac a paradise, and that river an Euphrates. He had been told it was a fine spot, and he sincerely wished those blessings might ever reside there.

SEPTEMBER 4

MR. AMES never intended that this question should be carried through the committee by the strength of a silent majority; he had confidence in the weight of the arguments to be urged in favor of the Susquehanna, and he was willing to put the decision of the question on that ground. He would now come forward, and give the reasons of his opinion, especially as gentlemen had entered fully into the reasons which guided their own to a different conclusion. He did not conceive it would be necessary for him, coming from the part of the United States from which he did, to disclaim the local views and narrow prejudices with which the subject teemed. He had feared, when the question was first brought forward, that the minds of gentlemen would be highly fermented, indeed so much, that he almost despaired of coming to a proper decision, nor did he think these apprehensions were illusive, if he judged from what had already taken place. He had observed that some gentlemen, whose discernments were clear and who were generally guided by the straight line of rectitude, had been most surprisingly warped on the present occasion; he was fearful that their wishes had misled them from a due regard of the real object of their pursuit, viz. the public interest and convenience. He was sensible, that he himself was liable to some improper impressions; but he trusted he did not feel them in that degree which he thought he saw in others.

He was willing to be led by the great principles which other gentlemen had laid down as the rule of their decision; but he thought they would lead to a different conclusion from what had been drawn from them; he admitted that a central situation is to be taken, and in considering this centre, the centre of a sea-coast line ought to be regarded, because it is more conveniently accessible, has more wealth, and more people than an equal area of inland country. Being more liable to invasion, government should be near to protect it. It is the interest of the back country to have the government near the sea, to inspect and encourage trade, by which their abundant produce will find an export. And lastly, he said the contingency of the separation of the western country was a reason for preferring the sea-coast.

He proceeded next to say, there will not be any contest where this centre of the sea-coast line is to be found: it falls between the rivers Potomac and Susquehanna. It will be found that there are good reasons why we should rather move East than South.

If the sea-coast line is to be preferred it will follow that the back lands, west of the Ohio, which the gentleman from Virginia has so often taken into his calculations, will be excluded; they are not peopled; they do not affect the sea-coast line; and that line has already been voted to be the proper one by the committee. As it is true that the sea-coast has more wealth and more people than the inland country in proportion to the extent, it is equally true that the eastern half of the sea-coast has more of both than the southern. If we reckon Maryland, which will be as well accommodated by the Susquehanna as by the Potomac, we shall find the population of the eastern part nearly two millions, and that of the southern only one million, and the population of free inhabitants still less in favor of the latter.

But, sir, instead of seeking a centre geographically we should consider the centre of common convenience. The place is the proper one where the greatest number of persons will be best accommodated. I will endeavor to show that that will be on the Susquehanna. Is the zeal of gentlemen, who oppose this design, influenced by their despair of removing the seat of government afterwards? I believe the people of America will not complain of it. If fixed there, I think it will be found convenient and will remain there.

The Susquehanna is the centre of the common convenience. At this moment there is more wealth and more inhabitants east than south of it. But the future population of America is calculated, and it is pretended that the balance of population is receding from the east. Surely the present inhabitants may be allowed principally to consult, their own convenience. West of the Ohio is an almost unmeasurable wilderness; when it will be settled, or how it will be possible to govern it, is past calculation. Gentlemen will pardon me if I think it perfectly romantic to make this decision depend upon that circumstance. Probably it will be near a century before those people will be considerable; if we fix the national seat in the proper place now, it would give me no inquietude to know that a hundred years hence it may be liable to be removed; but, in fact, the principle which is assumed by the committee, and which I have attempted to justify, of taking the centre of the sea-coast line, will, even in the event of that vast tract being settled, furnish abundant reasons for its remaining on the Susquehanna. I will not recapitulate those reasons. We must take some principle to guide us; and though some inequalities will appear, yet let gentlemen remember, that in so vast a country great inconveniences will attend the communications of the people with Government, be the seat of it where it may; and by taking the centre of the sea-coast line there will be less than any other principle. It will be found best to accommodate the greatest number; or, in other words, to be the centre of common convenience: indeed, this is not denied to be true at this moment; but the case is said to be changing. On the one hand, I think it is Utopian to calculate upon the population of the United States a century hence; and, on the other hand, I admit that it is impolitic at least, perhaps unjust, to confine our attention to the present population; a quarter of a century may be a medium. Will gentlemen deny that trade and manufactures will accumulate people in the eastern states, in proportion of five to three, compared with the southern? The disproportion will, doubtless, continue to be much greater than I have calculated. It is actually greater at present; for the climate and negro slavery are acknowledged to be unfavorable to population: so that husbandry, as well as commerce and manufactures, will give more people in the eastern than in the southern States. The very circumstance that gentlemen found their reasonings upon is pretty strongly against their calculations. They tell us of the vast quantities of good land still unsettled in their states; that will produce a thin population; for the old lands will not be crowded so long as new ones are to be had.

So far, therefore, as we may be allowed to look forward, the eastern half, from this central seat, will be far more populous than the other. In New England the settled parts are said to contain about forty-five to a square mile.

Much is said of the separation of the western country. At a remote period the junction of the British colonies with the Union might be taken into view.

The seat of Government on the Susquehanna will be nearly accessible by water to all the people on the sea-coast by the Delaware river on the one side, and Chesapeake bay on the other.

Let us next consider the inland navigation of this river. Pittsburg, on the Ohio, may be considered as the key of those waters, at least to the northward; it is a kind of common centre. Let us see how we shall approach it by the Susquehanna.

	MILES
From Havre de Grace, at the mouth of Susquehanna, and at the head of the Chesapeake to Wright's Ferry, is (and here the Federal Town probably will be)	40
To Harris's Ferry,	20
To the mouth of Juniata River,	15
Up Juniata River to the standing Stone	75
Portage to Conimaugh Old Town,	30
Down the Kiskaminetas River to the Allegany River,	60
Down that River to Pittsburg,	30
	270
And from the supposed Seat of Government at Wright's Ferry, only	230

Now, let us see what is the route by the Potomac. First, from the tide-water, on the Potomac, to Fort Cumberland, is two hundred miles.

Mr. MADISON thought the gentleman mistaken in his calculations.

Mr. CARROLL begged leave to give the Committee some information respecting the distance from tide-water to Fort Cumberland; from the tide-water to the Little Falls was three miles, to the Great Falls six more, from thence to the Seneca Falls was also six more, and from thence to Old Town one hundred and seventeen; which last place was fifteen miles from Fort Cumberland, making in all one hundred and forty-five miles, instead of two hundred, as stated by the gentleman.

Mr. AMES imagined his statement to be nearly right, and he found Mr. JEFFERSON stated in his *Notes* that the Falls of the Potomac were fifteen miles in extent, and a navigation extremely difficult to be made.

Mr. AMES then proceeded with his calculation; and, said he, let us compare this route to Pittsburg, with that by the Potomac.

	MILES
From the tide-water on Potomac to Fort Cumberland,	200
Portage to the three forks of Turkey-Foot,	30
Water-carriage and portage one mile at the falls of the Youghogany,	9
Down the Youghogany to the Ohio,	50
Up to Pittsburg,	15
	304

I have reason to confide in these calculations. The latter is said to be made by a distinguished person, whose authority no man will dispute. If it is true, or any thing near true, it will destroy the whole argument in favor of the Potomac. I have consulted the best informed persons out of the House, and believe the statement to be true, as it respects both rivers. If it is, the ponderous edifice which the gentleman from Virginia has erected with so much labor crumbles to powder. For it will appear, that it is more that 70 miles nearer by the Susquehanna and Juniata to Pittsburg, than by way of the Potomac. Neither should we forget, from the tide water on the Potomac to Chesapeake is near 200 miles. Of course the access by water is less convenient and direct.

The eastern branch of the Susquehanna is navigable to the head of Lake Otsego. A detachment of General Sullivan's troops came in boats from the lake quite down the river. This river stretches its long arms, and embraces a vast country, comprehending not less than twenty millions of acres.

Let us next consider the connexion through this water with the lakes. Its branches approach the Allegany river very near, and by a portage of only three miles, communicate with the waters of Lake Erie.

Reckoning from Fort Pitt, Lake Erie, and its waters, and the several branches of the Susquehanna, it will be found that more than fifty thousand square miles are accommodated with water carriage. Perhaps, out of America, there is not another such an instance in the world. Yet this is not all. The water communication by the Potomac is subservient to the argument for the Susquehanna; for if the western country is so wonderfully accommodated by it as a highway, then it is only sixty miles travel, a mere portage, to Wright's Ferry; they will be on a footing with those who came by sea, and they will have still greater advantages over many of those who travel by land.

However, Mr. Jefferson's account of the Potomac does not correspond with the praises now bestowed upon it. He says, the falls are fifteen miles long, and speaks very unfavorably of the interior navigation. In summer, the waters are very subject to fail. My informants prefer the waters of the Susquehanna. Admitting, however, that the Potomac is as commodious as the other, still there are weighty reasons in favor of its rival.

The advantage to the neighboring country, in point of trade, resulting from the federal town, is unessential in a national view. The people on the Potomac will not be injured, in the conveyance, or sales of their produce, by having it fixed on the Susquehanna. For the influence of the federal town, in this respect, will not extend far. And as to the convenient access to the government, it will make only sixty miles difference, which surely is not an object. But the great national point is, to fix the seat of government in that place where it will best secure the Union.

The Potomac is, in some degree, exposed to two dangers; by sea, and from the mountains, large vessels can go to Georgetown. The events of the late war have proved that there is a foundaton for this apprehension. The Western country is to be viewed under different circumstances. From Lake Erie, by Pittsburg, to the head of the Chesapeake, the people are naturally connected with us, they must send their produce through the states. But lower down the Ohio and the Mississippi the people have their exports by the latter river. If the latter should separate from the Union, they will not be willing to leave the southern states in the Union. The separation will not take place by the mountains, which are far from being impassable. The capital, if imprudently placed so far southwest, will furnish a temptation for this division, and strength and resources to maintain it. I will not debate on this idea, though I think it an important one. The more it is weighed, the more hazardous and preposterous it will appear to place the Capitol in a situation where gentlemen's own arguments admit, when they speak of the contingency of losing the western country, that we may need all our strength, and yet where we should be able to command but a small part of it.

Contrast this with the Susquehanna. The country is perfectly safe from both dangers of invasion by sea and from the mountains. If a division should happen, the seat of government will fall on the right side of the dividing line; and so much strength on the frontier of that line will prevent a division. For the country from Lake Erie to Fort Pitt, and from thence to Lake Champlain, vast in its extent, its soil is fruitful, its climate favorable to the production of a hardy race of men, and to sustain a vast multitude of them. This extensive country will be benefited, in some degree, and in a greater attached to the Union, by fixing the seat of government in this place; besides, nature has united them, by indissoluble ties, to the states, unless a feeble government should engender the anarchy of many separate sovereignties. It is a pleasing reflection, to trace the effect of the strength of this part of the Western Territory, towards securing the remaining Western region of the Union. At all events, the country east of a line, drawn from Lake Erie to the Chesapeake, will be safe from the force of any other part of America; will that other part be safe from this eastern part? Though national justice, and the wisest policy, should direct our councils, yet ambitious men will find a motive and a pretext for fomenting a division. But those near the line of the eastern half will be unwilling to be a frontier; those further south will be equally so; and what barrier, in case of a separation, have they to oppose to their northern neighbors? The mountains furnish none, and both parties live beyond them. The great rivers will expose them to hostile inroads, as they will afford a convenient passage to troops. In fact, the western people will secure the western people. If the separation should notwithstanding take place, it would not be because nature directs it. We should have the consolation of reflecting, that we have provided the best means of preventing its happening at all, and from it, after it has happened, the best security against the effects which will result.

I will not pretend to say, that any one of these arguments is conclusive; nor do I flatter myself that they will immediately produce conviction; I place dependence on the moderation and good sense of gentlemen who possess public spirit and private honor; I rely upon the calm review which they will make of my observations a week hence, when the fervor of this debate has subsided.

I appeal to their candor, at that time, to decide, whether, in point of centrality, accessibility, protection to the Union, salubrity, and safety from insurrection and invasion, there is not solid reason for establishing the seat of government on the Susquehanna. I will not say that the Potomac is insalubrious; but it is well known, that northern constitutions are impaired by moving to a more southern latitude. The air may be healthful, but the change is found to be pernicious to them. Whether there is any foundation for it or not, the eastern people would dread the experiment.

The preservation of the Union is the worthiest object of a patriot's wishes. The world has doubted our success. I feel a consolation in the opinion, that the measure I am contending for will best contribute to that end. An American legislature may seek true glory by such measures as will tend to secure the Union, to preserve peace, and to diffuse the blessings of science, liberty and good government over a greater extent of country, and in a higher degree than the world ever enjoyed them. Surely, this will interest the pride of every honest heart. It is the philosophy of ambition, or it is the religion of politics.

TO GEORGE RICHARDS MINOT

NEW YORK, SEPTEMBER 3, 1789

DEAR SIR,

You interest me by your account of the school politics of Boston. I will not give an opinion as to what ought to be done. The subject is important, and merits a more manly independency of conduct than you have described. These sneaking fellows are their own commentators. Art springs from fear, and that fear from weighing their own talents against other men's, and finding them wanting. I mean where the purpose is honest. For art is sometimes practised by able men. Then it is used to conceal the turpitude of the motive. I am sick of art. It requires too severe attention to keep it always guarded. And then the art of one is so overmatched by the art, and indeed by the simplicity of many, that it eternally miscarries. An honest, sincere conduct has to sustain an ordeal. The proudly mean are offended that a man dares to think and act in opposition to the *vox populi*. He appeals to the reasons for his conduct, and never acts without reasons. The same mean censurers will applaud his sense and firmness, and ever after leave him at liberty to act as he sees fit. Public clamor is employed as a means of effecting the removal of that resistance which the unpopular man makes to their will. When it is found that this end cannot be accomplished by such means, they will forbear. I would preach to the *pride* of these hunters after popularity, and show how they degrade themselves, to their love of ease, and make manifest their needless painstaking; and to their cowardice, and evince the peril they incur. You will ask,

And why do you preach to me? Forgive me. This is stuff, for a letter.

I believe that the New England people are better taught than any other, and Boston better than any other city. Since I have been here, I have thought of the advantage of our town corporations and town schools. I do not believe that any country has such judicious expedients for repelling barbarism, supporting government, and extending felicity. Boston might be an Athens, and I would wish to make it a London. *Apropos*, we are caballing about the permanent residence of Congress. The Pennsylvanians have made, or are about making, a compact with the southern people to fix it on the Potomac. They can carry this in the House if they think fit, and all unite from Pennsylvania southward. The Pennsylvanians abhor this in their hearts, but the terms are to remove the temporary residence of Congress to Philadelphia; and as the members east of the head of the Chesapeake outnumber the others, they are pretty sure of preventing the future removal to the Potomac. Mr. Morris, who wishes to fix at Trenton, disclaims and abhors the bargain. It is some proof of the nationality of his views. Possibly, however, it is the result of a more discerning selfishness. His opposition in the Senate will be weighty, and perhaps we may effect something in the House. The business is *in nubibus*, and in such dark intrigues, the real designs of members are nearly impenetrable. Reasoning will do no good. You will see, by the papers, what pace we move in the discussion of the judiciary bill. The question whether we shall have inferior tribunals, (except admiralty courts, which were not denied to be necessary,) was very formidably contested. Judge Livermore, and ten others, voted against them. You will see, in Fenno's Gazette, my speechicle on the subject. The lawyers will consider my idea of the exclusive nature of certain parts of the national judicial power (offences against statutes, and actions on statutes) in various points of light. If my distinction

714

between *jurisdiction* and the *rule of decision* in causes properly cognizable in a state court should be clearly understood,
they will have the means of judging on the merits of my
argument. The idea is not easy to make clear, and I feel
embarrassed to choose terms which will make my ideas as
clear as I perceive them myself. However, the public has
them, and I will not comment on them.

The recess will probably obtain at the time proposed, or
very near it. You politicians in Massachusetts say that we
are running away from duty. I think that some good will
ensue, and considerable inconvenience be prevented by it.
There is an interval between the organization of the government and the ordinary business, in which nothing should be
done. We shall return in better humor than we should
maintain together. We shall find business prepared by our
great officers, and a weight given to national plans, which
they have not at present.

It is now three o'clock, and we are debating about the
permanent residence of Congress. The Pennsylvanians and
southern people forced us, loath and supplicating delay, to
take it up this day. Now, it turns out that the Pennsylvanians
will not pursue the intended treaty with their intended allies,
but actual and natural rivals. The former offer to fix it in
Pennsylvania where the eastern people may choose, and to
stay in New York, till the proposed place is prepared to
receive the government. The minority, infinitely disappointed
and chagrined, are begging delay, though they denied us,
and to get one day, are talking the time out. Whose stomachs
will conquer, I know not. I must seal this, because I expect
to go out of town, to dine with the Vice. If so, I shall have
no time to tell the event.

I think Judge Dana will be District Judge. It is only guess
work. In any event my best wishes will attend you.

Your affectionate friend.

TO GEORGE RICHARDS MINOT

NEW YORK, SEPTEMBER 6, 1789

DEAR FRIEND,

THIS has been a week of incessant exertion, and this is not a day of repose. The world will wonder what inflames and busies Congress so much. Hear it. The eastern members had agreed that it was best to postpone the question of the permanent seat of government, and we had no doubt of being able to do it. We were deceived. All south of the Delaware had agreed to make Philadelphia the temporary residence, and the Potomac the permanent seat. To break this intrigue was then our and New York's object. We decided for the Susquehanna. The Pennsylvanians, though really divided, had agreed to act together, and in fact held the balance. After a day's deliberation, they complied with the proposition for the Susquehanna, and New York in the mean time. How they got clear of their allies is none of my business. Then the southerns, finding a majority against them, begged delay, though they had denied us. This was impossible, for Pennsylvania held the balance, and would have us fix in her limits. The minority, with great purity of virtue, exclaimed against the *bargain,* though observe, they had made one themselves, which failed; and now, failing in the committee of the whole, where our propositions for the Susquehanna passed, they make every exertion to embarrass and delay the business. To-morrow we resume the subject in the House, and as a minority is commonly well united, and this is violent, active, and persevering, and our majority is not

716

perfectly agreed as to the place, I think there is some danger of our final defeat. The recess is less certain on account of this vile, unreasonable business. But a majority are resolutely bent on having one punctually on the 22d. The Judicial slumbers, and, when it shall be resumed, will probably pass, as an experimental law, without much debate or amendment, in the confidence that a short experience will make manifest the proper alterations.

I must close. My compliments attend Mrs. Minot. Accept my best wishes, and believe me to be, as I really am,

Your affectionate friend.

TO THOMAS DWIGHT

BOSTON, OCTOBER 21, 1789

MY DEAR FRIEND,

No PRIVATE conveyance offering, this will go by the post. You see, by the date, that I am in Boston, which is busy with preparation and expectation. The President is to appear on a triumphal arch. The Governor[16] begins to take a part in the affair. The gout came so opportunely last Saturday, that it has been doubtful whether his humility would be gratified with the sight of his *superior.* Is it credible that doubts should have existed, whether *he* or the *President* should first visit?— that so much honor to one should be supposed to degrade

---

[16] *Hancock.* [S. AMES]

the other? This *inter nos*. Some of his folks have thrown cold water on the ardor of the town, to no purpose. I wish you and all my Springfield friends may be gratified with the sight and conversation of the great and good President. God bless him.

. . . .

I am, my dear friend,
affectionately yours.

TO BENJAMIN GOODHUE

BOSTON, OCTOBER 21, 1789

DEAR SIR,

ON SATURDAY the President will arrive in town—He is to lodge at Marlborough on Friday night. Mr. Lowel and some other of our mutual friends are of opinion that you and I should go out to meet him as far as Watertown. Your visit to this town will gratify me, because it will afford me an opportunity to see you, and if it is proper that we should meet him your attendance will be acceptable tomorrow, if convenient. Please to write unless you should think proper to come to town tomorrow. Mr. Dalton is here. The Vice President is gone to Braintree. They arrived today. I know you will wish to pay every suitable mark of respect to the President of the United States.

I am, sir, with affectionate esteem
your friend and very humble servant

FISHER AMES

TO THOMAS DWIGHT

BOSTON, OCTOBER 30, 1789

MY DEAR FRIEND,

I SHOULD be sorry to have any friend require of me an account of myself. Since my return from New York, I have seen many who were glad to see me, and many who were disposed to claim attention from me. I have dangled after the President, &c. He is gone, and I am glad of it, and I cannot find that I have done a single thing towards putting my affairs in a train to run away from them. Yet it is from such details, that I draw my excuse for not having written more particularly in my last, and for writing little now. I am going to Dedham to-day, and on Monday to Salem Court. I found it impossible to attend the Court in Middlesex. Ah, politics! how have they spoiled me for my profession. It is time, my friend, for me to consider what the noisy popularity of a public life will produce. It is a reward that wants value and permanency. Either I must become a mere politician, and think of my profession as a secondary matter, or renounce politics, and devote myself to the humble drudgery of earning bread. Pardon this egotism. You are not indifferent I think to the subject, and you will discern the risk of postponing the final decision, till the time when my head will be crazed with the chase, as other men's have been. No more of this.

Every-body, except Hancock and his tools, has been anxious to show more respect for the President, than he could find means to express. The good man has (I think) seen that the zeal for supporting government, and the strength, too, are principally on this side the Hudson. The Governor finally waited upon him. His friends say that he never doubted the point of etiquette, and that it was a mere falsehood invented to injure him. The popularity of the President seemed to bear every thing down, like a torrent. Comparisons are odious, they say.

When I took my pen, I did not imagine I was going to write such a letter as I have. I would burn it, but have not time to write one that would please me better. Take it as the accidental effusion of an heart that would not hide even its follies from you. I think I shall not see you at Springfield till December. My respectful compliments to friends, particularly of your house.

With affectionate esteem, I am, dear sir,
Your friend and humble servant.

FISHER AMES

DEBATES ON THE FEDERAL JUDICIARY

On August 24, 1789, the House considered a Senate bill to establish the federal judiciary. Some representatives wished to establish a system of federal district courts with extensive jurisdiction on federal issues, while others wanted to establish only a federal supreme court, leaving original jurisdiction on most federal cases to the state courts.

On August 29, Ames opposed a motion to strike out the clause establishing district courts. Ames argued that certain cases— those arising out of offenses against federal laws, and actions created de novo—*were of strictly federal jurisdiction and could not be tried in state courts.*

AUGUST 29, 1789

MR. AMES said, the remarks made by gentlemen on the importance of this question would be of some utility in deciding it. The judicial power is, in fact, highly important to the government and to the people; to the government, because by this means its laws are peaceably carried into execution. We know, by experience, what a wretched system that is which is divested of this power. We see the difference between a treaty which independent nations make, and which cannot be enforced without war, and a law which is the will of the society. A refractory individual is made to feel the weight of the whole community. A government that may make but cannot enforce laws, cannot last long, nor do much good. By the power, too, the people are gainers. The administration of justice is the very performance of the social bargain on the part of government. It is the reward of their toils; the equivalent for what they grant. They have to plant, to water, to manure the tree, and this is the fruit of it. The argument, therefore, *a priori,* is strong against the motion; for, while it weakens the government, it defrauds the people. We live in a time of innovation; but until miracles shall become more common than ordinary events, and surprise us less than the usual course of nature, he should think it a wonderful felicity of invention to propose the expedient of hiring out our judicial power, and employing courts not amenable to our laws, instead of instituting them ourselves as the Constitution requires. We might with as great propriety negotiate and assign over our legislative as our judicial power; and it would not be more strange to get the laws made for this body, than after their passage to get them interpreted and executed by those whom we do not appoint, and cannot control. The field of debate is wide; the time for consideration had been so ample, and that remaining for debate so short, that he would not enter fully into it. The gentleman from South Carolina (Mr. SMITH) had very ably proved the expediency of the motion. He would confine himself, he said, to another point; and if it could be established, it would narrow the discussion.

The branches of the judicial power of the United States are the admiralty jurisdiction, the criminal jurisdiction, cognizance of certain common law cases, and of such as may be given by the statutes of Congress. The Constitution, and the laws made in pursuance of it, are the supreme laws of the land. They prescribe a rule of action for individuals. If it is disputed whether an act done is right or wrong, reference must be had to this rule; and whether the action is compared with the rule of action in a state or federal court, it is equally out of the power of the judges, to say that right is wrong, or that wrong is right. If a man is restrained of his liberty, and for that sues the officer of the general government in a state court, the defendant shows that he was a marshal, and served a precept according to the law of the United States; then he must be cleared, otherwise the law of the United States would not be the law of the land. But there is a substantial difference between the jurisdiction of the courts and the rules of decision.

In the latter case the court has only to inquire into facts and the rules of action prescribed to individuals. In the former they do not inquire how, but what they may try. The jurisdiction of the court is the depositum of a truth. The supreme power in a state is the fountain of justice. Such streams are derived from this fountain to the courts as the legislature may positively enact. The judges, as servants to the public, can do that only for which they are employed. The Constitution had provided how this trust should be designated. The judges must be named by their Christian and sirnames, commissioned during good behavior, and have salaries. Causes of exclusive federal cognizance cannot be tried otherwise, nor can the judicial power of the United states be otherwise exercised. The state courts were not supposed to be deprived by the constitution of the jurisdiction that they exercised before, over many causes that may be tried now in the national courts. The suitors would have their choice of courts. But who shall try a crime against a law of the United States, or a new created action? Here jurisdiction is made *de novo*. A trust is to be exercised, and this can be done only by persons appointed as judges in the manner before mentioned. The will of the society is expressed and is disobeyed; and who shall interpret and enforce that will but the persons invested with authority from the same society? The state judges are to judge according to the law of the state, and the common law. The law of the United States is a rule to them, but no authority for them. It controlled their decisions, but could not enlarge their powers. Suppose an action was brought on a statute, declaring a forfeiture equal to the whole of the goods against him whoever shall unlade without a permit; before the law was made, no court had jurisdiction. Could a state court sustain such an action? They might as properly assume admiralty jurisdiction, or sustain actions for forfeitures of the British revenue acts. He did not mean any disrespect to the state courts. In some of the states, he knew the judges were highly worthy of trust; that they were safeguards to government, and ornaments to human nature. But whence should they get the power of trying the supposed action? The states under whom they act, and to whom they are amenable, never had such power to give, and this government never gave them any. Individuals may be commanded, but are we authorized to require the servants of the states to serve us? It was not only true, he said, that they could not decide this cause, if a provision was neglected to be made, by creating proper tribunals for the decision, but they would not be authorized to do it, even if an act was passed declaring that they should be vested with power; for they must be individually commissioned and salaried to have it constitutionally, and then they would not have it as the state judges. If we may empower one state court, suppose the Supreme Court, we may empower all or any, even the justices of the peace. This will appear more monstrous if we consider the trial of crimes. A statute creates an offence. Shall any justice of the peace be directed to summon a jury to try for treason or piracy? It was true the government would not direct a thing so wickedly absurd to be done; but who will believe government may lawfully do it? It would be tedious to pursue this, or even the ideas connected with it, very far. The nature of the subject rendered it difficult to be even perspicuous without being prolix. His wish was to establish this conclusion, that offences against statutes of the United States, and actions, the cognizance whereof is created *de novo*, are exclusively of federal jurisdiction; that no persons should act as judges to try them, except such as may be commissioned agreeably to the Constitution; that for the trial of such offences and causes, tribunals must be created. These, with the admiralty jurisdiction, which it is agreed must be provided for, constitute the principal powers of the districts courts. If judges must be paid, they might as well be employed. The remnants of jurisdiction, which may be taken away, are scarcely worth transferring to the State courts, and may as well be exercised by our own.

1 7 9 0

NEW YORK, JANUARY 13, 1790

MY DEAR FRIEND,

I SUPPOSE you are beginning, this day, your General Court labors. I wish you may have nothing to record, which a real patriot would not wish to find on the journals. If the spirit of hostility should expire in our state, the new government will not have much opposition to fear from any other quarter. A Mr. Hawkins, a Senator from North Carolina, has arrived. The letter of the Virginia Senators, addressed to that State (Virginia) legislature, was not received with approbation, on account of the antifederal sentiments which it expressed. They would not even order it to be printed, and it was conveyed to the press by a private hand. I suppose you have read it. It seems intended to prevent the amendments giving satisfaction, more radical ones being wanting. Patrick Henry, it is said, advises all his partisans to support the Constitution, and if they wish to be secure against its supposed ill tendency, to get into the government. This is a very ancient mode of proving the faith by the practice. In this state all is quiet. The legislature is federal. The people get too much by the new government to wish it overthrown. I wish the parties in Massachusetts may not wage war again. The question of excise and assumption of state debts may possibly furnish the fuel for fresh heats. I think the assumption will be a serious article of our business in Congress. I wish, from our state, coöperation, not resistance. Our people pay great taxes. In this, and every other state, they are more moderate. They have not raised twenty-five thousand pounds in this state these three years. Their dry taxes are very trifling. Why should our industrious people be crushed, to pay taxes to maintain state credit, and without maintaining it, too, when the United States by excises, &c., equally imposed, can do it effectually? Will they love their fetters so well as to contend against the hand that would set them at liberty? To-morrow the budget is to be opened. The report of the Secretary will excite curiosity, and produce, as every great object will, diversity of sentiment. How the business will issue, cannot be conjectured. I am positive there cannot be a safe and adequate revenue while the states and the United States are in competition for the product of the excises, &c. Wherefore the debts must be assumed.

I have written very dogmatically, and why should I affect doubts, when I entertain none? I am as dogmatical when I affirm that I am, with the esteem of my whole heart, your unfeigned friend, and humble servant.

FISHER AMES

726

TO WILLIAM TUDOR

NEW YORK, JANUARY 17, 1790

DEAR SIR,

THE REPORT of the Secretary of the Treasury has set curiosity in motion. It is allowed to be a masterly performance—is very long—is ordered to be printed, and taken up in the committee of the whole on Thursday week. The state debts are proposed to be assumed, and all the debts, except foreign, reloaned at four per cent. It is not to be presumed that any system, especially one so complex and important, can pass without great debate. Perhaps it ought not to be wished.

I hear that Mr. ——— is going to eat up the bar, not, as the opossum does her young, for protection, but as the turkey-cock eats grasshoppers.

An excise on spirits, wine, teas and coffee is proposed to furnish the cash. How will this suit the fair traders? The other sort of gentry I think will not be suited.

FISHER AMES

TO WILLIAM TUDOR

NEW YORK, FEBRUARY 7, 1790

DEAR SIR,

I THANK YOU for your esteemed favour by the mail. The attempts of Mr. ——— may not demolish the bar, but they serve to prolong the silly prejudice against them. His whimsical violence, and overdoing the matter, may perhaps disgust even prejudice, and turn the current a little the other way against the persecutors. I suppose the world will not allow the lawyers to compare their persecutions with those of the primitive Christians.

I perceive our General Court have a fondness for paying debts, and Mr. Edes's paper complains of the hardship and danger of having them paid by a foreign government, for whom, and at whose special instance they were contracted. No doubt these people would claim repayment of the United States. How is that to be reconciled to the project of keeping the debt alive, as good thing, and a nurse to the sovereignty of the state. Or would it be expected that the state should get paid by the U. S. and refuse to pay the creditors afterwards? For payment would destroy this good thing the debt. I should think our people mad if they should finally oppose the assumption of the state debts, which has clogged industry, kept the state poor and uneasy, and kindled one rebellion, and will banish the farmers to the western woods.

I have actually sought for the Bath Memoirs for Mrs. Tudor's memorandum, hitherto without success. The book is not in the New York library, where I went to inquire for it. If possible, I will send the information she desires. Please to present my most respectful regards to her. A young Mr. Martin Hoffman is now in Boston, and I promised to give him letters of introduction, but shamefully forgot it. You will see him, however, I presume, as his agreeable mother says she is acquainted with you. Permit me to hope that you will introduce him to the good folks, whom he may wish to see. I told him in particular that I would write to Gore.

To-morrow we are going to turn financiers—scarce a head in New York that is not ready to burst with a plan. The issue is very doubtful, as many oppose the assumption of the state debts, and others propose to offer the creditors three per cent. which I presume they would reject with indignation.

FISHER AMES

P.S. Were your witnesses militia, who opposed the regular allied troops in the—case? In case of an appeal, your troops may perhaps be taught the evolutions. I hope Judge N. is well, and the other judges; as the returning prosperity of their court may be supposed to keep them alive many years.

TO WILLIAM TUDOR

NEW YORK, MARCH 8, 1790

DEAR SIR,

WE HAVE NOT decided upon the assumption of the state debts. [Madison] hangs heavy on us. If he is a friend, he is more troublesome than a declared foe. He is so much a Virginian; so afraid that the mob will cry out, *crucify him;* sees Patrick Henry's shade at his bedside every night; fears so much the eastern confederacy, and perhaps thinks it unpleasant to come in as an auxiliary to support another's plan; that he has kept himself wrapt up in mystery, and starts new objections daily. I hope a favourable event. But the work goes on heavily and slowly.

FISHER AMES

TO GEORGE RICHARDS MINOT

NEW YORK, MARCH 23, 1790

DEAR SIR,

YOU WILL wonder at the slumber which the report of the Secretary has enjoyed for more than a week; and still more at the business which has waked in its stead, the Quaker memorial.[17] The absence of Messrs. Fitzsimmons, Clymer, and Wadsworth, who vote with us for the assumption of the state debts, has produced a wish to have the report postponed till their return. Clymer is expected to-day, and Wadsworth at the end of the week. This is some excuse for the delay— but it is not for the violence, personality, low wit, violation of order, and rambling from the point, which have lowered the House extremely in the debate on the Quaker memorial. You will read in the papers sufficient to confirm this representation; but it is scarcely possible to secure, by any description, the full measure of contempt that we have deserved. The Quakers have been abused, the eastern states inveighed against, the chairman rudely charged with partiality. Language low, indecent, and profane has been used; wit equally stale and wretched has been attempted; in short, we have sunk below the General Court in the disorderly moment of a bawling nomination of a committee, or even of country (rather Boston) town-meeting. The southern gentry have been guided by their hot tempers, and stubborn prejudices and pride in regard to southern importance and negro slavery; but I suspect the wish to appear in the eyes of their own people, champions for their black property, is influential—an election this year makes it the more probable;—and they have shown an uncommon want of prudence as well as moderation; they have teased and bullied the House out of their good temper, and driven them to vote in earnest on a subject which at first they did not care much about.

It remains to say something about the resolutions, which have been so many days in debate. They declare the Constitution in regard to the slave-trade, &c. I disapprove the declaring Constitution. It is risky; it is liable to error, by false reasoning, and to carelessness which will not reason

---

[17] *Upon the slave-trade.* [S. AMES]

at all. It is pledging Congress to dogmas which may be hereafter denied—it is useless, because it leads to no art. Upon the whole, I am ashamed that we have spent so many days in a kind of forensic dispute—a matter of moonshine. It is a question that makes the two southern states mad and furious.[18]

You will judge, my dear friend, how much of this is fit to be read to the club.

A motion was made just now by Mr. Madison, and decided by the yeas and nays, to enter the report of the committee of the whole House on the journals,—because it was understood that the subject would not be pressed further. But there did not seem to be much reason for it; for the whole discussion has been justified on two grounds; it was intended to form a result of the opinions on the points which were entertained, and to quiet the alarms, which have agitated the southern states, on account of the emancipation of the slaves. The opinion of the committee of the whole is sufficient for the first point, and public enough for the second purpose; and the insertion of dogmas relating to the Constitution on the journals is in my opinion highly exceptionable and imprudent.

MARCH 23, 1790, WEDNESDAY THE 24TH.

ANOTHER MEMBER from North Carolina is arrived—Mr. Ashe. We suppose that he will be against the assumption—though we are ignorant of his opinion.[19] The majority, till

---

[18] *South Carolina and Georgia.* [S. AMES]

[19] *Mr. Ashe very soon put an end to all uncertainty on this point. Mr. Ames used to say that it was a very great convenience to himself that their names stood so near each other on the roll. He was always quite sure that he had voted right, if Mr. Ashe, who came next, voted the other way.* [S. AMES]

the return of the absent of our side, will be small. All our state, and all New England (except Livermore, who is not violent and perhaps may concur with us) will vote for the assumption. While the states discover more and more jealousy of the national government, it seems to be proper to secure it against the many dangers which threaten it, and the multitude of such as are now unforeseen and will arise when the present state of harmony shall be changed. Neglecting to do good will be doing evil. In any country, a public debt absolutely afloat, will produce agitation. How necessary then for us to act firmly and justly!

TO JOHN LOWELL

NEW YORK, MAY 2, 1790

DEAR SIR,

SINCE I have been engaged in the business of this second session, I have considered my letters as a tax upon the time of my friends. They have been a transcript of my own mind, and accordingly have expressed my disgust against measures and my presages of the consequences. Like a valetudinarian, I have vented my spleen, and given useless pain to my friends—But since the assumption has been rejected I think I perceive that my friends are grown as valetudinary as I am. It has not been often [my] fortune to be a simple spectator of public affairs—At this time, I am almost sure you will feel as strong a sense of the hazard to which the Gov't may be exposed by our being so long doing nothing and at last doing wrong, as any person whatever. Those who see most clearly into the principles of gov't & the human character will most disapprove the non-assumption. You are acquainted with Mr. Madison, and of course you know that he possesses a most ingenious mind, and extensive learning. He has long been deemed a champion for the Constitution—I think you will be surprised therefore to read his speech against the assumption, pronounced the week before last. He spoke more than an hour, and seemed to have framed his argument with great care—The reasoning is specious, but will not bear a strict examination. He speaks of the assumption as increasing & perpetuating the *evil* of a debt—This word *evil* is always in his mouth when he speaks of our debt. He affirms that without assuming the debt may be paid more easily & speedily—North Carolina & R. Island have an expeditious mode—The former has a law for calling in their paper at 4 (shillings?) in the pound, and yet their members talk of the *exertions* of that state to keep up her credit. Madison says too that New Hampshire under the Confed. wd. have had to pay 1/20 of the debt—taking the present ratio of representation as the rule of contribution—& that she actually pays to the impost but 1/100. Therefore that state saves 4/5 of her quota & may take that saving & apply to her state debt. He reasons in the like manner about Connecticut & some others. Peter Pindar ought to answer this argument. It will not bear a serious refutation. He is totally silent on the topic of settling state acts—but enlarges on the burden that Virginia will bear—a creditor by the war—more favored than Masstts.— instead of being repaid she will be obliged to advance more, & for states wch. have been delinquent—she consumes more too than the other states, & has paid more since the peace towards her debt & to the union—This will have an inflammatory effect in Virginia—and as the Committee of the Whole was discharged soon after this speech, from the assumption, no opportunity was given to refute such bold vague & groundless assertions—

I see that the public mind is irritable in Boston. I have some fears that they will be intemperate. The enemies of the

733

gov't seem to be making use of the peevish humour of its friends to wound it—I wish that the antis could be made to clamour for the assumption more & agt. the gov't. less.

They scold about our tardiness, & perhaps with some reason—But last week was a very industrious one, & as much was done as I ever knew in any assembly—Delay has often been wished by the public for its own sake—in order to gain friends, or to have them return to Congress—and it has been the necessary consequence of those exertions which were made to carry measures conformably to their own wishes—No charge can be made with worse effect—for base people will readily believe that the members trifle away time to get more pay, because they feel conscious that they would do it themselves. People are least of all placable towards their own vices when practised by others. It strikes too at the root of popular confidence.

It gives me the truest satisfaction to hear that the District Court has proceeded with so much popularity. Brother Gore's account of the term at Salem makes me hope that the Judicial will gain ground while the legislative is certainly losing it— I have not wished to *impose* upon you the burden of an unprofitable correspondence. But if you would sometimes favour me with a line, it would be highly acceptable. For I think I value the share which you have been pleased to allow me of your friendship as I ought—I shall no longer deserve when I cease to value it—

Please to present my respectful compts. to Mrs. Lowell and the young ladies, and my regards to my friend, your brother, J. Lowell Junr.—I am dear sir, with sentiments of respect and affection, your very hble sevt

FISHER AMES

I hear that your neighbor Heath is trying to stir up the officers. I hope in vain—Is the assumption liked by our state rulers any better since it was rejected? If they shd. approve it, & it shd. pass finally, they will be estopd[?]—

734

TO GEORGE RICHARDS MINOT

NEW YORK, MAY 20, 1790

MY DEAR FRIEND,

IT IS a long time since I have heard from you. I wish to be assured by your own handwriting, that you have escaped the influenza, or if not, that you are well over it. The most dismal accounts of the prevailing sickness of the people in Boston have been given here. Our friend, Dr. Dexter, I am told has been very ill, and is but half recovered. I hope this is not true. You are going to be busy soon with the General Court, and after that kind of duty shall have begun, I shall despair of getting a word from you.

All my letters from our state assure me that Congress is becoming unpopular, and losing confidence as well as reputation. The impatience of the creditors to have their debt funded without delay has been mingled with the murmurs of the *antis*. I think I can see the policy of the latter, in forbearing to complain of the assumption as a piece of usurpation, and making use of the angry creditors to help their cause against the government. I was lately made apprehensive that the creditors were going to agree on a memorial, praying that the debt might be immediately funded, whether the assumption should be agreed to or not. Such a step would have blown up the whole assumption, and probably the funding system with it. But that memorial seems to be laid aside, and I am glad of it. For the cause of assuming the state debts has derived aid from the opinion, that the advocates of that measure would not suffer it to be separated from the funding system; but if the creditors at Boston had expressed a willingness to submit to such a separation on

735

any terms, the aid of those who have been lugged along, *vi et armis*, to approve of the assumption, would be withdrawn. We are now in committee on the bill for funding the debt, and debating about the old money. I am not sure that it is prudent to introduce it in this place. The success of any provision for the old money is problematical, and as it is now objected that it will delay and embarrass the funding business, it is attended with increased difficulty, to get the rate fixed at the scale of forty for one, which would confirm the promise made by the old government.

The assumption is not less to be hoped for than it has been for several weeks past. Mr. Sherman is indisposed, but in a day or two will renew his motion for assuming certain fixed sums. The success of it would be certain, if the Pennsylvania creditors were well disposed towards it. But they consider it as dividing their loaf with others, and they wish to have it all. I am surprised that men, who are to depend on government should be careless as to arguments, which seem to prove how much its strength will be impaired by a divided revenue system. They seem to be secure as to the permanency of the government, and mindful of nothing but the property of the debt. I hope we shall not finish the session without funding the whole debt; if not the whole, then as much as we can. For if we should not fund at all, I am apprehensive that the popular torrent, at a future session, would be found to be strong against funding. It might be said, we ought not to promise more than we know we can perform; that of consequence, temporary appropriations would be safe, and adequate to every purpose of justice, and the old game of preying upon the creditors would be played again. Without a firm basis for public credit, I can scarcely expect the government will last long. I own, my dear friend, I am sometimes ready to despond, when I think how great hazard attends those measures which are essential to its being. The President has been dangerously sick, and though much better, is still very weak. This circumstance has added something to our gloom. I hope in a few days, however, that I shall be able to say, the assumption is agreed to.

FISHER AMES

DEBATES ON MEASURES TO FUND
THE PUBLIC CREDIT

On February 9, 1790, the House began to consider a plan from Alexander Hamilton, Secretary of the Treasury, for supporting the public credit. The plan proposed that the Revolutionary War debt be provided for in full by a permanent funding system— effectively monetizing the debt.

In the first serious challenge to the plan, Representatives Samuel Livermore and Thomas Scott asserted that the domestic part of the debt had been artificially enlarged by citizens' overcharging the government for goods and services during the war. They recommended that Congress pare down the debt before funding it. Ames's speech of February 9 countered these arguments.

The next challenge to the plan concerned the question of discriminating between original and present holders of the debt, which Hamilton had opposed. When several members—including James Madison—came out in favor of discrimination, Ames answered with the February 15 speech.

The strongest challenge to the plan was over the assumption of state debts by the federal government. During the debate Alexander White proposed that the federal government assume only such debts as any state had incurred over and above its equal proportion of the war expense. Ames's speech of February 26 was in reply to this proposal. On May 25, after the question had been thoroughly examined and once voted down in the committee of the whole, Ames delivered his last major speech in favor of assumption.

*Another challenge to the plan centered on Hamilton's recom-
mendation that the debt be made redeemable by the government
only by a small proportion each year. The purpose of this measure
was to compensate the public creditors for the reduction of the
interest rate from six to four per cent. When on March 11 a
motion was made against irredeemability, Ames rose to explain
its connection with the reduction of the interest. He was again
on his feet on March 13, to show that the government gave up
little by delaying redemption of the debt, since to redeem it any
faster than the bill allowed was beyond the nation's capacity.*

MAY 25, 1790

MR. AMES.—I am obliged to obtrude my sentiments upon
the committee, under circumstances which stifle the hope of
procuring for them a welcome reception. The curiosity of the
Assembly, in the first stages of a public debate, will procure
some indulgence, and administer considerable aid to him
who has to support a part in it. But this subject has been
debated until it has become tedious; there is very little
remaining to be said which can excite curiosity or reward
attention. The feelings of the committee will procure me
belief when I say, that I obey the duty of attempting to
obviate the objections which have been urged by the gentleman from Virginia, and which I think is imposed upon me
by the nature of some of them, with unaffected reluctance.
I will hope, however, that a candid condescension to the
necessity of my situation, and a sense of public duty, will
overcome, or suspend for a time, the disgust which has
attended the revival of this debate.

The zeal of the gentlemen on both sides has led them to
draw aid to their cause from very remote sources. But all the

objections against the assumption may be comprised in these two—that the measure is against justice and against policy. Both sides of the question have been maintained with an uncommon warmth of conviction; in candor, and probably in strict truth, this ought to be mutually understood as the evidence of a sincere zeal for the public good.

To evince the justice of the assumption, I take, as the ground of my reasoning, a proposition which is admitted on both sides; that the expenses of the war ought to be made a common charge upon the United States.

It will illustrate my argument to observe, that this war was between this country and Britain, and not a war of particular states. All America, Congress in their resolves, the act appointing Commissioners to settle the accounts, the late amendment (Mr. MADISON'S) to the proposition for assuming the state debts, and the objections to that proposition, corroborate the idea that the expenses of the war ought to be equalized. Assume the debts, and settle the accounts, and this is effected. There is an end to the inequality as soon as this is done. This answer is so plain and conclusive, that it is attempted to take off its force by saying that the accounts will not be settled. If this assertion is true, the non-assumption is plainly unjust; for the burden is confessedly unequal now, and the only reason for refusing to take this burden off some of the states, is the certain assurance that they will be relieved from so much as shall be found to exceed their share, when the accounts shall be settled. But if the accounts are not to be settled at all, the states, which are now overloaded, have no justice to expect but from the assumption. It cannot be known with certainty which will be a creditor, or which a debtor state, at present. If the accounts should not be adjusted, we must remain in ignorance; we ought therefore, to exclude all consideration of the other claims, because it would be useless, and apply the principle of equality to the state debts. The debts to be assumed are either duly proportioned among the states, or they are not. If they are so proportioned, then it is certainly politic, and not unjust, because it would be equal to assume them. If they are now unduly proportioned, it is in terms even against equality to leave them upon the states.

If the war has made a random distribution of debts upon the states, it is best to make the amount which is to be left unsettled, as little as may be; for the probability is, that as you diminish the unsettled amounts, you make the inequalities less. This will serve as an answer to those also who say, that supposing a settlement to take place two or three years hence, a state may be relieved from a light burden of its own debt, and be obliged to bear, as its proportion of the assumed debt, one more weighty. For it is not certain that it will have, in that case, more to bear than its part; and if it should turn out to be more, the balance may be known almost as soon as the interest will commence. The assertion that the accounts will not be settled has been made with confidence. To judge how far we ought to guide our conduct by it, it is enough to examine what state it comes from. Let the gentlemen who make it ask their own hearts, let them look round and ask one another, whether their states are the more clamorous for their dues, or apprehensive for a settlement, which will expose their delinquency? In this place, where facts are known, this question will be an argument.

But what ground is there for saying that the accounts will not be adjusted? This was positively engaged by the former government. It is improper for Congress to act as if Congress was not to be trusted. Commissioners are employed in the business. A motion to extend their time and powers has met with no opposition, and it is maturing into a law. Who will oppose it? Not New England!—we wish it—we have pledged ourselves to support it; you ought to believe us, when it is so easy to bring us to the test. I have myself moved resolutions, the best I could devise, which I thought would facilitate—

would force a settlement. I am ready to revive them. Surely those who urge that the accounts will not be settled, do not propose to fulfil their own prophecy.

It is certain, therefore, that if there is a disposition in this House to prevent proper measures from being adopted to procure a settlement, it will be disappointed. I wish to remove this ground of objection, by urging the business of liquidation forward. If, then, provision is to be made for liquidating the accounts, the argument which I deduced from it remains in full force. All pretence of inequality is removed by it. It is a full answer to several other objections—it becomes unnecessary to ask whether state notes remain debts against this government, after they have been received into the state treasuries. Whether the United States are obliged to assume before the balances are found on a settlement: and whether the debts were wisely or unwisely contracted? It becomes immaterial to calculate how many parts in a hundred New Hampshire, and how many Connecticut will pay; and how much Virginia has paid, and will now have to pay. What was wrong in the distribution of the burdens of the war will be rectified; and as to future payments, all the citizens will be upon a footing. As the gentleman from Virginia reasons with great candor, I am sure he will be sorry that, in his observations, he has wholly neglected, certainly through inadvertency, to notice an argument which seems, on both sides, to be considerd as absolutely conclusive. When I say that both sides allow this argument to be conclusive, I presume my meaning is understood as I formerly expressed it. For the answer to it is, that the accounts will not be settled; which admits the force of the reason, and rests the decision upon a point of fact.

Perhaps, for the sake of simplicity and perspicuity, I ought not to pursue the inquiry as to the justice of the assumption any further. Though I mean to rely upon the argument I have stated, it will furnish an answer to some objections to furnish another. It is said these are state debts, Congress has nothing to do with them.

When the war commenced, Congress had neither money nor troops. They were so far from having a right to tax the states, that they had neither the powers of a government, nor a rule by which to require contributions. They appealed to the good-will and patriotism of the states, and entreated them to furnish supplies to the extent of their power. The calls upon the states were not taxes or debts, but advances or loans to the public. This is explicitly and formally declared by the resolves of Congress. I have made some attempt to examine the journals, in order to show from them how totally unfounded the assertion is, that these constituted debts against the states. But I found that the titles only of the resolves would fill a sheet of paper. Nothing can be more fully proved than the contrary, not only by the letter of the resolves, but by the conduct of Congress. In some cases no regard was paid to the conjectural ratio by which the states ought to furnish men and supplies. In other instances some of the states were wholly omitted, and not unfrequently a single state was called upon for supplies. One of the most signal proofs, however, is that in the resolves of February 9th, 1780, it is expressly stipulated, that if the states should furnish more than they are called upon for, the United States will stand charged with it. The resolve of January 5th, 1783, even in terms recognises the troops whom the states were to settle with as creditors of the Union, for whom good security must be provided.

This is an inquiry into the justice of the assumption. I reject, therefore, the forms of the transaction, and ask whether, if the war had been confined to a corner, instead of spreading over the continent, and one state had incurred the whole debt of eighty millions, it would be just to leave the burden upon that state? Consistently with the resolves I have mentioned, and the known sense of America, could it be called a state debt? I am sure of my answer, for the question extorts it. The difference between the case I have supposed, and that which is in debate, is only in degree—there is none in the principle.

It will be answered, perhaps, that it is true we owe the states. They are not finally to bear the burden; let them pay what they owe, and we will pay them. This is a dangerous concession to those who make it, if the accounts are never to be settled, as it is urged by those who contend against the assumption. For it amounts to this—the debt is binding, and yet it will never be paid. It presents them a choice of difficulties; it forces them to confess either that the assumption will not wrong you, or that the non-assumption will end in cheating such of the states as are your creditors.

It will be said, it is true, however, that the United States stand indebted to the states, but the creditors of the states have no just claim upon the United States. There is a great difference between the justice that will be done by the assumption to the states and to their creditors.

The states were called upon during the war to make advances. Accordingly, they procured something by taxes, and still more was procured by paper money, which died in the hands of the possessor. They have also paid some part since the peace. So far the states, as such, actually made advances; but the principal part was obtained either by borrowing, or seizing private property, or draughting men. So far the advances were made by individuals, and at periods so critical, and under such circumstances of violence and hardship, as to give a peculiar sanction to their claim upon the justice and honor of their country.

Justice plainly requires that these persons should be repaid their interest at least, in all events, and without delay. Their claims, in every view, are perfect; most of them are original holders. But neither the justice of the case, nor the engagements of Congress, require that the states should be repaid until the extent of their demand can be known. For I readily admit, that nothing more than the balances of their actual advances are due from the United States to the individual states. This has been urged against the assumption, but without foundation. If a state paid more than its proper share, the surplus should be repaid. But if a payment was only promised, and is still to be made, justice is due to the creditors and not to the state. The idea may be illustrated by considering the states as agents or contractors for the Union; what they paid, they claimed for themselves; what they barely promised should be paid, by their employers, who had the benefit of the debt, especially if the agent cannot or will not pay. I cannot think it necessary to give any further answer to the question so logically proposed with regard to the nature of the debts when redeemed, and in the state treasuries.

What remains due ought to fall not unequally upon states, but upon the whole society. It ought, if not paid sooner, to fall upon posterity. If some states should lose wealth and people, and others increase, if new states should join the Union, or spring up within it, and the Western wilderness be thronged with people, the burden will be equalized upon all the citizens. Liberty and independence were procured for the whole, and for posterity; why then should not all contribute to the price?

As it respects the army debt, the very terms of the bargain bind the United States. Congress promised to pay the men, but called upon the states to raise them. Afterwards, when the paper failed, the states were required to make up the depreciation. State notes were given for it, which remain due. Probably all the states cannot pay. In this instance not only justice, but your plighted faith, require you to pay them; you have asked their services, and had them; you have promised to reward them, and they remain unrewarded. I have already supposed the case of the whole debt being thrown upon one state. If, instead of the whole debt, its zeal, or the necessity of its affairs had pressed a state forward to exceed, and in its distress to disregard, its ability to pay, and, accordingly, had run in debt three times as much as it can pay—that the war had scattered its citizens and wasted its property—are the officers and soldiers who expelled the enemy, and who did not care which state line they served in, to be told, you served the United States, but you are the creditors of South Carolina? It is true, you shed your blood for us; by your valor we sit here; we have seen your wrongs, and when it would do you no good, because we had no power, we told the world how deeply we lamented them; but go home and starve. Would not this wring drops from their hearts, and plant thorns in our own?

The like reasoning will apply to another description of the debts to be assumed—to the certificates given by the commissaries and other officers of the United States, and since assumed by the particular states. You cannot deny your own, by calling them state debts. A great part of the debt of South Carolina is said to be a debt of that kind. Is that state to be crushed with a weight which it cannot bear, or are the creditors to be ruined because the state will be undone if they are not? Or how will this comport with the principle admitted on both sides, of equalizing the expenses of the war?

The best fund of the states, and hitherto the only one of the Union, the impost, has been taken away by adopting the Constitution. Let the debts follow the funds. Let the world judge whether the generous confidence of the state creditors in the public justice ought to be abused, and whether they ought to be made to repent the cordial support which they gave to the new Constitution. The force of this argument may be inferred from the uncommon pains which have been taken to destroy it. The fact is denied, and the issue of the question has been boldly rested upon this point, that the states most

urgent for the assumption were not incapacitated from providing for their debts by the surrender of the impost. The
impost collected in New Hampshire is called the amount of
that state's contribution to the Union, and the ratio by which
she ought to contribute is taken from her present representation. I waive, at this moment, all comment upon the
unfairness and fallacy of this mode of computation. I proceed
to observe that an uncommon use is made of the result.
According to her number of representatives, that state ought
to pay one-twentieth, and yet no more than a hundredth part
of the impost of the Union is paid by that state, or rather
collected in it; of course, it is gravely said, it will save four-
fifths of the sum which it would have had to pay if the debt
had been assessed upon the Union before the Constitution
was framed, and this saving to the state may apply to the
discharge of its debt. But, sir, such requisitions never were
paid, and never could have been paid by the states. Experience had taught us that it was not to be expected, nor was
it in their power. This, indeed, was one of the principal
reasons for adopting the Constitution. Are we seriously
addressed when we are told that the savings of a revenue,
which did not exist, that four-fifths of nothing, may be applied
to pay the state creditors? Without further regarding the
ridicule of the argument, let us trace the fact. The debt of
New Hampshire is said to be about 230,000 dollars; the
yearly interest, at four per cent., is upwards of 9,000 dollars.
The impost and tonnage collected in that state, from August
to December, is near 8,000 dollars. So that the impost of
that state, though far short of her actual contribution to the
common treasury, will, in the whole year, greatly exceed
their interest, which assuming her debt will throw upon the
United States. Here, then, the fund surrendered by that state
is more than adequate to the debt which ought to follow it.
The whole cause has been hazarded on the fact, and here
the fact is against him who appealed to it. May I be permitted

to ask, whether it is not to be lamented, that through inadvertency or mistake, the whole was not mentioned? May I demand why the non-importing states were preferred to the importing states for calculating the impost? Massachusetts collected, under a state law, near 150,000 dollars impost yearly. This falls short of her present collection under the law of the Union, which is nearly equal to the interest of her debt. The excise would have supplied the deficiency, and that fund you are about to invade. It would be wrong to take away funds, though inferior to the discharge of interest, and yet to leave the whole debt upon the state. If the funds surrendered were equal to the debts, it has been admitted that the Union ought to take the debts also. The injustice of rejecting the debts, and taking the impost to a less amount, differs only in degree. But why was New York passed over in silence? The interest of the debt of that state would not equal the impost collected within it. What will you say to that state?

The candor and impartiality of the committee will be exercised in deciding whether the arguments so often urged in favor of the assumption, that you ought to take the debts with the impost, has lost any thing of its force by this investigation of facts. What is asserted on one side, and denied on the other, after a strict inquiry, ends in the same point.

There is another view of the subject to be taken. It is allowed that the people pay duties in proportion as they consume dutied articles. The consumption in the several states is nearly according to the numbers of the people. It will be as fair in this as in the former calculation, to take the number of representatives as our rule to compute the proportions which the several states contribute by the consumption of articles charged with duties. The impost of New Hampshire and Massachusetts, collected within the period from August to December, and added together, was nearly one hundred and twenty thousand dollars. Allow the former three parts in eleven, according to her representation, and it will appear that her citizens paid thirty-two thousand seven hundred dollars of the whole sum. Less than eight thousand dollars were collected within the state. In case the debts should not be assumed, but should be provided for by state duties and excises, according to these principles, the citizens of New Hampshire would have to pay five thousand dollars a month, or at the rate of twenty-five thousand dollars from August to December, into the treasury of Massachusetts. Connecticut in like manner would pay within an equal period fifty-four thousand dollars, and Jersey, if reckoned with New York, would have to pay about sixty thousand dollars, and with Pennsylvania still more. In a whole year, this tribute which one state would exact from another would amount to very large sums. North Carolina is a non-importing state, and, in common with the others before mentioned, would have to pay for the debt of its neighbors, and then to provide for its own. Is there any justice or cause of discord or violence charged, or even imagined against the assumption equal to this? And yet we hear it said, let us leave the states to pay their debts for themselves.

Perhaps we shall never be fully agreed as to what is policy; on great questions, when the judgment should be cool, the passions most frequently interpose and disturb its decisions, and this is most likely to happen where public men are zealously faithful to their trust. But it is otherwise with our sense of justice; our pity, our gratitude, our resentments, may mislead us; but of all the operations of the moral sense, the most precise and infallible is our sense of justice. The heart acts as our interpreter, and guides us to certainty; injury or wrong is the opposite of justice. I appeal to that moral sense, to that law written upon the heart, and confidently ask, whether you can impose this burden upon the states, and call it equality? Whether you can reject the claims of their creditors, and call it justice? As to the policy of the assumption, to object is always easy. It is not hard to show how many little objections a great measure will be liable to; but, in a question of policy, we are commonly obliged to disregard little things for the sake of great ones; nor can complete proof be given of the affirmative; for, when it is asserted that bad consequences will ensue, time only can fully prove that they will not. I neither expect nor pretend to overcome every doubt when I undertake to show that it is more safe and prudent to assume than not to assume the state debts. When we speak of policy, what is meant by the term? A measure is said to be against wise policy, when it tends to prevent good, or to produce evil; it respects either the government or the citizens: as it respects government, will the assumption diminish its power, or embarrass the exercise of it? Or, as it regards the people, will it produce evil and not good?

This measure can neither increase nor diminish the power of the government; for the power to be exercised is expressly given it by the Constitution. Will it embarrass the exercise of power? The contrary is true; it removes impediments which will be in its way, if not assumed. Experience has taught us, to our cost, how very pernicious those obstacles are. The systems of state revenues, before the Constitution was formed, had crushed industry and almost ruined trade from state to state.

Will its tendency be to evil rather than to common benefit? This, it is true, is a vague as well as complex question; but its great objects are to establish justice; to produce equality of burdens and benefits, an uniform revenue system; to secure public credit by removing every example of bad faith, and to prevent all interference between the national and state governments, and the dangerous usurpation of the one upon the other, which would be the consequence.

How can it be said that policy is against the measure, if its tendency be such? Much has been said about consolidation.

Certainly it cannot be usurpation for Congress to pay the debts which were contracted either by itself, or, at its own request, by the states. The state governments are said to be in danger of a consolidation: that, however, is not the only, probably not the greatest, danger they have to risk; disunion is still more formidable. Nothing can shelter the small states from the greater ones but union: nor would any single state be safe against the combination of several states. All would be exposed to foreign foes. If you make the state governments strong by taking strength from the Union, they become exposed exactly in the degree you do it. For the principle of union ought to be strong in proportion to the strength of the members. In a compound ratio, therefore, you make the national government too weak to combine the whole together, and you expose governments and citizens to the caprice of accidents and to the fury of passions, which will confound laws, liberty, and governments.

It is true, a body of valuable citizens will be attached to the government; all good citizens should love the government, and they will do so, if government should deserve their love. Revenue powers are given to Congress without reserve. To say that it is dangerous and improper to exercise them is a charge against the Constitution.

There are but three points of view to consider the state governments in. Either as rivals for power, as watchmen, or as legislators within the state. To call them rivals would be an avowal of the principle of disunion, or rather of positive force, which is absurd. I do not know that either the state or national constitutions have given them the office to watch this government. The people are to watch us all, and I wish they always may. But if the state governments are still called watchmen, that office may be performed as well, perhaps better, without than with the incumbrance of their debts. It is equally difficult to see how it can impair the rights of internal legislation. The assumption and an uniform plan of revenue will take away not only all pretext, but every motive for encroachment upon them. If, by the non-assumption, an interference is produced, their danger will be the more imminent. For, if they prevail in the conflict, they will be ruined by disunion; if they fail, they will be swallowed up in the consolidation. I wish, among other reasons, to have the assumption take place, because I think it will give us the best security that our government will be administered as it was made, without suffering or making encroachments.

I hasten to notice some objections: a public debt is called an evil, and the assumption is charged with tending to increase and perpetuate it. I am not disposed to dispute about words, though I believe the debt, as a bond of union, will compensate the burden of providing for it. But I cannot admit that it is a greater evil to owe a debt, than to wipe it off without paying it; and if the whole debt is to be paid, at all events the assumption makes no increase; nay, if the modification first proposed should be made, the capital will be diminished near thirteen millions by this measure. It is said to be easier to pay eighty millions by leaving the state debts to be paid by the states, and paying the other debt ourselves, than to form the whole into one debt.

By this division of the debt, if there is any force in the objection, that we can pay more, or we shall pay what may be collected more easily, first, let us see whether this is true as to what the states will have to provide for. As it respects South Carolina, the contrary is confessedly true. So far is it from being a more easy way of paying, that they cannot pay at all. If Massachusetts can pay her interest, it will be with extreme difficulty. One gentleman observed that her efforts had raised a rebellion. It is certain that they have not succeeded. The price of the state paper in most of the states has been some proof of their incapacity to make effectual provision.

The state debts are to be paid, or they are not. If, by leaving them upon the states, they will be lost to the creditors, that cannot be supposed to be the most convenient mode of

751

paying part of eighty millions, which is intended by the argument. Besides the shock to public credit, it would be a loss of so much property. The disaster would probably be more felt than some of the greatest physical evils, such as inundation or blasting the earth for a time with barrenness. If then the debts are to be paid, by what means? The gentleman from Virginia has srongly reprobated excises. The states cannot touch the impost, what remains? Direct taxes only. This source will be soon exhausted. The land tax of England is not more than a sixth part of its income. They have carried it as far as they think prudent. Why should not labor and stock contribute as well as land? For these give their chief value to its products. It cannot be expected that the debt will be safe to rest upon a land tax. It is not even mortgaged at all in England. If our entire funds are barely sufficient, merely a single fund, and that not the best, will be inadequate. It is a better one in England than in America; for the wild land makes it impossible to impose very heavy taxes upon the old settlements, the oppressed people will fly beyond the reach of collectors. It is besides much more easy to procure the money in England than in America. Land taxes are not only insufficient, but liable to other objections. Land is to be taxed according to quantity or value. If the former, it will not produce much. If according to value, then you must resort to arbitrary assessments, more obnoxious than excises. Every farmer almost can attest the force of this objection. The expense, too, in England, is little; but in this country it is otherwise. Taxes on land have cost as much to collect as excises. In one of the states I am told that the collection has been estimated at thirty per cent. Experience, too, has proved that the states cannot pay their debts by direct taxes. It has been pushed to the utmost extent, and found insufficient.

The argument which has been urged by the gentleman from Virginia against excises, seems to exclude this mode of revenue; without it, the state debts cannot be provided for. The United States will be compelled to resort to it. It is absolutely necessary for drawing forth the resources of the country. As every man consumes, every man will contribute, including foreigners and transient people. Imposts cannot be carried far without defeating the collection. Duties on imported spirits would increase the use of homemade spirits, which cannot be reached without an excise. All taxes are in some degree unequal, but excises probably as little so as any. The rates are fixed, and very little is left to imposition and caprice. Besides every consumer taxes himself.

If, then, Congress should not lay excises, the best source of revenue will be lost. I am persuaded public credit cannot be supported without them. It seems to be a measure of equal necessity that the states should impose them. But the states cannot do it with convenience or much effect, for they cannot make them general. They will vary in the states, and hold out temptations to an infinity of frauds. The states are restrained from regulating foreign trade, or that from state to state; with such vast frontier lines to watch, and their powers on the importation and passage of goods by land so much restrained, and their laws obstructed and controverted by the laws of the Union, much of the collection will be defeated. The excise in Massachusetts and Connecticut, it is supposed, has not produced ten shillings in the pound of what it might be made to yield. I do not pretend that there is less wisdom in the states, but they labor under almost insurmountable difficulties. It is doubtful whether they will be able to collect much; and if they should, the burden of these rival laws has been found nearly equal to another tax.

Besides, one state will tax another. The consumers will go to the most convenient market. So that the attempt to make each state pay its own debt will be defeated, and the payments will fall as unequally as if the assumption should take place, and the accounts not be settled. New Hampshire,

Connecticut, New Jersey, and North Carolina would pay almost wholly into the treasuries of the neighboring states. The non-importing states will be obliged also to impose direct taxes to pay their creditors, so that their citizens will be doubly taxed. If state excises then yield so little, and are so unequal, where are those mysterious state resources which are inaccessible to Congress? If they are not of an incommunicable nature, we can judge better by hearing the subject of taxation named. It ought to appear that such exist, and that Congress could not draw them forth.

If you reject excises, you cannot have an adequate revenue; and if the states have also excises, the revenue will be impoverished and hazarded. For if an article can pay both duties, there is a loss to get but one, it might as well be collected throughout the United States as in one state; and if it cannot pay both, one or both treasuries will suffer for the loss. Besides, you incur a double expense in collecting them.

What revenues are left you if the excise is rejected? With such a slender sum you cannot offer new terms. The modification of the entire debt, as first proposed, makes a saving in the capital of almost thirteen millions. The debt to be assumed is about twenty-four. The interest on the difference, or on the real increase of debt by assuming, is less than five hundred thousand dollars yearly.

We depend upon two principles for the security of the revenues. One is that the trading people will not be disposed to offend, and the other is that all others will be inclined to watch and expose them if they should. Never was so popular a revenue system. But the violence to the just demands of the creditors, depriving them of the money they have been used to receive, and creating in the states an interest to have your collection fail, in order to make the state funds effectual, will produce a most disastrous change. It is setting men's interests as well as opinions against you. Nor will the landed interest have a different sentiment, for they will be murmuring under the load of direct taxes, and the more the state revenues can be improved by lessening the national, the less they will have to bear.

What reason is there, then, for asserting that more money can be obtained, and more easily, by several systems than by one? This bold assertion, which the sense of America would refute, if its experience had not done it already, is not true of imposts. I have endeavored to expose its fallacy with regard to state excises. They produce much evil and little money. Direct taxes, insufficient as they are, can be imposed by Congress to any amount which ought to be required, as well as by the states; and I do not know that they would be more obnoxious. It is true, just complaint is made of their unequal operation, and I trust that Congress will not be under the necessity to call for them. What advantages for taxation do the states possess over Congress? We ought not to admit that any such exist till the reasons and facts are made known to us; which has not yet been done.

Without adequate funds the states cannot propose to their creditors a modification of the debt. By the Constitution they are restrained from passing laws to impair contracts. The burden will rest upon the states, if not assumed, at six per cent., for without funds the creditors will not consent to take less; if assumed, upon Congress at four. Is this the more easy way of paying part of eighty millions? It makes a difference of several millions against the public.

If we commit an error by not assuming, it will be an expensive one. Have we funds so abundant and safe that we may divide and mangle with impunity? But we are told that probably there will be an assumption at the next session, and that it is improper to press a decision at the present, especially as immediate provision is not to be made, and as delay will reconcile men's minds to the measure. This is plausible, but at least it is yielding the great point as to the principle. If the business should be referred to the next session with intent then to assume, the states will not impose taxes and frame funding systems for half a year. In the mean time, this state of their paper will make it the subject of the most pernicious speculation. It will be engrossed for a trifle by foreigners, and at the same time aggravate the scarcity of money by employing what there is in purchases. In this state of suspense and loss, will the public mind become tranquil? Will it unite the two sorts of creditors? But though you delay the interest on the state debts to 1792, you pass the revenue laws as soon as possible. By delay you will lose the revenue which may accumulate prior to that time. Suppose a million and a half obtained before the payment of interest shall begin, that sum will secure the interest against any probable deficiency of the duties for two or three years. Will not the public; will not the creditors of every description, derive advantage from an immediate assumption and establishment of duties, and from the proposed delay of paying interest?

It is an unusual thing for a gentleman in a public assembly to assert, that four-fifths of the people are of his way of thinking. This, however, has been done. It is not strange for persons to mistake their own opinion for that of the public. These fond prepossessions may be received instead of evidence, but they cannot weigh much against evidence. My information may have been less diligently sought, and less carefully examined than that gentleman's; but I have compared it with what has been gathered by my friends, and I declare that I believe four-fifths of the wise and worthy men, in a very wide extent of country, look with strong disapprobation upon the injustice, and with anxious terror upon the impolicy of rejecting the state debts.

Little notice has been taken of an argument for the assumption, which, if just, is entitled to a great deal. I mean that which has been urged to show that it will strengthen the government. The answer given is, that instead of pecuniary influence, new powers are wanting to the Constitution. This is not denying the argument, but asserting a proposition, which, if false, is to be disregarded, and if true, is not inconsistent with the point in question. So far from denying, it seems to admit the utility of the assumption, and asserts the utility of some other thing. Which other thing he has not explained, and if he had, it is probably unattainable, nor will its attainment, be it what it may, be prevented by the assumption. But before we ask for new powers on paper, let us exercise those which are actually vested in Congress. What will new powers avail us, if we suffer the Constitution to become a dead letter? What has dropped from the gentleman on this point amounts to an important concession. Little topics of objection sink to nothing when it is allowed that the assumption will strengthen the government. Is the principle of union too strong? Do not all good men desire to make it perfect? What nation has more to hope from union, or to fear from disunion? Shall we make the Union less strong than the people have intended to make it, by adopting the Constitution? And do not all agree that the assumption is not a neutral measure? If its adoption will give strength to the Union, its rejection will have the contrary effect.

I have thought of this government with the fondest enthusiasm. I have considered it as tending to mend the condition of mankind, and to perpetuate the blessings of liberty. At this late period of the debate, it is hardly possible for gentlemen to exercise impartiality. It will be an act of virtue, of magnanimous self-command to do more—to place themselves for a moment in the situation of the advocates of the assumption, and to see with their eyes. They love their country, and mean to serve it; and I am sure they would shrink from the spectre of its misery which haunts us; they would not consent to undo the Constitution in practice, to realize the evils which are only apprehended under the

Confederation, and which were prevented by the total want of power in Congress. With this principle, however, it will be found that power enough is given to create division, and to make it fatal—it will beggar the government, and bind it in chains.

FEBRUARY 9, 1790

MR. AMES did not conceive it material to inquire, whether there be an equal obligation on the people of the United States to pay their foreign and domestic creditors, when they meant to pay both; but if it is intended to reduce the principal of either, it will lead us into a discussion of the principles on which such a measure ought to be founded. The honorable gentleman from Pennsylvania, (Mr. SCOTT) probably intends by the amendment, to have a reduction of the debt; I have, said he, so much respect for the good sense and upright intentions of that honorable gentleman, that I will not impute to him unworthy motives; nor do I believe that he governs his conduct in private life by maxims which I suspect to be contained in the amendment now before us. I would not be understood, by any means, to convey an improper reflection upon the opinions of any one. The science of finance is new in America; a gentleman may therefore propose the worst of measures with the best intentions. What, let me inquire, will be the pernicious consequences resulting from the establishment of this doctrine? Will it not be subversive of every principle on which public contracts are founded? The evidences of the debt, possessed by the creditors of the United States, cannot, in reason, justice, or policy, be considered in any other light than as public bonds, for the redemption and payment of which the property and labor of the whole people are pledged. The only just idea is, that when the public contract a debt with an individual, that it becomes personified, and that with respect to this contract, the powers of government shall never legislate. If this was not the case, it would destroy the effect it was intended to produce; no individual would be found willing to trust the government, if he supposed the government had the inclination and power, by virtue of a mere major vote, to set aside the terms of the engagement. If the public in such a case is, as I have said, personified, what conceivable difference is there, except in favor of the creditor, between the public and an individual in the case? If, then, the public contract is a solemn obligation upon us, we are bound to its true and faithful performance. What is the object for which men enter into society, but to secure their lives and property? What is the usual means of acquiring property between man and man? The best right to property is acquired by the consent of the last owner. If then, an individual is possessed of property, in consequence of this right, how can government, founded on this social compact, pretend to exercise the right of divesting a man of that object, which induced him to combine himself with the society; every gentleman may determine this question by his own feelings. Shall it be said that this government, evidently established for the purpose of securing property, that, in its first act, it divested its citizens of seventy millions of money, which is justly due to the individuals who have contracted with government! I believe those gentlemen, who are apprehensive for the liberties and safety of their fellow-citizens, under the efficiency of the present Constitution, will find real cause of alarm from the establishment of the present doctrine. I have heard, that in the East Indies the stock of the labor and property of the empire is the property of the Prince; that it is held at his will and pleasure; but this is a slavish doctrine, which I hope we are not prepared to adopt here. But I will not go further into a consideration of the idea of discrimination. I will ask, though, is this country ever to be in a settled and quiet state? Must every transaction that took place, during the course of the last war, be ripped up? Shall we never have done with the settlement and liquidation of our accounts? If this is the case, what kind of rights will the people have in their property? None but the will of the government. And will this tend to the establishment of public credit? What security will they derive from a new promise? None. They well know that this can be set aside equally with the other, provided it is deemed expedient. What mischief will follow this idea? The public faith destroyed, our future credit will be a mere vapor; and all this risk is to be run for the sake of—what? Of saving something to the public? No; the public will lose by the transaction more than they will gain; our justice will be impeached, and foreigners will feel themselves happy, that they have it in their power, by violence, to procure to themselves that which we deny to our own citizens. Such a mere arbitrary act of power can never be exercised on the part of government, but to the destruction of the essential rights of the people, and will finally terminate in a dissolution of the social compact.

FEBRUARY 15, 1790

Mr. AMES agreed with the gentleman from Virginia (Mr. MADISON) in regard to the validity of the debt. There was propriety in saying the nation is the same, though the government be changed. The debt is the price of our liberties and cannot be diminished a farthing, the gentleman from Virginia says; and why? Because the government, as one of the contracting parties, cannot annul, or vary the bargain, without the consent of the other. If the measure proposed by that gentleman corresponds with that sound principle, he should have the pleasure of agreeing with him on the ultimate decision; but if the measure should be found on a fair discussion, to be subversive of that principle, it would not merit the countenance of the committee.

A claim upon our justice is made, on behalf of the original holders of securities, who have transferred them. Does the plighted faith of the country stand charged to pay the difference between the price their securities sold for in the market and their nominal sum? In order to make the affirmative appear, the worthy gentleman has said, that the paper is the only evidence of a prior contract; and while the paper was sold, the residuary right to the debt still remained in the seller. Supposing this novel doctrine to be true, which cannot be conceded, it will not warrant any conclusion in prejudice of any purchaser of the Loan-office debt; for the paper was given when the loan was made: as no prior debt existed, the paper is the very debt. The gentleman ought, therefore, to confine his motion to the army debt, as his principle seems inapplicable to any other. And even on liquidating the army debt, the certificate extinguished the prior debt; otherwise the public would be twice charged. As when one man owes another an account, and gives his bond for the balance, the acount is no longer of force. By the terms of the certificate, the person transferring has lost his claim against the public. He has freely transferred; for if violence or fraud were practised, the law will afford him redress. In society, as well as in a state of nature, property is changed by the consent of the last occupant. He may dispose of it by gift or at half-price, and give a complete title. Nor will the pretence that this transfer was free only in appearance, avail; for the motives which disposed the owner to sell cannot affect the right of the purchaser. Every such creditor risked something; either that the government would not pay him at all, or not in due season. The risk, computed in free and open market, will be nearly right. It is a kind of insurance against these risks, and the insurers and insured will calculate the rate of insurance better than government can do it. If there is a new risk of government interposing, it seems that the purchaser, who may be called the insurer, did not rate his risk high enough. It seems pretty clear, therefore, that there is no claim on the stipulated justice of the country.

Another sort of justice is set up; a different sort from that which we were taught in the schools and churches; it is called abstract justice, and it is said to demand allowance for the loss sustained by the failure of public payments. No man respects more than I do the merit of the army; but the soldiers, at least, had something towards justice by their bounty.

Stock has sold in England at fifty per cent. discount, and yet no retribution has been made. Where then does this new line of justice begin? It can scarcely be denied, that their claim, if they have any, is not a debt. The arguments alleged by the gentleman are addressed merely to the compassion and generosity of the government. Nor do I know that there is any ground for saying, the public opinion is in their favor. It will be allowed, that if justice is to be done, it should be impartial justice. Partiality would be more cruel than total neglect. Will you refuse to make amends for paper money? For property taken by our army in Canada? For losses sustained during the war? For towns burned? In this last case, it is to be observed, that government has promised protection; and inability to protect is as much a debt as the case in question. The intermediate holders, who bought at six shillings and eight pence, and, despairing of government, sold at two shillings and six pence, have an equal claim. Are all these to be excluded? Let us not break contracts for half justice. The example of paper money is adduced to show that the public made up losses; but this is an example of the public fulfilling its contracts, not annulling them. Paper money is a bad source to draw examples from.

But is it true that justice requires the public to pay for all the losses sustained in times of calamity? I think not; for by fraud the government would be obliged to pay for more than was lost. The resources of the sufferers will more easily repair such losses than the government can make them good; and besides, in extreme cases, it would extend and prolong the evil. If an army should invade England, and the city of London should be burned, and the country laid waste by the order of the King, all Europe could not pay for it. What is justice? A line of public conduct which necessarily tends to utility. No pretence of abstract justice can be valid, if it tends to evil rather than good.

But if there subsists a claim on the public justice, it cannot impair the debt, in the hands of the present holder, for which the public faith is pledged. It is alleged that the seller, who sold for a trifle, will be taxed to pay the purchaser. He certainly ought to fare as other citizens do. But taxes are in proportion to property. If he has property, then the plea of necessity is destroyed; if he has none, then his taxes will be a mere trifle.

The project is not justice, even to those whom it pretends to relieve. If you allow less to the purchasers than they gave, it is downright robbery; if you allow them more, it is halfway justice to those who have sold. I would not risk everything to do justice, as it is called, and then not do it.

But this fragment of justice cannot be given to some, without wronging others; you impair the property in the hands of the present original holders. It is not supposed that the alienated property is nearly equal to that which is still in the hands of the first holders. Be that as it may, I believe, with confidence, that it would be cheaper for the present holders to pay the market price of the paper proposed to be given to the former holder, than to suffer the shock which this measure would give to the credit of their paper. I will not enter now into the merits of the Secretary's plan; but I think it not difficult to show that he proposes better justice to the present original holders than is contained in the motion, and that the debt, funded on this plan, would sell for more in the market. Great sums have been lent to the public by trustees, who acted for others, and only lent their names. Many original creditors were not first holders; supplies were furnished to contractors for the army, who got credit, and afterwards paid in paper, as they received it of the public. Many towns hired soldiers for a gross sum, and agreed to take the wages. Private debts have been paid at par. A man in embarrassed circumstances, instead of compounding with his creditors for ten or a dozen years' forbearance, paid them at par, or near it, in public money, which, in that period, was supposed to be as likely to be paid as his private note. No less a sum than two hundred and fourteen thousand dollars were paid in this way to one mercantile house, at about fifteen shilling in the pound. Compare the gross injustice of these cases with the pretended justice of the motion; consider what it pretends to pay the purchaser. But Loan-office certificates have sold from fifteen and eighteen shillings in the pound to five shillings. Foreign purchasers gave more than our market price. Before they bought, they got certificates of the nature of the debt, that it was not liable to any deduction, and that the transfer would be valid. People in the first offices in this country, and abroad, signed them. Five hundred thousand dollars were bought for one Dutch house, and registered, and the partners in the sum have divided the certificates by giving their own bonds. What will be the effect? Justice or injustice? In these cases, the gentleman will admit, that the rights of these people are perfect. The debt, he says himself, cannot be diminished a farthing; property is sacred; the right to a single dollar cannot be violated. Let the gentleman then acknowledge that he must give up his project or his principles.

I have endeavored to show what sort of abstract justice this is. But if it should be allowed that there is a claim of justice, what then? Let them claim justice of those who have done them injustice, not of the fair purchaser.

Let us examine the claims of the purchasers. The gentleman's argument on this point merits attention; if it is right, for its novelty in Congress; if wrong, for its tendency. Here I think it necessary to apologise, not for my sentiments, their apology must spring from their propriety, but for the manner in which I express them. My zealous conviction may seem to arraign the opinions of other gentlemen, whom I respect as I ought. I know that men of the best intentions entertain a favorable opinion of a discrimination. There is a wish to do more than justice to the one, and the heart, betrayed by its sympathy, consents to injustice to the other. But, sir, I cannot claim the merit of moderation on this point. I will not pretend that I doubted first, and then decided. The principles of my education, and the habits of my life, predispose me to believe, and my short experience and reading have confirmed it, that nations cannot admit cunning into their councils without its shedding a malignant influence on their affairs. Experience teaches government, as well as men, that nothing is safe that is wrong. We have endured tender-laws, and the pitiful expedients of a trickish policy. Our experience has cost us dear. The old Congress, however, were guided by other maxims; with little power, and scarcely retaining the mock representation of it during the whole year, they prosecuted the objects of an honest policy with a zeal which repulses and despair could not extinguish. They could say, with Francis the First, after the battle of Pavia, "We have lost all, except our honor." They resolved against discrimination, and foreigners, as well as citizens, bought securities under the public faith. But when the Constitution was framed, adopting the debts as valid, restraining *ex post facto* laws, and laws impairing contracts, who entertained any suspicion? The speech of the President, and the resolutions of the House in favor of public credit, banished it. Does this look as if public opinion was hostile to these purchasers? If it really is, it is more a duty on government to protect right when it may happen to be unpopular; that is what government is framed to do. If, instead of protecting, it assumes the right of controlling property, and disposing of it at its own pleasure, and against the consent of the owner, there is a cheat in the compact.

It will be admitted, that there is a right vested in the purchaser; government cannot diminish it a farthing, says the gentleman; but he says we cannot pay both. Then abide by your word of honor; prefer perfect rights, by solemn compact, to claims on your compassion. The claims of the present holders, you say, are just; are the others more than just? Treat all just claims alike, and do not rob on the highway to exercise charity. Why make one creditor pay another? He says, government is to get nothing by this; and yet he says, we owe these people, and our creditors shall pay them. Is paying a debt in this way not getting money? He talks of rival claims; there is no rivalry; the sellers agreed that there should be none. If government is bankrupt, compound with your creditors. Will this act of violence console the sufferers? Will they enjoy, as a favor, the violation of the rights for which they fought? The South Sea and Mississippi schemes have been adduced as examples. In the former, government interposed to fulfil the contract. The Mississippi is not parallel. What the gentleman calls public justice, I am sure he would not practise in his own case.

I have chosen to consider the principle of the motion; but it cannot be carried into execution. We have seen that justice, in the abstract, will not be done, nor can the measure proposed be effected. We may very well suppose that innumerable difficulties will arise in practice which cannot be foreseen. The detail will be endless; an account must be opened for each claimant, public offices must be opened, officers multiplied, and great expense incurred; there is no clew, by the records, to the cases of money deposited by agents for other people. I have inquired, and am told that it is not possible. Will you admit oral evidence, and of persons interested? Will you fill the land with discontent, corruption, suits, and perjury? The new paper, if not transferable, will be no great relief; if transferable, there will be a new harvest of speculation; the after-crop will be more abundant than the first cutting. A purchaser keeps his note for twenty shillings, by law you make it a note for ten shillings. How many frauds will be practised on the unwary? If the mind balances on these points, let policy turn the scale.

Will not this measure shake government? Instead of doing as it has promised, government is to do as it pleases. Right is to depend, not on compact, and sacred faith, and the Constitution; but on opinion, on a major vote, where nothing, not even right, is fixed, will not the government be liable to perpetual commotion?

How will it affect our national character? How will it affect public credit? We shall have to pay for meddling, if we in future should have any credit. The famous *Colonel Chartres* said, he would give one hundred thousand pounds for a character—not for its own sake, but because he could get two hundred thousand by it—*Henry VIII.* borrowed money on his personal security; and his base Parliament voted, that as he had done great things for the realm and church, he should be discharged from those obligations. *Charles II.* shut up the Exchequer. What was the consequence? *King William* paid fourteen per cent. on annuities, and at the rate of ten and twelve per cent. interest; but by good faith, in five or six years money fell to five per cent. interest. By breach of faith, we vote the government into a state of pupilage, and deprive it of its powers.

I have thus endeavored to show, that there is not a debt subsisting against the public, in favor of the original holders, who have sold out; that the motion is chargeable with partiality, and is inadequate to its pretended object; that it will do injustice to many, and violate the sacred rights of property; that the purchasers are secured by the contract, by the faith of government, and by the Constitution; that the measure is not practicable, and will produce confusion, corruption and expense; and that it will weaken, disturb, and disgrace the government, and impair its credit.

I have made this recapitulation of my argument, in order to bring it into one view—if it is just, or only plausible, let us ask, what will be the effect? Is this what was expected under the new Constitution? Did we expect it? Is there one here who has not told the people, that an end would be put to tender acts and paper money, and the ruinous effect of government's interposing in contracts? Who, in or out of Congress, did not suppose that the letter and spirit of the Constitution said as much? The spirit of the times said more. Will not the people charge us with violating the Constitution and the rights of property? If we plead necessity, they will demand, how came it that we were ignorant of it? And, if it exists, what is there that breach of faith can save that good faith would lose? Or, what will that be worth, which may be secured by a measure that will tarnish our national honor, and transmit to our children an inheritance of reproach? Is there no refuge but in dishonor? We have borne adversity before, and we had rather submit to the worst events of an honest policy—and this project is not to relieve any burdens; for government is to rob, not for plunder, but to get the reputation of justice.

If our own citizens say this, what will foreigners say? They will not be restrained, either by the opinion of their fellow-countrymen, or by attachment to our prosperity. They will detail their losses, and the arts by which their confidence was gained—they will think that we have been taught a species of immoral philosophy—that we administer government by a kind of cunning logic, which confounds right and wrong—they will rejoice that the Mahrattas and Americans are at a distance; the ocean has not hitherto proved a barrier against our depredations. An American abroad will be obliged to deny his country.

However, I still believe that justice is a law to Congress; but if justice, and public faith, and honor, have ceased to be things, let them cease to be names—let them be blotted from the vocabulary of our nation. If they have no being why should they be made use of to conjure up church-yard terrors, to haunt the hypochondriac imagination?

I will not be so uncandid as to charge the worthy gentleman with such intentions. I think so highly of his probity and patriotism, that if he can be made to see that these consequences will follow, or only be apprehended, he will give up his scheme. But if government has this right, what right of private property is safe? In the East, government is said to be the sole owner of property, and may resume it at pleasure. This absurd doctrine will not find advocates, for it would not do for practice, even where it may not be denied to be true; human nature revolts against it; it would shock the morality of Botany Bay; it would exasperate, beyond sufferance, the patient slavery of Indostan—and who can give a good reason why one sort of property should be more sacred than another?

If we pursue another kind of policy, such as the preamble to the Constitution declares to be the objects of the government, this government, and this country, may expect a more than Roman fortune. The government may have more credit, the people more knowledge, and the blessings of peace a longer duration than the world has ever experienced. That gentleman helped to frame the Constitution. I have no doubt it is the better for his eminent abilities; I hope that the love of his own work, and his zeal for the cause which he has so ably supported, will induce him to abandon a measure which tends so fatally to disappoint the first wishes of his own heart, and the hopes of his country.

FEBRUARY 25, 1790

Mr. AMES expressed great regard for the candor of the committee in proceeding to discuss a subject which some gentlemen considered as of the first importance. He presumed from it, and the consideration gave him the highest gratification, that they were disposed to persevere in that line of conduct towards each other, which had hitherto so notoriously contributed to preserve that harmony in their discussions and decisions which had hitherto prevailed.

He begged permission to state one or two reasons why the committee ought to proceed in the way they were in, which he was sure would not be considered as altogether foreign. I presume, in the first place, that it is pursuing the civil order of things; that is, we consider what is to be done, before we consider how it shall be done. It is perfectly natural to ascertain what the debt is, before we declare how it shall be paid. I can hardly contemplate a change in the order of proceeding, without incurring confusion.

But there is another consideration: the manner in which the provision shall be made for the discharge of the annual interest will, in a great measure, depend on the decision of this question; because, if the committee determine that they will assume the state debts, they may proceed without paying much regard to the existing and otherwise interfering revenue laws of the several states. They would then have a clear stage, and might fit it up as they judged most convenient. They might lay such duties as they supposed were most likely to be successfully collected. But if we do not assume them, it will then be worthy of inquiry, how far we are to regard the present laws of the states respecting excise? Whether we are content to take the residue of what is left after the state collection? This will also lead to the discussion of an invidious question between the pre-emption right of the state and of the United States, and the superiority of the general and particular creditors.

By pursuing order, we shall, I trust, come to satisfactory conclusions upon every proposition. The resolutions are simple; they do not enter too much into detail; nor are they expressed in too compact a manner. By their simplicity they are capable of fair discussion; it is what the honorable mover intended, and what I hope they will receive.

There is one other remark I would suggest; but then I would have gentlemen observe, that I barely suggest it. Perhaps if we do not assume the debts contemplated by the Secretary, we have no right to assume the funds; if we break into his general arrangement, the system is dissevered, and can hardly be again connected so as to preserve its symmetry, or give it efficacy.

FEBRUARY 26, 1790

MR. AMES said, that a jealousy was entertained of undue advantage being procured to particular states. In order to remove the impediments, which he supposed unworthy influence of state interests on his mind might place in his way, he was obliged, as well as disposed, to rest his arguments upon general principles. For these, like truth, upon which they are founded, have an unchangeable and uncontrollable authority.

Let the first inquiry be as to the justice of the measure. In 1775 the citizens of America, with a solemn appeal to heaven, made a common cause of their violated liberty. They agreed, as brethren, to expose property and life in its defence. If partial dangers and losses were to have fallen upon the sufferers, probably it would have discouraged many who were most immediately exposed, and yet displayed the most heroic fortitude.

Nor would those who were remote from the danger, and indeed from the quarrel, have become parties on any other principle than that it was the cause of all America. For instance, South Carolina, as happy as peace and wealth could make her, had little cause of complaint against Britain. He did not espouse the cause of South Carolina merely, but of America. That state gave an illustrious example of patriotism. But if her citizens, when they foresaw the evils of war, had foreseen that more than five millions of debt would be created against her, that the armies would live, as it were, on free quarters in her territory, and that a great part of the personal property would be destroyed or carried away, would they have drawn the sword if they had believed that the benefit would be common, but the burden partial? No, sir, the spirit of the people, and the resolves of Congress, spoke a different language. Let him who has not forgotten the spirit of 1775, deny that this is in conformity to its dictates.

But were the state debts contracted for the war? It appears by the books in the public offices that they were. Will any one say, that the whole expense of defending our common liberty ought not to be a common charge? Part of this charge was contracted by Massachusetts before Congress assumed the exercise of its powers. The first ammunition that repulsed the enemy at Lexington, and made such havoc at Bunker's

Hill, was purchased by that state, and appears in the form of their state debt. The war was chiefly a common charge, while paper money would defray it. But in 1780, when it became of little value, Congress called upon the states. The states which complied with the demand contracted debts, and that in proportion to their zeal. A state which totally neglected a requisition, or complied partially, would of course proportionally escape a debt. Is this justice? But the states were also exhausted, and to aid their feeble authority and slender resources, they called upon the towns, and these called upon classes, and these upon individuals; why not as properly say, that this debt is due from the town classes, or even individuals, as from states.

Nothing can more clearly evince the injustice of calling these state debts than this circumstance. Congress appointed persons to liquidate and settle public accounts, and some of the states did the like. If a state took early measures to receive and allow claims, of course many were exhibited and allowed. But where it was convenient to apply to the offices of the United States, and especially in case the state had not opened like offices, the claims chiefly appeared against the United States. Accordingly the commissioner from Congress allowed about two hundred and eighty thousand dollars in Massachusetts, and near one hundred and thirty thousand in New York, merely because the former state had incorporated them with her debt, and in the latter they were received by the officers of the United States. Congress delayed sending a commissioner to South Carolina till 1784; had he been sent in 1782, it was probable the debt of that state would have been of less magnitude. Are circumstances so merely adventitious and casual to constitute a plea for the Union to disown the debts? Formerly the state had the funds, and the creditors preferred their notes; they agreed to this Constitution, which was giving the funds to the United States; shall not the debts follow the funds? Shall we first disable the state from paying, and then refuse payment ourselves? Is it just, that officers, who fought side by side, should have a different recompense?

Let us examine this measure on the ground of policy. How would it strike the people of England to divide their debt upon several counties, and to establish independent revenue systems for its security? Habit has made an idea equally dangerous, and strangely familiar in our own country. It is unfriendly to the national and state governments, to make it absolutely inevitable for them to clash and interfere. Let us preserve the powers of both unimpaired; to combine our citizens in common views; to make the revenue laws uniform; to extend permanent protection to trade and manufactures; to relieve our husbandry from direct taxes; are objects worthy of the government. It is natural, too, to suppose, that the collection may be made less expensive, as it would make a double set of revenue officers unnecessary; it will relieve us from the confusion of so many sorts of paper, and by extending the market, and making the funds more certain, will increase the use of the state paper as money.

The southern states are supposed to possess a small share only of the present debt; but as Maryland, Virginia, North Carolina, and South Carolina, owe near thirteen millions of the state debts (more than half their amount) the assumption will produce a more equal distribution of benefits and burdens. Besides, the state duties operate to the injury of the revenue; an article that bears a low duty of import, is dutied high by the state, and there is danger that the temptation to fraud will impair both revenues; for the impost alone would not furnish such temptation, yet the state duty being superadded, the collection becomes insecure.

But state duties are not confined merely to their own citizens. The trade from state to state has been grievously burdened by their operation; the Constitution was intended to free our domestic intercourse from all restraint. Further, excise duties fall upon the consumer; one state will be tributary to another. Massachusetts has collected part of the duties from the citizens of New Hampshire; the operation of the New York impost is well known; when it is said, therefore, *let each state pay its own debt,* we ought to expect that this will not take place, if the debts should not be assumed; and it may be well doubted, whether, in that case, state duties would not prove a more grievous burden upon trade, and produce greater inequality and injustice, than has ever been urged against the assumption.

These arguments, independently considered, will probably be allowed to prove the justice and sound policy of the assumption. But in order to preserve their full force, it is necessary to obviate some objections.

The assumption, it is affirmed, tends to the consolidation of the states, and to the destruction of the state governments. The entire powers of peace, war, and treaty, are given to Congress; of consequence the power of raising supplies, and when they may fail, of contracting debts to carry on war, belonging to Congress. The entire debt was created by the war; it seems to be in strict conformity to the spirit, as well as letter of the Constitution, to assume it; for it cannot be improper to exercise that power in this instance, which, in all like cases, is exclusively vested in Congress. The states are restricted from raising troops and carrying on war; the power of contracting and providing for debts incurred by war, seems to be incident to it. It would not be safe to concede that the power of levying war belongs to Congress, and yet to assert that the power of providing for it is necessary for their security, to be vested in the states. If this, however, is not asserted, the objection will be untenable—for, if it is now necessary to the states, it will always be necessary. All future war debts will be contracted by Congress; the objection, therefore, supposes either that the state debts will be extinguished, in which case there is only a temporary security against perpetual danger, or that they will be kept perpetually in being to secure the states against it.

The objection plainly leads to this conclusion. If it is improper and unsafe for Congress to exercise this power, then the Constitution is wrong, and it ought to have been vested in the states. The power of providing for war necessarily draws after it the right of declaring it, and the whole power of the sword. The people of this country well know that this power, vested in more than one body, might soon be turned against themselves. There would be neither Constitution nor Union in that case. But we are to administer the government according to the frame of it. The real check against the abuse, and the security for the being of both national and state governments, is the knowledge of the people. The assumption will not render the Constitution obscure, nor strengthen the right of this government to raise armies, which is already given; nor will it make the state governments obnoxious, but rather the reverse, as it will throw upon the United States the odium of levying taxes. Besides, as soon as the accounts shall be settled, this danger will occur. The objection, then, applies equally against the liquidation of the accounts.

Let us, however, take the argument simply as it is stated. It proves too much. For if so much power follows the assumption as the objection implies, it is time to ask, is it safe to forbear assuming? If the power is so dangerous, it will be so when exercised by the states. If the assuming tends to consolidation, is the reverse, tending to disunion, a less weighty objection? If I am answered that the non-assumption will not necessarily tend to disunion, I reply, neither does the assumption necessarily tend to consolidation. An unreasonable clashing of jurisdiction cannot be friendly to the present frame of our republics.

We are told, that the accounts are in train of being settled. We are advised to wait that event. But, in the mean time, what is to become of the state creditors? Most of the states claim balances—will they provide for their creditors while they expect to receive those balances? Will their citizens submit to taxes cheerfully while this expectation lasts? The value of the debts would be fluctuating. If this settlement should be long delayed, their value would sink to a mere trifle; suppose, that by asuming, we bring the states, or some of them, into debt to the Union; by not assuming, the Union is certainly in debt to the states. Is it more wise or just to be debtors than creditors? But if the states are to have credit for what they have done and paid, and to be charged with what they have received from the United States, most of the states will be creditors; and as the war was a common charge, and ought to have been entirely supported by the Union, the debts of the states are debts which they ought never to have incurred, and, therefore, the assumption restores things to their just foundation.

It is said, leave the states to pay their own debts; are they to do it by direct taxes? It is well known that in estimating the product of taxation, as much depends on the mode of imposing and collecting, as on the wealth of the persons taxed. Perhaps direct assessments are of all taxes the most unproductive and uncertain. They are, besides, arbitrary and burdensome. Will any single fund, especially such as I have just mentioned, be sufficient? Or if it should, would it not banish the husbandmen from some of the states? Independence is a common acquisition, and ought to be enjoyed upon equal terms. But to some it will prove ruinous, while others, living in another state, and divided by an imaginary line, will enjoy their lands almost tax free.

Or shall the states fund the debts on excise? Have the states a right to excise imported articles? Without deciding that question, it is not supposed that they have the power of regulating the importation of goods. The checks upon the dealers in dutied goods, of consequence, will be imperfect.

Neither have they a right to prevent the transit of goods through a state. The extent of frontier is another impediment to state excises. Massachusetts has a frontier line to watch of many hundred miles, and it will not be possible to prevent the introduction of goods charged with less duties, or not dutied at all, from the neighboring states. If a state excise law should militate against the law of the Union, both cannot operate; perhaps neither. The right of the states to collect excises, if such right exist, is deduced from the silence of the Constitution; the right of Congress is expressed in positive terms. If, then, the right of laying excises by the states, either does not exist, or exists under several limitations and disadvantages, then the provision which they can make for their debt becomes proportionally inadequate and precarious. The burden, if equally borne, and under the wisest and most efficacious system of revenue, is supposed to be heavy enough; how, then, shall it be endured, if borne unequally, and under such inconveniences?

If it is urged that the United States cannot provide for the state debts, I answer, the states are still less able.

But with debts you take funds; and even on pecuniary calculations, the public will gain. Not assuming is paying twice over. For the people of a state will be unequally burdened to pay their debt; and then, as citizens of the United States, will be liable to be taxed to make retribution.

But how is this retribution to be made? Taxes must be uniform; you cannot, therefore, make a requisition upon the debtor states; you cannot sue for the debt in the federal court, for the money is due to the creditor states, and not to the United States. Will you wage war to enforce payment? The balances must be paid by the United States. If Virginia is found to be a creditor, the Union must pay it by taxing the citizens of all the states. The arguments urged against the assumption apply with equal force to the nonassumption.

The same answer will be equally proper to be given to those who object, that it will operate unjustly against the states which have advanced beyond their proportion, and now will have to bear a part of the debt of the other states, some of whom are debtors. The states are either creditors or debtors. If creditors, the assumption is a prompt payment of that amount of their claims; if debtors, the charge of inequality is absurd, even in terms. The debt is to be paid, or it is not: if not, the debate is improper; if it is to be paid, then equally or unequally. If the latter, abandon the plea of justice; if the former, then apportion it; if the debt were actually divided among the states, according to their quotas, the assumption would be unexceptionable; because it is manifest that the burden could be more conveniently borne by the people under one system. If it is unequally divided, why should the people be crushed by the inequality of the burden?

Congress have already agreed to pay the balances which may be found due to the states. This is virtually an assumption should we forbear to do that in the first instance which we are ultimately bound to do?

MARCH 1, 1790

ASSUMING THE STATES' DEBTS

MR. MADISON.—I conceive it now to be necessary to bring before the committee the fourth alteration in the proposition for assuming the state debts, which I suggested when I was up before—it is as follows:

"*Resolved,* That the amount of the debts actually paid by any state to its creditors, since the ——— day of ———, shall be credited and paid to such

779

state, on the same terms as shall be provided in the case of individuals."

.   .   .   .

Mr. MADISON admitted that it would not give effectual relief to the citizens of those states who had sunk a great part of the principal of their debt. His only object was to give every state an equal advantage as far as was practicable upon the plan of the assumption.

Mr. AMES.—Gentlemen have repeatedly told us, that they are not opposed to the assumption, provided the liquidation and final settlement of the accounts was speedily to take place. I give them credit for their intentions, and I will not presume to impute to any gentleman so unworthy a motive as a desire of throwing embarrassments in the way of this business. But the amendment now laid on the table seems to be grounded on an idea, that the assumption of the state debts will impede the liquidation and adjustment of the accounts; or, at best, that it will not tend to facilitate the accomplishment of that object. Upon the hypothesis that the accounts will not be settled, the gentleman seems desirous of doing what he thinks most consistent with equity, regardless of the inconvenience and oppression which must follow; but which, I presume, he would not contend for, if he was satisfied that proper measures would be pursued to attain that object.

Now, in order to answer the purpose which gentlemen seem to have in view, I have prepared some resolutions, which I mean to bring forward at a future period, when a fit opportunity presents, that is, after the other propositions are decided upon. I will read them, and then lay them on the table for the information of the committee.

Resolved, That effectual provision be made for the settlement of the accounts between the United States and the individual states.

Resolved, That in the said settlement the states respectively be charged with the advances to them severally made by the United States, liquidated to specie value, with interest thereon, at the rate of six per cent. per annum; and that they be also charged with the amount of their respective debts (which, with the consent of the creditors, shall have been assumed by the United States) with the interest thereon to the time from which interest shall be payable by the United States.

Resolved, That in the said settlement, the said states respectively be credited with all moneys paid, and supplies furnished to or for, and debts incurred on account of the United States, and, in general, with all expenditures whatsoever, towards general or particular defence, during the late war between the United States and Great Britain, with interest thereon at the rate of six per cent. per annum.

Resolved, That the said settlement be made under the direction of the Commissioners, whose authority shall continue until the said settlement shall be effected, and whose decisions shall be final and conclusive upon the United States, and upon the several states.

Resolved, That in case a ratio for adjusting the contributions of the respective states shall not be prescribed by Congress during the present session; the said Commissioners shall have full power to settle such ratio, and shall also have power to determine, in all other respects, the principles of the said settlement, in conformity to these resolutions.

Resolved, That the several states may exhibit their claims against the United States until the ———— day of ———— next, but not afterwards; and that the said Commissioners shall, as soon as may be after the said day, proceed to a final adjustment of the said accounts, whether the whole of the claims of the respective states shall have been then exhibited or not.

Under these resolutions, the commissioners are intended to be authorized to proceed *ex parte* if the states should be inattentive to its conditions; and the business must be completed by a given day. If Congress should be unable, or unwilling to ascertain a ratio, the commissioners will be empowered to fix one, independent of any other authority; by which means we acquire a moral certainty that a final settlement may soon take place, and equal justice be done to all.

Mr. SEDGWICK.—I do not know that I shall vote against the propositions offered by my colleague; but I am afraid of going into an investigation of a subject not immediately relative to that under consideration. I wish that all our attention should be confined to what appears to me to be of the greatest importance, until we have gone through with it. The amendment, which has been unanimously agreed to, I considered as, in some degree, improper to be connected with the original simple proposition; but as it appeared to have made a favorable impression on the gentlemen from Virginia, New York, and Pennsylvania, I readily withdrew my opposition. But to the one which is now brought forward, I cannot so readily acquiesce. If I understand it rightly, it goes to this, that each state shall have an immediate allowance for all the payments they have made, on the debts due by them at the conclusion of the war. I doubt whether it will not be as difficult to ascertain what has been paid since 1783, as it would be to ascertain all sums paid since the commencement of the Union. If this is the fact, I cannot see any good reason for stopping short; why is it not proposed to go to the commencement of the Revolution? Why is it supposed that the inequality of exertion is greater now than it was during the war? The most liberal presumption is, that the states which made the greatest exertions during the war are only equalled now by the exertions made by the other states since the peace. South Carolina and Georgia made great exertions during the war; but the exertions of South Carolina, having more exhausted her during the first period, she has been unable to do so much as her sister states during the second.

I believe, upon the fair adjustment of the exertions of the respective states, what I have supposed will be found to be the case. I am not influenced by the interest which Massachusetts has in the question, for, since the year 1783, I am confident she has contributed much beyond my apprehension of her ability. I fear that in attempting a partial equality, we shall destroy the principle upon which the original proposition rests; and, therefore, I wish to let all the advances made by the several states await the final adjustment of the accounts.

. . . .

Mr. AMES said, the gentleman's proposition went upon the idea that the exertions of the states were more equal during the war than they have been since the peace; but what evidence has been adduced to establish the fact? None. Then he was as much at liberty to deny the assertion as the gentleman to make it. He presumed, and it was a liberal presumption, that the exertions of the states were, at this moment equalized; it became the duty of Congress, then, to assume that part of the state debts which was yet outstanding. He thought they ought to await the final settlement. It would be making a provision *ex abundanti*, and undertaking to pay debts already discharged, to the injury of the real creditors of the United States. Let gentlemen consider, said he, whether the resolutions I proposed this morning are not more likely to produce a final settlement than the one now under consideration, and consequently more likely to bring about the equality which gentlemen solicit; but if they are desirous of truly equalizing the burdens already borne, I submit, whether it would not tend to produce that effect, by repaying the states all the money expended during the war? A reimbursement of this kind would do justice to all; this, like the proposition of the gentleman from Virginia, would make the state Treasuries rich, but it must be by making the citizens poor; this would be realizing the assertion of the gentleman, it would indeed be true, that a public debt is not a public blessing.

.   .   .   .

Mr. AMES said, he had no idea of funding more than the surplus of what the states had paid more than their quota, as the same should appear upon the final settlement of the accounts; for he imagined the debts paid by the states were subjects of liquidation and adjustment, but not of funding; neither did he think it necessary to anticipate a fraction on that account. But how would the measure operate? Is there a citizen in the United States who would be grateful to the government for taxing him, in order to pay money back to him again? Certainly he would be put to some inconvenience, besides losing the expense of the collection. How could it benefit the states? For my part, I cannot understand an interest of states subsisting, different from the interest of the citizens of the state. Will it do justice to our creditors? It will render the funds for that purpose precarious. Is it to fulfil the contracts of the United States? The United States have made no such contract. In short, it is a departure from the principles of the Secretary; after such a breach of his plan, he can no longer be responsible to this House for its consequences. It is an arbitrary grant without principle; it may increase, instead of diminishing the inequality. As to Massachusetts being a debtor state, Massachusetts never was afraid to meet the strictest investigation. She knows her exertions were not behind those of any state in the Union; we do for her nothing more than the equal justice she is entitled to. I firmly believe the same is true, as it respects

South Carolina. That state was stripped of her property, and ravaged from end to end; assume her debts incurred by superior exertions in the common cause; for her exertions were equal or unequal; if unequal, no doubt but they ought to be assumed; if they were equal, the arguments drawn from inequality vanish into air. Nor will the plea of inability excuse us; if South Carolina is able to struggle under an oppressive and unequal burden, the United States can bear it with greater ease.

MARCH 2, 1790

Mr. AMES contended that a certain description of the state debts was, in justice, due by the United States. The soldiers and officers of the late army were settled with, partly by the state to whose quota they belonged; how could the final settlement be more a demand against the United States than was the depreciation of pay? They were both given to the same person, and for the same kind of service against the common enemy. How can justice require us to pay the first, and acquit us of the rest? In many instances, if a discrimination of this sort is admitted, men who not only fought the same battles, but who fought side by side, and whose blood commixed and dyed in sanguine streams the horrid field of war, will meet a compensation from their country as different as sixteen is to nothing. One part of the debt of Massachusetts was contracted for the powder and arms which first repelled the enemy; how is it that justice does not require from the whole Union the repayment of such demands?

It is admitted that the state debts ought to be paid; but the question is by whom? If they are justly the debts of the Union, they ought to be paid by the Union. But, say gentlemen, the United States are perhaps not in condition to provide the necessary revenues. How do they expect, then, that the states which have been so long oppressed, and almost destroyed with them, can bear the grievous burden any longer? But there is no doubt of the ability of the United States, they have exclusively the command of a very productive revenue; what was laid in impost last year, with an addition on three or four articles of luxury, and a small excise, will be competent to provide for the payment of the interest, and gradual discharge of the principal of the whole foreign and domestic debt. A million and a half may easily be drawn from other sources, without having recourse to direct taxation, or subjecting the citizens of the United States to any oppression.

But this motion appears to be unseasonable. Why were we not called upon to go into a consideration of the ways and means, before we assumed the indents and interest on the domestic debt? If it was not necessary on that occasion, it is less so on this; if we are to be drawn aside from the main business by investigations of this kind, I see no end to our discussions. I hope, therefore, the House will reject the motion, and proceed to resolve themselves into a Committee of the Whole on the Secretary's report.

. . . .

Mr. AMES felt himself well authorized, on this occasion, to depend on the arguments which had been urged by the gentlemen on the other side of the question. It had been said, as a reason against the assumption, that we ought not to undertake to pay more than we are able, especially if the debt had never been contracted by the United States, and pay them in prejudice of those debts which were absolutely contracted and really due. Apply these principles to the present motion. Do we know that we do not undertake to pay more than we are able to pay, when we assume to pay the whole of the debtor side of the account instead of the balance?

Gentlemen who contend that we are not able to pay the state debts in the hands of individuals must have their imagination strangely warped when they suppose us capable of paying perhaps double the sum.

Is the government under a contract to pay the state debts? Gentlemen say there is no obligation. Apply their argument to the case in question, and you will be urged by them to vote against the motion.

But why shall we increase our load unnecessarily? If we leave the exertions of the states to be liquidated, and assume the balances, we may not have the one-third of this amount to pay. Interest paid by the several states since the peace may be calculated at twelve millions, and the principal sunk in the same period at fifteen millions; this will double the amount of the state debts. Now, if we respect their arguments, or our own principles, we must vote against the measure.

.   .   .   .

Mr. AMES denied being taxable with inconsistency. He said it must be apparent to every gentleman, that if states were to be recompensed for the exertions they had made since the peace, they ought to be recompensed for them in whatever form they were to be found; it was as great an exertion to pay the interest as it was to pay the principal; but there was another reason for his voting for the amendment—the proposition, as it was moved by the gentleman, was indefinite, by adding these words it became limited.

MARCH 12, 1790

MR. AMES.—It was moved to strike out the word "irredeemable" from the proposition of the Secretary. In order to judge of the expediency of adopting the motion, it will be necessary to take an extensive view of the whole subject. It will be proper to inquire whether it is necessary to effect a new modification of the debt, what ought to be the principle and terms of it, and whether the proposed amendment is or is not consistent with them?

Why do we not provide for paying six per cent.? Let us perform the contract as it was made. This has been frequently said. I answer, other terms to be agreed upon will better promote the interest of both parties.

Unquestionably the contract is binding on the government at six per cent.; nor can any thing short of the free consent of the creditors annul or change it.

We are to exclude from the discussion all suspicion of bad faith; government should not distrust itself, nor suppose that it is distrusted. The question turns, not on the willingness, but on the ability to pay; not merely the ability of the people, but of the government. We are not to regard alone the vigor and efficiency of government, for this is not to be trusted as the measure of its power to tax. For this power depends greatly on habit, and is the slowest growth of all the habits of a country. By often imposing taxes, government may be sure of their productiveness, and in what form they can best be supported. A new tax is more grievous than an old one; for the people form their habits of living to the permanent state of things. Experience only can teach the government what is practicable, and what is prudent; and habit not only makes public burdens less obnoxious, but less oppressive. I infer that Congress is not possessed of its entire capacity to form sufficient funds, nor of the evidence to satisfy the creditors that they will be sufficient for six per cent. The funds must be sufficient, otherwise they cannot be pledged, and known to be sufficient, otherwise they will not be trusted. We may say and believe, that the taxes will produce a sum adequate to six per cent., but it will be with a degree of doubt, and subject to contingencies equally unfriendly to the public and its creditors. Securities would fluctuate, for the doubt would be a subject of speculation. The creditors would lose much of their capital in the market, and the public would lose the use of the debt as money. Those who advocate a six per cent. provision, will please to point out the taxes which will ensure the payment at that rate. Straining the sources of taxation may make the product of the first year considerable; but that of the succeeding years will be impaired. Besides, is it consistent with prudence for a nation to pledge its funds to the extent of its capacity? Contingent expenses cannot be avoided. These would injure the funds, and war would totally destroy the whole system. This is doing, at best, but temporary justice to the creditors; but as the insecurity of the paper will effect the price, it will not merit even that title.

This leads to a view of the nature of this property. When the funds are sure and sufficient, the capital will rise in proportion to the rate of interest. The best condition of the paper is, when it has a fixed exchangeable value, and at the highest rate. For then the holder can dispose of it at pleasure, and without loss. He has no occasion to desire the public to pay off the loan, as he can get his money more conveniently at the time and in the place he may choose by selling at market. The paper is as good as the money lent. He may therefore be said to every useful purpose to keep his property while he is paid for lending. This is better and safer than private debts, and this is the natural state of public credit, and something must be found wrong where it is not so fixed. It is the interest of the creditors to concur with government in the means which will bring it to this desirable point. What are those means?

The Secretary has offered several proposals. Will these, or an adherence to the original contract, in exclusion of them, best promote the object?

One of the primary means proposed by the Secretary is funding the debt. Perhaps the strict claims of the creditors could not be extended beyond annual grants. But policy and liberal justice forbid the measure. Where this has been tried in some of the states, the securities have not risen above six shillings and eight pence in the pound. I do not pretend that government suffers any damage by funding; but the contrary. The creditors, however, acquire a new right and a valuable interest in the funds. For the appropriation is selling or mortgaging the public revenues, and making them private property. It is the delivery of a pawn for the security of the debt.

The great operation, however, to give permanency and value to this pledge, and in a sense to insure the funds against adverse contingencies, is the establishment of a sinking fund. It cannot be the interest of the creditors to receive perpetual annuities at any rate of interest which shall exclude this provision. For in that case, six, and possibly even ten per cent. would give them a bad bargain. In proportion as the rate of interest is raised, the securities ought to rise, but as the risk of a failure of payment is increased even more than in proportion to the rise of interest, it is scarcely to be doubted that the securities would sink below the value which they will acquire by the proposed loan. It will be proper to ask here, will any gentleman affirm with confidence that a sufficient and sure provision can be made at six per cent.? Will he go further, and designate adequate and proper subjects of taxation to insure the payment? No gentleman has yet attempted this task, nor do I believe that it can be done with any prudence. But even this task if accomplished by the advocates of six per cent. will not be sufficient. They must proceed and furnish a surplus revenue as a sinking fund. In proportion as the rate of interest is raised, the provision for it becomes hazardous; and in the degree that it is so, the sinking fund must be made more ample to secure it. It will be safe to rest the argument on this point, and to insist that as no evidence is offered to show that funds adequate to these objects can be provided, the interest of the public and its creditors equally forbids a dependence upon them. The sinking fund is an indispensable part of every system; it secures the capital loaned as well as the interest; for every million that shall be paid off will make the residue more safe. If the whole debt was reduced from eighty millions to eight, it could scarcely be so mismanaged as to want credit. The sinking fund will be constantly operating to bring it to that point. It is also a security against the danger arising from an increase of public expense; it will also prevent great fluctuation in the value of the paper; for when it shall be cheapest, the purchases of government will raise it in the market. Again, in our country, the quantity of money and other active property is not in proportion to real estate; a great national debt, when brought to market, may exceed the demand. The purchases of government will bring the demand to an equality with the stock offered for sale. Suppose the amount of money annually employed in buying up the public paper to be five millions; the discount is now sixty per cent., paper being at eight shillings in the pound. If government could throw into the market one million for the like purpose, it would increase the demand twenty-five per cent.; and the same money when in circulation may be calculated to be in part at least employed by individuals for the purchase of securities, which would further increase the demand. Perhaps the single operation of a sinking fund may be calculated to diminish the present discount one-half.

There is no subject so purely artificial as the science of public debts; whether I have assumed false principles, and drawn fanciful conclusions from them, will appear by resorting to facts.

Great Britain has repeatedly changed the form of her debt. George I. was scarcely seated on the throne before a rebellion broke out. This was suppressed, but doubts remained in regard to his title to the throne, and of the ability of the public to pay its creditors. To put the public credit on a stable basis, the Parliament proposed a new loan of the debt, amounting to more than thirty millions sterling at a reduced interest of four per cent. The South Sea Company were authorized to buy up the debts, or to suffer the creditors to take shares of the South Sea stock. This act passed in 1719, and the famous South Sea bubble happened the next year.

A still greater operation of the like kind was accomplished in 1749; and the interest on a debt near double the amount of the former (fifty-seven millions) was reduced from four to three per cent. The war of 1741, which was ended in 1748 by the peace of Aix la Chapelle, had greatly increased the public burdens. It was proposed to pay the former interest till the end of 1750, then three and a half till the end of 1757, and after that time three per cent. It will seem strange that the creditors should voluntarily accept a less rate of interest. We are well informed, however, that they consented to it for the sake of the increased security of the capital, and the stipulated interest; for by the saving of interest the sinking fund was increased; the conduct of creditors would be unintelligible otherwise; for as the interest was funded before, and regularly paid, the only motive to be discerned for consenting to the reduction is what has just been assigned. The sinking fund has been called the last hope of the nation, and the misapplication of it has been the subject of great complaint; and it may be demanded, was not this reasoning of the creditors just? For if the public revenue had stood charged to the exent of what it could produce, would not the credit of the debt have rested upon a very unsound basis? Britain had been frequently engaged in wars for extending commerce, or establishing the balance of power; and the unsuccessful war of 1741 had ended in a precarious state of armed peace. Unless the nation could be relieved so far as to prepare for new wars, the creditors foresaw the failure of the public faith.

I shall be told that the proposal of a new loan is not to be defended unless the terms are fair and free; and that, in the instances alluded to, Great Britain offered a new loan in one hand, and the money to redeem the debt in the other. Every thing regarding the public faith is so important as to be entitled to a full examination.

The first capital operation of the reduction of interest was in 1719. Was the offer to pay off the creditors made at the same time with the offer to pay four per cent.? It seems to be understood that the creditors were threatened, in case they should refuse to accept the reduced interest, with being compelled to receive their capital. This, however, is not true; no offer to pay off the capital was then made; the South Sea Company was expressly authorized to pay off the debts, or so many of them at a time as they, in regard to their own circumstances and ability, should think fit. Accordingly, the fact corresponded with the authority; and nothing but the stock of the Company was offered in payment for about five-sixths of the debt. It is true indeed that the stock sold at a great advance, and therefore was better than money; but it is also true, that the Company took advantage of the rise of stock to the utmost, and at the rate of three hundred and seventy-five per cent. except for about one-sixth part, which they offered to pay in money and their own bonds; but as stock continued to rise, they made new offers at five hundred per cent., and near two-thirds of the debt was subscribed in a few days; they afterwards renewed the offer, but at eight hundred per cent. It was provided in the act of Parliament, that the debts not subscribed or paid off, should remain upon their former footing, and not that the creditors should have their capital redeemed. But a circumstance absolutely conclusive against the reasoning urged in objection is, that the half of the debt was irredeemable, and of course the creditors were not liable to the threats of government, that on refusing the new loan they should be paid off. They had nothing to fear on that score, and of course could not regard any motive but the advantage in point of greater security which had been insisted on already.

In 1749, the fact is equally against the argument in question. There was not any offer on the part of government to pay off the creditors; indeed a second act was made extending the term within which the creditors might subscribe to the new loan. But so far from paying them off, the terms were made harder against them, and the reduction to three per cent. was appointed to a period two years earlier, 1755. In a third act it cannot be denied that means were used to pay off the non-subscribers. But the unsubscribed debt was then reduced to the moderate sum of one million and thirteen thousand pounds; and the bank was empowered to pay off that sum. The King, the Lords, and the Commons, speak of this transaction as highly beneficial to the nation, and not including the least violation of the public faith. Accordingly, the bills passed by large majorities, and with a great degree of popularity with the nation.

I am surprised that the opinion should have been so readily admitted, that such an offer ought to be made, or that it could be carried into execution. Could Britain have paid off seventy millions sterling? The existence of a national debt is proof that she could not. A nation that can pay the capital would not pay the interest. It is so far from being true that Britain could pay off her debt, that all Europe could not do it. America is at this moment more able to pay off than Britain, for two reasons; her debt is not so great, and the rate of interest is higher, so that she might procure new loans on better terms in Europe.

I cannot discern the obligation arising from the justice or reason of the case, to pay off on the refusal of the terms. I should suppose that if new terms were not to be approved, the old contract should continue; and that is precisely the language of the British statutes. It does no injury to the creditors to propose to mend their condition; the offer, if refused, leaves the parties on the former footing. When it was urged therefore that government ought to offer payment when new terms are offered, am I not at liberty to affirm that this opinion is not warranted by history, nor practicable in itself, nor required by the reason and justice of the case?

It is admitted, however, that the terms ought to be fair and free; are those proposed by the Secretary such, and will they give the highest value and most fixed quality to the debt? On some of the terms full payment is offered to such as may prefer land, on others an equivalent. Whether this offer is or is not an equivalent, remains to be inquired.

The debt is offered to be made irredeemable, except at the rate of one per cent. Government agrees to forego the advantage of the fall of interest. In times of war and calamity, nations are obliged to pay a high interest; but when peace and commerce have reduced the rate of interest, they are enabled, by new loans, to reduce the debt to its proper standard. It is now peace, and government may fairly offer to make the debt irredeemable at the due rate of interest. This is what the Secretary proposes. The question, however, recurs, is this arrangement beneficial to the creditor, and in what degree is it so?

It is urged that the creditors are rather disposed to consider the redemption of the debt as a desirable thing. They wish to get their money. How then, it is demanded, can the irredeemable quality of the debt be considered as a subject of compensation and advantage to the creditor? However paradoxical it may seem, all that is just stated may be conceded, and yet the irredeemable quality of the debt may be highly beneficial to the creditor.

A compendious proof of this may be found in this way: Suppose that the proposal was made to make the debt irredeemable at six per cent. interest. The burden upon the public would be manifestly unreasonable, and the advantage to the creditor equally so; and for this plain reason the public would be restrained from taking advantage of the fall of interest in this country, or of the present low rate in Europe.

Making the debt redeemable will not redeem it, nor will it be of any use to the creditor. If six per cent. irredeemable would be a hard bargain to the public, will the like stipulation at a less rate of interest prove mutually beneficial? This is a question for the public, on deliberation, to propose, and the creditors freely to decide.

It is necessary to premise that the Secretary has founded his report upon these two principles. On the idea that the entire mass of the debt constitutes a burden, which it is inconvenient to bear at once, he has proposed to divide it into two portions. The first portion of two-thirds is to be provided for at six per cent.; the other third is to be taken up after the period of ten years, when our strength may be equal to bearing it; and this postponement is proposed upon terms favorable to both parties. It is favorable to the public: first, because it relieves the public from the pressure of the present necessity; and secondly, the debt to be funded is nineteen per cent. less than the present debt; that is, the public receive one hundred dollars, and in consideration of the irredeemable quality stipulated in the loan, is burdened only with providing for eighty-one dollars. The amount of the nineteen per cent. upon the entire domestic debt is near thirteen millions.

The advantage to the public is so manifest that I entertain no fear of its being overlooked; a more formidable difficulty arises from the other quarter. It will be said the public, it is true, will gain; but it gains too much, it is a dishonest as well as an enormous gain, which is extorted from the creditor.

I respect this objection, and will endeavor, with proper candor, to obviate its force; and this will lead me to the second principle of the Secretary, that the reduction of the market rate of interest will make good to the creditor the release of nineteen per cent. of the capital loaned.

This question is submitted to the security holders. Is it better for you to receive a less rate of interest on the terms of receiving it a longer time, or a higher rate for less time? We propose to pay longer on condition of paying less yearly. Supposing the funds to be sure, the value of the capital will be regulated by the rate of interest. As interest falls, the capital will rise; if in five years interest should fall to five per cent., and in fifteen more to four per cent. the creditor will be compensated. The grounds of this reduction of interest are to be examined.

It is made probable by facts. Before the war interest was at the rate of five per cent. in the eastern part of America; then things were in their natural state, and as soon as the violent causes which have disturbed their equipoise have ceased to act, they will return to it. This is the more to be expected, as the rate of interest in Europe is low, and becoming still lower. Trade is still extending itself; wealth continues to increase; the surplus property which the owner cannot employ is offered on loan to those who can, and the market is more and more overstocked with the quantity. Precisely the contrary has happened in this country; a great part of our active property was destroyed by the war; but most evils tend to their own cure. Supposing a safe and firm government, the high rate of interest here naturally tends to draw the surplus capital from Europe, it will find its level; peace is diligently repairing the waste of war. I turn with pleasure from this barren disquisition to a scene that is interesting to our philanthropy as well as to our patriotism. My heart glows while I think of the contrast between the situation of this country in 1786 and now in 1790. No country ever made a more rapid progress towards opulence. Wherever we look, industry is working miracles, we may doubt whether interest will not fall even further than is calculated. Probably trade will not bear an interest so high as six per cent.; and the person who borrows must, after paying the interest, reserve a profit; and when few are disposed to borrow, many will be ready to lend, and interest will fall.

But a debt funded, as it is proposed, will be safer and more eligible than any private debts. Four per cent. from government will be nearly equal to six from individuals; and a debt so funded will itself reduce the rate of interest. For even if it should be all sold to foreigners, they will pay the value, and the property paid will increase the common stock and lower interest.

The debt is to be considered, when funded, as an increase of active capital. We have been often told that a public debt is not a blessing, but an evil. We are not to compare a debt with no debt; for it is a desirable thing to be free from debt; but the debt is already contracted, and we are to compare an unfunded fluctuating debt with a funded debt. Such a debt as the latter may be comparatively a blessing, for it makes the capital transferable as well as the income. We have but a small share of personal property; but this will make the very land and houses circulate. It is true it is an artificial capital, formed by a charge upon every other capital, but it is also true, that it is formed by small savings in expense, and if the taxes were not to be laid, there would not be an increase of wealth at the end of a year equal to the debt or the interest of it. A single cent in the price of an article cannot be said to impoverish the people, or to restrain them from enjoying their usual habits of living. Indeed it may tend in some degree to prevent excess, and to promote frugality, which will enrich the people. But at the end of the year these almost imperceptible sums, by their union into one mass, acquire a new power. The whole may be said to have properties which did not belong to the separate parts. The active circulation promoted by the debt will, in a considerable degree, compensate the burden of paying taxes. Those whose property is increased by possessing the debt will become greater consumers in proportion, and contribute largely to the revenue.

Another circumstance ought to be regarded: foreigners will be led to think the government safe when they think the funds so. Many will follow the property and come to live among us. Whether the advantages of a funded debt will balance the burden of having one is a question of mere speculation. We have a debt, and must provide for it. It cannot be denied, however, that these advantages will be considerable, and will tend to reduce the rate of interest. Such a reduction actually took place in England after the establishment of public credit. In about five years after 1693, interest fell from eight and ten per cent. to five.

Whether interest will or will not fall in the degree that the Secretary expects is a matter of fair calculation. Taking the reasons together which have been offered to evince the affirmative, there cannot be any impropriety in proposing to the creditors to consent to an arrangement which promises them such solid advantage.

Let this advantage be computed—eighty-one dollars are to be funded at six per cent. This is nearly £4 17s. 8d. per cent. The irredeemable quality of the debt may well be reckoned equal to one per cent. It will be worth near that to foreigners. Add to this, interest is to be paid quarterly. This is not only convenient, but actually makes some increase of the rate of interest.

The question may very properly be proposed to the creditors. Is this a fair equivalent? Is this as good as six per cent.? Nay, is it not better for them? Their debt is to be funded; revenues to be mortgaged for the interest; government agrees to continue paying, though interest should fall, and to provide a sinking fund to insure these advantages. Nor can it be said that the loan is forced, for government being at present in a condition to pay only four per cent., offers it equally to subscribers and non-subscribers. This also removes the pretext that advantage is taken of their necessities.

Was any reloan ever proposed in any country on terms more fair and beneficial to the creditors? We have examined the facts relating to the English funds. Their creditors sacrificed more, and for less. Of all the modifications of a public debt with which we are acquainted, is there one less exceptionable than that proposed by the Secretary?

However artificial this reasoning may appear, it is no longer considered as strange and visionary in Europe. In this transaction, government is to accommodate its proposals to the ideas which experience has established in other countries. I will not deny that I should have preferred a simple six per cent. proposition, redeemable at the pleasure of government. But we have seen the inexpediency of that measure.

Upon the whole, I submit it to the candid judgment of the committee whether if a Congress of debtors only should legislate, they could, with justice, or even policy, secure greater advantages to the nation; or whether a Congress of creditors only could, with any degree of prudence, provide better for themselves?

MARCH 13, 1790

M R. AMES.—The word irredeemable is made the subject of objection. It is said to convey a disagreeable idea, and to tend to excite popular prejudice against the debt as it implies that the public agrees to be saddled with a perpetual burden of debt. In a land of ignorance, where the people are not in the habit, and have not the capacity to reason, it may be proper to pay regard to this objection. I have too much reverence for the sober thinking people whom we represent, to believe that the mere sound of this word will work mischief, when their own inquiries will convince them that the substance is not only unexceptionable, but highly beneficial.

Making the debt redeemable will not redeem it. It puts not a farthing in the creditor's pocket. Making it irredeemable is no restraint upon the present or probable capacity of the public to redeem. It will not prolong the evil of a public debt a single day, but rather the contrary. All the money that can be provided for paying off the debt may still be employed for the purpose, though the irredeemable quality should remain.

The proposal to make the debt irredeemable is founded on the supposed gradual reduction of interest. But until the reduction has actually happened in a shorter period, or in a greater degree than is calculated, the paper will not bear a higher price than one hundred per cent. While the debt is at par, or below par, the creditors will not refuse to receive their money. The public has also the right to redeem at the rate of one per cent. against their will. But the value will not rise to par while the rate of interest keeps up. The government will therefore have full employment for all its surplus revenue to buy up the paper at a discount. Surely the public will not squander the public money to redeem the debt at par, when it is to be purchased at a discount. The latter is even more advantageous to the creditors. Buying at the market price, in fact, raises the price, and benefits those who do not sell. The greater the discount, the more paper a given sum will buy, and take out of the market. This not only raises the price, but increases the security of the unsold part. In these three ways, there is full exercise for the power of redemption, nor can it be supposed that the redeemable quality of the debt will increase the capacity of the public to redeem, or shorten the duration of the debt. The contrary may be proved by attending to these facts.

The government, in consideration of making the debt irredeemable, is allowed nineteen per cent.; one hundred dollars are to be lent, and eighty-one only to be funded. The aggregate of the sums saved to the public by this nineteen per cent. is near thirteen millions. The public is therefore paid beforehand for not redeeming. The right renounced is valuable to the creditors, as it has been formerly shown, but of no value to the public. For the right to redeem is worth nothing, if the public has not the means to redeem; and if money can be found, it appears that it can be better employed to buy up the debt than to pay it off. The capacity of the public is laid under no restraint. So far from it, thirteen millions will be already redeemed. Perhaps in a dozen years the public would not pay off that amount; and if it should prove able, it will have twenty years, according to the principles of the report, to buy stock on better terms than paying it off. Those who say we can redeem faster, and will not be satisfied with the argument I have just urged, will please to remember that by making the entire debt redeemable, we shall have more to redeem; with an imaginary increase of the power, will be an actual increase of the task to be performed. But will any one soberly assert, that the public will probably have the command of more money than it can find persons willing to accept for their stock; and unless this is asserted and really believed, I am sure the word irredeemable will not be struck out.

If, then, it is no burden to the public, is it any disadvantage to the creditor? If the debt is below par, the public will buy stock, and will not pay off the capital. If at par, the creditor will not thank government to do what he may get any individual, and in every great town, to do. If the debt should sell for more than par, it would be a loss to receive a less sum than the market price. This, indeed is not to be speedily expected. In every view of the subject the advantage to the creditor of making the debt redeemable is merely delusive.

Still it will be asked, if no good will flow from striking out this word, will any result from retaining it?

What is our object? To establish public credit—and that

is found when the stock will sell at par. The price of stock will depend upon the quantity offered to sale, and the demand.

In order to raise the price, we must provide means therefor to increase the demand; our own market for stock is a limited one; our citizens possess little money property, and that little is fully employed in active pursuits, and bears an higher interest than government proposes to give. We cannot expect that a poor market will give credit to a great debt; we must regard the great market—the trading and moneyed world. To qualify the stock for the great European market, it must be made irredeemable; interest is low in Europe and high in America, but even a higher interest than six per cent. would not compensate the European, if the property purchased want permanency. For if he has six per cent. for one or two years only, the charge of insurance, agency, &c., would reduce the net profit of his money below what he could get for it in Europe, where it would be under his eye, and subject to his control. You must give him a kind of estate, a freehold in the funds; for so long as he fears that you will borrow money and pay off his debt, after he has received interest a year or two, he will not buy stock at par. He will not deal in property which will yield a good interest, but of uncertain duration. If the debt should pass at par, it will be easy to borrow money in Europe, because the price will be a proof of the good state of our credit, and nothing but credit is wanting to enable us to borrow abroad. In proportion as it may be easy for us to borrow on better terms than six per cent. the buyers will have more cause to consider the debt as an improper subject of their permanent arrangements. The reasons already urged will evince, that if there should be a disinclination abroad to possess our stock, it will be liable to a reduction of value.

It is urged that the debt, if it shall be sold to foreigners, will be a drain of our wealth to foreign countries. This merits examination. I have already endeavored to show that the debt, if not suited to the foreign market by being made irredeemable, will pass below par. A great discount will hold out the strongest inducements to foreigners to purchase; they will buy more and for less; the discount will fully compensate the redemption, and this discount will be so much loss to the country. If, then, the drain of our wealth to pay interest to foreigners is an evil, this will aggravate the evil.

More will go out of the country, and less will be brought in to pay for it; we cannot help foreigners dealing in our funds. While our debt has any value, those who can best afford to run risks will deal in it. But if they will buy it, let us prevent their getting it for a trifle; let us make them pay for it. If they buy at par or near it, it may be questioned whether their purchases will be injurious; banish all doubts of your funds, and the sales will regulate themselves; when our citizens can better spare the property to buy stock than foreigners, they will buy it. It is bringing matters to the test of experience, whether the money can be employed more usefully in that or some other way. If a man can get more for his money than stock yields, it seems to be the interest of the nation to import money at four per cent. and employ its own at a higher rate. This is rather making a drain of foreign property into our country than the contrary. It is not to be forgotten that in the competition between American and foreign purchasers, the former will constantly have the advantage—for the latter, as has been before mentioned, will have agency and other charges to pay. We may expect, therefore, that the property paid by foreigners for our stock will yield a greater profit, and be more usefully employed in the country than the stock itself. It is true, that interest will be paid to strangers; but it is deducible from the principles which I have endeavored to establish, that the property paid by them for stock, will yield a profit more than sufficient to pay it—in that case, as a nation, we shall gain. It is probable, too, that a great portion of the interest money due to foreigners will be stopped in the country to buy articles, as these will bear an advantage in Europe; but money will be subject to the deductions of insurance and other charges.

If the purchase of stock by foreigners should, however, still be considered as injurious, let it be repeated that the motion in debate furnishes no remedy for the evil; for the greater the discount, the more they will purchase. We cannot prevent their buying; all that remains for us to do is, to oblige them to pay for what they purchase by giving a fixed and high value to the debt. This, we are told, will swell the wealth of stockjobbers. Those who make a science of speculation are gainers by the fluctuating state of funds. To banish speculation, give as certain a value as possible to your stock. My own belief is, that these things will be found necessary to effect this object—a national bank, and ample sinking fund, and considerable sales of stock to foreigners. It is allowed that the irredeemable quality of stock fits it for the last purpose, and as the nation is well paid for it by the nineteen per cent. on the capital, and will gain more as the stock shall sell for more; as it lays no restraint upon the application of all its surplus revenue to extinguish the debt, and will not increase the supposed evil of sales of stock to foreigners, and as it will prove mutually beneficial to the nation and its creditors, it is my desire that the word irredeemable may not be stricken out.

APRIL 23, 1790

A MOTION being made to take up the order of the day,

Mr. AMES rose and said, that previous to taking up the order of the day, he wished to introduce a motion for the consideration of the House. He observed, that it had been asserted in the course of the debates on the assumption of the state debts, that the State of Virginia had advanced for the common defence beyond her proportion; advantage appeared to be taken of such assertions; he thought it necessary that facts should be known, that the Committee might act with certainty in conducting this important question. He therefore moved the following, in substance, viz: "that the Secretary for the Department of War be directed to lay before the House a statement of the troops, including the militia, and ordnance stores furnished by the respective states for the general defence during the late war."

This motion was opposed, as tending to procrastinate the funding business, and as leading to excite invidious comparisons respecting the relative merits and exertions of the several states. It was, however, carried in the affirmative, with this addition proposed by Mr. BLAND, "and that the Commissioners of Accounts between the United States and individual states be directed to furnish an abstract of the claims of the several states against the United States, specifying the principles on which the claims are founded." On the above motion, the previous question was called for by Mr. LEE, which was lost, and the main question agreed to, 28 to 26.

MAY 1 AND MAY 2, 1790

————

MAY 1

TWO RESOLUTIONS were read: the first was, that five cents per hundred dollars be laid on every transference of stocks in the public funds; and the second, that five cents per hundred dollars be laid on the transference of stock in any of the other Banks of the United States.

. . . .

Mr. AMES, in a speech of some length, enlarged on the state of public credit, and the propriety and necessity of its being supported by government, since it had once been adopted. This tax on the transference of the public funds tended to injure it, by sinking their value. When we next want to borrow, and shall go to market, the lenders will rise proportionably in their demands, and refuse a loan on the terms which they before accepted. Hence we shall lose, instead of gaining by it. Let gentlemen reflect on the consequences of unsettling all ideas of property, which must be the result of this proceeding. He was not one of those who despised the Funding System because it was unpopular, for it was the property of a republic to set right above power. The Funding System had of late become a favorite topic of newspaper eloquence. As parties were inseparable from the nature of a popular government, so this subject had been employed as an engine to render that of America an object of contempt and abhorrence. It had been loudly said, that the Representatives in Congress from one of the New England states had immense property in the public funds, when, in fact, their whole income from that source was not sufficient for buying oats for their horses. To say, therefore, that they were under influence in their political conduct from such motives, was the merest bagatelle that can be conceived; and the groundless jealousy that it has excited may be considered as a very strong counter-balance to the interest of those members who were the objects of suspicion. People dream that Congress are voting money into their own pockets. The propagation of this idea promotes the dirty purposes of slander, abuse, and falsehood. By such unworthy means, the blossoms of public confidence in government are mildewed and blasted. This is more especially the case in the Southern states; and this dissatisfaction offers an apology for taking notice, in this House, of the abuse of newspapers. In the United States, taxation of the public funds is nothing more or less than the debtor taxing the creditor; and so questionable an expedient will recoil with tenfold force on the credit of government itself. The progress of this measure would degrade the public debt into a paper rag. It had been complained of in this country, that foreigners had too great a share in the funds, and Mr. A. was of opinion that it would be better if the money were all owing to American citizens. But, while things are in their present state, this tax would enable such foreigners to buy more debt out of the country and send less money into it in place of the debt. Public debt is a ground which cannot be trod with impunity. We may soon, on such a precedent, go still greater lengths; a few events may force us to apply to the moneyed men, and then will be seen and felt the miserable termination of this policy.

Mr. CLARK said, that the gentleman [Mr. AMES] had made a long speech with respect to newspapers. What was his meaning, or what he referred to, Mr. C. could not tell; but he supposed that the gentleman had an intention of publishing his speech in answer to these newspapers. It was to be hoped that he would make it so that it could be understood. If it contained arguments, they were above his reach, and there he should leave it. He closed with speaking a few words on a proposal for taxing bonds.

. . . .

Mr. AMES, in reply to Mr. CLARK, said, that the gentleman had complained of his being unintelligible. With regard to the defence that he had made of the character of members, reported to be creditors in the funds, the style of newspapers, of pamphlets, and of debates in that House, altogether justified the propriety of an explicit vindication. He appealed to every member who heard him that, excepting only the debate on the adjournment of Congress, there had not been a single discussion of any length, for a considerable time past, where there had not been some pointed allusion to this paper bugbear. This government, said Mr. A., has been painted as an object of suspicion and abhorrence. The gentleman [Mr. CLARK] complains that I am beyond his reach. He has made himself sufficiently intelligible, and has perhaps had his share in drawing such pictures. Recurring to the question before the Committee, he said that, when the Funding Act passed, no man will affirm that there was any notion of such a tax understood. No civilized nation can keep its credit while it taxes its public funds. Property is in general, to be sure, a fair object of taxation, but this tax cannot be levied with perfect equality, for it is beyond the knowledge of any government; and, were it even within the knowledge of a legislator, still it is beyond his power. There was no way to get at an exact acquaintance with the universal state of property, but by cutting off people's heads and searching their repositories.

. . . .

Mr. W. SMITH could not discover why tobacco might not be taxed, just as well as salt and other articles.

Mr. S. SMITH agreed that the tax would destroy the manufacture, and raise nothing. Every body would use a kind of unmanufactured tobacco, that has a well known name, as there was no mention of that article in the bill.

Mr. AMES approved the tax, as one of the best which he knew.

Mr. MADISON had always opposed every tax of this nature, and he should upon all occasion persist in opposing them. If we look into the state of those nations who are harnessed in taxes, we shall universally find that, in a moral, political, and commercial point of view, excise is the most destructive of all resources. He did not say this, because excise had been a frequent topic of popular declamation. He was not guided by that, but he knew, and was sensible, that it

produced almost in every case the most disagreeable consequences. Yet he admitted that the excise upon ardent
spirits was a very natural expedient in the American Government, who saw such immense quantities of foreign spirits
imported. Much of the collection of this tax on tobacco would
depend on the oath of the manufacturer, and this was but
another term for the multiplication of perjuries. The tax
would therefore injure the morals of the people.

Mr. AMES replied to Mr. MADISON, who spoke a few words
in explanation.

MAY 2

MR. AMES had a better opinion of government than the
gentleman who spoke last. He did not think excise a mark
of despotism. He did not think the people stocks and stones;
or their rulers knaves and fools. The member had spoke of
the citizens of this country, as if to rouse their attention it
was requisite to keep a flapper, like that of Gulliver, at their
ears. In some states, perhaps, the public were stupid enough
to require a flapper. In the part of the country which Mr. A.
represented, there was no need of artificial provocation to
keep alive the sensibility of the people to their rights. The
gentleman had said that a minister of state had no other
object in view but to fleece the public.

[Here Mr. SMILIE explained]

Mr. AMES replied, that, whatever were his words, *that* was
his exact meaning. It was perfectly understood, and was
exceedingly unjust. As to the resolution upon the table, is
there any comparison between a snuff tax and a land tax?
Land is the great *substratum* of American prosperity. Difficulties had been started, as to the *collection* of excise; an

oppressive law was a bad thing, but resistance was worse. Can any man think that a land tax does not open a much greater door to imposition than a tax on tobacco? In what way is a land tax to be laid, that can avoid inequality and injustice? Are we to tax the public funds, that last, and most desperate resource of national distress, and then to be told, that we dare not impose a duty on snuff and tobacco?

Mr. s. SMITH considered the observations of the member who had just sat down as amusing and ingenious, but they were not satisfactory. To him, it seemed a very odd scheme to crush American manufactures in the bud. Men of capital and enterprise advanced large sums of money in erecting snuff mills.

JANUARY 16, 1795

MR. AMES.—It would seem to be a trite, common-place inquiry to ask whether Congress is sincerely and earnestly engaged in the work of reducing the public debt? Most persons present would consider the question as the insinuation of a doubt equally illiberal and unwarranted. Every one would say, this article makes a part of my private creed, and of my public duty. Yet, mere speculative opinions and empty wishes for the object will leave it unaccomplished. The path to every great public good is obstructed with great obstacles, and, to surmount them, demands some vigor of exertion, some firmness of self denial. The debt, we are told, is unpopular, and this country would differ from every other in the world, if the imposition of taxes is not so too. Yet, without efficient revenues every one will see that the government cannot reduce the debt, and, therefore, we have only to choose between evils, or rather between the great evil of an undiminished public debt and the inconvenience of those clamors which taxes never fail to raise, though, happily, no country, I believe, acquiesces more cheerfully in the revenue laws than our own.

Gentlemen ought not to be surprised or offended, if we think it at least possible that the difficulties in the way of a powerful operation on the debt, may prove insurmountable. It is easy and natural to multiply doubts as to the plan of the reduction, as well as to inspire repugnance and apprehension of the taxes and other means of giving it effect. A plan for reducing the public debt certainly means a great deal more than paying off $600,000, the redeemable part of the six per cent. stock for once only, and then to drop it till another laborious and contentious effort of the legislature shall have provided for a second payment. Before we proceed to discuss points in which we disagree, I hope we may state this as one, and the groundwork of the whole, which, in theory, at least, unites all opinions, that we shall now settle a plan for applying year by year the whole strength of the revenues of the nation to paying off the public debt; that we shall sanction this plan by law, and give it energy by providing the funds for a sacred and unalterable application to the object. If the opposers of the report of the committee on the plan of reducing the debt are not willing to go this length, then they must confess they fall short of those with whom I am now acting, and who have usually, on questions of revenue and finance, had my vote; and I confess, this is one of the few occasions in which I had hoped to see an emulation in this House for measures of efficiency and permanency. But that hope, however pleasing, is somewhat checked by the alarming recollection that public debts are in all states the objects of public concern and dread. In Europe, their vast amount has at last terrified those who hold the supreme power, as well as those who pay taxes. Yet, although they have long portended convulsion and ruin, have not nations and governments nearly smothered their alarms, and, instead of rousing all their energies to subdue the evil, relapsed into a state of security and torpor? Nay, have they not, by madly rushing into war, as we might lately have done, augmented the danger and hastened the shock of that earthquake, which, for an age past, has threatened to throw Europe back again into chaos? The nations seem to have outgrown their fears, or to despair of the remedy, as the inhabitants of Italy whistle unconcerned on the sides of Mount Etna while it vomits fire, or plough the fields of Calabria while they shake under their feet.

These are remarkable facts, and show that, in spite of universal fears and wishes, there is some powerful obstacle in the nature of man, or in the structure of society, that baffles the attempts of a nation to break out of the circle of enchantment and ruin. What is it? Probably this: that wars which create public debts are almost always popular, and taxes that would speedily wipe them out, are no less obnoxious. I hope I shall be pardoned, if I say, and I would say it inoffensively, that the tone and sentiment of the opposition to the temporary taxes have not altogether convinced me that the United States are free from this common malady of nations.

It may be true, that we have less to dread from debt than some of the European nations. The amont is comparatively small, and the progress of wealth and people is every day lessening the share that falls to an individual to be answerable for. The taxes, it may be said also, powerfully stimulate manufacturing industry, as well as increase our shipping, by their operation as protecting duties. But, although the husbandry, arts, and trade of the country have prospered under both debts and taxes; although, while the interest is duly paid, the creditors have no claim to the principal, yet the motives for hastening the reduction of the public burdens are, notwithstanding, so cogent and powerful, they cannot be resisted. Indeed, to notice them ever so slightly, will, in a great measure, overpower the objections to the tax in question.

I am one of those who believe a nation ought to cherish public credit, for the same reason that it ought to have strength; for, in critical situations, credit is strength, and the want of it may happen to be not only weakness, but subjugation and ruin. And it is my belief, that, although it may answer for a time to pay the interest, and neglect the principal, yet, at last, and in the course of affairs; it will appear that a nation which neglects to pay its debts will have no credit. That would be the case with an individual. Besides, if we neglect the interval of peace and prosperity to pay off, lessen, and, if possible, to extinguish the debt, we cannot expect, for any length of time, to avoid the occasion of adding to it. We have had eleven years of peace, one half of which term, for want of a government, our debt was augmenting, at least twelve or fifteen millions of dollars. It has been funded four years nearly, and less than three millions are yet paid off. Are we to hope for peace always? A blessing so great has been hitherto denied, perhaps in benevolence as well as wisdom, to the prayers of devotion and the tears of philanthropy, and, from all we know of the nature and history of man, we have reason to believe, if not to desire, that war will sometimes fall to the lot of a nation. Peace is the time to prepare for it, by extinguishing the burdens of the last war, by exhibiting, as a basis of present exultation, and a ground of future confidence and credit, the novel spectacle of a great nation which has freed itself from debt.

There is an auxiliary motive, which I stated in the beginning of the debate. The funding of the debt has unhappily proved an occasion of division and jealousy in the country, and of acrimonious recriminations in public assemblies. The debt was not augmented, it was diminished by funding, and almost none of the first Congress declared themselves opposed to funding the debt. They resisted the assumption and some of the clauses of the bill. The sin and odium, therefore, of the Funding System, as a measure abstracted from the irredeemable quality, and the state debts, ought to have been shared among all the offenders, the southern as well as the northern members. Yet it has answered party purposes to represent the eastern members as the patrons of a system of paper influence, of Treasury corruption, of certificate nobility; that they have attempted and succeeded to pervert and stretch the Constitution, to organize, and uphold systems of concealed aristocracy; that they deem the debt, as it promotes these vile purposes, a blessing; that they made it to oblige one another, and will not part with it, lest the popular principles of our government should prevail over the artificial and treacherous schemes and corrupt connexions which, as they derive their life from the debt, must impart life to it. I forbear, indeed I am unequal to the recital of all the infamies which have been vented on this subject. The language of insinuation and invective has been exhausted. The dictionary and vulgar language can add nothing to the opprobrium which has been attempted to be thrown on the friends of the revenue and finance systems. Do not the ears of gentlemen still tingle with these disgusting recollections? Can they think, without mingled emotions of indignation and surprise, how the labor has been to represent the eastern members as the authors, the champions, of the advantages of a funded debt; while every vehicle by which the public could be misled has teemed with declamation that the members from another part of the Union were exclusively zealous to extinguish this devouring fire of public debt, that consumes the people and their liberties, that the same gentlemen were not consenting to the Funding System, and that all their efforts have been hitherto baffled by the interested arts of the friends of paper corruption?

I neither know, nor have the arrogance to pretend to know, the inclinations of men's hearts; but, when we are accused of keeping the debt for influence and corruption; when our accusers affect to lament that they cannot be allowed to prosecute a most powerful and even violent operation for reducing the debt, we have a right to say that we take the professions of these gentlemen as a ground for testing their consistency, if not their sincerity. When they proclaim their principles, we have possession of them, and have a right to indulge such comments, especially at the instant of bringing them to the touchstone, as I was induced to make on a former day's debate. I own it, sir, I rejoiced to see these professions brought to the test; for, if it should not criminate the sincerity of those who make them, it would at least exculpate those who have so long been the objects of the most licentious invectives. It will show, in the teeth of calumny, that the eastern members are advocates, and zealous ones, for the reduction of the debt.

It is true, the opposers of the resolution are not bound to adopt the plan, nor to continue these very duties, but they are bound by more than common sanctions to go even beyond the description of persons whom they have accused, in some plan, and to provide other taxes. No puny operation, no half-way measures will do. They stand pledged for some strong system, some efficient funds to bring into activity at least all the present revenue faculties of the country. It is, therefore, with the best reasons, and even on strong public considerations, that I repeat the observation which seemed to give offence on a former day. The present moment is the crisis of a political test. It gives an opportunity to one set of men, if they choose, to vindicate their consistency; and we, sir, on the other, actually use it, not by profession, but by our conduct, to confound the accusations which have been thrown upon us. I rejoice in this moment on public account. It cannot but undeceive the citizens who have nourished jealousies and prejudices. It cannot be unimportant to slay, with one stroke, the slanders, which the gentlemen from the southern states have assured us have sprung from this source. The confidence and affections of the citizens is the best defence of the Constitution; and we are told that this defence has been chiefly weakened by the misrepresentations which have been made of the intentions of government to keep the debt as an instrument of corrupt influence.

If the common object of both sides in this debate be really to reduce the public debt, what shall be the plan and the measure of the reduction? Is it to pay off the redeemable part of the six per cent. stock, and to stop there? If so, then we shall go far beyond them. For, why should not the unsubscribed debt be paid off, the registered debt, the foreign debt, the deferred and three per cent. and even the temporary loans or anticipation of the revenue, which, it is agreed, draw an interest of one hundred thousand dollars a year?

That bugbear, the irredeemable quality, so artificially conjured up to terrify the country, opposes no obstacle to the redemption of all this great amount—a mass of debt far exceeding the most extravagant conjectures of the product of the revenue for many years to come. And here let me observe, the argument almost solely opposed to the resolution is this: We have revenue enough, without the temporary taxes. Let it be allowed that we have, for argument's sake, what follows? That we have too much revenue with the temporary taxes. Will our money rust in the Treasury chest for want of debt to employ it upon? Shall we not make greater progress with all the present taxes than with only a part of them? Is it a time to refuse the aid of these temporary taxes when we are finding out a new way for employing the product? Shall we, with any color of wisdom, go on at the same instant to extend our expenses and to diminish the income of the taxes? The argument that these taxes are not wanted is utterly hostile to the professions we make of paying off the public burdens as fast as possible. If the statement to support this reasoning is true, it is not so much an objection as an encouragement to our progress in the plan, as it proves, by the documents adduced on one side, that the other has underreckoned the calculations of success.

It might seem, therefore, a superfluous labor to show that the Treasury will probably stand in need of the temporary taxes for this operation, since it is all the better if it should not. But, by showing it, at least, it will prove the necessity of assenting to the resolution, if we would have the public debt reduced.

It is infinitely to be regretted that the facts relating to the income and expenditure of the United States are so much in dispute. The law, and, because it is a law, it ought to be a rule of conduct for the House, requires it of the Secretary of the Treasury to digest and prepare plans for the improvement of the public revenue, and relating to the public credit; and, if such information had been called for, it would have thrown a strong light upon many points which have been contested, because they were in the dark. Indeed, at every step in business of revenue and finance, a deliberative assembly will find itself embarrassed; darkness will hide the path. I think as respectfully of this assembly as I ought, and perhaps as highly as any member of it, yet I hesitate not to say, that no assembly ought thus to reject the information which our own law makes it the duty of the Treasury Department to furnish. We often hear of the duty of a Republican to respect the law, and yet, in the teeth of this law, we are exhorted to stop our ears against all communications on these subjects from the Treasury. I am not ashamed to say, I have need of the information, and I see that others dispute on facts which show their want of it. It is strictly executive business, which, according to the correct theory of our Constitution, ought not to be usurped by this House. Executive officers, on their responsibility, ought to furnish it. The details of a great nation's money affairs are too complex, too vast, too much a science, for any committee to embrace in a report, if they should have the good fortune to understand them. I will not, therefore, under the disadvantages which I believe are common to others as well as myself, pretend to make a systematic parade of figures.

If we reckon on the revenue in 1793 as a ground of calculation for future years, we shall have some guide for our conjectures. Those who choose to imagine a vast increase of income from taxes, in future, may be answered in a word. It is conjecture—1793 was a year of uncommon importation. French property was brought here in almost every vessel, on account of the war with England and the troubles of the French Islands. This swelled the nominal amounts of our imports, and, as much of this property has been re-exported, it again diminished the supposed product of the duties by the allowance for drawbacks; yet, on the whole, it was a productive year, and it could not be thought unfair to reckon our steady yearly income, according to that year, 1793.

Mr. A. then produced a statement of income and expenditure, viz:

INCOME.

Duties on imports and tonnage, net	$5,500,000
On internal objects	780,000
Net produce of the Post Office	20,000
Surplus of dividends on bank stock	50,000
	$6,350,000

EXPENDITURE.

Interest on Public Debt, foreign and domestic	$3,100,000
On temporary Loans	100,000
Support of Government	500,000
Military Department, including military pensions	1,500,000
Naval Department	400,000
Light-House Establishment	24,000
Excess of income beyond expenditure	726,000
	$6,350,000

If (said Mr. A.) we apply six hundred thousand dollars to redeem the redeemable part of the six per cent. stock, we shall have only one hundred and twenty-six thousand dollars. Will any one deny that this dependence is unsafe? that, at any rate, the operation is frittered down to a contemptible scale? If trade should fluctuate, as it may to a very considerable degree, as much as it never fails to do after a raging war has terminated; if the reduced price of our exports, which, on the event of peace, is inevitable, should reduce our imports, and that is the most natural effect in the world? if new expenses, to which all affairs are liable, should arise, even this puny plan of reducing our debt would be arrested in its progress.

The statement I have submitted, rejects fractions, and makes no pretensions to absolute correctness. In substance, however, it exhibits such a view of our income and expenditure, as I believe cannot be invalidated.

It has been insisted that the question is not on the repeal of the temporary taxes, and therefore the argument is misapplied. This is merely an evasion of the force of it; for is it not the very question before us, whether we will adopt a plan for the reducton of the public debt, and whether we will apply to the yearly operation of that plan till the year 1801 these very taxes? The end is, at least, in appearance, agreed on, and we are now looking for the means of effecting it. This is, therefore, precisely the moment to choose or reject these taxes as the means; and in order to induce us to reject them, have not those who say the repeal is not in debate, insisted the taxes alluded to are unfit means; that they are dangerous to liberty, because they are in the nature of excises, dangerous to manufactures, which should not be taxed in their infancy; oppressive, and ruinous? and yet they urge the repeal is not brought ever so remotely under consideration; nay, they tell us, after all this, they were passed on experiment, and they reserve to themselves to wait the result of that trial. Are they who so loudly condemn the temporary revenues, and on such serious grounds, affecting to waver, and to keep in balance till the end of the term for which they were appointed to operate? One advocate for experiment assured us, in the last session, when they passed, that now liberty was lost forever. Does he desire time to bring himself to a liking of these assassins of liberty?

I waive the idea of the known condescension which produced the limitation of these acts to two years. Let the full force of the plea so often urged that they were passed on trial, be essayed. For whom was the experiment intended, for the public or for the sugar-refiners and snuff-makers, and was it to prove that they like or do not like the tax? Did any one who saw their committee expect they would in two years prefer the tax to no tax? Or was the experiment intended for other reasons? If the money was not likely to be wanted at all, it would be one good cause for dropping the taxes; or if the mode of levying the tax was new and uncertain, it would be proper to limit the act in order to produce a revision and improvement of it in that respect. Was the limitation tacked to the bills to see whether they were proper objects of taxation? And was it really doubtful whether snuff and loaf sugar were proper to be taxed? What could be more proper? One is the most trivial of all luxuries, and the other (loaf sugar) is almost if not quite exclusively consumed by the class of citizens who have some pretensions to wealth. Yet when we press hard for a substitute, instead of the snuff and sugar revenue, we are with a face of solemnity advised to tax the land. May I trust my senses? Is it possible for persons to call the taxes on snuff and loaf sugar oppression, and the land-tax relief? Is it possible to think of taking the tax from the snuff-box and the tea-pot, to put it on the plough?

If, however, that is intended, as gentlemen assure us it is, there is no time to be lost. It will take two years to organize such a tax, and get it into the Treasury. If a land-tax is to be the substitute, the question therefore really is, shall we repeal the taxes in question. If there had been any doubt before, there can be none in the opinion of those who prefer the land-tax.

The interests of the manufacturer have been strenuously urged, and no one would listen with more attention to any suggestion of injury on their part. If there is any point on which I am more an enthusiast than another, it is on the policy and duty of encouraging manufactures, and on every occasion where their interests have appeared to be affected, my voice has been heard.

But how is the suggested injury to happen? Is the capital of the manufacturer drawn from them to pay the duties? The case of those who pay duties is the reverse. The credits allowed are such as to leave the public money in their hands. Their complaints on that head, if they have any, may be easily satisfied by extending the term of credit.

Another allegation is, that the consumption of the articles is diminished in consequence of the duty. One of the snuff-manufacturers assured me they were not so weak as to imagine the consumers would not repay them. Will the consumers of loaf sugar be terrified by the exorbitant duty of two cents to do violence to their habits and deny themselves loaf sugar? Will they treat their friends with brown sugar? Of all tyrants fashion is the most inexorable. I tell the gentlemen who dread the brown sugar reform, it is not possible. It is not creditable to substitute brown sugar in place of loaf, in consequence of the price, any more than for the same gentlemen to wear frocks and trousers and leathern aprons on account of the impost on superfine cloth.

There is one other view of the interests of the manufacturers. Possibly the mode of levying the tax may be inconvenient and vexatious. If that be the case, who doubts the readiness of Congress to conciliate the interests and even the prejudices of the concerned? Surely not those who remember with what extreme solicitude Congress attempted to reconcile the country to the excise. Surely those who oppose the taxes will not expect the eastern members, where manufactures are the most extensive and numerous, to be opposers of any plan of accommodation of the manufacturers. They are perfectly sure, and ever have been, of our concurrence in such amendments, and why would they wish to keep the laws hung up in uncertainty for two years?

Is it to secure the power of the next Congress, and why not of the next Congress after that which perhaps may be better still? And why on that ground should any law be passed to continue longer than an almanac? Is this the idea to be inculcated of the reign of laws, that gentlemen tell us by passing an act for more than two years, we part with our power; and what is the import of this new-fashioned jargon of a power *over* the laws, instead of the power of the laws? The power to pass laws is not a personal prerogative, it is a public trust, and when the common good, when the attainment of a great advantage for our country, such as the progressive reduction of the debt, requires a law for ten years, or even longer, is it an argument to say that thus we may lose our personal importance and prerogative?

Shifting, unsteady laws, are a public evil, and they are always felt as such by the dealers in the taxed articles. The first effect of a tax is a little to stagnate and derange the business of the dealers, but soon the current finds its way again, and the tax becomes a part of the price, a part of the settled order of things, which a hasty repeal would derange anew. This argument, it is said, requires that all resource laws should be permanent. Where there is a permanent occasion for taxes, and the proper objects of taxation are known to be selected, the fluctuation of the revenue laws would be an evil, and therefore it would be proper to make them permanent. But when the call for taxes is temporary, or the mode of collection untried, the limitation of the bill to a short period may be no less proper. This objection therefore deserves little attention.

One objection is scarcely intelligible. Why will you urge the permanency of taxes for temporary objects, such as war establishments, frigates, &c.? The answer is, the appropriation is intended for the debt; for an object that will last, we fear, much longer than the year 1801, the term proposed for the taxes. The taxes are not to be made permanent, nor are the objects of their application temporary. The objectors are wrong in fact.

They are no less mistaken in principle. The temporary taxes were, during the last session, charged with an appropriation of twelve hundred thousand dollars, and one million of dollars also, for the foreign intercourse. These sums are to be satisfied out of the product of the temporary taxes, and the PRESIDENT is authorized by law to borrow on the credit of those funds. The public faith is solemnly pledged, and in express words, (see the appropriation act passed the ninth of June, 1794,) to provide for the principal and interest out of the proceeds of these very taxes, or to substitute other adequate funds in their stead. These taxes are charged in this manner by law, and if we refuse to renew the acts, we are sacredly bound to provide substituted revenues.

Every one knows that these taxes will not free themselves from the charge in the two years.

How then can gentlemen prevail upon their good sense to assert, that, by continuing the tax laws, the manufacturers are deluded and deceived, when the cause and necessity for such continuance appears on the face of the statute book? How, above all things, can they say, that it is a breach of the public faith to extend them to 1801, when, unfortunately for the sufferer, the public faith is in express words pledged to continue them, or to provide other funds? The assertion has been a subject of no little curiosity, under circumstances so singularly adapted to its confutation.

My own view of the importance of hastening the reduction of the debt, has led me to suggest answers to as many of the objections as I can recollect. I notice them as they happen to occur to me. One appeal to our pity is made on the score that sugars have risen, and that it is cruel to choose this time for the tax. Why not choose it if the tax will fall, as others do, on the consumers? Do the same objectors desire a relinquishment of the duty on molasses because it is dear, and yet the manufacture of New England rum is unfortunately, from various causes, in a languishing state? Foreign goods are dear, and yet they are taxed. All articles are become dear, and the blind rule contended for would be doubly wrong, if adopted on account of its necessary partiality.

If we regard the experience of other nations, we shall not find cause to dread the destruction of manufactures in consequence of taxes. Is England exempted from them, and yet where do they flourish more? The truth is, in an increasing, thriving society, the taxes are absorbed and distributed over the whole mass of the community. No problem has been oftener debated than where the taxes ultimately fell, and yet experience has invariably refuted the gloomy anticipations of interested theory. The language that infant manufactures are not to be crushed, is more declamatory than correct. They are not to be crushed; nor will the manufactures of snuff and loaf sugar fall, if the operation of the tax should be like that of other taxes, or of similar taxes in other countries.

But is it really desired wholly to exempt the loaf sugar from tax, now the duty on the foreign article has secured an effectual monopoly to the home refiners? Shall the four cents remain on the foreign loaf sugar, and nothing on the home made? If the price should in that event keep up, the consumers would still pay the tax, after its repeal, although the money would not go into the Treasury, but into the pockets of the refiners. I wish their prosperity, but they are too candid and patriotic to desire such an advantage.

A great object is before us, and if, after all, its attainment shall appear to be obstructed by much seeming and some real difficulty and embarrassment, still we owe it to our country, as well as to our own engagements, to proceed. Let us endeavor to overcome the prejudices of the overapprehensive, and to conciliate the interests of the manufacturers with that of the public. In our other taxes we suppose it is done, and why should it be despaired of in this case? Greater difficulties than any that a calm and unprejudiced mind will discern in the plan before us ought to be expected, and readily acquiesced in, rather than to abandon the great object of freeing the nation from debt. It is worth some exertion and sacrifice. If we should effect it, any hopes of the destinies of our government would brighten. There is nothing in the magnitude of the Debt to discourage us, and still less in the prosperous circumstances and good dispositions of our citizens. It depends on ourselves whether we realize their expectations by acting in conformity with our own professions.

TO THOMAS DWIGHT

———

NEW YORK, JUNE 11, 1790 IN THE FEDERAL HALL

MY DEAR FRIEND,

I AM GOING this afternoon to visit Passaic Falls, in New Jersey, with a party, and I write now, because I wish you to know the events of this day by the next post, which I shall not return in due season to write.

You have seen that *we* are sold by the Pennsylvanians, and the assumption with it. They seem to have bargained to prevent the latter, on the terms of removing to Philadelphia. It became necessary to defeat this corrupt bargain. We had voted in the House for Philadelphia. The Senate disagreed. The motion being renewed in the House, we have opposed it, first so as to gain time, and next to baffle the scheme *in toto*. Yesterday it rained, and Governor Johnson, who had been brought in a sick bed to vote in Senate against Philadelphia, could not be safely removed in the rain. It was supposed, that if the resolve to remove could be urged through the House, and sent up while it continued raining, that it would pass in Senate. They called for the question, but Gerry and Smith made long speeches and motions, so that the question was not decided till this morning. Rather than gratify the Pennsylvanians, and complete their bargain at the same time, *we* voted for Baltimore, which passed by two majority, to the infinite mortification of the Pennsylvanians. Philadelphia was struck out, and as, by the rules of the House, it could not be inserted again, it is a complete overthrow. But, my dear friend, we gain useless victories. I care little where Congress may sit. I would not find fault with Fort Pitt, if we could assume the debts, and proceed in peace and quietness. But this despicable grog-shop contest, whether the taverns of New York or Philadelphia shall get the custom of Congress, keeps us in discord, and covers us all with disgrace. How this resolve will fare in Senate, I know not. I trust the attempt will be made to turn it into a question of *permanent* residence. That would make the friends of the assumption the umpires, and enable them to dictate their own terms. I am, however, almost in despair of success. Yesterday it was moved in Senate to tack the assumption as an amendment to the funding bill. But Morris, Langdon, and another, declaring that they liked the assumption, said that they would not agree to it, as a part of that bill, lest the bill should be lost by it. Whereas the Pennsylvanians have both in their own power, and there is no ground for pretending danger to the bill, if *they* are disposed to vote for it. Their declaration is plain proof that Philadelphia stands in the way of the state debts. It is a shameful declaration for men to make, who have so solemnly asserted their zeal for the measure. Langdon is a partisan for Philadelphia. It is barely possible for any business to be more perplexed and entangled than this has been. We have fasted, watched, and prayed for the cause. I never knew so much industry and perseverance exerted for any cause. Mr. Sedgwick is a perfect slave to the business. Mr. Goodhue frowns all day long, and swears as much as a good Christian can, about the perverseness of Congress.

We are passing the ways and means bill. We do so little, and behave so ill in doing that, that I consider Congress as meriting more reproach than has been cast upon it.

I am gratified to know that your river is becoming important. I wish you could, by faith or otherwise, remove the rocks from its bed. I am pleased to find our General Court so much better than it was; but their sense, as expressed by their vote, will not help us to carry the assumption. It furnishes the others with a plea to delay, and get the sense of the other states, which would not be in the like strain.

My regards to friends. The first week of leisure, or rather of respite from urgent business, will carry me to Springfield.

I am, affectionately yours, &c.

The Pennsylvanians have hurried the removal of Congress, because (the) Rhode Island Senators are expected daily to join the New Yorkers.

TO GEORGE RICHARDS MINOT

NEW YORK, JUNE 23, 1790

MY DEAR FRIEND,

I DO NOT suppose you will wish my correspondence, while your duty in the General Court imposes so hard a task. However, you know that I do not pretend to exact an answer as a right.

I expect all the holders of securities in Boston will be alarmed, when they learn that on Monday the bill for excises, called the supply, or ways and means bill, was lost in the House, ayes twenty-three, noes thirty-five. Their anxiety will abate, when they know the circumstances that made it necessary to kill it. The perverseness of the Pennsylvanians has made them risk every thing for Philadelphia. One of them has often defied the friends of the assumption, to hinder the passage of the funding system. The Senate had become a scene of discord upon that subject, and partly from aversion to all funding, and partly from a desire to show that refusing the state debts would make the terms of the other debt worse, they have excluded the alternatives, and offer a simple four per cent. to the creditor. This is playing Rhode Island with one third of the debt, and I cannot think of it without indignation. In short, it was becoming probable that the whole would be postponed to the next session. The negative upon the ways and means, by opening the eyes of the advocates of the funding to a sense of their danger, really contributes to the security of the provision for public credit. It is rather paradoxical, I confess. Besides, a scheme has been ripening, and is agreed upon between the Pennsylvanians and the southern people, to remove to Philadelphia, stay fifteen years, and fix the permanent seat on the Potomac. To do this, and at the same time reject the assumption, is such an outrage upon the feelings of the eastern people, as I persuade myself they dare not commit;—and as our claim of justice has been expressed in a loud tone, and our reproaches and resentments have been reiterated since it was denied us, they have become afraid of consequences; and as our zeal and industry have not relaxed, and every instrument of influence has been tried, I think I see strong indications of an assent to the assumption. Those who love peace, and those who fear consequences, will naturally shrink from any side, and however unavailing the debates may have been to procure votes, they have at last silenced opposition. And it is, at the same time, in itself gratifying and a presage of success, that the justice and policy of the assumption, except as it regards the *vox populi* in the south, are no longer denied, or denied so faintly as to indicate merely the repugnance of pride to yielding a contested point. Mr. Morris is a zealous friend of the assumption, (though he has acted crookedly,) and he has strong motives to prevent the convulsions which would ensue, if a bargain for Philadelphia should be supposed the cause of losing the measure. His own wishes, shame, prudence, will concur to exact from all whom he can influence a vote for it, and taking all these things together, I begin to indulge a very confident hope of success. I believe that Congress will sit next at Philadelphia, and if we succeed in the assumption, we shall have nothing of bargain to reproach ourselves with. I confess, my dear friend, with shame, that the world ought to despise our public conduct, when it hears intrigue openly avowed, and sees that great measures are made to depend, not upon reasons, but upon bargains for little ones. This being clear, I should have supposed myself warranted to make a defensive or counter bargain, to prevent the success of the other. But even that would wear an ill aspect, and be disliked by the world. I repeat it, therefore, with pleasure, that we have kept clear of it.

I see by the papers that Mr. Gardiner's reform of the law is not quite extinct; but as our House is far better than the last, and the Senate absolutely federal, I hope no fresh disturbance will be given to the course of our judicial proceedings. Pray tell your brother Clarke, that I went to the President on his behalf, and made a strong representation of his losses and merits. The President is well disposed towards him, but I think he will not nominate him to the light-house, because Knox is there *locum tenens*. He will stand well for any vacant place. General Lincoln's vote would go far to serve him. Be so good as to say what I wish to have said to friends, Mr. Freeman, &c. My most respectful compliments to Mrs. Minot. Dear George, if you have leisure, and not else, write to me, for I have long been so vexed by the waves and storms of the political sea, as to wish, as much as the sailors do, for the port, and like them perhaps I shall be willing to quit it again.

Your affectionate friend.

TO THOMAS DWIGHT

NEW YORK, JUNE 27, 1790

MY DEAR FRIEND,

. . . .

YOUR FEARS are strong that we shall lose the assumption. Mine have been so, as I have often signified in my letters. Now, I am pretty confident of a better issue to this long contest. Conviction seems at last to have [won] its way to men, whose prejudices seemed to have barred up the passage. We hear no more about the injustice of the assumption; at last, it is tacitly allowed that it will promote justice; and it is asked, let it rest till the next session, and then we shall doubtless assume. This looks like coming over. Besides, consequences are feared. The New England States demand it as a debt of justice, with a tone so loud and threatening, that they fear the convulsions which would probably ensue. Further, they are going to fix the residence permanently on the Potomac, and by the apostasy of Pennsylvania will do it, removing, however, immediately to Philadelphia, and staying there ten years. Two such injuries would be too much. They dare not, I trust, carry Congress so far south, and leave the debts upon us. R. Morris, too, is really warm for the assumption, and as he is the *factotum* in the business, he will not fail to insist upon the original friends of it, and who have ever been a majority, voting for it. With five Pennsylvanians, our former aid from that delegation, we can carry it, or least obtain four fifths of the debts to be assumed. Accordingly, they begin to say, these violent feuds must be composed; too much is hazarded, to break up in this temper. Maryland is the most alarmed, as well as, next to Virginia, most anxious for the Potomac. I am beginning to be sanguine in the hope of success.[20] This week may decide. If so, the next will carry me to Springfield. But while such immense

---

[20] *The proposition to assume the State debts failed at one time in the House; but on being revived, and connected with the proposition to remove the seat of government to Philadelphia and, after the expiration of ten years, to the Potomac, it prevailed by a very scanty majority. Mr. Jefferson says that this log-rolling connection of the two measures was arranged by an express agreement. Accordingly, two gentlemen, "with a revulsion of stomach almost convulsive," voted for the assumption; and this change of votes secured its passage.* [S. AMES. See Jacob E. Cooke, "The Compromise of 1790," *William and Mary Quarterly*, vol. xxvii, 3d ser., pp. 523–45, 1970, and the discussion following in vol. xxviii, 3d ser., pp. 629–48, 1971. Ed.]

objects are depending, at the very crisis too, you will see that I cannot desert, without being chargeable with a breach of duty, and taking a risk of consequences and a weight of reproach I ought not to bear with my own consent. Please to give me your opinion upon these circumstances.

. . . Dear friend, I am in haste, going to spend the day abroad; and, at the hazard of writing nonsense, I have scribbled what I wished you to know without delay.

Your affectionate friend.

TO THOMAS DWIGHT

NEW YORK, JULY 11, 1790

MY DEAR FRIEND,

To-MORROW a committee will report in Senate in favor of the assumption, and on Tuesday I suppose it will be taken up. But we begin to relax in our sanguine hopes of success. It is plainly in our power. The game is in our hands. Last week the removal bill passed, in favor of Philadelphia and the Potomac. That encumbrance out of our way, it is not to be doubted that we could carry our long-contested point. But in Senate, some gentlemen advocate a simple four per cent. provision for the debt, making no compensation, as the Secretary has reported, for the two per cent. This has been agreed to as an amendment to the funding bill, which is still in that House. Several Senators, friendly to the funding and assuming, say that such a measure (four per cent. and no equivalent for the two per cent.) is against justice, against national policy, against eastern policy; for it is for giving, or rather throwing away, one third of the property now collected in the middle and eastern states,—disgraceful to the public,—weakens the attachment of individuals, &c.;—that if we can pay four per cent. now, we can pay two more in ten years. Even if we should fail, the evil would be foreseen and guarded against, and then we should have gained strength, and could bear it better. Four per cent., though dishonest, affords no relief; it is an unnecessary anticipation of an uncertain contingency, &c., &c. I confess I incline to this opinion. The other is, that as we may fail ten years hence, it is better not to promise. This difference of opinion is becoming serious. Those who insist on the Secretary's proposals, say that unless assurances are given that these offers shall be made to the creditors, they will vote against the funding, assumption, and every thing connected with what they call so improper a plan. Neither party seems to advance towards accommodation, and it now seems inevitable, that the assumption will, on Tuesday, be rejected in Senate. Thus, my friend, we hope and fear—we then become sanguine, and then absolutely despair. I begin to fear that we are but fifteen years old in politics, which is the age of our nation since 1776, and that it will be at least six years before we become fit for any thing but colonies. We want principles, morals, fixed habits, and more firmness against unreasonable clamors.

I shall give you the vapors. I finish.

Your affectionate friend.

TO THOMAS DWIGHT

NEW YORK, JULY 25, 1790

MY DEAR FRIEND,

$\cdot$ $\cdot$ $\cdot$ $\cdot$ $\cdot$ $\cdot$ $\cdot$ $\cdot$ $\cdot$

OUR POLITICS have been critical the past week. The funding bill having passed the Senate with amendments, on Friday the House took up the amendments, and instead of funding twenty-six dollars (on each hundred to be loaned) at the end of ten years, the House propose thirty-three and a third, at the end of seven years. The indents and interest on the debt of the United States to be raised from three per cent., as proposed by the Senate, and funded at four per cent. This being just, I wish it may pass in the Senate. Three per cent. seems to be abandoning all pretence of paying the creditors.

Yesterday we renewed the battle for the assumption—rather, we began it on Friday. Mr. Jackson[21] then made a speech, which I will not say was loud enough for you to hear. It disturbed the Senate, however; and to keep out the din, they put down their windows. Mr. Smith (S. C.) followed him, an hour. Yesterday, Mr. Gerry delivered himself. Jackson rebellowed. The motion by Jackson being that the House do disagree to the amendment of the Senate. Voted in the negative; thirty-two (not including the Speaker, who is of our side) against twenty-nine. Several motions were made to alter the sums to be assumed from the States, but were negatived. Thus, my friend, we again stand on good ground. We shall finish the amendments, I hope, to-morrow;

---

[21] *Of Georgia.* [S. AMES]

and as they are not likely to be founded on improper principles, I hope the Senate will concur, and relieve us from a state of solicitude which has been painful beyond any I ever suffered.

I do not see how the bill can be lost, as both Houses have agreed to its passage; and though the amendments may not suit both, I will not fear that they will be agreed to in some form or other. We are impatient for the end of the session. Should all go smoothly, we shall sit till near the middle of August.

I must conclude with my affectionate regards to friends, and especially to you, for I am truly

Your friend and humble servant.

[P.S.] The Indian chief, McGillivray, is here. He is decent, and not very black.

TO THOMAS DWIGHT

NEW YORK, AUGUST 8, 1790

MY DEAR FRIEND,

I HAVE NOT replied to your friendly letters, because I have hoped to give you absolute assurance that I should quit this place next Wednesday. A bill is ordered to be reported, and will be to-morrow, for employing a million of dollars which we have to spare, for buying up the debt. This will restore a great sum to circulation; raise credit and the price of paper; make foreigners pay dear for what they may buy, or stop their buying; produce good humor among the creditors, and among the people, too, when they see the debt melting away; create a sinking fund of near eighty thousand dollars yearly, and, by a little management, of upwards of one hundred thousand. Objects so great and so popular carry away every personal consideration. I think such an act of vigor and policy would restore all the credit and regard that the government has lost. This bill may, and I fear will, detain us two days longer, but no new business will be touched. Wherefore I think that on Monday week at the latest, and perhaps on Friday next, I shall reach Springfield, and help you help our fair friends keep house. I despise politics, when I think of this office. I shall forget, though you hint at it, that I am a candidate, and am to be gibbeted in Edes's newspaper. I am in haste, and why should I write a great deal, and spoil my pleasant task of telling you all I know?

Your friend, &c.

TO THOMAS DWIGHT

PHILADELPHIA, DECEMBER 12, 1790

DEAR FRIEND,

YESTERDAY I took lodgings at the house of a Mrs. Sage, where I begin to enjoy quiet, and to feel settled and at home. I arrived in the city the last Sunday evening, and lodged at the Indian Queen, a tavern, where I found it difficult to write you. We had no sooner landed our baggage in the stage-office, a place adjoining the tavern, taken a dish of tea, &c., than we learned that the room where it was left was robbed. Mr. Oliver Phelps's and Mr. Dalton's trunks were taken away, containing their linen, Phelps's notes of hand for his new lands, his title deeds, twenty thousand dollars securities he had brought for a friend, eight or ten thousand of his own, with many papers valuable only to Phelps. Dalton had forty dollars, and a dozen shirts, &c. The next day, the two trunks, with many of Phelps's papers, including the greatest part of his securities, which were wrapped in a letter, and so eluded their search, were found in a field. We were disturbed by this misfortune, as you may suppose, and kept up almost all night. My name was on my trunk. The partial rogues took that as a mark, that nothing was to be got by taking it away. But see my good temper; I have not felt angry at the slight.

Both Houses were formed on the second day of the session. We have had the speech from the throne, have answered it, and to-morrow we are to present our answer. Both contain some divine molasses.

Mr. Jackson, of Georgia, yesterday let off a balloon about the treaty with the Creeks, complaining that the speech was silent on that topic, and that he should move very furiously for papers, and an address to the President to know whether there were any secret articles, &c. *Ruat cœlum, fiat justitia.* We wish for Sedgwick, and shall want him soon. Virginia is teeming, we hear, with antifederalism. The excise will be opposed, and any other proper mode of provision for the state debts will rub hard. These are my fears.

This is a very magnificent city. Our accommodations to meet, &c., are good.

This cold weather admonishes you, that you are losing time. Why will you remain a forlorn, shivering bachelor a minute longer? I could preach on this subject in a manner that would edify you and all other negligent sinners, if I was not at this moment obliged to wind off. *Sat sapienti verbum.* Think of these things.

Pray read Sedgwick's letter.

TO THOMAS DWIGHT

PHILADELPHIA, DECEMBER 23, 1790

DEAR FRIEND,

I INCLOSE, in two newspapers, the plan of a bank reported by Mr. Hamilton. The late surprising rise of public stock is supposed to be owing in part to this report, because it affords an opportunity to subscribe three fourths paper and one fourth silver into the bank stock. In Holland, we are told, our stock sells above par.

The creditors in this State have sent us a huffing memorial, which I inclose. It came in when the price of debt affords an answer to it. No notice was taken of it. The Senate, I hear, have proposed to answer them by resolving that a revision of the funding act is improper. Please to let Colonel Worthington see the inclosed. I wish to be made use of to furnish any thing from hence that may amuse my Springfield friends. Please to signify as much at that house.

I think the public will be delighted to see the public credit rise, the debt reduced by two hundred and seventy-eight thousand dollars, which cost only one hundred and fifty thousand dollars, and still reducing more. The President has afforded them such evidence of our prosperous condition, as they will not controvert. I scribble in haste for the sake of inclosing the papers by this post. Instead of a letter, which I have not time to write, pray represent me at Colonel Worthington's.

The Senate have just voted, R. Morris only dissenting, in substance as I stated before. I wonder how the petitioners could overcome their Philadelphia modesty so far as to present such a . . . . memorial. You may fill the blank for yourself.

Sedgwick arrived, and took his seat this morning.

Pray let me hear from you. Are you married?

Your friend.

P.S. Old Mr. Edes's paper accused me of keeping aristocratic company at New York. I obey the admonition of my constituent. Instead of Sedgwick, Benson, and other bad company, I now lodge with Gerry, Ashe, Sevier, and Parker. Birds of a feather.

TO WILLIAM TUDOR

PHILADELPHIA, DECEMBER 30, 1790

DEAR SIR,

WE HAVE no want of business. The House at the first engrossed almost all the important objects of discussion, leaving the Senate a holiday season. But we have since sent up the bank, weights and measures, and other matters, to set them at work. Like good neighbours, we borrow and lend. The last session was managed as this began. The Senate were ousted of the greater part of the business. The bank is an important instrument in the hands of the government, and may be made to do a great deal of good. It will pass, it is said, in the Senate, though I do not know who has the means of knowing that it will. It has to encounter some prejudices and local institutions. The state banks apprehend injury. This did not happen it is said in England, when the national bank was established. Besides, room is to be left for incorporating those banks into the new one hereafter.—While I allude to things of this nature, I recollect a piece in Adams's papers recommending a canal through Cape Cod. I am an enthusiast on those points. While I see this place becoming a London in wealth, and more than a London already in arrogance, I long to see some plan of inland navigation effected, which alone seems adequate to the resuscitation of Boston. The public must be prepared gradually for such undertakings. The newspapers may be made use of to kindle some zeal for this purpose. Here every body is as forward to promote public objects as a Roman, and perhaps because, like a Roman, he thinks all the rest of the world barbarians. I own this is rather illiberal. You will make allowances. But they are in advance of us in public spirit and enterprise. It will however be allowed that our individuals are full of spirit and enterprise, and perhaps do as well at present as they do any where. But our public institutions are inferior. Our friend Mr. Breck is no doubt exulting in the reputation of his duck. Mr. Anthony here tells me its credit is very high, and that he cannot get so much of it as he wants. He cannot get a suit of sails for a New London ship in particular.

We have voted the principles of an excise bill, without much difficulty, and a bill like that which failed the last session is reported, and the order of the day for next Tuesday. This will complete the provision for the public credit, which is very high. It denotes health in the body politic.

FISHER AMES